THE LAWS OF ANCIENT CRETE *c.*650–400 BCE

Michael Gagarin is Professor Emeritus of Classics at the University of Texas at Austin.

Paula Perlman is Professor of Classics at the University of Texas at Austin.

The Laws of Ancient Crete c.650–400 BCE

MICHAEL GAGARIN AND PAULA PERLMAN

OXFORD
UNIVERSITY PRESS

OXFORD
UNIVERSITY PRESS

Great Clarendon Street, Oxford, OX2 6DP,
United Kingdom

Oxford University Press is a department of the University of Oxford.
It furthers the University's objective of excellence in research, scholarship,
and education by publishing worldwide. Oxford is a registered trade mark of
Oxford University Press in the UK and in certain other countries

First Edition published in 2016
First published in paperback 2020

Published in the United States of America by Oxford University Press
198 Madison Avenue, New York, NY 10016, United States of America

British Library Cataloguing in Publication Data
Data available

Library of Congress Cataloging in Publication Data
Data available

ISBN 978–0–19–920482–3 (Hbk.)
ISBN 978–0–19–883251–5 (Pbk.)

For
Henri van Effenterre
Scholar and Friend

PREFACE

The island of Crete was the center of Greek Bronze-Age civilization until at least 1400,[1] and continued to have a vibrant palace economy until around 1200, at which time this economy collapsed, palace buildings were largely abandoned, and the population declined significantly. With the demise of the palaces, the syllabic script known as Linear B, which had primarily been used to record the activities of palace bureaucracies, also disappeared, leading to several centuries during which writing was apparently unknown in Greece.

During these centuries (*c.*1200–800), the population remained widely dispersed, and although some continuity is evident from the Bronze Age to the Early Archaic period, the civilization that begins to develop in the tenth and ninth centuries is substantially new. It is characterized by the rise of small nucleated settlements with up to a few thousand inhabitants mostly located on the tops of hills, presumably for defense (Nowicki 2000; Wallace 2010a; see further Introd. 2A). As in other parts of the Greek world, a new form of writing, an alphabetic script was introduced, probably some time before 750. At first, this script was used for private writing, primarily personal expressions of gratitude or hope and other short graffiti, but in the second half of the seventh century it began to be used to write longer, public texts, the vast majority of which were laws (Gagarin 2008a: 39–44).

Inscriptions with archaic and classical laws are found all over the Greek world, but they are especially numerous on Crete. Thus far, inscribed laws have been found from ten poleis (city-states), all located in the central part of the island: Axos (**A**), Datala (**Da**), Dreros (**Dr**), Eleutherna (**Ele**), Eltynia (**Elt**), Gortyn (**G**), Knossos (**K**), Lyktos (**L**), Phaistos (**Ph**), and Prinias (**Pr**). New laws are continually being discovered and continuing excavation may add other poleis to this list, but many inhabited sites have now been excavated without yielding any trace of laws, either because these poleis did not write laws at the time or because they wrote them on more perishable materials which no longer survive.

The roughly two hundred texts in this volume represent only a fraction, probably quite a small fraction, of the total number of legal texts inscribed in Crete during this time; they represent a disproportionate percentage, however, of the total number of surviving Greek laws from this period. Gortyn, in particular, has yielded many more inscribed laws than any other city. It is very unlikely that this large number is purely the result of the accident of discovery, because at the

[1] All dates in this book are BCE unless the contrary is either indicated or obvious. The Note on Chronology (below) explains the various periods into which for convenience we divide Greek history.

same time, very few inscriptions have been discovered at Gortyn or elsewhere on Crete of the sort found everywhere else in the Greek world during this period, such as epitaphs. It seems, then, that the Gortynians, at least, both enacted more legislation than most other Greek poleis and inscribed more of their legislation on stone, the most durable material available.

Most of the surviving texts are now fragmentary; those that are complete range from single sentences to the Gortyn Code with more than 600 lines of text (**G72**). As far as we can tell, all but one (**Da1**, which is not a statute but an agreement between the city and an individual) were originally displayed in public spaces, some on terrace walls and on the walls of public buildings, others on freestanding walls or stelae (stone slabs). They are written in an epichoric (local) script, which is broadly similar across the island but varies a bit from city to city. Some of the letters in this script differ widely from their equivalents in the Ionic script familiar to most readers of ancient Greek and still in use today (see Introd. 3B). Interpretation of these texts is often not easy. In addition to the usual problems posed by fragmentary texts, we confront significant uncertainties about the dialect and vocabulary of these texts. More important, besides the laws, we have very few contemporary sources of information about Cretan life at the time other than what is provided by archaeological excavation and survey, and since about 1900, archaeological exploration on Crete has largely been concentrated on Bronze-Age sites, to the neglect of archaic and classical sites. This is beginning to change, but at present we still must reconstruct the legal system and the social and political order of the period mostly on the basis of the laws alone.

Although many of the texts in this volume are included in one or both of the recent collections of archaic Greek laws—Koerner 1993 and van Effenterre and Ruzé 1994–5, with German and French translations respectively—they are still not widely known, especially in the English-speaking world. The main publication of most of the texts is the four volumes of *Inscriptiones Creticae* (*IC* = Guarducci 1935–50); this is a superb work of scholarship but its Latin commentary is not easily read by many who might otherwise be interested in these laws. New texts discovered since the publication of *IC* have appeared in a variety of journals and for the most part have been little studied. For these reasons, we are presenting here a collection of all significant archaic and classical legal texts from Crete that have thus far been published, together with an English translation and commentary. Our aim is to make these laws more accessible to scholars and students, including those who know no Greek. We have not included any previously unpublished inscriptions.

Many of the texts published in *IC* are very fragmentary; some contain only a letter or two. We include here only those texts in which some significant content can be identified. Thus we include some texts in which only one significant word survives but omit other texts where two or three very common words survive (such as *ai de ka*). We are more likely to include a very fragmentary text if it is not in *IC*, and we regularly provide more detailed notes concerning texts not in *IC*, because many of them are published in works that are not readily available and, perhaps because of this, have generally received less discussion than those in *IC*.

Since the beginning of the twentieth century, the study of these texts from the Archaic and Classical periods has taken second place to the study and excavation of Bronze Age Crete. Interest in the later periods has, however, increased considerably in the last two decades, as have excavations and studies of the material from earlier excavations from these periods. As a result, recent scholarship has begun to challenge some long-standing views, and the picture of post-Bronze-Age Crete will undoubtedly continue to evolve. We have tried to take account of work published through 2013, but have undoubtedly overlooked some of it.

Our present work, then, is not intended to be the final word. We seek in the first place to provide Greek texts that are as complete as possible, with enough epigraphical evidence that readers can form their own judgments about uncertain or incomplete texts. The translations are intended to clarify our understanding of the text, and are thus often more literal than elegant. In the Introduction we have tried to note the range of existing views on various issues, but we do not hesitate to express our own views, even when they are controversial. When we are uncertain, we say so. Our hope is that others will study these texts, and challenge, revise, and probably disprove some of what we write here. Our goal is not to present a definitive account of the laws of Crete but to provide a foundation for others to build on.

Because of the difficulty in establishing firm dates for these inscriptions, we have not used a fixed chronological cut-off point for the texts we include; instead, we have included all suitable texts written in the epichoric alphabet, before it was replaced by the Ionic (and ultimately pan-Hellenic) alphabet. The latter was officially adopted in Athens in 403, and the transition in Crete probably took place around the middle of the fourth century; after this date laws continued to be inscribed but in much smaller numbers. We take a broad view of what qualifies as a law, using the term to include all texts that record authorized public actions; thus, among our laws are interstate agreements (e.g. **G80**) and other sorts of agreements or contracts (e.g. **Da1**) entered into by the polis, as well as many fragmentary texts whose nature cannot be determined with certainty. However, because only a handful of the Cretan inscriptions on stone from this period are clearly not laws, and because many of the fragmentary texts we include contain language that either is legal or occurs often in laws of the period and none contains language that is inconsistent with its being a law, we are fairly confident that virtually all the texts in this collection are legal in nature.[2]

[2] We have not included two legal texts with possible relevance for our period, the oath of the Drerians (*IC* 1.9.1) and the agreement between Argos, Knossos, and Tylissos (*IC* 1.30.1 + 1.8.4; M&L no. 42; VER I.54; Rhodes and Lewis 1997: 308, 310). The former dates from the late third century and is thought to

To assist the reader, we first present an Introduction to the material found in the texts. This is intended to provide background, including our approach to the question of unity or diversity in archaic and classical Crete (Introd. 1), the archaeological and historical context for written law in Crete (Introd. 2), and information about more technical matters, such as dialect (Introd. 3), as well as a more extended discussion of some of the issues raised in the texts than is possible or desirable in a commentary (Introd. 4–10). The reader may wish to read parts or all of the Introduction first, or just refer back to it in the course of reading the texts. We refer to its different sections by number: e.g. 'Introd. 5B', referring to the section on women.

The texts are arranged by city. Those that have been published in *IC* are numbered with the abbreviated name of the city of origin (for which see above), followed by the *IC* number, all in bold face; thus *IC* 2.5.1 from Axos is **A1**, *IC* 2.5.4 is **A4**, and between **A7** and **A9** we do not include an **A8**, because too little of *IC* 2.5.8 survives. After the *IC* texts from a city come any texts from that city not included in *IC*. To distinguish these from the texts in *IC*, they are identified by the full name of the city and are numbered consecutively, beginning with 1 (e.g. **A12** is followed by **Axos1** and **Axos2**). When we include no *IC* texts for a city, we use the abbreviated name for all that city's texts (**Da1**, **Dr1–7**, **Ph1**). Our hope is that any confusion this may initially cause will be outweighed by the benefit of preserving the *IC* numbers with which some readers are familiar—e.g. the Gortyn Code (*IC* 4.72) is numbered **G72**, even though fewer than seventy-one texts from Gortyn precede it.

Except for two large texts, **G41** and **G72**, where for convenience we divide our discussion into columns or sections respectively, we present each text in its entirety, with a translation either next to or below it depending on the length of the lines, followed by notes and then a commentary, somewhat after the model of van Effenterre and Ruzé 1994–5. The translations are intended to explain our understanding of the Greek; where possible, we try to stay close to the word order of the Greek, even if this is slightly awkward in English. The notes are more technical and assume knowledge of classical Attic Greek; in them we primarily discuss epigraphical and linguistic matters. The Introduction and commentary are devoted especially to historical and legal matters, and assume no knowledge of Greek (except for parts of 3B and 3C). In cross-references we use n. for notes and comm. for commentary; where these are omitted, it is understood that cross-references in the notes are to other notes, those in the commentary to other parts

incorporate some archaic language, but we are not confident that we can reconstruct an actual archaic text. The latter, usually dated to *c.*450, is written in the Argive dialect, and thus may reflect the thought and language of Argos rather than of the two Cretan cities. We also omit the so-called Eteocretan inscriptions from Praisos (*IC* 3.6.1, 3.6.3), both sixth century, and from Dreros (van Effenterre 1946b), *c.*650.

of the commentary. We include photographs or drawings of all inscriptions published since *IC*; for those in *IC*, we only include a photograph or drawing where we want to illustrate a specific point.

We have ourselves seen and studied all the texts that we have been able to find (see Locations). Some stones were lost long ago, others disappeared more recently, and still others may be in museum storerooms or elsewhere though we have not been able to find them. A systematic inventory of all inscriptions on the island would be very helpful. Despite our autopsy, we only rarely suggest new readings, especially for texts discovered long ago. Some of these older inscriptions, especially those still *in situ*, have deteriorated since they were first recorded to the point where some are nearly illegible today. We thus rely heavily on the work of earlier editors, especially Halbherr and Guarducci, who fortunately were very fine epigraphers. For this reason, we have also consulted the notebooks of Halbherr and De Sanctis together with a few notebooks of Guarducci, which are located in the archive of the Italian School in Athens.

Although this work is a joint product, and we take joint responsibility for everything in it, we initially distributed the work between us as follows: the section on Gortyn was first prepared by MG; those of all the other cities were first prepared by PP. We then read and revised each other's work more than once. The Introduction was written in different pieces and has been revised several times by each of us.

ACKNOWLEDGMENTS

Our work was initially supported by a collaborative grant from the National Endowment for the Humanities, and has been further supported by the University of Texas, the College of Liberal Arts, and the Department of Classics.

It was our intention from the start of this project in 2006 to study firsthand as many of the laws as we were able to locate and to consider them in their archaeological and historical contexts. To advance these objectives we made seven trips to Crete, most recently in 2014. Our fieldwork would have been impossible without the cooperation of the French, Greek, and Italian directors of excavations of the sites whose communities enacted the laws and the Greek archaeologists and staff of the 23rd, 24th, and 25th Ephorates of the Greek Archaeological Service who graciously made available for study the inscriptions under their authority. We are deeply indebted to many. They are far too numerous to name them all, but we must mention in particular the wonderful individuals in Crete, who welcomed and assisted us at all the sites and museums. We gratefully acknowledge the assistance of the archaeologists and staff of the 23rd Ephorate (central Crete) and the Archaeological Museum of Heraklion, and in particular Nota Dimopoulou-Rethemiotaki, Athanasia Kanta, Ioanna Serpetsidaki, Giorgos Rethemiotaki, Danae Kondopodi, and Maria Kyrimi. We also thank Maria Englesou, Popi Galanaki, Yanis Giaourakis, Michalis Karouzakis, Evi Kourouthianaki Papadaki, and Chrysi Tsichlaki for their assistance and warm hospitality at Gortyn. We thank as well the archaeologists and staff of the 25th Ephorate (west Crete) and the Archaeological Museum of Rethymno, particularly Maria Andreadaki-Vlasaki, Anastasia Tzigounaki, Nikolas Stampolidis, Eva Tegou, and Giorgos Droudakis, for their assistance in our study of the inscriptions from Axos and Eleutherna, and Stavroula Apostolakou, Chrysa Sofianou, and Vaso Zographaki of the 24th Ephorate (east Crete) for their assistance with the inscriptions from Dreros. We are particularly indebted to Eva Tegou and Vaso Zografaki, not only for their assistance with our study of the laws from Axos and Dreros respectively, but also for their generosity in sharing with us the results of their fieldwork and for their warm hospitality.

We have discussed different aspects of this project with many additional scholars. Three colleagues in particular have been especially helpful in reading sections of our work: Monique Bile has read most of the Catalogue, parts of it more than once, and given us invaluable advice on matters relating to the Cretan dialect; Alberto Maffi has read the entire section on Gortyn and has offered many useful comments and criticisms; Antonis Kotsonas provided much-appreciated feedback on sections of the Introduction and Catalogue that rely heavily on the archaeological record.

Other colleagues have also helped us by answering questions or advising us on specific points. We are grateful to Nicola Cucuzza and Vance Watrous who shared with us their knowledge of ancient Phaistos and the western Mesara. Florence Gaignerot-Driessen discussed with us questions concerning the archaeology and history of settlement in the vicinity of Mirabello bay and Dreros in particular. Donald Haggis introduced us to ancient Azoria and discussed with us the implications of this remarkable settlement for our understanding of archaic Cretan society. Charilambos Kritzas shared with us his knowledge of laws from Eltynia and Lyktos. Jenny Moody discussed with us questions concerning the climate and geology of Crete and aspects of production on the island.

Other individuals have contributed to this volume in a variety of ways. We thank Ilaria Simiakaki, archivist at the Scuola Archeologica Italiana di Atene, who provided invaluable assistance in our study of the notebooks of Federico Halbherr and other early Italian archaeologists and epigraphers, and Charles Crowther, Assistant Director of the Centre for the Study of Ancient Documents (CSAD), Oxford, who answered our questions concerning *Poinikastas: Epigraphic Sources for Early Greek Writing*, the archive of the papers of Liliane (Anne) Jeffery, and provided us with access to materials that are not available on the website of CSAD. Judith Swaddling and Alex Truscott at the British Museum made it possible for us to study the bronze mitra inscribed with **Da1**. Maria Pilali and Ioanna Damanaki of the American School of Classical Studies in Athens deserve special mention for their invaluable assistance with permit applications. We especially thank Deena Berg and Chris Williams, who patiently created, made legible, or redrew all of the figures in this volume, for their artistry and advice. Finally, we thank Hilary O'Shea at Oxford University Press for her continuing support of this project, even when it may have seemed as if we would never finish. Also at OUP, we are grateful to Commissioning Editor Charlotte Loveridge, Assistant Editors Taryn Das Neves and Annie Rose, Production Editors Kizzy Taylor-Richelieu and Caroline Hawley, and copy-editor Heather Watson for their assistance in producing this volume. David Pelteret provided invaluable help with the difficult proofs.

MG and PP

Our work is dedicated to Henri van Effenterre, whose path-breaking studies have influenced our work at almost every step. From the time I first met him in 1985, we discussed my work (and his) on many occasions in Paris and Austin and at conferences around the world. We disagreed on many points of detail (as will be evident in our comments throughout), but he always encouraged our work, and in particular this project, which pleased him greatly. Regrettably, we did not complete it soon enough for him to see it published.

MG

CONTENTS

LIST OF FIGURES

ABBREVIATIONS

(Abbreviations for journal titles can be found at the head of the Bibliography)

Bile	= Bile 1988.
Blass	= Blass 1905.
C	= Comparetti.
FGrH	= Jacoby 1923–58.
G	= Guarducci 1935–50.
H	= Halbherr.
IC	= *Inscriptiones Creticae* (Guarducci 1935, 1939, 1942, 1950).
IG	= *Inscriptiones Graecae.*
IK Knidos	= *Die Inschriften von Knidos* (Blümel 1992).
IvM	= *Die Inschriften von Magnesia am Maeander* (Kern 1967).
IvO	= *Die Inschriften von Olympia* (Dittenberger and Purgold 1896).
J-MD	= Jeffery and Morpurgo-Davies 1970.
JP	= Jeffery, Poinikastas: Epigraphic Sources for Early Greek Writing (web site for the Jeffery archive: http://poinikastas.csad.ox.ac.uk).
K	= Koerner 1993.
Kerameikos	= Peek 1941.
LSJ	= Liddell, Scott, Jones 1940.
LGPN I	= Fraser and Matthews 1987.
M	= Magnelli 2008.
M&L	= Meiggs and Lewis 1969.
OCD	= *Oxford Classical Dictionary* (Hornblower, et al. 2012).
SEG	= *Supplementum Epigraphicum Graecum.*
Syll[3]	= *Sylloge Inscriptionum Graecarum* (Dittenberger 1915–24).
VER	= van Effenterre and Ruzé 1994–5.
W	= Willetts 1967.

In cross-references, comm. = commentary, n. = note—either footnote or a note in the text concerning the Greek text.

'Dialect' followed by a number (e.g. 'Dialect 13') refers to the subsection of Introd. 3C on 'Dialect'.

NOTE ON CHRONOLOGY

All dates in this book are BCE unless the contrary is either indicated or obvious. The periodization and absolute dates assigned to the Bronze Age and Early Iron Age in the chronological table follow those of Gaignerot-Driessen (2013: 19–20).

Main Periods	Subdivisions	Absolute Dates	Traditional Subdivisions of the Bronze Age
Bronze Age	Protopalatial	*c*.1900–1600	Middle Minoan IB–Middle Minoan III
	Neopalatial	*c*.1600–1360	Late Minoan IA–Late Minoan IIIA1
	Postpalatial	*c*.1360–1190	Late Minoan IIIA2–Late Minoan IIIB
	Final Palatial or Postpalatial	*c*.1190–970	Late Minoan IIIC–Subminoan
Early Iron Age	Protogeometric	*c*.970–810	
	Geometric	*c*.810–700	
	Orientalizing	*c*.700–630	
Iron Age	Early Archaic	*c*.630–575	
	Archaic	*c*.575–480	
	Classical	*c*.480–330	
	Hellenistic	*c*.330–67	

The rubric 'Orientalizing' reflects the view of many archaeologists that during the period *c*.700–630 Crete appears to have been remarkably (and precociously) open to Near Eastern and Levantine products and influences. Recent scholarship has, however, begun to examine the 'orientalizing phenomenon' more closely and to contest the appropriateness of both the rubric and the termini assigned to the period (e.g. Kotsonas 2013; Whitley 2013). Kotsonas, for example, argues that 'orientalizing' styles were produced and circulated in Crete throughout the Early Iron Age (eleventh to seventh centuries), but it is wrong to refer to any archaeological phase on Crete as 'orientalizing'. He proposes the rubric 'Proto-Archaic' for the diverse styles (especially in vase painting) of the seventh century.

The chronological termini of the Archaic period are particularly resistant to scholarly agreement. Morris (1998), for example, follows Snodgrass (1980: 15–84) in identifying the eighth century as the time when the important structural changes that characterize the seventh and sixth centuries begin—a sort of 'Proto-Archaic phase' in historical rather than archaeological terms, although neither Morris nor Snodgrass refers to the eighth century in this way. The material record of Crete strongly indicates that significant cultural changes occurred around 600, starting a generation or so earlier in some places (*c*.630) or somewhat later in others (*c*.575). The changes, which result in decreased archaeological visibility in several contexts (e.g. cemeteries and sanctuaries), are apparent throughout the island by the middle of the sixth century (below, Introd. 2A). We refer to this transition (*c*.630–575) as the early archaic cultural horizon and the chronological phase during which it took place as the Early Archaic period.

The end of the Hellenistic period on Crete is traditionally assigned to the year 67 BCE when the Roman Q. Caecilius Metellus completed Rome's subjugation of the island.

Introduction

1. ARCHAIC AND CLASSICAL CRETE: UNITY OR DIVERSITY?

Any study of archaic and classical Cretan society must confront the fact that our two main types of evidence present conflicting, and at some points irreconcilable, pictures. On the one hand, the traditional view of Cretan society presented by ancient Greek writers, which derives ultimately from Ephorus, Aristotle, and others living in the fourth century or later, sees the Cretans as Dorians, who largely shared the customs and institutions of other Dorian states, notably Sparta (Perlman 2005). On the other hand, the inscribed laws and the archaeological material provide little evidence for this view and in important respects contradict it. As Maffi has succinctly stated in reference to the relation between the literary sources and **G72** (the 'Code'): 'si l'on se fie à Aristote et à Dosiadas, on n'arrive pas à comprendre le Code; si on suit le Code, le témoignage des historiens n'est pas confirmé par les inscriptions'.[1] The essential difference, as Chaniotis puts it (2005: 175–6), is between the picture of homogeneity presented by the literary sources and the clear sense of heterogeneity found in the documentary sources and the material culture.

Most scholars nonetheless assert or assume that the literary picture of homogeneity in the Archaic and Classical periods is accurate to a considerable degree. Thus, they argue (or imply), it is appropriate to extend information from the laws concerning one polis at one time to other poleis and other times. We disagree and offer here a brief discussion of the *startos* as an example of the methodological problems that we find in this approach (see further Introd. 4B3). Some scholars take the fact that Kyllos was *kosmos* with the *startos* Aithaleus in fifth-century Gortyn (**G72**.5.5–6) as evidence for a rotation of tribes (which are assumed to be equivalent to the *startoi*) in the selection of a *kosmos* in all Cretan poleis at this time, as appears to have been the case in many of the poleis during the Hellenistic period.[2] The *startos* is assumed to be a military unit (possible but by no means certain) and the *kosmos* its leader; the *startagetas* ('*startos* leader') mentioned in

[1] 'If one trusts in Aristotle and Dosiadas, one cannot manage to understand the [Gortyn] Code; if one follows the Code, the testimony of the historians is not confirmed by the inscriptions' (Maffi 1997b: 446). Dosiadas was a third- or early second-century historian of Crete.

[2] For the Hellenistic evidence, see Perlman 2002: 207–9.

G80.4–5 is then taken to be a more specialized military commander. Although in the archaic and classical texts the *startos* is mentioned only at Gortyn (**G72**.5.5; **G80**.7), the appearance of *startos* in a second or third century CE text from Lyktos (*IC* 1.18.11) is taken as evidence that it was a pan-Cretan institution in earlier periods. Some scholars further conclude that the *kosmos* was a military leader throughout Crete, and that one of the areas where homogeneity existed was a martial ethos and societal focus on military training—this despite the absence of any clear reference to military training in the texts (Introd. 8).

We would not argue that no areas of homogeneity existed. The *kosmos* was likely the main official in every polis (Introd. 4C1), though we know almost nothing of his specific duties at this time except at Dreros. In our view, however, we should not allow the influence of later ancient writers, who are not known to have had any direct knowledge of archaic and classical Crete, to lead us to find homogeneity wherever possible, no matter how slim the evidence for it. Another example of this approach will be seen when we examine the polis (Introd. 4A).

In this work we take a different approach: the evidence of the contemporary inscriptions is our starting point, supplemented only by that derived from archaeological finds, and we question any conclusions based on the later tradition for which there is no contemporary evidence.[3] We are also hesitant to ascribe the institutions or practices documented for one polis to other Cretan poleis where no evidence of them has been found. In addition, we do not take for granted any kind of unity among the Cretan poleis before the Hellenistic age. Only in areas where we have contemporary evidence for it, therefore, will we speak of Crete as a unity.

Of course, Crete is an island and thus a geographical unit, but the topography of the island may work against other sorts of unity. Large mountain ranges effectively divide the island into three main regions, East, West, and Central.[4] The large central region is further divided by other mountains, producing smaller regions including Gortyn, Phaistos, and Prinias (the settlement on Patela Priniàs, possibly ancient Rhitten) in the south, Axos and Eleutherna in the north-west, Knossos, Datala, and Eltynia in the north-central, and Dreros and Lyktos in the north-east. After the collapse of Bronze-Age civilization, the population dispersed, living in many small communities all over the island (Introd. 2A3). By the beginning of the Archaic period the number of settlements had decreased and many of those that survived had grown larger.

The nature of settlement hierarchies within a region and of the inter-state relations of the larger communities have only recently begun to be explored. Cooperation among neighbors seems to have occurred in the area of cult practice, especially in the mountain sanctuaries, such as on Mt. Psiloritis (ancient Mt. Ida) (**G80**.2–3), that have been identified on Crete beginning in the Bronze Age; but significant regional

[3] A fuller argument for this approach is presented by Perlman 1992.

[4] A slightly fuller account is given by Whitley 2009: 275–6.

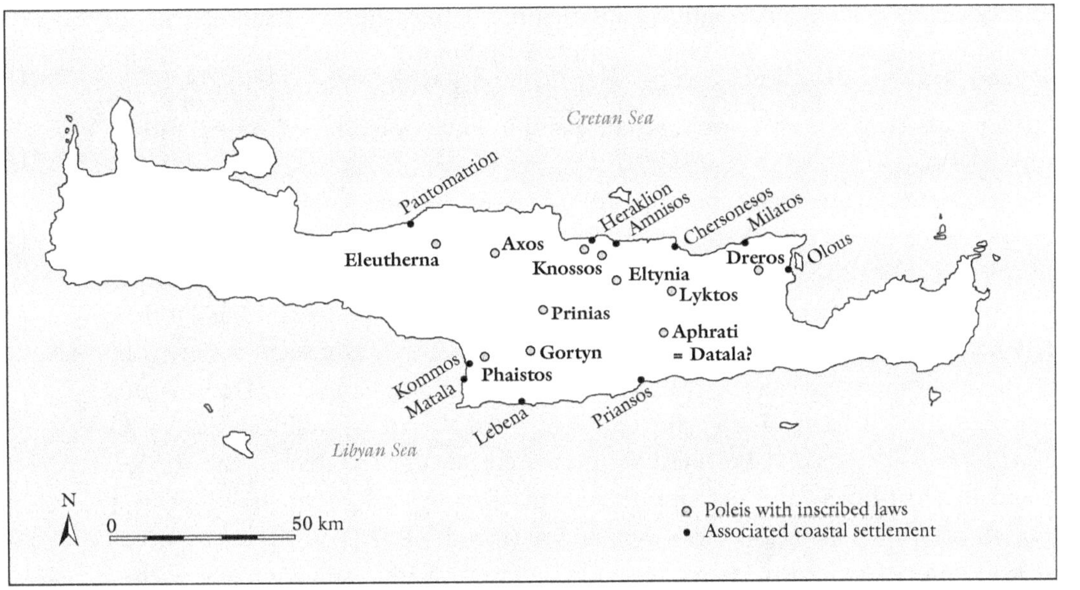

FIG. 1. Map of Crete

differences are apparent, notably for us in the practice of inscribing laws on stone for public display. Poleis elsewhere on the island, especially in the East, were well developed in the Archaic period, but with one possible exception only the poleis in the central region have yielded archaic or classical legal inscriptions.[5] Continuing excavation is making it increasingly unlikely that the poleis in the other two regions wrote legislation that has not yet been discovered, but whether they did not write legislation at this time or wrote it on materials that have perished is uncertain.

Homer may speak of Crete as a single military unit under the leadership of Idomeneus (*Iliad* 2.645, etc.), but he also knows Crete as composed of a hundred poleis (*Krētēn hekatompolin, Iliad* 2.649), several of which are named in the course of the epics. Herodotus too alludes to Crete as a military unit (3.59), and as a military/political unit when Greek envoys come to Crete to ask their help against Xerxes (7.169); the Cretans, according to Herodotus, consulted Delphi and then said no. But none of these passages indicates any clear knowledge that two or more poleis acted together politically or militarily. We know that in the Hellenistic period several Cretan poleis formed an alliance (the *Krētikon koinon*), and Greek scholars from the fourth century (Ephorus, Aristotle) and later often assume the existence of a specifically Cretan society beginning in the Archaic period, but we

[5] The possible exception is *IC* 3.6.1, an inscription from Praisos (east Crete) written boustrophedon in an epichoric alphabet resembling that of Lyktos but in the language dubbed Eteocretan. The text, dated to the sixth century, is carefully inscribed between horizontal guidelines on a wall block. Its monumentality suggests that it is a public enactment of some kind.

have no actual evidence of political unity before the third century (Perlman 2005). The inscriptions contain no hint of political unity and even the words 'Crete' and 'Cretan' are completely absent from the archaic and classical inscriptions. Agreements between two poleis are rare and involve only immediate neighbors (Introd. 8).

The absence of any formal political unity or close cooperation between poleis in this period, however, would not preclude the sort of unity that consists in having common political, social, or legal institutions that might have been part of the common cultural background of the Cretan poleis, often categorized as Dorian. As with dialect (Introd. 3C), however, the Dorian character of Cretan society is an oversimplification. Across the island, the mixtures of populations of Dorians and others appear to have varied, and to judge from the texts, political and social institutions also varied. The one common political office is that of the *kosmos*, found in most poleis and perhaps present in all; only at Gortyn, however, is a specialized *kosmos* named (*ksenios kosmos*, see Introd. 4C1b). Of the many other officials named at Gortyn, moreover, only one is explicitly named anywhere else, namely the *dikastas* (judge), mentioned more than twenty-five times at Gortyn but otherwise probably only once at Lyktos (**L3**B2–3). None of the other officials found at Gortyn—*mnamon*,[6] *gnomon*, *titas*, *startagetas*, *epottas*, *esprattai*, *karpodaistai*—is found in any other polis (Introd. 4C3, 4C5). With respect to the personnel of government, then, the inscriptions suggest unity only with respect to the leading official, the *kosmos*; otherwise they document considerable diversity.

Similarly, the only evidence for common social institutions is the mention of an *andreion* ('men's hall') in several different poleis (Introd. 6C). Little information is provided about this place, but it appears that meals were served in it: in **A1** sustenance (*tropa*) is provided there, in **Da1** a specific amount of meat must be provided to the *andreion*, and **G4** may mention drinking in the *andreion*. But we can only speculate about the function of these meals—when they were served and to whom. The later institution of common meals (*syssitia*) attested at Lyktos in the Hellenistic period is never mentioned in the laws (see Introd. 6C). We do know that there were 'produce-distributors' (*karpodaistai*) at Gortyn, who collected and presumably distributed produce, but we do not know whether this was done within the context of the *andreion*. The mention of sustenance in the *andreion* (**A1**.15) reminds one of the Athenian *prytaneion*, where certain officials and special honorees were given free meals, but this is only one of many possibilities.

[6] It is possible that Spensithios might have been called a *mnamon*, since his duties are 'to record and remember' (*poinikazen kai mnamoneuwen*, **Da1**A5–6); but he is identified throughout the agreement as the *poinikastas* and is never called a *mnamon*.

Besides the sharing of common meals in the *andreion*, other institutions commonly ascribed to classical Crete are also conspicuously absent from contemporary inscriptions. The rigorous military training, the separation and training of boys in age-groups,[7] the tightly controlled requirement for citizenship (limited to a small group of landowners), the inalienability of land—all these are missing from the inscriptions. Silence, of course, does not provide a secure basis for concluding that an institution is absent, and new discoveries could completely change our understanding; nonetheless, in our view, the picture presented by ancient writers of a substantial degree of Cretan unity and homogeneity in the Archaic and Classical periods is a mirage. Only in the few areas for which the inscriptions provide clear evidence is it legitimate to speak of Cretan unity or common Cretan institutions.

2. SETTING THE STAGE

In the absence of the kinds of ancient literary sources that might assist us in understanding the historical context of the advent of written law on Crete and provide a framework for interpreting the laws (Introd. 1), we are dependent on archaeological evidence, including the laws themselves, for both. The earliest of the Cretan laws have been dated to the second half of the seventh century, with the greater part inscribed in the sixth and fifth centuries (Introd. 3E).[8] Archaeologists have identified the late seventh and early sixth centuries (*c.*630–575) as a significant cultural horizon on Crete that is reflected in the archaeological record for burial customs, sanctuaries and ritual activity, and the organization of polis-towns,[9] and more generally in a qualitative transformation in material culture resulting in a much lower 'archaeological profile' in sixth- and early fifth-century Crete.[10] The causes of these changes and their political, social, and economic implications for sixth- and fifth-century Crete are the subjects of lively scholarly debate.

[7] The word *agelaos* apparently signifying an age-group occurs at Eltynia, but we know nothing more about it; see Introd. 6B.

[8] Far fewer laws survive from the fourth century on. Whether Cretans stopped enacting new legislation or abandoned the practice of inscribing their laws on stone and displaying them in public is an interesting question, but lies beyond the scope of this study.

[9] In addition to these internal cultural shifts, the material record of sixth-century Crete suggests a reorientation of overseas trade routes. For a detailed review of the evidence, see Erickson 2010a: 273–308. We discuss trade below (Introd. 7E2). Cross 2011: 126–71 offers a stimulating account of an 'emerging mercantilism' in late archaic and early classical Crete that emphasizes aspects of trade with low archaeological visibility.

[10] This reduced archaeological profile has been understood in the past as an actual gap in the material record. See Introd. 2B.

The likelihood that the practice of writing laws for public display[11] in Crete begins within this early archaic cultural horizon has not gone unnoticed. Scholars by and large agree that the laws were the product of socially complex communities and that they reflect the development of public institutions and the vesting in those institutions of authority over all members of the community. The role of the polis as the enacting authority in **Dr1**, possibly the earliest of the Cretan laws (and after the Gortyn Code (**G72**) the one most often cited by scholars), has encouraged the association of the changes that denote the early archaic cultural horizon with the 'emergence' or 'crystallization' of the polis in Crete (e.g. Kotsonas 2002). Less attention has been paid by archaeologists to what the content of the many other laws might contribute to their interpretation of the material record and by historians to the implications of the material record for their interpretation of the laws. Scholars of both disciplines have instead resorted to the later literary traditions in interpreting their respective data sets.

We have made an effort to consider the full range of archaeological evidence for the topics that concern us in the Introduction and when relevant in our discussion of the laws themselves, but do not claim to have achieved anything close to an adequate synthesis. Our main objective is the presentation of the laws. In order to establish a context for the laws we provide here a selective overview of the material record of early Crete, considering first the developments that define the early archaic cultural horizon and then some of the implications of the sixth-century archaeological record for the historian of archaic Crete. It is important to note that what archaeologists perceive as general trends in the material record vary, sometimes considerably, in their expression at the regional and local levels. We include brief discussions of the history and topography of the ten communities that enacted laws at the beginning of each of the individual sections of the Texts.

A. The Early Archaic Cultural Horizon

Significant change during the Early Archaic period (*c.*630–575) is particularly evident in three areas: burial practices, sanctuaries and related activity, and settlement patterns.

1. Burials

Recent studies of Cretan burial practices during the Early Iron Age (*c.*970–630) identify considerable regional variation,[12] locally in the practices of a single

[11] The majority of the inscribed laws from all periods were written on the walls of public buildings in the polis-towns of central Crete.

[12] Eaby 2011 identifies on the basis of burial methods and architecture six Early Iron Age 'burial regions' and three 'border zones' between burial regions. Two of the ten communities that inscribed laws on stone

cemetery, and diachronically.[13] Burial practices included inhumation and cremation,[14] single and multiple burial, and a variety of tomb types.[15] Burials were organized in both large cemeteries and smaller plots and are found singly. In some regions burial practices are quite homogeneous, providing little evidence of social stratification until quite late in the Early Iron Age;[16] in others there is considerable variation in the size and type of tomb and in the richness of the grave offerings.

Early Iron Age burials have been found in the vicinity of the later polis-towns of all of the communities that inscribed laws on stone apart from Gortyn and Lyktos. Particularly large and well-defined Early Iron Age cemeteries have been excavated at Aphrati (ancient Datala?), Dreros, Eleutherna, Kounavi (ancient Eltynia), Knossos, and Prinias.[17] Eaby (2011: 185–90) observes that during the Early Iron Age, these and other settlements that became poleis generally constructed large, well-defined cemeteries that were used for centuries and employed a variety of tomb types. By the ninth century inurned cremation was one of the most common forms of burial in central Crete. The funerary vases and the associated grave gifts (objects of ivory, metal, faience, and ceramic; both locally produced and imported exotica) were deposited in rock-cut and rock-built tombs.

Two characteristics of the burial practices of Early Iron Age Crete deserve special comment. First, collective burial was common. The earlier tombs, with a small number of individuals (typically one to five), have been understood as family tombs;[18] but in the Protogeometric period (tenth and ninth centuries) particularly large and rich tombs began to appear, which were used for several generations and held the cremated remains of many individuals (Wallace 2010a: 286–311; Eaby 2011). These have been taken to reflect increasing social complexity and the emergence of an elite that was organized in supra-familial associations,

in the Archaic and Classical periods (Axos and Eleutherna) are located in Eaby's West-Central region, one (Dreros) in the burial region designated Mirabello/West Siteia Mountains, one (Aphrati = ancient Datala?) in a border zone to the west of Mirabello/West Siteia Mountains, and the remaining six in the Central burial region.

[13] In addition to changes in burial practices that take place in the Early Archaic period (*c.*630–575) Wallace (2010a: 150–61, 286–311) discerns a shift beginning in the tenth century.

[14] Cremation is first attested in LM IIIC (*c.*1200–1100). See Wallace 2010a: 150–1.

[15] The most common tomb types are the tholos tomb, the chamber tomb, caves and rock shelters, pithos burials, pit graves, and burial enclosures. See Eaby 2011.

[16] The greatest degree of homogeneity in burial practices during the Early Iron Age is found in the Lasithi plateau (tholos tombs) followed by the Far Eastern region (tholos tombs and pit/pithoi tombs). See Eaby 2011.

[17] Some scholars have understood the coexistence of several distinct cemeteries at Knossos as evidence that the Early Iron Age community comprised several nuclei each with its own burial ground, although the settlement evidence does not appear to bear this out (see Introd. 2A3a). The North Cemetery at Knossos was perhaps the main cemetery.

[18] See Wallace 2010a: 150–63, who identifies the small collective tomb as a characteristic of Cretan burial practices during the twelfth and eleventh centuries.

often referred to without further definition as 'clans' (Introd. 4B3).[19] Secondly, scholars have noted the likely symbolic function of the large collective tombs with their monumental façades, rich offerings, and in seventh-century Eleutherna and Prinias impressive grave markers (Stampolidis 2004c: 134–6; Lebessi 1976). Eaby (2011) understands these burials in terms of competitive display among the extended families of an emerging elite. Wallace (2010a: 286–311) views them instead as a mechanism for creating and maintaining a coherent group of powerful and wealthy families that dominated public life in the large communities of central Crete during the Early Iron Age.

Beginning in the later seventh century, however, and continuing through the early sixth many Cretan communities abandoned their Early Iron Age cemeteries and changed their burial habits. New cemeteries were established, and henceforth most burials were modest, less archaeologically visible individual inhumations.[20] The dead were interred with few grave gifts and for the most part without grave markers.[21] Local expressions of this pattern vary in the communities that inscribed laws during the Archaic and Classical periods. Burials in this new style were introduced into the Early Iron Age cemetery of Patela Prinià̀s at Siderospilia shortly before the abandonment of both the settlement and the cemetery in the first half of the sixth century (Introd. 2A3; Prinias Site). At Knossos, the Early Iron Age cemeteries were abandoned *c.*630. Burials in any number do not resume until the fifth century; for the sixth century there are just two burials, both *c.*525 (Erickson 2010a: 249), and almost no settlement evidence. **K2** and other small fragments of epichoric inscriptions have been dated to the late sixth century at the earliest.[22]

At Aphrati (ancient Datala?) a new cemetery was established on the slope of the hill below the largest of the earlier (ninth to seventh centuries) cemeteries (Levi

[19] For the association of the large collective tombs with extended kinship groups or clans, see e.g. Wallace 2010a: 286–311. Cf. Kotsonas 2011, who cautions against assuming that the burial groups in collective tombs necessarily represent kinship associations. The 141 individuals identified in the cremation vases from tomb A1K1 at Orthi Petra, the Early Iron Age cemetery at Eleutherna, were almost all adult males (Agelarakis 2005: 30–40). Stampolidis (2004c: 116–38) suggests that this form of burial was reserved at Eleutherna for young adult males who formed the core of the community's political and military class. Their real or fictive kinship affiliation, if any, is not known.

[20] Individual cremations become popular in the seventh century and continue on into the sixth. See Kotsonas 2002: 42. For a review of archaic and classical burial practices with attention to local variation, see Erickson 2010a: 249–57.

[21] Sixth- and fifth-century grave markers are known from Eleutherna (one example), Stavromenos on the coast north of Eleutherna (one example), Achlada in north-central Crete (one example), Eltynia (one example), and perhaps Gortyn (*IC* 4.71). Three stelae with epigrams in what is possibly the Aiginetan script come from Kydonia. See Erickson 2010a: 7–8, 292.

[22] There is considerable debate about the history of sixth-century Knossos; see Introd. 2A3; 2B; Knossos Site. For a recent survey of the material record of sixth-century Knossos and assessment of the historical implications of the 'Knossian recession', see Erickson 2010a: 235–49.

1927–9: 381–7; Datala Site). At Eleutherna, whose cemetery is one of only five Cretan cemeteries of the Archaic period that have been excavated,[23] the move towards a more austere material culture is detectable already in the seventh-century burials at Orthi Petra (Kotsonas 2008: 340–1). Clusters of locally produced ceramics with an occasional import identify sixth-century burials in the disturbed levels above the Early Iron Age cemetery; the location, if not the burial practices, indicates 'a higher degree of continuity than documented at any other Cretan site' (Erickson 2010a: 43–51, 250 for quote). Lastly, at Axos an archaic (burial?) pithos is thought to have come from the cemetery located at the southwestern foot (at Teichio) of the settlement hill (Tegou 2013: 89; FIG. 4).

This early archaic transformation (*c.*630–575) in funerary practice suggests a significant change in mentality: rejecting what had been the traditional patterns of location and practice, the Cretans developed significantly new ones. If the earlier forms of collective burial emphasized membership in associations of some kind (e.g. kinship, age, social status, gender), the relocation of cemeteries and the de-emphasis on collective burial has been understood to indicate a decreasing desire (or need) to mark groups and reinforce membership claims. Wallace (2010a: 286–311) argues that by the late seventh century the authority of elite families was so firmly established that they no longer found it necessary to mark their coherence and status in their burial practices. Kotsonas (2002: 43) and Erickson (2010a: 255–6), on the other hand, suggest that the shift from collective to individual burial reflects the representation in death of a new, more inclusive corporate identity. We shall return to this subject and discuss the implications of the shift from material exuberance in burial practices to a more restrained or austere style below (Introd. 2B).

2. Sanctuaries and Ritual Activity

The rich evidence for Cretan sanctuaries and cults during the Early Iron Age (*c.*970–630) attests not only considerable diversity but also formal and regional patterns as well as diachronic development.[24] Prent (2005) discerns four patterns in the archaeological record of sixty-nine possible Early Iron Age sanctuaries and suggests specific social, political, and to some extent economic functions for the

[23] Sixth-century cemeteries have been excavated in west Crete at Phalasarna (where most of the burials date to the fifth century), Chania (ancient Kydonia), and south of Chania at Kastello Varypetrou (ancient name?), and in east Crete at Praisos (three tombs) and Itanos (Erickson 2010a: 250–3). The very low archaeological visibility of sixth-century burials has no doubt contributed to the fact that so few have been discovered. Erickson (2010a: 254) observes that on current evidence it does not appear that sixth-century burials were dispersed (e.g. on family farms) rather than gathered together in community cemeteries. See **G46B**.

[24] Two recent monographs focus on Cretan sanctuaries and cults during the Early Iron Age (Prent 2005) and the Classical and Hellenistic periods (Sporn 2002). Neither treats the sixth century or comments specifically on the early archaic cultural horizon.

cults associated with each of the four. These are in brief: urban sanctuaries with freestanding hearth temples associated with the construction and consolidation of adult male aristocratic identity; sub-urban sanctuaries situated in conspicuous locations near their settlements with more inclusive cults (age, gender, and social status?) that focused on social integration; sanctuaries established amidst the remains of Bronze Age palaces and towns that served to appropriate the past and in some cases establish territorial claims; and regional extra-urban open-air and cave sanctuaries established in the Minoan Neopalatial period (*c.*1700–1370/60) if not earlier that drew pilgrims from a number of Cretan communities and in some cases visitors from abroad as well.[25] Examples of each of these four types of sanctuaries are attested for the settlements, agricultural hinterlands, and frontiers of one or another of the ten communities of central Crete whose written laws are studied here.[26] We briefly explore two aspects of Early Iron Age record, freestanding hearth shrines/temples and dedicatory practices, that are particularly germane to the cultic expression of the early archaic cultural horizon (*c.*630–575).

The freestanding hearth shrine/temple, defined as a freestanding cult building consisting of one to three rooms in linear arrangement with a rectangular hearth in the centre of the main room, had replaced the 'bench shrine/temple' as the principal form of communal urban cult building by the eighth century.[27] The freestanding form of the earlier 'bench shrine/temple' can be traced back to the Postpalatial period (fourteenth–thirteenth centuries) and understood within the context of the disappearance of palatial control over ritual practice. The characteristic furnishings of this earlier building type were benches set against the interior of one or more walls of the main room of the shrine/temple and used for the presentation, display, and storage of votive objects. During the twelfth–eleventh centuries the bench shrine/temple was the standard form of communal cult building in newly founded settlements of the inland/upland defensible type.

[25] Prent (2005: 627) identifies a fifth pattern, viz. small rural largely open-air cult places with modest terracotta votives. Unlike the sanctuaries and cults of the other four patterns, these sanctuaries do not appear to have functioned within the social and political framework of the developing Iron Age polities.

[26] The distinction between urban and sub-urban sanctuaries is problematic in part because so little is known about the organization of settlements during the Early Iron Age. For example, the so-called 'temple of Aphrodite' at Axos, which Prent (2005: 248–50, B.6) identifies as a sub-urban sanctuary, was located on the eastern slope (not high up) of the settlement hill within (i.e. west of) a stretch of defensive wall that runs north–south along the gentler east slope of the settlement hill (FIG. 4). The date of the fortification is unclear. Coutsinas (2013: 229, 429 no. 33) admits the possibility that the wall is archaic on the basis of epigraphic evidence, but to the best of our knowledge none of the blocks with archaic inscriptions has been associated with this wall. We also note that at least some of the walls atop the west acropolis at Dreros (Prent 2005: 283–4, B.31) and high up on the settlement hill at Axos (Prent 2005: 248, B.5), which in the past have been attributed to temples, may be terrace walls (Axos Site; Dreros Site).

[27] For bench shrines/temples, see Prent 2005: 188–200, 424–41, 616–18; for hearth shrines/temples, see Prent 2005: 441–76, 627–33.

They are not attested at the continuously inhabited sites of central Crete where evidence for occupation by incomers is strongest. This observation together with the Bronze Age origin of the architectural form and the Minoan ancestry of the associated cult equipment (terracotta figures of the 'goddess-with-upraised-arms' type, terracotta stands known as 'snake tubes', and terracotta baskets (*kalathoi*) used for offerings) have been understood as evidence of a regional and historical pattern of cultural or even ethnic difference distinguishing the population of east Crete from that of the center.[28]

The substitution of the central hearth for the bench was not total; some Early Iron Age temples have both and in others fixtures identified as tables or the like, often placed next to or near the hearth, continue to provide a locus for the presentation and display of offerings. The recalibration of emphasis (from surfaces for display to hearths for sacrifice/cooking), however, surely reflects a shift in ritual focus and meaning, with the shared activities of sacrifice, food preparation, and feasting overshadowing that of votive ritual. Many of these buildings are small, however, indicating that only a few people could gather together inside; perhaps they attended on behalf of a larger group or the community as a whole (Klein and Glowacki 2009). The hearth temples at Kommos and Dreros are illustrative not only of these developments but also of the characteristic variety in form and presumably function and meaning of cult equipment and furniture of the Early Iron Age.

The sanctuary at Kommos, located on the coast at the western edge of the Mesara plain,[29] was established late in the eleventh or early in the tenth century when the first of two early temples (Temple A) was built in the midst of the ruins of a significant Minoan harbor town that had been abandoned around 1250 (Prent 2005: 323–30, B.57). Temple A had a bench and evidence for feasting (faunal remains), but no hearth; all three phases of Temple B (late ninth/early eighth to *c*.600) had benches, a hearth, and evidence of roasting and eating meat indoors. Temple B is the only extra-urban hearth temple thus far securely identified on Crete.[30] The focus of the cult during the eighth century was a tripillar structure, resembling in form a Phoenician tripillar shrine.[31] Evidence of Phoenician activity

[28] See Prent 2005: 616–19, who nonetheless cautions against reductionist oppositional explanations (e.g. Minoan descendants vs. Mainland Greek incomers) of a very complex picture. See Perlman 2014.

[29] The establishment of the sanctuary at Kommos has been understood to reflect the process of territorial expansion and consolidation on the part of the settlement at Phaistos and the revival of overseas communication in the tenth century. See Prent 2005: 523–37.

[30] For another possible extra-urban hearth temple (at Sta Lenika in east Crete), see Prent 2005: 348–9, B.67.

[31] Cf. the recently discovered 'trilithic structure' in room VD of the monumental building (eighth–seventh centuries) south of the so-called 'Temple B' at Prinias. See Palermo in Palermo, Pautasso, and Gigli Patanè 2008: 195–206.

at Kommos (the tripillar structure and Phoenician pottery, especially storage jars), beginning as early as the late tenth century, decreases after *c.*650 by which time the tripillar shrine appears to have been partially covered by a new hearth.

The so-called 'temple of Apollo Delphinios' at Dreros is possibly the earliest urban hearth temple thus far discovered on Crete (mid-eighth century?). In addition to its central hearth, this one-room temple was equipped with a complex installation comprising a tall stone platform or bench with a stone enclosure containing numerous wild goat (agrimia) horns, and a freestanding offering table. Small finds, primarily of the seventh century but also some earlier and later material (including Hellenistic), attest the activities of drinking, sacrifice, feasting, votive display, and storage (Prent 2005: 284–9, B.32). Theories about the function of hearth-temple cult identify different antecedents for the architectural form,[32] equipment (i.e. hearth), and the associated activities of sacrifice, cooking, and banqueting, but agree in associating the cult with political authority and an emerging elite.[33]

There are a few other eighth-century buildings of the sort described above (freestanding one-room buildings or more complex structures with two or three rooms in linear arrangement),[34] but the seventh century appears to have been the heyday of temple-building on Crete, and temple-building is generally acknowledged to be one of the notable features of seventh-century Cretan culture. Cult buildings (temples and more modest buildings or shrines) dating to the seventh century have been identified in central Crete at Aphrati,[35] Axos,[36] Dreros,[37]

[32] e.g. palatial Mycenaean megara and Early Iron Age domestic architecture. See Prent 2005: 442–50; 2007.

[33] Prent (2005: 441–76, 627–33; 2007) discerns functional and symbolic similarities in the practices of sacrifice and communal feasting inside these buildings with communal dining in other elite venues, i.e. the *andreion* and the *prytaneion*. For the *andreion*, see Introd. 6C. The term *prytaneion* is not attested in the early inscriptions from Crete.

[34] e.g. a three-room structure built perhaps as early as the mid-eighth century in the midst of an open-air sanctuary established on the southeast slope of Prophitis Elias (Aphrati) in the ninth century (Prent 2005: 279–80, B.28; Datala Site) and the monumental building VA/VD (later eighth–early seventh century) on Patela Priniàs. The function of the latter is uncertain, but ritual activity certainly took place in the westernmost room (VD). See Palermo in Palermo, Pautasso, and Gigli Patanè 2008: 195–206.

[35] A single rectangular benched room replaced the earlier three-room structure (above n. 34) in the seventh or early sixth century. Prent 2005: 279–80, B.28.

[36] Several fragments of limestone sculpture and several fragmentary blocks inscribed with archaic letters found in the area of the Hellenistic 'temple of Aphrodite' suggest the presence there of a late seventh- or early sixth-century predecessor (Prent 2005: 248–50). For the stone sculpture, see Rizza 1967–8: 285–9, figs. 55–7; D'Acunto 2001: 61–2. The inscribed blocks include *IC* 2.5.12–14 and possibly **Axos1**. *IC* 2.5.14c was found reused in a wall of the Hellenistic temple. See Axos Site with Fig. 4.

[37] Recent excavations on the west acropolis of Dreros have uncovered a seventh-century temple/shrine in the vicinity of an earlier (eighth-century?) open-air sanctuary (Dreros Site).

Eleutherna,[38] Gortyn,[39] Phaistos,[40] Prinias,[41] and Smari.[42] Most of these buildings were located in the urban centers of communities that enacted laws and inscribed them for public display, in several cases on the exterior of these buildings (see Introd. 3A). Sixth- and fifth-century temples are attested, with examples at Phaistos[43] and at locations where earlier temples have not been identified, in central Crete at Kounavi (ancient Eltynia),[44] Kalamaki (west of Phaistos),[45] and Knossos.[46] But there is a noticeable decrease in temple-building after the early archaic cultural horizon.

Turning next to dedicatory practices, the dedication of bronze armor (particularly helmets and mitras or loin guards) at urban sanctuaries, a votive practice of

[38] Two seventh-century buildings, possibly temples, have been identified at Eleutherna: one on Pyrgi, the eastern acropolis of Eleutherna (Kalpaxis 2004: 110–13; with 209, figs. 158–9); the other beneath the Hellenistic–Byzantine remains to the east of Pyrgi at Katsivelos (Themelis 2009a: 50–3, fig. 3). See Eleutherna Site with FIG. 36.

[39] Two seventh-century temples have been identified at Gortyn: the temple on Agios Ioannis (the so-called acropolis) attributed to a female deity who in the Classical period was probably identified as Athena Poliouchos (Prent 2005: 267–73, B.23; D'Acunto 2002); and the temple of Apollo Pythios located in the plain *c.*650 m. southeast of Agios Ioannis (Prent 2005: 274–5, B.24). The date of the construction of the latter temple is based solely on the date of the inscriptions, about which scholars disagree with suggestions ranging from the seventh century to *c.*600 at the earliest (Gortyn. Texts **G1–40**). See Gortyn Site with FIG. 45). A third structure tentatively identified as a temple is located about three kilometers northeast of Agios Ioannis on Mt. Vourvoulitis. The nature of the structure and its date are both uncertain. Prent 2005: 275–6, B.25.

[40] Cucuzza (1993) attributes the so-called 'temple of Rhea' (*c.*625–600) southwest of the Minoan palace to Leto. Fragments of architectural terracottas found near the church of Agios Georgios at Phalandra, in the saddle between Christos Effendi and Acropoli Mediana, indicate the probable location of a second temple. Cucuzza (2005: 299) associates these fragments with the small seventh-century structure that was partially excavated by Levi in 1958. See Phaistos Site with FIG. 68.

[41] Temple A (seventh century) and the slightly earlier neighboring building dubbed Temple B. For a description with bibliography up to 2000, see Prent 2005: 253–9, B.14–15. For Temple A, see also Pautasso 2013 and Pautasso in Lefèvre-Novaro et al. 2013 (with additional bibliography).

[42] Votive objects and sacrificial debris indicate the cult function of a small freestanding building (the so-called 'House of Athena') built amidst the remains of a small Minoan and Early Iron Age settlement on Smari Prophitis Elias (about six kilometers northwest of the polis-town of Lyktos) that was abandoned not long before its construction (Chatzi-Vallianou 2000, 2004).

[43] Terracotta and stone architectural elements indicate the location of a small public building, possibly a temple, on Acropoli Mediana (Cucuzza 2005: 299). Cucuzza dates the structure to the sixth or fifth century.

[44] See Eltynia Site.

[45] Cucuzza (1997: 64–70; 2005: 315–16) suggests that the church of the Panagia Evangelistria (near the village of Kalamaki about 2 km. north of Kommos) was the location of the temple of Artemis Toxia near Amyklaion (**G72.3.7–9**). If so, a temple was established there no later than the mid-fifth century. Cf. Sporn 2002: 210–11.

[46] A temple, attributed to the goddess Demeter, was erected late in the fifth century on the north slope of the Gypsadhes Hill in the midst of a sanctuary that goes back to the eighth (or late ninth?) century (Prent 2005: 262–3, B.19). A small shrine (of the local hero Glaukos?), consisting of a one-room structure with an attached courtyard, was established *c.*500 at the foot of Monasteriaki Kephala (the so-called acropolis) west of the Minoan Palace (Callaghan 1978).

the late seventh and early sixth centuries,[47] marks a shift in Early Iron Age dedicatory habits associated with large bronze votives.[48] In the preceding century (and possibly already in the late ninth) bronze shields and vessels, especially tripod-cauldrons, often in conjunction with other costly and exotic objects, were dedicated mostly at large, extra-urban regional sanctuaries.[49] Prent suggests that whereas the earlier eighth-century practices were characteristic of 'a process of ritualized competition between aristocratic members of incipient city-states... votive behaviour in the seventh century BC was aimed less at the articulation of an aristocracy, probably because of the full development of the polis and concomitant changes in ideology' (Prent 2005: 420, 422). Yet, the dedication of costly bronze armor most likely remained the privilege of the aristocratic members of the political community.

What changed in addition to preferences in what bronze objects were dedicated was the audience, from the supra-local audience of the extra-urban sanctuaries to an audience of local elite and presumably others from the community. The contrast between the costly and exotic objects dedicated in the eighth century along with bronze shields and tripod-cauldrons at extra-urban sanctuaries and the seventh-century votive types associated with bronze armor (e.g. anthropomorphic (especially female) terracotta figurines and plaques and miniature bronze and terracotta armor) at urban sanctuaries reflects a more diverse community of worshippers. This late seventh-century pattern of associated votive types (bronze votive armor and terracotta plaques and figurines) is attested in central Crete at Aphrati (in the disturbed fill of the seventh-century benched structure),[50] Axos (in the vicinity of the temple on the east slope of the settlement hill),[51] Dreros (associated with both temples, but in greater quantity on the west acropolis),[52] and Gortyn (in the votive dump on the east slope of Agios Ioannis).[53]

[47] Dating is largely on stylistic grounds (Hoffmann 1972).

[48] Prent 2005: 383–8; Erickson 2010a: 385–7.

[49] Prent 2005: 368–83. Cf. the bronze shields and cauldron found beneath the floor of the late seventh-century temple of Rhea/Leto at Phaistos. Cucuzza (1998: 67) suggests that the bronzes, although earlier than the date of the temple, were associated with ritual activity carried out in it.

[50] Prent 2005: 280. In addition to fragments of armor found at the site, a group of twenty-four pieces of late seventh- to early sixth-century bronze armor that appeared on the international art market may have been looted from this building complex (Hoffmann 1972). The inscriptions on fourteen of the pieces indicate that they were seized as booty (*SEG* 52.829–42). For the possible votive nature of this armor, see Perlman 2010: 101–2.

[51] The bronze armor was found in three deposits. Four deposits of terracotta figurines and plaques (mostly female) dating from the Protogeometric period (tenth/ninth centuries) to the fourth century were found in the same area (Prent 2005: 249–50 with Pilz 2011: 163–7 for the date of the terracottas).

[52] Prent 2005: 284. In addition, a deposit with vases (*kalathoi*) and animal figurines dating to the late eighth and seventh centuries was discovered in 2010 in the vicinity of the temple on the west acropolis (Dreros Site).

[53] Prent 2005: 269–71. The votive dump is associated with the sanctuary on top of Agios Ioannis.

The evidence for votive practices across the island and in all votive contexts attests a remarkably consistent and abrupt change in the first half of the sixth century. The offering of one-off objects made of bronze and other costly or exotic materials (e.g. ivory), rich in symbolism and worthy of display, ceases at every Cretan sanctuary, and is replaced by gifts of inexpensive, mass-produced objects of clay, especially utilitarian objects (e.g. cups and lamps) associated with the shared activities of sacrifice, feasting, and drinking.[54] Various explanations have been proposed for the abrupt disappearance of bronze offerings from sanctuary contexts and for the generally 'restrained' or 'austere' character of many of the clay objects deposited in sanctuaries and burials. Three aspects of the early archaic votive pattern—the decrease in the dedication of rich offerings worthy of competitive display, the increase in the mass-production of clay votives, and the dedication of utilitarian objects associated with shared ritual activities—may be understood to imply greater inclusivity in cult communities. We will consider further the social implications of Cretan 'cultural restraint' below (Introd. 2B).

Other aspects of the late seventh- and early sixth-century record suggest an increasing focus on the civic dimension of urban sanctuaries. The hearth shrine at Azoria in east Crete provides a concrete example of this. The construction of the shrine was part of a large-scale reorganization of the urban core of the settlement that took place late in the seventh or early in the sixth century (Haggis et al. 2011a; see Introd. 2A3b). The shrine occupies an upper terrace immediately north of the large benched hall (D500) of a building dubbed the Monumental Civic Building. The roughly rectangular main room of the two-room shrine (D900) is equipped with a central hearth and a table/altar apparently used for the presentation and display of a variety of objects, both natural and man-made. The only certain point of access to the shrine's terrace was via a stepped doorway in the north wall of the main hall of the Monumental Civic Building, indicating that although topographically discreet the shrine was conceived as an extension of the Monumental Civic Building. A corridor or porch, now eroded away, is believed to have extended along the western side of the shrine and access from the west may also have been possible (Haggis et al. 2011a: 30).

The small size of the shrine suggests that only a few individuals participated in the ritual activities performed within. Yet, those gathered in the Monumental

[54] Erickson 2010a: 264–6. Erickson (2010a: 262) observes that the discovery of several sixth-century life-size terracotta busts from the vicinity of the temple on the east slope at Axos suggests that 'at least some worshippers made a token effort to distinguish themselves from the pack'. Furthermore, **Da1**, inscribed on a bronze mitra and dated *c.*500, and the fragmentary bronze crest from a helmet discovered in the sixth-century Communal Dining Building at Azoria (Haggis et al. 2011a: 4–16) indicate that at least some bronze armor continued in circulation after the structural changes that occurred in the Early Archaic period (Introd. 2A3b).

Civic Building[55] and perhaps others assembled to the west of the shrine's terrace could have witnessed the comings-and-goings of the cult officials. Although it is not possible to define precisely the groups that met in the Monumental Civic Building, the evidence of communal feasting indicates that it 'apparently served functions that we normally associate with a variety of typically Greek civic venues (and associated polis institutions) that combined cultic, social, and political activities in contexts of public commensality' (Haggis et al. 2011a: 40).

The inscribing of laws on the walls of urban temples beginning late in the seventh century is perhaps the clearest expression of their civic dimension. The practice is securely attested only at Gortyn where the earliest laws (**G1–40**) were inscribed on the walls of the temple of Apollo. The blocks bearing the laws from Dreros (**Dr1–7**) were discovered in a Hellenistic cistern below and to the east of the eighth-century hearth temple. It is not certain that they came originally from the walls of the temple, but it is likely that they did. The situation at Axos is somewhat different. Although there probably was an archaic predecessor of the Hellenistic temple on the east slope (the so-called temple of Aphrodite) it is not certain that laws were inscribed on its walls (Axos Texts). Many of the laws of Axos, including **A1–7** and **11**, were probably inscribed on the massive terrace walls of an open-air sanctuary established in the seventh century if not earlier on the middle peak of the settlement hill (Axos Site, Texts).

It is not possible to claim with certainty that the sanctuary at Axos or the temples at Gortyn and Dreros were located near venues—buildings or open-air spaces—where members of the political community met on public business as we can in the case of the hearth shrine at Azoria.[56] It may be significant, however, that laws were not published, or at least the majority of them were not published, in sanctuaries strongly associated with the dedication of large bronze objects.[57] The pattern is most clearly attested at Axos, Dreros, and Gortyn,[58] and probably holds

[55] The excavators estimate that the benches along the walls of the main room would have seated sixty to eighty individuals, with standing room in the central space for up to 150 (Haggis et al. 2011a: 39).

[56] The large area with steps along its south and west sides that lies northeast of the hearth temple at Dreros, often referred to as the archaic agora and interpreted as a place of public assembly, may have been laid out in the Hellenistic period at the same time as the construction of the cistern (see Introd. 2A3, Dreros Site).

[57] It is worth observing that the inscriptions from the east Cretan polis of Praisos that are written in the Greek alphabet but in a language dubbed 'Eteocretan' were found in the vicinity of the sanctuary on Altar Hill (or 'Third Acropolis') where bronze votive armor (both full size and miniature) was also found. The earliest of the texts is inscribed in epichoric letters on a wall block and has been dated to the sixth century (*IC* 3.6.1). If it records a law, as is usually assumed, this is the only certain exception to the pattern attested in central Crete.

[58] Large bronze votives have not been discovered in association with sanctuaries at Eleutherna, Eltynia, Knossos, Lyktos, and Prinias (nor is it possible to conclude with certainty where the inscribed laws of these communities were displayed). At Aphrati (= Datala?) only one of the criteria (large bronze votives) is attested. In this connection it is worth noting that **Da1** is engraved on a bronze mitra (loin guard), a type of

for Phaistos as well, although the assemblage of bronze votives more closely resembles the earlier pattern of the late ninth and eighth centuries. While it is not possible to determine with certainty where **Ph1** was displayed, it was found at Chalara in the plain to the south of the Bronze and Early Iron Age settlements on the ridge and is most likely to be associated with the remains of monumental buildings found there (Introd. 2A3, Phaistos Site). It may be that the strong association of these sanctuaries with the exclusive practices of the communities' elite members made them inappropriate venues for the publication of laws that were meant for the entire community regardless of an individual's social or even civic status.

Finally, it is important to note that the inhabitants of Phaistos and Gortyn appear to have abandoned their Early Iron Age settlements in the course of the seventh century and moved down to the plain. There is little evidence of ritual activity in association with the temple of Rhea/Leto at Phaistos or the temple on Agios Ioannis at Gortyn after the early sixth century.[59] The reorganization of the polis-towns of these communities may well also have been a factor in the choice of location for the display of their laws.

3. Settlement Patterns and the Organization of Urban Centers

Scholars have detected signs of a significant shift in the pattern of Cretan settlement in the seventh century on the scale of the LM IIIC (twelfth-century) transformation. Characteristics of the LM IIIC transformation include a decrease in the number of settlements, a significant shift in settlement location from the lowlands (plains and coast) to inland and upland defensible sites, and the transition from a hierarchic pattern—with palaces and palace-towns serving as regional political, economic, and religious centers—to a non-hierarchic pattern of dispersed or clustered settlements.[60] The settlement pattern in central Crete (defined as the area between Mt. Psiloritis and the Lasithi mountains and from the north coast to the Mesara) differs somewhat from the west and east. Nowicki (2000: 14–15) attributes this to geography (no obviously defensible hills) and more populous settlements and better inter-site communication, which would have contributed to better defence.[61]

armor that occurs in votive contexts at Aphrati and elsewhere. However, **Da1** is not strictly a law but rather an agreement between the polis and Spensithios, and the nature of the text (very small letters which would be impossible to read at a distance) makes it almost certain that it was not intended for public display.

[59] Cf. D'Accunto 2002: 212–14, who argues that the sanctuary on Agios Ioannis was not abandoned during the Archaic and Classical periods. For the meager ceramic evidence for continued use of the sanctuary during these periods, see Johannowsky 2002: 103.

[60] Nowicki 2000. See further Introd. 2A3a.

[61] See also Wallace 2010b: 67; Haggis 2013: 68. The ten communities that enacted laws in the Archaic period are located in this central zone.

For the seventh century, when, as we have seen (Introd. 2A1), Early Iron Age cemeteries were abandoned, attention has also focused at the regional level on the abandonment of settlements and at the local level on urbanization, notably the construction of stone temples, and the relocation or reorganization of the urban core of the settlements that survived. Both have been understood to reflect a period of settlement aggregation with residents of one or more interdependent villages relocating to a village within the same cluster/region and a restructuring of the aggregated settlement, although it is not clear if the restructuring was a response to the aggregation process or preceded it.

The processes of settlement aggregation and urban core reorganization during the seventh century are nowhere more clearly observed on Crete than in the vicinity of the modern village of Kavousi in eastern Crete. Archaeological survey of the Kavousi region and excavation at Vronda, Kavousi Kastro, and Azoria document the establishment of these three settlements, each comprising about ten to twenty households (*c.*150–200 people), in the twelfth century.[62] The settlements were by no means static during the centuries following their foundation; excavators have tracked a number of significant developments that occur during the Early Iron Age.[63] Yet overall they present a picture of considerable stability. Around 600, however, the Early Iron Age settlement at Azoria was obliterated and rebuilt on a radically new plan that integrated several large residential structures with monumental public buildings and structures devoted to primary and secondary agricultural processing and storage as well as food preparation and consumption at a supra-household scale.[64] The settlements at Vronda and Kastro were abandoned by the early sixth century, the inhabitants presumably relocating to Azoria. At the time of the violent destruction of Azoria late in the sixth or early in the fifth century the settlement occupied an area of about fifteen hectares, significantly larger than its Early Iron Age predecessors in the Kavousi area.[65]

Elsewhere on Crete, the processes of settlement aggregation and urban core reorganization are not as clear as they are in the Kavousi region, nor does what evidence there is produce as consistent a picture of the early archaic cultural horizon as does the evidence from burials and sanctuaries. Kotsonas (2002: 48–50) attributes this at least in part to uneven archaeological exploration. Of the ten communities known to have enacted laws during the Archaic and Classical

[62] Haggis 2005; 2013. For twelfth-century Vronda, see Day, Klein, and Turner 2009; Day and Glowacki 2012. There was a second cluster of small settlements, also implicated in the aggregation process, nearby in the vicinity of the modern villages Avgo and Monasteraki.

[63] In addition to population growth that is reflected in domestic architecture at Vronda and Kastro (Haggis 2013: 74 fig. 4.4), Kastro underwent a major reorganization in the tenth century (Nowicki 2000: 99 with earlier bibliography).

[64] Haggis et al. 2007; Haggis et al. 2011a; Haggis et al. 2011b; Haggis and Mook 2011; Haggis 2013.

[65] Haggis 2013: 68. The EIA settlements are estimated to have occupied *c.*0.6–1.5 hectares.

periods, systematic excavation has revealed significant portions of the areas where the polis-towns of six were located: Dreros, Eleutherna, Gortyn, Knossos, Phaistos, and Prinias. For the others, only small-scale excavations, focusing for the most part on cemeteries and sanctuaries, have been conducted. Beyond the immediate area of the polis-towns archaeological exploration has by and large been limited to survey. A detailed understanding of the *longue durée* is, of course, beyond our grasp for a number of reasons.[66] Yet it is instructive to compare the archaeological evidence for the processes of settlement aggregation and urban core reorganization at the ten communities whose laws provide the focus of this study. In evaluating the historical context of the laws it is important to keep in mind the general patterns of settlement aggregation and urban core reorganization, the considerable diversity in settlement history, and the variety of expressions at the settlement level of the early archaic cultural horizon that the archaeological record suggests.

To understand developments in the early Archaic period, however, we must first briefly consider the earliest evidence of occupation in the vicinity of the later polis-towns *c.*1200–800 (Introd. 2A3a). We will then discuss the evidence for settlement aggregation and urban core reorganization in the period *c.*800–600 (Introd. 2A3b).

a. EARLIEST OCCUPATION IN THE VICINITY OF THE LATER POLIS-TOWNS, *C.*1200–800

Settlement close to the remains of the Minoan palaces and palace towns at Knossos and Phaistos was probably continuous (but not static) from the end of the Bronze Age. Knossos appears to have been strongly nucleated throughout the Early Iron Age (Coldstream 2000: 296–9; 2006; 2013: 346–51; Kotsonas et al. forthcoming). Notwithstanding the concurrent use there from as early as the ninth century of several separate cemeteries extending over a distance of five kilometers (from the cemetery at Mastamba in the north to the one on Gypsadhes Hill in the south), there is little evidence of outlying villages or isolated houses, apart from a house (tenth and ninth centuries) found beneath the Villa Dionysus northeast of the Minoan palace.[67] Postpalatial settlement was concentrated first in the immediate vicinity of the palace, extending right around its periphery without, apparently, extending over the remains of the palace itself.[68] Coldstream (2013: 348)

[66] e.g. the lack of excavation data from an extended period of time, significant overbuilding at several of the larger sites (notably Knossos and Agios Ioannis at Gortyn), human and natural processes that profoundly affect the archaeological visibility of the surface material on which survey analysis depends, and others.

[67] Coldstream and Hatzaki 2003. Cf. Kotsonas et al. forthcoming, who view these remains as evidence for the northern limit of the nucleated settlement.

[68] As Coldstream (2000: 296) puts it, the palace was 'a sacred island . . . surrounded by a busy and prosperous town'. There is some evidence of postpalatial activity (tenth–seventh century) in the palace's

estimates on the basis of excavated deposits that by the ninth century the urban nucleus occupied an area of *c.*12.5 hectares.

The core of the twelfth-century settlement at Phaistos appears to have been located on the summit of Acropoli Mediana where a massive wall may have added to the natural protection that the hill afforded.[69] Traces of ninth-century habitation extend from the hill Christos Effendi in the west to Chalara at the southern foot of Palace Hill in the east, an area of *c.*50 hectares (FIG. 68).[70] A significant residential quarter (ninth to early seventh centuries) developed to the southwest of the palace.[71] Burials (twelfth to eighth centuries) on the northern slopes of the ridge and in the hills to its northeast at Liliana and Kalyvia are associated with the settlement. The location well beyond the ridge of several others (both individual burials and cemeteries) also dating from the twelfth to the eighth centuries is understood to reflect a dispersed pattern of settlement.[72]

The settlement at Gortyn on the hill Agios Ioannis was established in the twelfth century or possibly late in the thirteenth. A second settlement was founded at Gortyn in the eleventh century to the east of Agios Ioannis on the hill Prophitis Elias (FIG. 45). Very little is known about the organization of either of these communities in their earliest phases (twelfth to ninth centuries), including where they buried their dead (Bejor and Sena Chiesa 2003; Allegro 1991). There is some evidence (pottery) for settlement in the plain by the tenth or ninth century, both from the area of the Roman Odeion and south of the Basilica of Agios Titos.[73] A third nucleated settlement was established sometime during the twelfth to tenth centuries high up on the hill Vourvoulitis, about three kilometers as the crow flies northeast of Agios Ioannis.[74] Although the area is unexcavated, it is possible to make out the walls of small structures on a terrace and higher up the hill the walls of a rectangular structure of uncertain date that has been identified as a shrine or temple on the basis of votive material visible on the surface.

West Court and Theatral Area. Coldstream (2000: 272–9; 2013: 349) imagines that these open areas were used by the postpalatial community for public gatherings.

[69] Borgna 2003: 317–53. The wall has been dated from the fourteenth to the eighth century (Cucuzza: 2005: 292–3; La Rosa 2013: 53–4; Coutsinas 2013: 279).

[70] Watrous and Hadzi-Vallianou 2004b: 342. If the entire area was densely settled, which is by no means certain, Wallace (2010a: 236–8) estimates a population of 6,000 to 13,000. La Rosa (2013: 55) cautions that much still remains to be learned about the organization and development of the Early Iron Age settlement(s).

[71] Levi 1961–2: 377–448. For the chronology, see Rocchetti 1974–5; Palermo 2001. A paved ramp provided access from the quarter to the palace's west court, presumably then visible (La Rosa 2005; 2013). The parallel with the evidence for the visibility of the West Court and Theatral Area at Knossos is worth noting.

[72] Bredaki, Longo, and Benzi 2009: 938–9, 968. But cf. Knossos.

[73] Pottery from the area of Roman Odeion: Pernier 1925–6: 7–9, 14–15 (stratified deposit); Erickson 2001 (residual pottery); from south of the Basilica of Agios Titos: Papadopoulos 1988.

[74] At Charkià Pervoli. La Torre 1988–9: 290–7; Prent 2005: 275–6.

The settlement at Prinias on the flat-topped hill Patela Priniàs also dates to the twelfth century (or perhaps slightly earlier?) as attested by the earliest burials in the cemetery at Siderospilia (thirteenth/twelfth–sixth century), *c.*500 m. northwest of the hill (Rizza 1991; Rizza and Rizzo 1984: 234–8) and by the significant quantity of twelfth-century material found in the deepest layers at many points on top of the hill and on the terraces cut into its southern slope (Perna 2007; Rizza 2008: 295–300; Pautasso 2013). Material dating to the following two to three centuries is scarce on the hilltop (Pautasso 2013: 84); the implications of this for the history of the settlement are not clear as burials appear to have continued at Siderospilia. If there was a recession, it appears to have ended by the ninth century when, in addition to an increase in material from the hilltop, a small cemetery was established near the Church of the Twelve Apostles, 250 m. north of the necropolis at Siderospilia.[75] A better understanding of the chronology of the extensive residential areas on top of the hill to the east of Piazzale TZ and below on the south terrace must await the second part of the publication of the excavations conducted in 1969–2000 (FIG. 70).[76]

Evidence for the establishment of the remaining settlements as early as the twelfth century is much less secure. Nowicki reports the presence of some twelfth-century pottery visible on the surface of the summit of the hill where the polis-town of Axos was located[77] and eleventh- or possibly twelfth-century pottery on the surface of the hill Aphrati Prophitis Elias (= Datala?).[78] The earliest material recovered from excavation at both sites is considerably later: tenth-century (or possibly late eleventh?) in the case of Axos; late ninth-century in the case of Aphrati Prophitis Elias.[79] The earliest burials in the cemetery at the northern foot of the east acropolis of Dreros date to the twelfth century (Dreros Site), but the evidence for contemporary habitation on the hill Agios Antonios where the

[75] Biondi (2011) observes that the cemetery may have been a decentralized part of the larger cemetery at Siderospilia or may have served a small settlement in the agricultural zone controlled by Prinias.

[76] Rizza (2008: 295–302) provides a brief discussion of the chronology.

[77] Nowicki 2000: 193. Taramelli (1899: 314) identified 'Mycenaean' potsherds on the summit.

[78] Nowicki 2000: 180. It is important to keep in mind that the identification of Aphrati with ancient Datala is by no means certain (Datala Site). Tombs dating to the eleventh or possibly even the twelfth century are located near Aphrati Prophitis Elias at To Kephali tou Kophina (Halbherr 1901a: 283–7). It is unclear if this cemetery should be associated with the settlement on Aphrati Prophitis Elias or with an unidentified settlement closer to it (Nowicki 2000: 180; cf. Wallace 2010a: 296).

[79] Axos: burials in the cemetery at Teichio and the earliest terracotta figurines from the deposits associated with the later temple on the east slope of the settlement hill (the so-called temple of Aphrodite) appear to be Protogeometric (tenth to ninth centuries). See Axos Site. Aphrati Prophitis Elias: ninth-century burials from the cemetery on the upper west slope of Aphrati Prophitis Elias (Levi 1931: 78–400 for the geometric and orientalizing cemetery) and ninth-century material from what appears to have been an open-air sanctuary on the southeast slope several hundred meters from the summit (Lebessi 1970).

polis-town was located is scanty.[80] Gaignerot-Driessen (2013: 96, 107–12) suggests that the twelfth- (and eleventh-?) century burials were associated with the contemporary settlement on Kephali Limnes, a hill located just east of the cemetery. The settlement there was abandoned in the ninth century; it seems likely that the residents relocated to the far more spacious hill of Agios Antonios. At Eleutherna a significant quantity of twelfth-century pottery was excavated on the summit of Pyrgi, where the civic center of the archaic polis-town may have been located, but the nature of the activity that this material represents is unclear.[81] The ninth-century burials from the cemetery at Orthi Petra on the west slope of Pyrgi provide the earliest excavated evidence of settlement at Eleutherna (Eleutherna Site).

The settlement history of the area where the polis-town of ancient Eltynia is thought to have been located (near the village of Kounavi) is largely unknown apart from some chance finds of the late Archaic and Classical periods and the rich cemetery with burials dating from the eleventh to the eighth centuries that was excavated near Kounavi (Eltynia Site). Even less is known about Early Iron Age Lyktos. Nowicki (2000: 177–8) identified pottery dating from the twelfth to the eighth centuries on the surface of the ridge with the chapels of Agios Giorgios and Timios Stavros where the polis-town is believed to have been located (Lyktos Site), but the earliest excavated remains are much later (seventh century).

b. SETTLEMENT AGGREGATION AND THE REORGANIZATION OF URBAN CENTERS, C.800–600

Not much can be said about the settlements at Axos, Aphrati Prophitis Elias (Datala?), Kounavi (Eltynia), and, surprisingly, Dreros during the eighth and seventh centuries. Votives attest the continuation of ritual activity at the open-air sanctuaries at Axos (east slope), Aphrati (southeast slope), and Dreros (west peak), and burials continue to be made in the Early Iron Age cemeteries. Structures, probably temples, were built in the vicinity of the earlier open-air sanctuaries at Dreros and Aphrati in the seventh century. The hearth temple in the area of the so-called agora at Dreros is usually assigned to the mid-eighth century, largely on the basis of the famous triad of bronze figures that was found in it, but the new excavations may change this (Dreros Site). The cemetery at Kounavi appears to have been abandoned at the end of the eighth century; those at Aphrati and Dreros reflect the pattern of abandonment in the seventh.

[80] Nowicki (2000: 173) reports the presence of potsherds (twelfth to ninth centuries) 'at many spots on the summit and highest slopes of the hill'. See Dreros Site.

[81] The twelfth-century pottery was concentrated in a rather small area (*c.*30 m.^{2}) and included prepalatial potsherds (late fourth–late third millennium) as well. Kalpaxis (2004: 106–7), who excavated the area, does not indicate if the material was stratified or mixed; he identifies the archaeological context as a deposit ('repository') associated with 'an isolated installation'. Kanta (1994: 72) interprets the material as evidence for the location of a refuge settlement. Cf. Nowicki 2000: 193–4.

There is very slight evidence for the process of aggregation in the eighth century at Dreros (abandonment of the early settlement at Kephali Limnes) and Prinias (abandonment of the cemetery near the Church of the Twelve Apostles). The more compelling examples are seventh century. We begin, however, with Eleutherna where on current evidence it is not possible to determine if the community ever coalesced into a strongly nucleated polis-town (FIG. 36). The preliminary publications of the excavations of The University of Crete, which document traces of habitation and ritual activity at several locations on the ridges Pyrgi and Nisi, seem to suggest that occupation was dispersed during the seventh century,[82] although to date only one early cemetery (at Orthi Petra) is known, just the opposite of Knossos, where the concurrent use of multiple cemeteries belies the strongly nucleated character of the settlement! Although Pyrgi is usually identified as the center of the polis-town, the evidence does not appear to be particularly strong (Eleutherna Site). The dramatic shift in burial practices attested at Orthi Petra at the beginning of the sixth century, if not the abandonment of the cemetery, marks the early archaic cultural horizon at Eleutherna.[83]

Gortyn provides the strongest case for settlement aggregation in the seventh century. Little is known about the development of the settlement on Agios Ioannis during the eighth and early seventh centuries apart from the construction towards the middle of the seventh century of the temple in the vicinity of the early (ninth century?) sanctuary (Introd. 2A2; Gortyn Site). The settlement on Prophitis Elias flourished during the eighth and early seventh centuries; its parallel terraces bounded by east–west roads and blocks of houses separated by spacious courtyards exhibit clear signs of urban planning (Allegro 1991; 2010; 2012). With the abandonment of these settlements and the one on Vourvoulitis in the seventh century,[84] the core of the aggregated settlement is presumed to have developed in the plain east of the Mitropolianos river and south of the hills, although traces

[82] Stampolidis 2004a: 85; 2004c: 117; Kalpaxis 2004: 107–10. Traces of the early settlement at Eleutherna include small pits (possibly industrial) and walls that may belong to a habitation at Xeniana (Stampolidis 2004a: 84–5), the 'Geometric-Archaic megaron' at Katsivelos (Themelis 2002: 25–31; 2004: 48–9), walls belonging to the large building (a temple?) on Pyrgi (Kalpaxis 2004: 110–13), and votive offerings attesting the location of other early sanctuaries on Nisi (Stampolidis 2004a: 83–4; Kalpaxis 2004: 109) and Pyrgi (Kalpaxis 2004: 111).

[83] The sixth-century material from Orthi Petra comes from disturbed levels above the Early Iron Age cemetery. Erickson (2010a: 43–51) associates the material with sixth-century burials, but it could reflect post-funerary cult, in which case there is no evidence for burial in the cemetery after the seventh century.

[84] Significant overbuilding on Agios Ioannis makes it difficult to develop a clear picture of its settlement history. Di Vita (2010: 37) questions the view that habitation on the hill ceased after the seventh century. As at Kavousi Vronda, some habitation may have continued on Prophitis Elias into the early sixth century. Allegro (2012) tentatively identifies an enclosure built on the ruins of houses on an upper terrace of the settlement as the temenos wall of an open-air sanctuary; pottery from the terrace's fill dates from the seventh century to the Hellenistic period. The view that the settlement on Vourvoulitis was abandoned in the seventh century is based on surface material.

of the seventh- and sixth-century settlement in the plain are very scanty.[85] In addition to the construction of the temple of Apollo Pythios, usually dated to the later seventh century, a small amount of pottery of this period is documented from the recent excavations in the area of the Odeion, the number of potsherds increasing slightly across the eighth, seventh, and sixth centuries, with a notable concentration *c.*525–500.[86] And a pottery workshop contemporary with the final phase of the settlement on Prophitis Elias (*c.*650–575) was discovered on the lower south slope of the hill, about one kilometer east of the area that Di Vita identified as the core of the archaic settlement.[87]

The process of aggregation arguably played a role in the development of the polis-towns of Lyktos and Phaistos, although the evidence is less compelling than in the case of Gortyn. Small-scale excavations attest habitation from the seventh century on the ridge where the polis-town of Lyktos was probably located (Lebessi 1975a; 1980), but the area has not been explored systematically, and the organization and development of the settlement during the Archaic and Classical periods remain largely unknown. The abandonment in the mid-seventh century of the Early Iron Age settlement on Smari Prophitis Elias, located about six kilometers northwest of Lyktos, has been ascribed to the aggregation process, the inhabitants relocating to the more spacious ridge to the southeast.[88] The surface remains at Kalo Chorio Maza, about a kilometer northeast of Smari Prophitis Elias, suggest a similar settlement history, although the date of its abandonment (eighth century or later?) is uncertain.[89]

The pattern of dispersed settlement in the western Mesara, the hinterland of archaic and classical Phaistos, attested by burials for the twelfth to ninth centuries

[85] Di Vita (2010: 37) suggests that the urban center of archaic and classical Gortyn occupied the area from the hills south to the temple of Apollo Pythios and from the Mitropolianos river east to the bed of a stream that flows down from Pervolopetra about 100 m. east of the temple of Apollo (FIG. 45).

[86] Erickson 2001. It is important to note that the pottery comes from later contexts and that the numbers overall are very small: one sherd from the eighth century; seven from the seventh; nineteen from the sixth. Erickson implies that the 525–500 bump may represent a significant phase in the development of the area, possibly as civic space.

[87] Santaniello 2004. The workshop was discovered during remodeling of the campus of the Italian School at the northern edge of the modern village Agii Deka. Santaniello compares its location—at some distance from an area of dense habitation—with the settlement on Patela Priniàs and the associated pottery workshop at Mandra di Gipari, but it is unclear if she associates the workshop at Agii Deka with the settlement on Prophitis Elias or the settlement that was developing at the edge of the plain to the west.

[88] At Troulli tis Korifis (Chatzi-Vallianou 1980; 2000; 2004). Three adjacent megaron-like buildings occupied the central area of this fortified settlement; additional rooms/structures were built against the interior of the circuit wall. In the seventh century, apparently after the abandonment of the Early Iron Age structures, a small freestanding cult building was erected within the fortification wall. Wallace (2010a: 269) identifies the sanctuary as a territorial cult place of Lyktos.

[89] Nowicki 2000: 175–7, no. 75. Nowicki (2000: 177, no. 76) implies that Kalo Chorio Maza was a dependency of Lyktos.

is further documented by settlement evidence for the eighth and early seventh centuries, e.g. in the vicinity of the modern village of Agios Ioannis in the plain to the south of the ridge and at Marathovigla on the far side of the plain to the southeast (FIGS. 2, 68; Bredaki, Longo, and Benzi 2009: 938–9, 968; 2012: 939). Occupation of the ninth-century residential areas southwest of the palace and at Chalara at the foot of Palace Hill continues through most of the seventh century. Late in the seventh century, however, the significant residential area southwest of the palace was abandoned once and for all. Habitation continued at Chalara and possibly at Agia Photini (above eighth-century pottery kilns) (FIG. 68).[90] Beyond the ridge the archaeological record has been interpreted to indicate two seemingly contradictory developments: the end of dispersed settlement in the western Mesara marked by the absence of securely dated sixth-century burials and surface evidence of settlement[91] and the establishment during the period *c*.625–550 of a ring of small sites (farmsteads?) at the edge of the agricultural catchment within one to two kilometers of the ridge (Watrous and Hadzi-Vallianou 2004a: 313–14; 2004b: 343).

The absence of sixth-century burials and settlement evidence at some distance from the ridge might be understood to reflect settlement aggregation. Watrous and Hadzi-Vallianou (2004b: 343) tentatively interpret the ring of small sites closer to the ridge as newly created farms (*klaroi*) associated with a political reorganization of the community and a redistribution of land. It is important to emphasize, however, the difficulty in identifying the sixth-century pottery of Phaistos and the western Mesara from survey in the absence of relative chronologies developed through excavation (Bredaki, Longo, and Benzi 2009: 939). The core of the settlement is presumed to have moved down from the ridge to the plain. As in the case of Gortyn there is little positive evidence for this or mutatis mutandis for the organization of the polis-town, although there are reasons to recommend the area south of the village of Agios Ioannis as a possible location of the civic center (Phaistos Site).

The change in the settlement pattern in the western Mesara late in the seventh century, if correctly perceived, appears to be reflected as well in the sanctuaries at Kommos and Agia Triada where excavation evidence, terracotta figurines and imported vases in particular, are of fundamental value in clarifying the history of

90 For the temple built in the later seventh century over the remains of the residential area southwest of the palace, see Introd. 2A2, Phaistos Site; for archaic and classical architectural fragments indicating the existence of other public buildings, probably temples/shrines, on the ridge, see Phaistos Site.

91 Bredaki, Longo, and Benzi 2009: 939. Seventh-century burials have been identified north of the Ieropotamos river at Taphos tou Loghiou and Lilianà (Cucuzza 2011: 363–5) and possibly at Petrokephali west of the eighth-century settlement at Marathovigla (Watrous, Hadzi-Vallianou, and Blitzer 2004: 533, no. 51).

the sanctuaries. Control of the sanctuary at Kommos, located on the coast six kilometers southwest of Phaistos, during the Early Iron Age and the Archaic and Classical periods is unclear.[92] Activity at the sanctuary increased during the second phase of Temple B (*c.*750–650). Prior to its abandonment around 600, Temple B appears to have suffered from neglect and vandalism. Around 550 the focus of ritual activity shifted to a newly built open-air altar (altar H), but activity overall appears to have fallen off thereafter until early in the fourth century.

At Agia Triada, situated on a low hill three kilometers west of Phaistos, an open-air sanctuary established in the midst of the ruins of the Bronze Age town in the twelfth century was abandoned early in the seventh. D'Agata (1998) assigns the Early Iron Age votives from the sanctuary to two phases: twelfth to eleventh centuries and late ninth to early seventh centuries. Agia Triada must have lain within the territory of Phaistos during the Archaic and Classical periods. Wallace (2010a: 315) suggests that Phaistos appropriated this open-air sanctuary during its second phase, reactivating the dormant cult place in connection with the process of territorial consolidation, but uncertainty about the nature of settlement on and in the vicinity of the ridge (small dispersed villages or a large town with outlying hamlets) during this period makes this no more than a guess. D'Agata (1998: 24) attributes the partial abandonment of the sanctuary at Agia Triada in the seventh century to the completion of this process and a new focus on civic cult at Phaistos (e.g. the construction of the temple southwest of the palace).

Gypsadhes Hill, where an open-air sanctuary was established in the eighth century (FIG. 57), appears to have marked the southern limit of the post-palatial settlement at Knossos. Wells discovered in the vicinity of Venizeleio Hospital, *c.*900 meters north of the Minoan palace, indicate habitation in the area during the late eighth and seventh centuries (Coldstream 2000: 297). It is unclear whether the settlement extended north from the palace all the way to the wells or the wells represent a small outlying settlement to the north of the urban core. The few fragments of early inscriptions that appear to be public enactments come from the area of the Roman Civil Basilica located between the palace and the hospital (Knossos Site, Texts), suggesting that the civic center of the polis-town was nearby. Much of the area between the palace and the hospital is planted in vines and so archaeological exploration has been minimal; even so, the preliminary results of the Knossos Urban Landscape Project indicate that the Early Iron Age settlement was much larger than has been appreciated heretofore.[93] The

[92] Shaw 2000b and Phaistos Site. Postpalatial activity in the vicinity of the important Minoan harbor town begins in the late eleventh or early tenth century when Temple A was built.

[93] Bennet et al. 2008; Bredaki et al. 2010; Kotsonas et al. 2012; Kotsonas et al. forthcoming. Kotsonas et al. (forthcoming) estimate the size of the urban nucleus of the early Greek city at *c.*40 hectares, although at what point before the sixth century the settlement reached this size is not clear.

archaeological record seems to point to sustained expansion from the initial postpalatial nucleus northwards until late in the seventh century when the rich Early Iron Age cemeteries were abandoned (by *c.*630–620) followed within a generation by an interruption *c.*590–525 in the material record from all other contexts.[94] None of the scenarios proposed in explanation of this gap in settlement (i.e. temporary abandonment) or recession (i.e. temporary contraction, but not necessarily abandonment) answers all of the possible objections.[95]

Four monumental buildings dominate the top of the hill to the west of Piazzale TZ at Patela Priniàs. From the south these are Building VA/VD, the structure with Room VE, Temple B, and Temple A. The first three of these buildings, the walls under Temple A, the residential areas to the east of Piazzale TZ, and the residential area on the southern slope of the hill all seem to share the same orientation (FIG. 70).[96] The chronological implications of this are not clear. Building VA/VD and the building with Room VE appear to have been built in the later eighth century or early in the seventh;[97] the same is probably the case for Temple B and the structures that lie under Temple A. Building VA/VD combines an anteroom and a large hall with a central hearth (VA/VB) with what appears to be a two-room cult complex (VC/VD).[98] The remodeling of room VB and repurposing for an industrial use in its final phase (late seventh–early sixth century?) has made it difficult to understand the interior layout and function in its first phase. Room VE, part of the structure that lies immediately to the north of Building VA/VD, appears to have served as a repository for cups, cooking utensils, and dining debris associated with banqueting (Gigli Patanè in Palermo et al. 2007: 288–92; Gigli Patanè in Palermo et al. 2008: 188–94). The structures in the two residential areas are organized in blocks bounded by wide paths running perpendicular to one another (N–S and E–W). Temple A was built in the seventh century to the north of and with a slightly different orientation than the earlier monumental structures to the west of Piazzale TZ in an area where there is evidence of ritual activity, eating, and drinking for all phases of the life of the

94 Coldstream and Huxley 1999: 289–92 (for the abandonment of the cemeteries); Erickson 2010a: 115–64 (for the material record from other contexts).

95 Erickson (2010a: 235–45) rehearses previous attempts to explain the archaeological record (e.g. failure to recognize sixth-century pottery, environmental crisis, human agency). He favors human agency, identifying Gortyn as the agent, noting in support the abandonment of Patela Priniàs, which commands the principal route from the Mesara to the north coast east of Mt. Psiloritis. It is worth pointing out that the abandonment of Patela Priniàs has been dated as late as *c.*550, considerably later than the date proposed for the failure of the material record at Knossos.

96 For the walls under Temple A, see Pautasso in Palermo et al. 2008: 179–86.

97 Palermo in Palermo et al. 2008: 205. The pottery workshop east of the plateau at Mandra di Gipari was also established *c.*700 (Rizza, Palermo, and Tomasello 1992).

98 Palermo et al. 2007: 292–9; 2008: 195–206. A trilithic structure at the rear of VD resembles the tripillar monument in Temple B at Kommos (eighth–early seventh century).

community (Pautasso in Palermo et al. 2007: 267–78; Pautasso in Palermo et al. 2008: 179–88; Pautasso 2013; Pautasso in Lefèvre-Novaro et al. 2013). The settlement was abandoned, apparently without any signs of recession, sometime in the first half of the sixth century, remaining uninhabited for the duration of the Archaic and Classical periods. As in the case of Knossos, the cause is at present unclear.

With the lens set at its widest aperture the settlement histories of these ten communities during the Early Iron Age and early Archaic period appear quite similar: settlements are either founded by the twelfth century or established in the eleventh, tenth, or ninth centuries in areas where twelfth-century activity of some kind is attested; they undergo significant growth and urbanization in the eighth and early seventh centuries; and some are abandoned in the later seventh and early sixth century and the urban centers of those that survive are reorganized. Yet the spotty state of the archaeological record notwithstanding, it also suggests significant differences in the settlement history of these communities and cautions against assuming a shared Cretan or even central Cretan experience to the exclusion of important settlement-specific ones.

Settlement in the vicinity of the Minoan palaces at Knossos and Phaistos was continuous following the collapse of palatial society. Postpalatial Knossos appears to have been strongly nucleated from the start, whereas at Phaistos, burial and settlement evidence suggests a dispersed pattern through the seventh century in what would later comprise the hinterland of the archaic polis-town and perhaps on the ridge as well where the palace and palace town had been located. The settlements on Agios Ioannis (Gortyn) and Patela Priniàs were founded in the twelfth century at the beginning of the unstable period following the collapse of palatial society. Several settlements were established by the tenth century within a few kilometers of one another on the hills above the plain where the polis-town of Gortyn later developed. There is scant evidence for a similar settlement cluster in the vicinity of Patela Priniàs during the Early Iron Age.

Despite their different early histories, a strong argument can be made for settlement aggregation in the cases of Gortyn and Phaistos and for the urban core reorganization that presumably accompanied the abandonment of the villages and hamlets on the hills and in the plain, but there is disappointingly little evidence on the ground for the organization of the new towns. The laws refer to some of the components that may have been provided early on—the agora (market/civic center), the gymnasium, the *andreion* (men's hall), new urban and country houses, temples and so on—but we know next to nothing about the location and plan of the public centers, the location of residential areas or the plans of houses, the locations and types of burials, provisions for defense, or the spatial relationship of these parts to the whole (see Introd. 2C).

It is tempting to turn to the newly-built town at Azoria as a model in imagining the towns of archaic Gortyn and Phaistos, but we should be cautious in doing so.

Prinias offers the clearest picture we have of the organization of a large Early Iron Age settlement in central Crete, but it was strongly nucleated from the time of its foundation in the late thirteenth or twelfth century and may have experienced its most significant phase of (re)building in the later eighth or early seventh century, well before the early archaic cultural horizon. The townscape that we should probably imagine at the time of the enactment of **Pr7** is that of a mature town, with large probably public buildings, which were about one hundred years old at the time (*c*.600), opening onto a central plaza where a stone temple (Temple A) was built sometime in the seventh century. Its construction must have caused considerable disruption, requiring as it did the remodeling of the northern part of the plaza and the destruction of some buildings that used to occupy this prime real estate. New stone temples were erected at about the same time at Gortyn and Phaistos in the vicinity of earlier residential areas (on Agios Ioannis and southwest of the Minoan palace respectively), but the remodeling and construction at Prinias do not compare with the radical transformation, involving the creation of new blended communities and new urban centers, that Gortyn and Phaistos may have experienced at the end of the seventh century.

B. *Sixth-Century Cretan Austerity and Exceptionalism*

In broad outline, then, the early archaic cultural horizon (*c*.630–575) attests some population mobility, discernible mainly in the abandonment of settlements whose former inhabitants presumably relocated to a neighboring town. Where habitation continued, the residents established new cemeteries in the late seventh and early sixth centuries and established new forms of modest, less archaeologically visible burial (individual pithos cremations or individual interment in simple cist graves with at most a few vases as grave gifts). At a few places, these new forms of burial are attested in Early Iron Age cemeteries at about the same time. Signs of activity at extra-urban sanctuaries, both those that were established in the Minoan Neopalatial period (*c*.1600–1360) if not earlier (e.g. the cave sanctuary of Zeus on Mt. Ida) and others established at the start of the Early Iron Age amidst the remains of Minoan settlements (e.g. the sanctuaries at Agia Triada and Kommos) decrease. Ritual activity intensifies at some urban and sub-urban sanctuaries where sixth-century preferences in votive objects—mass-produced and utilitarian objects associated with shared ritual activities—may be understood to imply more inclusive cult communities.

1. Sixth-Century Cretan Austerity

The changes in the types of goods deposited with the dead and objects dedicated at sanctuaries are characteristics of sixth-century Cretan culture that many scholars have considered as signs of economic recession, cultural 'revolution', or both. The observation that grave gifts and votive objects alike indicate a dramatic and island-wide decrease in imports and inspiration from the east has been understood to support the view that Crete suffered an economic and artistic recession during the sixth century. Attention has focused on the decline and collapse of the Assyrian empire late in the seventh century and the effects of Nebuchadnezzar's subsequent campaigns in Syria on the Phoenician-controlled trade routes that brought copper, tin, and eastern luxury goods to the island.[99]

The discovery of imported pottery (Corinthian, Attic, Laconian, and Cycladic) in Crete during the sixth century proves that Cretans were not cut off from foreign markets (or inspiration) following the early archaic cultural horizon. Scholars are beginning to understand better the sixth-century overseas exchange networks in which the communities of Crete participated and to recognize complex intra-island patterns of exchange and consumption (Introd. 7E2). Furthermore, it is clear that the knock-on effects of the collapse of the Assyrian empire are not sufficient to explain several characteristics of sixth-century Cretan artistic production and consumption, e.g. the failure to substitute objects made from locally available iron for imported bronze, the preference for imported black-glazed pottery rather than more elaborately decorated figural styles, and perhaps most notably the failure to continue earlier local traditions of linear and figural decoration of pottery.

Ceramic tableware produced on Crete during the sixth century is characterized by its simplicity in decoration (linear and figural decoration, both narrative and non-narrative, on locally produced tableware is virtually absent),[100] its narrow range of shapes (archaeologists identify the one-handled, high-necked drinking cup as the most common shape), and its significant homogeneity across the island.[101] In all three respects sixth-century tableware contrasts with earlier

[99] Aubet 2001: 343–5 (Assyrian collapse and Phoenician trade). Erickson (2010a: 279–81, 298–9) acknowledges the likely impact of the Assyrian collapse and subsequent disruptions on Crete's access to eastern goods, but points out that such a model both exaggerates the role of Phoenician-controlled shipping in trade networks that included Crete and ascribes unwarranted cultural and social effects to the loss of access to eastern goods and influence.

[100] A Cretan workshop, possibly at Aphrati, produced some black-figure pottery in the sixth century. Most of the examples come from Tocra and Cyrene, but a single fragment is attested at Eleutherna. See Erickson 2010a: 79–80, 324.

[101] Erickson 2006: 72–4. Erickson (2010a) identifies seven possible sixth-century ceramic production centers on Crete (from west to east): Kydonia, Eleutherna, Gortyn (certain from *c.*525 BCE), Knossos (beginning *c.*525 BCE), Aphrati, Praisos, and the Vrokastro region (Gulf of Mirabello). Erickson (2010b:

production (ninth to seventh centuries) on Crete and contemporary trends in some other regions of Greece (notably Corinth and Athens). This island-wide preference for plain tableware is perhaps the most pervasive expression of what has come to be called archaic Cretan 'cultural restraint' or 'cultural austerity'. But it is not the sole expression. Restraint or austerity has been ascribed as well to the simplicity of sixth-century burials, the scarcity of stone sculpture (free-standing sculpture, architectural sculpture, and grave markers) datable to the sixth century,[102] and the alleged scarcity of narrative imagery, if not figural decoration, in all media.

Some of the claims made in discussions of Cretan cultural restraint are probably overstated. For example, the view that the Cretans produced *no* narrative imagery after *c.*600 BCE is based largely on the absence of architectural and funerary sculpture, both important vehicles for narrative imagery in other parts of Greece, and the scarcity of figural decoration on vases, without question the most pervasive medium for narrative imagery in archaic and classical Greece. Narrative imagery, however, is found in Crete on sixth-century terracotta plaques. Oliver Pilz (2014) documents its use on terracotta plaques from Krousonas Koupo, an ancient settlement located about twenty kilometers southwest of Heraklion in the eastern foothills of Mt. Psiloritis, and Agios Ioannis (Gortyn) in central Crete, and on plaques from Praisos, Lato, Sitia, and Azoria in east Crete. The few plaques from central Crete are seventh-century; in east Crete, however, the production of terracotta plaques with narrative imagery continues throughout the seventh and sixth centuries and perhaps into the early fifth. Furthermore, the archaeological record gives the impression that restraint was not expressed uniformly across the island; significantly for us, cultural restraint in central Crete appears to have been both more severe and longer-lasting than was the case in the west or east.[103]

336–9) suggests that this unusual homogeneity, which cuts across local (i.e. polis-level) and regional (i.e. west, central, and east Crete) divisions, indicates the development of a 'Cretan' identity in certain social contexts (e.g. communal drinking).

102 D'Acunto (2001) identifies a local workshop at Axos, active during the period *c.*650–550 BCE, to which he attributes three fragmentary limestone reliefs and a limestone head. A second concentration of possibly sixth-century sculpture comes from Knossos, including a fragmentary limestone kouros and a limestone head (of a female?), as well as two monumental limestone birds, usually identified as eagles, from the coastal sanctuary of Zeus Thenatas at Amnisos in the territory of Knossos. A fragmentary pentelic marble kouros of uncertain date from Gortyn and a fragmentary limestone kouros from Eleutherna (Orthi Petra) completes the dossier of significant archaic stone sculpture from Crete. See Erickson 2010a: 7; Whitley 2003: 81–2, fig. 134 (limestone head from Knossos).

103 In addition to the continuation of narrative imagery on east Cretan plaques, sixth-century burials in west Crete (Phalasarna and Kydonia) and east Crete (Praisos) contain a greater number of grave goods including imported vases. See Erickson 2010a: 256–7, 331–4.

2. Cretan Exceptionalism

Notwithstanding objections to particular points or the likelihood that the archaeological expression of cultural restraint was more complex than appreciated at present, there is no question that the phenomenon was both real and significant. The causes of the shift and the implications of the characteristics that define it for our understanding of Cretan society in general and the laws in particular are far from clear. It lies beyond the scope of our study to grapple systematically with either of these central questions; but we need to explore briefly both sixth-century Cretan cultural restraint and the alleged peculiarity of archaic Cretan culture and society, which has figured prominently in much of the recent scholarship, because both issues carry implications for the practice of writing law in archaic Crete and for the substance of these laws.

Prior to the surge of interest in the archaeology of archaic and classical Crete beginning in the final decades of the twentieth century the inscribed laws were seldom understood to contest what the literary traditions claimed. At the broadest level, the literary construction of a Cretan identity with shared social, political, and cultural institutions appears to have encouraged scholars to emphasize similarities among the laws enacted by different communities (Introd. 1; cf. 10E). In detail as well—from the organization of the *andreion* to the restriction of eligibility for the office of *kosmos* to certain *genē* (clans)—the laws were interpreted through the lens of the literary traditions.[104]

Recent discussions of archaic Crete include the characteristics of sixth-century cultural restraint in a catalogue of features that allegedly distinguish 'Cretan' culture from a mainstream (i.e. mainland) Greek culture.[105] A few examples will suffice to illustrate the role cultural restraint plays in this discourse on Cretan exceptionalism. We begin with the alleged scarcity of narrative imagery, which Whitley (e.g. 2001: 251–2; 2009: 286–7) attributes to Crete's rejection of symposium culture, a major context for the use and display of vases with narrative imagery. Crete's elite developed instead (he argues) a tradition of state-sponsored communal dining in the *andreion* where birth and wealth, not performance and display (i.e. competition), were the marks of the elite.[106] Not only did Cretan

[104] The literary traditions have exerted an influence on the interpretation of the archaeological record as well, notably for us in the identification of such structures as *andreia*. See Introd. 6C.

[105] Whitley, the most consistent advocate of Cretan exceptionalism, has developed his views in a series of studies: Whitley 1997; 2001: 243–52; 2005; 2009; 2013).

[106] It is worth noting that descriptions in the literary sources of Cretan political and social institutions imply competition for prestige and authority as judged by performance in the contexts of male initiation rituals, dining, military training, the battlefield, and politics. See e.g. Aristotle, *Pol.* 2.10, 1272b4–16—competition among the powerful (*dynatoi*) for the office of *kosmos* leading to factional strife and the dissolution of the political association (*hē politikē koinōnia*); Ephorus *ap.* Str. 10.4.20–2—competition among coevals for leadership of an *agela* (20), among adults for adolescent lovers (21), among *kosmoi* for

consumers by and large reject narrative imagery, but we cannot be certain that any of the few scenes that were depicted in metalwork and clay refers to a standard Greek myth. Instead, both the iconography of Cretan figural (i.e. emblematic) imagery and the names and epithets of divine figures attested in epigraphic and literary sources suggest that the Cretans worshipped a 'distinct Cretan pantheon that is being gradually assimilated into the Olympian' (Whitley 2009: 278).

Furthermore (it is argued), the preference for simple burials and for the use of mass-produced utilitarian objects as votive gifts implies the suppression of elite competition in sanctuaries and cemeteries as well. The scarcity of personal or informal writing in these contexts in the form of inscribed grave markers and dedications on votive objects is also noteworthy, as is the low proportion of informal writing in comparison with public writing, especially laws, in Crete during the Archaic and Classical periods (Whitley 1997; 2005). Finally, although decreased archaeological visibility and a shift towards a more restrained or austere cultural expression have been observed in other regions of Greece during the seventh and sixth centuries, in this regard as well Crete is understood to have been exceptional, experiencing its shift at the beginning of the sixth century rather than at the beginning of the seventh as appears to have been the case elsewhere with the possible exception of Sparta.[107]

Some scholars have begun to contest this view of the Cretan polis as an alien type. Erickson, for example, adduces sixth- and fifth-century evidence from likely or certain residential and burial contexts at Aphrati, Azoria, Eleutherna, and Knossos consistent with private parties along the lines of the mainland Greek symposium (Erickson 2011: 388–91; see Introd. 5C1). He argues for a specifically Cretan form of the symposium (e.g. one that preferred the use of black-glazed pottery to pottery with figural decoration) and for the accommodation of both private parties and communal feasting in various contexts, noting that nowhere in the ancient traditions concerning Cretan dining practices is it claimed that the Cretans did not hold private feasts at home. Pilz 2014 identifies a number of certain or very likely references to standard Greek myths in late seventh- and sixth-century Cretan metalwork and terracotta plaques, including episodes from

appointment to the council or *gerousia* (22); Dosiadas *ap.* Athenaeus 4.22, 143D—praise in the *andreion* for members who have excelled in battle. See Introd. 4C1 for the *kosmos*, 6B for the *agela*, and 6C for the *andreion*.

107 An early seventh-century archaeological horizon has been noted in central Greece and the Peloponnese (Attica, Corinth, Argos, and Eretria). For a brief discussion with bibliography, see Erickson 2010a: 15. Recent scholarship on archaic Sparta tracks the decline of its artistic production across the sixth century. See in particular Hodkinson 1998. Erickson (2010a: 334–45) explores the similarities in the archaeological records of sixth-century Crete and Sparta and, adducing evidence of sustained contact between the Peloponnese and Crete during the first half of the sixth century, raises the possibility that Cretan cultural restraint may have inspired Spartan practices.

the Heracles cycle, the Trojan War cycle, the myth of Bellerophon, and possibly the rape of Persephone. Haysom (2011) concludes that broadly speaking Cretan cults and rituals exhibit many of the characteristic features of Greek polis religion, noting that the co-existence of these characteristic features with highly localized religious phenomena is in fact characteristic of Greek polis religion. Johnston (2013) notes that while the Cretan epigraphic habit is in some respects exceptional (e.g. the scarcity of writing on votive dedications and in particular the scarcity of the term *anethēken*, 's/he dedicated'), there are parallels for e.g. the scarcity of inscribed grave stelae. We would add that apart from Gortyn, which *does* seem to be exceptional in this regard, the number of inscribed laws that survive from the other nine central Cretan communities is not all that unusual (Introd. 10A). On current evidence, then, it is not so much a *Cretan* epigraphic habit that is distinctive but rather the practices of a small group of central Cretan poleis, Gortyn above all, in comparison with the poleis of west and east Crete.

The picture of a distinctively 'Cretan polis', at once shared by all Cretan poleis and quite unlike the mainland Greek type (however the latter is defined), concerns us insofar as it has served as a filter through which the laws—their content, the circumstances of their inscribing, and their use—have been examined. The extent to which this perception of the archaic and classical Cretan polis is *historical* is still far from clear. We conclude with a brief consideration of several aspects of the discourse concerning Cretan exceptionalism, including sixth-century cultural restraint, having to do with social structure and identity.

The large, collective Early Iron Age burials have been understood to reflect kinship associations that are commonly referred to as clans and loosely imagined as supra-(nuclear) household kinship affiliations that served not only as a source of social identity and authority but also of economic and, at least in the Early Iron Age, political and probably religious authority as well (Introd. 2A1). The changes that distinguish sixth-century from Early Iron Age burials, viz. individual rather than collective graves, unmarked burials in plain pithoi rather than elaborate tombs and tomb markers, and austere rather than rich burial offerings, have been understood to denote a transformation in the way that the burial groups chose or were obliged to represent themselves in death. Some scholars suggest that as membership in the presumably somewhat more inclusive political class of the polis became the dominant ideology, there was less to gain by demonstrating other kinds of affiliation (e.g. clan) and status (e.g. elite) through communal burial, monumental tombs, and costly grave goods in death.[108] Others suggest instead that the new forms imply the domination of an established elite who no longer found it advantageous to emphasize kinship affiliations or wealth and

[108] e.g. Erickson 2010a: 255–6. Sjögren (2008: 153–4) emphasizes the potential role of sixth-century funerary ritual in articulating elite group identity.

prestige in their burials. In other words, rather than implying a decline in the significance of the burial groups—elite clans or what have you—at the beginning of the Archaic period, the changes mark their self-confidence and the consolidation of their social, political, and economic authority in the polis.[109]

Domestic architecture and the epigraphic record provide some context for interpreting the social implications of sixth-century burial practices. The settlements in the Kavousi cluster offer the clearest picture of domestic architecture before (Vronda and Kavousi Kastro) and after (Azoria) the early archaic cultural horizon.[110] Each of the Early Iron Age housing complexes at Vronda and the Northwest Building at Kavousi Kastro consisted of several house or household units. The excavators interpret renovations (adding new rooms, tearing down walls or adding new ones to expand or divide rooms, blocking some doors and adding new ones, etc.) as responses to the changing size and composition of the co-residential groups, defined as extended families.[111]

The sixth-century houses at Azoria (South Slope, Northwest, and Northeast buildings) were conceived as part of the new town plan at the time of its radical reorganization *c.*600 BCE.[112] The Azoria houses are much larger than the individual house/household units at Vronda[113] and unlike their Early Iron Age predecessors they appear to have experienced remarkably little renovation throughout the life of the settlement (late seventh–early fifth century), indicating perhaps that the size and composition of the co-residential groups changed little (Haggis et al. 2011b: 481). The excavators suggest that the urban houses at Azoria represent one node of multilocal elite households, comprising the nuclear family, dependents,

[109] e.g. Wallace (2010a: 327) who observes, 'The monolithic wealthy kin group had, I think, by now become so well established within the state structure that it no longer needed to advertise or promote itself in burial in the same way.'

[110] We must await detailed studies of the eighth- and seventh-century residential areas at Prophitis Elias (Gortyn) and Patela Priniàs. Very few sixth-century houses have been excavated and none, apart from the ones at Azoria, has been published in any detail. Others include what is possibly a sixth-century house at Aphrati (Lebessi 1970), houses at Onythe Goulediana near Rethymno (Platon 1954; 1955; 1956), and houses identified through archaeological survey of the Meseleroi Valley (Isthmus of Ierapetra) (Hayden 1995: 128–9). See Haggis and Mook (2011: 372–3) for a comparison of the Azoria houses with these.

[111] Glowacki 2007: 134; Haggis 2005: 81–6, 150–1; Mook in Haggis et al. 1997: 388. Building A on the east slope of Kastro does not resemble the others. It is both larger than the Northwest Building and does not appear to have been renovated during its lifetime (eighth to early seventh centuries). Evidently a residence, the excavators suggest on the basis of its size and its high-quality construction that it was the home of 'an important member of the Kastro community' (Tobin in Haggis et al. 1997: 332–3).

[112] Haggis and Mook 2011: 369–70, 373, with figure 31.1 p. 368; Haggis et al. 2011b: 432, 434.

[113] Interior space of Northeast building at Azoria, *c.*164 m.^{2}; the lower of the Southwest Buildings, *c.*109 m.^{2}; the North Acropolis Building, *c.*84 m.^{2} (Haggis et al. 2011b: 478). Interior space of house/household units at Vronda, approximately 30–40 m.^{2} (Glowacki 2007: 135–6 with table 14.1).

and multiple houses (Haggis et al. 2011b: 484; Introd. 5C1). The shift from the agglutinative housing complexes at Early Iron Age Vronda and Kavousi Kastro to the multilocal households at Azoria seems to reflect the fragmentation of co-residential groups identified as extended kinship associations into units comprising the nuclear family and its dependents. We cannot, of course, be certain that sixth-century residential architecture at Azoria resembles sixth-century residential architecture elsewhere in Crete. But it is noteworthy that neither the co-residential unit of the houses at Azoria (i.e. the nuclear family) nor sixth-century burial practices in Crete appears to reflect supra-(nuclear) household kinship affiliations (aka clans).

There is very little evidence in the epigraphic record of archaic and classical Crete, the laws included, for the existence of supra-(nuclear) household kinship associations of the sort that eighth- and seventh-century burials and residences suggest, not even where we might most expect to find it (e.g. in the fifth-century laws of Gortyn on marriage, adoption, and inheritance).[114] The only possible evidence for the clan in the sense of a formal private and/or public association is the term *startos*, a local Cretan term referring to a group of some kind. *Startos* is not attested before the Classical period and then only at Gortyn. It has been variously identified as a local term for clan or tribe or as a military unit (Introd. 4B3). Apart from the *startos*, whose nature remains obscure, we find neither terms for formal groups such as e.g. the *genos* or phratry nor names of the sort that might be identified as names of such groups, apart from two—*Prepsidai* at Dreros (**Dr2**) and *Kydanteiois* at Axos (**A9**)—where the contexts recommend other meanings. The only kinship affiliations that appear with certainty in the epigraphic record are the nuclear family (Introd. 5C2), the extended family (Introd. 5C3), and the *pyla* (*phylē*) or tribe, if kinship was the basis of tribal organization as seems plausible (Introd. 4B3).

In conclusion, supra-(nuclear) household kinship associations are less visible in sixth-century burials and in sixth-century houses, at least those built at Azoria following the obliteration of the Early Iron Age settlement, than they are in the burials and houses of the centuries preceding the early archaic cultural horizon. Furthermore, in contrast to the nuclear family and the tribe, such mid-level kinship associations do not appear to have played a significant role in the public life of the polis or in those private matters that the polis regulated. Taken together, the evidence of the burials, houses, and public enactments suggests that the shift from more exclusive to more inclusive sources of corporate identity was one of the significant social correlates of the early sixth-century archaeological horizon.

[114] For a more detailed discussion of the issues presented here, see Perlman 2014.

C. *Polis-Town and Territory: The Communities that Inscribed Laws on Stone*

The traditional picture of patterns of settlement and land use in the early Cretan poleis relies heavily on assumptions deriving from the literary record and parallels with early Sparta, according to which the landowning political class resided in town while their serfs lived in the countryside on the farms of their owners. A provision of the Gortyn Code concerning the distribution of an estate supports this picture in that it gives the sons of the deceased the contents of a house that is not occupied by a *woikeus* (serf?) residing in the country (see commentary **G72**.4.32–5). The qualification 'residing in the country', however, implies that some *woikeis* resided in town. Moreover, as noted above (Introd. 2A3), the picture that is emerging from surface surveys on Crete suggests that there was very little rural settlement during the Archaic and early Classical periods. Several factors, notably the impact of erosional and depositional processes and of human activity on archaeological visibility as well as uncertainty concerning the identification of local ceramic production during these periods, may disguise what was a much more robust occupation of the countryside, but on current evidence sixth- and early fifth-century settlement on Crete appears to have been markedly nucleated.[115]

The polis-towns of six of the ten communities that inscribed their laws on stone were located on high ground (at altitudes ranging from *c*.375 m to *c*.675 m), in the foothills of two of the mountain ranges dominating the island's topography: Eleutherna and Axos in the northern and Prinias in the eastern foothills of Mt. Psiloritis; Lyktos and Datala (= Aphrati?) in the western foothills of Lasithi (ancient Dikti?); and Dreros on a southern spur of Mt. Kadiston in northeastern Crete. The spacious flat-topped hills or ridges that the earliest settlers of these communities appear to have favored provided a good line of vision on at least three sides, with the fourth often protected by higher land that probably would have fallen within their territory. Defensibility was clearly a concern, but so too was ease of access to a large and fertile agricultural hinterland. The polis-towns of Eleutherna and Axos overlook the fertile plain of Crete's north coast. The settlement on Patela Priniàs dominated a vital route linking the north coast and the Mesara that ran along the western edge of central Crete's fertile heartland. The polis-town of Lyktos lay at the southeastern corner of the Pediadha, a region of rolling hills and rich farmland, in north central Crete. That of Datala, if correctly identified with the ancient settlement at Aphrati (see Datala Site), dominated the eastern end of the Mesara plain. The polis-town of Dreros commanded the coastal

[115] Erickson 2010a: 11–12. Cf. Wallace 2010a: 327–38, who identifies a phenomenon of 'rural spread' beginning in the seventh century.

plain of the Gulf of Mirabello to the east and south and the valley that lies between Mt. Kadiston and the northern foothills of Lasithi.

Although the location and organization of the polis-towns of the remaining four communities have not all been clearly defined archaeologically, the towns were not built on the high flat-topped hills that were characteristic of the others. The early polis-town of Gortyn was located at the northern edge of the Mesara plain. At Phaistos, where settlement on the ridge amidst the remains of the Minoan palace and town continued through the Early Iron Age, it appears that a more complex process than the nearly complete abandonment of the hilltop towns at Gortyn led to much the same result, the establishment of the late archaic polis-town in the plain (Gortyn Site, Phaistos Site). The polis-town of Knossos was located in the vicinity of the Minoan palace and town at the northwestern edge of the Pediadha where it meets the coastal plain (Knossos Site). Eltynia was located at the western edge of the Pediadha, six kilometers southeast of Knossos. Its polis-town was somewhere in the vicinity of modern Kounavi, but whether the modern village is built upon the remains of the ancient town or the ancient town lay on one or more of the gentle ridges that ring the modern village is not known.

As noted above (Introd. 2A3) very little is known about the organization of the polis-towns. Urban defenses dating to the Archaic and early Classical periods, including circuit walls that would have served to define a settlement's urban core, appear to have been very rare on Crete.[116] The use of the term *polis* in Crete (and elsewhere) to designate a community's more densely inhabited urban space (the polis-town or city) in contrast with the rural area, as in the expression 'in the country (*apamia*) and in the city (*polis*)' (**Ele16**Ab2–3) indicates that the two were conceptually distinct. How clear the physical demarcation of the city was probably depended to some extent on its location: a hilltop site like Dreros would have had a more clearly demarcated urban area, whereas at a site like Gortyn, the demarcation between city and countryside may have been vaguer. But the 'houses in the polis' at Gortyn (**G72**.4.32) must have been distinguishable from houses in the country; and although there is as yet little archaeological evidence for dispersed settlement in the countryside, in practice the limits of the polis must have been discernible. In the country, cultivatable plots were owned by individuals,[117] but the higher slopes of hills, used for grazing, were apparently communal space (**Lyktos1B**).

[116] Coutsinas (2013: 275–88) identifies two archaic defensive walls: a section of a wall below and to the west of Patela Prinià̀s and a circuit wall protecting a small settlement in the Meseleroi valley in east Crete. Sections of walls at Gortyn (Agios Ioannis) and Dreros (west peak) have been identified as either defensive or terrace walls and dated to the Archaic period; the Byzantine circuit wall protecting the top of the east peak of Agios Antonios (Dreros) may rest on earlier foundations (see Gortyn Site; Dreros Site). For the difficulties in identifying and dating archaic and classical defensive walls on Crete, see Coutsinas 2013: 131–47.

[117] See e.g. **G46**B7–8: 'through another person's land.'

Polis is found in its geographical sense of the city most clearly in **Ele16**Ab2–3 (cited above). The same sense is found at Gortyn and perhaps at Axos.[118] Within the polis, the Gortynian inscriptions often mention an agora, or 'gathering place' where public business is conducted, such as adoption 'with the citizens gathered' (**G72**.10.34, 11.12), and some commercial activity takes place (**G72**.7.10–11);[119] and **G9**a–m twice mentions an *agrēion*, perhaps a smaller or earlier gathering place. An agora is also mentioned at Phaistos as a place where someone speaks (**Ph1**.1). We also hear of an *andreion* or 'men's hall' in Axos, Datala, Eltynia, and Gortyn (Introd. 6C).

No other location in the city receives more than occasional mention. We hear of a gymnasium (**G64**.6), a *synbolētra*, and a *koros* (both **Elt2**.6), but we can only guess at where these were; nor is anything said of the activity in these places, though presumably the gymnasium was a place for exercising, the *synbolētra* perhaps for meetings of a council, and the *koros* for dancing. Finally, Spensithios is required to perform certain public sacrifices, for which he will receive *temenia* or 'revenue from the sacred precinct (*temenos*)' (**Da1**B6; cf. **A20**).

Although little is known about the nature of settlement in the agricultural and pastoral hinterlands of much of Crete during the sixth and fifth centuries, survey archaeology is bringing into focus the history of occupation in the western Mesara beyond the ridge and its immediate vicinity where the polis-town of Phaistos was located.[120] As noted above (Introd. 2A3), settlement in the plain appears to have been dispersed during the Early Iron Age (eleventh through seventh centuries), although the pattern of settlement that the evidence reflects (farmsteads, hamlets, villages) is not clearly understood. There appears to be an increase beginning late in the seventh century in the number of small sites (farmsteads? hamlets?) established at the edge of the agricultural catchment of the ridge where the Minoan palace and Early Iron Age village(s) were located that is more or less contemporary with the evidence for reorganization of the polis-town (*c.*625–550). Scholars have understood both phenomena in political terms: the apparent reorganization of the town as a sign of the birth or rise of the polis and the pattern of use of the

[118] **G72**.4.32 and 8.1–2 (a house 'in the polis'), **G79.10** ('those who live in the polis', the same text in *IC* 4.144.9), and perhaps in **G45**B1 ('to the polis'—*es polin*—without context). In **A1**.10–11—'is not to put in the city' (μὴ ἰνθέμεν | τᾶι πό[λ]ι)—it is unclear whether 'put in' has a physical sense, 'place [something] in the city', in which case polis is the urban area, or means 'impose [charges] on the polis [that employs them]', in which case *polis* is probably used in its political sense.

[119] **G13**h–g2 (probably); **G43**Bb5–6; **G72**.7.10–11, 10.34, 11.12; **G75**A8; **G80**.14 (at Rhitten); **G81**.11; **G102**.2.

[120] For the final report of the Greek–American survey, see Watrous, Hadzi-Vallianou, and Blitzer 2004; for initial reports of the ongoing Greek–Italian survey, see Bredaki, Longo, and Benzi 2011; 2012. Bredaki, Longo, and Benzi (2012: 275–6) compare the objectives and methods of the two surveys.

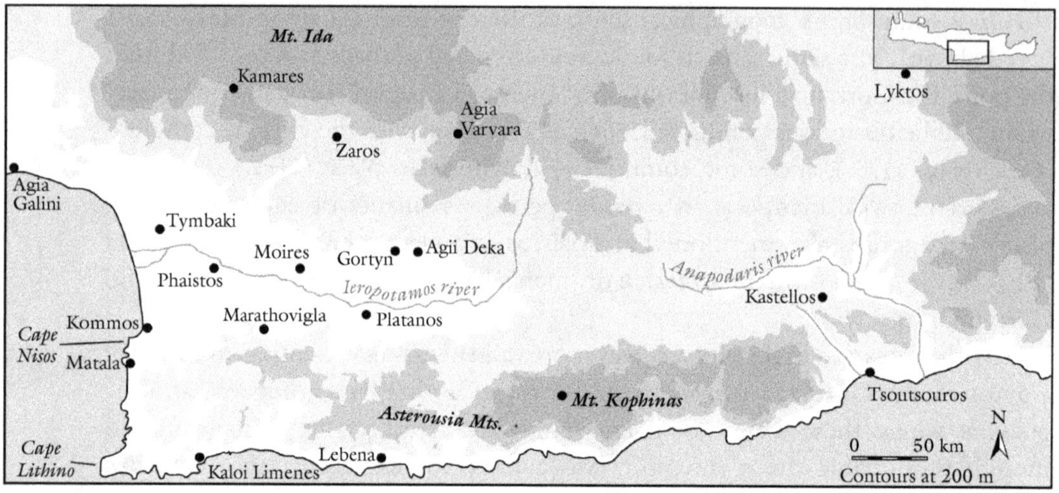

FIG. 2. Map of the Mesara

agricultural hinterland as symptomatic of state-formation (Cucuzza 1998: 67; Watrous and Hadzi-Vallianou 2004a: 315–17; 2004b: 342–4).

During the Archaic and Classical periods Phaistos probably controlled the Mesara plain from the coast in the west to its border with Gortyn in the east, although there is no evidence for the precise location of this border.[121] References in the *Odyssey* and in **G72** complicate what we might otherwise imagine to have been a straightforward division of the fertile plain with Phaistos controlling the west end and Gortyn the east. In *Odyssey* 3.293–6 Nestor relates how on Menelaus' journey home from Troy, after getting blown off course rounding Cape Malia, part of his fleet was driven to Crete. 'There is a sheer and steep cliff (*lissē aipeia te petra*) at the shore of the misty sea, at the end (*eschatiēi*) of Gortyn. There the south wind pushes a large wave toward a reef on the left, toward Phaistos, and a small rock holds back the great wave.'[122] The 'sheer and steep cliff' has been identified with either Cape Lithino at the extreme southwest of Crete or Cape Nisos to the south of Kommos (FIG. 2).[123] For a ship sailing towards the coast, Phaistos would have been to the north of this cliff ('on the left'). If so, these verses indicate that Gortyn controlled the Asterousia mountains and the south coast of Crete from at least as far east as Leben (**G63**) to the west coast south of the Mesara.

121 For a detailed account of the relations between Phaistos and Gortyn, see Cucuzza 1997; 2005: 314–20.

122 ἔστι δέ τις λισσὴ αἰπεῖά τε εἰς ἅλα πέτρα
ἐσχατιῇ Γόρτυνος ἐν ἠεροειδέι πόντῳ·
ἔνθα νότος μέγα κῦμα ποτὶ σκαιὸν ῥίον ὠθεῖ
ἐς Φαιστόν, μικρὸς δὲ λίθος μέγα κῦμ᾽ ἀποέργει.

123 Cucuzza 1997: 74; Shaw 2000b: 709–10. Cf. D'Acunto 2008 who locates the *lissē aipeia te petra* and Amyklaion on the south coast of Crete in the vicinity of Kaloi Limenes (FIG. 2).

The *Odyssey* is not, admittedly, compelling evidence for the geo-political organization of archaic Crete (or for anywhere else, for that matter) nor is there widespread agreement on its historical context, although the early sixth century is gaining some currency. Even so, **G72**.3.5–9 suggests that Gortyn exerted control of some kind over the southwestern corner of the Mesara in the first half of the fifth century. This passage provides that a divorced woman accused of having taken property belonging to her ex-husband swear an oath of denial by the goddess Artemis before (the statue of) the Archeress at Amyklaion. We assume that Amyklaion lay within the territory of Gortyn (comm. ad loc.). Cucuzza (1997: 64–72; 2005: 315–17) identifies one of two sanctuaries with the one at Amyklaion: either the sanctuary at Kommos or the sanctuary of Artemis at Kalamaki several kilometers to the north.[124] If *Odyssey* 3.293–6 preserves an accurate description of the territories of Gortyn and Phaistos at some point in the Archaic period, the location of either of the two sanctuaries proposed for the one at Amyklaion suggests that it was located near the border of Gortyn and Phaistos (Cucuzza 1997: 79). Phaistos, in short, was for some time in the sixth and fifth centuries boxed in by Gortyn to the south.

There is little evidence for rural habitation in the Western Mesara during the sixth and fifth centuries, suggesting either its desertion or at most the seasonal use of rural farmsteads without permanent occupation.[125] When habitation in the countryside returns (*c*.375), rather than re-occupying the earlier archaic sites the people preferred to establish new farms and hamlets, although even then rural settlement during the remainder of the late Classical period (*c*.375–300) is sparse, with an increase by three residential sites over the Archaic period. Both the apparent decrease in rural settlement during the period *c*.550–375 and the preference for new, previously unoccupied sites for the location of new farms and hamlets suggest a discontinuity of rural settlement during the period *c*.550–375. It is not until the final quarter of the fourth century that rural settlement within the survey area increases significantly (Watrous and Hadzi-Vallianou 2004a: 326–8).

The Mesara Plain is, admittedly, unlike any other part of Crete in both the extent of its arable land and the fertility of its alluvial soils.[126] Thus, patterns of settlement and land-use elsewhere on Crete may not resemble those in the Mesara Plain. Furthermore, competition with Gortyn for control of the plain might have influenced where people lived. Indeed, the reference to serfs residing in the country in **G72**.4.32–5 (discussed above) indicates that we might expect to find

[124] Neither site suits all of the ancient evidence for the location of Amyklaion and scholarly opinion on this question remains divided. See Shaw 2000b: 709–11 with nn. 61–8.

[125] Cucuzza 2011: 369; Bredaki, Longo, Benzi 2011: 939. For the scarcity of evidence dating to the period *c*.525–375 from the ridge and its immediate environs, see Phaistos Site.

[126] The Mesara Plain includes two-thirds of the best arable land on Crete (40,485+ hectares) consisting of rich alluvial farmland with ample groundwater drained by the Ieropotamos river.

more evidence for rural habitation in Central and East Mesara, at least during the first half of the fifth century, than has been found in West Mesara. Yet it remains the case that on current evidence habitation appears to have been strongly nucleated in the late seventh and sixth centuries and we should resist discussions of settlement, society, and land-use that assume or imply otherwise.

Crete's agricultural zone ends at an altitude of about one thousand meters. Above this, the uplands of Mt. Psiloritis and Lasithi provided seasonal pasture, but possibly not equally so for all six of the communities whose town centers occupied the foothills. Nowicki (2000: 23) observes that communication with the upland pastures on Mt. Psiloritis was easier for settlements located, as were Eleutherna, Axos, and Prinias, in the northern and eastern foothills. Access to the upland pastures of Mt. Psiloritis from the west and south was far more difficult. Nowicki concludes that communities to the north and east were likely to have depended to a greater extent on herding in their economy than were those to the south and west. Access to Lasithi is more difficult from the north, south, and west than it is from the east where the transition between the coastal plain and the mountain is gentler. A series of steep and craggy ridges along the western side of Lasithi forms an effective barrier between the uplands and the Mesara plain and the Pediadha. These natural barriers may be expected to have reduced the contribution of herding to the economy of Datala and Lyktos by making it more difficult for members of these communities to access the summer pastures on Lasithi. Yet **Lyktos1B**, which probably concerns the seasonal movement of livestock, suggests to the contrary that animal husbandry may have played a significant role in the economy of Lyktos (Introd. 7C).

The territory of six of the poleis probably extended to the coast, although it is rarely possible to determine with certainty the location of the archaic and classical ports. The polis-towns of Knossos and Phaistos were about five kilometers as the crow flies from the coast. Archaeologists have proposed two candidates, both at the mouths of rivers, for the harbor of Knossos: Poros-Katsambas at the mouth of the ancient Kairatos river (present-day Katsambas) and Amnisos at the mouth of the ancient Amnisos river (present-day Karatos). Communication with Poros-Katsambas was probably easier and the recent discovery there of Minoan ship sheds confirms its use as a harbor during the Neopalatial period (*c.*1500–1200), but the small bay at Amnisos, also a Bronze Age harbor, offered somewhat better protection than the more open coastline at Poros-Katsambas and there is evidence of activity there during the Archaic period.[127] Kommos and Matala on the west coast have been identified as harbors of Phaistos, although there is little

[127] For the recent discovery of Minoan ship sheds at Poros-Katsambas, see Vasilakis 2010. For the remains at Amnisos, including the Minoan villa, walls associated with the Bronze Age harbor, and the substantial Early Iron Age and later open-air sanctuary, see Schäfer 1992a.

archaeological evidence for activity at Kommos during the period *c.*600–375 or at Matala earlier than the fourth century.[128] The small bay at Matala offers better protection than the more open coastline at Kommos.

The fifth-century agreement between Gortyn and Leben (**G63**) may be evidence that this small settlement on the south coast served as a port for Gortyn. However, Leben was *c.*14.5 km. south of Gortyn as the crow flies and the arid highlands of the Asterousia mountains barred the way, making the trip both long and difficult. This perhaps explains why Gortyn appears to have sought access to a more convenient, if more distant, harbor on the west coast (Phaistos Site).

For Eleutherna, the reference to 'Dion Akron' ('Zeus's promontory/peak' or 'divine promontory/peak') in **Eleutherna1**.3 likely refers to a cape on the north coast of Crete between Rethymno and Heraklion (comm. ad loc.). If so, the context of the reference (a rule concerning sympotic drinking at Dion Akron) suggests that the territory of Eleutherna extended to the north coast. The ancient settlement, archaic and later, at Stavromenos, on the north coast ten kilometers north of Eleutherna (eleven kilometers east of Rethymno), is a likely candidate for a harbor of Eleutherna (Schiering 1982: 17–47; Perlman 2004b: 1159).

Almyrida, located on a small bay on the north coast near the modern village of Sisses, provides the most convenient coastal access for Axos. Earlier and later remains have been found there, but nothing between the end of the Bronze Age (*c.*1200) and the Hellenistic period. If Almyrida is the location of ancient Kytaion as Stefanakis (1998) suggests, numismatic evidence indicates that it was a polis in the late fourth century. The route (*c.*11 km. as the crow flies) between Axos and Almyrida is reasonably clear, but the pass through the Kouloukonas mountains was difficult.

The coastal settlement of Chersonesos has been identified as the harbor of Lyktos. Remains at Chersonesos are no earlier than the fourth century, although fragments of a sixth-century funerary stele were discovered one kilometer to the south of Chersonesos near the village of Koutoulophari (*LSAG* 316 no. 20). Chersonesos is attested as a polis in the third century and appears to have joined politically with Lyktos in the second century (Perlman 2004b: 1155). Viviers (1994: 252–4) argues on the basis of **L1** that the union dates to the sixth century, but this is very uncertain (comm. ad loc.).

The remaining four poleis—Datala (Aphrati?), Dreros, Eltynia, and Prinias—were probably cut off from direct access to the coast by the territory of another polis: Prinias by Tylissos to the north, Datala (= Aphrati?) by Priansos to the

[128] For the partial abandonment of the Early Iron Age and later sanctuary at Kommos during the period *c.*600–375, see Shaw 2000a: 36–7; for Matala, see Perlman 2004b: 1177–8.

south, Dreros by Olous to the east and Milatos to the north, and Eltynia by Knossos to the north and Priansos to the south. This does not, of course, mean that these land-locked communities did not negotiate the right to use the harbor of a neighboring polis, as Tylissos apparently did with its neighbor Knossos (M&L 42B).

3. THE INSCRIPTIONS

A. Inscription and Display

The writing on archaic and classical Cretan inscriptions varies considerably, but is generally notable for the large size of the lettering.[129] Perlman (2002: 214–16) has catalogued all the inscriptions of sufficient size inscribed on the Pythion at Gortyn, most from the Archaic period, and has found that the height of the letters on 29 out of 31 of them varies from 4 to 25 cm.[130] The two whose lettering is smaller (2–4 cm.), though still very legible, are both from the fifth century (**G78**, **G79**), suggesting perhaps that by then masons had become more skillful in their writing or more confident in their readers' ability to read (or both), and could thus make their letters smaller. Other fifth-century inscriptions are similar; e.g. the letters on both **G41** and **G72** are 2.5–3.0 cm. Even then, however, as anyone who has looked at the Code or other Gortynian inscriptions can testify, the letters are large enough to be easily viewed at some distance, and the letters on some of the early inscriptions are enormous. The only text in which the lettering can truly be called small is the agreement with Spensithios; its letters are only about one-tenth the size of those inscribed on stone, and the worn parts are truly difficult to read.[131] But this was probably a private copy of the agreement, perhaps made for and even by Spensithios himself and not intended for public display (**Da1** Introd.). With this exception, the size and legibility of the letters indicate that all the texts in this edition were intended for public display.

To be sure, the current legibility of these texts also depends on the condition of the stones, but inscriptions that have been well preserved, such as **G72**, are among the most legible inscribed texts we have from the Greek world. In addition, most

[129] Wilson (2009: 558) asserts that 'the lettering is often small and barely legible, and there is no punctuation'; this conclusion may have some validity for other parts of Greece, but it is not applicable to archaic or classical Cretan inscriptions.

[130] For comparison, the letters on Athenian inscriptions of the fifth century are regularly less than 2 cm. in height and sometimes less than 1 cm.

[131] J–MD 120 give the height as 0.03–0.06 cm. for side A and 0.04–0.08 cm. for side B. These impossibly small figures are evidently a misprint for 0.3–0.6 cm. and 0.4–0.8 cm. The text was certainly more legible (despite the small lettering) when first inscribed than it is today.

of the archaic inscriptions (like many from other parts of Greece) contain lines or dots separating words or groups of words (Introd. 3D1). It appears, then, that the masons[132] who inscribed these texts made an effort from the beginning to make them as legible as possible; if by the Classical period they dispensed with word division and generally reduced the size of their lettering, it was probably because they were writing for a more experienced readership. The result, however, was still eminently readable.

We do not know who these masons were, but some of them must have been professionals by the fifth century, at least, and may have been from the beginning. Although anyone could learn to scratch a few letters on a pot, it would require some training, together with special tools, to carve dozens of words on a stone. The earliest masons were clearly still learning their trade. The size of letters often varies considerably, lines of writing are often not straight,[133] and masons sometimes run out of room and have to squeeze the end of a text into a space that is too small or carry over a few letters to another stone. It goes too far, however, to speak of the 'ineptitude' of archaic scribes (Wilson 2009: 558). This might accurately characterize some private writers scratching letters on a pot (whom we would not identify as 'scribes'), but it does not apply to the masons who carved Cretan laws. Similarly, Wilson's claim that 'scribes' continually shifted the orientation of letters and the direction of writing may be valid for some private writers or for other parts of Greece but not for the masons who inscribed the Cretan laws.[134]

With the exception of **Da1** (see above), all the texts in this volume were inscribed on stone and were, as far as we can tell, displayed in a public space. Some, especially in the earliest period, were inscribed on the walls of temples or other buildings; others were inscribed on freestanding walls or stone slabs (stelae). A few of these stelae (e.g. **A10**) are inscribed on two sides, **Lyktos1A** and **1B** are inscribed on two sides of an Ionic column capital, and one text (**IC** 1.28.1) is inscribed on four sides of a stone pillar. **Da1** is inscribed on both sides of a thin sheet of bronze. We do not know where it was found. As mentioned, it may have been Spensithios' own copy (perhaps even written by him), in which case another copy on stone may have been displayed in a public space somewhere in the city.

132 We use 'mason' instead of 'scribe' to avoid some of the connotations of the latter term. Scribes in many ancient cultures belonged to elite professional groups; they were highly trained, controlled most of the writing in the society, and often had considerable authority in other matters, whereas masons in Greece probably existed in small numbers and do not seem to have had any special authority. Even if the verb *poinikazen* means 'inscribe' in addition to 'write', Spensithios' role (**Da1**) is to accompany the *kosmos* and write down texts that are provided by others. He is an employee of the polis with no evident authority to influence the content of the texts he is supposed to write.

133 To be fair, some of the crooked lines (e.g. **Dr1**) were undoubtedly caused by irregularities in the stone's surface which would have required the mason to carve around them.

134 We assume Wilson is not simply thinking of boustrophedon writing.

FIG. 3 Chart of Cretan Letter Forms

B. *Alphabet*

All the texts in this collection are written in a local (epichoric) Cretan alphabet that differs significantly from the classical Greek alphabet used in Athens after 403 and in most of the Greek world (including Crete) in the Hellenistic period and later. There are also a few variations in scripts among the Cretan poleis themselves; these may have developed as a means of promoting the poleis' self identities (Luraghi 2010); and there appear to be some regional similarities among scripts from Axos and Eleutherna, and among those from Datala, Lyktos, and Eltynia.

The letters that are most likely to confuse readers of Attic Greek are *iota* (which in most Cretan alphabets looks like a Roman *S*), *pi* (which takes several different forms), and the sibilant, for which the inscriptions use the letter *san* rather than *sigma*; the letter *san* resembles a four-stroke *mu* (Cretan *mu* usually has five strokes[135]) or Roman *M*. In addition, the letters *xi*, *psi*, *chi*, and *phi* are missing (except for *xi* in **L4**.2), and are expressed by *kappa san*, *pi san*, *kappa*, and *pi* respectively. *Zeta*, in the form of a Roman *I*, is used in some periods but not others. The Cretans preserved *digamma* throughout this period, and before the fifth century used *qoppa* for *kappa* before *omicron* and sometimes before other letters (except at Dreros).

Finally, the vowels and diphthongs that in Attic Greek express long *o* and *e* sounds (*eta*, *omega*, *ei*, and *ou*) are often missing in Crete, in which case these sounds are commonly expressed by *epsilon* and *omicron* (see below Dialect 2). *Eta* is used in some periods but in others is expressed by *epsilon*; *omega* is regularly expressed by *omicron*, but at Lyktos, Datala, and Eltynia in addition to the standard *omicron* we also find a 'doughnut' (two concentric circles), which seems to represent a lengthened *o* sound (see further Introd. to Lyktos). Unlike most other editors, we do not add a macron to *epsilon* and *omicron* when they represent *eta* and *omega*, because it is sometimes unclear whether these vowels are in fact lengthened.

[135] In some inscriptions from Axos, *mu* is written as a single vertical stroke.

C. *Dialect*

Descriptions of the Cretan dialect,[136] such as Willetts 1967: 6–7 (based on Buck 1955: 154–5, 169–72) are generally quite technical. There are good reasons for this and some technical terminology is unavoidable. Our aim here, however, is to present the main features of the dialect as clearly as possible to readers who may not be well versed in historical linguistics. Thus, we try to minimize the use of technical terms and concentrate on those dialectical features that in our view are most important for understanding the texts in this volume. Most of the rules we list below are intended to elucidate the most common features, or those that are the most unusual and thus least likely to be understood intuitively. Further information about dialectical forms is given in the textual notes.[137]

Cretan is commonly classified as a West Greek and more specifically a Doric dialect, and it does in fact have much in common with certain Doric dialects of the Greek mainland. But it is clear that as early as the Bronze Age several different languages were spoken on the island, and in historical times the population included descendants of immigrants belonging to several dialect groups as well as non-Greeks (such as the so-called Eteocretans).[138] As Odysseus says of the island, 'Languages mingle, one with another; there are Achaeans, and great-hearted Eteocretans, and Kydonians, and Dorians in three divisions, and illustrious Pelasgians' (*Odyssey* 19.175–77)—a passage most scholars accept as having some historical basis, though the details are disputed (see Russo, et al. 1992: 83–5). All these languages and dialects undoubtedly influenced the dialect as we find it in these legal texts, with the result that Cretan is not a purely Doric dialect.

The features listed below represent common occurrences; in many cases our descriptions could be further expanded with exceptions and other qualifications, but this would not have served the needs of the majority of our readers, who are not trained linguists. At the end we list some words with unfamiliar meanings, and unfamiliar words that either are not phonologically equivalent to their Attic counterparts or whose relationship is phonologically so complex that it would be unhelpful to try to explain it for most readers. Anyone who wants more detail can consult Buck 1955 or Bile's magisterial study (1988). Finally, because readers who know Greek will be familiar with the Attic dialect, we usually give Attic equivalents (in parentheses), and for convenience will sometimes speak of how Cretan diverges from Attic, though this should not be taken to imply any particular historical relationship between the two dialects.

[136] For convenience, we will generally speak of Cretan as a single dialect; geographical and historical variations are evident, however, which would make it more accurate to speak of Cretan dialects (see Bile 9–15).

[137] Bile 1988 has been an indispensable help in writing this section and for our notes and comments on the texts.

[138] See especially the studies in Brixhe 1991.

1. Phonology

1. The Attic-Ionic use of η for long α is not found in Cretan—δικαστάς.
2. The 'spurious diphthongs' (ει, ου) are written as ϵ and ο;[139] η is often written as ϵ, and ω almost always appears as ο. Many editors write these vowels with a macron (ϵ̄, ο̄) when they are long, if they are not already marked as long by a circumflex accent, but because in some cases the length is uncertain, we have left all such words unmarked, though in some cases the accentuation indicates vowel length—κσένιος (ξείνιος), πονε̂ι (φωνῇ); δόλοι (δούλῳ), cf. δο̂λοι (δου̂λοι).
3. The main vowel change is ι from ϵ before a vowel (but not if originally followed by a Ϝ); Indo-European (IE) vowel gradations also differ from the Attic equivalents—ἰόντος (ἐόντος), ἀδελπιός (ἀδελφου̂, see below 5); τράποι (τρέφοι), ἰαρός (ἱερός).
4. Closely related is the transposition of the liquid ρ when the IE zero-grade form vocalizes—καρτερός (κρατερός), πορτί (προτί = πρός).
5. Aspiration is absent, both initially (psilosis) and in combination with the consonants κ and π; in the fifth century θ occurs before vowels and τ before liquids and nasals (Bile 140)—ὀς, κρόνος (χρόνος), τράποι (τρέφοι), θιοί (θεοί), τνατός (θνητός).
6. Intervocalic νς and final νς before a vowel are retained—ἔκονσα (ἔχουσα), τὸνς ἐλευθέρονς (τοὺς ἐλευθέρους), but τὸς μαίτυρανς (τοὺς μάρτυρας).
7. Original -ντ- in verb endings is retained—ἡβίοντι (ἡβω̂σι < ἡβάουσι, see below 19).
8. Initial *digamma* (Ϝ) is commonly retained; also in compounds—Ϝοίνο (οἴνου) ἀποϜείποντι (ἀπείπωσι, subjunctive, see below 22).
9. Final consonants are regularly assimilated before a consonant, as are also consonant groups within words (including ζ = σδ), and occasionally consonants that are separated—τα̂δ δίκας (τη̂ς δίκης), τὸμ μάτροα (τὸν μήτρωα), νυττί (νυκτί), ἔγραττται (γέγραπται), πρόθθα (πρόσθεν), δικάδδεν (δικάζειν), νύναμαι (δύναμαι).
10. Final consonants are sometimes doubled before a vowel—τὸνσς (or τὸνς) ἐπιβάλλονtανς.
11. Double consonants may (or may not) be simplified; accordingly, initial *zeta* (see above 9) may become a single *delta*—δόοι (ζόοι). This sometimes results in variant forms in the same text—ἄλος, ἄλλος (**G72**.1.44, 53), κρε̂θθαι (χρη̂σθαι) and κρε̂θαι.[140] Much more rarely there is variation

[139] In some early inscriptions some types of compensatory lengthening of ϵ are written with a special sign (Ꮻ), which is usually taken to be η.

[140] In the Gortyn Code (**G72**) the proportion of -θαι to -θθαι is roughly 3:1.

between single and double vowels even in the same text—ἀπλόος and ἀπλός (in **G41**).

12. The prepositions ἀνά and παρά undergo apocope, both alone and in compounds—πὰρ τὸν ἄνδρα, ἀνδεκσάμενος (ἀναδεξάμενος). ἀν- may or may not become ἀμ- before π—ἀμπί or ἀνπί.
13. If σ was originally IE *tį*, it appears as ττ—ἴαττα (ἔουσα, οὖσα), μέττος (μέσος), ὅττος or in early texts ὅζος (ὅσος).
14. The prepositions ἐκς (ἐκ) and ἐνς (εἰς) both shorten to ἐς before a consonant (ἴος in **A1**.12); thus, before a consonant ἐς with a gen. = ἐκς, but ἐς with an acc. = ἐνς. In forming compounds, ἐσ- can stand for either ἐκ- or εἰσ-.
15. The future and aorist of ζ-stem verbs are formed with κσ—δικάκσαι.
16. λ is sometimes expressed as υ after a vowel—ἀδευπιαί and ἀδελπιαί.

2. Morphology

17. The reflexive pronoun is formed by the personal pronoun and αὐτός, each inflected separately—Ϝὶν αὐτôι (ἑαυτῷ), τὰ Ϝὰ αὐτᾶς (τὰ ἑαυτῆς).
18. Only one half of the relative pronoun is inflected—ὅτις, ὂτι, ὅτιμι, ἄτι (= ὅστις, οὗτινος, ᾧτινι, ἅτινα).
19. Verbs in -αο are conjugated like verbs in -εο, with ε shortening to ι (see above 3).
20. Active infinitives of thematic verbs (including contract verbs) end in -ἔν or for verbs in -αο (see above 19) in -ε̄ν; infinitives of athematic verbs end in -μεν, which may be long or short (and can be ambiguous in texts which lack *eta*)—κρίνεν, νικε̂ν, ὀπῆλεν (ὀφείλειν), ὀμνύμην and ὀμνύμεν, ἤμην and ἦμεν (εἶναι, both in **Dr1**.3). Bile 239–42.
21. Three Attic deponent verbs—πεύθομαι, ὠνέομαι, ἐλεύσομαι—have active forms (πεύθο, etc.).
22 Short-vowel aorist subjunctives are retained—δικάκσε̆ι (see above 15), δείκσο̆ντι (= δείξωσι, see above 7).
23. Present and perfect subjunctives of some athematic verbs are formed by adding personal endings directly to the (long) stem—νύνᾱται (δύναται), ἐστετέκνο̄ται (ἐκτετεκνωμένος ᾦ).
24. The 'Doric future' in -σεο (which becomes -σιο, above 3) is the rule—ἐκσίοντι (ἕξουσι).

3. Vocabulary—unfamiliar meanings

25. ἀμπί/ἀνπί (see above 12), alone or in compounds, means 'concerning', as in Homer—ἀμπὶ δόλοι.
26. ἀντί means 'in front of' (Lat. *ante*)—ἀντὶ μαιτύρον.

27. *καρτερός* (above 4) with *ἔμεν* (= *εἶναι*, above 20) means 'in control of'—*τôν κρεμάτον καρτερòνς ἔμεν.*
28. *κόσμος* = ***kosmos***, the leading official of most Cretan poleis.
29. *πονέο* (*φωνέω*), used of litigants, and *ἀποπονέο*, used of witnesses, = 'speak in court'.

4. Vocabulary—unfamiliar dialect forms

30. *αἰρέω* (= *αἱρέω*) is standard in the sixth century but takes the form *αἰλέο* in the fifth century (Bile 121).
31. *Ϝίκατι* = *εἴκοσι* < **ἐ-Ϝίκοσι.*
32. *ἡμίνα* = *ἥμισυ.*
33. *ὄκα, τόκα* = *ὅτε, τότε.*
34. *πρεῖγυς* = *πρέσβυς.*
35. *τôνυ, τôινυ* = *τοῦδε, τῷδε.*

5. Vocabulary—unfamiliar words

36. *ᾶι* (*ᾗ*) and *-αι* (e.g. *ὄπαι*) = 'where' or especially 'as'.
37. *ἀκεύο* = 'take care of'.
38. *ἀμπαίνομαι* (*ἀναφαίνομαι*) = 'adopt'.
39. *ἄπατος* = 'immune from penalty'.
40. *δρομεύς* = 'adult' (lit. 'runner').
41. *ἐ̃* = 'where' or 'when'.
42. *ὀ ἐπιβάλλον* = 'claimant', either to an estate (as an heir) or to the hand of an 'heiress' (Introd. 5C4).
43. *κα* = *ἄν.*
44. *καρταῖπος* = 'cattle' as distinct from *πρόβατα* = 'small animals' (sheep and goats).
45. *λαγαίο* = 'release' (but see comm. ad **G78**.4).
46. *λείο*= 'wish' (*θέλω*).
47. *μωλέο*= 'contend in court'.
48. *πάομαι/πάστας* = 'own'/'owner'.
49. *πατροιôκος* = 'heiress'.
50. *πεδά* = *μετά.*
51. *στέγα* = 'house'.

D. Punctuation

Greek inscriptions do not use punctuation (in our sense) or distinguish small and capital letters until a much later period. But Cretan and other Greek inscriptions from the Archaic and Classical periods do make use of several features that serve some of the functions of modern punctuation and paragraphing, namely, word-division, asyndeton, gaps, and the direction of writing.

1. Word-Division

Before the fifth century, most Cretan inscriptions have a rudimentary form of word-division, in which a vertical line—or in three texts two dots (**Ele13**; **Ele15**) or small circles (**G62**), one above the other—separate words or small groups of words. The use of word-division is neither consistent nor systematic, though it generally does not occur between natural groupings of words, such as article and noun or preposition and noun. The effect of word-division can be seen in the first line of **Dr1**, which in translation would look something like this:

thepolis | hasdecided | whensomeonehasbeenkosmos | withintenyears | thesameperson.

This would undoubtedly be easier to read than:

thepolishasdecidedwhensomeonehasbeenkosmoswithintenyearsthesameperson.

These division marks would have provided assistance for readers, who at this early time might not have much experience reading longer texts, and it seems likely that this was in fact their purpose.

2. Other Signs

In addition to these forms of word-division, a few other signs are inscribed in the space before an asyndeton; these reinforce the implication of asyndeton that a new clause or new section is beginning. Most notable is the 'hourglass' sign (⧖) in **Dr1**.4, which separates this line from the first three; it is also found in **G72**.9.43, **L5**.7 (⋈), and perhaps in **G72**.7.4. We also find an inscribed *folium* or 'leaf' (Ʊ) in **G47**.10 and a *ligo* or 'mattock' (⟻) in **G72**.10.25.

Besides these inscribed signs, painted decorations of various sorts fill some of the gaps in **G72** (e.g. in 1.12, 5.9); drawings of these can be found in Guarducci 1950: 125, and a complete list in Willetts 1967: 4. Several of those that appear in older drawings of **G72** are no longer visible today because the paint has worn off; it seems likely that all the gaps in this inscription (and perhaps in others) were originally painted, but that the paint has disappeared from most of them.

3. Asyndeton

Since most Greek sentences contain a particle indicating a connection to the sentence that precedes (commonly 'and' or 'but'), a sentence without a connecting particle is notable. This phenomenon, called asyndeton (lit. 'non-connecting'), commonly indicates the beginning of a new subject, rather like the beginning of a new paragraph today. Usage varies over time and is never entirely consistent, but asyndeton can often alert readers to the organizational structure of a text that treats several different subjects.

4. Gaps

Many of these texts also contain gaps, usually one or two letters wide but sometimes wider, where nothing was written on the stone even though the surface was smooth enough for writing. Like asyndeton, gaps commonly indicate the switch to a new topic or sub-topic. Gaps may occur together with asyndeton. In the Gortyn Code (**G72**), gaps are more frequent than asyndeton, and seem to mark subdivisions within the larger subjects, which are marked by asyndeton. Gaps may also indicate the end of a text, in which case they may be quite long. These gaps are traditionally indicated by the notation *vac.* (*vacat* = 'it is empty'). The use of asyndeton and gaps in the Gortyn Code is fairly systematic (see Gagarin 1982); elsewhere it seems to vary widely.

5. Direction of Writing

The direction of writing in most of these inscriptions is *boustrophedon* or back-and-forth (lit. 'as the ox turns'). It usually begins from the right and runs to the left (retrograde) in the first line and then left to right in the second line, and so forth, though a few texts begin from the left. On Crete the writing may be boustrophedon even in the rare cases where the letters are written vertically (e.g. **Pr1**). Sometimes a new line will begin in the same direction as the one above it; in most cases this indicates that a new provision is beginning, though the provision may be related to what precedes (see further Jeffery 1990: 43–50). We follow Jeffery in referring to this practice as 'archaic paragraphing'.

E. Dating

The primary method of dating these texts is by letter forms. Where we have enough material from one site (as at Axos, Eleutherna, Gortyn, and Lyktos), these may provide a rough relative chronology (see Ikonomaki 2010). Another factor that is sometimes useful is the date of the building on which a text was inscribed, though this argument is often circular since the date assigned to the building can be influenced by the supposed dates of its inscriptions. We must emphasize, therefore, that the dates assigned to all these texts are approximate and tentative. Jeffery (1990: 311) warns that 'any attempt at precise dating of Cretan inscriptions before the fifth century is most uncertain'; we would add that even fifth-century dates must be used with caution.

F. Literacy

1. The Issue

Questions about the degree of literacy in archaic and classical Greece have stirred considerable debate in recent years, as scholars disagree about how many people could read or write, at what level, and what kinds of people. The debate was stimulated by Harris (1989), who argued that in Greece generally literacy was more restricted than had previously been thought. His conclusions have been accepted by many, but have also encountered significant opposition, especially regarding Athens, for which we have more evidence than for anywhere else (see Pébarthe 2006, Missiou 2011).

In an influential study specifically examining Cretan literacy, Whitley has argued that, in contrast to the other parts of Greece, in Crete, private inscriptions are plentiful in the eighth and seventh centuries, but they almost disappear in the sixth century. From this he concludes that the level of literacy on the island in the late Archaic and Classical periods was significantly lower than it was earlier, and that Crete in the sixth and fifth centuries knew only 'scribal literacy'. Therefore, only a small number of Cretan elites could have read the texts collected here. The ruling elite would thus have been able to impose laws favorable to themselves on the rest of the population, who would not be aware of the inequalities contained in such legislation. Public inscription, especially when it was monumental like the Gortyn Code, would have conveyed the authority of these laws to the common people without letting them know their content (Whitley 1997: esp. 649–61).

One might wonder why the many Cretans who learned to read and write in the eighth and seventh centuries suddenly forgot this skill in the sixth at more or less the same moment when large quantities of legislation began to be written and displayed publicly, and indeed Whitley's evidence for private writing in the Archaic period has been disputed by Perlman, who concludes that private writing actually increased after 600.[141] Perlman's data (which have increased with recent finds) cast doubt on the view that in the sixth and fifth centuries reading and writing were confined to the elite members of the community, so that few outside of the ruling elite could have read the archaic and classical legislation of Crete. The inscriptions themselves (see below) also suggest a larger reading audience than Whitley's conclusions would allow.[142]

The fact that so much legislation was publicly displayed, moreover, suggests that these laws were intended to be widely communicated. The purpose of a single

[141] Perlman 2002: 194–6 with table pp. 218–25; see also Gagarin 2008a: 68–71 and Johnston 2013.

[142] On literacy, see also Papakonstantinou 2002: esp. 137–40. More recently Whitley himself has left open the possibility that the evidence may have different explanations: 'either fewer individuals were literate than elsewhere in the Aegean, or personal expression through writing was in some way discouraged' (2009: 289).

monument like the Gortyn Code (**G72**) could perhaps have been to convey authority by making a visual impact, but if so, this one inscription should have sufficed by itself to achieve this aim. Yet the Code was not a one-off collection like the inscribed stele with the laws of Hammurabi now in the Louvre; it was surrounded by dozens of earlier and later legal inscriptions, some on the same wall, others on nearby walls or stelae, that were considerably less monumental. It is hard to believe these would all have been displayed in public purely for the sake of their visual impact.

2. The Inscriptions

Apart from the level of literacy, certain features of sixth- and fifth-century inscriptions appear intended to make the texts easier to read, suggesting that the legislators who drew up the laws and the masons who carved them were aiming to make them available to a fairly wide audience. The letters are generally large and deeply incised; some, at least, and perhaps all were originally painted red, which would have increased their legibility.[143] At Gortyn the practice of writing some of the earliest inscriptions in long rows of text covering many blocks gradually gave way to inscriptions with shorter rows organized into columns of text that would have eliminated the need to walk along the side of a building while reading a law.

Punctuation in the texts also seems aimed at helping readers. As noted above (Introd. 3D1), word-division is a feature of most early texts; this feature disappears around 500, suggesting that as readers became more proficient, this aid was no longer needed. At Gortyn after 500, masons began to group more laws together on the same inscription, and readers may have had difficulty finding the ones they needed to read. Masons then often used asyndeton or small gaps (or both) between sentences or groups of sentences to help readers see where a new provision or group of provisions began. And the direction of writing that began on a new line could sometimes indicate a change of subject ('archaic paragraphing'); this too would have helped readers locate the provisions they wanted to read (see further Perlman 2004c; Gagarin 2008a: esp. 39–66, 122–75).

It seems reasonable to conclude, therefore, that those in charge of enacting and displaying these legal inscriptions were trying to make them accessible to a broader segment of the community than just the elite. We are not suggesting anything approaching universal literacy, but at least some non-elite members of the community could probably have read the laws if they wanted to know how to proceed when they had some dispute with a neighbor or thought they had been harmed in some way. Families with property might want to read an inheritance

[143] Just as some of the painted signs in the gaps in **G72** have vanished since earlier drawings were made (Introd. 3D2), many of the letters that were originally painted red may no longer show any traces of color.

law, and families with only daughters would be especially interested in the law pertaining to heiresses. We will never know precise numbers, but it is likely that many, perhaps most of those who were or might expect to be involved in litigation would have been able to read the relevant laws, some perhaps with help from friends, and that many of these would actually have done so. Presumably, the wealthier members of the community, who would be most interested in many of these laws (many of which concern property), would be best able to read them, but the poorer citizens and even slaves would also have been interested in some laws, and some of these probably learned to read well enough to understand these texts.

4. GOVERNMENT

Following Aristotle, Cretan society has traditionally been seen as an aristocracy with an oligarchic form of government, in which the leading official of each polis was the *kosmos*, a position open only to members of the elite. The evidence of the laws confirms the prominent role of the *kosmos*, but otherwise reveals a more complex picture of the political structures of Cretan poleis, one in which several parts of the community participate in decision-making. In particular, the inscriptions reveal significant participation in civic affairs by groups that include a relatively large share of the population.[144] Just what the relationship was between these larger bodies and other groups and officials is not entirely clear, and may have differed in different poleis; but it does seem clear that the label 'oligarchy' without qualification is misleading as a general characterization of Cretan government. In fact, the concept of oligarchy and the clear opposition between democracy and oligarchy, which are so well established in Greece by the end of the fifth century (especially in the context of the Peloponnesian War), were largely unknown in the sixth.[145] We are not suggesting that the government of any of these poleis was democratic, but rather that governments were composed of a mixture of elements, with the *kosmos* having clear authority in some respects but also being subject to constraints imposed by the broader community, as well as subject to the rule of law.[146]

[144] Given the nature of our evidence, it is impossible to be more precise about the percentage of the population that would have been designated by the term 'polis' or the city ethnics, but we are confident that it would have been larger than that designated by the modern term 'elite', however this is defined (and it usually remains undefined, which may account for its recent popularity among scholars).

[145] Neither term, 'oligarchy' or 'democracy', is found before the fifth century. It is perhaps also worth stating that the Cretan laws make no mention of monarchy or kingship.

[146] See Gehrke 2009: 399: 'there is no doubt that the formal power of decision-making (in archaic Greece) rested with the people, that is, the popular Assembly, which our sources usually call *damos/demos* or

A. *The Polis*

The word *polis* is found in texts from (in roughly chronological order) Dreros, Axos, Datala, Eltynia, Gortyn, and Eleutherna. In addition to its political uses (state in the abstract and the decision-making authority of the state), it can refer to the union of hinterland and urban center, to the urban center alone, or more specifically to the citadel (Hansen and Nielsen 2004: 39–46). At Eleutherna, Gortyn, and perhaps at Axos the word is clearly used in the sense of the urban area or 'city',[147] but it is also well attested in archaic Crete in the sense of political community. The most debated issue with regard to this last sense is, how inclusive a community the word *polis* designated at this time.

The origin and development of the Greek polis have been the subject of many studies in recent years,[148] some of which seem to assume that the process was fairly uniform across the Greek world. Even if there was a single pattern for the rest of Greece, the archaeological evidence seems to suggest that not only was development in some respects different in Crete (e.g. archaic Cretan 'cultural restraint') but that it may have varied across the island.[149] The following remarks are therefore limited to Crete, specifically to those poleis in central Crete from which inscribed laws survive from the Archaic and Classical periods.

Traditionally, scholars' understanding of the Cretan polis, just as of other Cretan institutions, has been heavily influenced by the reports of later Greeks beginning with Plato and Aristotle (Perlman 1992; Introd. 1). Typical of this approach is a recent paper by Youni, who takes it as 'well-established' that 'the regime of Cretan cities had been aristocratic from the Archaic through the Hellenistic period', and that 'supreme power' was exercised by the *kosmoi*, who were 'military leaders and governors' with judicial authority, who 'took all essential decisions with the assistance of the Council, which consisted of ex-*kosmoi*' (Youni 2010: 154, citing Aristotle and Ephorus). The only alternative to this picture that she considers is that of a sovereign polis with a relatively powerless *kosmos*, but she rejects this alternative, arguing instead that decision-making at Dreros and other poleis was restricted to members of the elite.

In our view, however, the epigraphical evidence suggests a middle ground between 'oligarchic' rule by the *kosmos* and the 'elite' and 'democratic' rule by a large share of the community, or the polis. The inscriptions suggest, rather, that from the earliest time (as in **Dr1**), both groups participated in governance. In what

simply *polis*'. For Gehrke, however, 'the people' are primarily land-owners and those who were active as soldiers. Whitley (2009: 274, 291) calls the form of government 'oligarchic republicanism'.

147 We generally translate *polis* 'city' or 'polis-town' whenever it is used in this geographical sense, but when *polis* refers to the political community, we will speak of the 'polis'.

148 See Mitchell and Rhodes 1997, Davies 2009: 11, with further references.

149 Morris 1998, esp. 58–68, Whitley 2009. For archaic Cretan 'cultural restraint', see Introd. 2B.

follows we examine all the evidence for the polis in our texts, beginning with those from Dreros, which are the earliest. We leave aside the information provided by fourth-century and later writers in their accounts of the 'Cretan *politeia*'. As much as possible, moreover, we confine ourselves to the terminology of the inscriptions rather than later terms like 'assembly', which carry connotations that may not be applicable to early Crete; and we caution that even if we translate a term like *poliatas* as 'citizen', this does not mean that it necessarily carries the implications of 'citizen' in the modern world, or even of *politēs* in classical Athens.

1. Dreros

Both **Dr1** and **Dr5** open with a clause proclaiming 'it pleased the polis' (*ewade poli*), the standard expression for 'the polis decided'. To this **Dr5** adds 'the tribes having been assembled' (*dialeisasi pylasi*).[150] The force of this expression is not certain. It could mean that the tribes assembled and then a separate (smaller) body, the polis, decided, and thus that the tribes had only an advisory role—'with the tribes assembled, the polis decided'. Because the participial phrase is in the same case (dative) as *polis*, however, it is more likely that 'tribes' stands in apposition to *polis*—'it was pleasing to the polis, that is, to the tribes assembled' (comm. ad loc.). This suggests that when the whole polis met, it assembled by tribe, and that the polis was thus roughly equivalent to all those who belonged to one of the tribes in Dreros.[151]

The enactment clause in **Dr1** (line 1) mentions only the polis, but later it mentions the polis again in a way that may be informative (line 4): 'The oath-swearers [are] the *kosmos* and the *damioi* and the twenty of the polis.' It is not certain exactly what oaths are sworn or when, but since the oath-swearing was presumably accompanied by a certain amount of ritual, the best explanation for the participation of just twenty members of the polis is that total membership of the polis was too large for all members to participate in the ceremony. The law thus enlists a smaller group, 'the twenty of the polis', who represented the full polis in the oath-swearing ceremony. Some take the expression to be equivalent to the polis (i.e. 'the twenty who comprise the polis'), but if this were the case, *polis* alone would suffice, as it does in line 1.[152] Thus, we conclude that for the oath-swearing ceremony, the polis was represented by twenty persons; and from this we may speculate that the full polis consisted of at least 200 members (1:10) and

[150] This is the most likely sense of the participle, but it is not certain; see n. ad loc.

[151] 'Possibly there were separate meetings of the tribes in addition to the meeting of the assembly, but more probably there was simply a meeting of the assembly at which the tribes voted separately' (Rhodes and Lewis 1997: 390). We should not assume, however, that the decision was reached by voting.

[152] Superfluous words are rarely included in these early texts; rather, early Greek laws are more commonly elliptical, sometimes to the point of obscurity. Moreover, the genitive would be difficult to explain on this reading.

perhaps many more than this. The oath was also sworn by the *damioi*, who were presumably somehow connected with the *damos* (Attic *dēmos* = 'people' or 'common people'); and it is reasonable to suppose that they were similar to the twenty of the polis—a small group representing a larger membership.[153] The oath was thus sworn by three separate elements comprising the community of Dreros: the *kosmos* as the highest official, the *damioi* who represented the *damos*, and twenty members representing the polis.

The precise composition of *damos* and the polis is unclear. Van Effenterre (1985) has argued that the polis consisted of the urban inhabitants of Dreros and the *damos*, who must have been different, consisted of the rural inhabitants of the territory of Dreros. With regard to the polis, this conclusion may draw some support from semantic considerations: one of the meanings of *polis*, perhaps its most basic sense, is the 'urban area', that is, a fairly well-defined geographical space with a relatively dense population, such as is found on the two hilltops at Dreros (Dreros Site). It would be a natural extension of this meaning that *polis* then came to designate the population inhabiting this area, understood as the free adult males, of course. The *damos* might then be those residing in the countryside around the polis. It is not clear, however, that there was very much habitation in the countryside (Introd. 2A3b and comm. ad **Dr1**.4). Another possibility might be that the polis consisted of all those who owned property (or met some other qualification), and that the *damos* consisted of the rest of the inhabitants (the common people).[154]

2. Datala

A similar clause specifying enactment by the whole community begins the agreement with Spensithios: *ewade Dataleusi*, lit. 'it was pleasing to the Dataleis'.[155] The text then continues 'and we the polis promise to Spensithios, from the tribes five from each, etc.' (**Da1**A1–2).[156] Here 'Dataleis' are the body that enacts the agreement, and another group, 'we the polis', formally promise to execute it. Like the oath in **Dr1**.4, the act of pledging (the verb literally means 'we pour a libation') presumably involved a certain amount of ritual, and thus, as with oath-swearing at Dreros, a smaller group composed of five men from each tribe carried out the ritual action on behalf of the entire polis. It is possible to interpret the sentence to mean that the polis at Datala consisted of five men from each tribe, but in that case 'we the polis promise' would not need the additional qualification

[153] It is possible that either 'the twenty of the *polis*' or the *damioi* (or both) formed a council of some sort, but if so, we know nothing about their activities other than their role in this ceremony.

[154] Youni explains the polis as consisting of 'the powerful chieftains of the local elite' (2010: 157), but this sense has no connection to any other meaning of the word *polis*.

[155] For more on the Dataleis and other collective bodies, see Introd. 4B1.

[156] *ἔϜαδε Δαταλεῦσι καὶ ἐσπένσαμες πόλις Σπενσιθίϴι, ἀπὸ πυλᾶν πέντε ἀπ' ἐκάστας*, etc.

'five from each tribe'. The qualification thus implies that the five from each tribe were a representative group drawn from the tribes and assembled to represent the polis at this pledging ceremony.

A more difficult question is whether the Dataleis, who enacted the agreement, are equivalent to the polis. As we will argue below (Introd. 4B1), it is hard to understand the collective city-ethnic 'Dataleis' as anything but the members of the political class of Datala, however that territory was defined (and presumably limited to free-born adult males). As for *polis*, the term occurs twice in the specification of Spensithios' duties as 'writing and remembering for the polis in public matters (*ta damosia*), divine and human' (A3–5, repeated in 5–7). Spensithios was thus a public servant, working for the polis. And since he was employed by the Dataleis, the community, who are providing substantial benefits to him and his offspring, he must have been working for the benefit of that community, not just for part of it. Thus, it appears that here too the polis is equivalent to the political community, which can be identified as either a single political entity (the polis) or a collective consisting of all members of the community (the Dataleis).

3. Other Poleis

Besides enactment clauses,[157] other mentions of the polis in the sense of a political community show it acting in financial or economic affairs.[158] **G43**Ba, for instance, begins 'the polis have given (*edokan a polis*) the land at Keskora and Pala for planting' and goes on to prohibit selling or mortgaging the land; interestingly, the singular noun *polis* is used with a plural verb indicating a collective sense to the noun;[159] evidently Gortyn had public land that the polis collectively gave to individuals to cultivate while it retained ownership. **A1** shows us the polis as an employer: lines 6–7 prescribe that certain people will work for five days for the polis without pay, and 10–11 may prohibit the imposition of additional charges on the polis (comm. ad loc.). The role of the polis as employer is also evident in **Da1**, and is probably reflected in texts like **G79** and **Ele9** that regulate the employment of workers. In addition, **G78**.8, **G79**.16 and 21, and **Elt2**.3 all specify that a fine is to be paid to or deposited with the polis (Introd. 7E3). Finally, a sixth-century fragment from Gortyn (**G13**e2) has the phrase *poli pansai*, 'the whole

[157] Enactment clauses that survive from poleis other then Datala and Dreros designate the body enacting the laws as those people associated with the location rather than by the term *polis*: 'Gortynians' (*Gortynioi*) **G78**, 'Lyktians' (*Lyktioi*) **Lyktos1A** and **1B**, and perhaps Eltynians (*Eltynioi*) **Elt2**.2. See Introd. 4B1.

[158] In addition to the sixth- and fifth-century texts, two fragmentary fourth-century texts from Gortyn appear to use *polis* in the sense of the political community: *IC* 4.146.6 has the expression 'if the polis sacrifice [something] on Ida' and *IC* 4.148.2 has 'on behalf of the polis' (*uper poleos*) without context.

[159] Cf. **Da1**A1–2; also *IC* 4.146.6.

polis' (in the dative) perhaps followed by a form of the verb for exacting payment, probably of a fine.[160]

These texts from Gortyn and other poleis are entirely consistent with the sense of *polis* as the entire community, which is suggested by semantic considerations and supported by the laws from Dreros and (to a lesser extent) Datala. They show that the Cretan polis, as a political body, owned and leased out public land, received income and spent its funds on sacrifices, public works, and other public matters, in much the same way as the classical polis in Athens and elsewhere.

B. Public Bodies

1. Collective Bodies

The Greek word for assembly (*ekklēsia*) is not found in our texts, and so we try to avoid speaking of an assembly in Crete, as this term may evoke the specific circumstances of the classical Athenian Assembly. We do find in Crete, however, the widespread use of city-ethnics, often in contexts where the body seems to be acting as a kind of assembly.[161] In addition to the Gortynians, we find the Dataleis, Lyktians, and Eltynians, and also the Itanians (at Lyktos), Rhittenians (at Gortyn), and Prepsidai and Milatioi (at Dreros). Occasionally one of these collectives is used in the singular to denote an individual from that particular place.[162]

These collective bodies appear in a variety of roles, including that of enacting legislation. We have already noted the enactment clause at Datala (**Da1**A1, Introd. 4A2), which is dated to the late sixth century. In addition, both faces of **Lyktos1** (**A** and **B**) begin with this same enactment clause, preceded by *thioi* on **A** and probably also on **B**: 'Gods. The Lyktians decided these things.' **Elt2** may have begun with a similar clause.[163] The only example of an enactment clause from Gortyn, **G78**.1, is particularly interesting: 'the Gortynians, voting, decided these things' (*tad' ewade tois Gortyniois psapidonsi*).[164] The specific mention of voting

[160] Three letters, πρα, follow πόλι πάνσαι, and several editors supplement this as πόλι πάνσαι πρά[ζεσθαι] ('is to exact [payment] for the polis'); see further ad loc. The same expression perhaps appeared in **G59**.3.

[161] City-ethnics are discussed (together with other sorts of ethnics) in Hansen and Nielsen 2004: 58–69. We cannot be certain that their use at this time on Crete was the same as it was elsewhere in classical Greece, but we have no reason to think otherwise; see Perlman 1996.

[162] The Latosians (**G58**.4–5, **G78**.2) may be different from the others in that the name does not appear to be derived from the name of a polis. Note also the expression 'all Gortyn and those living in Aulon' in **G64**.2–3, where 'all Gortyn' may be equivalent to 'the Gortynians'.

[163] The first preserved words in **Elt2**.2 are *tois Eltyniousi*; they may originally have been preceded by *ewade*.

[164] *Psapidonsi* is the phonetic equivalent of Attic *psēphizousi*, derived from *psēphos*, a 'voting pebble'. This suggests that the Gortynians voted by means of pebbles or similar tokens, rather than by a show of hands.

suggests that it was not the regular procedure for making collective decisions at Gortyn, since if it were, there would be no need to mention it here.[165]

Another text, **G80**, which is an agreement between Gortyn and Rhitten is notable for its repeated use of collectives. It begins, 'On the following terms, the Rhittenians are to have their own laws and their own judicial system independent of the Gortynians' (line 1). 'The Rhittenians' are mentioned again in line 7, followed by a specific prohibition—'a Gortynian is not to go and take security from a Rhittenian' (8–9); consequences are then specified for those who violate this rule (9–12). Then comes the final provision of the preserved text: 'whatever matter the Rhittenians as a community (*to koinon oi Rhittenioi*) again fight about with the Gortynians, the herald is to summon (?) [the Gortynians], either they themselves or others on their behalf, to Rhitten in ten days to answer (the charge) in the agora with the people gathered' (12–15). This last expression leaves the identity of those who gathered vague, and it is also unclear whether this assembled group merely observed the judicial proceedings or participated somehow (comm. ad loc.). Regrettably, the next clause (beginning in line 15), which apparently specified how a decision would be made in the case, breaks off before providing this information.

The composition of these collective bodies which are designated by a city-ethnic is never specified, as it was presumably evident to anyone reading the texts, but it is hard to escape the conclusion that they comprised all the appropriate inhabitants (i.e. free, native-born, adult males) of the polis in question, that is those living permanently in both the hinterland and the urban center. The uses of the collective, however, indicate that these inhabitants were also considered to be the political community of the polis in question. It is possible, but far less likely, that city-ethnics were used to designate a more narrowly defined group—for example, 'those owning a certain amount or kind of property' or 'those from certain elite families'. The difficulty with understanding the city-ethnics in this way is that they are never qualified or limited in any way that might indicate a smaller body than the whole political community. The only way in which an unqualified city-ethnic could come to be used to designate a smaller group of elites would be if this smaller group were well known in the community as 'the Gortynians', 'the Dataleis', and so on, and it is hard to see how any smaller group would be so designated.[166]

[165] The common method of making decisions may have been by consensus and acclamation, as it was in Homer and in Sparta even in the fifth century (Thucydides 1.87); see Larsen 1949.

[166] There is a possible parallel in the historical process that led to the term 'Spartiates' designating a smaller group within the community of the Lacedaimonians. But as far as we know, the historical process in Sparta that resulted in this smaller group of elite citizens was unparalleled in the Greek world, and it seems highly unlikely that a similar series of events occurred in (at least) six different Cretan cities, particularly without leaving any trace in the archaeological or textual record.

Two further arguments may support our conclusion. First, the reference in **G78**.1 to 'the Gortynians voting' indicates that the group must be fairly large or else there would be no need to vote, especially by means of voting pebbles as the verb suggests (above, n. 164). A stronger argument can be made on the basis of the provision in **G80**.8–9: 'A Gortynian is not to go and take security from a Rhittenian.' This prohibition would make little sense if these two city-ethnics designated only members of a small elite class, since then any of the other (non-elite) members of the Gortynian community would be free to take security from any person at Rhitten and even elite 'Gortynians' could take security from anyone else in Rhitten except for these elite 'Rhittenians'.[167]

Finally, in the rules for settling conflicts between the communities of Gortyn and Rhitten in lines 12–15, one might wish to argue that because the expression *to koinon oi Rhittenioi* apparently designates 'the Rhittenians as a community', the collective alone ('the Rhittenians') must designate something less than the whole community; it is more likely, however, that *to koinon* is added to the collective here to emphasize that it concerns conflicts between the entire communities, not conflicts between their individual members, which have already been addressed in 8–12.

Whatever other roles these collective bodies may have played in the governance of Cretan poleis, **Da1**, **G80**, **Lyktos1A**, and **Lyktos1B** show that they did enact legislation, and in this regard they functioned like the Drerian polis and the popular assembly at Athens. And since the only other body that apparently enacts legislation are the (otherwise unattested) *thystai* in an early inscription from Dreros (**Dr4**.1), we can conclude that the word *polis* and the city-ethnic for that polis were equivalent ways of designating the political community and that this was the primary legislative body in these Cretan poleis at this time.[168]

2. Council

Closely connected to the traditional idea that Cretan government was oligarchic is the assumption that every polis had a council or council of elders; but although such a council is part of the traditional literary picture of Cretan government (Aristotle, *Politics* 1272a7–8), it gets very little notice and seems of little importance in the laws (Wallace 2013: 195). We have one certain occurrence of the noun *bola* (*boulē*), at Axos, where the council is directed to give money for certain

[167] Singular city-ethnics are also used in **G63**.3, which apparently regulates litigation between 'the Gortynian' and 'the Lebenian', and in **L4**.5–6, where we find 'the Lyktian'.

[168] In addition to examples discussed in the text, city-ethnics are also found in **G23**.8b (*ton Gortynion*—perhaps acc. sing. but more likely gen. pl.), **G62**.2 (*oi Go*[*rtynioi*]), **Gortyn5**.2–3 (*tois Gortyni*[*ois*]), and possibly **G10**x–y, where all that survives are the letters *ynia*, which could be supplemented as [*Gort*]*ynia*[*i*] (or -*a*[*is*]), 'women of Gortyn'. We also find Itanians in **Lyktos1A**, and (in the singular) both Gortynian and Lebenian in **G63**.3 and 4.

sacrifices 'in the same way' (**A9**.13); there is also a possible instance at Lyktos, where the text may mean 'by enactment of the council' (*hyper wolas wadas*, **Lyktos1A6** with notes and commentary). The qualification at Axos seems to indicate that this was not the only sacrifice for which the council provided funding, and suggests that providing public funds for sacrifices was one of the regular duties of its council (comm. ad loc.); otherwise, we have no information about other duties or functions it may have had. At Lyktos, the council may have enacted legislation concerning the harboring of aliens. A council may also be mentioned in two Gortynian inscriptions, but in both cases other interpretations of the very fragmentary text are possible.[169] Finally, the agreement between Knossos and Tylissos may provide evidence of a council in each city in the mid-fifth century, with each *bola* apparently authorized to fine the *kosmoi* in the other city; but much is unclear in this passage.[170]

Besides *bola* we also find *pre(i)sgēia* in a text from Prinias (**Pr7**D1, D3).[171] The sense of this noun is unclear: it could be a body of elders or an embassy (the fragmentary text provides no context).[172] In addition, the agreement between Gortyn and Rhitten provides that in certain cases the Rhittenian *kosmos* is to exact the fine and 'if they do not, there is to be immunity for the elders (*tons preigistons*) who exact it from them' (**G80**.10–12). 'The elders' may be a reference to a council of elders, and the possible identification of Rhitten with Prinias makes it tempting to conclude that this polis (and perhaps only this polis) had a council of elders; but 'the elders' at Rhitten may also have been a small group with administrative duties rather than a council.[173]

All in all, the meagerness of these references suggests that a council of some sort may have existed in one or more Cretan poleis, and that it may have had some sort of financial duties (collecting fines, providing funds for a sacrifice), but it evidently played a less important role in the affairs of the polis than did the collective body of all members of the political community. This group, whether referred to by a

[169] In **G23**.4 the letters *esbolan* may be a noun (= *ekbolēn*, 'removal') or the phrase *es bolan* (= *eis boulēn*), 'to the council' (see above, Dialect 14); in **Gortyn3**.6 the letters *mbolai* may represent the noun [*s*]*ymbolai*, but perhaps more likely represents the phrase [*e*]*m bolai* (*en boulēi*); see n. ad loc. In both cases the absence of a definite article with *bola* would be puzzling (as it would also in **Lyktos1A**.6).

[170] See Preface, n. 2. In lines B38–42 we read, 'If the Knossian summons an embassy (*presgea*) in Tylissos, it is to follow wherever he wishes, and if the Tylissian [summons an embassy in Knossos], the Knossian [is to do] the same. And if he (?) should not provide hospitality, let the *bola* immediately impose a fine of ten staters on the *kosmoi*. And in Tylissos, the Knossian [is to do] the same.'

[171] It is possible to restore *pre(i)sgeia* in **A7**.1 but the text there is very uncertain; see n. ad loc.

[172] Note that in the passage from the agreement between Knossos and Tylissos cited above, n. 170, *presgea* must have the sense of 'embassy'.

[173] The only other possible mention of a council-like group is at Dreros, where among the oath-swearers in **Dr1**.4 are the *damioi* and the twenty of the polis; either of these groups might possibly have been some sort of council-like body; see Introd. 4A1.

city-ethnic or as 'the polis', clearly played a larger role in governance and had greater authority in general than did any council. To be sure, the textual evidence is not conclusive, but the relative scarcity of mentions of any council or council-like body in contrast to the much more abundant references to the polis or to the collective body designated by a city-ethnic is striking, and at the very least, poses a substantial obstacle to the conclusion that the *kosmoi* made 'all essential decisions with the assistance of the Council' (Youni 2010: 154).

3. Tribe and *Startos*

Two other groups mentioned in the inscriptions, the tribe or *pyla* (*phylē*) and the *startos* may have played some role in governance on Crete, though we have little information about either.

The tribe is attested in the archaic and classical inscriptions of Dreros (**Dr5**.1), Datala (**Da1**A1–2), and Gortyn (**G19**.3; **G104**.1; **G72**.7.50–8.36). We cannot demonstrate their existence elsewhere on Crete during the Archaic and Classical periods, but we assume that most if not all of the Cretan poleis had tribes.[174] **Dr5**.1 and **Da1**A1–2 suggest that all the members of the polis belonged to one of the tribes into which the polis was divided (see below). Tribal names provide a further clue as to the basis of their organization. The only possible tribal name in archaic and classical Cretan texts is the '*startos* Aithaleus' at Gortyn, which may or may not refer to the tribe Aithaleis (below), but the dating formulas of Hellenistic inscriptions from Crete preserve the names of fourteen tribes (Perlman 2014). We cannot, of course, claim with certainty that any or all of these date back to the Archaic period or earlier. On the other hand, there is no reason to suggest that they did not. Jones observes that with very few exceptions the Cretan tribal names belong to the category he terms *Landsmannschaftlich* names, that is names that reflect the members' place of origin.[175] Aithaleis, for example, is one of two tribal names from the island which suggest mainland Greek Aeolic–Thessalian origins,[176] but the historical implications of these alleged connections are complex.[177]

[174] Hellenistic inscriptions attest tribes at twelve of the Cretan poleis including Axos, Dreros, Gortyn, and Knossos. See N. Jones 1987: 219–31; Perlman 2014.

[175] Jones 1987: 219–22. For the organization of public associations in ancient Greece and the distinction between territorial and personal units, with *Landsmannschaftlich* units a category of the latter, see Jones 1987: 4–14.

[176] Maiuri 1911: 663–6 understood the tribal name as apocope of **Αἰγιθαλεῖς*, 'sucklers of goats', and on the basis of the use of other forms of the name posited for it Aeolic–Achaean origins. The other, Ainaones, also occurs at Gortyn (*IC* 4.196 partially restored). Maiuri 1911: 666–8 linked this name to the Thessalian Ainianes who represented an Aeolic–Achaean pre-Dorian segment of the population.

[177] For a detailed study of the implications of tribal names and month names for the deep history of the population of archaic and classical Crete, see Perlman 2014.

In any event, it is likely that tribal membership was not determined by where one resided (or where an ancestor resided at the time of the 'creation' of the tribe) but by kinship with a group or notional ancestor. The fact that tribes had a significant private role in the marriage of heiresses at Gortyn (**G72**.7.15–8.36), providing a kind of 'safety net' (Kristensen 2002: 79) for heiresses who, if they could not find a husband among the closer relatives, could look to their tribe for a larger selection of candidates (Introd. 5C4), suggests that at Gortyn the tribe was loosely thought of as a kinship association. There is, however, very little evidence for a formal relationship between tribes and supra-(nuclear) household kinship associations.

The tribe's public role is only mentioned in two texts we have already examined in connection with the polis (Introd. 4A), **Dr5**.1, where the assembled tribes appear to constitute the polis, and **Da1**A1–2, where the polis in the form of 'five from each tribe' formally ratifies the agreement with Spensithios. If the *startos* Aithaleus is the same as the tribe Aithaleis (below) this might suggest a tribal organization and possibly tribal rotation of the *kosmoi* at Gortyn.[178] Whether the tribes had any other public function is unknown.

The *startos* is an obscure body known only from Crete, and in the Archaic and Classical periods only from Gortyn (**G72**.5.5; **G80**.7).[179] The word is usually translated either as 'clan' (Willetts)[180] or as a military 'troop', 'company',[181] but since we have next to no evidence for the group's composition or function, we can do no more than speculate. The military sense depends on the assumption that *startos* is a metathesized form of Attic *stratos*, whose primary meaning in the Classical period is 'army'. The phonetic change is plausible, though not certain, but because *stratos* can mean any large body of people, not just an army (see LSJ *s. v.* 2–3), we must allow that *startos* at Gortyn could have either a military or a civilian meaning.

A civilian sense is clear in the dating formula in **G72**.5.5–6: 'when the *startos* Aithaleus, Kyllos and his colleagues, were *kosmoi*'. This formula seems to mean that the Aithalian *startos* as a whole had the office of *kosmos* but that it was Kyllos and certain other members of the *startos* who actually served as *kosmoi*, perhaps

[178] Cf. the very fragmentary **G104**, which mentions the tribe and perhaps also says something about a *kosmos.*

[179] *IC* 4.142.2, probably from the fourth century, ends with the letters OAI[.]A[, which, on the basis of **G72**.5.5, Comparetti supplemented as ὀ Αἰ[θ]α[λεὺς σταρτὸς (*o Ai[th]a[leus startos*). Guarducci cautiously accepts this supplement, but it is only one of many possibilities.

[180] So too Guarducci (*gens*). These translations are based on Aristotle's report (*Politics* 1272a33–5) that the Cretans choose *kosmoi* from certain clans (ἐκ τινῶν γενῶν).

[181] So Chaniotis, who states that the *startos* consists of the warriors in the tribe: 'all the members of the tribe's military assembly that elected its officers' (2005: 181). Kristensen too (2002: 71–4) argues for a military sense for *startos.*

with Kyllos as the chief *kosmos* (Introd. 4C1). Since there is no evidence that the *kosmos* was a military leader—possibly a role filled by the *startagetas* (Introd. 4C5)—there seems no reason why a military company would be serving with him as *kosmos*. The expression also implies that the Aithalian *startos* was only one of several *startoi* which could serve as *kosmos* in Gortyn, and the office may somehow have rotated among these several *startoi*. Similar formulas from other Cretan cities in the Hellenistic period that use the names of known tribes (e.g. the Dorian Dymanes, Hylleis, and Pamphyloi) are understood by most scholars to imply a system of tribal rotation (presumably annual) for the office of *kosmos*.

In addition to the fifth-century mention of the *startos* Aithaleus, the occurrence of the plural Aithaleis in three Hellenistic dating formulas from Gortyn raises the difficult question of the relationship between the *startos* and the tribe. *IC* 4.259, for example (second century), begins 'when the Aithaleis, Erasōn, son of Antiphatas, and his colleagues, were *kosmoi*'.[182] This indicates that Erasōn was the chief *kosmos*, perhaps a kind of chairman of a board of ten or eleven *kosmoi* all of whom belonged to the Aithaleis. Because other Cretan cities use the names of known tribes in such dating formulas, Aithaleis was probably the name of a tribe in the Hellenistic period, and we believe that many if not most of the tribal names attested in later inscriptions from Crete are early. It is thus a reasonable conclusion that the tribe Aithaleis existed at Gortyn in the fifth century, and that the *startos* Aithaleus was connected with the tribe Aithaleis. Presumably, there were several other tribes, and thus several other *startoi*, at Gortyn as well.

Just what the connection was between *startos* and tribe is unclear. It seems unlikely that the two were identical, or that, as Kristensen (2002: 66) proposed, the *startos* consisted of the male adult citizens of the tribe, because whenever the tribe is mentioned, whether in its public role (enacting laws) or its private role (providing a husband), it almost certainly goes without saying that only adult males are involved, so that no special term to designate this sub-group was needed. But the *startos* was probably some sort of sub-unit of the tribe, in which case the *startos* Aithaleus would presumably have been a sub-unit of the tribe Aithaleis. The *startos* Aithaleus might consist of those members of the tribe Aithaleis who were eligible to serve as *kosmoi*, though this would tell us nothing about the composition of the *startos*, and other criteria for inclusion are also possible.

The position and function of the *startagetas* ('leader of the *startos*') is equally uncertain. He is mentioned together with the *kosmos* in **G80**.4–8, where he and the *kosmos* who go to Rhitten are to serve as *kosmoi* with the Rhittenian *kosmos*, where they can levy certain fines which are to be used 'with the *startos* and with the Rhittenians.' The *startagetas* then is not the *kosmos*, though here he serves as a

[182] The other two are *IC* 4.167.3 and 184.1. For *IC* 4.142.2, see above, n. 179.

kosmos, and the *kosmos* is a member of the *startos* (**G72**.5.5–6) but is not its leader. Both must be Gortynians and both presumably belonged to the same *startos*. It is possible that the *startagetas* is a military leader, but his role in **G80**, like the role of the *startos* in **G72**.5.5–6, is entirely civilian.

C. *Public Officials*

1. Kosmos

The one official attested in almost all Cretan poleis in the Archaic and Classical periods is the *kosmos*. He is mentioned in texts from every polis from which legislation survives except for Knossos, Phaistos, and Prinias, and since only one short fragmentary text survives from each of these, the absence of a *kosmos* is of no significance. No text says explicitly that the *kosmos* (whether one or several) is the leading official in the polis, but the amount of attention paid to this office strongly implies this, and on this point, at least, later authors (e.g. Aristotle, *Politics* 1272a4–b11) agree with the inscriptional evidence. Beyond this, however, there are many uncertainties regarding the position. Some texts imply a single *kosmos*; others clearly indicate the presence of two or more. Occasionally the word is qualified by *ksenios* (*xenios* = 'the *kosmos* for foreigners'?) or some other term ('the presiding *kosmos*'). Whether these differences are the result of the haphazard survival of evidence from different poleis, or whether the office was, in fact, organized differently in different poleis (or at different times in the same polis) is impossible to determine with certainty. Both of these factors may be involved.

a. NUMBER OF *KOSMOI*

The earliest evidence seems to imply a single *kosmos*. **Dr1**, probably our earliest text, states: 'When someone has been *kosmos*, the same person is not to be *kosmos* for ten years.' This might be taken to mean that anyone who serves as one of several *kosmoi* cannot serve again for ten years, but the wording seems rather to imply a single *kosmos*. This implication is even stronger in the last provision of the law, which specifies that the oath-swearers are '*kosmos* and the *damioi* and the twenty of the polis'. *Kosmos* here might be meant to designate the *kosmos* in question on each occasion, or perhaps the *kosmos* who is beginning his term in office, or it might even mean 'a *kosmos*', i.e. any of several *kosmoi*; but here too it seems much more likely that the mention of *kosmos* in the singular together with two groups indicates that there was just one *kosmos* at the time and that he would be one of the oath-swearers. We might also note that no other official is mentioned in the seven surviving laws from Dreros, though several other groups are mentioned—the *thystai* (**Dr4**), the *agretai* (**Dr5**), and probably the *hetaireiai* and the *agelai* (**Dr3**).

After Dreros, most of our information comes from Gortyn, where the earliest text contains a provision similar to that at Dreros that even more strongly implies a single *kosmos* (**G14**p–g2): 'the same person is not to serve as *kosmos* for three years, the *gnomones* for ten years, and the *ksenios*[183] for five years'. As at Dreros, this law might apply to any one of several *kosmoi*, but it seems much more likely that it designates a single *kosmos*, and that by contrast, the plural *gnomones* indicates that there were several of these officials. The same inscription also contains another provision involving a *kosmos* (**G14**g–p1): 'he is to pay fifty cauldrons in each case. The *kosmos* in charge (*kosmos o epistas*), if he does not exact payment, is to owe it himself, and the *titas*, if he does not exact payment, . . . ' Here the expression 'the *kosmos* in charge' might designate the chief *kosmos* among many, but could also mean 'the *kosmos* in charge of the case', that is, the case that is regulated by the clause that precedes. If this is so, the *kosmos* may have been the judge in the case (Introd. 4C1c), or he may have had some sort of supervisory role. The expression may still imply that there is more than one *kosmos*, since if there were no others, there would be no need to specify 'the *kosmos* in charge'. But it is also possible that the qualification is meant to be explanatory: the *kosmos*, because he is in charge, is to exact payment or owe it himself.

The next significant information about the *kosmos* at Gortyn comes in the Code (**G72**), which contains several mentions. Best known is the dating formula in 5.5–6 (discussed Introd. 4B3): 'when the *startos* Aithaleus, Kyllos and his colleagues, were *kosmoi*'.[184] This expression informs us that at the time of this provision (which is probably the time that the Code was enacted) the position of *kosmos* was held by members of the *startos* Aithaleus, specifically 'Kyllos and his colleagues'. This expression seems to imply that there were several *kosmoi* from this *startos*, of whom Kyllos was apparently the most important, but this implication may be misleading. In any case, the clause provides no information how a plurality of *kosmoi* may have worked.

A passage later in the Code (**G72**.8.53–9.1)—'if anyone marries the heiress otherwise than is written, the claimants are to bring information to the *kosmos* (*porti kosmon*)'—seems to imply a single *kosmos*, though it might perhaps mean that the claimants are to inform 'a *kosmos*', that is, any one of several *kosmoi*. Even stronger evidence for a single *kosmos* comes in the agreement between Gortyn and Rhitten, which states that 'the *startagetas* and the person serving as *kosmos* (*ton kosmionta*) who go to Rhitten are to serve as *kosmos* together with the Rhittenian *kosmos*' (**G80**.4–8). The two Gortynian officials are pictured as working together, and there is no hint of another *kosmos*. But the expression could also

[183] For the possibility that the *ksenios* was a specialized *kosmos*, see Introd. 4C1b.

[184] This expression may be echoed in a fragment of a later text (*IC* 4.142.4): 'those with . . . were *kosmoi*' (*ekosmion oi s*[*yn* . . .).

mean 'the one person [out of many] serving as *kosmos* who goes to Rhitten'. Thus, although much of the evidence suggests that Gortyn (and also Rhitten) had a single *kosmos* in this period, a plurality of *kosmoi* is also possible at Gortyn (see further on Rhitten below). Interestingly, the person who 'serves as *kosmos*' at Gortyn (*ton kosmionta*, line 5) goes to Rhitten and 'serves as *kosmos*' there (*kosmen*, also line 5) together with the *startagetas*,[185] even though the *startagetas* appears not to be a *kosmos*.

Some of the mentions of *kosmos* in **Da1**, the agreement with Spensithios, suggest there was just one *kosmos*, but others may indicate that there was more than one in that polis. The agreement requires Spensithios, as *poinikastas*, to be present at all sacred and secular activities 'wherever the *kosmos* is present' (B1–4). Since Spensithios probably could not serve more than one *kosmos* at a time in this way, the passage strongly suggests that there is only one *kosmos*, for whom the *poinikastas* is a kind of assistant. But the agreement later mentions 'the presiding *kosmos*' (*kosmos epestakos*) in a section where most of the text is now lost (A16–17). As with 'the *kosmos* in charge' in **G14**g–p1 (discussed above), this expression might designate the *kosmos* who presides over other *kosmoi* or the *kosmos* who presides over the situation at hand; in either case, it seems to suggest that there are other *kosmoi*. Then, in **Da1**B9–10 we find the letters *kosmoi*. Different interpretations of the text have been proposed:[186] for some (e.g. VER I.22) the *poinikastas* who is facing trial is to be tried 'like the other *kosmoi*'; in our view (n. ad loc.), the text allows a *poinikastas* who is facing trial to be tried 'in the presence of the *kosmos*' (*en kosmoi*) if he wishes. This might imply a single *kosmos*, but the text is too insecure to use this passage as evidence.[187]

References to the *kosmos* in other poleis besides Dreros, Gortyn, and Datala are scattered and relatively uninformative. At Rhitten: the agreement with Gortyn specifies that 'the Rhittenian *kosmos* is to exact payment; and if *they* do not exact payment' (**G80**.10–11). The singular noun followed by a plural verb may indicate more than one *kosmos* at Rhitten, but perhaps more likely the plural implies that the Rhittenian and Gortynian *kosmoi* work together. A plurality of *kosmoi* is clearly indicated in one text, **Ele9**.2, where we find the words [*k*]*ai Timarkos ekosmion*; this was probably part of a dating formula from which the name of another person (or other persons) has been lost: '[when X] and Timarkos were *kosmoi*'. The plural verb makes clear that two (or more) *kosmoi* served together at this time in Eleutherna. Besides this, we simply note that the *kosmos* is mentioned

185 Since the regular meaning of *kosmen* as 'serve as *kosmos*' is clear in *ton kosmionta* ('the one serving as *kosmos*') two lines earlier, it would be very difficult for the verb in **G80**.5 to mean something more general, such as 'bring order to' *vel sim.*

186 J–MD print the letters without attempting to interpret them.

187 We also omit two passages in **Da1** where *kosmos* is possible but not secure: *toi kos*[*moi*] ('for the *kosmos*'), A19–20 and *ko*[*sm* . .], A21.

five times at Axos, three times certainly in the singular (**A5+6**.7, **A9**.9, **Axos1**.13–14) and twice where the number is uncertain (**Axos1**.17–18, **Axos2**A8). Finally, an inscription from Eltynia directs the (singular) *kosmos* to exact a fine for the polis (*kosmon de praden tan es polin timan*, **Elt2**.3) but later speaks of *kosmoi* in the plural, the only certain use of this noun in the plural in our texts (**Elt2**.8): 'the *kosmoi* having sworn the oath are to decide, the one for? the polis, and the one . . .'[188] Here we clearly have more than one *kosmos*; they decide cases, each perhaps with a specialized jurisdiction, though the text is too fragmentary to reveal how their duties were divided. In any case, Eltynia too seems to fit the pattern we seem to see at Gortyn, of both a single *kosmos* and plural *kosmoi*.[189]

b. THE *KSENIOS* (*KOSMOS*)

Since the evidence we have considered thus far from Gortyn and Eltynia (and perhaps other poleis) seems to point to both a single *kosmos* and several *kosmoi*, we must look for another route to a solution, and the mention in two texts from Gortyn of a *ksenios kosmos* or 'foreigners' *kosmos*' may provide the clue we need. The first of these occurrences (**G30**.4) records only the words *ksenion kosmon*,[190] but the second (**G78**.4), which offers protection for those who settle in Gortyn as Latosians, calls on 'the foreigners' *kosmos*' (*ton ksenion kosmon*) not to allow these residents to be enslaved or plundered. Thus, the *ksenios kosmos* was evidently, as the name indicates, an official concerned with matters relating to foreigners, and since the phrase occurs in both an early inscription and a fifth-century text, it seems that the *kosmos* and the *ksenios kosmos* coexisted during most, if not all, of the period. But we must also recall that the non-iteration law at Gortyn (**G14**p–g2) prohibits the *ksenios* (without qualification) from holding office again (for five years), as well as the *kosmos* (for three years), and the *ksenios* (without *kosmos*) is also mentioned in **G72** 11.16–17 and **G79**.15, and perhaps also in the fragmentary texts **G53**A2–3, **G89**.7, and **G98**. In the last two of these texts, *ksenios kosmos* is also possible, but in **G53**A2–3 [*k*]*senios* is followed by *pan*[, which seems to exclude this possibility.

[188] κόσμος γ[ι]γνοίσκεν ὄμνυντας τὸν ἐπὶ πόλεος τὸν τ' ἀṛ[—].·

[189] Other possible occurrences of *kosmos* at Gortyn that we do not discuss, many of them fragmentary, have either a noun that could be singular or plural, or some form of *o kosmion* ('the one who is *kosmos*'), which likely designates a single *kosmos* but could also designate one of several *kosmoi*. See **G10**.*i*; **G14**.*f*1(?); **G25**.*s*; **G29**.3; **G41**.4.10–11 and 13; **G53**A4–5 (almost certainly singular); **G62**.5; **G72**.1.52, 52–3; **G104**.3. The uncertainty stems mainly from the ambiguity of several forms in the Cretan script, where *kosmos* could be nom. sing. or acc. pl., *kosmoi* could be dat. sing. or nom. pl., and *kosmon* could be acc. sing. or gen. pl. In addition, note the word *apokosmos* at Lyktos (**Lyktos1A5**), perhaps with the sense '*kosmos* elect' (see comment ad loc.).

[190] These words could be a genitive plural, but in view of **G78**.4, where the same words must be singular, and because there is no certain instance of the noun *kosmos* in the plural at Gortyn (and the plural is very rare anywhere else), the singular is much more likely.

The question then naturally arises, were the *ksenios* and the *ksenios kosmos* the same official? If so, why the variation in name? If not, what was the difference between the two positions? Since it seems unlikely that the foreign population of Gortyn was so large that the city needed two main officials to handle their affairs, we suggest that they are the same official and that the variation in name was arbitrary: at Gortyn there was an official called simply the *kosmos*, but there were also other high officials, one of them the *ksenios*, who had the rank of *kosmoi* and could be considered *kosmoi*, but each had his own separate title too. The situation would be somewhat similar to the Athenian archons: there was an archon, sometimes referred to as the eponymous archon because like the Gortynian *kosmos* his name was used in the dating formula; but there was also a *basileus*, a polemarch, and six *thesmothetai*, all of whom had the rank of archon and were considered to be such.

At Gortyn, we suggest that, although there may at first have been a single *kosmos*, as the need arose (quite early), other officials were created, each of whom had his own designation but in addition was considered to be a *kosmos*. The *kosmos* pure and simple, who might be called 'the presiding *kosmos*', would be the eponymous *kosmos*—Kyllos at the time of the Code—and would have other specified duties, perhaps including protection of heiresses. He could be designated simply 'the *kosmos*'. Others like the *ksenios* or *ksenios kosmos* (we have no explanation for the variation in name) had other specified duties. Thus, just as one could speak of the archon or the archons at Athens, at Gortyn one could speak of the *kosmos* or of several people 'serving as *kosmos*', with the latter expression designating all the officials who held the rank of *kosmos*; these other officials would be called either by their individual title (the *ksenios*) or by this title together with the title of *kosmos* (the *ksenios kosmos*). An expression like 'when the *startos* Aithaleus, Kyllos and his colleagues, were *kosmoi*' (**G72**.5.5–6) would then indicate that although Kyllos was the (eponymous) *kosmos*, other *kosmoi*, all from the *startos* Aithaleus served with him. And although not enough evidence survives from other cities, it is possible that some such combination of singular and plural *kosmoi* existed elsewhere, perhaps with some differences in detail.

c. THE *DIKASTAS* AS *KOSMOS*

This solution may point the way to solving the problem of the identity of the *dikastas* or 'judge' (see further Introd. 4C2). Several scholars (most recently Thür 2010a: 147–8) have argued that the *dikastas* was the *kosmos*, looking in the first place to **Dr1**, where judging appears to be a primary task of the *kosmos* at Dreros. As we noted (Introd. 4C1a), moreover, the *kosmoi* also decide cases in **Elt2**.8 and possibly at Datala (**Da1**B7–10). At Gortyn the *dikastas* (never *dikastas kosmos*) and the *kosmos* are both mentioned many times but their duties never overlap (Gagarin 2010b); the *dikastas* decides cases, the *kosmos* has other duties but never decides cases. It is possible, however, that the *dikastas* had the rank of *kosmos* and could be referred to as a *kosmos*, even though he is never so designated in our texts, and it is also possible that in the sixth century, when we have no mention of a *dikastas* at Gortyn, the *kosmos* functioned as a judge there. Thus, it is possible that in the beginning the *kosmos* at Gortyn judged all cases, but by the fifth century, as the number of cases grew, a separate official with the status of *kosmos*, the *dikastas*, was appointed, thereby relieving the *kosmos* of this task.

d. FUNCTIONS

Laws provide evidence that *kosmoi* in different cities had the following functions: judging cases at Dreros, Eltynia, perhaps at Gortyn in the sixth century, and maybe at Datala; exacting payment for violations at Gortyn, Rhitten, and Eltynia; protecting heiresses at Gortyn; serving as the eponymous official at Gortyn and probably at Eleutherna; and overseeing the affairs of foreigners and other non-citizens (the *ksenios kosmos*) at Gortyn. Presumably they had other duties as well.

Despite the relatively small amount of evidence in the laws, it seems from this brief summary that there may have been a fair amount of homogeneity in the duties of the *kosmoi* in different cities. If the explanation we have offered for multiple *kosmoi* at Gortyn is correct, this pattern may perhaps be generalized—namely that in early times the *kosmos* (perhaps just one) was the executive official in charge of most of the affairs of the city, but that as time went on, especially in the larger cities, his duties grew to the point where other officials were appointed, some with the rank of *kosmos*, to take on some of these duties. This process might also, over time, have increased the differences among the different poleis in this respect, as each polis appointed new officials according to its needs and modified the duties of its *kosmos* accordingly.

e. LENGTH OF TERM AND SELECTION

It is generally assumed that the term of office for the *kosmos*, and probably for most other officials, was one year. No text explicitly states this—the non-iteration laws from Dreros and Gortyn specify only an interval (in years) between terms—but annual offices were the norm in Greece. The provision governing a fugitive slave who belongs to a *kosmos* in **G41**.4.10–14 might imply that his term of office was longer than one year, but interpretation of this provision is problematic (n. ad loc.). All in all, we are inclined to accept the prevailing view that a *kosmos* served a one-year term.

We have almost no information about how *kosmoi* were chosen, but the dating formula in **G72**.5.5–6 ('when the *startos* Aithaleus, Kyllos and his colleagues, were *kosmos*') suggests that at Gortyn all the positions with the rank of *kosmos* were selected from the same *startos*. This information is of limited use, however, because we do not know the number of *startoi*, whether each *startos* had a turn in a rotation, or whether *startoi* were involved in the selection of *kosmoi* in other poleis. Scholars assume on the basis of the later literary tradition (Aristotle, *Politics* 1272a33–4) that *kosmoi* were chosen from a small group of elite families. They may have been, but nothing in our texts indicates this. If the *startos* at Gortyn played a role in the selection (as it seems it did), and if, as most scholars think, the *startos* was either a clan of some sort or a military troop (Introd. 4B3), both of which would have been considerably larger than even an extended family, then the pool from which *kosmoi* were selected must have been quite large—certainly larger than just the elite (however they are defined). Elite competition is cited by some scholars to account for the non-iteration laws and other political developments in archaic Greece,[191] but there does not seem to be any place for this in the selection of *kosmoi* by *startos* (unless we imagine that there was rivalry among the members of a *startos*).

If the fifth-century reference to the *startos* Aithaleus holding the office of *kosmos* at Gortyn (**G72**.5.5–6) indicates a rotation of *startoi* or tribes in appointing a *kosmos*, as seems likely, such a procedure would appear to render the sixth-century non-iteration law in that city (**G14**p–g2) moot. It is possible that a similar rotation was in effect in other cities in the Classical period, as seems to have been the case in the Hellenistic period, but evidence for this practice in earlier periods is lacking everywhere but Gortyn.

The non-iteration laws are generally thought to have been intended to prevent the accumulation of power by a single individual (Perlman 2002, Link 2003a); as written, however, they might not prevent the accumulation of power by a family or a *startos*, if the individual members worked together. At Gortyn, for example, where the interval between service was only three years, a family with three sons could put up a different member for the office each year, and thus remain in power indefinitely.[192] At Dreros, on the other hand, the ten-year interval and the severity of the punishment prescribed for a *kosmos* who returned to office too soon would probably have been a stronger deterrence to any accumulation of power. It may be that Dreros had had direct experience with *kosmoi* who abused their position, and thus treated such abuse with particular severity. It is also possible that fear of a possible tyranny, such as those that had begun to sprout up elsewhere in Greece, motivated these laws. For whatever reason, however, we hear nothing about tyranny in any Cretan polis.

[191] e.g. Forsdyke 2005; see p. 26 for the non-iteration laws (contra Gagarin 2008a: 878–89, with n. 32).

[192] The laws could easily have been written to prevent iteration by the same family or *startos*, if that had been their intent.

2. *Dikastas*

With one fragmentary exception,[193] the *dikastas* ('judge') is attested only at Gortyn. As discussed above (Introd. 4C1c), the *dikastas* at Gortyn may have had the rank of *kosmos* and been treated as a *kosmos*, but his work is entirely separate from that of the *kosmos*. His duties are entirely judicial: he decided cases[194] and occasionally testified about an earlier case that he had judged. The simple noun *dikastas* is always found in the singular, suggesting perhaps that there was only one *dikastas* at Gortyn; but there were also specialized judges, including 'the *dikastas* of the *hetaireiai*' (**G42**B11–12), 'whoever judges in cases of sureties' (**G42**B12–13), and 'orphan-judges' (*orpanodikastai*, **G72**.12.6–19); the last of these is the only certain example of the plural in our texts. It seems unlikely that these specialized positions required full-time work; perhaps the specialized judges were also ordinary judges the rest of the time. It may thus be likely that there were several *dikastai* at Gortyn and that the law almost always uses the singular to designate the one who is judging the particular case in question.[195]

3. *Mnamon*

The main duty of the *mnamon* ('rememberer', Attic *mnēmōn*) is, as the name implies, to remember. He attended trials, and probably other events too, that were conducted orally and remembered what happened in case any question should arise in the future. He was thus a kind of living record of the legal cases or other events he attended.[196] A good illustration of this comes in a section of the Gortyn Code (**G72**.9.24–40) that addresses litigation over debts that were incurred by a deceased person or were owed to a deceased person by someone else. If the debt was the result of a penalty that resulted from an earlier lawsuit, then the judge and the *mnamon* should testify.[197] Presumably the reference is to the judge who had judged the earlier case and the *mnamon* who had attended the trial as the official rememberer. The *dikastas* and the *mnamon* are also paired in **G42**B6, where they may swear oaths that not more than fifteen days had passed between someone making an accusation and obtaining a judgment, events at which both were presumably present. Similarly, in **G72**.11.52–3, the two are

[193] **L3**B2–3, where we read [δ]ικαστâι; there is no context, so the *delta* is not certain, but seems likely.

[194] For the two methods of judgment, ruling as directed by the law and deciding with reference to the pleadings, see Introd. 10D1.

[195] There may be some similarity in the use of *kosmos* in the singular, if this was used to designate the one (out of many) who was concerned with the particular matter in question.

[196] The knowledge of *mnēmones* served as a record of public activities outside of Crete as well. In disputes over property at Halicarnassus, the *mnēmones* were to testify about what they knew (*eideosin*) and their testimony was to be authoritative in court (M&L 32.20–2, fifth century). See Gagarin 2008a: 119, 215.

[197] The *mnamon* must testify 'if he is alive and fulfilling civic duties (*poliateuen*)'; for the meaning of this condition, see Introd. 5A4.

present when a divorced woman is officially accused of taking property that is not hers; these officials would then be available to judge and remember exactly what the woman was accused of taking that did not belong to her.

A *mnamon* could also be attached to other officials. The rules on adoption include a provision for renouncing an adoption: the renouncer must deposit ten staters at the court (*dikasterion*), 'and let the *mnamon* of the *ksenios* give it to the renounced person' (**G72**.11.16–17). Nothing is known of the duties of the *ksenios* in this regard (Introd. 4C1b), and it is odd that the *mnamon*'s task here seems to have nothing to do with remembering. More typical, if the passage is correctly restored, is the role of the *mnamon* of officials called the *esprattai* or 'collectors' (**G87**.7–8): 'with the *esprattai* and the *mnamon* of the *esprattai* present'. If the *esprattai* were debt-collectors, then the *mnamon* would have been present when they collected or attempted to collect a debt. Later, the *mnamon* would remember and could testify authoritatively to the various details of the debt that the *esprattai* were charged with collecting, especially whether it had been paid.

In the Classical period, the *mnamon* is not found in any Cretan polis besides Gortyn. The agreement with Spensithios (**Da1**), however, requires him 'to write and remember' (*poinikazen te kai mnamoneuwen*) and it seems likely that as an assistant to the *kosmos*, he would be fulfilling the same function as the *mnamon* at Gortyn, though he would also have the additional duty of writing. For whatever reason, in this agreement he is never given the title of *mnamon* but is always referred to as *poinikastas* ('writer'); but he may also have been called a *mnamon* in some circumstances.

4. *Poinikastas*

The agreement with Spensithios requires him 'to write and remember' (*poinikazen te kai mnamoneuwen*) for the polis all public matters, divine and human (**Da1**A4–5, 5–7). In specifying his further duties and the benefits he will receive, the law designates him a *poinikastas*, generally translated 'writer' or 'scribe'.[198] These further duties include being present at all human and divine events whenever the *kosmos* is present (B1–4), performing public sacrifices whenever there is no priest for a god (B4–6), and contributing to the *andreion* (B11–12). Finally, the agreement may specify that if the *poinikastas* is involved in litigation, he is treated 'just as the other *kosmoi*',[199] implying that he has the rank of *kosmos*, though he is not a *kosmos*.

[198] See Gagarin 2008a: 119–20, n. 33. The noun occurs six times in **Da1** (and nowhere else). The new inscription from Eltynia (**Eltynia1**.2) with the words *poinikēia tade* ('these letters') sheds little light on the office of *poinikastas*.

[199] B7–10; there are many obscurities in the text at this point; see comm. ad loc.

5. Other Officials

In addition to those already discussed, a number of other officials are mentioned in these texts, most of them only once. Their duties are often obscure. At Gortyn we find *titai*, 'collectors of fines', (from *tino*, 'pay or collect a fine', **G14**p–g1; **G15**a–b2; **G78**.5, 7; **G79**.20; **G102**.3; **G107**.1), *gnomones* ('investigators'?, **G14**p–g2),[200] *esprattai* ('collectors'?, **G75**D2; **G87**.1, 7–8, 11; **G91**.4), *karpodaistai* ('produce distributors', **G77**B5), *startagetas* ('company commander', **G80**.4–5, see Introd. 5B3), and *epottas* ('overseer', **G84**.4).[201] Outside Gortyn, relatively few officials are named. An *ephor* may be mentioned twice at Rhitten (**G80**.6, 10), but in both places interpretation of the Greek is problematic. An otherwise unknown group of officials, the *eszikaiōteres* ('controllers' or 'exactors'?) is mentioned at Lyktos (**Lyktos1A**8). At Prinias, *pre(i)sgēia* (**Pr7**D1, 3, without context) may be a council of elders or an embassy. At Eleutherna a *thiaros* may be a sacred envoy (**Ele11**.1).

The texts from Dreros present many problems concerning the presence of other officials. For example, the *damioi* in **Dr1**.4 could perhaps be a permanent group of officials or merely a group assembled for the oath-swearing ceremony. Another law states: 'whoever ministers (*ostis propolewseie*), the *agretas* will not punish him' (**Dr5**); the *agretas* is almost certainly an official of some sort, and the clause *ostis propolewseie* may point to another official, a *propoleus* ('minister'?). And **Dr4** opens with an enactment clause: 'the *thystai* ('sacrificers') decided', where the *thystai* may be priests of some sort.[202]

We may conclude from this survey that apart from the *kosmos*, who is found almost everywhere, only the *dikastas* is (probably) mentioned in more than one polis, and he is only named once outside of Gortyn; otherwise, no official of one polis is mentioned in the texts from any other polis. Of course, more evidence might reveal more instances of overlap, and some of these officials are named in post-classical inscriptions from other poleis; but the evidence we have is sufficient to make it very likely that, except for the *kosmos*, there was no set of officials common to more than one Cretan polis in archaic and classical Crete. This conclusion would be consistent with the suggestion made above (Introd. 4C1d), that in the Early Iron Age, as communities were forming, one person emerged in each community, who conducted the small amount of administrative business required and came to be called the *kosmos*; but as these communities

[200] Because the verb *gignosko* occurs in **Elt2**.8 in the sense of 'decide (a case)', it is possible that the *gnomones* are 'deciders' or 'judges' of some sort.

[201] Our translation of these officials' names is based on the meaning of the Greek or the nature of their duties, if discernible.

[202] A priest (*iareus*) is mentioned at Axos (**A9**.2–3), Datala (**Da1**B4), Eleutherna (**Eleutherna1**.6), and Gortyn (**G65**.6), but we do not consider this generic term the title of an official. There probably were various priests in all Cretan poleis. See further Introd. 10.

grew, each developed its own additional officials depending on its needs and named them according to their duties, without consulting with or imitating other poleis (and without drawing on any common Cretan heritage). The one name (besides *kosmos*) found in more than one polis, *dikastas*, would have easily been derived from his function of judging (*dikadden*). But it does not seem possible that these local officials formed part of a shared 'Cretan' form of government.

5. PERSONS

Almost all our evidence for civic status and the family in early Crete comes from Gortyn, and it is easy to generalize unthinkingly from this polis to the rest of Crete. But although we may probably assume that certain features of status or the family, such as the fundamental distinction between free and slave, were common to all of Crete, we must be very cautious in ascribing most of the features we find at Gortyn to poleis for which we have no evidence.

Because of the legal nature of the texts in this collection, very few individuals are named in them. The only exceptions are the *kosmoi*, Kyllos (**G72**.5.5–6) and Timarchos (**Ele9**.2), Dionysios (the recipient of honors at Gortyn, **G64**), and Spensithios (the *poinikastas* of Datala, **Da1**).[203]

A. Status

1. Free Persons

The most basic distinction in the laws is between free and slave—*eleutheros* and *dolos*. The distinction is the focus of disputes about status that are the subject of the first column of the Gortyn Code, where we find the remarkable rule that in disputes about whether a person is free or slave, witnesses who testify that the person is free are to prevail. At Gortyn, at least, the judicial system had a bias toward freedom. But the laws also show how much more highly free persons were valued than slaves. In the provisions governing sexual offenses, for example, rape of a free person draws a fine of 100 staters (200 drachmas), whereas in most cases rape of a slave incurs a fine of only 5 drachmas.[204] And slaves incur twice as large a fine for committing rape or adultery as do free persons. Finally, not only in this section but probably in

[203] Other possible names are [—]*nikoi* in **A7**.2, and [—] . νιπα[—] (Enipas?) in **L3A7**.

[204] We are assuming the legal equivalence of slaves and serfs in the laws on sexual offenses; see further Introd. 5A7 and Gagarin 2010a: 16–18.

most (if not all) of the laws from Crete, the generalized subject ('someone', 'whoever', etc.) is a free person. Thus, the law beginning 'if someone rapes' in **G72**.2.2–3 applies only to free persons; it is followed two lines later by a separate law 'if a slave (rapes)'.

2. Age Distinctions

The laws distinguish between adults, minors, and post- and pre-pubescent children.[205] Although in most cases laws drawing on these distinctions were probably aimed primarily at free persons, they may have also applied to slaves. This is clearest in the case of the *dromeus* (lit. 'runner'), who was a legally competent adult: a number of provisions require that witnesses be *dromeis*, and three of these also specify that they be free *dromeis* (**G72**.1.41–2, 3.22, 5.53–4); this strongly suggests that when *dromeus* is not so qualified, it may include those who were not free. Besides the requirements for witnesses, *dromeus* also occurs in a law that prohibits a father from selling or using as security the property of his deceased wife without the approval of her children, who must be adult (**G72**.6.36).[206] And in Eleutherna, a *dromeus* is allowed to drink to the point of intoxication (**Eleutherna1**.2–5). Finally, *dromeus* occurs in the regulations concerning heiresses at Gortyn (**G72**.7.15–8.20), where most of the other terms indicating age-categories are also found. There *dromeus* (7.41) is contrasted with *apodromos*, 'not adult' (**G72**.7.35–6). We do not know the exact age of majority at Gortyn, but it was probably about the same as in Athens, namely eighteen. At Eltynia (**Elt2**) the law distinguishes between a man (*aner*), a child (*pēiskos*), and a third category, *agelaos* or 'member of an *agela*', which may designate someone between childhood and adulthood.

The other significant age marker, puberty, was important for marriage. Heiresses could marry at the age of twelve (**G72**.12.17–19), which presumably was considered the onset of puberty, and there is no reason to think the age was different for girls who were not heiresses. The rules concerning heiresses also imply that boys were subject to the same age restriction. The terminology of pre- and post-puberty at Gortyn is fairly clear: *anoros* (**G72**.7.29–30, etc.) and *anebos* (**G72**.11.19) designate one who has not yet reached the age of puberty, whereas *ebion*, *ebionsa* (**G72**.7.37, etc.; also **G51**.6, 8) and *orima* (**G72**.8.39) designate someone past puberty.[207]

[205] In a study of the evidence for 'age-class societies' in ancient Greece, Kennell examines Crete at some length (2013: 42–62). He finds evidence for 'universally-applied official age designations' but 'without any indications that citizens belonged to age sets or [that] age-grade scales were systematically arranged'.

[206] In Datala, the office of *poinikastas* was reserved for Spensithios and his offspring, unless Spensithios himself or 'the majority of his offspring who were adult (*dromēs*)' chose otherwise (**Da1**A8–10).

[207] See Willetts 1967: 10–11, Bile 343–4. For terms denoting 'child, children' more generally, see Introd. 5C2.

3. *Apetairos*

In our period, the status of *apetairos* (lit. 'not of a *hetaireia*') is only mentioned at Gortyn and, apart from a fragmentary text where there is no context (**G84**.6), only in the Code in the rules on sexual offenses (**G72**.2.2–45). An *apetairos* is apparently a free person, but of lower status than other free persons, since the rape of an *apetairos* draws a fine of only 10 staters, compared with 100 staters for the rape of a free man and 5 drachmas (2 ½ staters) for the rape of a serf. It is possible that serfs without a master and freed slaves belonged to this class (comm. ad **G72**.5.27).

4. Citizens

As we saw above (Introd. 4B1), city-ethnics denoting the members of the political community are fairly common in Crete, and we may probably presume that 'the Gortynians' as a collective did not include people from other places who were living in Gortyn temporarily. On the other hand, the laws of Gortyn and other poleis, with their generalized subjects ('someone', 'whoever', etc.), almost certainly applied to all free persons who were in the city, including foreigners. Certainly foreigners would not be free to rape or seize property with impunity, nor is it likely that a Gortynian could injure a non-Gortynian with impunity. But legal procedure was another matter, and references to both a citizen's trial and a foreigner's trial (see below on foreigners) suggest different procedures and perhaps different trials for these two groups at Gortyn.

As at Athens, besides the city-ethnics two different terms appear to have been used to designate those who belonged to the city, *astos* (person of the *asty* or 'town') and *poliatas* (person of the polis). In Greece generally it seems that *astos* 'invariably designates a person of citizen birth (whereas *polites* usually designates a person with citizen rights)' (Hansen and Nielsen 2004: 47), but this distinction may not hold for Crete, especially in the Archaic period when the concept of 'citizen' was probably less strictly defined than it later became in classical Athens.

The more common term indicating some sort of citizenship, though occurring only at Gortyn, is *poliatai*.[208] It is found twice in the section on adoption (**G72**.10.35–6, 11.14).[209] In both passages the citizens are gathered in the agora, apparently as a kind of assembly; and both the adoption and the renunciation of an adoption must take place at a gathering of this group, which perhaps must give its approval.[210] Along with the noun, we also find the verb *poliateuen* in two texts, apparently used of someone fulfilling his civic duties. In **G51**.7, sons who swear

[208] However, the contrasting term, *allopoliatas*, 'citizen of another place', is found in other cities (Introd. 5A5).

[209] The variant *politai* occurs in **G83**.1–2 without context; see also **L2**.5 (discussed below, n. 213), also without context, which may be restored as *poliatas* or *allopoliatas*.

[210] A similar gathering seems to be specified in **G80**.14–15 (*kat'agoran weumenan*).

certain oaths must be active as citizens, and in **G72**.9.33 the *mnamon* who is called to testify must be alive and 'active as a citizen' (if that is the correct sense; see comm. ad loc.). The requirements for someone to be 'active as a citizen' are unknown. Apart from these passages, we have no evidence about the qualifications for citizenship, the rights and duties of citizens, or what activities they were expected to engage in.

The personal noun *astos* may occur once in Crete in our period, in **A5+6**.6, where the feminine plural *astai* ('citizen women') is a possible interpretation of the text (n. ad loc.); even if this is correct, however, there is no context that might clarify the precise meaning of *astai*. More securely, at Gortyn we find the expression *wastia dika* (a 'citizen's trial'), *wastia* being equivalent to Attic *astikos*.[211] The expression *wastia dika* may imply that *astoi* had a special status beyond simply being Gortynians, but more likely it only distinguished Gortynians from foreigners (see below). And if the feminine noun does occur in **A5+6**.6, it indicates that at least at Axos, women were included in this category. We have no evidence, however, to indicate whether *astai* were also considered *poliatai*, or in what specific ways these women may have participated in any activities of the polis, but if **A5+6** concerns the ritual use of booty from war (comm. ad loc.), then the Axian *astai* may have participated in these public rituals.

5. Foreigners

Gortyn and other poleis distinguished between foreigners and those native to the polis. The adjectival form *ksenios* ('foreign') occurs several times at Gortyn, but there is no clear instance anywhere in Crete of the corresponding noun *ksenos* (Attic *xeinos*), which is common elsewhere in Greece.[212] A special Cretan term, *allopoliatas* ('citizen of another place'), occurs in **Ele3**.1 (without context) and in **Lyktos1A**1–2, in a law that probably prohibits harboring foreigners.[213] But most often, it appears, foreigners are referred to by the city-ethnic (e.g. 'the Itanians', **Lyktos1A**4).[214]

Despite a law at Lyktos that apparently prohibits harboring a foreigner (**Lyktos1A**), foreigners were not without rights at Gortyn, where there was a special

[211] Note *hai astikai dikai* in Lysias 17.3, though the meaning of this expression is obscure.

[212] Occasionally letters occur which could be supplemented as either the noun or the adjective (e.g. **Ele4**.4 and **G89**.7, where κσεν[- or κσε[- could be supplemented κσε[νο-] or κσε[νιο-]).

[213] In **L2**.5 [—]πολιαταν | could be a form of *allopoliatas* or of the simple *poliatas*; also cf. *eks allopolias* ('from another polis?') in **G72**.6.47. For a fuller discussion see Perlman 2004a: esp. 124–7.

[214] For 'the Latosians' see above n. 162.

official, the *ksenios* (or *ksenios kosmos*, for discussion see Introd. 4C1b), who probably was assigned to oversee and protect foreigners, and his very existence indicates that foreigners must have been present in fairly large numbers in Gortyn and were given certain protections. Among these was a provision for a *kseneia dika* (**G80**.8)—a foreigners' trial (or perhaps foreigners' justice), a procedure already implicit in the provisions for a citizen's trial, *wastia dika*, in earlier texts (**G13***h–g2*; **G64**.4). And whatever the correct supplement at the end of **G78**.1, that law seems to offer protection to Latosians in Gortyn against being enslaved or plundered.[215]

6. Temporary Servitude

Evidence for the practice of temporary servitude comes only from Gortyn, where a person, free or slave, could be pledged to another person for a certain period of time in a kind of indentureship or debt-bondage. The person so pledged, the *katakeimenos* ('the one who lies under [an obligation]') must serve the *katathemenos* ('the one who has put him under [an obligation] to himself') until the debt is paid. A free person so pledged became a quasi-slave to his temporary 'master', but he had more rights than an indentured slave (compare the rules in **G41**.5–6 with those in **G47**), who would continue to be enslaved to his permanent master during and after the indentureship. There is no evidence for the normal length of such indentureships.

7. Serfs and Slaves

In the laws we find two terms for Cretans who are not free, *dolos* and *woikeus*, commonly translated 'slave' and 'serf'.[216] *Woikeus* is the older term, occurring in inscriptions that probably date from the sixth century (**L5**.14; **G23**.3); in the fifth century it occurs only in **G72** and **G41**.4.6–17, and is not found in later texts. *Dolos* first occurs in the fifth century but later becomes the common term for 'slave' throughout Crete. The precise relationship between the two terms is difficult to determine. At times they appear nearly synonymous, but there also seem to be certain differences in the way each is treated. We will address this issue first, and then examine the position of both groups relative to free persons.[217]

[215] The provision in **G78**.1 specifically protects either 'freedmen' or (as we think more likely) 'those who left' (see comm. ad loc.). The law further provides that members of this group can live 'as a Latosian' (line 2); this implies that Latosians already have protection.

[216] We translate *woikeus* by 'serf' for convenience, without claiming an exact correspondence. Although a serf may be defined as 'an agricultural laborer bound under the feudal system to work on his lord's estate' (*The New Oxford American Dictionary*), the term is often used more broadly. By the eighteenth century, for example, serfs in czarist Russia worked in many non-agricultural areas—in households (rural and urban) as domestic servants and also in industrial enterprises, such as mining. They could also be bought and sold rather like chattel slaves, though they are still commonly referred to as serfs.

[217] See Gagarin 2010a for a more extensive discussion of the issues in this section.

Like the rest of the Greek world, Crete recognized a fundamental distinction between free persons and slaves, *eleutheroi* and *doloi*, notably in the first section of the Gortyn Code on illegal seizure (**G72**.1.2–2.2). This section addresses as two kinds of disputes, those about status, whether a person is free or a slave, and those about ownership or belonging, that is, to which master a particular slave belongs.[218] Serfs are not mentioned in this section, but we must assume that the rules governing the status or ownership of a slave would apply equally to serfs. In other sections of the code, however, for example in the laws concerning sexual offenses (**G72**.2.2–45), both terms are found but the laws never address exactly the same situation for both groups. One rule will mention slaves, another serfs, without any evident reason for the difference. Despite this, as far as we can tell, serfs and slaves are treated identically in the laws.

Offender the same

Offense and Offender	Victim	Fine (in drachmas)
Rape by an *eleutheros*	*eleutheros*	200
	woikeus	5
Rape by a *dolos*	*eleutheros*	400
Rape by a *woikeus*	*woikeus*	10
Adultery by a *dolos*	*eleutheros*	400
	dolos	10

Victim the same

Offense and Victim	Offender	Fine (in drachmas)
Rape of a *woikeus*	*eleutheros*	5
	woikeus	10
Rape of an *eleutheros*	*eleutheros*	200
	dolos	400
Adultery with an *eleutheros*	*eleutheros*	200
	dolos	400

As this table (based on **G72**.2.2–45) shows, relative to the fines for free persons exactly the same fines apply to both serfs and slaves, whether as victim or offender. When the offender is the same (whether free or slave), the fine is always forty times as large when the victim is free. On the other hand, when the victim is the same, the fine is always half as large when the offender is free. The conclusion seems to be that for legal purposes, serfs were treated in the same way as slaves.

On the other hand, certain laws may have applied to serfs but not to slaves. The Gortynian law on inheritance protects houses in which serfs are living and certain

[218] Vlassopoulos 2011 makes the good point that the Greeks themselves before Aristotle tended to see slavery as a relationship of power—the subordination of one person to another—not ownership.

animals owned by serfs (**G72**.4.31–7), and in the absence of any relatives, it is possible that serfs inherited a free person's estate (**G72**.5.25–8); these rules almost certainly did not apply to slaves. On the other hand, although a law regulating the purchase of slaves in the agora might apply equally to serfs, it seems likely that serfs were not normally bought and sold like slaves. All this suggests that, although treated as slaves for most legal purposes, serfs had a somewhat higher status than ordinary slaves; they were primarily agrarian workers, who may have been working the land before chattel slaves were introduced to Crete, and thus continued to have certain rights not available to slaves. Eventually serfs became assimilated to the status of ordinary slaves; in our period, however, the two groups were not identical, and there were probably reasons (not apparent to us) for mentioning one and not the other in specific laws. But if the law mentioned one group, and members of the group not mentioned were in the same situation, then they were probably treated according to the same rules.[219]

Relative to free persons, both serfs and slaves at Gortyn appear to have had a significantly higher status and greater legal protection than slaves in classical Athens (the society about which we have the most evidence).[220] First, not only could slaves[221] almost certainly marry and divorce in much the same way as free persons,[222] but marriages between slaves and free women are explicitly recognized in the laws (**G72**.6.55–7.10), and it is reasonable to suppose that free men could also marry slave women (comm. ad loc.). It is also possible that free men could adopt slaves as their own children (**G72**.10.33–4, with commentary). To be sure, slaves, including serfs, had masters, and (as noted above) could be bought and sold, though this may have been rare in the case of serfs.[223] On the other hand, serfs certainly, and probably slaves too, could own property, though it is possible that they could not own land (Introd. 7B).[224]

219 There may be some similarity to the use of the Athenian terms *doulos* and *oiketēs*, 'slave' and 'household servant'. All *oiketai* were *douloi*, but many *douloi* were not *oiketai*. *Doulos* is the general term, always used in contrast to *eleutheros* ('free'), but when appropriate, *oiketēs* is normally used instead of *doulos*.

220 In a long article Lewis 2013 argues that slaves at Gortyn did not have the 'right' to marry or own property and that their position with regard to marriage and property was not significantly different from that of Athenian slaves. Furthermore, Lewis introduces cross-cultural evidence to show that similar 'unions' existed in many slave societies, and argues that the position of Gortynian slaves was not legally different. Much of his argument rests on speculation about what (he claims) the Gortynian texts 'mean', which in many cases is not the same as what they 'say'.

221 In the following discussion, 'slave' should be assumed to include 'serf' unless otherwise specified.

222 The verb for 'marry' in the case of free persons (*opuien/opuiesthai*) is also used for slaves, for serfs, and for free/slave couples; and *aner*, the common term for a free 'husband' is also used of serf husbands in **G72**.3.54 (see commentary). Scholars generally assume that at Athens unions between slaves, which may have produced children, nonetheless had no juristic validity, though this is not certain (Harrison 1968: 177).

223 If serfs were attached to the land, they may have been transferred to other masters only in connection with the alienation of land (by sale or inheritance), though there is no clear evidence on this point.

224 If a *woikeus* inherited his master's estate, as seems to be allowed in **G72**.5.25–8, he would then own land, but he would also have no master, and thus would no longer be a serf.

Finally, the laws offered a good deal of protection for slaves (or for their masters), notably with regard to sexual offenses, though the fines were smaller for offenses against slaves and larger for offenses by slaves than they were for free persons. Slaves also could be witnesses, unless explicitly excluded, and in one extraordinary case of rape, a domestic slave woman is given preference in her oath, so that evidently her oath would prevail against that of a free person (**G72**.2.15–16). Whether or not slaves could litigate is unclear. Some laws specify that masters litigated on behalf of slaves (e.g. **G47**.1–16), but others imply that slaves themselves litigated (e.g. **G72**.3.40–4). Even if slaves were never allowed to litigate, however, it is clear that they had significantly more rights than their counterparts in classical Athens.

B. Women

Virtually all our evidence for women comes from Gortyn (and specifically from the Gortyn Code). An isolated word for 'maternal estate' (*matroia*) in **Ph1**.3 suggests that the treatment of women at Phaistos, at least, may have been somewhat similar to the treatment of Gortynian women, but whatever the case in other poleis, women at Gortyn had significantly more control over their own lives and property than women in classical Athens.[225] Not only is there is no sign of the *kyrieia* ('guardianship'), which prevented an Athenian woman from owning more than a nominal amount of property in her own right and required her to conduct her affairs through a male *kyrios* ('lord'), but there is clear evidence that Cretan women owned property, including land, in the same way as men did (comm. ad **G72**.2.48–50), and could manage it themselves, though they may often have allowed their husbands to manage it for them. In addition, daughters in Crete inherited a share of their father's and mother's estates directly, just as sons did, though their share was only half as large as their brothers' shares (**G72**.4.37–43). They could also receive gifts from their fathers, brothers, and sons, gifts that many scholars have likened to the dowry in Athens, though unlike Athenian women, Cretan women themselves owned the property that was given to them as a gift. In a divorce women left their husbands, taking with them their own property, and when they died they left their property to their heirs.

A woman's estate was called the *matroia* ('maternal estate'), a word found in this sense only in Crete at this time and clearly coined as a counterpart to *patroia* ('paternal estate'), which is widespread throughout Greece from the time of

[225] See Gagarin 2008b, 2012b for a more extensive discussion of the issues in this section. Archaeological evidence for private houses also suggests less gender segregation in Crete than in other parts of Greece; see Introd. 5C1.

Homer.[226] In Crete, a *patroiokos* or daughter without brothers (conveniently referred to as an 'heiress') was subject to certain rules prescribing her marriage to a paternal relative, just as her Athenian counterpart (an *epiklēros*) was, and would apparently share her father's estate with her husband; but she had more control than her Athenian counterpart over whom she would marry (if anyone), and in certain circumstances she retained control over all of the estate (**G72**.7.15–9.24).

In addition to owning and managing property, women could engage in litigation as plaintiffs (**G72**.6.12–31) or defendants (**G72**.2.54–3.9, with **G72**.11.46–55), and they could make decisions about such things as distributing their property among their children. A woman could choose a husband, who could even be a slave (**G72**.6.55–7.10), though her choice may often have been influenced by family considerations. She seems to have been able to choose whether or not to stay married to her present husband (**G72**.2.45–3.16, 8.22–4). And an heiress had some ability to reject the person designated for her by law and choose another husband (**G72**.7.50–8.20). In all these areas, Athenian women would not have been able to act at all (marrying a slave), or could have acted only through the agency of a *kyrios*.

This greater amount of freedom accorded women at Gortyn did not, however, put them on an equal basis to men. We have already noted the provision that women inherit half as much as their brothers (actually less than half since the brothers first inherit city houses and cattle), and other provisions imply that men owned or controlled significantly more property than women. For example, the law restricts gifts from men to women (**G72**.10.1–25) but those from women to men are not mentioned. The law on divorce (**G72**.2.45–3.16) states that the wife is to keep 'her own things' and provides for cases where she might take something of her husband's; it says nothing about a husband keeping his own property, though he must have done so. Both these laws imply that men will have more property than women. And the prohibitions on misuse of the property of others (**G72**.6.12–31, 9.7–24) are directed only at males who misuse a female relative's property. We may thus suspect that many, perhaps most, Gortynian women let their husbands or brothers or sons manage their property for them.

It also appears that women's ownership of property and freedom to do as they wished with it had been increasing during the Archaic and Classical periods. This is implied by some of the non-retroactivity provisions in the laws (see on **G72**.5.7–9), and it would also account for the very large number of laws (about half of all laws in **G72**) that concern women and their property. As we have seen very clearly in our own time, when the rights of women and their control over

[226] *Matroia* is also found several times in a late-fourth-century decree from Tegea concerning the return of exiles as ordered by Alexander (*SIG* 360; see Thür and Taeuber 1994: no. 5, Heisserer 1980: 205–29).

property increase, some members of the society, women as well as men, feel threatened by the situation and may have difficulty accepting it. Others may look for an opportunity to profit from new conditions. This may explain why the Gortyn laws so often emphasize that a woman should have 'her own' property—an expression never used for men's property. The legislator wanted to remind people, emphatically, that a woman did indeed own property of 'her own', independent of her father or husband, even if in some cases these men managed this property for her.

An increase in women's ownership of property at Gortyn during the sixth and fifth centuries would also account for the increased protection of women's property that we see in the rules about misuse. These rules are explicitly said not to be retroactive. This must mean that the rules are different from the earlier rules, or that there were no earlier rules. In any case, the Code must be providing more protection for the property of women, again a sign that as women gained more property, threats to that property also increased. The assumption seems to be that men will often manage women's property and thus will have opportunities to misuse it but that men's property does not need similar protection against misuse by women. Nothing in the laws specifically prevents women from managing their husband's property, but the implication is that this was probably quite rare.

We should also note that although we have laws from this period from nine poleis in Crete besides Gortyn, with one or two possible exceptions, none of those from other poleis concerns women.[227] The argument from silence is not conclusive, but it does suggest that the Gortynians were more concerned about the rights of women and their ability to control their own property than were the inhabitants of most other Cretan poleis. We can only speculate why this was the case (if it was), but the location of the city may offer an explanation. As noted above (Introd. 2C), unlike many of the other poleis that wrote laws, Gortyn abandoned several defensible hilltop sites in the seventh century before it began to write laws and moved down to a new site at the edge of the rich Mesara plain. This indicates that the polis felt secure from the threat of attack, and this feeling of security was apparently accompanied by an increase in economic prosperity derived from the Mesara. We tentatively suggest that this sense of security was accompanied by a reduced need for military preparation and also an increase in the value and respect accorded to women, who consequently were granted greater freedom and more opportunity to own and control property.

[227] As noted above, **Ph1** contains the word *matroia* without any context, and 'citizen women' may be mentioned in **A5+6**.6, perhaps in connection with ritual.

C. Family

There is no word in the laws (or in Greek generally) that corresponds precisely to 'family', which to be sure has a range of meanings in English and other modern languages. We will therefore consider three different groups, the household, the nuclear family, and the extended family.[228] We will then discuss inheritance, which as elsewhere in Greece was always treated as a family matter.

1. House and Household

Like Attic *oikia*, Cretan *woikia* denotes the physical 'house' (**G64**.4[229] and almost certainly in **G81**.1), but seems also to be used to designate the 'household', namely those living in the house (or in one of the family's houses), including slaves and serfs. This meaning occurs only in **G72**.5.26, where in our view 'those of the household' in which there are no claimants to an estate (i.e. no living family members) must be the serfs (*woikeis*) who were owned by the deceased.[230] A second term for 'house', *stega* (lit. 'roof'), is attested in the Code (**G72**.3.46; 4.15; 4.32–3, 47; 7.31; 8.1–4) and in other fifth-century laws from Gortyn (**G73**A7; **G80**.3; **G81**.16–17; **G97**). It is not possible to determine if the two terms denote different kinds of buildings or were used interchangeably. Finally, it is not possible to determine the precise meaning of *doma* ('house', 'hall') although it was apparently a roofed structure with a smoke-hole (**G46B**2–3).[231]

With regard to the physical house of the Archaic and Classical periods, archaeological evidence for the ten poleis that wrote laws is almost entirely lacking.[232] Indeed, only a few fifth-century houses have been excavated anywhere on the island.[233] We are in a better position to evaluate the form and function of

228 Bile 332–5 has a concise discussion that is generally good, though we take issue with a few of her conclusions. Willetts' remarks on the family (1967: 18–22, 1955: 59–100) are vitiated by his quasi-Marxist views of the primitive household, tribal kinship, cross-cousin marriages, etc., which are now generally discredited (see Morris 1990). As in the case of women, virtually all the evidence for the family comes from Gortyn.

229 Guizzi (2011: 397–8) suggests that the gift of *woikian kai woikopedon* in **G64** bestows the *right to possess* a house and a building plot (comm. ad **G64**).

230 This interpretation of **G72**.5.26 is not shared by most scholars. See our notes and comments on **G72**.5.25–8, where we discuss this and other difficult problems in this passage; and see further Gagarin 2010a: 26–9.

231 The 'hearth room', a single room with a central hearth that functioned as an all-purpose space for storage, cooking, eating, and other activities, is a common feature of Cretan houses of the Early Iron Age and Hellenistic periods, but not of the sixth-century houses at Azoria, where fixed hearths and portable braziers are restricted to spaces identified as kitchens. See Westgate 2007 for the Hellenistic houses; Haggis et al. 2011b and Haggis and Mook 2011 for the sixth-century houses at Azoria.

232 See Westgate 2007: 445–6 for the scanty remains from Gortyn and Knossos.

233 For the fifth century, Westgate's important study of house and society in classical and Hellenistic Crete mentions only the house at Aphrati (Introd. 6C) and the largely unpublished remains of the small settlement (fifth–first centuries) at Xerokambos in southeast Crete (Westgate 2007: 441).

sixth-century houses thanks in large part to the excavations at Azoria in east Crete. We cannot, of course, generalize with any certainty from the sixth-century houses at Azoria to contemporary houses elsewhere on Crete, but several aspects of the houses at Azoria are worth noting in connection with the laws. The urban houses excavated so far are large[234] and, while exhibiting considerable variety in their plan, belong to two basic typological categories: a roughly linear axially-aligned plan and a roughly square plan identifiable as an early form of the archaic Aegean 'corridor' type house (Haggis and Mook 2011).

Despite the differences in the size, plan, and location of the houses in the town center, Haggis and his colleagues have identified general patterns of room use that distinguish these houses from houses of the Hellenistic period.[235] The main living area of the house (the 'hall') was a large square or rectangular room without any discernible built features (e.g. benches, hearths). Floor assemblages indicate that at a minimum the activities that took place there included eating, drinking, and possibly weaving. Access to the halls was either through a vestibule or from an exterior corridor or courtyard. The halls in turn provided access, often exclusive access, to one or more large storerooms or corridors used for storage. Food preparation was confined to a space (i.e. a kitchen) that was always separated from the hall by a courtyard or corridor and was normally without direct access to storerooms.

Several patterns of use suggest that these large urban houses represented one node of a multilocal household, defined as a system incorporating kin and serf populations residing and working elsewhere in the town center (Haggis et al. 2011b: 484), an attractive model in light of the provisions in **G72** implying that an estate might include more than one house in the city (Introd. 7A). First, despite the space devoted to the storage of agricultural produce, there is surprisingly little indication of large-scale storage of grain. Second, the 'kitchens' attest the preparation for consumption of a great variety of foods and methods of preparing food (grinding, mixing, baking, boiling, roasting), but almost no evidence for primary butchering of livestock or primary processing e.g. of grain into flour, olives into olive oil, or grapes into wine. Third, the large amount of stored agricultural wealth suggests reliance upon a labor force exceeding in number those possibly residing in a single house. These observations suggest that some agricultural products were stored elsewhere and that primary butchering and processing took place elsewhere, either at other houses in the town center or on farms belonging to the multilocal household.

[234] The internal area of the Northeast Building is *c.*164 m^2; the lower of the Southwest Buildings is *c.*109 m^2; the North Acropolis Building is *c.*84 m^2.

[235] Haggis et al. 2011b: 477–85 *et passim*. For the Hellenistic houses, see Westgate 2007.

Also worth noting is the discovery of paraphernalia appropriate to male drinking parties (black-glaze kraters and drinking cups) in the halls of private houses, suggesting that at least in some Cretan communities, contrary to what is often claimed concerning archaic (and classical) Cretan society, men held drinking parties at home (Introd. 6C). Haggis and his colleagues suggest that visitors to the halls were possibly meant to look through the doorway into the storeroom and see the rows of impressive and ornately decorated storage pithoi that held the host's stores of agricultural produce, symbolic of the wealth and status of the household (Haggis et al. 2011b: 482–3). If so, the owners of the large urban houses of Azoria engaged in competitive display contrary to what the ancient literary traditions and the austere material culture of the poleis of central Crete might lead us to expect.

2. The Nuclear Family, Marriage, Adoption

Many passages at Gortyn show that the core group of parents and their children was central to family organization. The vocabulary for this group was the same as elsewhere in Greece: father (*pater*), mother (*mater*), daughter (*thygater*), son (*uiys*), sister (*adelpia*), brother (*adelpios*). *Teknon* is the regular term for a 'child' of unspecified age and gender; *paidion* is also used for 'child', and appears interchangeable with *teknon* in **G72**.3.44–4.23.[236] Finally, in contrast to *antropos*, which designates any 'person', *aner* and *gyna* ('man', 'woman') are almost always used in the context of a family, where they refer to husband and wife or (occasionally) father and mother (e.g. **G72**.2.45–6, 5.9–10).[237]

Several laws treat marriage, most often with reference to the heiress (**G44**; **G72**.7.15–9.1). The verb *opuien* is used in the active voice for the male, who 'marries', and in the middle voice for the woman, who 'gets married' or 'is married'. The same verb is used of serf and slave marriages (e.g. **G72**.3.54–5, 4.4, 7.1). No information is given about the procedure for marrying, which probably was arranged between families, but the prospective bride may have had a say in the decision.[238] There is no mention of a dowry at Gortyn, and the provisions for gifts to a daughter in **G72**.4.48–5.9 indicate that a different method could be used to transfer wealth to a bride, rendering the dowry system unnecessary (Schaps 1979: 86–7). These gifts became the woman's own property; upon marriage she brought them with her to her husband's house, and took them with her if she was divorced. Divorce appears to have been freely available to either spouse without the need to show cause (**G72**.2.45–3.16, 3.40–4; cf. 3.44–4.23,

[236] Cf. also **G8**m, where there is apparently a form of *pais*, and **Elt2**.5 and 7, where the word is *pēiskos*.

[237] In **Elt2**.5 *anēr* may designate an adult male or 'man' in general, but it could also designate a father; see comm. ad loc. and also on **G41**.7.12.

[238] The heiress was allowed to refuse marriage with certain claimants (**G72**.7.52–8.7).

11.46–55), though if the husband was judged responsible for the divorce, he was obliged to give his wife an additional five staters (**G72**.2.52–3.1).

Adoption (*anpansis*)[239] was allowed 'from wherever one wishes' (**G72**.10.33–4); it is unclear whether this means that a man could adopt any Gortynian, or that he could adopt a foreigner or even a slave (see comm. ad loc.). Women and children were probably not allowed to adopt (**G72**.11.18–19, with comm.). All adoptions were *inter vivos*; there is no provision for testamentary adoption. As at Athens, the primary purpose of adoption seems to have been to provide an heir. A person could also renounce an adoption, paying compensation to the renounced person; such renunciation may have occurred most often when the adopter had natural children (*gnesia tekna*) after the adoption.

3. The Extended Family

There is no vocabulary in the laws specifically designating individual relatives outside the nuclear family (such as cousin or nephew). There are general terms for maternal or paternal relatives (*matros*, *patros*), but when a legislator wanted to specify an uncle or cousin or niece, he used precise combinations: 'father's brother', 'father's brother's son', 'sister's children', etc.[240] *Matros* and *patros* (found only in **G72**) are often translated 'maternal uncle', 'paternal uncle',[241] but these terms appear to be broader, denoting (loosely) 'close maternal/paternal relatives', who of course might often be uncles (see 9.3–5 and 8.44 with commentary).

Two other terms, *epiballontes* and *kadestai*, are the subject of much dispute. Some scholars (e.g. Bile 333–4) argue that the *kadestai* (found only in **G72** and **G46B**12–14) are the maternal relatives, as opposed to the *epiballontes* (found only in **G72**), who are the paternal relatives. But the *epiballontes* ('claimants') cannot be restricted to paternal relatives when they are claimants to an estate (e.g. in 5.28–34) because women were among those who could claim an inheritance. Examination of the uses of the two terms suggests a different distinction, that they are 'relatives regarded from different aspects' (Sealey 1994: 58): *epiballontes* are those who, by virtue of being relatives, have a claim to something, either to an inheritance or to the hand of an heiress (which was another means of inheritance), whereas *kadestai* are those who have certain obligations with respect to their relatives (comm. ad **G72**.2.18).

239 The rules for adoption are in **G72**.10.33–11.23. For more on the vocabulary of adoption, see note on **G72**.11.21–2.

240 Some have suggested that *anankas* in **G72**.6.47–8 are 'ties of kinship', but we understand the term as 'necessity'; see n. ad loc.

241 So Bile 332, who immediately adds 'except in **G72**.12.13–14'.

4. Inheritance

Inheritance at Gortyn, and probably elsewhere in Crete, followed clear rules concerning the distribution of an estate.[242] Wills are not mentioned in the laws and were apparently unknown. As at Athens, direct descendants were first in line to inherit; at Gortyn, however, daughters inherited together with sons, the rule being that, after excluding some property, each daughter received one-half the amount of each son's share (**G72**.4.31–43). The same rules held for the maternal estate (*matroia*) as for the paternal (*patroia*). If there were no direct descendants, the law ranked other groups who would inherit in order: brothers of the deceased and their descendants, followed by sisters and their descendants, and then the more distant relatives (**G72**.5.9–25); lastly, as we interpret a highly controversial passage (**G72**.5.25–8, see comm. ad loc.), it appears that in the absence of relatives, the estate would go to the serfs who lived on it. The estate of a woman who had married a slave would go to her children, if they were free (that is, if the couple were living in her house), but to her other relatives if she was living elsewhere with the slave, in which case any children they had would be slaves (**G72**.6.55–7.10).

An adopted son could inherit in the same way as a natural child, but if he wished, he could also choose not to inherit, in which case the estate would go to other relatives in order (**G72**.10.39–48). If he did inherit, his natural children would inherit from him in turn, but an adopted son of an adopted son did not inherit any of the first adopter's estate (**G72**.11.6–10). If there were natural children together with an adopted son, then the latter received a share of the estate that was equivalent to a daughter's share (**G72**.10.48–11.1).

Finally, the most elaborate rules governed inheritance by an heiress, a woman who had no brothers when her father died (**G72**.7.15–9.24). These required that she marry one of her father's relatives, who were listed in order of priority (7.15–29), but if these relatives or the heiress did not wish to marry, she was then directed to marry someone from the tribe if she could, and if she could not, then anyone at all (**G72**.8.8–20). It appears that in most situations she inherited half the estate and her new husband received the other half, but the rules provide various outcomes depending on the age and willingness of the two parties.

[242] All the surviving rules for inheritance are in **G72**, but other fragmentary texts from Gortyn, such as **G20**, may have also dealt with the topic. We have no evidence for inheritance in other Cretan poleis at this time, though it seems very likely that some of the fundamental rules, such as inheritance by direct descendants, also applied elsewhere.

6. SOCIAL INSTITUTIONS

Only two or possibly three social institutions appear clearly in the laws of this period, the *hetaireia*, the *agela*, and perhaps the *andreion*; and none of these is mentioned often. They are all known from other parts of the Greek world, but we must not necessarily assume that their composition and functions were the same in early Crete as at other times and places or were the same in all Cretan poleis.[243]

A. Hetaireia

The *hetaireiai* ('associations') at Athens were groups of aristocratic young men who shared social and political interests. In Crete our evidence for them in this period comes from Gortyn, where one law reveals that there were judges of the *hetaireiai* (**G42**B12), and another requires that a person who adopted someone give a sacrificial animal and a jug of wine 'to his own *etaireia*'(**G72**.10.38).[244] The latter provision implies that membership in a *hetaireia* (= *etaireia/etairēia*) was widespread among free adult males (Maffi 2003a: 163), though *apetairoi* (those 'not belonging to a *hetaireia*') were presumably excluded. Since no other legislation at Gortyn mentions the *hetaireia*, it seems that the group may not have had a large role in Gortynian affairs.

B. Agela

Although the *agela* ('band, troop') at Sparta was an age-group of pre-teen and teenage boys, whose highly-structured education emphasized military training, our texts provide no reason to think that anything similar existed in Crete at this time. The word is only found once for certain in our texts, where it appears to be a place, perhaps the residence or headquarters of an age-group (**Elt2**.6: 'or in the *andreion* or in the *agela*').[245] We also find the noun *agelaos*, presumably meaning 'member of an *agela*', in the same text: 'if an *agelaos* shames (?) a child as is written . . . ' (**Elt2**.7); this may imply that members of an *agela* were older than children, perhaps in their mid or late teens. Whether *agelai* existed at this time elsewhere in Crete besides Eltynia is unknown.

[243] See the brief summary in Bile 343–4, with references to later texts. The descriptions of these institutions in Willetts 1955 and Lavrencic 1988 are based almost entirely on later sources and analogies with other non-Cretan poleis (primarily Sparta).

[244] *Hetaireiai* (and *agelai*) were probably mentioned in **Dr3**, but the reading and interpretation of this text are disputed; even if they were mentioned, **Dr3** provides no information about the composition or functions of either institution.

[245] *Agelai* were probably mentioned in **Dr3**; see preceding note.

C. Andreion

The *andreion/antreion* ('men's hall') is attested in texts from Axos, Datala, Eltynia, and Gortyn (**A1**.8, 15; **Da1**B11; **Elt2**.6; **G4**.4; **G75**B7–9), always in the singular without qualifying language of the sort e.g. 'his own' that might imply the existence of more than one men's hall in a community (cf. e.g. **G72**.10.37–8: *tai etaireiai tai wai auto*, 'to his own *hetaireia*'). Traditionally, the *andreion* has been connected with the institution of common meals for which the Spartans were famous. Aristotle (*Pol.* 2.10, 1272a1–4), Ephorus (*FGrH* 70F149.10), and Dosiadas (*FGrH* 458F1) all agree that the Cretan word for these Spartan-style communal dining clubs was *andreion*, and modern scholars, relying on these ancient literary traditions, generally conclude that the institution of communal dining was a cornerstone of early Cretan society.

The ancient accounts all seem to imply that free native-born males, including boys, adolescents, and adults, regularly took their meals in the *andreion* to which they contributed a share of their agricultural produce.[246] The accounts differ in many details, however, particularly on the question of the role of the polis in supplying the *andreion* with food and drink for these common meals. The texts from Axos (**A1**) and Datala (**Da1**), both contracts between the city and public workers, indicate that the *andreion* served as a dining hall. Both compensate the workers with *tropa/thropa* ('sustenance'), the contract from Axos specifying that the sustenance would be provided in the *andreion* (**A1**.15). We suggest that the sustenance Datala promised its *poinikastas*, Spensithios, and his offspring implies consumption in the *andreion* as well (see **Da1**A2–3 with commentary). Both Axos and Datala also granted their public workers tax exemption in all things; but both also required them to make certain payments. In the case of Axos, it is clear that these payments were ritual in nature (see **A1**.12–14 with commentary). Datala required its *poinikastas* to give 'to the *andreion* ten axes of meat[247] as *dikaia* when the others offer first fruits (?) and the yearly obligation' (**Da1**B11–14). We suggest that the *dikaia* was an annual ritual obligation, not, as some argue, a one-time entrance fee upon admission to an *andreion* (comm. ad loc.).

Besides these laws from Axos and Datala, two laws from Gortyn (**G4**; **G75**) mention the *andreion*; the earlier possibly refers to drinking in the *andreion* (**G4**.4); the other identifies an official (*o arkos*, 'the leader') as someone who contributes something to the *andreion* (**G75**B7–9). Finally, the provision in the law from Eltynia envisages the *andreion* as a building where an assault might take

[246] The economic aspects of the *andreion* are discussed at Introd. 7E1.

[247] The ax was a unit of weight; see comm. ad loc.

place (**Elt2**.6). Taken together, these laws indicate that the *andreion* was a locus of dining and public ritual.[248]

Scholars have associated two further laws from Gortyn with the *andreion*. The first, **G77**, the law of the *karpodaistai*, is often adduced in connection with the *syssition* (communal meals). The law appears to set forth rules for the collection from individuals of set shares of produce which were then distributed, perhaps to the *andreion*. Other uses for the produce are possible, however, including as payments in kind to public workers (see Introd. 7E1). The second (**G72**. 10.37–9) is the provision from the Code requiring an adopter to give to his own *hetaireia* a sacrificial animal and a jug of wine, which we cited above (Introd. 6A) in connection with the *hetaireia*. Davies (2005: 166) takes this as an 'explicit reference' to the *andreion*, perhaps relying on statements of Dosiadas that the Cretan word for one of the houses (*oikoi*) where the *syssition* took place and for the *hetaireia* was *andreion*.[249] This would require us to assume that each *hetaireia* at Gortyn held a common meal (*syssition*) in a building called an *andreion*. This is not impossible, but the laws give no indication that the *andreion* functioned as a meeting place of a *hetaireia* or that there was more than one *andreion* (though the *hetaireiai* might have shared one *andreion*). Nor is there any reason to take the provision from the Gortyn Code concerning the role of an adopter's *hetaireia* in an adoption as evidence for other activities associated with the *andreion*. We prefer, therefore, to take the two terms *hetaireia* and *andreion* on their own, the former referring to a collectivity of free men (Introd. 6A), the latter to a public building or specific space. Whether the two were connected and what exactly the function of the *hetaireia* was cannot be determined.

The laws do, however, attest to dining and possibly drinking in a public building called *andreion* in several communities, to public contributions of food to some individuals for meals taken in the *andreion*, to the performance of rituals in association with the *andreion*, and to the existence at Gortyn of an official ('the leader') associated with the *andreion*. Apart from the public worker at Axos and the *poinikastas* of Datala we do not know who dined in the *andreion* or under what terms, or who supplied their food and drink. It is possible that all free native-born males dined there, or perhaps only those who belonged to a particular sub-group (based e.g. on age, wealth, or kinship). If there was broad participation in the activities of the *andreion* we should imagine that those eligible in even a small community would have numbered in the hundreds. Another unknown is how

248 For a review of opinions concerning ritual activity in the *andreion*, see Erickson 2011: 386–8.

249 Dosiadas *FGrH* 458F2.8–15 (= Athenaeus 143b): διῄρηνται δ' οἱ πολῖται πάντες καθ' ἑταιρίας, καλοῦσι δὲ ταύτας ἀνδρεῖα, . . . εἰσὶ δὲ πανταχοῦ κατὰ τὴν Κρήτην οἶκοι δύο ταῖς συσσιτίαις, ὧν τὸν μὲν καλοῦσιν ἀνδρεῖον, 'All the citizens are divided into *hetairiai*, but they call them *andreia* . . . Throughout Crete there are two buildings for the *syssitiai*, one of which they call *andreion* . . .'.

often individuals dined in the *andreion*. Some scholars appear to have assumed that it was daily, but it could have been less frequently, perhaps only on special occasions.

The archaeological evidence from the seventh and sixth centuries is consistent with the practice of communal dining, though the identification of any particular building as an *andreion* has proved to be elusive.[250] Several poleis appear to have had buildings associated with communal dining, but the evidence is clearest from the seventh- and sixth-century settlement at Azoria, where a large structure that the excavators call the 'Communal Dining Building' and an even larger 'Monumental Civic Building' both contain remains testifying to dining and drinking activities: the storage of agricultural produce; the processing of food and drink; feasting and drinking; and the performance of sacrifices as part of feasting behavior.[251] The Communal Dining Hall with several large rooms could have accommodated a few dozen banqueters; the Monumental Civic Building, on the other hand, could have accommodated perhaps one hundred and fifty individuals in one room. This suggests that small groups, presumably of elites, dined in the former, whereas a much larger, less restrictive, group used the latter; whether either (or both?) of these buildings was an *andreion* cannot be determined.

7. ECONOMY

Most discussions of the economy of late archaic and early classical Crete are greatly influenced by the accounts of ancient authors who compared the social and political organization of the Cretan poleis with that of Sparta. According to these accounts, the Cretan economy was based on subsistence agriculture with a Dorian landowning class supported by a class of dependent serfs, the descendants of the pre-Dorian inhabitants of Crete, who supplied the agricultural workforce through a system of share-cropping (e.g. Chaniotis 1999b: 182). Modern scholarship devotes particular attention to the economic implications of the institution of the *syssitia*, dining clubs of the political class, that convened in public buildings called *andreia* ('men's halls', Introd. 6C). Ancient authors describe in considerable detail a redistributive system for supplying the *syssitia* with food and drink that linked the dependent class, the political class, and the state in a complex local network of agricultural production and consumption. Modern discussions

[250] For the dangers involved in using the inscriptions and the much more detailed later literary construct of the *andreion* as models for the interpretation of the archaeological record, see Erickson 2011: 383–9; Haggis et al. 2011a: 4–6. Whitley (2011: 40–1) adduces three criteria in his identification of the late classical/early Hellenistic 'Almond Tree House' at Praisos as an *andreion*: a 'considerable quantity' of drinking vessels and animal bones; 'emphatically masculine' iconography; and 'architectural sophistication'.

[251] Haggis et al. 2007; 2011a.

do indeed look beyond the ancient accounts in recognizing the contributions, albeit limited, of pastoralism, hunting, piracy, and service abroad as mercenary soldiers to the Cretan economy. But they still generally accept that the Dorian political class, at once provincial and conservative, inhibited both market production and trade. Thus, accounts of the economy of archaic and early classical Crete for the most part sideline the epigraphic evidence for monetization, capital, the creation of a specialized workforce, and trade, both intra- and off-island.

This is changing, however, as archaeological exploration, both excavation and survey, adds to the traditional picture based largely on the literary record. For example, the identification of late archaic centers for ceramic production on Crete and the establishment of chronologies for their ceramic sequences not only have led to a better understanding of local ceramic traditions and intra-island exchange networks, but also imply a workforce of specialist craftsmen. Furthermore, intensive excavation of the urban centers of poleis, notably those of Eleutherna in the west and Itanos in the east, have brought to light ceramic evidence of Crete's participation in off-island trade that is otherwise almost invisible.

Of wider significance is the recognition that what was once perceived as a gap in the archaeological record of Crete during the late Archaic period (roughly the sixth century) is instead 'a major departure from earlier periods in the inherited forms and structures of the archaeological record' (Erickson 2010a: 249). Admitting considerable local and regional variation in material culture among the communities of late archaic Crete, one can nonetheless trace an island-wide shift in mortuary practices, ritual behavior, the production of monumental architecture and sculpture, and the circulation of elite exotica to a lower archaeological profile characterized as 'austere' (Introd. 2B1). Furthermore, this material and cultural austerity is particularly pronounced in central Crete where the communities that enacted laws were located. The factors contributing to this shift and its implications remain unclear, but this late archaic transformation of the material culture of Crete should be kept in mind in assessing the epigraphic evidence for the Cretan economy.

The following discussion explores the contribution of the inscribed laws to our knowledge of the economy of late archaic and early classical Crete without appeal to the later literary tradition as an explanatory tool or to supplement the epigraphic record. We do draw, however, on archaeological correlates from time to time in assessing the evidence from the laws, and we follow the recommendation of Davies (2005: 160) in defining our business as that of 'seeking to understand how real men and women extracted a living from a real landscape'.

The inscriptions, of course, are not evenly distributed across the ten communities nor is the light they shine on the economies of the communities that enacted them equally bright. What are understood to be the earliest of the laws, including the laws from Prinias, Dreros, and the first forty or so laws from Gortyn, provide very little information of economic interest. The rest, including the laws of Datala, Eleutherna, Eltynia, Knossos, Lyktos, and Phaistos dating to the late sixth or early fifth century and in particular the fifth-century laws from Gortyn provide the lion's share of the evidence. Whether this reflects social developments that made the economic sphere larger and more complex, and thus a source of greater anxiety and contestation beginning in the latter half of the sixth century, or is a consequence of legislative or epigraphic habit (more laws were enacted and published on stone), or results from other factors cannot be determined. Although much of our evidence comes from late archaic and classical Gortyn, it is nonetheless possible even with such a lopsided data set to identify local peculiarities. The laws from Gortyn, for example, have a great deal to say about property, including land, and agricultural production and distribution, but less about animal husbandry, and have almost nothing to contribute concerning other kinds of production. The laws from Lyktos and Eleutherna, on the other hand, are a particularly rich source of information concerning pastoralism and, in the case of Eleutherna, specialized craft production, while several of the laws from Axos seem to concern labor of some kind.

A. Property

Although the Cretan economy was primarily agricultural and landownership was thus the primary form of wealth on the island, the laws seldom refer to land per se. Two general terms for land, *ga* (Attic *gē*) and *kora/korion* (Attic *chōra/chōrion*), are attested at Gortyn. The former occurs twice: in a provision of a law concerning a dispute involving the boundaries of *ga* (**G42**B2, *ai akriai atera ga*, 'where the other's land ends') and in a decree for a benefactor of Gortyn granting him a house in Aulon inside of Pyrgos and a 'a plot other than (agricultural) lands' (**G64**.5, *woikopedon eksoi gan*; for the sense of this expression, see comm. ad loc.). The terms *kora/korion* were used throughout Greece to refer to the hinterland of a polis, including not only land suitable for cultivation, but also land fit only for pasturing livestock. Like *ga*, the use of *kora/korion* suggests that at Gortyn the terms referred to farmland (*kora*: **G72**.4.34–5; *korion*: **G46B**7–9; cf. **G52A**6–7). Two of the provisions that refer to *ga* and *korion* (**G42**B2; **G46B**7–9; cf. **G73A**) and several others that require the measuring of what we assume was farmland (**G75A**; **G81**.7–11) indicate that the borders of an individual's land were clear, and that the area of individual plots must have varied. There is no clear evidence for disputes concerning the location of the boundaries of a property, though this does not mean that such disputes were unknown.

In addition to these general terms for agricultural land, four terms refer to specific categories of farmland: *pytalia* (Attic *phytalia*), 'orchard' or 'vineyard' (**G43Ba**); *apamia*, a term that in origin perhaps referred to lands, possibly of marginal utility, worked by a dependent class called *aphamiotai* (comm. ad **Ele16Ab**); *kerson* (Attic *cherson*), 'barren or fallow land' (**Ele15**); and *moros*, a term that may possibly refer to a vineyard (comm. ad **Da1**A14–15). Finally, the phrase *athanata kremata*, 'immortal things', occurs in an incompletely preserved provision of a law from Gortyn: 'If...he works immortal things or trees or—' (**G76B**8–9); in this context, property that is in some sense 'undying' is likely to be 'land' (cf. below for *tnata* (*kremata*), 'mortal things').

The general term in the Gortyn Code for property of all kinds including land was *kremata*.[252] A provision of the Code on disputes among the heirs over the division of an estate provides a glimpse into the formal classification of personal property in fifth-century Gortyn (**G72**.5.39–44). The provision lists four kinds of property that might be divided among the heirs: *tnata* ('mortal things'); *karpos* ('agricultural produce'); *wemas k' anpidemas* ('clothing and footwear');[253] and *epipolaion krematon* ('movable property'). Neither land nor improvements to land (e.g. buildings) are included in these categories (comm. ad **G72**.5.28–54).

What might each of these categories include? The term *tnata*, 'mortal things', undoubtedly covers human property, i.e. *doloi* and *woikeis* (Introd. 5A7) and animals. The laws attest the ownership of horses, mules, and donkeys (**G41**.2.3–4), cattle (**G3**; **G41**.1.12–17; **G65** *boïan* 'cow hide'; **G75**.B6), sheep and goats (**G1**; **G3**; **G4**; **G65**), pigs (**G4**; **G26**; **G41**.1.12–17; **Lyktos1B4**), birds (**G41**.3.8), and dogs (**G41**.2.16).[254] There is no evidence in the early laws for the public ownership of livestock, and all these animals were probably owned privately; the polis would then purchase or otherwise acquire from individuals (as taxes or voluntary contributions) the animals required for sacrifices and other public uses.[255]

The term *karpos* occurs in the laws of Axos, Eleutherna, and Gortyn. Its context in the inscriptions from Axos and Eleutherna is unclear (**A12**, **Ele5**, **Ele13**). At Gortyn, *karpos* in **G72**.5.39–44 (discussed above) is one of the categories of property that might be divided; *karpos* is also mentioned in provisions concerning the property of divorced (**G72**.2.48–50), widowed (**G72**.3.27–9), and childless wives (**G72**.3.35–6), and of heiresses (**G72**.7.35–40; **G72**.8.47–50). In these examples *karpos* is paired with *kremata*, i.e. land and (its) produce. The term

252 On *kremata* as including land, see further Introd. 7B.

253 For the meaning of *anpidemas* ('footwear'), see comm. ad **G43Ab**.11–12.

254 The term *kartaipoda* ('stout-footed') probably refers to cattle (**G41**.1.12–17; **G72**.4.36 with commentary; **Lyktos1**B3) and *probata* (animals that 'walk in front') to sheep and goats (**G72**.4.35; **Lyktos1**B2–3).

255 Chaniotis 1999b: 194–7.

occurs in one further law from Gortyn (**G77**) where it is clear that *karpos* included figs (*dierosykon*, 'fresh figs') and grapes (*gleukios*, 'grape must').[256] Grapes are attested as well at Datala (**Da1**: *kleukos*, 'grape must') and figs at Eleutherna (**Ele15**: *sykia*, 'fig trees'). The only other agricultural product that the laws mention specifically is barley (**Ele9, Ele13, G63, G79**). There is no certain mention of the olive, unless the term *dendrea* ('trees') in the laws from Gortyn means olive trees, but this is far from clear.[257] Finally, the law concerning the *karpodaistai*, 'distributors of *karpos*' (**G77**) and the phrase *to karpo to endothen moira laken*, 'to have a share of the produce from within' (**G72**.3.27–9) indicate that *karpos* referred in particular to the actual produce that has been harvested (*karpoomai*, **G43Aa**) and stored away. The term *epikarpia*, attested only at Gortyn, may refer to the total value of all that the land produces on a continuing basis, i.e. the revenue from the land.[258]

The distinction between 'clothing and footwear' and 'movable property' may seem curious to the modern reader, but is probably an expression of the view that clothing, unlike other movable property, was distinctively personal, a view also reflected in e.g. rules concerning an Athenian bride's trousseau. The phrase 'clothing and footwear' occurs in two other laws from Gortyn: one setting the fine for stripping a *dolos* at three times the value of the stolen 'clothing and footwear' (**G43Ab**); the other recording various objects including 'clothing and footwear' in a list in **G75**B that also includes '*tnaton* and movable objects', although the precise nature of the list is not clear (comm. ad loc.). The other items in this list include household equipment (a loom, worked wool,[259] perhaps a vessel of some kind, a marriage bed), agricultural equipment (a plow, iron tools), a yoke of oxen, and millstones (both lower millstones and an upper grinding stone). Taken together these objects might be described as the basic 'starter-kit' for a family of subsistence farmers.[260]

Absent from both lists (**G72**.5.39–44; **G75**B) are improvements to land, or what the Gortynians might have referred to as 'immovable property' (e.g. houses, threshing floors). The term *stega* occurs in the sense of 'house' in inscriptions from Gortyn (Introd. 5C1), including a provision of the Gortyn Code concerning

[256] For both crops at Gortyn, see also **G79**.

[257] In **Ele14A**3, G and VER restore [*e*]*laion*, 'olivier', but other restorations are possible (see n. ad loc.).

[258] **G43Ba**; **G72**.7.29–35, 8.45, 12.9–17.

[259] Provisions giving a wife half of what she has woven when she divorces or is widowed imply that textiles had significant value (**G72**.2.50–2, 3.24–7).

[260] The first object mentioned in **G75**B is military equipment (*opla*) belonging to a free man. The relationship between the *opla* and the list of items that follows is not clear. Also unclear is the relationship between the specific objects in the list and the indefinite 'whatever' that the leader provides for the *andreion* (**G75B**7–9).

inheritance where mention of 'houses in the city' implies that there were also houses in the country.[261] The use of the plural in this provision indicates that an estate might include more than one town or country house. *Stega* also occurs together with *dendrea*, 'trees', in a provision giving an individual who builds a house (*ton woikodomesanta*) or plants trees ((*ton*) *pyteusanta*) the right to sell these improvements (comm. ad **G80**.3–4). A term that is commonly used for 'house' elsewhere in Greece, *woikia*, is also attested at Gortyn (**G64**.4; **G81**.1), although it appears to mean 'household' in its single appearance in the Code (Introd. 5C1). It is not possible to determine with certainty the meaning of *woikia* ('household', 'house', or 'right to possess a house') in the phrase *dendreon kai woikias* (**G81**.1), but the provision concerning house (*stega*) and trees in **G80** recommends 'house' in **G81**.1. If so, *woikia* and *stega*, which occur in the same law (**G81**.16), would mean the same thing.

Several inscriptions from Gortyn in addition to **G80** and **G81** refer to trees. Trees appear to have been regarded as a separate category of property, not subsumed under e.g. land. This is suggested by the juxtaposition of *athanata kremata* ('land'?) or trees in **G76**B8–9. Thus, it seems that an individual might exercise complete control over, i.e. own, trees and their produce (planting, sale, use to secure a loan) without owning the land on which they grew.[262] Similarly, threshing floors (**G43Aa**) also appear to have been regarded as an improvement to land; they could in some sense be separated from the land they occupied and pledged to secure a debt.

B. *Ownership*

The evidence for ownership comes almost entirely from the fifth-century laws of Gortyn; very little can be said about ownership before the fifth century or elsewhere on Crete. One of the earliest laws from Gortyn (**G4**) includes the provision *me priasthai me amewsasthai*, 'not to buy not to exchange', but the context of the prohibition and the nature of the property cannot be determined. Bile 328 suggests that the verb *amewusasthai* (Attic *ameibesthai*) denotes a pre-monetary transaction (i.e. barter). If so it is important to observe that it occurs here as an alternative to purchase. The same verb occurs in one other text, a sixth-century law, perhaps the earliest, from Lyktos (**L1**), but here it is unclear whether the thing exchanged was property or something else entirely, such as a declaration of some kind. The terms for purchase and sale occur in uncertain contexts at Lyktos (**L4**) and Eleutherna (**Ele16Aa**), as do terms associated with the pledging

[261] **G72**.4.31–7 with comm. ad loc. For a house in the city, see also **G72**.7.52–8.7.

[262] **G43Ba**: planting trees and their use as security; **G80**: planting trees and their sale.

of property as security at Eleutherna (**Ele16Aa**; **Ele16Ac**) and Axos (**Axos1**.7–8), again in uncertain contexts.

Traditionally scholars have thought that land at Gortyn was indivisible and inalienable; it belonged to the extended family and could only be passed down intact within the family. Recently, however, this view is changing and most scholars now more plausibly conclude that, at least in the case of fifth-century Gortyn, land could be bought, sold, and mortgaged, and at a person's death would be divided among the heirs.[263] Moreover, these heirs could include women, who could inherit land and leave it to their heirs (Introd. 5B). In the unlikely event that a person died without any heirs at all, his property (*kremata*), including land, was inherited by members of the household who were the *klaros*, who in our opinion were probably the serfs or perhaps a select group of them (**G72**.5.25–8, with comm.).

One argument in support of the view that *kremata* included land is that if *kremata* does not include land, then land per se is not mentioned in any of the laws pertaining to family property and inheritance at Gortyn.[264] It might be argued that it was understood by all that land remained with the family, and that the laws could thus be silent on this point, but several passages make clear that *kremata* could refer to land and that land could be bought and sold and pledged as security (i.e. mortgaged). First, a divorced woman is allowed to take 'half of the *karpos*, if there is any, from her own *kremata*' (**G72**.2.48–50, cf. **G72**.3.35–6). Since *karpos* is agricultural produce, *kremata* must be a reference to land which the woman owns, having either inherited it, bought it, or acquired it when a debtor who had pledged his land as security defaulted on the loan (Gagarin 2008b). Furthermore, the provision in **G43**Ba.3–7 preventing the sale or mortgaging of certain land given by the polis implies that ordinarily land could be sold and mortgaged, since otherwise there would be no need for such a prohibition. Taken together, these provisions leave little doubt that in fifth-century Gortyn land could be bought and sold and mortgaged, and was divided among the heirs in an inheritance.

In addition to private ownership of land, it appears that sanctuaries owned land that produced revenue (**Da1**B6 with note), and the fifth-century laws of Gortyn indicate that some land was owned by the polis. **G43**Ba explicitly and **G64** implicitly refer to a gift to individuals of land belonging to the polis, orchard-land (*pytalia*) and a building plot (*oikopedon*) respectively. In the case of **G43Ba** it is clear that the recipients of these lands did not own them; they

263 Link 1994a: 80–2; Maffi 2003a: 175–80 (with a good summary of earlier scholarship); Davies 2005: 160–1; Gagarin 2010a: 24–5.

264 Thür 2006: 30–2 has speculated that *klaros* (**G72**.5.27) designates land and that an estate at Gortyn was divided into the *klaros*—real property—and *kremata*—movable property, but this interpretation of *klaros* seems impossible (comm. ad loc.).

could, apparently, pledge the revenue (*epikarpia*), but they could not sell or pledge the *pytalia*, the land itself. **G43Ba** does not specify to whom the polis gives orchard-land. Although it was highly unusual in archaic and classical Greece for a foreigner to farm public lands and control its agricultural produce, the agreement of Gortyn with Rhitten (**G80**) appears to envisage precisely this privilege (see below).

The agreement of Gortyn and Rhitten permits a Gortynian who builds a house or plants trees, presumably on land within the territory of Rhitten, to sell the house and trees, and gives a Rhittenian the same rights on lands within the territory of Gortyn (**G80**.3–4). Although this provision does not specify whether this land was public or private, it was likely the former. It seems unlikely that private landowners would give away their land to others without receiving anything in return. It would be to the advantage of the polis, on the other hand, to cultivate unused public lands thereby increasing its tax base (for taxes in kind, see Introd. 7E3). If we are right, it appears that Gortyn and Rhitten had a surplus of public land that they brought under cultivation by offering such land rent-free to their citizens and on occasion to their treaty partners.

What was true of privately-owned land at Gortyn was also true of all kinds of private property: it could be bought and sold, pledged as security, and inherited. The ownership of people deserves special treatment. It should be noted at the outset that there is no explicit evidence for state-owned slaves (Introd. 7C). The purchase and sale of both a *dolos*, 'slave', and a *woikeus*, 'serf', was allowed, at least in certain circumstances.[265] **G41**.4, prohibiting the sale of a fugitive serf for one year while he takes refuge in a temple, implies that in other circumstances the sale of a fugitive serf was permitted. Whether or not a serf who was not a fugitive could be sold is unclear. Evidence for the purchase and sale of slaves at Gortyn concerns the buyer's ability to terminate a purchase rather than his ability to buy a slave in the first place. The provision (**G72**.7.10–15) limits the liability of someone who has bought a slave from the market (*eks agoras priamenos dolon*) for a wrong committed by the slave around the time of his purchase. The new owner had sixty days following the purchase within which 'to terminate' (*peraiosei*) and avoid liability for the slave's wrong. The provision does not specify the procedure for terminating the purchase of a slave, but the ability of the new owner to do so implies an interest in protecting consumers, at least in the purchase of slaves. The ownership of a slave could also be temporarily transferred to a new master in order to secure a debt (**G47**, see Introd. 5A6). There is no evidence for the pledging of

[265] **G72**.7.10–15 may suggest that unlike slaves, serfs could probably not be sold by themselves (in the agora) but only in connection with the sale of the land to which they (in a sense) belonged. For the differences in status between *doloi* and *woikeis* (which are not always clear), see Introd. 5A7.

serfs, but since a free man could indenture himself to secure or pay off a debt (**G41**.5–6), it is reasonable to assume that someone could also indenture his serf (comm. ad **G47**).

Whether serfs or slaves could own real property is unclear. If the phrase 'those of the household who are the *klaros*' refers to serfs, in the unlikely situation that there were no heirs serfs could inherit whatever property belonged to the estate, including, presumably, other slaves as well as serfs who were not 'those of the household who are the *klaros*'. However, the status of a serf who inherited an estate in this way likely changed, perhaps to that of an *apetairos* (Introd. 5A3). Otherwise serfs probably could not own land, improvements to land, or people. The rule that a serf wife 'is to have her own things' (*ta wa autas eken*) if she separates from her husband (**G72**.3.40–4) implies that serfs could own movable property (*epipolaion krematon*), including livestock (**G72**.4.31–7); but unlike the case of a free woman who divorces, no mention is made of produce in connection with a divorced serf woman, presumably because she could not own any land that might yield produce. We have even less information about the property rights of slaves. Gagarin (2010a: 26) observes that the rules setting fines for sexual offenses (**G72**.2.2–45) are written 'in a way that implies that the *dolos* or *woikeus* paid the fine himself', but this implication might be misleading. An individual could not strip a slave of his clothing and footwear (**G43**Ab), but this does not make clear whether the slave owned the clothing and footwear.

For a free native-born person to indenture himself to pay off a debt (see Introd. 5A6) must have been an act of last resort by someone who had no other form of wealth to pledge. We hear as well of a free man who has no house (**G72**.4.14–17) and of a free woman who marries a slave (**G72**.6.55–7.10), possibly because her family is impoverished, because her slave husband has accumulated some wealth, or both. Other Gortynians appear to have possessed considerable property: town and country houses, farmland and stores of agricultural produce, livestock, furnishings and equipment, and, as we shall see, money. It appears, in short, that there was a significant inequality of wealth among both the free and the dependent populations of fifth-century Gortyn.

C. *Production and Labor*

References to fig trees and fresh figs, grape must, and barley, to trees, gardens, and produce, to orchards and barren land, to houses in the country, plows, yokes of oxen, threshing floors, and iron tools, to planting and harvesting, to the collection of manure and ash, and to irrigation and the control of water vividly evoke agricultural production; rarely, however, is agricultural production the focus of regulation.[266] Exceptions to this general observation include two laws from Eleutherna that possibly regulate aspects of agricultural production (**Ele13** and **Ele15**), and three of the four texts of **G43** that more clearly do so: **G43Aa** on the use of threshing floors; **G43Ba** on the use of public land for cultivating orchards; and **G43Bb** on the diversion of river water, presumably for irrigation.[267]

Animal husbandry is amply attested in the laws, widely so in sacrificial regulations specifying offerings of cattle, goats, sheep, and pigs,[268] but also at Gortyn in rules concerning liability for damages to animals,[269] and at Lyktos in a law regulating the location for 'pooling together' (*koinaonia*) and 'separating out' (*synkrisis*) *probata* (sheep and goats), *kartaipoda* (cattle), and pigs (**Lyktos1B**). Some scholars have understood the law from Lyktos to concern the reassignment of livestock from private to public ownership, associating the communal herds with a system of communal dining,[270] but we think Chaniotis' interpretation (1995: 46–8; 1999b: 192–7) is more likely, namely that the provision marked out the area where privately owned herds came together and intermingled in preparation for seasonal migrations.[271] A poorly preserved fifth-century law from Gortyn may also concern the pasturing (*nemontai*) of animals, in this case sheep judging from the term *pilosis*, 'compaction' (from *pilos*, 'wool'),[272] although the rule is usually understood to concern distribution (*nemontai* in the sense of 'distribute' rather than 'pasture').

The size of herds cannot be determined. Davies (2005: 165) cautions that 'there is no warrant for attributing a specialist pastoral regime to (Gortyn)', implying that the Gortynians maintained small herds for household and ritual use. In the case of Lyktos, however, animal husbandry may have represented a greater share of the economy, and tensions between shepherds and farmers perhaps occasioned the law in **Lyktos1B**, which, by specifying the paths marking the boundaries of the area for pooling together and dividing the herds, may have served to control

266 Fig trees (**Ele15**); fresh figs (**G77**); grape must (**Da1**A14–16; **G77**); barley (**Ele9**; **Ele13**; **G63**?; **G79**); trees (**G10**c–e; **G69**; **G76**B; **G80**; **G81**); garden (**Ele15**; **G20**); orchards (**G43Ba**); barren land (**Ele15**); plow (**G75**); yoke of oxen (**G75**); threshing floors (**G43Aa**); iron tools (**G75**); planting/cultivating (**G43Ba**; **G80**.3); harvesting (**G43Aa**; **Ele11**); collection of manure and ash (**G73**A); irrigation and the control of water (**G5**.2?; **G43Bb**; **G52**; **G73**A1–6). The specification of 'houses in the city' implies the existence of country or farm houses (**G72**.4.32, 8.1–2).

267 For discussion of the relationship of the four texts of **G43**, see commentary.

268 Cattle: **G3**; **G41**.1.12–17; **G65**; goats: **G2**; sheep: **G1**; **G2**; **G4**; **G65**; pigs: **G4**; **G26**; **G27**; **G41**.1.12–17; animal sacrifice in general: **A1**.12–13; **Dr6**; **Dr7**; **G72**.10.38–9; **G80**.

269 **G41**.1 and 2 concern an owner's liability for injuries his animal causes an animal belonging to someone else; **G41**.3.7–17 concerns liability for failure to return an animal to its owner.

270 H. and M. van Effenterre 1985: 184–5; VER I.12B; Guizzi 1997: 48.

271 For the fairly recent (late nineteenth- and early twentieth-century) practice in the Mesara of pooling flocks of sheep and goats to form one large herd that was cared for by a single individual, see Blitzer 2004: 198.

272 Perhaps a reference to the process of felting wool (**G53**B3–6 with comm.).

the movement of animals to and from their individual grazing grounds so as to avoid damage to fields, orchards, and gardens (Introd. 2C).

Herds of animals left free to roam were a threat to fields, orchards, and gardens, but the use of horses, donkeys, mules, and oxen to transport goods to and from the fields, to pull plows, and to help with the threshing, and of their manure as fertilizer were indispensable to agricultural production. Cattle together with sheep and goats contributed as well to non-agrarian production. Rules from fifth-century Gortyn concerning the ownership of the cloth (woolen and perhaps also linen)[273] that a wife produced (**G72**.2.50–2; **G72**.3.24–7) and the reference to a loom (**G75**) attest the household production of textiles, as does the discovery of loom weights in sixth-century houses at Azoria.[274] Moreover, in a divorce the woman took half of what she had woven with her (**G72**.2.50–2). In many cases (especially if she had children), her share would be far more than she could use herself, which implies that some means, presumably a market, must have existed for calculating the value of these woven goods.

Two laws from Eleutherna (*c.*525–500) perhaps concern the production or sale of leather goods by specialist craftsmen: the *sisyropoios*, a maker of goatskin or sheepskin cloaks, *sisyrai* (**Ele9**); and a leather worker, *skyteus*, or perhaps his leather product, *skytos* (**Eleutherna3**A). These two laws provide the only textual evidence for the existence of specialist craftsmen in late archaic Crete, although we should perhaps include here the evidence from the laws for textile production, performed by wives within the house but not necessarily for household use alone. It is not, of course, possible to determine if these leather products were produced for the local market or for more distant trade, although demand for leather cloaks at home was probably too limited to support a specialist craftsman if that were his only product (Introd. 7E2).[275]

Many scholars assert (once again, largely on the basis of late classical and Hellenistic literary traditions based in large part on a Spartan model) that most productive processes were in the hands of non-citizens or members of the unfree subordinated population of serfs (*woikeis*) and slaves (*doloi*), whereas free native-born members of the community engaged in occupations appropriate to members of the political class, which included participation in governance, military training and service, performing religious rituals, and taking part in the activities of the *andreion*.[276] There is no good evidence for such assertions, however. The reference to serfs living in the country indicates that some, perhaps the majority of

[273] The cultivation of flax for its fibers (for linen and cord) is attested at Mycenaean Knossos (Rougement 2007) and in the western Mesara during the late nineteenth and early twentieth centuries CE (Blitzer 2004: 127).

[274] Haggis et al. 2011b: 479.

[275] See further Chaniotis 1995: 49–51; Perlman 2004a: 103–8.

[276] See e.g. van Effenterre 1979 for the identification of wage-earners as non-citizens.

them, lived on their masters' farms, at least in fifth-century Gortyn (**G72**.4.34–5), but neither this passage, the only one that actually locates *woikeis* or *doloi* in the *chora*, nor any other provision in the laws suggests that free men did not work their farms alongside them.

In addition to doubting the participation of members of the political class in agricultural labor, scholars have rejected out of hand a role for them in non-agrarian labor or as wage-earners. Thus, the few references in the laws to the specialist craftsmen discussed above and to wage-earners have all been understood to refer either to foreigners or to unfree members of a dependent class; but the laws themselves suggest otherwise. Four laws refer to wages (*mistos*) (**A1**; **Da1**; **Dr4**; **G79**). The recipients of *mistos* in **A1** and **Da1** were skilled workers, a builder? (*o inymenos*) and a writer (*poinikastas*), who contracted to work for the polis in exchange for wages, tax exemption, and sustenance in the *andreion*. There is nothing in either law to indicate that these individuals were foreigners, serfs, or slaves. To the contrary, the observations that they were provided sustenance in the *andreion* and were required to participate in sacrificial ritual strongly suggest that they were members of the political class of Axos and Datala. Nor is there any reason to conclude that the specialist craftsmen discussed above or the kithara player mentioned in **Ele16**Ab.1 were foreigners, serfs, or slaves.

G79 is an agreement between the polis and public workers who are defined as those 'who live in the city, both free men and slaves (*dolois*)'; wages are paid in produce as they are at Datala, but there is no reference in what survives to tax exemption or sustenance in the *andreion*, and there are provisions for fines for those who refuse to work, which the *ksenios* was responsible for exacting. The large quantities of produce suggest that the wages were intended for a crew of workers. Van Effenterre (1979) concluded from the role of the *ksenios* and the qualification of the wage-earners as those living in the city in **G79** that the free men were foreigners, but it is quite possible that the *eleutheroi* included members of the political class. Apart from **Dr4**, where the employer appears to be an individual although a clear understanding is not possible, there is no evidence for wage-earners working in the private sector.

In his discussion of the material evidence for the economy of late archaic Greece, Osborne (2007: 288–9) observes that the large-scale public building projects that characterized the sixth century required Greek poleis both large and small to support a labor force that was at best part-time food producers. Although the material culture of sixth-century Crete was in many ways austere, it is nonetheless clear that at least some of the Cretan poleis participated in the phenomenon of large-scale public building that was characteristic of Greek communities elsewhere. The evidence for this is particularly unambiguous at Azoria where the urban center was completely reorganized in the late seventh or early sixth century, an undertaking that must have required a substantial workforce

(Haggis et al. 2011a: 1–4; 2011b: 432–4). The contract of Gortyn with a crew of workmen and of Axos with *o inymenos* ('builder'?) may be signs of this phenomenon as well. The occurrence of terms for work or workers is a notable feature of the laws from Axos (**A1–A4**; **Axos1**), although in these cases it is not possible to determine if the rules concern wage-earning public workers or not.

D. Money

The laws from Crete preserve several of the earliest attestations of pre-coinage monetary instruments in the Greek world.[277] Cauldrons (*lebetes*) were used as a recognized measure of value in provisions prescribing fines in laws from the Pythion at Gortyn.[278] The amounts occur in multiples of five: five *lebetes* (**G1**.1d–f; **G21**); ten (**G8**i, a–f); twenty (**G10**s–t; **G11**); fifty (**G10**f–h; **G14**); and one hundred (**G1**.4d–f; **G5**; **G7**).[279] In one of these provisions from the Pythion, the fine is set at 'a tripod sworn to be (worth) ten *lebetes*' (**G8**i, a–f with commentary). In this case it seems likely that 'tripod' refers to the actual metal object rather than to a measure of value; otherwise it would have been sufficient to express the amount in terms of *lebetes*. It is perhaps significant that here the fine is referred to as *poina*, the term used in archaic poetry for a compensatory payment or blood money in a case of homicide. A fine expressed in *lebetes* (one hundred) also occurs at Lyktos (**Lyktos1A6**).[280] A third metal object, a *pelekys* or double-edged ax, is attested as a standardized unit, probably of weight rather than of value, at Datala (**Da1**B11–14 with commentary).

In the mid sixth century, at the same time as Gortyn and Lyktos were using the cauldron and tripod as measures of value or monetary instruments, the first mints in the Greek world were established.[281] The earliest of the Cretan mints, those of Gortyn and Phaistos, commenced production of silver coins around 470.[282] Their

[277] For a recent discussion of pre-coinage monetary instruments in the Greek world, see Kroll 2012.

[278] Cf. Von Reden (1997: 157–8) who implies that the fine was paid in cauldrons rather than in property worth so many cauldrons. We do not exclude the use of cauldrons as money, but it seems very unlikely that someone would hand over as many as one hundred actual cauldrons as payment of a fine.

[279] In the majority of the provisions the term occurs in the accusative plural (*lebetas*), 'he is to pay so many cauldrons (in value)', but it occurs in the genitive plural (*lebeton*) in **G8**i, a–f and in the genitive singular (*lebetos*) in **G6**. In the latter case, the context is unknown; perhaps we should understand (a specific item) worth one *lebes*.

[280] A fine expressed in cauldrons is also attested in what is perhaps an early provision from Knossos that was reinscribed in the Ionic alphabet but Doric dialect in the third century: *IC* I.8.5B, lines 1–3, 'If a man breaks the horns of an ox he shall pay five *lebetes* to the owner of the ox.'

[281] For recent discussions of the start of coinage in the Greek world, see Osborne 2009: 237–46; Kim 2001.

[282] Price 1981: 464; Stefanakis 1999: 257–60; cf. Le Rider 1966: 194–8, who proposes a later date (*c*.450–425) for the start of minting on Crete. Stefanakis (1999: 257) attributes the start of minting on the island to the reduced supply of new Aiginetan coinage after 479.

coinage, like that of all subsequent Cretan mints, was produced on a standard that ultimately derived from the much-imitated silver coinage of Aigina, one of (if not the earliest of) the Greek mints (from *c.*560–540).[283] Examples of four denominations are attested at Gortyn during the period *c.*470–360: stater (*stater* = two drachmas), drachma (*darkna* = six obols), triobol (*triodelon* = three obols), and obol (*odelos*).[284] The mints of Gortyn and Phaistos did not, however, introduce coinage to Crete. Aiginetan traders, some of whom appear to have settled at Kydonia in northwest Crete, are likely to have introduced the use of coined money, for the most part coins minted on Aigina, to the island during the final quarter of the sixth century (Stefanakis 1999: 249–57). It has further been suggested that these settlers established a mint, perhaps at Kydonia, for the production of 'pseudo-Aiginetan' coins in small denominations (triobols and obols) shortly before Gortyn and Phaistos established their own mints (Stefanakis 1999: 257).

The name of the smallest of the denominations, 'obol' (*odelos* in the Cretan dialect) was in origin the word for 'iron spit', another metal implement with monetary significance in early Greece (Kroll 2012: 34–6). The term is first attested on Crete in three small fragments from the Pythion at Gortyn where it most likely serves as a measure of value or possibly weight, although we cannot rule out reference to iron spits or even to coins (**G25**u; **G26**a; **G26**b). On the other hand, although it is not impossible that the terms obol, triobol, drachma, and stater in laws dating to the period *c.*500–450 refer to units of weight (of silver bullion), since coinage had been introduced to Crete almost a quarter century earlier, there is no good reason to doubt that they refer to coins.[285] The terms occur in the laws from Axos (stater), Eleutherna (triobol, stater), Eltynia (drachma), Gortyn (obol, drachma, stater), Knossos (drachma), and possibly Phaistos (stater?). At Datala we find the otherwise unattested compound adjective *ikatidarkmios*, 'twenty-drachmas worth'.

The word silver (*argyron*) occurs in several laws to refer to an unspecified sum of silver, which could be either silver bullion or silver coin. In either case, silver was lent (**G72**.9.1–2; **G72**.10.21; **G72**.11.31–2, 39–40), given away (**G72**.10.19), and exacted as a fine (**G77**B11). Possible evidence of its use in a commercial context is limited to a single inscription (**Ele16Aa**4–5).

By far the most common context for the mention of coins in the laws is in the assessment of fines. In almost all cases where the amount of the fine is preserved it

[283] The standard of the Cretan mints was between 6% and 12% lighter than the Aiginetan standard (± 11.10 grams of silver in a Cretan stater in comparison with ±12.20 grams of silver in an Aiginetan stater). Stefanakis (1999: 260–2) explains the debasement as an effort to save bullion.

[284] See Le Rider 1966: 194–5, pl. XI, 8–19.

[285] For the monetary use of silver bullion in archaic Greece, see Kroll 2008.

is either a single unit or a multiple of five. Fines, especially single-unit fines, are sometimes assessed on a per diem basis (e.g. **G72**.1.33; cf. **G63** five staters per day and **G72**.2.12 two staters per day) or for each occurrence of an offense (e.g. **A9**.5–7; cf. **G79** ten staters for each offense). Most of the fines are between two and one-half and ten staters. The smallest recorded fine of one obol was assessed for the daytime rape (two obols if at night) of a female household slave who has already had intercourse (**G72**.2.11–16); the largest of one hundred staters (double this if the offender was a slave) were for the rape of a free man or woman (**G72**.2.3–4) and possibly for the 'plunder' ([*suli*]*oien*) of an individual (**G78**). We assume that the fine was paid to the injured party in almost all cases, except where it is explicitly specified that the fine should be paid to the polis (Introd. 7E3). Apart from the assessment of fines, sums in coin were specified for gifts to women (**G72**.2.52, 3.38–40, 10.1–25) and former adoptees (**G72**.11.15), and for public contributions for sacrifices (**A9**.11–14; **G80**.2–3). In only two instances are amounts in coin specified for what is possibly the price of a commodity or payment of wages (**Ele9** triobol; **G63** five staters per day).

Fines, either simple or double (and in two cases triple),[286] were also assessed in terms of the value of the injury that the plaintiff suffered. The intention of fines assessed in terms of the simple value (*to aploon*) presumably was to restore the injured party to his *status quo ante*. Examples include the value of an animal, diminished through injury or loss (**G41**.1.5–7, 3.6), and the value of an indentured slave whose current master, while claiming that the slave has died, neither shows the corpse to the former master nor swears to the slave's death (**G47**). Fines of double or triple the value of disputed property were intended not only to restore the injured party to his *status quo ante*, but also to punish the wrongdoer. If the current master is found guilty of selling or hiding the indentured slave, he is fined double the value (*dipleia*) of the slave; someone who asserts that he is not liable for the simple value and then loses at trial is fined the double value (**G41**.3.14–17); and if someone convicted of illegal possession of another person refuses to release him after a year, the fine is tripled (**G72**.1.35–8).

A 'punitive' penalty of this sort is also found in the earliest law from Crete (**Dr1**.2). An unlawful *kosmos* owed double 'whenever he should give judgment', presumably meaning that he was to pay twice the amount of any fines he assessed against another. We assume that in the unlikely event that this provision was actually enforced the party who had paid the original fine and the polis shared 'the

[286] For a fine set at triple the value, see **G43Ab**.9–11 and **G72**.1.37, with comm.

double'; otherwise someone who may well have been guilty would profit from his wrong-doing. Later laws imposed a double penalty for the misuse of the property belonging to another (**A9**; **G72.3**.12–16, 5.35–9, 6.18–23, 9.11–14; **G78**.3–6), including wrongful seizure of goods pledged as security (**G43Aa**.4–9; **G80**.9–11). In the laws dating to the period *c*.500–450 the values were perhaps assessed in terms of silver coin, although payment may have taken other forms (e.g. the replacement of the property in question).

Support for the assessment of value for different sorts of property may be found in the two provisions concerning the wrongful seizure of goods pledged as security (**G43Aa**.4–9; **G80**.9–11). In both it appears that the state regulated the valuation of property pledged as security and published a record of the state-approved values,[287] perhaps in order to prevent unscrupulous creditors from seizing property that was worth more than the debt or unscrupulous debtors from pledging property that was worth less than what they owed. References to measuring land that was pledged indicates that the size of the parcel was one of the criteria for assigning it a value (**G75**A1–8; **G81**.1–11). We do not know the basis for the valuation of property in other contexts (property that was stolen or was not returned according to agreement), but market-value is certainly a likely basis.

Several laws suggest the concurrent use of various objects (including metal, coined or uncoined) as money.[288] **Ele13**.1–2 stipulates payments in barley in conjunction with debts calculated in staters (silver bullion or coins). We may compare it with the collocation of triobol and barley in **Ele9**, the law concerning the maker of cloaks. Of note is the fact that in both texts the ratio of silver to grain is identical: one-half unit of silver (one-half stater) to one unit of grain (*medimnos*).[289] The occurrence together of grain and silver in the same ratio in two different inscriptions suggests that in each case the law may have provided alternative forms of payment either in silver or in barley. Equivalences between metals (coined and uncoined) and other products in rules concerning payments and gifts are attested as well in laws from Datala (**Da1**A13–14 'twenty-drachmas worth of bronze') and Gortyn (**G8** 'one tripod (worth) ten cauldrons'; **G72.3**.37–40 'twelve staters or something the value of twelve staters'). Such evidence for the use of 'monnaie multiple' almost certainly reflects accommodation, albeit incomplete, of money in day-to-day transactions, both private and public, that were conducted without it in the not too distant past.

287 This is implied by the references to writing in **G43Aa**.4–9 (*ai wekasto egrattai* 'as is written for each'), and **G80**.9–11 (*ai en tai porai egrattai* 'as is written in the ephor's place?').

288 For the concurrent use of various objects (including silver) as money, see Descat 2001.

289 A *medimnos* is a dry measure of grain a bit larger than a bushel.

E. *Distribution and Consumption*

1. Beyond Subsistence

The late archaic and early classical laws support the assumption that the inhabitants of the Cretan *poleis*, like those of almost all other Greek communities, depended on a largely agrarian subsistence economy. We catch a glimpse of the domestic storage of produce in one of the several rules in the Code (**G72**.3.24–7) concerning the distribution of property at the dissolution of a marriage: when a husband dies leaving his wife childless, she is to have her own things, half of whatever she has woven, and a share of the 'produce within' (*to karpo to endothen*). A similar clause occurs in two other provisions, but these passages specify that either the wife (in the case of divorce, **G72**.2.45–52) or her heirs (in the case of her death, **G72**.3.31–7) receive a share (one-half) of the produce 'of her own property if there is any'. Like most other scholars, we understand the qualifying 'within' (*to endothen*) of the first passage to refer to produce 'stored up'. Unlike the other two provisions, this neither limits the source of the produce to the wife's property nor implies that there may not be any produce for her. Rather she is to get a share of the household's stored produce, whether it came from her husband's property or her own, perhaps a share equal to that of the other heirs.

The few sixth-century houses that have been excavated on Crete attest the domestic storage of agricultural produce on a considerable scale. Five of the substantial town houses at Azoria and the two large country houses at Onythe Goulediana were equipped with storage areas (rooms or corridors) adjacent to what appear to have been the main halls of the houses.[290] Fragments of large storage jars (*pithoi*) were discovered in each of the storage areas; in three of the houses from Azoria the fragments belong to at least five *pithoi* (North Acropolis Building and Southwest Building) and in one case to at least seven (Northwest Building), well within the range of the six to ten *pithoi* that Ebbinghaus (2005: 57) estimates were required to store a yearly supply of basic foodstuffs for a household of around six members. Large storage jars were themselves valuable. Datala may have included jars, perhaps for the storage of grape must, or their equivalent value in bronze, in the wages promised to the *poinikastas* (see **Da1**A12–14 with notes and commentary). Drinking, pouring, and serving vessels dominate the ceramic assemblages from the halls of the Azoria houses. Haggis and Mook 2011 note that the proximity of hall and storeroom enhanced the accessibility to and perhaps even

[290] For the houses at Azoria, see Introd. 5C1; for the houses at Onythe Goulediana, see Platon 1956; Sjögren 2003: 18–21; for their comparison, see Haggis and Mook 2011.

visibility of the family's valuable *pithoi*, reminders of the agricultural produce stored in them and of the household's landed wealth.

Although the late archaic and early classical laws reflect an agrarian subsistence economy, we have observed that they also provide an exceptional body of contemporary documentary evidence for craft specialization and wage-earners, for the introduction of coinage and the first steps toward monetization, and for significant inequality of wealth in fifth-century Gortyn. The evidence for estates of considerable size, at least at Gortyn, for craft specialization, and for the private use of money in day-to-day transactions (e.g. purchases and the payment of debts and fines) suggest that at least some families were able to accumulate property beyond what was needed for domestic use.

In addition to the distribution of wealth between individuals and from individuals to the polis in payment of debts and fines, provisions in the laws of Axos, Datala, and Gortyn granting certain individuals 'tax exemption in all things' imply that the *poleis* imposed upon their members taxes of various kinds (**A1**.2, 15; **Da1**A3; **G64** with 'in all things' restored). The law from Axos indicates the purpose of one kind of tax on individuals, payments for sacrifices (**A1**.12–13): 'They pay for the following: for the Great Hekatomb and the sacrificial offering.' The preserved text does not specify the amount of the payment or if the payment was to be made in money or in kind, perhaps suggesting that the obligation was a familiar one. A similar tax is implied in the provision requiring the people of Rhitten 'to furnish every third year 350 staters for sacrifices on Ida' (**G80**.1–3). Rhitten may have met this obligation by imposing a special tax on individuals, or it may have paid for the sacrifices from its public treasury. If the obligation was 'sacrifices worth 350 staters', not '350 staters *for* sacrifices', as translated above, then payment was perhaps made in kind rather than money.

Payments in kind are attested in the law from Gortyn regulating payments of fixed shares of produce (two of fresh figs, three of grape must, and two of one other product) presumably by individuals to public officials called *karpodaistai*, 'distributors of produce' (**G77**B). It appears that provision is made for payment of a half-share in the event that the payee did not (or could not) pay the full amount (**G77**B3–4). Figs and must, together with barley, are listed in **G79** as payment for workers, and it is possible that the collection that was regulated by **G77** was intended for that purpose. Most scholars, however, connect the regulations of **G77** with the *syssition*, the system of communal dining in the *andreion* that late classical and Hellenistic writers describe (Introd. 6C). Davies (2005: 166–7) adduces a model of this institution drawing on the much later literary tradition and the early laws from Gortyn to assert that distributions of produce to the *syssition* had the effect of preventing the generation of private capital and the development of robust market-based exchange:

any growth in market-based exchange and distribution will have been impeded by the requirements of what all the literary sources see as the prime institution, alike of male citizen brigading and of economic redistribution, namely the *andreion* or *syssition*... The basic step is that a tithe of all agrarian produce was levied (with provision against concealment to be enforced by public officials) and is supplemented by levies in kind or in coin from non-citizens and from public lands. After some has been top-sliced for cult and public administration, these resources are then redistributed by the city to the *andreia* and can in their turn be supplemented by members.

As we indicate above (Introd. 6C) we do not have sufficient information concerning the organization of the archaic and classical *andreion* (who dined there, how often, and the nature of an individual's obligations to the *andreion*) to calculate the impact of the *andreion* on the ability of a household to generate capital for use in market-based exchange. If, for example, individuals dined in the *andreion* on a daily basis and were obligated both to support the members of their household who did not dine in the *andreion* (at least wives, daughters, and slaves) and to contribute to the *andreion*, the drain on private production would have been substantial. But since our evidence cannot rule out more limited or occasional participation in the *andreion*, as seems to have been the case for the Communal Dining Hall at Azoria (Introd. 6C), the economic impact of the activities associated with the *andreion* on many households may not have been as significant a factor in the Cretan economy as Davies and others conclude.

2. Market-Based Exchange and Trade

Since it appears that the obligations of individuals to the *andreion* may not have significantly reduced their ability to accumulate capital, we can now turn to the laws and examine what light if any they shed on market exchange during the sixth and fifth centuries. The development of market-based exchange (i.e. 'trade'), defined as exchange that obeys the rules of supply and demand where capital is risked in the search of profits, has long held center stage in debates concerning the nature of the ancient Greek economy. We have already noted the epigraphic evidence for specialist craftsmen and wage-earners who were at most part-time farmers, for a slave market, for the possibility that the polis used market values in establishing values for property used as security, and for monetization. None of this necessarily implies market exchange beyond the local level, but there are a few inscriptions from this period that attest supra-local trade. The most explicit of these is the mid fifth-century agreement of Knossos, Tylissos, and Argos (M&L 42).[291] Scholarship on the ancient Cretan economy has largely ignored the implications of its three provisions concerning export (lines B11–14).

[291] For the text see also *IC* 1.30.1 + 1.8.4; VER I.54; and Rhodes and Lewis 1997: 308, 310. We do not include this agreement in our texts because the dialect is Argive, not Cretan (see above Preface, n. 2); but

The first permits export from Knossos to its neighbor Tylissos and from Tylissos to Knossos (B11–13). The promise not to interfere in trade between these communities implies that in the absence of such agreements poleis did regulate the export of goods across their borders. Viviers (1999) understands the provision as the earliest example of a stipulation found in several later inter-state agreements from Crete granting customs-free trade between Cretan poleis. The details of the movement of goods between Knossos and Tylissos that this provision implies are unknown. We imagine that the lion's share of exports were agricultural products, either unprocessed or minimally processed, that leave scant trace on the archaeological record. Yet Erickson's studies of pottery production and style on Crete during the sixth and fifth centuries have traced the intra-island movement of locally produced black-glazed pottery, suggesting very localized patterns but also broader regional and even island-wide networks.[292]

The provision permitting the movement of goods between Knossos and Tylissos is followed by one concerning the export of goods *perande* (B13–14): 'If he exports *perande*, let him pay just as the Knossians.' The general meaning of the adverb *perande* is 'beyond', and this is the sense that Viviers (1999: 221), among others, understands here, i.e. '(if he) exports goods to areas beyond'. The provision appears to regulate a Tylissian who exports goods beyond Knossos, allowing the Tylissian to pay the same fees as a Knossian. The adverb *perande* thus seems to mean 'abroad' here, and refers explicitly to export by sea or transshipment through the harbor at Knossos.[293] In this case the rule is not reciprocal, suggesting that export by a Knossian 'beyond' Tylissos was likely not a concern, perhaps because Knossian exports 'beyond' were already well established and did not need to pass through Tylissos. The harbor of Knossos (just east of modern Heraklion, see Introd. 2C) probably attracted more traffic than the much smaller anchorage at Agia Pelagia (ancient Apellonia?) located six kilometers north of Tylissos and eighteen kilometers west of Heraklion.[294] Although the latter was much closer to Tylissos, a Tylissian may well have found it advantageous to ship his goods from his neighbor's harbor. The provision not only suggests that in the absence of a special agreement Knossos charged foreigners higher transit fees than it charged Knossians, but also implies that these fees represented a valued source of revenue for poleis that controlled harbors with good anchorages.[295] As observed above

there is no reason to doubt that its provisions concerning export reflect actual conditions in the two Cretan cities.

[292] Erickson 2002; 2004; 2010a: 184–7, 225–8, with maps of the movement of pottery from Lyktos (p. 36, figure 2.2) and from Gortyn (p. 185 figure 6.8), to the Ierapetra Isthmus (p. 197 figure 7.4) and to Itanos (p. 232 figure 9.6), and to and from Knossos (p. 226 figure 9.2) and Eleutherna (p. 227 figure 9.3).

[293] This is the sense in which Vollgraff 1948: 46–9 and VER I.54II understand the term.

[294] For Apellonia, see Perlman 2004b: 1150–1.

[295] Cross (2011: 133) includes such fees among other largely invisible revenue streams of maritime trade.

(Introd. 2C), the majority of the communities whose laws we study here appear to have had direct access to the coast or to have been linked to coastal settlements with good anchorages; the exceptions are Datala, Dreros, Eltynia, and Prinias, which do not appear to have had direct access to the coast.

The third provision (B14) allowing Tylissians to export goods wherever they wish probably has in mind exports to other Cretan poleis as well as abroad, since goods moved by sea might just as well be destined for distribution at Cretan ports as off-island ones.

In addition to the Knossos–Tylissos agreement, evidence for commerce abroad comes from a provision at Gortyn (**G72**.9.43–10.1) that attests both individuals who traveled abroad (*es peran*) on commercial ventures and investors who funded them. The provision, which envisages loans as large as one hundred staters or more and as small as ten staters or less, arguably had the effect of encouraging investment by giving an investor who was not repaid his choice of procedure for deciding his case in the event that he had no witnesses to the transaction. Another law from Gortyn (**G72**.6.46–51) provides that a person who has gone abroad (*perande*) may be ransomed 'from another polis' (*eks allopolias*); although often understood as addressing the ransom of persons captured while fighting abroad, this provision may rather indicate that Gortynians traveled overseas on business that risked putting them in harm's way (see commentary). We cannot determine the nature of the business, but trade is one of the possibilities.[296] The same adverb (*perande*) occurs in a law from Eleutherna (**Ele11**) concerning someone who sails abroad either as a *theoros* ('sacred envoy') or on some other business that is not preserved. It is tempting to suggest that the business was commercial in nature, but again there are many other possibilities.

We have no reason to doubt that the individuals who were the subject of these regulations from Gortyn and Eleutherna concerning sea travel and commercial ventures were free native-born members of the communities that enacted the laws. It is worth noting, however, that at least in Athens many of those engaged in maritime trade in the fifth and fourth centuries were metics (resident aliens).[297] In Crete, there is evidence that at Gortyn, and perhaps at Eleutherna (**Ele4**.4 with note), there was a foreigners' *kosmos* (*ksenios kosmos*), as well as special judicial

[296] See also **G72**.8.36–40, a rule providing that if a claimant to an heiress is 'not at home' (*me epidamos*), she is to marry the next claimant in line. Presumably this refers to a long-term rather than temporary absence, and in many cases at least, the claimant must have been able to anticipate the heiress having enough property that he would not need to hire himself out as a mercenary for service abroad. Thus, the most likely reason for his absence is a commercial venture.

[297] For recent discussions of the role of Athenian metics in overseas trade, see Reed 2003; Möller 2007: 368–70. In Athens foreigners (*xenoi*) and metics were distinct categories, the latter being long-term residents as opposed to visitors. In Crete, there is no clear evidence for a category of 'resident alien' (as distinct from 'foreigner') in the late archaic and early classical laws.

procedures for foreigners (Introd. 4C1b, 5A5). In any case it seems likely that among the *allopoliatai* ('citizens of another polis') and individuals who came under the jurisdiction of the *ksenios* (*kosmos*) and *kseneia dika* were some, Cretan and non-Cretan, who traveled for the purpose of trade.[298]

In short, the early inscriptions from Crete reflect, if not always explicitly, Crete's involvement in overseas trade. They provide clear evidence for public control of maritime export through the assessment of fees. They suggest that the poleis of Crete were porous communities with special public officials and judicial procedures for non-citizens among whom we imagine both Cretans and non-Cretans. They indicate that Cretans traveled abroad for various reasons including commercial ventures. They suggest that problems arose as a consequence of overseas travel and poleis enacted laws in response: to help investors in commercial transactions whose loans went unpaid; to ensure the repayment of ransom by individuals who had been held hostage overseas; and to determine the legal status of property belonging to the long-term absentee owner and the legal rights of heiresses to marry before the return of an absentee claimant. The enactment of these laws in itself implies that travel and long absences were not uncommon.

One obstacle to imagining the early development of market-based exchange on Crete is the fact that there is little archaeological evidence either for Cretan exports during the late Archaic and Classical periods or for imports to the island.[299] Again, as in the case of intra-island trade, ceramics are an exception, with Cretan pottery found e.g. at Tocra and Cyrene in North Africa and in the Levant in mostly fifth-century contexts at Al Mina, Shiqmona, Dor and Apollonia (modern Herzeliya)[300] and a greater quantity of imported ceramics found on Crete. Eleutherna may have served as a gateway community for the import of pottery (Laconian, Corinthian, and Attic) into Crete during the period *c*.600–460 and the principle hub for its distribution across Crete, as Erickson suggests (2004; 2010a: 287–9). Cycladic pottery dominates the archaic and early classical import record from Itanos, Olous, and Azoria in east Crete (Erickson 2010a: 294).

Although it cannot be denied that overall the archaeological record of Crete's participation in off-island trade during the late Archaic and early Classical periods is scanty, two points that mitigate the significance of archaeologically visible trade are worth mentioning. First, what we suspect was the case for intra-island trade may also have been the case for off-island trade: much of the trade was in

[298] The jurisdiction of the foreigners' official was not necessarily confined to people who came from elsewhere, but, depending on the context, appears to have included others who were not members of the political class—free or slave, native-born or foreign (Perlman 2004a: 109–18).

[299] See Erickson 2010a: 273–308 for a recent discussion of the archaeological evidence.

[300] Study of the Cretan material from the Levant is being done in the framework of a Ph.D. dissertation of Yiftah Shalev (University of Haifa), and a research project supported by an Israel Science Foundation Grant awarded to Ayelet Gilboa (University of Haifa) and Gunnar Lehmann (Ben-Gurion University).

agricultural products with low archaeological visibility. Second, Crete lay at the center of sixth-century trade-routes linking southern Greece, the Cyclades, Asia Minor, and Egypt and Cyrenaica (Erickson 2010a: 281–95). Recent scholarship on the participation of the island in maritime trade has emphasized the convenience of the island's harbors for transshipment, shelter, and provisioning and this, rather than Crete's own products, may have been the principal draw for Mediterranean traders.[301] The economic advantages the island's location offered both the poleis controlling the harbors (in the form of harbor, customs, and transshipment fees) and the individuals involved in their operation (from produce-sellers to dock workers to shipwrights) should not be overlooked.

Another factor that distorts many scholars' estimate of the significance of market-based exchange on Crete is the emphasis they place on the contribution of warfare and violent acquisition to the economy of archaic and classical Crete. The early laws and the contemporary archaeological record, however, unlike later tradition and modern scholarship, do not suggest that early Cretan society was exceptionally martial (Introd. 8). Despite the dearth of evidence in support of the view of early Cretan society as an 'armed camp', its proponents emphasize the role of booty and mercenary pay in the movement of goods to and from Crete as well as intra-island. Chaniotis, for one, understands whatever trade occurred on Crete as a side-effect of warfare and other forms of violent acquisition (1999b: 184–5):

> Exchanges on and with Crete were primarily trade in captured persons, slaves, and foreign luxury items, which usually found their way to the island as the booty of mercenaries or raiders or in the cargo of foreign ships. For the Cretans, trade was to a large extent a side-effect of war: bringing home luxury items, selling captives, trading with booty, and transporting these goods abroad on their ships.

As the evidence introduced above makes clear, however, trade was far broader and more complex than this.

3. Public Revenue

Mechanisms other than market-based exchange played a significant role in ancient Greece in the near and distant movement of goods as e.g. gifts, votive offerings, mercenary pay, and the influx of money and goods purchased abroad, and booty from war, piracy, and brigandage. The agreement of Knossos, Tylissos, and Argos (M&L 42, see above n. 291) confirms for the mid fifth century that Cretan poleis regulated the acquisition and distribution of booty: 'Whatever we both (Knossos and Tylissos) capture [from the enemy?], (Tylissos?) is to have the third portion of everything (taken on) land, and the half of everything (taken) at sea' (B4–7). Tylissos (and Knossos) presumably were responsible for determining what if any

[301] Erickson 2010a: 279–81; Cross 2011: 131–54, 166–71.

per capita distributions to make from the polis's share. A tithe (*dekaten*) of the booty was skimmed off and set aside for the gods: 'Whatever we capture (*elemes*) jointly, Knossos is to have the *dekaten*; the finest of the booty we both are to bring jointly to Delphi, and the rest (of the booty) we both are to dedicate jointly to Ares at Knossos' (B7–11). The same verb 'capture' (*airen* = Att. *hairein*) occurs in six of the fourteen inscriptions, possibly dedicatory, that were written on late seventh- or early sixth-century bronze armor (five mitrai or groin protectors and one corselet) said to have come from Aphrati (ancient Datala?).[302] The public dedication at Aphrati of arrows, possibly seized in battle, to the goddess Athena is securely attested in an epichoric inscription on stone (*IC* I.5.4). This early evidence from Aphrati for the dedication of booty, including armor and possibly arms, supports the suggestion that **A5+6**, with its references to 'things from the war', 'tithes', and a 'spearhead', concerns similar practices at Axos.[303]

In addition to booty the laws attest two other sources of public revenue: fees or taxes of various kinds, including harbor fees and export taxes, and judicial fines. Grants of tax-free status in all things (*ateleia panton*) imply that the poleis imposed a variety of taxes (**A1**.3, 14–15 and **Da1**.A3; cf. **G64**.3 where *panton* is restored). We have already had occasion to note the inscriptions that appear to refer to particular taxes: the payment, presumably to the polis, in full or of 'the half' of standard measures of fresh figs (two measures) and grape must (three measures) (**G77**B1–3); payments by individuals, possibly to the polis, for sacrifices (**A1**.12–13); and the payment of customs-fees for goods moved by sea (M&L 42B13–14).

The payment of judicial fines to the polis, probably in coinage, is attested in the laws of Eltynia (**Elt2**.3) and Gortyn (**G41.3**.14–17; **G78**.5–7; **G79**.12–16; **G84**). The laws from Gortyn suggest that judicial fines were paid to the polis in extraordinary cases: when a 'simple' fine (i.e. the value of the contested property) was doubled following the conviction of an accused who had denied his guilt, the double fine was likely divided equally between the plaintiff and the polis (**G41.3**.14–17); when someone robbed a member of a group (the Latosians) that the polis declared inviolable, the robber paid the victim double the value of the stolen property and a fine of one hundred staters to the polis (**G78**.5–7); and when someone under contract to work for the polis refused to do so, the worker paid a fine to the polis of ten staters for each work stoppage (**G79**.12–21). Several public officials were involved in the collection and deposit of fines for the polis: the *kosmos* (**Elt2**.3), the *titai* (**G78**.5–7), and the *ksenios* and *titai* (**G79**.12–16). In other laws, these officials appear to have been concerned largely with the exaction of judicial payments, a function that they are attested performing already in **G14**g–

[302] Mitrai: *SEG* 52.835, 837, 838, 840, 841; corselet: *SEG* 52.834. **Da1** is inscribed on a *mitra*-shaped sheet of bronze. See comm. ad loc.

[303] Perlman (2010) discusses in greater detail the evidence for the dedication of booty in early Crete.

p1. The Gortynian *karpodaistai*, whose title suggests that they functioned as distributors of produce, were tasked with securing produce that had been withheld or stolen and with exacting fines in silver (i.e. coinage) equal to the value of the mishandled produce (**G77**).

Poleis used their revenue to pay wages (*misthos*) and sustenance (*tropa*) to their employees (**A1**; **Da1**; **G79**) and to pay for sacrifices. Wages were paid in kind—grape must and (ceramic vessels?) worth twenty drachmas or bronze (**Da1**A11–14), barley, figs, and grape must (**G79**.1–8)—as presumably was 'sustenance in the *andreion*' (**A1**.15). The picture the laws paint of public revenue and expenditure implies that the poleis stored produce on a grand scale. The sixth-century Service Building at Azoria, a sprawling complex of multiple rooms located adjacent to the Monumental Civic Building, provides evidence for the storage and processing of food at the scale that the laws suggest (Haggis et al. 2007: 274–95; 2011a: 43–62).

In conclusion, the archaic and classical laws are practically silent about the very aspects of the economy that are the focus of the later literary traditions concerning early Cretan society (and the modern scholarship that has relied so heavily on those traditions), namely serf labor, the *syssition*, and the role of institutionalized violence in the production and distribution of wealth. To be sure, the agreement of Knossos, Tylissos, and Argos regulates the distribution of booty seized in warfare, including the share for the gods, practices that the laws and the archaeological record confirm. But there is nothing exceptional in this, and the agreement also provides evidence for trade wholly unconnected with warfare. We know that Cretans were among the men who went abroad to serve as mercenaries in the late Archaic and Classical periods, but it is clear that Cretans also traveled abroad for other reasons including commercial ventures. And Aiginetan merchants, not Cretan mercenaries, introduced coinage to Crete probably to pay for Cretan exports.

Cretans made use of dependent labor, to be sure, but the laws of fifth-century Gortyn also suggest a familiarity on the part of landowners with the day-to-day running of their farms—e.g. where to dispose of manure and locate irrigation ditches, the use of mortgaged threshing floors, securing one's livestock so that it not injure a neighbor's animal—that is strongly suggestive of hands-on experience. To assume that free native-born Gortynians did not spend their time farming is to disregard these implications. The *andreion*, by contrast, is widely attested. We can be confident that eating was one of the activities that took place there and that among the diners were a few skilled public workers whose sustenance was supplied by the polis. But to suggest that an individual's obligations to the *andreion* limited his ability to accumulate capital and participate in market-based exchange is to assume a Spartan model for the social and political organization of the institution that neither the laws nor the archaeological record support.

8. INTER-POLIS RELATIONS

The laws focus on regulating the lives of the members of the individual communities, both residents and visitors, including free native-born individuals, serfs and slaves, and foreigners. The fifth-century agreement of Knossos, Tylissos, and Argos is the only certain example of a treaty between fully independent Cretan states that predates the Hellenistic period (M&L 42A and B, see above, Preface, n. 2, and Introd. n. 291). We discuss its provisions from time to time in this volume, but the role that Argos appears to have played in the enactment of the agreement and its continuing influence on the relations between Knossos and Tylissos that many of the provisions imply make it difficult to assess to what extent it was typical of interstate relations in early Crete.

Besides this agreement, five laws from Crete possibly or certainly concern relations between communities.[304] **A5+6** provides the closest parallels to the provisions in M&L 42 concerning the distribution of booty, but nothing in the surviving provisions suggests that it is the text of an agreement between Axos and another community rather than a law affecting Axos alone. **Dr2**, the earliest of the five laws, is extremely elliptical: '[It was decided] as the Prepsidai and the Milatioi initiated.' If the text is complete, as we suggest it is, it could only have made sense in reference to another text, now lost, or to a public decision that was not recorded in writing. We are fairly confident that Milatioi refers to the community Milatos, whose town center, at least during the Classical and Hellenistic periods, was probably located on the coast about nine kilometers northwest of Dreros. The Prepsidai are not otherwise attested, but the coordination of Prepsidai and Milatioi suggests that they too were a community located somewhere in the vicinity of Dreros. We cannot know what the Prepsidai and Milatioi initiated, but we might speculate that **Dr2** confirmed the participation of Dreros in an agreement of some kind among all three communities.

[304] A relationship between Gortyn and Phaistos may perhaps be indicated by their coinage. Le Rider (1966: 161–2) understood similarities in the fifth-century coins of Gortyn and Phaistos (*c.*470), distinguished by the name of polis written on the reverse (*Gortynos to paima*, 'stamp of Gortyn'; *Paistion to paima*, 'stamp of Phaistos'), as evidence that the poleis had formed a political union (*sympoliteia*). Cucuzza (1997) suggests that they had joined together already in the sixth century.

Two enactments of Gortyn clearly regulate its relations with other communities. **G80**, an agreement between Gortyn and Rhitten, presumably located somewhere in or near the Mesara,[305] addresses several sources of tension plaguing relations between the members of the two communities: the ownership of improvements to land (buildings and orchards), lines 3–4;[306] the behavior of magistrates, 4–8; the maintenance of order, 4–5; and the seizure of property as security, 8–12 (comm. ad loc.). The conciliatory tenor of two further provisions evinces Gortyn's interest in having good relations with the Rhittenians. The agreement begins by affirming that the Rhittenians are to have their own laws (*autonomoi*) and their own judicial system (*autodikoi*) independent of the Gortynians (**G80**.1), and at the end it provides for the resolution of future disputes between the two communities, requiring a Gortynian whom a Rhittenian has accused of wrongdoing to go to Rhitten to answer the charges against him in the agora before the assembled Rhittenians (**G80**.12–15). The observations that Gortyn appears to be dictating the terms of the agreement and that its officials are authorized to go to Rhitten, a community that is otherwise *autonomos* and *autodikos*, to help maintain order there strongly suggest that Rhitten was a dependent polis of Gortyn, *viz.* a polis that was not fully independent or autonomous in the modern sense of the term (Hansen and Nielsen 2004: 87–94; Perlman 1996).

The other text from Gortyn, **G63**, is an agreement between Gortyn and Leben, a coastal community directly to the south of Gortyn (Introd. 2C).[307] Two or three of its six fragmentary lines contain procedural language: '[the Lebenian?] against the Gortynian and against the Lebenian the G[ortynian?]' (line 3); 'for the Lebenian the witness [is to] prevail' (line 4); and 'five staters per day' (line 5), a reference to a fine or possibly to wages (comm. ad loc.). What is striking about both these Gortynian agreements is the attention paid to the peaceful resolution of disputes between members of the two communities, hinted at in the poorly preserved agreement with Leben, but a focus of attention, both in resolving present disputes and in anticipating future conflicts, in the agreement with Rhitten.

Finally, **Lyktos1A** exempts two groups from a general rule concerning the reception of *allopoliatai* (alien citizens): *allopoliatai* who are held by force (*kartei*)

[305] Many scholars identify Rhitten with ancient Prinias, but there is reason to question this; see Prinias Site.

[306] **G80**.3–4 allows members of either community to buy and sell improvements to land located in the territory of the other, but not, apparently, to own the land itself. Cf. M&L 42B.23–5, a provision permitting a Tylissian to acquire *chremata* (land?) in Knossos, but prohibiting a Knossian from doing so in Tylissos.

[307] By the Hellenistic period Leben appears to have been a political dependency of Gortyn. The same may have been the case earlier, but nothing in **G63** implies as much (Perlman 1996: 248, 251). For the possibility that Aulon (**G64**) was a dependent polis of Gortyn, see Perlman 1996: 266–8.

and *allopoliatai* who are Itanioi (lines 1–4).[308] It is not possible to determine whether the general rule permitted or prohibited the reception of alien citizens, but we agree with the majority of scholars that it was probably prohibited. Lyktians could, then, 'receive' Itanioi, an exemption from the general rule prohibiting the reception of foreigners, which implies a special relationship between Lyktos and Itanos. Perhaps the two communities were bound by an agreement that provided for the security of individuals from one community within the territory of the other.

Other possible evidence for inter-polis relations includes the noun *ksenodokos*—'host' in the sense of 'one who receives (*-dokos*) strangers (*kseno-*)'—which occurs with a verb meaning 'seize' in one of the earliest laws from Gortyn: '[if] he should be taken for (by?) the host' (**G13**b2 with commentary). Several fifth-century provisions from Gortyn may also indicate that personal security was a concern: **G72**.1.2–2.2 has to do with the seizure of someone before a judge has determined his status, though there is no reason to think that such seizures were commonly carried out by persons from other poleis; **G72**.6.46–51 concerns someone who is being held abroad for ransom; and **G78** prohibits the enslavement of a Latosian.[309]

Taken as a whole, the evidence from these early inscriptions together with the evidence from Gortyn for the establishment of special officials and laws for foreigners (Introd. 4C1b, 5A5) contrasts with the common characterization of Crete as continually engaged in military training and warfare,[310] for which there is strikingly little evidence in the laws from our period.[311] 'Arms of a free man which he has for war' are mentioned once (**G75**B1–3), and in **A5+6**.2–4 'things from the war' and a spear are mentioned, perhaps as dedications of booty,[312] but otherwise any allusion to war is purely speculative.[313] **G64**.2 is commonly restored on the basis of three partial letters (*ole*) to read 'valor in war' ([*aretas em p*]*ole*[*moi* . . .]),

[308] We believe that the Itanioi are more likely the citizens of the east Cretan polis, Itanos, than the inhabitants of an otherwise unattested community in the vicinity of the modern village *ta Aïtania*, located fifteen kilometers west of Lyktos, as Faure 1993: 69–70 suggested (see comm. ad loc.).

[309] For the identity of the *Latosios*, mentioned also in **G58**.4–5, see comm. ad **G78**.

[310] 'A territorial army on permanent standby' (Davies 2005: 161); for Gehrke the lives of Cretans were marked by extreme competitiveness and war (1997: 29); cf. Chaniotis 2005: *passim*. For the scarcity of fortification walls dating to the Archaic and Classical periods, see Introd. 2C.

[311] For the assumption that *startos* at Gortyn designates a military unit, see Introd. 4B3.

[312] Inscriptions on bronze armor believed to have come from Aphrati indicate that the armor was booty seized in battle (Introd. 2A2). The armor has been dated on stylistic grounds to the late seventh and possibly early sixth centuries, the inscriptions slightly later (*c.*600 and after).

[313] Representations of warriors in sixth- and fifth-century art are rare (Introd. 2B). Notable exceptions—mold-made plaques datable to *c.*575–525 depicting a hoplite abducting a youth and another type showing a hoplite at rest—come from several open-air spring sanctuaries in the vicinity of the east Cretan polis, Praisos (at Agios Giorgios, Roussa Ekklesia, and Vavelloi near Praisos). Erickson (2009) interprets the former (hoplite with youth) as a scene of ritual abduction associated with a male maturation rite.

but this is simply a guess that probably owes its general acceptance by modern scholars to the tradition of Cretan militarism. **G72**.6.46–55, which speaks of ransoming someone who has gone abroad, might concern prisoners of war captured outside of Crete, but just as likely concerns traders or others captured by pirates (or in the course of piratic activity).[314] The laws from our period, however, provide no explicit evidence for private (i.e. piratic) violent acquisition by Cretans.[315] Nor is there evidence in the laws for the service of Cretans as mercenaries in foreign armies, although we know that Cretans served as hired warriors at least as early as the final quarter of the fifth century.[316] This final observation reminds us that the laws cannot possibly provide a comprehensive picture of Cretan society. Yet, as noted above (Introd. 2C), on current evidence the construction of fortifications (defensive walls and fortresses) appears to have been very rare during the Archaic and Classical periods, and while many of the archaic and classical settlements continued to occupy the defensible hill-top locations preferred during the Early Iron Age, others including Gortyn and Phaistos moved down from the hills at the beginning of the Archaic period.

On the other hand, the agreement of Knossos, Tylissos, and Argos is referred to as a treaty (*spondē*) (M&L 42A6–7), implying that two or possibly all three of the communities had been at war, and it includes provisions common to fifth-century treaties and alliances: rules for declaring war and concluding peace (M&L 42A6–11); for the conduct of joint expeditions (M&L 42A17–28); for the distribution of booty (M&L 42B4–11; 31–4); and for the sending of embassies (M&L 42B38–42). Furthermore, the abrupt desertion of some Cretan settlements may be evidence of coercive or violent relations between Cretan poleis during the late Archaic and Classical periods. For example, while the remains of the final phase of the late archaic/early classical settlement at Prinias appear to reflect a voluntary or negotiated relocation of the community (Pautasso 2014: 63), evidence for the early

[314] See Perlman 1999 and Luraghi 2006 on the thin line between maritime trade and piracy in ancient practice.

[315] Brulé (1978: 66–7) lists twenty-six piratical raids by Cretans beginning in the final quarter of the fourth century. Evidence for Cretans engaged in piracy before then is exiguous at best.

[316] Eighty Cretan archers served as mercenaries in Athens' ill-fated expedition to Sicily in 415 (Thuc. 6.43; 7.57.9) and Cretan *epikoroi* in the service of Amyrtaios scrawled their names on the funeral temple of Seti I at Abydos (Jeffery 1990: 316, nos. 30a–b). Jeffery (1990: 314) dates the graffiti to *c*.400. Accounts of Cretans serving in foreign armies before then may or may not be historical. Pausanias (4.19.4) reports that mercenary archers from Lyktos and other Cretan poleis fought with the Spartans against the Messenians in the second Messenian war (second half of the seventh century); according to Ktesios (*FGrHist* 688F13.146–8) Cretan archers came to the aid of the Greeks at Salamis in 480. Snodgrass (1974) identifies miniature bronze arms and armor from the archaic phase of the sanctuary of Apollo at Bassai as dedications left by victorious Cretan archers. Viviers (1995: 257) sees no reason to reject Ktesios' account, although most scholars deny the historicity of the claim. For a votive dedication that may have been brought back to Crete as booty from Persia (a Persian bridle ornament from the sanctuary of Demeter at Knossos), see Coldstream 1973a: 157, no. 221, pl. 93.

fifth-century destruction at Azoria suggests a more violent process and relatively rapid abandonment (Haggis 2014: 132). It is reasonable to suppose that Cretans, like all Greeks, did at times engage in combat, but not that Crete was exceptional in this regard or that continual military training and readiness on the model of fifth-century Sparta was characteristic of any Cretan community in the sixth and fifth centuries. The picture of Crete as engaged in constant warfare in this period appears to be a mirage, spawned by the more plausible picture of interstate relations on Crete, Cretan mercenaries, and Cretan pirates during the Hellenistic period.

9. RELIGION

A. Sacred and Secular

Several laws denote a conceptual distinction between divine matters (*ta thina/thiēia*) and human matters (*ta anthropina*) in public activities and in private life. The phrase 'public matters both divine and human' (*ta damosia ta te thiēia kai tanthrōpina*) defines the scope of the authority of Spensithios and his successors in their activities *qua poinikastas* for the polis Datala (**Da1**A4, 6–7; **Da1**B2–3). At Gortyn, an adoptee is required to fulfill the adopter's divine and human obligations (*ta thina kai ta antropina*) in order to inherit (**G72**.10.42–4). *Ta thina* and *ta thiēia* are attested on their own (e.g. **A5+6**.6; **Da1**B16; **G53**B1);[317] *ta anthropina* is not. This conceptual distinction between sacred and divine, however, is not often discernible. The subject matter of a few of the laws appears to pertain wholly or largely to religion (see below); the enacting authority of one law in this small group of what we might call 'sacred laws' is probably a priesthood (*thystai*, **Dr4**).[318] But for the most part 'divine matters' and 'human matters' are woven together in the fabric of the legislation, and although we do not know what authority enacted the other 'sacred laws', we imagine that in most of these cases, as in all but one of laws for which an enactment clause survives (**Dr4**), it was the polis (Introd. 10B) or the civic body (e.g. the Gortynians).

Although many other laws mention gods or rituals such as oath-swearing that had a religious component, we can designate six as 'sacred', in the sense that religious matters are their main focus. Of these six, five concern sacrifice. **G3** is a sacrificial calendar, recording the month, the days, the types of sacrificial animal,

[317] In **A2**.4 *ta thina* is probably followed by *kai*, allowing for the possibility that the original text also contained *ta anthropina*.

[318] For the concept of 'sacred law' as it pertains to Cretan legislation, see Gagarin 2011.

and the divine recipients.[319] **G65** and **Dr6** also list sacrifices, although neither of them preserves any calendric information. **Dr6** lists offerings according to the location where the offering is made; it possibly refers to a date (fifth), but this is far from certain. **G65** lists sacrifices with details concerning the offerings, the divine recipients, and the priestly emoluments. The distribution of the sacrifice is a central concern of two other laws (**A9**.2–8 and **Dr4**; see below). **Eleutherna1** provides rules concerning the consumption of wine by adult men at Dion Akron (1–5) and probably for priests (6–10).

B. Gods and Goddesses

The invocation '*thios/thioi*' occurs at the beginning of many of the laws where enactment language is preserved (**Da1**A1; **Dr1**.1a; **Lyktos1**A1 and **Lyktos1**B1; **G64**; **G78**; **G80**), and of a few where the invocation stands alone (**G43Ba**.1 and **G43Bb**1; **G65**; **G72**). Only at Dreros do we find enactment language without the invocation (**Dr2**; **Dr3**; **Dr4**; **Dr5**). It appears that the laws from Dreros were each inscribed on a single block; perhaps the invocation was omitted as a space-saving strategy (Introd. 10B). In any case, apart from its use as an invocation, *thios* does not occur very often in the laws. Instead, most of the references to gods are to particular divinities either as the recipients of offerings or as oath gods. A notable exception is the rule assigning the *poinikastas* to perform the public sacrifices for whatever god (*otimi thiōi*) has no priest (**Da1**B4–5).

Almost all of the deities mentioned in the legal texts are common Greek gods. Oath gods include Artemis (**G72**.3.4–9) and Apollo, Athena, and Hermes (**G51**.2–3).[320] Demeter and Hera (**G3**.3), Zeus and Helios (**G65**.2, 7–8), and Poseidon (**A5+6**.1; **G66**.3) are attested as recipients of sacrifice. The month names Dionysios at Eleutherna (**Ele9**.1) and Welkanios at Gortyn (**G3**.1) suggest the celebration of festivals in honor of Dionysus and Welkanos, a pre-Dorian or pre-Greek god (or possibly Apollo Welchanios or Zeus Welchanos) at Eleutherna and Gortyn respectively.[321] Divine epithets are very scarce. The month name Boazromios (**Axos1**.16) perhaps reflects a cult title Boēdromios, possibly of Apollo with whom late literary sources associate the title in Athens and Boeotian

[319] For the prescriptive force of the phrase [*ia*]*ra tetelēmena* '(these) rites have been performed' (**G3**.1), see comm. ad loc.

[320] **L3**B3–4 possibly refers to Hermes, but the context is unknown.

[321] Welchanos is depicted on the obverse of late fourth-century coins of Phaistos as a youth seated in a tree and holding a rooster (Le Rider 1966: 149, pl. IV.6). Hesychius glosses Gelchanos (= Welchanos) as 'Zeus according to the Cretans' (Hesychius s.v. *Γελχάνος· ὁ Ζεὺς παρὰ Κρησίν*). Apollo Bilkōnios occurs at Eleutherna (*SEG* 41.743, line 11, early third century; *IvM* 20.3–5, third–second century). The month name is also attested at Hellenistic Gortyn, Knossos, Lyktos, and Golgoi, Cyprus (*IC* 4.184, line 3; *IC* 1.16.3, line 2; *IC* 1.28.11, line 3; and Masson 1983: 298–9, 417 no. 299). For the month name and the god, see Trümpy 1997: 189–90; Sporn 2002: 202–3.

Thebes.[322] Toxia ('the Archeress') is probably the epithet of Artemis at Amyklaion (**G72**.3.4–9).[323] Finally, the sanctuaries attested in **Dr6**—Agoraion and Pythion—should probably be understood to reflect cult titles of Zeus and Apollo (Agoraios and Pythios respectively, comm. ad loc.). Apart from the implications of the month name Welkanios, the gods attested in the laws are the Olympians. This emphasis on the pan-Hellenic pantheon of gods belies the representation of Cretan religion as unlike the mainland or Aegean Greek pattern, 'a land of suckling and dying gods', at least in the case of civic or public cult.[324]

C. *Rituals*

References to ritual in the laws give a similarly conventional impression. We have already noted invocations of the divine (*thios/thioi*) at the beginning of laws. Oaths are referred to often in provisions concerning procedure, usually without details as to the specific form of the oath, the timing and location of the oath ceremony, or the identity of the oath god(s) (Introd. 10D2). Notable exceptions to this include the rule that a divorced woman swear an oath of denial by Artemis, before (the statue) of the Archeress at the Amyklaion (**G72**.3.4–9) and the rule that a litigant swear an oath by [Zeus?], Apollo, Athena, and Hermes and 'a curse on himself to die [the worst?] death (if he perjures himself)' (**G51**). The curse (*ara*) is also attested in the context of oath-swearing at Eleutherna (**Ele3**).

Purification rituals and ritual purity are indicated in the contexts of preparing a corpse for burial (**G76**B) and probably the suitability of offerings for sacrifice (**Dr7**). The terms *amyoton* (= *amyēton*, 'uninitiated'?) at Gortyn and *emwesthai* ('to be initiated in'?) at Eleutherna may perhaps refer to initiation ritual of some kind (**G14**b1; **Ele16A**b4–5). The offering of a share (*dekaton*) of booty won in battle is attested at Axos and (with less certainty) an offering of first-fruits of some kind ([*ap*]*arkontai*) at Datala (**A5+6**.4–5; **Da1**B13). Consumption of wine in ritual contexts is attested at Eleutherna (**Eleutherna1**) and Gortyn (**G72**.10.39: an adopter is to give a sacrificial victim and jug of wine to his *hetaireia*) and is implied by the term *espensames* ('we promise') at Datala (**Da1**A1) and perhaps also *epi spowddan* ('for a libation'?) at Axos (**A2**.9).

The laws' primary interest in religion, however, concerns sacrifice, for which the laws preserve a rich lexicon: the substantives *iareion* and *thyma* ('sacrificial

[322] Athens: *Etymologicum Magnum* 202.49; Thebes: Pausanias 9.17.2.

[323] Toxia is not attested elsewhere as an epithet of Artemis. Artemis Toxitis occurs at Cos (Sokolowski 1969: 154AI.16, *c*.270–260) and Apollo Toxias is attested for Sicyon (Hesychius s.v. *Τοξίας*).

[324] The quote is from Haysom (2011: 95) who critiques the view that Cretan religion was exceptional. Welkanos is a youthful male divinity, but we do not know if he was a god who dies and is reborn, as, of course, was Dionysus.

victim'), *parthymata* ('additional sacrificial victims'?), *thysia* ('sacrificial ritual'), and *thystas* ('sacrificial priest'?), and the verbs *thyo* ('sacrifice') and *diïereuo* ('sacrifice'? or more generally 'perform cult'?).[325] We have already noted that four of the laws appear to be concerned wholly with sacrificial ritual. The animals specified for sacrifice are the standard fare—goat, sheep (rams, ewes), and cattle (a bull)—as are the requirements concerning their age, gender, and color.[326] Two laws from Dreros specify the upper portion of the leg of the sacrificial animal (**Dr6** and **Dr7**: *mēros* and *hypermēridia* respectively). In addition to sacrifice, offerings of a *medimnos* of something (barley? figs?) and cheese are attested at Gortyn (**G65**.13–14).

Many of the sacrifices referred to in the laws probably belong to the category of public sacrifices, performed by public officials at public expense on behalf of the entire community. The law concerning the *poinikastas* of Datala refers explicitly to *damosia thymata* ('public sacrifices') (**Da1**B4–6). Payment for the sacrifice at the Kydanteia by the council of Axos and for the sacrifice on Mt. Ida by the Rhittenians indicate that these belong to the same category (**A9**.11–14; **G80**.1–3). The difference in the costs of these sacrifices, twelve staters at Axos and 350 staters (an enormous sum) for the sacrifice on Mt. Ida, suggests a range in the scale of sacrifices that is worth noting. The Axians also sacrificed at a grand scale, if, as its name suggests, the Great Hekatomb (*tan ekatomban tan megalan*) was a sacrifice of one-hundred animals (**A1**.12–13). The public workers who are the subject of this agreement are required to pay a kind of tax for the Great Hekatomb. This might be taken to imply that all members of the community (or a large part of them, e.g. all members of the political class) paid a tax to fund this sacrifice, but certainty is not possible. **Dr4** perhaps refers to voluntary contributions to defray the costs of public sacrifices ('whoever gives pay'), but again we cannot be certain.

In addition to the ritualized eating that sacrifice implies, several of the laws attest ritualized drinking: by adult males of the political class (*dromeis*) possibly at a rural sanctuary (**Eleutherna1**.1–5); by priests in performing their priestly functions (**Eleutherna1**.6–12); and by the members *hetaireia* on the occasion of an adoption (**G72**.10.37–9).

We have very little information about festivals apart from the ones already mentioned, *viz.* the Great Hekatomb and Kydanteia at Axos and the grand sacrifice on Mt. Ida that Gortyn and Rhitten celebrated. The month names Boazromios (Axos), Dionysios (Eleutherna), Hyperboios (Dreros), and Welchanios (Gortyn) imply the celebration of homonymous festivals: the Boazromia,

[325] *Iareion*: **G72**.10.38–9; *thyma*: **A1**.13; **A9**.13–14; **Da1**B5; **G80**.1–2; *parthymata*: **G65**.9–10; *thysia*: **A9**.6; *thystas*: **Dr4**; *thyo*: **Da1**B5; *diïereuo*: **Eleutherna1**.6–7.

[326] Goat: **G3**.2; **G3**.4?; ram (*krion*): **G65**.7; male sheep: **G65**.7–8; ewes: **G3**.2–3; pregnant ewe: **G3**.3; white female sheep: **G65**.3–4; ewe lamb (*ammna*): **G65**:5, 11–12; bull: **G3**.2.

Dionysia, Hyperboia, and Welchania (**Axos1**.16; **Ele9**.1; **Dr3**; **G3**.1). Of these putative festivals, only the Hyperboia ('raising the ox') is attested in Crete during the Hellenistic period at Malla and Hierapytna.[327]

D. Sanctuaries

The archaeological evidence for sanctuaries is discussed above (Introd. 2A2); here we examine the evidence of the laws.

The verb *naeuo* ('take refuge in a temple') occurs in several provisions from Gortyn concerning individuals who attempt to avoid capture or litigation, as does the noun *naos* ('temple') from which it derives;[328] no other word meaning 'temple' or 'sanctuary' is attested. We do not know if in practice one or another temple in the urban center or in the countryside was preferred for seeking refuge. The earliest laws from Gortyn and probably the laws from Dreros were inscribed on the walls of urban temples (Introd. 2A2). Most of the sacrifices that the laws mention probably took place at urban sanctuaries (e.g. the Agoraion and Pythion at Dreros), though we hear twice (**G80**; **A5+6**) of sacrifices on Mt. Ida.[329] Most scholars identify the Amyklaion of Artemis Toxia as another extra-urban sanctuary, although its location remains uncertain.[330] Dion Akron ('divine promontory' or 'Zeus's promontory'), where the *dromeis* of Eleutherna are allowed to drink wine together, perhaps refers to another rural sanctuary (**Eleutherna1**.3).

E. Personnel

The common Greek term for priest (*iareus*) is attested in several laws, always in the context of sacrificial ritual (**A9**.2–3; **Da1**B4–6; **Eleutherna1**.6–10; **G65**.5–6). The *thystai* at Dreros are clearly priests of some kind (**Dr4**). Hesychius glosses *thystai* as a Cretan term for priest without further qualification, but it is also possible that the *thystai* were associated with a particular cult at Dreros or were assigned specifically to perform sacrificial rituals for the community (comm. ad loc.). The *poinikastas* of Datala was required to perform the public sacrifices for one or another of the polis gods when a priest was not available (**Da1**B4–6). The

[327] Malla: *IC* 1.19.1, lines 22–3; Hierapytna: *IC* 1.8.13, line 13; *IC* 3.3.4, line 42. For the festival, see Chaniotis 1996: 125.

[328] *naeuo*: **G41**.4.5–10; **G47**.31–3; **G72**.1.39–44; **G73**B2; **G83**.3–7; **G86**.3–4; *naos*: **G6**; **G41**.7; **G72**.1.43; **G73**B. For *temenia*, see below.

[329] The archaeological record of the cave sanctuary of Zeus on Mt. Ida seems to dry up during the sixth and fifth centuries, but sacrifices must have been celebrated at the altar outside of the cave, unless the laws refer to another location on or off the mountain. See Erickson 2010a: 266–7.

[330] **G72**.3.7–9. For the identification of the Amyklaion with the ancient remains at Kommos or at Kalamaki, both in the western Mesara, see Phaistos Site.

city did not, apparently, give him the title of priest although it anticipated that he would perform this important priestly function: yet another indication of the complex relationship between the divine and the human.

In payment for performing the sacrificial function of priest, the *poinikastas* was to receive the revenue from the precinct (*temenia*) of the god(s) he served. The nature of the payment is not specified here as it is at Axos, where a priest is entitled to carry away (from the sacrifice) only what is prescribed in writing and what someone, presumably someone who receives a share of the sacrificial animal, gives him voluntarily (**A9**.2–5). The priest at Gortyn receives the hide of the sacrificial animal (**G65**.5–6); an individual, not necessarily a priest, who contributed to the cost of the sacrifice at Dreros may receive a share of the slaughtered animal (**Dr4**).

The laws attest the communities' wide-ranging interests in and oversight of the performance of public rituals. The *thystai* of Dreros enacted a law that presumably concerned their purview, but there is little reason to suppose that similar groups were responsible for enacting the other 'sacred laws' (Gagarin 2011: 105–6). The *kosmos* of Axos was responsible for exacting the fine from a priest who broke the law concerning sacrificial perquisites **A9**.2–8; it is probably right to assume that in many if not most cases of unlawful behavior in religious matters civic officials were charged with the job of setting things right. On the other hand, the laws have very little to say about rituals that pertained more to private life. In addition to oaths sworn in litigation concerning private matters (e.g. the oath of a divorced woman at the Amyklaion) we note the rule that an adopter must provide a sacrificial victim and wine to his *hetaireia* (**G72**.10.37–9) and the provisions concerning purification of a corpse (**G76**B1–7). Even here, though, public interests are discernible: inheritance and the perpetuation of the community in the cases of divorce and adoption; community-wide contagion in the case of the purification of corpses.

10. LAW

A. Legislation in Crete

The tradition that Crete excelled in legislation was widespread in the Classical period, and probably took shape even earlier. Plato's Athenian stranger remarks that 'the laws of Crete are especially highly regarded (*diapherontōs eudokimoi*) by all' (*Laws* 631b), and as early as Homer, the legendary King Minos of Crete is portrayed as a judge in Hades (*Odyssey* 11.568–71).[331] Cretan laws, however, did

[331] Morrow (1960: 19) surveys other classical references to the excellence of Cretan legislation and legislators.

not spring up in isolation. Although an inscription from Dreros (**Dr1**) may be the oldest Greek law yet discovered, dating from perhaps 650–600, inscribed laws dating from the late seventh and especially the sixth and fifth centuries have been found in many other parts of Greece. Moreover, ancient tradition reports that laws were being written in the seventh century in parts of the Greek world where no inscriptions from this period have been found. These include Athens, where Draco wrote a homicide law (and perhaps others) in about 621.[332] Whatever the cause of this pan-Hellenic legislative impulse, Cretan poleis were active participants. As we have noted, inscribed laws dated to *c.*650–400 have been found from ten poleis in the central part of the island and may have been enacted by others as well.

It is often noted that Crete enacted more legislation than other parts of Greece in this period, but in fact it is only Gortyn that was exceptional in this regard. Gortyn has more laws than all the other Cretan cities combined, and the Gortyn Code (**G72**) in itself contains more legislation than the total output of any single Cretan city. If we exclude Gortyn, however, the quantity of legislation from the other Cretan poleis is not especially remarkable. Other Greek cities such as Argos and Elis have just as many archaic and classical laws as Axos and Eleutherna, if not more.

B. Writing and Enacting Laws

Several theories have been proposed to explain the propensity of the Cretans, and especially the Gortynians, to enact and display legislation on this scale. There is some evidence that artists from the Near East together with traders and merchants were present in Crete from the tenth century on, and Westbrook (2010: 7–13), pointing to the Gortyn Code (**G72**) as the prime example, argues that Greek law before Aristotle was derived from Near-Eastern law. But despite the absence of lawyers in both systems, and a few superficial points of similarity between **G72** and the Code of Hammurabi, which are roughly the same length and treat many of the same subjects, the evidence Westbrook presents for this 'revolutionary' view is either misleading or simply wrong, and it seems very unlikely that the Cretans took anything more from the Near East than (perhaps) the idea of writing down laws. The differences between Near-Eastern written laws and early Greek legislation are vast and fundamental, and the Code, Westbrook's main evidence for Near-Eastern influence, was clearly the end result of local developments in the

[332] The evidence is collected in Gagarin 1986 and is discussed more briefly in Gagarin 2005b. Although there are undoubtedly legendary aspects to the tradition (Szegedy-Maszak 1978), the basic elements are confirmed by other good evidence.

Gortynian practice of writing legislation on an increasingly large scale that began at least a century earlier. No outside influence is required to explain the Code's existence or its form. The impulse to write true legislation (which Westbrook acknowledges the Code of Hammurabi is not), and to display it in public spaces accessible to the community owes nothing to the Near East but appears to be a purely Greek phenomenon (Gagarin 2008a).

Gehrke takes a different approach, attributing the large amount of legislation to 'the concentration of potential conflict and violence', and to 'processes of imitation and emulation' (2009: 407). But the laws themselves, especially at Gortyn with its heavy concentration of laws on family and property, provide no evidence of any special concern with conflict and violence, nor (as far as we can tell) was Gortynian legislation significantly influenced by the laws of other Cretan cities (see Introd. 10E).

A more significant factor, in our view, is the evident involvement of non-elite groups in the governance of Cretan poleis (Introd. 4A, 4B). The inscriptions themselves provide strong evidence that the laws were intended to be read and used by a relatively large segment of the population, not just by a few officials and elite members of the community (Introd. 3A, 3F; see also Perlman 2004c; Gagarin 2008a), and Gortynian legislation as a whole shows that legislators became progressively more sophisticated in the organization and display of their laws in order to make them easier to read and use. It seems hard not to connect the involvement of larger segments of the community in governance with the desire for wider dissemination of the laws, and wider dissemination was only possible if the laws were written.

In this connection, the evidence for population mobility and settlement aggregation in the Early Archaic period (*c.*630–575) presented above (Introd. 2A3b) suggests that the communities that were writing laws in this period had mixed populations that had come together from different Early Iron Age settlements. And as Gagarin has argued in connection with Draco's homicide law (2008a: 100–1), the growth and increasing diversity of the population would provide another motive for specifying in detail rules that had formerly been orally preserved in the customs and traditions of a homogenous community, and this could only be done by enacting written laws, which allow detailed rules to be recorded with greater precision than oral means of preservation would have allowed. Precision of detail would have been especially necessary if a complex legal system like that at Gortyn was to function smoothly.

We should also note that a law like **Dr1** suggests a certain communal pride on the part of the polis for its role in legislation; this raises the possibility that an additional reason for displaying this law, and perhaps those of other poleis, was to celebrate the growing sense of confidence and importance that was felt by the entire community in these early poleis. The enactment formulas in themselves suggest this sense of communal pride and importance. In those that survive, the enactor is never an individual but always a group, and with one or two possible exceptions always a large group, probably representing the entire civic community. The polis enacts in **Dr1** and **Dr5**, and the civic collective enacts in **Da1A** (the Dataleis), **G78** (the Gortynians), and **Lyktos1A** and **1B** (the Lyktians). In **Dr4** the enacting group are the *thystai*; it is not clear who these are, but if they are 'sacrificers', they are presumably a small group (Introd. 9C; comm. ad loc.). The regulation in **Dr4**, however, may only apply to specific circumstances that arise in the course of their sacrifices.[333]

This sense of civic pride may have played a role in displaying all legislation, particularly at Gortyn. As mentioned, we know that toward the end of the seventh century, the Gortynians evidently felt secure enough to move down from their defensible locations on several low hilltops overlooking the Mesara plain to a site at the edge of the plain below. Gortyn appears to have gradually come to dominate most of this fertile plain, the largest in Crete, bringing a number of other villages under its sway in the process. With this seems to have come greater prosperity and stability and a growing sense of security, which would have allowed the Gortynians to turn their attention to maintaining a smoothly functioning economic order and to writing rules concerning inheritance, property, and other commercial activity, which make up a large percentage of the legislation at Gortyn, in contrast to the rest of Crete, where these subjects are barely mentioned in the surviving legislation. And the growth and increased diversity of population that resulted from absorbing other smaller communities would have provided another reason why Gortyn would want to put its legislation in writing, as it would be increasingly difficult to rely on a communal sense of customs and traditions in maintaining order.

At Gortyn in particular, the impulse to legislate and to inscribe and display legislation on stone seems to have been a defining feature of civic life. During the course of the sixth and fifth centuries, laws of varying lengths were written on different subjects at many different times. Later legislators evidently built on the work of their predecessors, for we can trace a clear development in the consistency of the script, the organization of legal texts, and the clarity of their display on stone. In the fifth century the Code (**G72**) was published, together with several other laws, in a central public space in the city, on a curved wall, probably covered by a roof—a highly unusual (perhaps even unique in this period) architectural structure probably intended specifically for the display of a large number of

[333] In **Dr3**, *ewade* seems to be used without a dative indicating the enactor, as it is also perhaps in **Dr2**, where the fragmentary text could be restored to give *ewade* but there is no dative object in the rest of the surviving text. The most likely explanation is that the Drerians shortened the enactment formula, perhaps so that these short texts would fit on the stone, and that we are meant to understand *poli* with *ewade*.

laws.[334] This special space is clear testimony to the civic pride that the Gortynians took in their legislative achievement.

C. Substantive Law

The archaic and classical legislation from the Greek world treats many different subjects, and it is not uncommon for a subject to be treated in more than one polis. As far as we can tell from the surviving texts, however, in the laws from Crete there is little substantive overlap among the different poleis, either in their general subjects or in the details of their regulations. For example, inheritance, especially as it affects 'heiresses', occupies roughly one-third of the Gortyn Code (**G72**) and was apparently also treated in **G44** (and perhaps in **G56** and **G74**), but inheritance is not mentioned in the preserved laws of any other Cretan polis.[335] Nor, as far as we can see, does any other polis treat other aspects of family or property law.[336] Nonetheless, there are a few areas of substantive overlap among the different poleis, which we need to examine.

The obvious starting point is the earliest law from Dreros (**Dr1**) on the non-iteration of the office of *kosmos* and a similar provision at Gortyn (**G14p–g2**). To our knowledge, no other archaic Greek polis enacted a non-iteration law. The Dreros law provides that a person who has been *kosmos* may not serve again within ten years and specifies heavy penalties for violations of this rule. At Gortyn, the provision is part of a longer text with several different rules concerning magistrates. The last of these prohibits a person from becoming *kosmos* again for three years, and also prohibits the *gnomones* from serving again for ten years, and the *ksenios* ('foreigners' magistrate') for five years. At this point the law ends, apparently without specifying any penalty for violations.

The similarity between these two laws is obvious: both impose an interval between successive terms for those holding the office of *kosmos*. But many differences are also evident: the intervals between terms are different for no apparent reason (three years vs. ten),[337] the Gortyn law includes two offices not mentioned

[334] For the physical setting of the Code see Di Vita 2005. The Code's excellent state of preservation has led to the conclusion that it was probably roofed.

[335] One isolated word in **A10B** may suggest that the subject is inheritance, and five letters in **A11** have been supplemented as three words concerned with inheritance, but in neither case is inheritance the likely subject (see notes ad loc.). Inheritance was also one of the subjects treated by Solon in Athens.

[336] To be sure, we find isolated occurrences of the names of family members ('brother' in **L5**.3), or other terms suggesting property or inheritance ('maternal property' in **Ph1**.3), but these in themselves do not necessarily indicate the main subject of the legislation.

[337] The purpose of these laws has often been thought to be the reduction of inter-elite competition: leading families agreed to reduce competition for these offices by restricting access. If this is correct (and we think it unlikely), the interval required may reflect in some way the number of potential candidates (or families). But then one would expect Gortyn, which was probably larger than Dreros, to have more

at Dreros (or anywhere else), the *gnomones* and the *ksenios*; and no penalties are imposed at Gortyn. Moreover, the Dreros law stands alone, is preceded by a formal enactment clause and followed by an oath-swearing ceremony, all of which would have given the law a prominence that the Gortyn law would not have had, coming as it does at the end of two long rows of provisions treating other matters. Thus, if the Gortynians took the idea of prohibiting successive terms in office for certain magistrates from Dreros, they enacted a significantly different law for their own polis.

Besides non-iteration, the only subjects on which laws from more than one polis are preserved are sacrifice and regulations concerning workers. Laws on sacrifice were common in Greece and are found at Dreros (**Dr6**), Gortyn (**G3**; **G65**), and Axos (**A9**).[338] **G3** and perhaps **Dr6** are fragments of sacrificial calendars. The former is typical of Greek laws on sacrifice: it specifies a day of the month, an animal (to be sacrificed), the number of animals, and a divine recipient of the sacrifice.[339] The latter specifies a place, a number (of animals?), and a part of an animal, but no date (at least in what survives). Thus, although both calendars take the form of a list, they present different kinds of information, suggesting that the idea of inscribing a public record of sacrifices was widespread (probably because these represented a financial commitment on the part of the polis), but also that there was no standard format for such lists. A later law from Gortyn, **G65**, appears to be similar to **G3** in that it names a victim and a divine recipient. The law from Axos (**A9**), however, is quite different: it apparently specified the amount of meat the priest could take for himself from a sacrifice and adds penalties for any priest who takes more. It also specifically commits the council (*bola*) to paying for certain sacrifices. Neither of these issues—a priest's share of the sacrifice or payment by the council—is included in the laws from Dreros and Gortyn.[340] To be sure, all these laws are quite fragmentary, but judging from what remains of them, it appears that each of these Cretan poleis—Gortyn, Dreros, and Axos—wrote different kinds of rules concerning sacrifices; and the likelihood that one of these poleis influenced another thus appears small.

The same appears to be the case with laws concerning public workers, which we also have from three poleis, Axos (**A1**), Eleutherna (**Ele9**), and Gortyn (**G79**).[341] The first of these apparently provides sustenance and tax exemption to someone

candidates in competition and therefore a longer interval between terms rather than a much shorter one. Moreover, the *kosmos*, being the highest office, was presumably the one most sought after and thus should have the longest interval, not the shortest, as it does at Gortyn.

338 Sacrifice is also mentioned in **Da1** and **G80**.

339 'A typical entry in a sacrificial calendar includes the month, the recipient, and the type of victim to be offered; the date within the month may or may not be indicated' (Lupu 2005: 65).

340 It is possible that regulations now lost in **G65** specified what part of the sacrifice the priest was entitled to, but even if it did, the rest of the text is quite different from **A9**.

(perhaps children of workers), specifies daily fines for something, requires five days of work for the polis without pay, prohibits additional charges for the polis, says something more about taxes and then exempts someone from all other taxes and gives them sustenance in the *andreion*. **Ele9** provides a wage for the maker of cloaks. And **G79** (apparently) provides wages for some group, specifies that the work is to be done by inhabitants of the polis, free and slave, and fines those who do not want to work. The three laws can all be classed as work contracts, and as such can also be compared to the agreement between the polis of Datala and the writer Spensithios (**Da1**), which specifies the writer's duties and the compensation the city is to provide in exchange. All these documents specify that certain work be done in return for which workers will receive remuneration, which can take the form of money, produce, free sustenance or tax exemptions, or some combination of these. As in the case of sacrifices, these poleis were faced with a certain need—to manage work that is done for the polis—and they passed laws or wrote agreements providing specific benefits in return for that work. Because the agreements committed the poleis to spending public funds, the texts were all written and displayed in public. There is considerable variation among the poleis, however, in both the form of these agreements and their details. Significant influence from one city to another thus seems unlikely.

In sum, three subjects, non-iteration of office, sacrifice, and public work, are treated in the legislation of more than one Cretan polis, and in each area the laws of different poleis show some similarity but also display considerable difference.[342] In these cases, one polis may have been influenced by the legislation of other poleis, but any influence one finds is fairly general, since in each case the details differ significantly from polis to polis. It thus seems more accurate to conclude that these poleis faced certain common situations or problems and in response enacted legislation that unsurprisingly took a certain common form or approach. Besides these three subjects, however, the vast majority of the archaic and classical legislation in any one Cretan polis has no parallel in the laws of any other polis. All in all, the degree of possible influence from one polis to another appears small. There may, of course, have been more similarities than we see today, but enough legislation survives that if there was a significant amount of direct influence among the laws of different Cretan poleis, we ought to see clearer evidence of this. Instead, we find almost entirely different laws from different poleis.

[341] Several other texts and fragments of texts contain some form of the word 'work' or may allude to some aspect of paying workers, but these are the only three which provide any significant information on this subject.

[342] We are not including cases where the same few words may occur in laws from two different poleis (e.g. 'twelve (or ten) medimnoi of barley... five staters' in **G63** and **Ele13**), which appear to be chance similarities in texts with different purposes.

Within their common cultural heritage, then, the Cretan poleis appear to have legislated independently. Undoubtedly there was some contact among those who wrote laws in these poleis, but as was generally true in Greece, individual poleis prided themselves on their independence. This may be one reason for the use of scripts that despite having enough similarity that we can speak of a Cretan script, are noticeably different in some respects. In any case, the texts suggest that each polis enacted legislation to meet its own specific needs and made little or no attempt to imitate legislation elsewhere.

D. *Procedural Law*

Many Greek laws contain procedural regulations either as their primary focus or as part of a substantive regulation, and in this respect they differ significantly from most early legislation in other parts of the world, which may address many of the same substantive areas but say very little about procedure.[343] In this regard, Crete was similar to the rest of Greece. Although relatively few laws have legal procedure as their primary subject, procedural regulations are common throughout the laws at Gortyn, and are also found in laws from Axos, Eleutherna, Eltynia, and Lyktos (**A9**.8–9; **A10**A; **A11a**; **Ele3**; **Ele11**; **Ele12**; **Ele13**a+b; **Elt2**; **L3**?; **L5**).

The evidence for legal procedure in archaic Greece suggests that most poleis continued the Homeric tradition of submitting disputes to a public process in which litigants plead before one or more judges. As far as we can tell, the Cretan poleis never developed additional procedures besides the basic suit, similar to the Athenian *dikē*, which one litigant would bring against another. There is evidence at Gortyn for different types of specialized judges (Introd. 4C2), but there is no indication of any specialized procedures, such as the *graphē* or *eisangelia* that we find in Athens. Nor is there any evidence for different categories of ordinary *dikai*, such as the Athenian *dikē blabēs* or *dikē aikeias*. Indeed, the procedural language is simple and fairly consistent. A Gortynian who had a grievance summoned his opponent to court (*kalen*) and the two litigated their dispute (*molen*). They delivered their pleas (*ponen*) and presented witnesses who testified (*apoponen*) before a judge. If the system was procedurally more complex, there is no hint of it in the texts of the laws.

A few areas of procedure, however—giving judgment, swearing oaths, and presenting witnesses—have some unusual features and require more discussion. The following summary is based almost entirely on the laws from Gortyn. None of the laws from other poleis provides the kind of details that might enlighten us further about procedure.[344]

[343] See Gagarin 2001, comparing the laws at Gortyn to the collection of Hammurabi.

[344] See Gagarin 2010b for a more extensive discussion of the issues in the following sections.

1. Judgment

The basic rule concerning judgment at Gortyn in the fifth century is stated in an Addendum to the Code (**G72**.11.26–31): 'Whenever it is written that the judge (*dikastas*) is to rule (*dikadden*) according to witnesses or an oath of denial, he is to rule as is written; but in other matters he is to swear an oath and decide (*omnynta krinen*) with reference to the pleadings.' The distinction between these two methods is strictly adhered to in **G72** and most other fifth-century texts at Gortyn. In some cases, the vocabulary of judgment makes clear which method must be followed: *dikadden* (or *katadikadden*) requires the judge to 'rule' according to the method or terms specified by the law; *krinen* requires him to 'decide' freely. In many cases, however, the law says nothing at all about the method of judgment; in these cases, as the general rule cited above makes clear, 'swear and decide (*omnynta krinen*)' is the default method.

The provision in **G72**.1.18–24 illustrates both methods: 'If they contend about a slave, each affirming that he is his, if a witness testifies, [the judge] is to rule according to the witness; but if they [witnesses] testify either for both sides or for neither, the judge is to swear an oath and decide.' Here, if there is a witness for only one side, the judge must rule in favor of that side; otherwise, he must swear an oath and decide the case on his own; presumably his decision will be based on the arguments of the two litigants and the testimony of their witnesses, if any.

The clearest example of ruling according to an oath of denial is in divorce cases where the woman is accused of taking property that belongs to her husband and denies it (**G72**.3.5–12): 'But with regard to things she denies, (the judge) is to rule that the woman is to take an oath of denial by Artemis, before (the statue of) the Archeress at Amyklaion. And whatever anyone may steal from her after she has sworn an oath of denial, he will pay five staters and the thing itself'. In other words, if she swears the oath, the judge must rule that the disputed property is hers. There are also several provisions which specify that someone is to be *orkioteros* (lit. 'more oath-worthy'), that is, if the person swears an oath (*orkos*), the judge must rule in his or her favor. On the other hand, if the person is unwilling to swear, in most cases the judge must rule against him or her.

The strict distinction between these two methods of ruling is confined to fifth-century laws from Gortyn. Earlier laws and a few fifth-century texts from Gortyn, as well as the laws in all other Cretan poleis (e.g. **Dr1**.2), use the verb *dikadden* in a more general sense, 'decide the case', without specifying a particular method of judgment. Only once outside of Gortyn is a method of judgment specified, in **Elt2**.8, where the *kosmoi* are directed to swear and decide, though here a different verb (*gignosken*) is used for this method than at Gortyn (*krinen*). Finally, the judge (*dikastas*), an official mentioned repeatedly in the Gortyn laws, is only found once outside of Gortyn in a fragment without context (**L3**B2–3).

2. Oaths

As we have seen, judges at Gortyn were regularly required to swear oaths before they decided a case; presumably they swore that their decision would be fair, or just, or lawful, etc. Litigants were sometimes required to swear an oath of affirmation or denial in order to win a case; in some cases they had to swear first, before they were allowed to bring a case or in order to prevent a case from being brought against them (**G41**.2.12; **G72**.3.49–50, 4.6–7). Witnesses are explicitly required to swear along with the plaintiff in one case (**G72**.9.38–40), and it is possible that they were routinely required to swear oaths, though we have no clear evidence of this. Other laws at Gortyn and elsewhere mention oaths and oath-swearers either without context or in a context where it is not clear what sort of oath is being sworn (**Dr1**.4). Finally, we have two mentions of 'co-swearers' (*omomotai*) without context (**G4**.3; **L5**.13), but these may refer to a process such as that depicted in **G81**, a law concerning land pledged as security. At several points in this law oaths are required either from the litigants or from a group of nine neighbors, people who presumably would be knowledgeable about the land in question. At one point the law specifies that the case is to be decided by a majority of those who swear, but on another point only three of the nine are required to swear in order to establish a fact.

3. Witnesses

References to witnesses are common in the laws at Gortyn at all periods, but witnesses are only mentioned once in the laws from other Cretan poleis (**L5**.10), and outside Crete they are not mentioned in legal inscriptions before about the middle of the fifth century (see VER II.75), though they are mentioned in literature as early as Hesiod (*Works and Days* 371). This does not necessarily mean that the Gortynians used witnesses more often than other Greeks; it is possible that their laws are more concerned with procedural matters and thus mention witnesses more often. Whatever the explanation, the large number of references to witnesses at Gortyn is striking.

Two kinds of witnesses are mentioned there, formal and accidental (Gagarin 1989). A 'formal witness' is someone who is asked to be present at some event or transaction, such as a sale. Later, if a dispute arises, he may be asked to testify about the transaction but the law generally does not mention formal witnesses testifying; it only specifies that they are to be present at the event in question. At Gortyn, the laws always specify qualifications for formal witnesses, that there be one, two, three, or 'three or more' (**G72**.5.52–4), or that they be of age or adult or adult for fifteen years or more, or that they be free. Often more than one of these requirements is specified.

In addition to formal witnesses, the laws refer to some witnesses who testify in court on matters about which they happen to have relevant knowledge, such as the ownership of a disputed person (**G72**.1.18–24, cited Introd. 10D1). These 'accidental witnesses', as we call them, are always mentioned in connection with testimony in court, and the law simply refers to 'a witness' or 'witnesses' testifying without further qualification. These witnesses presumably testified in court to whatever they happened to know, and their testimony is always designated by the verb *apoponen* (lit. 'speak out'), in contrast to the pleading of a litigant, for which the simple verb *ponen* (lit. 'speak') is used.

E. *The Unity of Cretan Law*

The same questions arise about the homogeneity of early Cretan law as about the general issue of homogeneity among Cretan poleis (Introd. 1). All Cretan poleis shared with the rest of Greece a common cultural heritage, expressed most obviously in the poems of Homer and Hesiod. This heritage included traditional substantive rules (*themistes*) that are often alluded to in the poems and must have played a role in the litigation portrayed in the poems. Writing is evidently unknown in the epics and plays no role in the legal process portrayed in them; thus, the *themistes* must have been orally preserved and transmitted. These unwritten rules appear to have been fairly general, consisting essentially of the customs and traditions of the community. In addition, a legal process is portrayed or alluded to in many places—most notably on the shield of Achilles in the *Iliad* (18.497–508). As portrayed there, and also in other passages in Homer and Hesiod, the process involved two litigants pleading their case in a public space (usually in the agora) in the presence of other members of the community before one or more judges, with the ultimate goal of achieving a resolution of the dispute that would be broadly acceptable to all.[345]

Beyond this common cultural background, however, can we speak more specifically of Cretan law? That is, do the laws from different poleis treat the same subjects or specify similar procedures, or can we see the influence of legislation of one polis on that of another?[346] With regard to substance, we have noted only three subjects on which legislation from more than one polis can be identified, non-iteration of office, sacrifice, and the payment of workers, and have also noted that on each of these subjects there are clear differences among the laws from different poleis. More important, as far as we can tell, the areas of family, property, and inheritance, which comprise such a large part of the legislation from Gortyn were not treated in the legislation from any other Cretan polis. The absence of

[345] For more on the legal system portrayed in Homer and Hesiod, see Gagarin 2008a: esp. 13–38.

[346] The following discussion is based on Gagarin 2012a. As is noted there, the question is not unlike the larger question of the unity of Greek law (see Gagarin 2005a).

such legislation elsewhere, at least in the surviving texts, is striking, and may perhaps be explained by supposing that Gortyn was far more prosperous, and thus more concerned about property and inheritance, than the other Cretan cities in this period. This is not impossible in view of the apparent productivity of the Mesara plain, and if true, suggests that Gortyn stood apart from these other cities in its legislation as in its prosperity. Whatever the explanation, there is little evidence of substantive unity in the laws of Crete. Each polis, it appears, legislated on matters of concern to it, and each devised its own rules as it saw fit.

With regard to procedure, the situation is more complex. There are certainly differences among the different poleis: whereas judgment is the task of a judge (*dikastas*) at Gortyn and a judge is otherwise (probably) mentioned only in one text from Lyktos (**L3**B2–3), it is the *kosmos* who judges at Dreros (**Dr1**.2) and Eltynia (**Elt2**.8) and possibly Datala (**Da1**B9–10). Witnesses, too, although common at Gortyn are only mentioned once elsewhere (**L5**.10). The strict separation of free decision-making by the judge after swearing an oath and rulings directed by law is found only at Gortyn in the Classical period, though a similar distinction may have existed at Eltynia (**Elt2**.8, see Introd. 10D1). On the other hand, oaths are not only common at Gortyn but are mentioned in texts from Dreros (**Dr1**.4, **Dr7**.2), Eleutherna (**Ele3**.2; **Eleutherna4**.1; and perhaps **Ele17**.4 and **Eleutherna2**.4), Eltynia (**Elt2**.8), Lyktos (**L5**.13), and perhaps Axos (**A3**.4). Moreover, various terms that normally designate aspects of procedure at Gortyn, are also found in isolated contexts elsewhere (e.g. *ponen*, 'affirm' in **A1**.11, *antimolos*, 'opposing litigant' in **A10**A4, *apoweipen*, 'deny' in **A11**a3 and **Pr7**A1). All of this suggests that there may have been some broad similarities in judicial procedures in the different Cretan poleis.[347]

Two other aspects of Cretan legislation may be relevant to the question of unity. First, with regard to the methods of inscribing legislation, Gortyn developed a method of writing legislation in columns that is found nowhere else in Crete (and is quite rare outside Crete at this time). On the other hand, other Cretan poleis sometimes inscribed legislation on both the front and back of a stele. There is one example of this from Axos (**Axos2**) and one from Eleutherna (**Eleutherna3**). We do not, however, find any such stelae among the almost 150 inscriptions from the Archaic and Classical period at Gortyn (though they are not uncommon outside Crete). Using two sides of the stele is a perfectly natural development, as is writing in columns, but evidently some poleis took the former route while Gortyn took the latter. It is possible, of course, that the poleis with two-sided stelae influenced one another in this respect (Axos and Eleutherna

[347] Gagarin 2008a argues that Greek law more generally exhibits procedural unity but not substantive unity.

are located quite close to one another), but Gortyn apparently went its own separate way.

One other feature of Cretan legislation, however, appears to be common to virtually all poleis, namely use of expressions with the verb *grapho* ('write'), especially (but not only) the perfect passive participle, in cross-references to another legal text or law. Thus, phrases like *kata ta gegrammena* (lit. 'according to the things that have been written') are regularly used to mean 'according to the law'. Common forms of this expression are found in inscriptions from Axos, Eleutherna, Eltynia, Gortyn, and Lyktos.[348] Such expressions are not unknown in archaic laws from other parts of Greece, and so we cannot consider their use distinctively Cretan; but the fact that they are so common in Crete, together with the fact that neither of the other archaic terms for 'law' (*rhētra*, *thesmos*) occurs in Crete,[349] may suggest that Cretan poleis shared a common understanding of the importance of writing to the whole idea of law, an idea perhaps supported by the quantity of written law on the island, even if they developed the substance of their legislation independently of one another.[350]

F. Reason and the Rule of Law at Gortyn

Of all the Cretan poleis only Gortyn provides enough legislation for us to get a sense of the underlying principles or spirit of their law. Whether all these principles were shared by other poleis is impossible to say. Gortyn, however, is clearly committed first, to the fundamental idea of the rule of law in the full sense of that expression (Gagarin 2004: 173), and second, to rational, practical solutions to legal problems.

With regard to the rule of law, the very quantity of Gortynian legislation in itself suggests widespread agreement that it is beneficial for the polis to regulate many areas of human conduct, and this view certainly implies a commitment to the rule of law. The most explicit statement of that commitment comes in the first lines of the Code (**G72**.1.2–3): 'Whoever is going to dispute concerning a free person or a slave is not to seize him before trial.' This provision orders Gortynians to settle this type of dispute in court, and it is followed by sanctions in the form of fines for anyone who might resort to self-help rather than follow the law, fines that increase daily if the seized person is not released within three days (**G72**.1.4–12). It is probably not by chance, moreover, that this provision is placed first in the Code. Surely the legislator (or legislators) began this monumental collection with a

[348] See e.g. **A9**.3–4; **Ele13**.7; **Elt2**.7; **L4**.9; **L6**.8, and many examples from Gortyn (Gagarin 2008a: 146 n. 5 lists 34 in **G72** alone). We should also note the expression 'these writings (*poinikēia*)' in **Eltynia1**.2 ([τὰ] ποινικήια | τάδε); this phrase has no context, but it is possible that it is a similar expression meaning 'this law'.

[349] For expressions for 'law' in archaic Greek law, see Gagarin 2008a: 91.

[350] The concept of law as 'what is written' is almost certainly not part of Crete's Minoan heritage, since to our knowledge no laws were written in the Bronze Age.

provision that was judged to be one of the most important pieces of legislation in the polis, if not the most important. By implication, therefore, the strong affirmation of the rule of law in **G72**.1.2–3 probably would have been taken to apply to all disputes in Gortyn, as if to say, 'whatever the issue, don't take matters into your own hands but go to court'. That is, respect the rule of law.

As for enforcement, though we have no evidence for actual trials, the laws provide a considerable amount of information about procedures in court that would have contributed to the fair and certain enforcement of these rules. It is clear that litigants brought suit in front of a judge to whom they pleaded their case and presented witnesses if they had any. In some cases the judge was required by law to prescribe a certain penalty or to follow a certain procedure (Introd. 10D1). In all other cases the judge listened to the pleadings, swore an oath, and decided the case himself. We have no information about this judicial oath, but it is very likely that he swore to decide in accordance with law and justice.

Gortyn also adheres to the rule of law in another respect which is commonly understood by this expression, namely that no one is above the law. In fact, the provisions just discussed, prohibiting seizure before trial, provide explicitly for violations of this rule by a *kosmos*, the highest official in the polis: if a *kosmos* seizes someone, or if someone belonging to a *kosmos* is seized, the case will be delayed until after he leaves office, but it will then be tried and if the *kosmos* is found guilty, the fine he will have to pay will be calculated from the day of the seizure (**G72**.1.51–5). Presumably the trial of a *kosmos* was delayed in order that he could attend to his duties, but he would eventually be tried and if convicted, would pay the same fine as an ordinary Gortynian. Other indications that officials at Gortyn were not above the law appear in the many provisions penalizing officials who do not carry out certain duties. One of the earliest laws (**G14**g–p1) states that if the *kosmos* does not exact payment (probably of a fine assessed by a court), he is to owe the fine himself, and fines for officials are also found in **G42**B6–9 and **G80**.10–12. Thus, all officials at Gortyn, including the highest, were subject to the law; and the *kosmos* is also subject to fines for violating the law in **A9** and **Dr1**, which suggests that these poleis too adhered to the rule of law in the sense that no one was above the law.

In addition to promoting the rule of law, Gortynian legislators clearly strove to enact laws that were rational and practical and, at least in the Code, to present them in a clear, rational, and well-organized manner. To be sure, the meaning of some laws is not clear, even when a complete text survives (e.g. **G22**), but in most cases the difficulty lies in the meaning of one or more words; such laws would presumably have been clear to Gortynians at the time. In other cases uncertainties remain that are not addressed by the laws, but this is inevitable in any legal system. On the whole, however, the sense of complete texts is almost always clear.

Furthermore, where several laws on a topic occur together, it is often clear that the legislator made an effort to organize the provisions in a rational manner. The effort to organize groups of laws appears to have begun with the earliest legislation (e.g. the list of sacrifices in **G3**), but legislators clearly became more skilled at this over time. Their organizational ability seems to have reached its height in the Code, where good examples of it are **G72**.1.2–2.2 on disputes concerning the status or ownership of persons, and **G72**.10.33–11.23 on adoption.[351]

The rationality and practicality of Gortynian legislation is evident in many texts. If one person's animal was injured by someone else's animal, for example, the former could sue the latter for damages but he first had to bring his animal to the other animal's owner in order to show him the damage (**G41**.1.7–12), presumably to give him a chance to dispute the severity of the injury. If, however, the injury was so severe that the animal died or for some other reason could not be moved, then its owner had to summon the other owner in the presence of witnesses to view the injuries for himself (**G41**.2.6–16). These conditions appear both reasonable and practical. Similarly, a landowner must allow people who are bearing a corpse to a rural burial site to cross his land if there is no road to the site; if there is a road, however, he need not allow it (**G46**B6–14).[352] Many other such examples could be cited, and indeed it is hard to find a provision at Gortyn that is clearly unreasonable. Finally, we should note that there is no trace of the kind of formalism that characterizes some other early legal systems (such as we find in early Roman law); at Gortyn, as elsewhere in Greece, the focus was on practical solutions to problems facing the community.

[351] For discussion of these examples, see Gagarin 2008a: 159–62, 165–70; see also his Index s.v. organization.

[352] The provision breaks off before the end, but this was almost certainly its sense.

Texts

Site

Ancient Axos was located in north-central Crete in the foothills of Mt. Psiloritis (ancient Mt. Ida) roughly midway between the modern cities of Heraklion and Rethymno. Its territory probably extended north to the coast, bordering on that of Tylissos and Knossos to the east, Gortyn to the southeast, and Eleutherna to the west. The polis-town occupied a hill (alt. *c*.600 m) above the modern village of Axos that commanded ancient routes to Panormus and Almyrida on the north coast and south to the sanctuary of Zeus on Mt. Ida.

The earliest evidence of occupation on the hill (burials and terracotta votives) appears to date to the tenth or possibly the late eleventh century.[353] Rescue excavations have uncovered several cemeteries (Subminoan/Protogeometric to Roman) west of the hill along the modern road to Rethymno.[354] Excavation on the hill has been limited to a single campaign in 1899 by Halbherr and De Sanctis who uncovered two archaic structures: one at the northwest part of the hill's plateau (henceforth the 'acropolis structure'), and one below and to the southeast of the acropolis structure (FIG. 4). Levi, who published the first account of these excavations, records four walls of the roughly rectangular acropolis structure (which he identifies as a temple), a stepped altar carved directly out of the bedrock in an open area to the east of the structure, and a layer of black earth mixed with animal bones, terracotta animal figurines, and fragments of storage jars near the structure's west wall (Levi 1930–1: 44–7) (FIG. 5). Further evidence of sacrifice or dining in the vicinity of the acropolis structure was recovered from a cistern containing a great quantity of animal remains—deer and gazelle antlers, the jaw bones and horns of wild goats (agrimi), and boar and cow bones (Levi 1930–1: 47–8).

The second structure, which occupies a terrace on the east slope of the hill, is clearly a temple (Levi 1930–1: 49–57), but both its chronology and the identity of the deity worshipped there are unclear. The structure excavated by Halbherr and de Sanctis is no longer visible, but it appears to be Hellenistic, with a second phase of remodeling in Roman times (Prent 2005: 248–50, B.6; Aversa and Monaco 2006). Several deposits of bronze and terracotta votive objects indicate that the terrace was the location of a sanctuary from at least the tenth century.[355]

[353] Taramelli 1899 reports the discovery of Mycenaean sherds at the north end of the hill in the vicinity of an unexcavated structure. See below.

[354] Tegou 2013: 89. There is very little evidence of archaic and classical burials. Tegou (2014) reports the discovery by a villager of an archaic (burial?) pithos from the vicinity of the cemetery at the southwestern foot of the hill (Teichio).

[355] For the terracotta votives (Protogeometric to Hellenistic), see Rizza 1967–8; for the bronze votives (late seventh to early sixth centuries), see Hoffman 1972.

FIG. 4. Plan of Axos

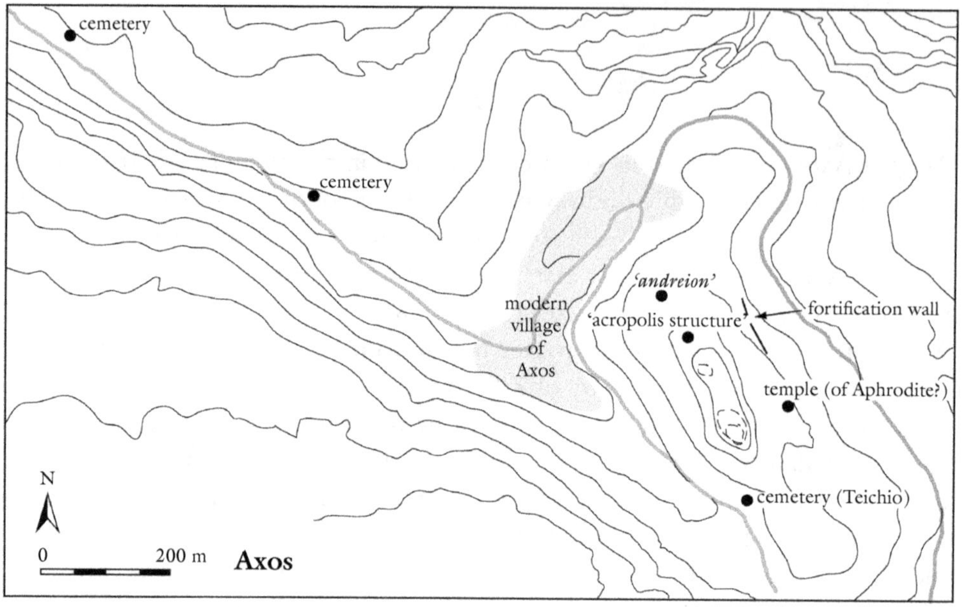

Fragments of archaic limestone (architectural?) sculpture and several fragmentary blocks inscribed with archaic letters found in the vicinity of the later temple indicate that there may have been an archaic predecessor.[356] The patron deity has been identified as a goddess, often identified in the literature as Aphrodite-Astarte, on the basis of the votive types (see e.g. Levi 1930–1: 50; cf. Rizza 1967–8: 293).

The unexcavated remains of a third structure of unknown function are located about fifty meters to the north of the acropolis structure. Taramelli 1899: 312–14 identifies this variously as an *andreion* or a 'Mycenaean *megaron*' (for the *andreion* at Axos, see **A1**; *IC* 2.5.25).

New exploration of the polis-town and territory of Axos, which began in 1999 under the direction of Eva Tegou, is revising our understanding of the topography, dating, and function of the remains on the hill and adding to our knowledge of the organization of its territory (Tegou 2010, 2013, 2014). Of greatest significance for us is Tegou's observation that the acropolis structure comprises only two walls (north and west). She suggests that they served to support a terrace and that **A1**, and possibly other epichoric inscriptions found in its vicinity (see below), may have come from its walls. A sizeable open area (*c.*100 m^2) suitable for public gatherings lay to the west of the terrace walls. The bed-rock cuttings that Levi identified as a stepped altar more likely preserve the traces of quarrying.

[356] For the stone sculpture, see Alexiou 1952; Rizza 1967–8: 285–9, figs. 55–7; D'Acunto 2001; Tegou 2014. For the blocks with archaic inscriptions, see below.

FIG. 5. Drawing of the Acropolis Structure, Axos

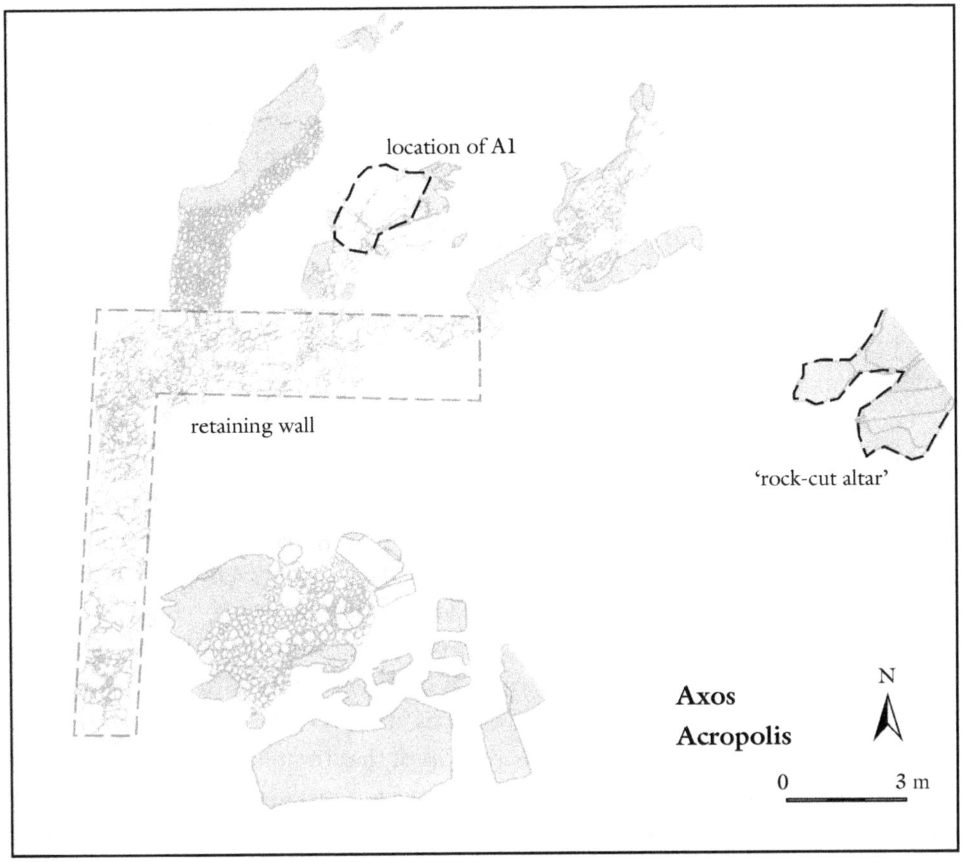

Rather than evidence of ritual activity associated with a putative temple, she proposes a largely civic context for the animal and ceramic remains found in the vicinity of the acropolis structure. Tegou tentatively identifies Taramelli's *andreion* as a cistern, and observes that a fortification wall of uncertain date appears to enclose the temple on the east slope of the hill within its circuit.

Texts

We include eleven of the epichoric inscriptions that appear in *IC* 2.5 (**A1–7, 9–12**) and two later discoveries (**Axos1–2**). Of these, Guarducci notes that she examined **A12**. We located and studied **A1**, **A12**, **Axos1**, and **Axos2**, but were unable to find the others. Thus, our knowledge of the majority of the texts we discuss relies ultimately on the autopsy of Halbherr and De Sanctis. We have therefore devoted considerable attention to the unpublished notebooks of these scholars (compiled in 1884–1914) and to their publications as well as to the publications of Comparetti and Haussoullier. Where their drawings differ from those of Guarducci we include facsimiles. We know of two epichoric inscriptions from Axos that remain unpublished: one is part of the epigraphic collection of the Archaeological Museum of Heraklion (Inv. no. 320a); the second is located on the site of ancient Axos.

The majority of these texts were inscribed on blocks of local limestone. **A1–4, 6–7**, and **11** were found in the vicinity of the acropolis structure and may originally have come from its walls (see above). The block bearing **A5** was found in a home in the modern village of Axos. If **A5** and **A6** belong to the same inscription (see below **A5+6**), then it too should be associated with the acropolis structure. The size (0.07–0.09 m) and forms of the letters of **A1–7** and **11** are very similar. Jeffery dated them as a group to the period *c.*525–500.[357]

The letters of **Axos1**, said to have come from the acropolis, are similar in form to the inscriptions associated with the acropolis structure, but the stone is considerably thinner than the blocks from the acropolis structure (0.093 m vs. 0.23–0.64 m) and the letters are considerably smaller (0.015–0.02 m vs. 0.07–0.09 m). The observation that **Axos1** continues down to the lower edge of the block suggests that it came from a wall rather than a free-standing monument. Jeffery 1949: 36 proposes that the block may have come from one of the walls of the temple on the east slope of the hill. She dates the inscription to the late sixth or early fifth century. Halbherr and De Sanctis discovered the four fragments of **A12** (a + a^1 and b + b^1) during the excavation of that temple. The letter forms are clearly earlier than those of the inscriptions on the blocks from the vicinity of the acropolis structure. Jeffery suggests a date for them early in the sixth century.[358]

A9 was located on the summit of the acropolis in the sixteenth century, but by the nineteenth century it had been transported to the modern village of Axos.[359] **A9** shares several orthographic peculiarities with **A10** and **Axos2**: a single vertical line is used for *mu*, there is no word division, and all *iotas* face left. These inscriptions do not appear to have been cut by the same mason,[360] but the shared orthographic features (e.g. the open *etas* in **A9** and **Axos2**), and the apparent use of the letter *xi* in **Axos2** suggest that these texts are later than the ones associated with the acropolis structure. Jeffery dates **A9** to the early fifth century.[361]

[357] Jeffery 1990: 316 no. 22. Cf. Ikonomaki 2010 who suggests that the inscriptions from the acropolis structure range in date from *c.*600 to the early fifth century, with **A11** (fragments a–d) the earliest and **A5** the latest in the series.

[358] Jeffery 1990: 316 no. 20. Cf. Ikonomaki 2010 who dates **A12** to the second half of the eighth century.

[359] For the sixteenth-century account of Francesco Barozzi, a Venetian who found **A9** 'in terra nella sommità della collina' and was the first to transcribe the text, see Teza 1883. For its nineteenth-century reuse, see Spratt 1865: 77–8.

[360] e.g. Barozzi and Spratt record the *iotas* of **A9** as curvy; those of **A10** and **Axos2** are angular.

[361] Jeffery 1990: 316 no. 24. Ikonomaki 2010 dates **A10** to the third quarter of the fifth century.

The form of **A10** and **Axos2**, two of the monuments that bear inscriptions with late features, differs markedly from the group from the acropolis structure in that they are inscribed on the 'front' and 'back' of limestone stelae. It is not possible to determine where these free-standing monuments were displayed. The early editors found **A10** in a home in the modern village; as for **Axos2**, we have no information concerning its provenance.

With two exceptions (**A6** and **12**B), the first line of all of the multi-line epichoric inscriptions from Axos that are inscribed on blocks with a preserved upper edge begin at the left (**A1**, **4**, **7**, **9**, and **10**) as do three texts that appear to consist of a single line only (*IC* 2.5.8, 11b, and 15). The earliest of the epichoric inscriptions, **A12**A, consisting of a single line, and **A12**B, consisting of two lines, begin at the right. Although certainty is not possible, it does not appear that any text was inscribed above **A12**A. It may be that scribal preference determined the direction of writing at Axos. Or perhaps a change in the convention that a text should begin with a line from the right took place some time after the inscribing of **A12** and before the inscribing of the texts associated with the acropolis structure towards the end of the sixth century.

Jeffery suggests that the archaic inscriptions of Axos belong to one of three 'codes': **A12** and *IC* 2.5.13–14 (tiny fragments from the early sixth century, inscribed on the temple on the east slope); **A1–7** and **11** (*c*.525–500, inscribed on the acropolis structure); and **Axos1** (*c*.525–500, also inscribed on the temple). It is not clear what she means by 'code', but without autopsy strong claims based on the evidence of letter forms—such as the suggestion that all of the inscriptions associated with the acropolis structure were written by the same mason or by masons from the same workshop as part of a single inscribing program—cannot be supported.

On the other hand, it is worth pointing out that five of the thirteen inscriptions included below (**A1–4**, **Axos1**) preserve various forms, both nominal and verbal, of the root *werg-. These include *wergastas* 'worker' (**Axos1**.3–4, 5), *wergon* 'work' (**A2**.9, **A4**.5), and *wergazomai* the verb 'work' (**A1**.6–7, **A3**.4). For the economic implications of these provisions, see Introd. 7C.

A1 (K 101; VER I.28; Genevrois 2012 = Gen.). Law concerning salaried workers, *c*.525–500. Blocks Aa and B are located on the hill of ancient Axos near the 'acropolis structure'. FIGS. 5, 6, 7

Fifteen lines of text inscribed boustrophedon beginning at the left on two joining polygonal blocks of limestone: block A at the right consisting of two joining fragments (Aa and Ab) and block B at the left. The upper and lower edges of A +B are preserved as are the left edge of B and the lower right edge of A. Block A has suffered considerable damage since its was first recorded in 1885. Ab (the upper right corner) is now lost, as are 1–6 letters from the left edge of Aa3–12.

FIG. 6. **A1** (drawing after Comparetti 1893: 381–2)

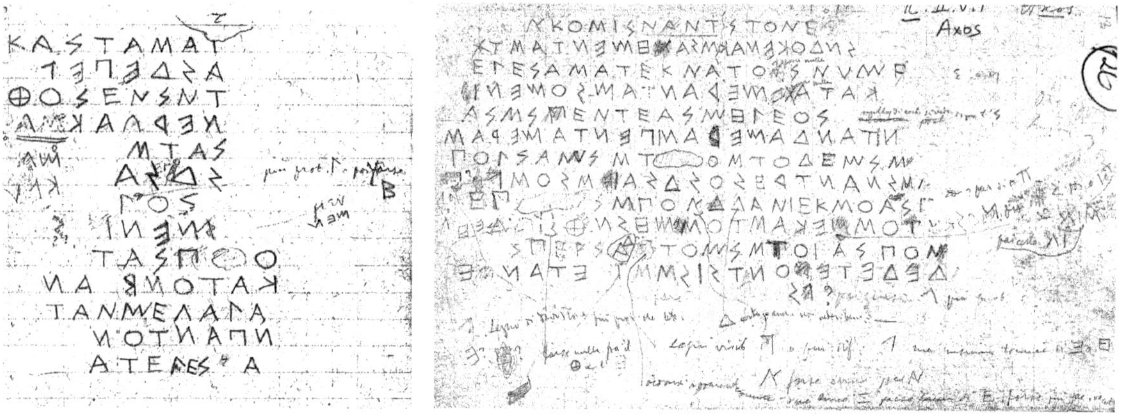

. **A1**B, left (drawing after Halbherr 1885: 17); **A1**A, right (drawing after Halbherr 1885: 13)

Lines 3–15 are complete at the left; the text probably continued onto an additional block (or blocks) to the right of A. It is possible that line 1 is the first line of the inscription. The uninscribed band across the bottom of A+B indicates that line 15 is the last line, unless perhaps a partial line 16 was inscribed below it to the right of A on a stone now lost.

Pitting in the surface of the blocks appears to have caused the mason to leave uninscribed spaces within lines (see on lines 7, 9, 12, 15) and to stop inscribing before reaching the left edge of B. Furthermore, until quite recently the inscribed face of the blocks was exposed to the elements; consequently the letters are very difficult to make out.

Comparetti (1893: 397–8, Comparetti and Halbherr 1888: 141–2) suggests that **A1** and **A2** perhaps belonged to the same inscription.

[—]ϝκος | ἴναντι τôν ẹἰ[—] →
[—]ιν δοκêν ἀκσία ἤμεν τâς τ[ε τροπâς]
καὶ τâς ἀτελείας ⟨τ⟩ὰ τέκνα τô ἰνυμẹ́[νο —]
[—] κατ' ἀμέραν ζαμιôμεν. | αἰ δ' ἐπέλ-
θοιεν ἰν ταῖσι πέντε, αἰ μὴ λέοι[εν —]
[—]ν, | τâν δ' ἀμερâν | πέντ' ἀμέρας ϝεργακσα[c.2?]
[c.5]ς τâι πόλι ἀμίστος. τô δὲ μισ[τô —]
[— τ]ậς ἰν ἀντρηίοι διάλ̣σιος | [.] *ΙΔΙΑ*
Δ̣ΟΙ ẹ̓πὶ σποϝδδὰν | *ΕΚΣΟΑΙ* . [—]
[— ἀ]ϝ̣τὸς | ϝεκάστος μὴ ἰνθẹ́μεν |
τâι πό[λ]ι. περὶ δẹ̀ τô μιστô | αἰ πον[—]
[—. τά]δε δὲ τελίοντι· | ἴσς τε τὰν ἑκατόνβαν
τὰν μεγάλαν | καὶ τὸ θῦμα | καὶ̣ [. .]δ[c.3–5]ν[—]
[—]ρηιον διδόμεν· | τôν δ' ἄλον πάντον
ἀτέλειαν καὶ τροπὰν ἰν ἀντρηίοι κα[—]
vacat

1 — in the presence of the —
2–3 — the children of the (?) are deemed to be worthy of both [sustenance] and tax exemption —
4–5 — is to fine per day. If they should come forward within five (days), unless they should wish —
6–7 —, and of these days, work (?) five days for the city without pay. Of the wage —
8–9 — of the *dialsis* in the *andreion* . . . . 8. . . . for serious work (?) —
10–11 — each one himself is not to give to the city. Concerning the wage, if —
12–13 — They pay the following: for the Great Hekatomb and the sacrificial offering, and —
14–15 — to give; but (they are to be) tax exempt from all others and (are to receive) sustenance in the *andreion* —.

Unless otherwise indicated:

H = Halbherr 1885: 13–14, 17; Comparetti and Halbherr 1888: 129–40 nos. 1 and 2; Halbherr *ap.* Comparetti 1893: 381–94 no. 183.

C = Comparetti and Halbherr 1888: 129–40 nos. 1 and 2; Comparetti 1893: 381–94 no. 183.

1 ẹ: H records faintly, adding 'piu difficilmente *N* o *Λ*'.

[—]ϝκος: [γλέ]ϝκος C, Van Effenterre 1979: 290; [λε]ϝκός G. There are other possibilities, such as a perfect participle.

Perhaps [—]ϝκος | ἴναντι τôν ε̣ἴ[κοσι] '[having done something] in the presence of the twenty (?)', cf. **Dr1**.4.

2 [—]ιν: C's [—σπ]ὶν δοκêν 'seemed to them' is unlikely.

τ[ε τροπᾶς]: τ[ροπᾶς] G, but if the mason continued line 2 about as far to the left as the lines that follow, there are *c*.7–8 letters missing. *Tropa* and *ateleia* occur together in line 15.

3 ⟨τ⟩ἀ τέκνα. The relative pronoun ἅ is possible, but an indefinite relative pronoun (ἅτι) would probably be used instead (for the form, see Dialect 18). Blass #5125a, G, K, VER, and Gen. prefer ἁ τέκνα = ἡ τέχνη 'art'. VER begin a new sentence with ἁ τέκνα, which the nom. appears to require. If this is correct, it is the only certain example of asyndeton in this text.

ε̣: H records the vertical and upper two horizontal strokes; *eta* is also possible.

τô ἰνυμε̣[νο]. Most editors (e.g. Blass #5125A, G, K, VER) restore [τ]ινυμε̣[νο—], from τίνομαι. There is room for a letter before the *iota*, but the drawings of H and G record a rough spot on the stone and Halbherr 1885: 13 notes '*forse nulla*' in the space. C suggests ἰν ὑμε[ναίοι] or ἰν Ὑμη[ττίοις].

For the sense, see Hesychius s.v. ἰνύεσθαι· κοσμεῖν, ἱδρύνεσθαι. The term may be related to the denominative verb ἐντύω, a rare biform of ἐντύνω, 'equip, harness', derived from (τὰ) ἔντεα, a noun referring to various kinds of equipment (e.g. arms and armor, harnesses, and furniture). Chantraine s.v. ἔντεα posits *sen as the stem and identifies -τος/τυς as a suffix. Psilosis yields the stem *en. On Crete the verb without the suffix might have taken the form ἰνύω/ἰνύομαι. For e > i, see Dialect 3, Bile 85–6. The middle could mean 'cause to provide the ἔντεα', possibly in the sense of produce equipment of some kind or oversee others in its production. For the causative middle in Cretan, see Bile 248–51.

4 κατ' ἀμέραν. There is room for 1–2 letters between *alpha* and *mu*. H and G record faint traces of an *epsilon* in their drawings, but Halbherr 1885: 13 notes '*forse nulla*' in the space.

ζ̣: the vertical and upper horizontal strokes are visible.

6–7 ϝεργακσα[*c*.2 | *c*.5]ς: ϝεργακσά|[μενο]ς Blass #5125a; ϝεργακσα|[μένο]ς (acc. pl.) G, K, VER. H records no letters following the *alpha* in line 6 or before the *sigma* in line 7), which may suggest ϝεργάκσα|σται (= ἐργάσασθαι ?), but the mid. inf. always has a *theta* (Bile 239–40).

7 ἀμίστος = ἀμίσθους or, less likely, ἀμίσθως.

8 α̣: H records the lower tip of the left oblique stroke.

λ̣: H records the vertical stroke; the oblique stroke is faint.

διάλ̣σιος: for most editors the gen. of δίαλσις (e.g. C, G, K, VER, Gen.), attested only here. The etymology and meaning are disputed. We follow the scholars (e.g. K, VER, and Gen.) who associate the noun with the root ἀλ- 'to feed/nourish' (cf. ἀλδαίνω 'nourish'). Cf. C who prefers ἅλ-; δίαλσις is a 'dance with jumping across' (cf. ἅλλομαι 'jump').

8–9 [.] *ΙΔΙΑ*|*Λ̣ΟΙ*: [α]ἰ διά|λ̣οι or [α]ἰ δ' ἰά|λ̣οι? Most editors restore [α]ἰ and understand διάλοι as a verbal form (aor. opt.?) from the same root (ἀλ- or ἅλ-) as δίαλσις. C (followed by G) suggests *διάλλω (= διάλλομαι) or *διάλω (= διασιτέω). Gen. proposes an absolute or intransitive sense for *διάλω ('take nourishment'), but noting the absence of a conjunction or particle in the conditional clause, he prefers [α]ἰ δ' ἰάλοι, pres. opt. of ἰάλ(λ)ω 'send forth' or 'depart' (for the intransitive use of ἰάλλω, see Gen. p. 292). Van

Effenterre 1946a: 592 associates διάλοι (and δίαλσις) with ἀλ- of ἐάλην (aor. pass. of ἴλλω) in the sense 'assemble' (n. and comm. on **Dr5**.1), but VER tentatively translate δίαλσις as '*entretien*' and do not translate διάλοι. K's [.]δια[- - -]λοι is probably wrong (no letters appear to be missing between lines 8 and 9).

9 λ̣: H records the *lambda* faintly.

ε̣: H records the *epsilon* faintly.

ἐπί H records an un-inscribed space (a rough spot on the stone) between *pi* and *iota*.

σποϝδδάν = σπουδήν 'enthusiasm, zeal' (K, G, Bile 138, Gen. 294, and tentatively VER). For the replacement of *upsilon* with *digamma* in diphthongs on Crete, see Bile 105–7, 118. C suggests σπουδήν 'libation'.

ἐπί σποϝδδάν (=σπουδήν). The meaning is not clear. Gen. 295 suggests 'for something important' ('*pour un travail sérieux*'); ἐπί σποϝδδάν (=σπονδήν) 'for a libation' makes sense, but is difficult (Gen. 294 '*impossible*') phonetically.

ΕΚΣΟΑΙ . : ἐκς ὃ αἰ, meaning? C, VER. Possibly ἔκσο (ἔξω). Gen. 295 takes ἔκσο to mean 'outside', but it can also mean 'except for, other than'. See n. on **G64**.5 where the spelling is ἔκσοι.

H and G record a stroke, very slightly off from vertical after the final *iota*. H suggests *mu*, *nu*, or *pi*; a vertical stroke (word division) is also possible.

10 ϝ̣: H records the tail and upper part of the left oblique of the *digamma*.

ε̣: H records the *epsilon* faintly.

[ἀ]ϝ̣τὸς ϝεκάστος: acc. pl. The plural is awkward, but in keeping with the plural verbs (4–5 ἐπέλθοιεν and λέοι[εν], 12 τελίοντι); and as the subject of μὴ ἰνθέμεν, the accusative is required.

ἰνθε̣μεν = ἐνθεῖναι. There is an un-inscribed space of *c*.2 letters after *theta* where the surface of the stone is rough.

10–11 μὴ ἰνθέμεν |τᾶι πό[λ]ι. Cf. θέμημ πόλι (**G41**.3.17).

11 πό[λ]ι. There is an un-inscribed space after the *pi* where the stone is rough.

ε̣: H records the upper and lower horizontal strokes of the *epsilon*.

πον[—]: πον[ίοιεν]? πονε̂ν, 'assert (a claim)', used of litigants (see n. on **G72**.1.14); cf. **A9**.8 πορτιπονε̂ν 'bring a charge against someone'. The singular πον[ίοι] is also possible. VER connect πον[ίο] with πονέω 'work', but this verb is not attested in Crete at this time, where 'to work' is ἐργάζεσθαι (see above 6–7 and **A3**.4).

12 τελίοντι = τελοῦσι.

ἴος = εἰς. See Dialect 14.

13 ι̣: H records the *iota* faintly.

καὶ̣ [. .]δ[*c*.3–5]ν. The stone appears to be damaged after *delta*. H records *ΠΕ* following καί̣ and two letters—*P*, *Λ*, or *N* + *A* or *F*—before *nu*.

14[—]ρηιον: [ἰα]ρήιον C, VER; [ἰς ἀντ]ρήιον Blass #5125a, van Effenterre 1979: 291; [πο]ρήιον G.

A1 belongs to a small group of archaic inscriptions from Crete (**Da1**; **Ele9**; **G79**) that establish the conditions of employment for workers hired by the city (van Effenterre 1979). These texts include provisions defining the workers' compensation and specifying procedures in the event that one of the parties to the agreement finds fault with the performance of the other. The use of the plural (4–5, 10, 12) suggests that the law concerns a group of workers. Despite our general understanding of the nature of **A1**, the loss of an unknown number of letters to the right and the use of several rare or otherwise unattested terms make it impossible to determine the identity of the workers or the nature of their work.

1 We cannot tell if the text began higher up, but the partially preserved prepositional clause 'in the presence of the' (*inanti ton ei*[—]) may indicate an enactment clause (cf. **Dr5**, 'with the tribes assembled'?). The first four letters (*FKOΣ*), however, defy interpretation as enactment language.

2–3 The general sense of these lines is fairly clear: the city grants tax exemption (*ateleia*) and probably sustenance (*tropa*, restored on the basis of line 15) to certain individuals. There remain, however, significant difficulties in interpretation. The infinitive 'to seem' (*doken*) depends on a verb that is missing. We suggest something like, 'the city decided that X seems to be worthy'.[362] Furthermore, the antecedent of 'worthy', that is, the recipients of the grant, is uncertain. The only possible candidate in the preserved text is 'children' (*tekna*, line 3), although this reading requires either assuming a scribal error (⟨τ⟩ά) or, in the absence of an error, a very doubtful construction (see n.). We take the letters following *tekna* (*to inume*[—]) to belong to a nominal phrase in the genitive, possibly the participle *to inume*[*no*] ('of the *inumenos*'), a rare verb meaning 'to arrange, build' or perhaps 'to make equipment' (n. *ad loc.*). The opening of the agreement of Datala with the *poinikastas* Spensithios (**Da1**) is similar in structure and content to what we suggest here. Its enactment formula (**Da1**A1–2) is connected syntactically with the award of sustenance and tax exemption for Spensithios and his descendants (*genias*) (**Da1**A2–5).

Most editors, however, understand *technē* 'craft' rather than *tekna* 'children' (n. *ad loc.*). This reading necessitates punctuation after 'tax exemption' and the start of a new sentence with 'The craft'. Asyndeton would mark the beginning of a new subject (Introd. 3D3).

4 The subject of 'to fine' is likely to be an official of Axos. The person subject to the fine is perhaps the one who receives sustenance and tax exemption. The fine was calculated on a per diem basis, probably for as long as the unlawful activity continued (see **G52**B1–5; **G72**.1.7–11, 29–35; **G73**A4–6).

4–5 The provision perhaps provides an exception to the preceding rule. The verb 'come forward' (*epelthoien*) is otherwise unattested in our texts. It is found frequently in treaties in Hellenistic Crete, where it is used to describe foreign ambassadors who appear before the council or assembly of the host polis, e.g. from Axos *IC* 2.5.17, lines 7–8. The legal sense proposed here ('proceed against,

362 The phrase 'to seem to be worthy' (*doken aksia emen*) is common in later honorary decrees, although not on Crete. It occurs as part of an indefinite relative clause, e.g. 'of whatever [sc. other honor] he appears to be worthy'. See e.g. *IG* II² 360, 75–6 (Athens, 325/4); *IG* XII 5 714, 12–13 (Andros, *c.*350).

challenge') is attested in Athens and in Hellenistic papyri (see LSJ I.1.d.). The clause may be giving the accused five days to assert something or present evidence. Limits on the amount of time within which an action may be taken are common in the laws from Gortyn (see e.g. **G72**.2.28–31, 11.46–50; **G82**.5–6).

6–7 The five days of work without pay may have been a penalty imposed for some offense. If so, this would be one of two penalties attested on Crete that takes a form other than the payment of a fine (for the other, see **Dr1**). Alternatively, the provision perhaps imposes corvée (unpaid) labor upon the worker. If so, as far as we know, this is the only example of corvée labor attested in the Greek world during the Archaic and Classical periods (cf. **Ele9**, but the context is very uncertain).

7 The details of the *mistos* are not preserved, but probably consisted at least in part of food (e.g. grape must, figs, barley), as was the case at Datala (**Da1**A12–14) and Gortyn (**G79**.1–6).

8 *Dialsios* (from *dialsis*) occurs only here and its meaning is not known (n. ad loc.). Gen. presents a strong case for 'provision/distribution of food' ('*la répartition de ces vivres*'), but we can be certain only that the term refers to something that took place or was kept in the *andreion*.

8–9 The readings at the end of lines 8 and 9 are not secure and the sense of these lines cannot be determined with certainty (see n.). Most editors suggest that a conditional clause follows *dialsios* and that *spouddan* (line 9) means 'haste, enthusiasm' (= Attic *spoudē*). Gen. proposes that the provision concerns a worker who has left the polis ('if he should go outside', *ai d' ialoi ekso*) on a matter of importance (*epi spouddan*), presumably before completing the task he has been hired to perform.

10–11 'Place in the city' (*inthemen tai poli*) could mean 'impose additional charges upon the city' or possibly 'pay to the city'. There are no close parallels in our texts for the use of the verb in either of these senses, but for the former ('impose additional charges'), cf. **G79**.7–9 stipulating that work shall be performed for the wages as defined, implying that the city will not pay anything additional. For the phrase in Hellenistic treaties, see Chaniotis 1996: 81–2.

11 preserves part of a conditional clause concerning wages. The verb in the condition (*pon*[—]) is possibly a form of *ponen* 'to assert a claim', used of litigants.

12–13 The workers are liable for two contributions either of sacrificial victims or of money for the purchase of victims—the 'Great Hekatomb' and 'the sacrificial offering'; a third obligation may perhaps have been named after the 'and', the last word that can be read in line 13. Scholars identify the triennial sacrifice to Zeus on Mt. Ida, perhaps also attested in **A5+6**, as the occasion of the Great Hekatomb (VER; Sporn 2002: 227; cf. **G80**.1–3). Another hekatomb offering at Axos is attested in a late classical or early Hellenistic text (*SEG* 23.566, line 16).

14 The partially preserved word at the beginning can be restored [*ia*]*reion* 'sacrificial victim' or [*ant*]*reion* (for the latter, cf. **Da1B11**, 'he shall give to the *andrēion*'), but other restorations are possible.

The civic status of the workers in **A1** is uncertain. H. and M. van Effenterre 1985 and 1988, K, and VER identify the workers as non-citizens, either members of a dependent class or free foreigners. Yet, their participation in two of the essential civic institutions of the polis, the *andreion* and sacrificial ritual, strongly suggests that they were members of the political class of Axos (Perlman 2004a). In this regard it is also worth observing that Axos and Datala compensate their workers with wages (*mistos*) and food (*tropa*) for the *andreion*, while Gortyn compensates its workers, who included both free men and slaves, with wages alone. See Introd. 7C.

A2 (K 102; VER I.28). Law concerning workers?, *c*.525–500. Current location unknown. FIG. 8

Twelve lines of text inscribed boustrophedon beginning at the left on two joining fragments of a limestone block that was recut into a drum shape for reuse, perhaps as a millstone. The curve of the drum appears to straighten out below line 12, possibly preserving part of the original lower edge of the block. A considerable amount has probably been lost, though we cannot determine exactly how much.

Comparetti (1893: 397–8; Comparetti and Halbherr 1888: 141–2) suggests that **A2** and **A1** may have belonged to the same inscription.

[—] . *ONAT*[—] →	
[— τὰ] δὲ τέκνα σ̣[—]	— but the children —
[—]οια πάσταν [.]ι . [—]	— master —
[—]μεν τὰ θῖνα κ̣αὶ ἰ[—]	— the sacred matters and —
[—]ιηιο | μὴδ̣' ὀνυμ̣[αι —]	— nor name (?) —
[—]τ̣ο̣ς ἦμεν, ἐλθὲν | ἐδε̣[—]	— are to be [—], to come —
[—]εν καταμετρὲν | ἀ̣[—]	— to measure completely —
[—] πλίας | αἰ λέοι ὀ[—]	— more, if he should wish —
[—]αλ̣ε τὸ Ϝέργον ἀν[—]	— the work —
[—]ιο̣ν | ἀβλ̣οπία[ι —]	— without fault —
[—]εν τôν τέκ[νον (?) —]	— of the children (?) —
[— α]ἰ λ̣έοι ἐπο[—]	— if he should wish —

Unless otherwise indicated:

H = Halbherr 1885: 20; Comparetti and Halbherr 1888: 139–42 no. 3a and b; Halbherr *ap.* Comparetti 1893: 395–8 no. 184.

C = Comparetti and Halbherr 1888: 139–42 no. 3a and b; Comparetti 1893: 395–8 no. 184.

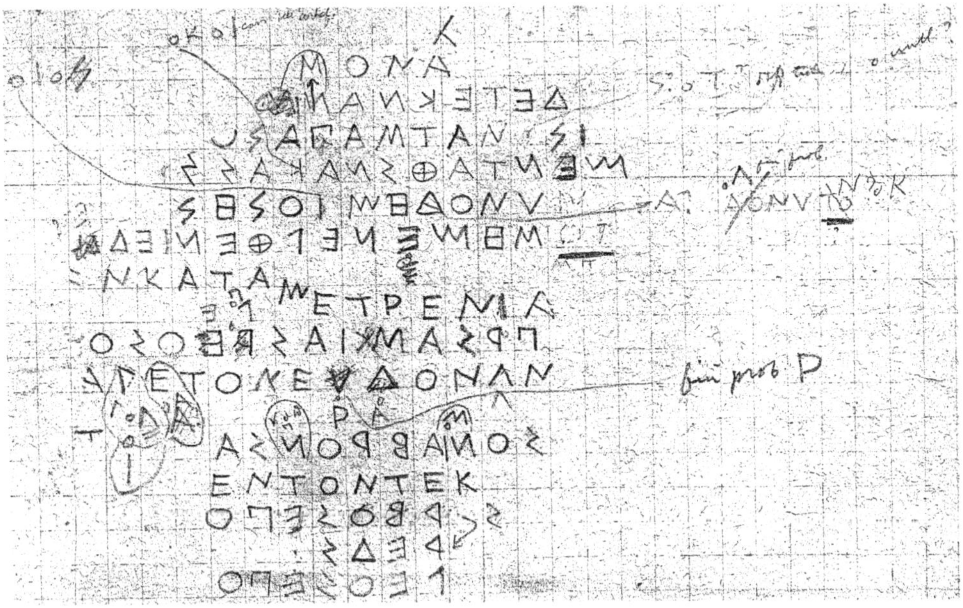

FIG. 8. **A2** (drawing after Halbherr 1885: 20)

1 G records the tip of a vertical stroke before *omicron*.
Halbherr 1885 records *AT*; all other drawings record faintly the left oblique and crossbar of the *alpha* and the lower tip of a vertical stroke to its right.

2 σ̣: Halbherr 1885 records the final letter as *san* or *nu*.

[—τὰ] δὲ τέκνα: all other editors prefer a form of τέχνη: τέκναν or τεκνᾶν C; τέκνας G, K, VER (cf. **A1**.3).

3 [—]οια πάσταν: C, G, K, VER; [—]οι ἄπας 'everyone' is also possible, although the intensive form ἄπας is not otherwise attested in the epichoric inscriptions from Crete.
Halbherr 1885 suggests *iota*, *tau*, or possibly a *vacat* after *nu*.
Halbherr 1885 records a vertical stroke at the right edge of the stone.

4 κ̣: H and G record the vertical stroke and faint traces of what could be two short oblique strokes, but H notes that what he records as *kappa* is possibly punctuation (vertical line), i.e. τὰ θῖνα | αἰ ἰ[—]; JP records only the vertical stroke.

5 ιηιο: ['Ασκλαπ]ιηίο or ['Ολυμπ]ιηίο C.
δ̣: H, G, and JP record the two oblique strokes; *gamma* is possible but unlikely.
μ̣: H, G, and JP record the vertical stroke and the ghost of 2–4 short oblique strokes; H notes that *nu* is also possible.
ὀνυμ̣[—]. For ὀνυμαίνο ('name'), see **G75**C7–8.

6 τ̣: H records the vertical stroke and faintly records the horizontal stroke.
ο̣: H records the ghost of a circular letter.
[—]τος: [ἀπά]τος (?) ἦμεν 'they are to be immune', most often neuter sing., but cf. **Ele1**1.5.

7 α̣: all drawings record the oblique stroke at left and the cross-bar.
καταμετρε̃ν. For the force of κατα- (completion), see Bile 276.

8 πλίας = πλείονας. See Bile 203.

9 λ̣: H and G record the vertical stroke, an upper oblique stroke, and faint traces of a lower oblique stroke (could be *rho*, but cf. the rounded head of the *rhos* in 7 and 9).

τὸ Ϝέργον: cf. **A4**.5 [—]ṭαλει το Ϝεργ[—]).

10 ṿ | : H notes that *san* is also possible.

λ̣ Halbherr 1885 records *rho*; all other drawings record *lambda*.

ἀβλοπία = ἀβλάβεια.

11 τôν τέκ[νον]: τὸν τεκ[νίταν] C (τôν τεκ[νιτâν] is also possible).

12 λ̣: H prefers *rho*, but notes that *lambda* is possible; G and JP record *lambda*.

Most editors read 'craft' (*tekna* = *technē*, line 2) and 'craftsman' (*tek*[*nitan*], line 11); we suggest (with reservations) 'children' in both lines (*tekna* and *tek*[*non*]). *Pastas* refers to the master of slaves in **G47**.6 and **G72**.2.32–45, 3.52–4.24, and to a master of oxen in **G41**.1.16 (also in a later law from Knossos, *IC* 1.8.5B3). Its appearance here together with 'the work' (*to ergon*, line 9) suggested to C, G, K, and VER that the law concerns dependent (slave?) or non-citizen (foreign?) craftsmen. However, the reference to 'sacred matters' (*ta thina*) seems to us to be out of place in provisions concerning relations between citizens and non-citizens, and nothing else in **A2** suggests that it pertains to livestock.

That said, with at most three words preserved in any of the lines it is not possible to determine the subject of the law.

4 'Sacred matters' occurs here and in two other laws from Axos: **A5+6**.6 and *SEG* 23.566, line 6 (late fourth or early third century). In both of the latter a ritual context is likely. Elsewhere on Crete it occurs in the expression 'sacred and civic matters' (e.g. **Da1**A4, **Da1**B2–3; **G72**.10.41). See Introd. 9A.

5 'To name' (*onumaino*) occurs in a provision of **G51**.4–5 prohibiting the litigants from swearing by gods other than those listed.

7 'Measure completely' (*katametren*) is not otherwise attested on Crete. 'To measure' (*metren*) refers to measuring the area of a parcel of land (**G75**A3, 5 = **G81**.6, 8) and 'to calculate' (*epimetren*) refers to measuring the value of crops produced on a parcel of land (**G43**Ba8). The context here may be a dispute concerning land or its produce.

10 'Without fault'. The plaintiff in the dispute concerning land used to secure a loan (see comm. above) is to swear that the size of the parcel is as measured 'without fault' (**G75**A9–10 = **G81**.12–13). The term occurs in the later law from Axos (*SEG* 23.566, line 17), perhaps in reference to the purity of sacrificial cattle.

A3 (K 103). Law concerning workers? *c.*525–500. Current location unknown. Fig. 9

Seven lines of text inscribed boustrophedon beginning at the left on a limestone block. No original edge is preserved.

FIG. 9. **A3** (drawing after Halbherr 1885: 19)

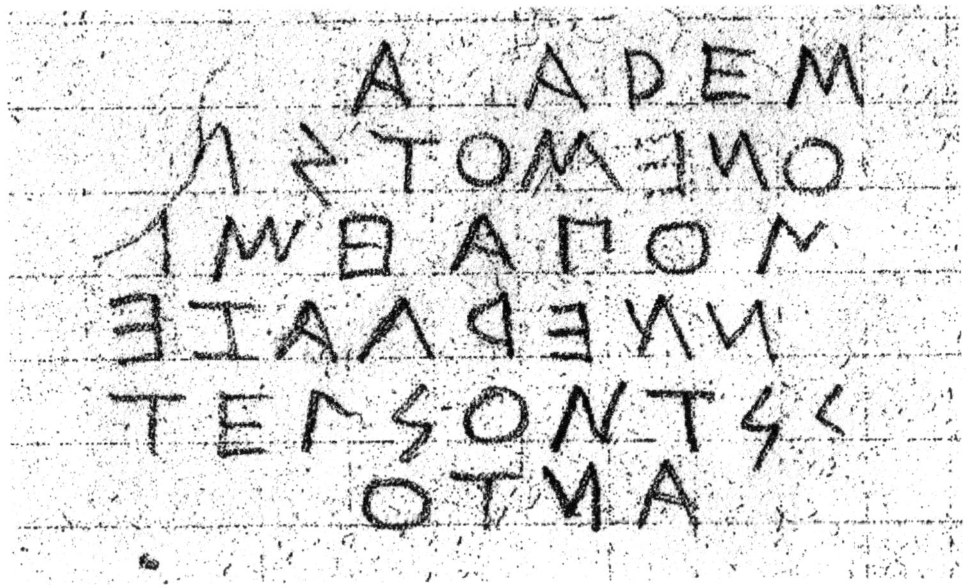

[—]αραρεν̣[—]	→
[—]ονεσοτι . [—]	
[—] |̣ μὴ ἀπο . [—]	— not —
[—]ν Ϝεργαζε[—]	— work —
[—] τελίοντι ι̣[—]	— they pay —
[—]αντο[—]	
[—]Ϝ̣ . [—]	

Unless otherwise indicated:

H = Halbherr 1885: 19, 52; Comparetti and Halbherr 1888: 141–2 no. 4; Halbherr *ap.* Comparetti 1893: 397–8 no. 185.

C = Comparetti and Halbherr 1888: 141–2 no. 4; Comparetti 1893: 397–8 no. 185.

1 ν̣: Halbherr 1885 records *san*; all other drawings (H, G, JP) record *nu* or traces consistent with *nu*.

2 Following *iota*, all drawings record the first two strokes of a letter consistent with *lambda*, *mu*, *nu*, *san*, or possibly *digamma*.

[—]ονεσοτι . [—]: [—]ονες ὀτιμ̣[ι —]G, JP; [πλί]ονες ὀτιμ̣[ι —] C.

3 \|̣: H records the vertical stroke (punctuation); G and JP do not.

Following *omicron*, all drawings record three strokes consistent with *mu*; *nu* and *san* are also possible. C, G, and JP prefer *san*.

5 ι̣: H records two short oblique strokes resembling the upper part of *iota*. G and JP record the upper tips of the two intersecting oblique strokes of a triangular letter (*alpha*, *gamma*, *delta*, *digamma*).

7 Ϝ̣: Halbherr (Comparetti and Halbherr 1888; Halbherr *ap.* Comparetti 1893) and JP record the upper tips of two intersecting oblique strokes and a third oblique stroke that resembles the tail of a *digamma* followed by the upper tip of a vertical stroke. G and JP prefer *nu*.

The verbs ‘work’ in 4 and ‘pay’ in 5 suggest that like **A1** and possibly **A2** this law may concern workers.

A4 (K 104). Law concerning workers? *c.*525–500. Current location unknown. FIG. 10

Eleven lines of text inscribed boustrophedon beginning at the left on a limestone block with all edges preserved. The text continued to the right and the left and possibly above. An un-inscribed band along the lower edge of the block indicates that there was at most one additional line of text from right that ended to the right of **A4**.

[—]σ . [. . ἰ]σελθε[ν (?) —]	→	— come in (?) —
[— ἀβλ]οπίαι [.] . τ̣ασδ̣[.]τε[.] . [—]		— without fault (?) —
[—]ν̣ τ̣ρ̣ὶ̣ς̣ ἀμέρας [—]		— for three days —
[—]ετρ̣ε . [.] . αν̣[.]οιδ̣ατα̣[—]		
[—]τ̣αλει το Ϝεργο[—]		— the work —
[—] . [.]δ̣ . [3–4]ι̣τον̣π . [—]		
[—]ν̣αρσιας | τον ν̣[—]		
[— ν]υνατὸν ἦμεν [—]		— is to be able —
[—]δ̣α̣[5–6]ελοντ[—]		
[—]η̣[3–4]οσ̣[—]		
[—]ν̣α̣[—]		
vacat		

Unless otherwise indicated:

H = Halbherr 1885: 47, 52–5; Comparetti and Halbherr 1888: 143–4 no. 5; Halbherr *ap.* Comparetti 1893: 399–400 no. 186.

C = Comparetti and Halbherr 1888: 143–4 no. 5; Comparetti 1893: 399–400 no. 186.

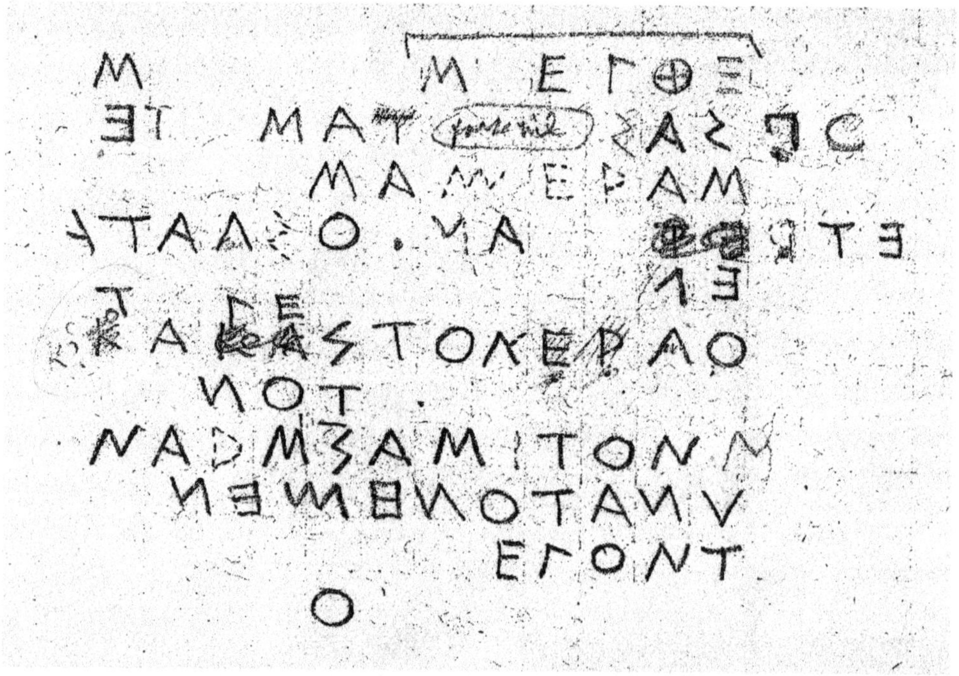

FIG. 10. Drawing of **A4** (after Halbherr 1885: 47)

1 G records the faint trace of a vertical stroke after the first *san*.

2 Halbherr 1885 suggests nothing was inscribed between the second *iota* and the first *tau*.

τ̣: all drawings record the vertical stroke.

δ̣: Halbherr 1885 does not record the dotted *delta*; Halbherr (Comparetti and Halbherr 1888; Halbherr *ap.* Comparetti 1893), G, and JP record the *delta* as visible but faint.

G and JP record the faint trace of a vertical stroke at the left edge of the stone.

[— ἀβλ]οπίαι: C, G, and JP on the basis of **A2**.10.

τ̣ασδ̣[.]τε[.] . [—]: τ̣ᾶς δ̣[ἐ] τ̣έ[κ]ṿ[ας]? G on the basis of **A2**.2.

3 [—]ṿ τρ̣ὶς̣: H records no traces before the *san*; all others record the first three letters clearly and the *iota* faintly. H records the *san* clearly; all others record the first two strokes faintly and the second two clearly.

Possibly [τᾶν δ' ἀμερᾶ]ν τρ̣ὶς̣ ἀμέρας (cf. **A1**.6 τᾶν δ' ἀμερᾶν | πέντ' ἀμέρας), but this is only a guess.

4 ρ̣: recorded by Halbherr 1885, G, JP.

Halbherr (Comparetti and Halbherr 1888; Halbherr *ap.* Comparetti 1893), G, JP record a *lambda* following the second *epsilon*, but the string of letters *ΤΡΕΛ* is very rare, attested only in the personal names Τρέλλος/Τρέλλων (see Chantraine s.v.) and in the names of ointments formed with ἔλαιον (e.g. κιτρέλαιον, νιτρέλαιον, πετρέλαιον). Halbherr 1885 appears to record very faintly the third stroke of a *nu*, and so instead of *lambda*, we suggest *nu* or possibly *san* (e.g. [μ]ετρε̂ν or [μ]ετρεσ̣[—]).

Halbherr (Comparetti and Halbherr 1888; Halbherr *ap.* Comparetti 1893), JP, and G record a vertical stroke before the first *alpha*.

ṿ: all drawings record the *nu* faintly.

δ̣: all drawings record at least one or both of the obliques clearly and the other oblique and the horizontal faintly.

α̣: Halbherr 1885 records the *alpha*; all other drawings record a faint oblique line.

5 τ̣ Halbherr 1885 seems to have hesitated between *kappa* and *tau*; all other drawings record the *tau* faintly. Perhaps [— αἴ] κ̣α λε̂ι?

το Ϝεργο[—]: τὸ Ϝέργο[ν —] C; τô Ϝέργο [—] is also possible.

6 JP records the upper part of a triangular letter at the right edge of the stone.

G and JP record the *delta* followed by a vertical line, the *iota*, and the fourth stroke of a *san* (instead of *nu*); all are recorded faintly.

H records only τοṿ.

Halbherr 1885 records no traces of letters after the dotted *nu*. The drawings of Halbherr (Comparetti and Halbherr 1888; Halbherr *ap.* Comparetti 1893) and G differ on the last three letter spaces. Halbherr: *nu*, nothing, *pi*; G: possibly *san*, *pi*, rectangular letter.

7 ṿ: H records the first *nu*; G and JP record the final two strokes consistent with *mu* or *nu*.

[—]ṿαρσιας | τον ṿ[—]: [—ἀ]ναρσίας | τôν σ̣[—] C without explanation; ἀρσίας possibly the acc. pl. of ἄρσις ('lifting, removing')?

8 νυνατόν = δυνατόν. See Dialect 9.

9 δ̣: Halbherr (Comparetti and Halbherr 1888; Halbherr *ap.* Comparetti 1893) records the two oblique strokes of a triangular letter (*alpha* and *gamma* are also possible); G and JP record only the faint traces of the right oblique stroke.

α̣: Halbherr (Comparetti and Halbherr 1888; Halbherr *ap.* Comparetti 1893), G, and JP record the first oblique stroke clearly and the other two strokes faintly.

Halbherr 1885 records no traces of letters before the *epsilon.*

[—]ελοντ[—]: perhaps *τὸν*] *ἐλόντ*[*α* —] 'the captor' (cf. **G72**.2.37–8).

10 Halbherr 1885 records only the *omicron*; all other drawings also record faintly the dotted *eta* and *san.*

11 G and JP record faintly the dotted *nu* and *alpha.*

Apart from the term 'work' (**A4**.5), suggesting that **A4** has something to do with labor, and several possible lexical parallels with **A1–3**, nothing more can be said about the subject of **A4**.

A5+6 (Perlman 2010). Law or treaty with provisions concerning booty. *c.*525–500. Current location unknown. Figs. 11, 12

Eight lines of text inscribed in boustrophedon beginning at the right on two limestone blocks. For their association and proposed join along the left edge of **A6** and the right edge of **A5**, see Perlman 2010. The text probably began higher up on the wall and continued onto a block or blocks to the left of **A6**. **A5** probably preserves the right edge of the text. It cannot be determined if line 8 is the final line of the text. For the texts as they appear in G, see Fig. 11.

[ἐν] Ϝ̣ίδ̣αι, κα[ὶ] Ποτειδᾶνι ο[—]	←	— [on Mt.] Ida, and to Poseidon —
[—]ε̣θεν ἦμεν | τô πολέμ̣[ο].		— from the war are to be —
| τὰ ἀϜτῆ μὲν τô πολέμο | [—]		The things here from the war —
[— τ]ô δ' ἄλο δεκάτο Ϝ̣ιεν ἢ λογ̣κί̣-		— of the other *dekaton* a *wien* or a spear
ον ὂνς αἰέ | τὸ μ̣ὲν δέκατον [—]		the ones which at the time the *dekaton* —
[—]εν τὰ θῖνα. | αἰ δ' α[ἰ] ἀσταὶ ἢ ἄ-		— the sacred things. But if the citizen
λ̣οιτο α̣π̣ε̣[.]πεσπ̣α̣ι̣ ὀ κόσμο[ς —]		women, after it was seized, [. . . . . . .],
σ̣ . ατ[—]		the *kosmos* —

Fig. 11. Texts of **A6** (left) and **A5** (right) as they appear in *IC* 2.

A6	A5
——	——
— Ποτειδᾶνι ὀ— ←	— α̣ι δ̣' αι κα̣— ←
— τ]ε̣θὲν ἤμεν | τ[—	—τ]õ πολέμ[ο—
—εν τõ πολέμο | —	—| τὰ ἀϝτη μ̣[—
—τ]õ δ' ἄλο δεκάτο ϝ[—	—]κ̣εν · λοϝ̣κ · [—
— · τὸν ἐνδέκατον —	—]ονονς αιε[—
—]ε̣ν τὰ θῖνα. | αἰ δα—	—]ασται ἠ α—
—]πεσπα̣ι̣ ὀ κόσμο[ς —	—]οιτο · α̣ · πε̣[—
— · · · α̣τ[—	——
——	

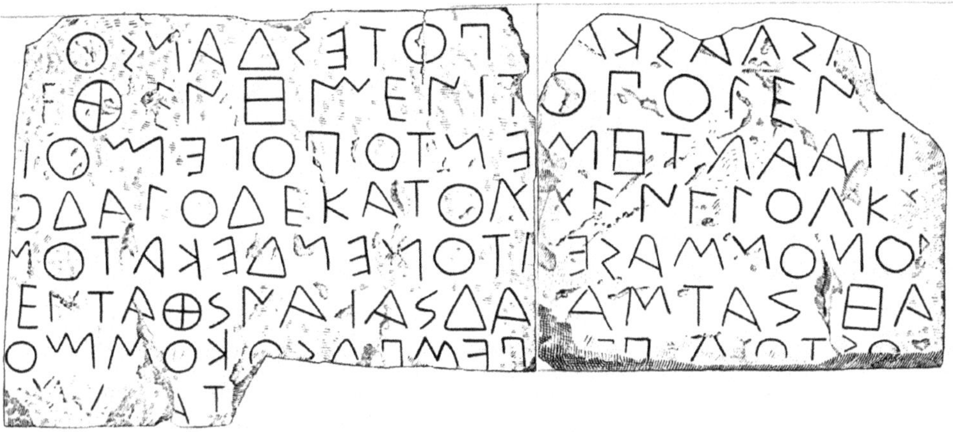

FIG. 12. Drawing of **A6** (left) + **A5** (right). Perlman 2010: 86 FIG. 2.

For a detailed epigraphical and linguistic commentary, see Perlman 2010.

---

1 ὄ[ιν—]? For sheep as sacrificial animals see, e.g. **G3**.2, 3.

2 Perlman 2010 suggests [— τὸ ἐκσαιρ]ε̣θὲν (μέρος) ἤμεν τõ πολέμ̣[ο] ‘the (share) that has been set aside from the war shall be[—]’ or perhaps [—μ]ε̣θὲν ἤμεν τõ πολέμ̣[ο] ‘from the war is to be invalid’, although μεθέν = μηδέν is not attested on Crete before the Hellenistic period (*IC* 2.12.20.6). For μηδὲν ἦμεν ‘is to be invalid’, see **Dr1**; **G72**.10.24–5.

3 ἀϝτῆ = αὐτοῦ adv. ‘(just) there/here.’ See **G87**.9.

4 For the hapax ϝ̣ιεν (a projectile weapon, i.e. arrow or javelin), see Perlman 2010: 88.

4–5 λογκίον ‘(small) spear’. For the -ιον suffix, rare before the Hellenistic period (Bile 171–2), cf. παιδίον (**G72**.4.5); ἐπενιαύτιον ‘yearly obligation’? (**Da1**.B13).

ὄνς = οὖς; ὄνσαι = οὖσαι might be possible, but there is no possible antecedent, and it seems impossible to construe ὄνσαι ε as the end of a sentence.

αἰέ = αἰεί/ἀεί; the only other occurrence in early Crete is spelled αἰεί (**G72**.11.25).

ὄνς αἰέ: if our reading is correct, the phrase is not easy to construe. The acc. relative pronoun requires a verb to follow for which it is the object, so it seems that despite the *men* that follows, the sentence continues. The *men* does however suggest that a second subject also followed: perhaps something like ‘(the arms) which the *dekaton* [and the X] provide’.

6 [—]εν: perhaps an infinitive ending, e.g. [—τέλλ]εν τὰ θῖνα ‘fulfill the sacred obligations’ (**G72**.10.42), [— μὴ ἰνῆ]μεν τὰ θῖνα ‘is not to be eligible to participate in rituals’ (*IC* 2.12.22 with Chaniotis 1996: 402–3).

This is the only example of ἀσταί or other *ast-* words without an initial *digamma* in the epichoric alphabet. But we find ἀστάς in a fourth- or early third-century inscription from Axos (*SEG* 23.566, line 7), so perhaps this form was known earlier.

ἤ = temporal adverb ‘after’/‘when’ or adverb of place ‘where’. Bile 211–12. In its temporal sense ἤ usually appears with κα + subj. See Willetts 1967: 67–8.

For the use of the optative (ἄλοιτο) through assimilation in temporal clauses, cf. e.g. **Dr1**.3, **G72**.4.10 with Willetts 1967: 63 ad loc., Bile 256–7.

---

1 **A5+6** begins with a provision concerning offerings, perhaps an animal sacrifice or votive objects, to Poseidon and to Zeus, the latter indicated by the reference to the god's cave sanctuary on Mt. Ida. For sacrifices on Mt. Ida, see also **G80**.1–3 and *IC* 4.146.6. The cult of Zeus Idatas is attested at Axos in a public document, perhaps a decree, dated to the first century (*IC* 2.5.35). A cult of the god Poseidon is not otherwise attested there.

2–7 The remainder of the text may concern the disposition of property (*dekaton* 'booty' or 'tithe', 4–5) seized in battle (*polemos*, 2–3). As suggested here, the inscription treats goods that have been taken to Axos (3) and two or more *dekata* (shares of the booty or sacred tithes) from one of which a weapon (a *wien* or a spear) is singled out for special handling of some kind. Bronze arms and armor (two spear-butts, one helmet, one corselet, nine abdominal guards) dating to the late seventh or early sixth century were recovered from votive deposits in the vicinity of the same temple on the east slope of the settlement hill at Axos where **Axos1** may have been displayed (Perlman 2010: 101–2). For a roughly contemporary (*c*.500) communal dedication of weapons (arrows) from the central Cretan village of Aphrati, see *IC* 1.5.4. The mention of 'the sacred things' (*ta thina*, 6) may indicate that *dekaton* here refers to the sacred tithe, although it is not certain that the *dekaton* in 5 belongs to the same provision. The text provides for repeated action in the future, probably by officials of the state (5), and for action that takes place after the battle, perhaps involving *astai* ('citizen or resident women', 6–7).

The term *dekaton* ('tenth') occurs twice in the neuter singular (4, 5). The feminine singular *dekatē* was commonly used to refer to the portion of goods (e.g. booty from war, agricultural produce) set aside for the gods. *Dekaton* may refer to booty (e.g. 'tenth share') suggesting that the booty was divided into at least ten shares, presumably for distribution, or it may be used for *dekatē* (tithe for the gods), in which case the phrase 'from the other *dekaton*' suggests that there were at least two sacred portions. Provisions concerning the distribution of booty seized in war occur in several Hellenistic alliances of the Cretan poleis, but are so far attested in only one earlier inscription, the mid fifth-century agreement of Knossos, Tylissos, and Argos (M&L 42, Introd. 7E2). This inscription, with its references both to the distribution of booty (B.4–11), including the disposition of the *dekatē*, and to blood sacrifice, including one made by priests of the Knossians to Poseidon on Mt. Iutos (B.14–17), provides the closest parallels for **A5+6**. The observation that **A5+6** refers to several portions of booty or two or more sacred tithes may suggest that the provision concerns two or more communities. If so, **A5+6** perhaps preserves part of an alliance (as G proposes for **A6**), one of the earliest interstate agreements from Crete, if not the earliest (cf. **G63**, **G80**). Alternatively, Axos alone may have reserved the two sacred tithes for two gods, e.g. Zeus and Poseidon. In the absence of other firm evidence for the worship of Poseidon at Axos, it is tempting to speculate that the inscription might record an alliance between Axos and Knossos, requiring that each of the treaty partners sacrifice to the god of the local extra-urban sanctuary—the Axians to Zeus on Ida and the Knossians to Poseidon on Iutos (= Mt. Juktas?)—and to receive a sacred tithe of the booty. See Perlman 2010: 108–9.

6 If we are correct about *astai* it could mark either the women's civic status (i.e. 'citizen women') or their domicile (i.e. 'townswomen'). The observation that the cognate adjectival form *wastios* appears to have been used at Gortyn to distinguish 'citizens' trials' (*wastiai dikai*, **G13**.h–g2 and **G64**.4) from 'foreigners' trials' (*kseneiai dikai*, **G80**.8) suggests that something more than residency is meant. Confirmation of this comes from Axos itself where the phrase [*kse*]*nas e astas* ('foreign or citizen woman') occurs in the late fourth- or early third-century law (*SEG* 23.566, line 7), suggesting, if rightly restored, that at Axos as at Gortyn the term and its cognates marked civic status.

If 'war', 'tenths', and 'citizen women' all belong to the same context, then **A5+6** provides evidence for the participation of citizen women in the rituals attendant to war. Scholars have noted the connection between goddesses and warriors that the Early Iron Age and early archaic votive assemblages of bronze weapons and armor from several Cretan sanctuaries attest (Perlman 2010: 103–7, 109). The coincidence of votives of female figures indicating that the divinity worshipped was female, and in the case of Gortyn of armed and armored ones, at many of the same sanctuaries, including the temple at Axos where bronze arms and armor were dedicated, has occasioned comment, but no direct connection between the female worshippers who are assumed to have dedicated these figures and the martial interests of the goddesses to whom they were offered has been suggested (Introd. 2A2). If our interpretation is correct, this provision concerning the citizen women may provide a more direct link between the warrior function of the goddess and her female worshippers than has previously been proposed.

A7. *c.*525–500 Current location unknown. FIG. 13

Six lines of text inscribed boustrophedon from the left on a rectangular limestone block.

The block is broken along the right edge and at the lower left corner. The drawings of Halbherr (1884a, Comparetti and Halbherr 1888, Halbherr *ap.* Comparetti 1893) and G appear to record the faint traces of a few letters above line 1, but we are not certain that there was writing there. The text continued to the right, the left, below, and possibly above.

[—]γ̣ηίαι καὶ τ̣ὸσ[—]	→	— and —
[—]ου̣ικοι καὶ μϵ[—]		— and —
[— κ]αθονυμαινϵ[—]		— name (?) —
[—] μὴ ἰόντα . . . [—]		— not going —
[— ἀπ]οδοίη | ἰσ[—]		— he should give back —
[—]ϵ̣μημ[—]		

FIG. 13. Drawing of **A7** (after Halbherr 1884a: 28)

Unless otherwise indicated:

H = Halbherr 1884a: 28 no. 27; Comparetti and Halbherr 1888: 149–50 no. 8; Halbherr *ap.* Comparetti 1893: 405–6 no. 189.

C = Comparetti and Halbherr 1888: 149–50 no. 8; Comparetti 1893: 405–6 no. 189.

Haus. = Haussoullier 1885: 2 no. 2.

1 γ̣: all drawings record two oblique strokes; H records faintly the horizontal stroke of a *delta*. If *gamma*, C's [—πρε(ι)σ]γ̣ηίαι (= πρεσβεία) is the only word attested in Crete ending in *-gēia*. If *delta*, perhaps [— δικά]δ̣ηι· αἰ κα ΙΤ̣ΟΣ[—], '— he should judge; but if —'.

τ̣: H and Haus. record the vertical stroke; C and G record an undotted *tau* in their texts. The letter in Halbherr 1914: 9 resembles *lambda*.

2 ν̣: H, G, and JP record three clear strokes and a faint short fourth stroke; Haus. records *mu*.

Halbherr 1884a: 29 notes that the second *omicron* was inscribed over another sign, possibly a word division (vertical line), and that there is room for a small letter between the final two preserved letters, but that the stone is damaged and no trace survives.

[—]ον̣ικοι: C suggests the end of the name of a *kosmos*.

3 [—κ]αθονυμαινε[—]: from κατονυμαίνομαι? Bile 102–3 attributes the spelling with *theta* to confusion over the use of *tau* and *theta* for the aspirated dental. Hesychius s.v. τᾶλις records the use of the middle for a girl who 'is promised' to someone.

4 Following the *alpha* H suggests an oblique stroke belonging to a triangular letter, a vertical stroke at the right of the letter space, and the upper part of a triangular letter; G's drawing records traces of an oblique stroke belonging to a triangular letter or possibly the first leg of *mu* or *nu*, an *iota*, and the upper part of a triangular letter.

5 Halbherr 1884a: 31 notes that the word division (vertical line) was inscribed over another sign, possibly an *iota*.

ἰσ[—]: possibly ἰς or ἰσ[ς—] (cf. **A1**.12). For ἀπ]οδοίη ἰς, cf. **G72**.1.34–5.

6 ϵ̣: all drawings record the vertical and upper two horizontal strokes of the *epsilon*.

[—]ϵ̣μημ[—]: [θ]ϵ̣́μημ G is possible (aor. inf. of τίθημι or a compound).

It is not possible to draw any conclusions about the subject of **A7**, but two possible words deserve comment.

1 [*Pre*(*i*)s]*gēia*, if correct, is a common term in Cretan interstate agreements of the Hellenistic period where it always means 'embassy'. It is attested in only one early Cretan text (**Pr7**), where it occurs twice (D1, D3); cf. M&L 42.B38–9, where Bile 341 suggests it means 'embassy', but G and VER (I.63) take it to mean 'council', which seems preferable. See Introd. 4B2.

2 [—]*nikoi* is possibly the dative of a personal name ending in -*nikos*. Personal names are rarely attested in our inscriptions; for those that are, see Introd. 5 *ad init.* We cannot determine the context of this possible reference to a personal name.

A9 (K 106 (lines 1–11) & 107 (lines 11–14)). Law concerning sacrifices. *c.*500–450. Current location unknown

Fourteen lines of text inscribed boustrophedon beginning at the left transcribed in 1865 by Colonel T. A. B. Spratt and Churchill Babington. Spratt describes a slab of black marble bearing a 'very curious inscription in characters partially reversed and of very early date' (Spratt 1865: II.77–8; Babington 1865: 424–5). If the block bearing **A9** is marble, it is the only inscribed marble block from archaic Crete. The dimensions of the stone are not recorded, but Spratt's use of the term 'slab' to describe it suggests that it may have resembled a free-standing monument (e.g. a stele) more than a wall block. Spratt's is the last recorded sighting of **A9**. Several years later, Emilio Teza came across a transcription of this text in an account of Crete by the Venetian Francesco Barozzi (Teza 1883; Barozzi 1577: 118). G includes the drawings of both Barozzi and Babington.

At the time of Barozzi's visit to Axos, **A9** was located on the summit of the acropolis; by the nineteenth century it had been transported to a spring in the modern village of Axos where its use as a surface for scrubbing linens appears to have abraded considerably the inscribed surface, making the letters significantly more difficult to read than they were in the sixteenth century.

The text is complete at the right and the left. Babington's drawing (Babington 1865: pl. 2.5) suggests that the lower, left, and upper left edges were preserved, but the first preserved line is clearly not the start of the inscription. Babington's drawing records one additional letter (*tau*) at the end of line 14 that Barozzi does not include. If Babington's drawing is accurate, the text continued below line 14.

A9 uses a vertical line for *mu*; Comparetti (1893: 411; Comparetti and Halbherr 1888) interprets the form as an abbreviation. Other orthographic oddities of **A9** are the apparent use of ο not only for the long and the short vowel sounds, but also for θ (although Barozzi and Babington may not have noticed an inscribed cross-bar or central dot, or the cross-bar or a central dot may have been painted originally), an open rather than a closed *eta*, and a curvy *iota* that always faces left.

ον ἀπ̣ο̣δόμ̣εν ἠ[c.10–13]	→	— to give back [—]
σ̣υνγνοίη αὐτός. τοῖς δ̣' ἰαροῦσ-		he should agree. As for the priests,
ι, ὅτι κα πέρ̣ονται πὰρ τὰ ἠγ-		whatever they should carry off contrary to
ραμένα, αἰ μή τις αὐτὸς δ̣οίη μ-		what is written, unless someone himself
ὴ ὐπ' ἀνάνκας, τιτουϜέσθ̣ο σ-		should give not under compulsion, let him
τατῆρα κατὰν θ̣υσίαν Ϝεκάστ-		pay a stater for each sacrifice
αν καὶ τô κρίος τὰν διπ̣λ̣εία-		and twice the value of the meat.
ν. πορτιπονε̂ν δ' ἆιπερ τôν ἄλ-		One is to declare against (him) just as for
ον. αἰ δ' ὀ κοσμίον μὴ ἀποδοίη τ-		the others. If the *kosmos* should not give
ὰ ἐπιβάλοντα Ϝίσα̣νς τιτ̣ου-		back things that are claimed, let him pay equal.
Ϝ̣έσθ̣ο. κατὰ τὰ αὐτὰ τοῖς		In the same way for the
Κυδαντείοις διδόμεν τρ̣ίτο-		Kydanteia the council is to give in the
ι Ϝέτει τὰν βολὰν ἰς τὰ θ̣ύ-		third year for the sacrifices
ματα δυόδεκα στατῆρανς.		twelve staters.

Barozzi appears to have recorded accurately letters that must have appeared very peculiar to him (e.g. *digamma* and the curved *iota*). Nowhere is it necessary to override what he recorded in order to produce the edited text. The same cannot be said for the transcription of Spratt and Babington; the inscription had clearly deteriorated considerably since Barozzi studied it.

The dotted letters are ones that we read from Barozzi's transcription, although because he was unfamiliar with Cretan letters, some of his transcriptions are wrong, but consistent. These wrongly transcribed signs and the letters that they most likely represent are: *gamma* for *pi* (frequent); *omicron* for *rho* (lines 3, 12); || for *digamma* (line 11); *lambda* for *delta* and *alpha* (frequent); *nu* for *san* (line 2); *omicron* for *theta* (throughout); *pi* for *lambda* (line 7); *tau* for *mu* (line 1).

1–2 Barozzi recorded several dots following the *eta* at the end of line 1—probably to indicate that he could not read any more letters in the line—and then transcribed the end of line 2 (*ΟΙΣΔΙΑΡΟΥΣ* reading from the right), to the right of the dots. The first part of line 2 (*ΣΥΝΓΝΟΙΗΑΥΤΟΣΤ*), the start of which should be aligned with the right edge of the transcription, is instead shifted to the left so that it aligns at the left with the left edge of the transcription. We have no explanation for this.

3–4 The construction πὰρ τὰ ἠγραμένα is not otherwise securely attested on Crete. Cf. *IC* 4.201 πὰρ τὰ ἐ[γραμμένα] and *IC* 1.5.52, line 36 πὰρ τὸ γραφὲν δόγμα.

5 τιτουϝέσθο = τιτευέσθω from *τιτεύομαι 'pay a fine' (Bile 327).

6 κατάν = κατὰ τήν.

7 κρίος = κρέας 'meat' (Bile 200–1).

8 πορτιπονε͂ν = προσφωνεῖν.

τὸν ἄλον: Blass #5128 and K take this as neuter (other offenses), but we prefer the masculine (other offenders). In either case, the construction with the genitive is unusual.

10 ἐπιβάλοντα: 'things that are claimed'. See n. on **G72**.5.23–6.

12 τοῖς Κυδαντείοις: either neuter designating a festival or masculine designating perhaps a tribe or college of priests. The noun should probably be associated with the root κυδα- (from κῦδος 'renown'). Adjectives derived from this root (κυδάλιμος, κύδιμος, κύδιστος, κυδρά) appear frequently as divine and heroic epithets in poetry, although no such epithet is attested as a cult title on Crete. Personal names based on the root κυδα- are common on Crete, e.g. from Axos Τηλέμναστος Κύδαντος (*IC* 2.5.35).

K divides **A9** into two distinct laws (lines 1–11 and 11–14) both of which treat cult. The asyndeton in line 11 does suggest the beginning of a new provision, but the expression *kata ta auta* 'in the same way' (11) ties the two together. We interpret the inscription as a single law. It is one of the few inscriptions included here that appears to be wholly concerned with the performance of sacred ritual. See Introd. 9C.

1–2 preserve a few words from the last two lines of a provision the details of which are not retrievable but perhaps concern the return of sacrificial meat that someone other than a priest (2–3) has misappropriated.

2–8 provide the penalties for priests who carry off portions of the sacrifice contrary to (presumably larger than) what is written unless someone—perhaps the butcher or another official charged with distributing the sacrificial animal—willingly gives the portions to them.

3–4 'Contrary to what is written' could refer to a different law or to a provision that is lost in the missing portion of the inscription.

5–8 If the priest was found guilty, he was to pay one stater for each sacrificial victim and 'the double'. Sokolowski (1962: 184 no. 113) and K 107 understand 'the double' as a double portion of meat, either double the portion of meat to which the priest was entitled (Sokolowski) or double the portion of meat that the priest unlawfully carried off (K). The latter is more likely; elsewhere 'the double' refers to a fine based upon the value of the goods at issue (e.g. **G72**.6.41–3; **G78**.6). In either case, if the state funded the sacrifice it is likely that the fines were paid to the state (11–14).

8–9 The procedure for bringing a case against a priest accused of misappropriating sacrificial portions is to be the same as 'for the others', probably other people (i.e. non-priests?) similarly accused of misappropriating portions of the sacrifice.[363]

[363] A law from Chios concerning the priesthood of Eileithyia provides a useful parallel for this situation (*SEG* 35.923, lines 22–3): a priestess who takes a portion of the sacrifice other than that prescribed for her in

9–11 The *kosmos* was responsible for executing the judgment and was liable for the full amount—a stater per sacrifice plus the value of the meat—in the event that he did not exact payment from the priests. The implication of the formulation with the participle 'the one serving as *kosmos*' (*o kosmion*) rather than the noun '*o kosmos*' is not clear.

11–14 Although asyndeton in 11 indicates that 11–14 is in some sense distinct from 1–11, 'In the same way' (11) most likely refers to provisions in the missing portion of the text.

11–12 *Kydanteiois* is not otherwise attested (see n.). It could designate either a festival ('for the *Kydanteia*') or a group of some kind ('to the *Kydanteioi*'), e.g. tribesmen or priests. Certainty is not possible, but we think the former is more likely.

12–13 'In the third year' most likely indicates a sacrifice that is celebrated every third year. For the same formulation, see **G80**.2–3.

13 The council (*boulē*) is very rarely attested in the epichoric inscriptions from Crete. See Introd. 4B2.

A10. Law possibly concerning inheritance? *c.*500–450. Current location unknown. Fig. 14

A10 is inscribed on the opposite faces of a limestone block. 10A consists of seven lines and B of eight lines of text inscribed boustrophedon beginning at the left. The block is broken across the top and the bottom. The text is complete at the right of A (left of B), but incomplete at the left of A (right of B).

The letters of B are larger and appear to be more widely spaced than those of A, but the shapes of the letters on both sides are very similar. A and B share several orthographic oddities with **A9**: all *iotas* face left (although the *iotas* of 10 are angular rather than curvy as in **A9**), a vertical stroke is used for *mu*, and there is no occurrence of a word division. The text could be continuous; if so, it is not possible to determine on which face the text begins.

A	[—]δ̣ε̣π̣αι[1–2] →		
	[.]ε τον μο[—]	— the —	2
	[—]παι· τὸν δ̣’	— the opposing litigant —	3–4
	ἀντίμολο[ν —]		
	[—] ἐπὶ δὲ τ-	— upon the —	5–6
	οῖς τε[—]		
	[—]σεσε		

the law is to be fined the same as butchers who misappropriate part of the victim. For a discussion of this and other laws with penalty clauses for cult personnel, see Lupu 2005: 314.

FIG. 14. **A10A**, left (drawing after Haussoullier 1885: 3); center (drawing after Halbherr 1884a: 22); **A10B**, right (drawing after Halbherr 1884a: 22).

B [—] . οι . ϵ . [—]	→	
[—] ἀ̣ναιρε̂-	— he should inherit —	2–3
ται σ . [—]		
[—]ιοτο[1–2]		
τοινϵ[—]		
[—]ι̣ϵμϵν κ-	— and —	6–7
α̣ὶ . [1–2] . [—]		

Unless otherwise indicated:

H = Halbherr 1884a: 22–3; Comparetti and Halbherr 1888: 159–62 no. 11a and b; Halbherr *ap.* Comparetti 1893: 416–18 no. 192a and b.

C = Comparetti and Halbherr 1888: 159–62 no. 11a and b; Comparetti 1893: 416–18 no. 192a and b.

Haus. = Haussoullier 1885: 3

A

1 δ̣ϵ̣π̣αι: after the drawing of Haus.

2 μο[—]: perhaps a form of μολϵ́ο, e.g. τὸν μο[λίοντα?] C, but there are many other possibilities.

3 δ̣: Haus. records the upper tip of an oblique stroke at the right edge of the stone.

5–6 τοι̂ς τϵ[—]: perhaps τοι̂ς τϵ́[κνοις—?], but there are many other possibilities.

B

1 H and G record the lower tips of three vertical strokes before *omicron* and before and after *epsilon.*

3 H and G record the lower tip of a vertical stroke at the right edge of the stone.

6 ι̣: H and G record the top stroke of *iota*; *nu* is also possible.

[—]ιϵμϵν: perhaps [—]ι̣/ν̣ ἔμϵν or [—ἰ]ν̣ϵ́μϵν, but there are other possibilities.

7 α̣: H and G record an oblique stroke at the left edge of the stone.

A The term 'opposing litigant' (*antimolon*, line 4) and possibly a form of 'to plead' (*mo*[*l*—], line 2) suggest that A perhaps concerns judicial procedure.

B possibly concerns inheritance, as 'take up for oneself' (*anairetai*, lines 2–3) occurs elsewhere in the early laws from Crete only in the context of inheritance (n. ad **G72**.5.24–5).

If the texts on the two faces belong to the same inscription, this last observation may provide some support for reading *epi tois te*[*knois*] ('in the hands of the children') in A5–6 above (see n.).

A11. *c.*525–500. Current location unknown

A11 consists of six fragments (a–f) of inscribed limestone blocks discovered in 1899 by De Sanctis and Halbherr on the acropolis of Axos in the vicinity of the acropolis building. Only fragment 'a', with a few letters from each of seven lines inscribed boustrophedon beginning at the right, preserves some meaningful text.

Apart from the circumstances of their discovery and the general appearance of the letters and the stones on which they are inscribed, there is no good reason to argue that any two of the fragments belong to the same inscription.

Frag. 'a' is broken across the upper edge. The drawings of Halbherr 1899–1900: 67 and G indicate that the original edges of the lower right corner of the block are preserved, but the text does not wrap around at lines 4–5 or 6–7. It probably continued onto another block to the right. A wide un-inscribed band along the lower edge indicates that there was at most one additional line of text running from left to right that stopped before the left edge of frag. 'a'.

[—]ν ἢ παϝ̣[—] ←
[—]μον | τον[—]
[— α]ι[.] μ̣ὴ ἀποϝεί[π —] — not declare? —
[—]ιας | ἐλιο . [.] | ὀβ̣[—]
[—]ροσ̣[. . .]ηι | ἀλο̣[—]
[—]α̣σσ[.]ς κα[—]
[—]νο[.] . ολ[—]

---

1 α̣: H and G record the lower part of the right oblique.
ϝ̣: H and G record clearly the two oblique strokes and faintly the 'tail'.
3 μ̣: H and G record the final two strokes; *nu* is also possible.
[— α]ι[.] μ̣ὴ: [— α]ι[.]ν ἢ is also possible.
4 H and G record the upper tips of two oblique strokes after the first *omicron*; *gamma*, *digamma*, *lambda*, *mu*, *nu*, and *san* are possible.
β̣: H and G record clearly the vertical stroke and G faintly the loops.
ὀβ̣[—]: ὀβ̣[ολο—]?
5 σ̣: H and G record the four strokes of *san*, but *mu* appears to be possible.
ο̣: H and G record the upper part.

6 α̣: H and G record the lower part of the right oblique.
7 H does not record any traces of letters after line 6. G records space for two letters after the first omicron with no traces in the first space and the final two strokes of *mu* or *nu* in the second.

---

3 The verb for 'declare' (*apoweipen*) occurs in several different senses in the early laws of Crete: 'renounce', 'refuse', or 'declare'; see n. on **G72**.9.37–8. The meaning here cannot be determined.

A12. Early sixth century. Heraklion Museum (Inv. nos. 97 and 98). Fig. 15

A12 is inscribed on four fragments (A = a + a^1, B = b + b^1) of limestone that were re-cut for reuse as a basin of some kind. Halbherr 1899–1900: 70 noted that the fragments were found 'tempio in basso', presumably in its vicinity rather than reused in the construction of the temple, as was *IC* 2.5.14c (Levi 1933: 51). The upper and right edges of **12**A are original; the left edge has been re-cut. The upper edge of **12**B is original; the right and left edges have been re-cut. The original shape of the blocks cannot be determined, but they appear to have been fairly large,[364] suggesting their initial use as wall blocks. The four fragments are currently cemented together to form a rectangular monument.

12A is a single line of text inscribed from the right across the center of the face. B has two lines of text, the first from the right across the top, the second from the left across the lower portion. The text in B2 dips down in the middle, presumably to avoid a rough spot on the block that was later trimmed off for reuse; the lower half of the letters *ΙΟΠ* are missing, either because they were trimmed off when the blocks were re-cut, or because they were inscribed on a block below.

The letters in A and B2 appear very similar both in form and height (0.70–0.75 m., omicron: 0.45 m.). The letters in B1 are approximately half the size of the others, but the angular head of the *rho* and the *epsilon* with a long tail are similar to those in A and B2. If A and B originally belonged to the same monument, it is not possible to determine their position relative to one another.

A	[—] ὀ καρπὸς | ἐπ̣ο̣γ . [—]	←	— the produce —
B	[—] . [.]ερ . [—]	←	
	[—] | μήτι ὀ̣πήλεν̣	→	— is to owe nothing —

A
π̣: the lower part the vertical stroke is visible.
ο̣: a faint trace of the lower arc is visible.
There is a vertical stroke following *gamma*.

364 The dimensions of **A12**A (a + a^1): alt: 0.19 m., w: 0.78 m.; dimensions of **A12**B (b + b^1): alt: 0.19 m., w: 0.64 m., max. th: 0.37 m.

Fig. 15. **A12**

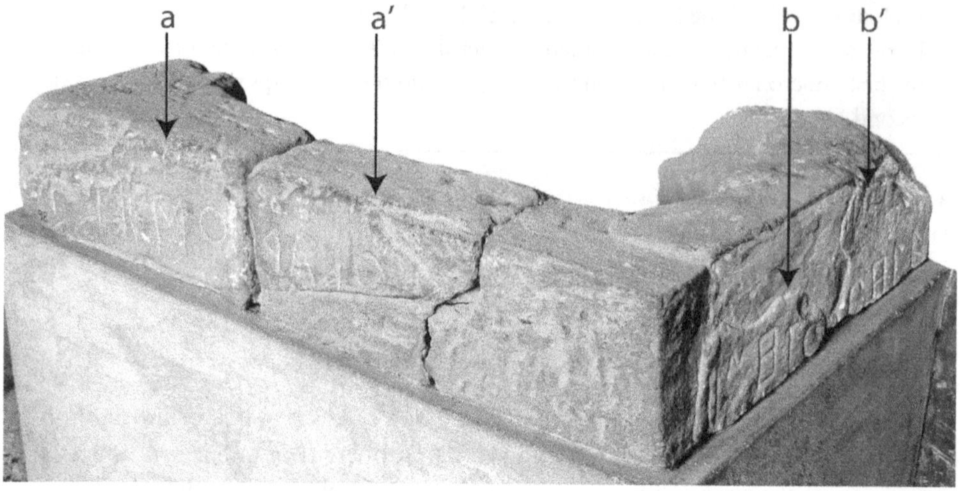

B

1 Before *epsilon* there is a space without any traces followed by the lower part of a vertical stroke.

The lower tip of a vertical stroke is visible after *rho*.

2 ο̣: the ghost of the upper curve is visible.

ν̣: the left leg is visible.

Opēlen ('owe') permits the identification of B as a part of a provision from a law concerning the assessment or payment of debts. 'Produce' and 'owe' occur together in **Ele13**.3.

Axos1 (Jeffery 1949: 34–6 with Figs. 10–14, K 105, VER I.29). Law regulating workers. *c.*525–500. Heraklion Museum (Inv. no. 279a + b). Fig. 16

Seventeen lines of text inscribed boustrophedon beginning at the right on two joining fragments of a smoothly dressed limestone block (a = 1–7; b = 7–18), acquired by the Heraklion Museum in 1947. The local families of Axos who had discovered the fragments reported that both were found on the acropolis. The left and lower edges of b are preserved. The text is complete at the left; it is not possible to determine if 18 is the final line of the inscription. Jeffery 1949: 36 suggested that the block may have come from the corner of an exterior wall of the temple on the east slope of the acropolis.

[—]λ̣ε̣τ̣[. . . *c.*6 . . .] ←		
[. . *c.*4 . .] . ς ταυ[τ —]		
[—]εν | τὸν ϝ̣[εργ-	3–4	— the worker and —
α]στὰν καὶ τ[—]		
[—] ϝεργαστὰς̣	5–6	— if X and] the worker agree —
συνγνοῖεν̣ [—]		
[— ϝε]ργαστᾶ ἦ ἰ-	7–8	— of the worker in the event that he
νεκυράκ̣[σει —]		should accept a pledge —
[—]όμεθα ἦ ἀ-	9–10	— if] we [. . .] or we sell —

ποδιδόμ̣[εθα —]
[—]άκοντα σ-
τατῆρας [—]
[—] τôι τόκα κ-
οσμίον̣[τι —]
[—]ς̣ | αἰ μὴ
βοαζρο[μι —]
[—]ε κόσμ-
ος πεν̣[τε (?) —]

11–12 —]ty staters —

13–14 — to the one who is *kosmos* at the time —

15–16 — if not *Boazro*[*mios* (?) —

17–18 — *kosmos* five (?) —

FIG. 16. **Axos 1**

1 λ̣: Jeffery suggests that *rho* is also possible, but the oblique stroke does not resemble the upper part of the head of the *rho* of this mason.

ẹ: all four strokes of the *epsilon* are visible, but Jeffery notes that the rectangular shape of the letter resembles more an *eta*.

ṭ: the lower half of a vertical stroke is visible; *kappa*, *pi*, and word division (vertical stroke) are also possible.

2 The lower tip of an oblique stroke is visible before the *sigma*.

Jeffery records traces of a letter after *upsilon*, but we do not.

3–4 τὸν ϝ̣[εργα]στάν: τôν Ϝεργαστâν is also possible.

5 ṣ: three oblique strokes are visible. Jeffery 1949 prefers *nu*, but because the second and third strokes extend to the bottom of the letter space, *san* is preferable.

7 ἤ: adv. 'where' or 'when', but the temporal meaning 'when' seems to be required here; for the use of ἤ + subj. without κα, see Willetts 1967: 67–8.

8 κ̣: the lower part of the vertical and the lower oblique of *kappa* are visible.

7–8 ἰνεκυράκ̣[σει] = Att. ἐνεχυράσῃ; ἰνεκυράκ̣[σοντι] is also possible. ἰνεκύρα | [—] Jeffery.

9–10 ἀποδιδόμ̣[εθα]: ἀποδίδομ̣[εν] is also possible; see com. on **G41**.4.7–8.

13 τόκα = τότε (Dialect 33).

16 βοαζρο[μίο μηνός?] Jeffery. The absence of the definite article recommends the restoration of the term as the month name rather than as the festival name τὰ βοαζρο[μία].

17 [ὀ δ]ὲ? Jeffery.

It appears that a considerable amount of text has been lost at the right, thus making it impossible to conclude very much about the subject, but the law clearly regulates the activities of workers, who are mentioned three times in 3–7.

5–6 imply that a worker has the legal standing to enter into an agreement with someone else (the polis? a security-holder?) and so is probably a citizen, either of Axos or perhaps of another polis, rather than an individual of dependent status; but the possibility that a slave or serf could make an agreement on his own cannot be ruled out (Introd. 5A7).

7–8 These lines (which do not necessarily belong to the same provision as 5–6) provide for the securing of a debt. For the meaning of *inekurazo* ('accept a pledge'), see comm. ad **G43Ba**7–8. The verb could be restored as either singular or plural, and if the former, the subject could be the worker, the one with whom the worker came to an agreement (3–4), or someone else entirely.

9–10 The first-person verbs are puzzling. Jeffery concludes that they suggest 'the wording of some kind of testimony or oath'. Elsewhere such verbs occur only in the enactment formula of **Da1** and in an uncertain context in **G87**, neither of which sheds much light on their use here.

11–12 prescribe a monetary amount of at least thirty staters. Jeffery suggests restoring '[thir]ty'; 'fifty' is also possible.

15–16 preserve the only reference to the month *Boazromios* (*Boedromios*) on Crete. It is possible that the month establishes a temporal limit for some activity, as does the occurrence of a month name in **Dr3**. If 17–18 belong to the same provision, the *kosmos* was perhaps required to do something before the beginning of or during the month.

Axos2 (*SEG* 23.565, Manganaro 1965, Bile 51 no. 45, VER II.18). Law concerning payment of fines. *c.*500–450. Rethymno Museum (Inv. no. 39). FIG. 17

Axos2 is inscribed on the front and back faces of a grey limestone stele. No original edge is preserved. Both are inscribed boustrophedon, 2A beginning at the left and B at the right. B3 preserves the only example of archaic paragraphing from Axos (Introd. 3D5).

The shapes of the letters on both faces are very similar and may well have been inscribed by the same mason; if so, A and B may belong to the same text. They also share two orthographic features: all *iotas* face left and a vertical stroke is used for *mu* (A8). The letter *xi* is represented here for the first time at Axos (A3, 6); its peculiar form (three parallel vertical strokes with a horizontal stroke across the top) may be compared with the *xi* that appears in several inscriptions from Argos that date to the period *c.*475–450 (Jeffery 1990: 151–2).

A [—]ονταπ[—] →	
[—] ἔκηι τὸν [—]	— he should have the —
[— μ]ἢ̣ πράξαι[εν —]	— they should not (?) exact payment —
[—]το τον πυ[—]	
[—]ινασθ̣α[—]	
[— π]ράξαι[ε]ν̣ [—]	— they should exact payment —
[—]α̣ι τôι ἐ[—]	— to the —

FIG. 17. **Axos2A**

[—] κόσμοι̣ [—] — to the *kosmos* (?) —
[— ο̣?]τ[.]ο[—]

B [—]νισ[—] ←
[—]δ̣υοδ̣ϵ[—] →
[—] τόκα [μ (?) —] → — then —
[—]ασθ̣ον[—] ←
[—] . οντι[—] →

A

VER publish only side A.

1 [—]ονταπ[—]: ζο̣ντα VER, but the *zeta* is not visible. Perhaps a number, e.g. [τριάκ]οντα.

3 [— μ]ἠ̣: [—αἰ δὲ μ]ή̣ Manganaro. μή is likely, but not certain.

5 θ̣: the complete circumference of the circle is clearly visible, but there is no trace of an interior dot or cross-bar.

[—]ιναсθ̣α[—]: [— ἠμ]ίνας θ̣α[—] Manganaro.

7 α̣: the lower part of the left oblique is visible.

[—]α̣ι τôι ἐ[—]: [—]αι τὸ ἰϵ[—]Manganaro, Bile; [—]α̣ι τοὶ ἐ[ρευταί] or ἐ[σπράτται] VER are only possible if the terms are dat. sing. (the nom. pl. article is οἰ not τοί, Bile 205 n. 192).

8 ι̣: the lower part of *iota* is visible.

κόσμοι dat. sing. or nom. pl.

9 Manganaro records a dotted *omicron* before the *tau*.

B

2 δ̣ύο δ̣ὲ [—] or δ̣υόδ̣ϵ[κα —]?

3 τόκα = τότϵ: also possible are [—]το κα[μ (?) —] or [—] τὸ/τô κα[μ (?) —].

Manganaro records a *mu* after the *alpha*.

4 θ̣: nothing of the interior dot or cross-bar of *theta* is visible.

5 A short oblique stroke at bottom right of the letter space before *omicron* is visible, perhaps *kappa*?

Site

Datala was situated in north central Crete between Knossos and Lato, but its precise location remains uncertain. The toponym has been restored in a late second-century description of the border of Lato where the majority of the landmarks used to trace the border are natural features (*IC* 1.16.5, line 64 *Datt*[*alla*]). Faure (1967: 99–100 and map) identifies this *Datt*[*alla*] as a peak on the border between Lato and Lyktos high up on the east side of the Lasithi massif. The toponym has also been restored in **Lyktos1B**4–5 (n. and comm. ad loc.) where it appears to be a place to the west of the Lasithi massif in the vicinity of Lyktos. Watrous 1982: 39–40 suggests that the ancient settlement at Agios Giorgios Papoura in northern Lasithi was Datala. Evidence for habitation there dates from the Early Iron Age through the Archaic period (*c*.970–480), when it was the largest settlement in this area. Viviers 1994 identifies Datala with the ancient remains at Aphrati where Levi 1927–9 located one of the nucleated settlements of ancient Arkades.

The remains at Aphrati (Prophitis Elias) include a small classical or Hellenistic fortress at the summit of the hill that was supplied with water from a cistern (Levi 1927–9: 32–7; Coutsinas 2013: 419, no. 22), residential districts on the protected eastern slopes of the acropolis dating from the sixth century to *c*.400 (Levi 1927–9: 38–57, Lebessi 1973: 458–60), and an archaic hearth building with benches along its interior walls located on the southeast slope of the acropolis that was in use during the seventh and sixth centuries. Lebessi, who excavated the building, identified it as a temple (Lebessi 1970: 415–18, 1973: 455–8). Viviers 1994: 244–9 suggested instead that it was an *andreion* or *bouleuterion* (for the *andreion* at Datala, see **Da1**B11–14 and comm. ad A2–3). Early Iron Age cemeteries (*c*.970–630) were located on the upper western slopes of the acropolis (Levi 1927–9: 78–400; for a tomb of the sixth century, see Lebessi 1983).

Text

Da1 (*SEG* 27.631, J–MD, VER I.22). Agreement concerning the appointment of a *poinikastas*. *c*.500. British Museum 1969. 4–2.1. Figs. 18, 19

Da1 is inscribed on the two faces of a semi-circular bronze plaque, resembling in form a mitra (abdominal guard). If in its original use the object was a functional mitra, the mitra's typically convex form appears to have been hammered flat prior to inscribing (Raubitschek 1972). Most of the right edge of A (left edge of B) and the upper left edge of A (upper right edge of B) are preserved. A few letters have been lost at the left edge of A (right edge of B) and along the bottom of A. The upper edge appears to have been trimmed prior to inscribing, removing the upper half of two of the three holes that were punched along the upper edge (the central hole is completely preserved) and used for attaching the mitra to a belt (if functional), hanging the object for display, or both.

The provenance of this inscribed bronze mitra or mitra-like object is not known. The alphabet, particularly the use of two concentric circles for *omega* (rendered here with the sign ⊙), suggests that it comes from somewhere in the vicinity of Lyktos and possibly Aphrati (J–MD 122–3). For the sign at Aphrati, see *SEG* 52.830–1, 834–5 (inscribed bronze armor believed to have come from Aphrati, seventh to sixth centuries). VER assert that the object comes from the archaic hearth building at Aphrati (see above Site) where fragments of bronze armor were discovered. This is possible, but by no means certain.

The text on A, which begins at the right with an enactment formula (A1–2), consists of twenty-two lines written boustrophedon. It is possible that one line of text has been lost at the bottom of A. B consists of seventeen lines of text written boustrophedon beginning at the right. There is a *vacat* at the end of B17 and sufficient space below B17 for the upper parts of letters to be visible were there another line of text. It appears, then, that the end of the text on B is preserved.

The letters on the two sides are quite similar. Only in the case of *gamma*, inscribed as a nearly vertical long stroke with a very short oblique head on A and, in the single example on B (B6), as a triangular letter with two long oblique strokes, do the letter forms on the two sides differ. J–MD 119–20 noted that the text on B gives the overall impression that it was produced by a more accomplished writer than the text on A, suggesting that there were two writers and that the texts on the two faces, though clearly related, may not have been continuous (cf. van Effenterre 1973: 45–6 and Koerner 1981: 188–9 who identify B11–17 as an addendum). We imagine instead that the writer realized as he started writing on B that he would have ample room to complete his assignment and so he began to form slightly larger letters (A: 0.003–0.006 m; B: 0.004–0.008 m), which in turn enabled him to shape them better. We believe that the text on B continues that on A (comm. ad B1).

It is difficult to envisage **Da1**, with its small letters written on a thin and fragile sheet of bronze, as a public document in the same sense as the laws and agreements that were inscribed on stone. We suggest that **Da1** may have been written for and possibly even by Spensithios as a personal copy for himself and his family, perhaps copied from a public inscription in the city.

The letter forms, morphology, and the absence of word division indicate a date of *c.*500 (J–MD 120–2).

We have autopsied the inscription. Even with the aid of magnification (a hand lens) the letters are very difficult to make out. In dotting letters, we follow for the most part J–MD 122–3.

A

Θιοί. ἔϜαδε Δαταλεῦσι καὶ ἐσπένσαμες̣ πόλις ←
Σπενσιθίʘι, ἀπὸ πυλᾶν πέντε ἀπ᾽ ἐκάστας, θροπά-
ν τε καὶ ἀτέλειαν πάντʘν αὐτʘ̑ι τε καὶ γενιᾶι ʘ̆́-
ς κα πόλι τὰ δαμόσια τά τε θιήια καὶ τἀνθρʘ́πινα
ποινικάζ̣εν τε καὶ μναμονεῦϜην. ποινικάζεν δὲ
[π]όλι καὶ μναμονεῦϜεν τὰ δαμόσια μήτε τὰ θιήι-
α μήτε τἀνθρʘ́πινα μηδέν᾽ ἄλον αἰ μὴ Σπενσίθ[ι]-
[ο]ν αὐτόν τε καὶ γενιὰν τôνυ, αἰ μὴ ἐπαίροι τ-
ε καὶ κέλοιτο ἢ αὐτὸς Σπενσίθιος ἢ γενιὰ
[τ]ôνυ ὅσοι δρομῆς εἶεν τʘ̑ν [υἰ]ʘ̑ν οἰ πλίες.
μισθὸν δὲ δόμεν τὸ ἐνιαυτὸ τʘ̑ι ποινι[κ]-
[α]στᾶι πεντήϙοντά τε προϙόος κλεύκιο-
ς κηνδυ̣[.]ε[. .]ς ἰκατιδαρκμίος ἢ καλ̣[ϙ]-
ό̣ς· δόμεν δὲ τὸ κλεῦϙος ἐς τô μόρο ὄ-
πʘ κα λῆι ἐλέσθαι. αἰ δὲ μὴ δοίη τὸ κλε[ῦϙ]-
[ο]ς̣ αιδε̣ . . . σ̣[c.3–4]α[.]εσδ . . . ς ϙόσμ-
ο̣ς ἐπεστ̣αϙʘ̀ς ἀ[c.4]ι[c.4]λ̣ε[.]εκ[.]
[1 ?]σαι ἀπλοπία̣[ι .]α̣[.]α̣ι μὴ αὐτοῖσ-
ι . . . πολ[. .]αν̣εσ̣η̣μ̣εν τʘ̑ι ϙόσ-
[μʘι c.7]ε̣[.] τεμένια πε[.] . ϙ-
[c.2] τὸ Ϝῖσον λακὲν ϙό̣[σμʘι ?]ασ[c.4]
[. . . . . c.17 . . . .]α̣[. . . c.6 . . .]

1–5 Gods. The Dataleis decided and we the polis promise to Spensithios, from the tribes five from each, rations and full tax exemption to himself and his offspring so that they both write and remember for the polis public matters both sacred and secular.

5–10 No one other than Spensithios himself and his offspring is to write and remember for the polis public matters, neither sacred nor secular, unless chosen or bidden by either Spensithios himself or his offspring, the majority of his sons who are adults.

11–15 As an annual stipend it (the polis ?) is to give the *poinikastas* fifty *prokooi* of must, [—] worth twenty drachmas (?), or bronze; it is to provide the must from whatever portion he should wish to take (the must).

15–16 If he (?) should not give the must [—]

16–17 [—] the *kosmos* who is in charge [—]

18–19 [—] without fault [—] not to them [—]

19–20 [—] to the *kos*[*mos* —] revenue from the sacred precinct [—]

21 [—] is to obtain the equal to the *ko*[*smos* ? —]

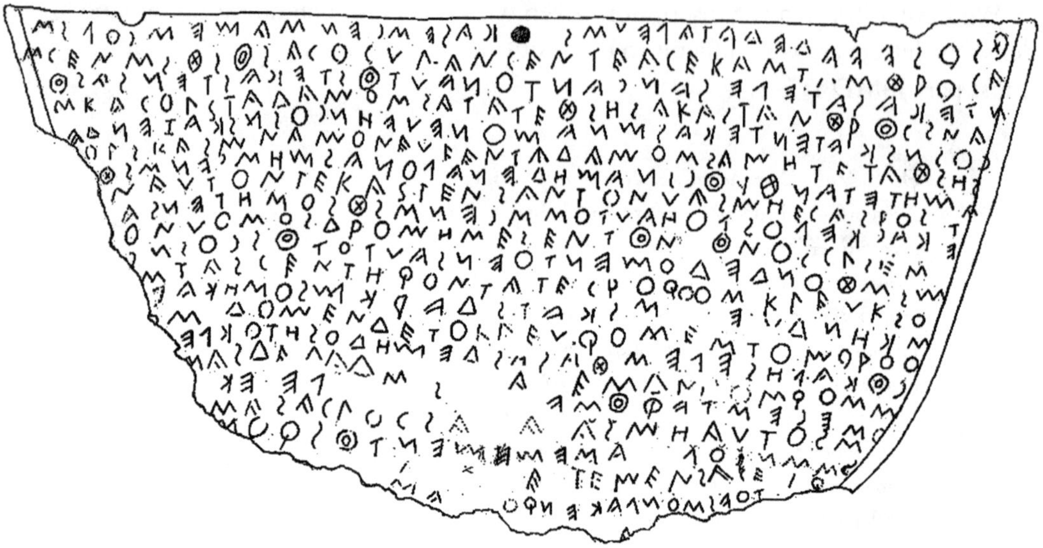

FIG 18. Da1A (drawing after JP)

B

τὸ Ϝῖσον λακὲν τὸν ποινικαστάν· καὶ παρῆμε- ←
ν καὶ συνῆμεν ἐπί τε θιηίʘν καὶ επ' ἀνθρʘπί-
νʘν πάντε ὅπε καὶ ὁ ϙόσμος εἴη καὶ τὸν ποινι-
καστάν· καὶ ὅτιμί κα θιʘ̑ι ἰαρεὺς μῆι δίαλο-
[ς] θύεν τε τὰ δαμόσια θύματα τὸ⟨ν⟩ ποινικαστὰ-
ν καὶ τὰ τεμένια ἔκεν. μήδ' ἐπάγραν ἦμ[ε]-
[ν] μήδε ῥύτιον αἰλε̑ν τὸν ποινικαστάν. δ-
ίκα δέ, ὅτερόν κα λʘληται ὁ ποινικασ[τ]-
[ὰ]ς, αἶπερ οἰ ἄλοι κρήσεται, ἦν ϙόσ[[π]]-
μοι ἀ δίκα Ϝοι τέλεται, ἄλε δὲ οὐδὲ
ἔν. δίκαια ἐς ἀνδρήιον δʘσει δ-
έκα πέλεϙυς κρέʘν ἆι κα ϙʘ̑ι ἄλọ[ι]
[ἀπ?]άρϙʘνται καὶ τὸ ἐπενιαύτιον· τὸ
δὲ λάκσιον συνϜαλεῖ. ἄλο δὲ μ[ηδ]-
[ὲ]ν ἐπάνανϙον ἦμεν αἴ κα μὴ λῆι
δόμεν· ἦμεν δὲ τὰ θιήια τ[ʘ̑ι]
[c.4]ίστʘι. *vacat*

1–6 The *poinikastas* is to obtain the equal; wheresoever the *kosmos* should be, so too the *poinikastas* is to be present and attend at both sacred and secular (activities), and for whatever god there should be no clear (?) priest, the *poinikastas* is to perform the public sacrifices and to have the revenue from the sanctuary (?).

6–11 There is to be neither seizure of the person nor of the property of the *poinikastas*. As for a trial, whichever the *poinikastas* wishes, he is to use, just as the others, or his trial will be before a *kosmos*, but not any other way.

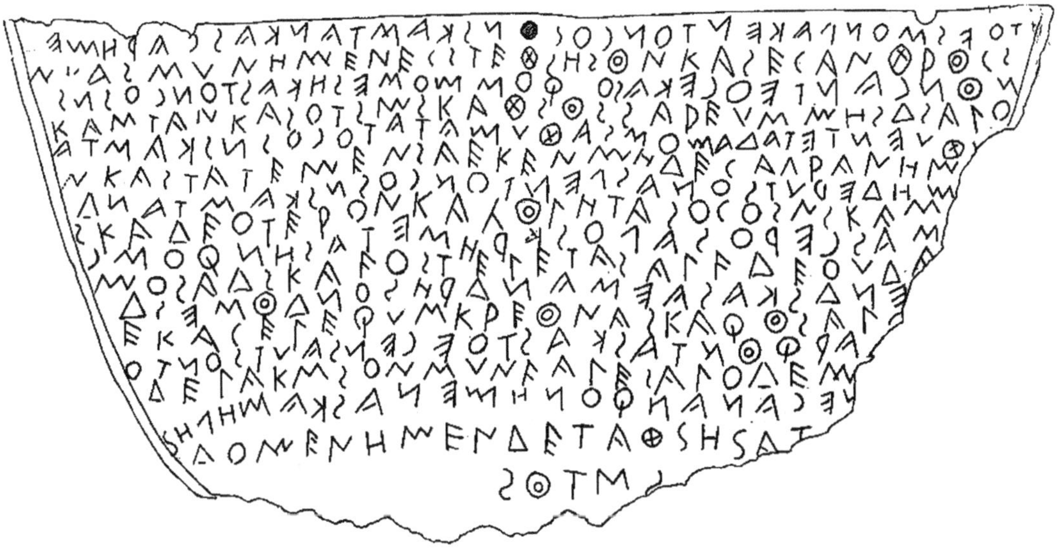

FIG 19. Da1B (drawing after JP)

11–16 (As) *dikaia* to the *andreion* he shall give ten axes of meat when the others offer the first fruits (?) and the yearly obligation (?); but he will collect (?) the *laksion*. Nothing other is to be required unless he should wish to give.

16–17 The sacred matters are to be for the [—].

A

1 ἔϜαδε Δαταλεῦσι· καὶ ἔσπενσ' ἀ μὲν πόλις, 'The Dataleis resolved. Whereas the city poured a libation for Spensithios' (Raubitschek 1972); but the sense would be very strained and, as Beattie 1975: 11 notes, there is no answering δέ.

Δαταλεῦσι: the ethnic also occurs in the signature written on the ring-handle of a sixth-century bronze vase from the sanctuary of Hermes and Aphrodite at Kato Syme Viannou, Δαμόθετος ἐπόεσ' ὀ Δαταλές (Lebessi 1975b: 191).

ἐσπένσαμες̣ = ἐσπένσαμεν (σπένδω). The first three strokes of the final *san* are visible; J–MD and JP record the fourth stroke of the *san* faintly in their drawings. For the first-person plural, cf. **G87**.2.

2 For the personal name Σπενσίθιος, which is not otherwise attested, see comm. ad A2, B4–6.

2–3 θροπάν = τροφήν; Dialect 1, 5.

3 γενιά = γενεά; Dialect 3.

3–4 ὅς κα: this is the only occurrence of the conjunction ὡς in our texts. J–MD 148 propose that it belongs to a pre-Doric substrate and was replaced elsewhere on Crete by ἆι. We understand ὡς as indicating both purpose and condition ('in order that he might', 'on the condition that he'). κα (= ἄν) is rare with ὡς (= ὥστε). It is also possible that ὥσκα = ὥστε (but cf. J–MD 131).

4 τά τε θιήια καὶ τἀνθρόπινα: the same expression in **G72**.10.42–3 with τὰ θῖνα.

5 ζ̣: the vertical and upper horizontal strokes are legible.

ποινικάζεν: most scholars understand the verb to mean 'to write' and derive it from *φοίνιξ* ('purple-red'), but its precise formation is uncertain (see J–MD 133). Beattie's 1975: 26–31 association of *ποινικάζεν* with *ποινή* ('blood-money', 'requital') has few adherents. Cf. **Ele11** *ποινικα[κσίε (?)]* and **Eltynia1** *π̣οινικήια*.

μναμονεῦϝην: cf. *μναμονεῦϝεν* in the next line. The latter is the standard form (Dialect 20), and J–MD 133 and others conclude that *-ην* is an error; but more likely it is 'another example of the occasional variation we find between *epsilon* and *eta*' (Bile 236).

8 *τôνυ* = *τοῦδε* (Dialect 35); see also **Ele11**.3, 4 and **Lyktos1B**. J–MD 133–4 attribute this form to a pre-Doric, Arcado-Cyprian substrate, rather than to later influence. They observe that if **Da1** comes from Aphrati, where the pronoun *ὅδε* is attested in the same sense as Attic *οὗτος*, the pronominal system at Aphrati was the same as that of Arcadian where *ὅνυ* looks backward and *ὅδε* looks forward. For the use of *ὅδε* at Aphrati, see *SEG* 52.831–5, 837–40 (inscribed bronze armor believed to have come from Aphrati, seventh–sixth century).

ἐπαίροι: the derivation is uncertain; see note on **G21**.7, where we discuss the possible meanings 'persuade' or 'choose' (someone else to write and remember).

10 *δρομῆς* = *δρομείς*; see Dialect 40 and Introd. 5A2.

12–13 *κλεύκιος*: a variant spelling of (the gen. sing. of) *γλεῦκος* 'must', 'new wine' (cf. **G77**B3).

13 *υ̣*: J–MD record the upper tips of the two oblique strokes.

κηνδυ̣[.]ε[..]ς: J–MD 137 suggest that the *τε* (in 12) points to a *καί*, here crasis of *καί* and a word beginning in *ἐ-/ἠ-*, i.e. *καὶ ἐνδυ̣-* (or *ἠνδυ̣-*). Beattie 1975: 32–3 suggests *καὶ ἐνδυτῆρας* and the otherwise unattested meaning of 'storage jar' for *ἐνδυτήρ*; cf. Hesychius s.v. *ἐνδύτας· αὐλωτὸς στάμνος*, possibly a storage jar fitted with pipes for drawing off liquid. The form may be a genitive with *ἰκατιδαρκμίος* ('twenty-drachmas worth of') or an accusative plural (figs or storage jars 'worth twenty drachmas').

13–14 *καλ̣[ϙ]ό̣ς* (= *χαλκούς*): *λ̣*: we read the two oblique strokes that resemble a *lambda* or the first two strokes of *nu*, *san*, or *mu*. J–MD 138 read *rho* (or *lambda*? 138 n. 23), although the *rhos* in **Da1** have rounded heads; *ο̣*: J–MD record the upper right curve of the *omicron*.

J–MD 138 read *καρ̣[π]ό̣ς*, although as they note, the plural would be unusual. They also suggest *καλ̣[π]ό̣ς*, a variant of the receptacle *κάλπις* or *κάλπη*. Beattie's suggestion (1975: 34), *κάρ̣[ο|ν]ο̣ς* from *κάρρων* 'of greater value', appears to be too long.

14 *ἐς* = *ἐκ*; Dialect 14.

μόρο: here in the sense of 'plot of land', especially a vineyard; see J–MD 139, Bile 134 n. 240.

14–15 *ὅπΘ* = *ὁπόθεν*; see **G72**.5.23 and Willetts ad loc.

16 *[ο]ς̣*: J–MD record the last three strokes of the *san*.

αιδε̣...σ̣: J–MD record the vertical and upper two strokes of the *epsilon*, traces of three letters between *epsilon* and *san*, and four oblique strokes of *san* or *mu*.

αιδε̣...: *αἴ δε̣̄[ται]* = *δέηται* (Beattie 1975: 35) 'as he may request', but the recorded traces are not consistent with the *tau* and *iota* of *ται*.

εσδ...ς: J–MD record the traces of three letters between *delta* and *san* including possibly a circular letter before *san*.

17 *ο̣*: the left portion of the curve of the *omicron* is visible.

τ̣: J–MD record the vertical stroke and the horizontal stroke at the left.

λ̣: the *lambda* appears to be complete in J–MD's drawing.

ἐπεστ̣αϙός: cf. **G14g–p1**, ϙόσμος ὁ ἐπιστάς, and Introd. 4C1a.

18 ἀπλοπία̣[ι .]α̣[.]α̣ι: J–MD record faintly the three *alphas.*

ἀπλοπία = ἀβλάβεια 'without fault' (also in **G75**A9–10; **G81**.12–13; **A2**.10; **A4**.2?).

18–19 αὐτοῖσι or αὐτοῖς ἰ[*c*.3–4] are possible.

19 ι . . . π: J–MD record traces of three letters between the *iota* and the *pi* consistent with *mu*, *nu*, and *san.*

αν̣εσ̣η̣μ̣εν: J–MD's drawing suggests that the first *nu* could be *san*, and the second *san* could be *mu*; the *eta* and *mu* are recorded faintly.

εσ̣η̣μ̣εν: possibly ἐσ̣ῆ̣μ̣εν = ἐξεῖναι, but we would expect εκσ- before the vowel (J–MD 141).

20 ε̣: J–MD record the *epsilon* faintly.

τεμένια: see n. on B6.

πε[.] . ϙ: JP records an *alpha* before *qoppa*; J–MD record only the left oblique stroke.

21 ὀ̣: J–MD record the *omicron* faintly.

22 α̣: J–MD record the vertical stroke and upper two oblique strokes of the *alpha* (*epsilon* is also possible).

B

1 τὸ Ϝῖσον λακὲν τὸν ποινικαστάν: probably continues from the bottom of A, which would supply a context for understanding τὸ Ϝῖσον.

3 πάντε is not otherwise attested.

4–5 μῆι δίαλο[ς]: J–MD and most others read μὴ ἰδιαλο[.] and understand the second word (or words) as some sort of verbal expression. J–MD suggest ἴδια λο[ίη] or λοῖ, but note that λέοι is attested as the optative of λῶ (see Bile 227–9). VER apparently think the verb is understood and take the second word as an adjective, '(for all the gods for whom) there is no special ('particulier') priest'. We agree with this general sense, but follow Beattie 1975: 36 in reading μῆι. We then understand δίαλο[ς] as 'clear', following Hesychius, s.v. δίαλον· φανερόν; διάλας· τὰς δήλας καὶ φανεράς. Other suggestions include ἰδίαλος (Merkelbach 1972: 102), but the trace he reads at the right edge of B5, if accurately recorded by J–MD, cannot belong to a *san*, and δι' ἄλο[ν], 'through a deputy' (Beattie), which is possible, but the formulation strikes us as odd.

6 τὰ τεμένια: we follow VER in taking this as a derivative of τέμενος ('sanctuary'), meaning 'sanctuary things' (i.e. revenue). J–MD suggest it is the plural of τέμενος, but it is difficult to understand in what sense an official could 'have' a sanctuary.

6–7 Among the uncertainties in this sentence are the force of μήδ' . . . μήδε, the meanings of ἐπάγραν and ῥύτιον and the syntactical role of τὸν ποινικαστάν. We take up the first three here; for the fourth, see the comm.

μήδ' . . . μήδε. The first μήδε could be a conjunction, in which case the double prohibition is likely to refer to the role of the *poinikastas* as priest, or, as we prefer, it could be an adverb, in which case the sentence is in asyndeton and addresses a new topic.

ἐπάγραν: the noun is not otherwise attested, but ἔπαγρος means 'in quest of prey' (Aristotle *HA* 616b34 of herons; Callimachus, *Hecale* F74.23–4 (Hollis) of thieves' hands), and ἀγρέω means 'capture/take'. J–MD 142 suggest 'capture/seizure', and this seems most likely, though a derivation from ἀγείρω 'gather/collect' cannot be excluded.

ῥύτιον (= ῥύσιον) has a range of meanings relating to seizing or holding property owed to one: in M&L 42B41 (a fifth-century agreement among Knossos, Tylissos, and Argos) it means a 'fine'. Most scholars understand it as distraint of property, perhaps to enforce a legal obligation (Koerner 1981: 187–8).

αἰλῆν = αἰρῆν; Dialect 30.

7–11 We follow the reading of Gschnitzer 1974: 271–3; for J–MD the sentence 'remains almost completely obscure'.

7–8 δίκα: either (as we prefer) a *nom. pendens* used as a heading ('as for a trial'), or with 'to be' understood ('there is to be a trial').

8 ὄτερον = ὁπότερον adv. 'in whichever way'.

ʎόληται = βώληται or possibly Ϝώληται (= βούληται). The sign ʎ is not otherwise attested on Crete, but it resembles a *beta* attested on Thera (Jeffery 1990: 308, *B*4). *Beta* does not occur elsewhere in **Da1** for comparison. *Digamma* for *beta* is not securely attested in Crete; for a possible example, see n. ad **Lyktos1A6**.

9 κ̣: J–MD record the vertical and upper oblique strokes of the *kappa*.

κ̣ρήσεται = χρήσεται, with δίκαι understood ('use the trial' = 'stand trial'); VER read κρησεταιην, but this form is impossible.

ἢν = ἢ 'ν = ἢ ἐν. As Gschnitzer notes, ὄτερον implies two alternatives joined by ἤ, and if we read ἤ, ἐν seems to be the only possible interpretation of the *nu*; see **Elt2**.6 and Bile 93 n. 83. However, the use of ἐν + dat. to identify the presiding magistrate at a trial is not otherwise attested in Crete.

[[π]]: the π appears to be an error.

10 τέλεται: τέλομαι serves as the future of εἰμί (Bile 248).

ἄλε = ἄλλῃ: 'otherwise' (cf. πάντε ὄπε, B3).

11 ἐς for εἰς before a vowel is exceptional. See J–MD 143–4 and Dialect 14.

12 ἆι is probably temporal. The comparative ('as') cannot be ruled out (so Beattie 1975: 40–1), but is never attested with the subjunctive. The temporal sense is otherwise attested on Crete in *IC* 1.9.1, lines 104–8 (Dreros, third–second century); see note on **G72**.6.15–16. J–MD read the conditional ἄι κα, but it would be odd to make his contribution depend on all the others contributing. VER also read ἄι but translate 'when'.

ϙὸι = καὶ οἱ.

ο̣: J–MD record the upper left portion of the *omicron*.

13 [ἀπ?]άρϙονται: J–MD; [ἐν]άρϙωνται 'inaugurate' Beattie 1975: 41; [ἐπ]άρϙονται is also possible as is the uncompounded verb ἄρϙονται.

τὸ ἐπενιαύτιον is not otherwise attested; for the meaning 'annual offering', see J–MD.

14 λάκσιον is not otherwise attested. J–MD suggest that it might be connected with λαγχάνω and its derivative λάξις 'a share/portion of land'; Beattie 1975: 43 derives it from λῆξις 'ballot'; van Effenterre 1973: 43 suggests a connection with λάχνος 'wool', perhaps the woolly hide from the sacrificial animal.

συνϜαλεῖ: perhaps a form of συνειλέω meaning 'press together/collect' (J–MD). Beattie 1975: 42–3 reads συνβ̣αλεῖ.

17 [*c*.4]ίστοι: [πρειγ]ίστωι (= πρεσβευτάτῳ) J–MD.

Da1 records an agreement between the polis of Datala and Spensithios and his offspring. J–MD 148–9 observe that this is the earliest detailed record of the creation of an important public office, that of the *poinikastas.* It is possible that the office already existed and we have here only a new appointment to it, but the amount of detail included in the agreement suggests that it is new.

The text written on side A records the main terms of the agreement: the principal activities that Spensithios and his offspring will perform for the polis (writing and remembering all public matters, both sacred and secular), the tenure of the office (for life, heritable, and exclusive to Spensithios and his descendants), and the compensation that the polis promises to provide Spensithios and his successors (rations, tax exemption, and an annual salary). The agreement continues onto B where the text further defines Spensithios' official duties, grants him certain rights at law, and states his obligations to the *andreion.*

As regards Spensithios' civic status, we are persuaded by J–MD 149 that because he offers sacrifices on behalf of the polis (B4–6) and belongs to an *andreion* (B11–14), he was very probably a citizen of the community where he served as *poinikastas.*[365] Van Effenterre (1973: 37–9, 1979) takes the fact that he receives a salary together with rations and tax exemption as proof that he was an alien.[366]

A

1–2 The enactment clause refers to two or possibly three groups: the Dataleis, the polis, and a group consisting of five men from each tribe. Scholars have debated at great length the identity of the Dataleis, their relationship to the polis, the implications of the transition from the third person 'the Dataleis decided' (literally 'it pleased' the Dataleis) to the first person *espensames* 'we promised', and the role of the tribal representatives in the legislative process. Among their suggestions are that the Dataleis are the politically authoritative members of the polis (Datala) that passed this decree (Gschnitzer 1974, Viviers 1994), the members of a civic subgroup (*startos*, tribe, or clan) of the (unknown) polis that passed this decree (J–MD 1970, Ruzé 1983), or the inhabitants of Datala, an outlying hamlet dependent upon the (unknown) polis that passed this decree (van Effenterre 1973: 35–7, who suggests that the enacting polis was Lato). Parallels from Lyktos (**Lyktos1**) and Gortyn (**G78**) for the collective use of the city-ethnic with *ewade* (*ewade Lyktioisi*; *ewade tois Gortyniois*) strongly support the first alternative (see further Introd. 4B1).[367] If the Dataleis are the members of the political class of the polis of Datala,

[365] J–MD 149 (and 135) also note that Spensithios' sons could be *dromēs*, 'adults', a term they take to include citizenship, but this is not certain; see Introd. 5A2.

[366] Cf. Gorlin 1988 who took this as an indication of the interest of the polis in ensuring that the *poinikastas* maintained his citizen status by guaranteeing that he was able to meet his obligations to his *andreion*, on the assumption that in this requirement Datala resembled Sparta. See further Introd. 7C.

[367] Note also the sixth-century artist's signature, 'Damothetos the Datales' (n. ad A1). In Crete the use of a city-ethnic as part of a person's name is more likely than the use of the name of a civic sub-unit. See Perlman 1996: 245–52.

what, then, is the role of the tribal representatives? The phrase 'from the tribes five (men) from each' appears to be used in apposition to the term *polis*, i.e. 'and we the polis, (represented by) five (men) from each of the tribes'.[368] For the tribes in Crete, see further Introd. 4B3.

1 'We promise': the verb *espensames*, from *spendo* 'to pour a libation', is not otherwise attested in the laws from Crete, although the compound *epispendo* occurs several times in **G72** in the sense of 'pledge/promise',[369] perhaps referring to the practice of offering a libation to seal the promise. Here the tribal representatives may have poured a libation on behalf of the entire polis to secure their promise to uphold and enforce the provisions of the agreement. The process, then, included a decision by the politically authoritative body to make this agreement with Spensithios, followed by a libation and a promise performed by representatives of the tribes that bound the community to uphold the decision. We may compare **Dr1** where the *kosmos*, the *damioi*, and the 'twenty of the polis' swore an oath as part of the enactment process.

2 The name of Spensithios may have special significance (Willetts 1972). It is formed from the root *spend-* 'to pour a libation' (see above on A1) and the noun *thios* 'god'. Such names often reflect the occupation of the person's father or his paternal ancestors more generally, and may indicate that Spensithios' ancestors held a priesthood, as indeed Spensithios himself might have.

2–5 The first provision states the essence of the agreement: the duties of Spensithios and his offspring and the obligations of the polis in return.

2–3 The polis promises rations (*thropa*) and full tax exemption; cf. **G87**, which mentions the rememberer (*mnamon*) of the *esprattai* and the receipt of rations by someone, but it is not possible to determine if it is the *mnamon* who receives them. *Thropa* here may refer to the food that a citizen was required to contribute for consumption in the *andreion* as it does in **A1**.15 (*tropan in antreioi*); it is distinct from the annual salary (*misthos*) described here in **Da1**A11–15.

4–5 Spensithios is hired to write and remember public matters, both sacred and secular, for the polis. How did these two activities function in practice? So far as we know, the early Cretan poleis used writing in an official capacity primarily to record public laws and agreements. It is possible, as J–MD 149 suggest, that the office of *poinikastas* was new and that a growing need to record public documents in writing led to its creation. Either more documents were being created or perhaps documents that had earlier been remembered were now to be written

[368] See J–MD 129 for parallels from Chios and Eretria. Cf. Beattie 1975: 23, who understands polis here to indicate an executive council and 'from the tribes five from each' appositively, i.e. 'and we the council, consisting of five men from each tribe, ratified (the decision of the Dataleis)'. But if the polis was an established body (a council), then there would be no reason to specify its composition.

[369] **G72**.4.52–3, 5.3–4, 6.11, 6.13–14, 6.19–20, 6.21–2, 10.28–9, cf. **Gortyn5** (?).

down. In any case, the *poinikastas* would be the one to put all such documents in writing. He was obliged to accompany the *kosmos* in all of his official duties (B3–4), and it is reasonable to suppose that he was tasked with remembering what happened as the *kosmos* conducted the business of the polis and writing down any legislation or other documents that resulted from this business. In sum, Spensithios for the most part remembered the details of official public business (which made him an authoritative witness of that business), and recorded public enactments in writing. See further Gagarin 2008a: 119–21.

4 'Both sacred and secular': the same expression, with a minor difference in wording (see n.) occurs in **G72**.10.42–3.

5 'Write': neither *poinikazen* nor *poinikastas*, the agent noun derived from it, is otherwise attested for certain, though either of them might have originally stood in **Ele11** (*poinika*[—]). Most scholars (e.g. J–MD; Edwards and Edwards 1974) associate the verb with the noun *phoinix* in one of its two senses, 'Phoenician' or (the color) 'purple-red', and understand it to mean 'write'.[370] *Poinikastas* would then mean either 'writer' or 'colorist'.[371] The historical connection between the Phoenician and Greek alphabets was recognized already in antiquity. Herodotus (5.57–8) claims that Ionians living around Cadmean Boeotia at first called the Greek letters *phoinikeia* after the Phoenicians who had introduced them. The entrenchment clause of an early fifth-century inscription from Teos in Ionia recording curses to be pronounced by public officials each year against anyone who defaces the text by cutting out the letters (*phoinikeia*) or making them illegible supports his claim (*SEG* 31.984, B37–9). The term *poinikēia* is attested on Crete (**Eltynia1**), though without context.

'Remember': Datala also assigned Spensithios and his descendants the job of 'remembering' (*mnamoneuwen*) public matters, both sacred and secular. The verb is not otherwise attested on Crete, but the noun *mnamon* (Attic *mnēmōn*) occurs in several laws from Gortyn (Introd. 4C3), where he usually accompanies or is attached to other officials (*dikastai*, *ksenios* (*kosmos*?), *esprattai*). He attended trials and other quasi-judicial public proceedings (e.g. renunciation of adoptions in **G72**.11.14–17) and could later testify about what he remembered. In similar fashion, Spensithios must accompany the *kosmos* on public business (B3–4).[372]

[370] The widespread practice of accentuating letters inscribed on stone with red paint has left traces that are still visible in, e.g. **G72** (and were even more evident when MG viewed this inscription in 1981). Even if derived from a color (e.g. Chantraine 1972: 'color (letters) red'), however, the verb would still mean 'write' since it is inconceivable that Spensithios was merely obliged to color letters that had already been inscribed. Thus, *poinikazen* may have combined both senses, writing and writing in red.

[371] Beattie's ingenious view that both terms were associated with the noun *poinē*, 'blood-money/ requital', is refuted by Edwards and Edwards 1977; and the mention of *poinikēia* in the recently discovered **Eltynia1**, which certainly means 'writing' elsewhere, poses an insurmountable obstacle to it.

[372] In later times *mnēmones* used writing to record matters and might better be described as writers or secretaries. Thus, in Aristotle, *Politics* 6.8, 1321b the *mnēmōn* is one of several officials who recorded (sc. in

5–10 The job of 'writing and remembering' was heritable and exclusive to Spensithios and his offspring. The choice of a successor in the event that there was more than one possible candidate appears to have been left up to the family. Only Spensithios or the majority of his adult male sons (in other words those eligible for the job of 'writing and remembering') could allow someone from outside the family to fill the position. The exclusivity of Spensithios' appointment, its heritability, the absence of a term limit, and the apparent inability of the polis to modify or rescind the agreement are extraordinary and differ markedly from the (probable) one-year tenure of the *kosmos* and the limitation on his (and other officials') holding successive terms (see **G14**; **Dr1**; Marginesu 2006: 387–9). Unlimited tenure makes sense, on the other hand, for a *mnamon*, whose memory serves as an archive of the public business of a community. We do not know the details of the tenure of a *mnamon* at Gortyn, but in one case, at least, he was required to testify to what he remembered so long as he was 'alive and performing his civic duties' (**G72**.9.31–4), which appears to amount, in essence, to life-time tenure.

Vesting a public office with a particular family is also unusual. Herodotus (6.60) notes that at Sparta heralds, butchers, and flute players were hereditary. All three of these offices may be regarded as quasi-religious. Hereditary priesthoods were also common and in some cases the *poinikastas* served as priest (B4–6). There may be a common thread here (comm. ad B4–6).

11–14 Spensithios' title, *poinikastas*, is introduced in the first of several provisions concerning his annual salary, and from this point on, the agreement refers only to the *poinikastas* (A11–12; B1, B3–4, B5–6, B7, B8–9); neither Spensithios nor his offspring are mentioned again by name. Why the title conveys only one of his two responsibilities (writing) is unclear. It may be that he was already *mnamon*, or *poinikastas* may have been shorthand for '*poinikastas* and *mnamon*'. It is likely that a 'rememberer', whatever he was called (we have no evidence of the name *mnamon* from any Cretan polis besides Gortyn), existed long before there was a need for a writer.

The salary of the *poinikastas* consisted of fifty *prokooi* (a liquid measurement of unknown volume) of grape must and something worth twenty drachmas or the equivalent value of bronze. **G79**.6–7 also provides alternative forms of payment of wages. Beattie 1975: 32–3 suggests restoring the partially preserved term after 'must' as an otherwise unattested name for a type of storage jar (n. ad A13).

writing) private agreements, judicial decisions, indictments, and initiations of judicial proceedings. This has led several scholars to see *mnamoneuwen* and *poinikazen* as synonymous or nearly so (Beattie 1975: 26–31; Edwards and Edwards 1977: 139; van Effenterre 1973: 38); but there is no hint of writing in the activities of *mnamones* in Crete, and there would be no point in assigning Spensithios two duties that were essentially the same. Cf. Marginesu 2006: 393–6, who emphasizes the importance of memory to recording in writing.

If a *prokoos* was roughly the same as an Attic *chous*, the *poinikastas* received about 164 liters per annum. Storage jars sufficient to hold this amount would have been quite valuable; it would not be surprising if a storage jar or the equivalent in money (bronze bullion or coin) was included in Spensithios' salary. More surprising would be that his wages, unlike those that Gortyn paid for the labor of free men and slaves (**G79**), do not appear to have included other food staples such as barley or figs. This may indicate that unlike the laborers of Gortyn, the *poinikastas* owned land and could be expected to provide food for his family from it, while the polis provided rations (*tropa*, A2–3) for the *poinikastas* himself. Or perhaps the rations that the polis provided were intended for Spensithios' whole family, with the must being a special extra.

14–15 The *poinikastas* determines from which portion (*moros*) his grape must was to come. The term *moros* is not otherwise attested in Crete. In a third-century inscription from Mytilene (*IG* XII 2.74) it refers to a portion of land, sometimes further defined as land cultivated in grapes. Here *moros* may refer to a plot of land cultivated in grapes, or perhaps to the share of produce that an individual paid in taxes to the state, as is understood in **G77**B3 'three (shares) of grape must'. There is no reason to suggest that *moros* refers to public land or to its produce as J–MD 139–40 suggest. Why the polis allows the *poinikastas* to choose from where his grape must comes eludes us, unless certain plots were known to produce superior grapes!

15–16 'If he (?)': the responsible party could be the owner of the *moros* or perhaps an official of the polis.

16–17 If the grape must is not given to the *poinikastas* the '*kosmos* in charge' is apparently obliged to intervene, presumably by seizing the must for the *poinikastas*. The expression '*kosmos* in charge' (also in **G14**g–p1) suggests that there was more than one *kosmos* at Datala at this time, but it is not possible to determine if the expression means 'chief *kosmos*', the *kosmos* who was responsible for this particular kind of business, or more generally the *kosmos* who happened to be on hand or on duty at the time (Introd. 4C1a).

17–18 If the term 'without fault' (*aplopia*) (18) is connected with the preceding provision, it may be that the *kosmos* was protected from charges being brought against him for his actions in securing the grape must on behalf of the *poinikastas*.

20 'Revenue from the sacred precinct' (*temenia*): see below on B4–6, where the word recurs.

21 'Is to obtain the equal': see below on B1, where this clause recurs; here we can only guess at the context. The restoration of *ko*[*smos*] is likely but not certain.

B

1 'Is to obtain the equal': the sense is not clear to us but would probably have been clarified by the text, now lost, at the bottom of A. Many scholars understand it to

mean 'equal share' (e.g. van Effenterre 1973, Koerner 1981, VER; cf. J–MD 150 'equal allotment of rights'); this is possible, but it might also mean something like 'equal authority'. J–MD 141, 146 explain the repetition of the clause here as 'an elaboration of an over short statement... at the end of A, which did not make clear what the "equal share" meant' (141 n. 28).

2 'Be present and attend': Both *paremen* and *sunemen* can mean 'to attend' or 'to be present at' without implying participation in the activities attended. *Sunemen*, on the other hand, can also mean 'to take part in' (J–MD 149). This has suggested to some that the *poinikastas* was not only a recorder of but also a more active participant in the work of the *kosmos* (though we do not know what this official's duties were in Datala), and was perhaps himself a specialist *kosmos* (e.g. Raubitschek 1972). But if the restoration of *ko*[*smos*] in A21 is correct, the expression 'the equal to the *kosmos*' (A21) implies that the *poinikastas* was not himself a *kosmos*, and that his participation was therefore as a *poinikastas*, nothing more.

4–6 The provision is comprehensible despite some uncertainty concerning the letters in 4–5, which we understand to mean 'is not clear' (n. ad loc.). The *poinikastas* is to perform the public sacrifices for any god whose cult is without a priest, and he is to receive the revenue from that god's sacred precinct. This enlargement of responsibilities is remarkable, and goes well beyond the writing and remembering he has already been charged with (for the possible connection of Spensithios' family with priesthoods, see comm. ad A2). We cannot know how many cults this might involve or why a cult may lack a priest; perhaps the regular priest was unavailable (had died, was not at home, had temporarily lost his citizen status). Or the polis may have created a new cult or may have added new public sacrifices to an existing cult.

6–11 As the comments below indicate, interpretation of this section is problematic. In our view it prohibits certain actions either by or (more likely) against the *poinikastas* (6–7); in either case, it provides him a choice of legal procedures for adjudicating any dispute (7–11). The first sentence (6–7) probably begins with asyndeton (Introd. 3D3) indicating a new topic not directly connected with Spensithios' priestly service.

6–7 'Neither seizure of the person (*epagran*) nor of the property (*rhytion*)': these are the most likely meanings, though both words are obscure. *Epagran* might instead mean 'collection', but if *rhytion* applies to property, it makes more sense for *epagran* to apply to persons. The seizure could be intended as a means to collect an unpaid debt or fine.

Grammatically, 'the *poinikastas*' could be the agent doing the seizing or the victim whose person or property is seized. The latter is preferable, for it seems much more likely that the *poinikastas* would be protected because of the important role he plays in the community and the interest of the polis in maintaining his services without interruption than that he (alone) would be prohibited from seizing other persons or property. So Merkelbach 1972, Gschnitzer 1974: 273–4, Bravo 1980: 767–9, and VER; cf. van Effenterre 1973: 43–5 and Beattie 1975: 37, who understand *ton poinikastan* as the subject of the two infinitives.

7–11 This provision probably applies to a trial arising out of the prohibitions in 6–7. If the *poinikastas* is the victim, as we think likely, he may choose to have the case tried either by the same court as 'the others', or by the *kosmos*. This extraordinary privilege indicates the high regard the polis has for his office. It is not clear who 'the others' are here or which court they use, but in B12 'the others' contribute to the *andreion* and thus are most likely the members of the political class of Datala. The same group is probably meant here and reference is thus to the ordinary court. The provision implies that the *kosmos* was not the regular judge for the citizens of Datala (Introd. 4C1c, 4C2). The frequent association of the *poinikastas* and the *kosmos* in managing the day-to-day affairs of the community might result in a close relationship that the *poinikastas* could use to his advantage at trial.

10–11 '. . . but not any other way': Bravo 1980: 768–9 takes this as an implicit reference to a foreigners' trial (*ksenia dika*), and an indication that Spensithios is not a citizen, though he is treated like one in some respects. But foreigners' trials are only mentioned at Gortyn (**G80**.8), and 'not any other way' might more likely imply not using self-help.

11–17 Asyndeton marks the beginning of a new subject, the obligations of the *poinikastas* to the *andreion*. For the *andreion*, see further Introd. 6C). The unspecified subject ('he shall give') is almost certainly the *poinikastas*.

11–13 The *poinikastas* must contribute meat as *dikaia* ('what is rightful'?) and the *epeniaution* (on which see below). Most scholars understand *dikaia* as a reference to the dues (especially food) that members of a dining club periodically contributed to their *andreion*, but if the rations Spensithios receives are intended for the *andreion* (see above on A2–3) then the contribution mentioned here should be something different. See further below on 12–13.

12 The use of the ax as a standard unit of weight is also attested for Boeotia, Olynthus, and Idalion (Cyprus). Although it is not possible to confirm the statement of Eustathius (p. 1878, 50 ad. *Od.* 19.572) that the Cretan *pelekys* weighed six or ten minas, calculating on the basis of the Aiginetan standard of weights (the standard that was later used for Cretan coinage), ten axes would be the equivalent of 37.8 kg. (six minas) or 63 kg. (ten minas) (see J–MD 144, Kroll 2011: 34).

12–13 'When the others offer the first fruits (?)': the particle *ai*, which we translate as temporal ('when'), could also be conditional ('if') or comparative ('as'); see n. ad loc. It is hard to see the point of a comparison, however, and a conditional would indicate that the *poinikastas* was obliged to give meat only if others should do something, making the donation contingent rather than required, which seems unlikely. We thus prefer the temporal sense, though it is less common in general; it presumably refers to a well-established date on which other contributions to the *andreion* were made.

13 'Offer first fruits (?)': if the verb is only partially preserved (see n.), several different prefixes can be supplied in the available space. The resulting compounds can all refer to ritual actions: *aparchesthai* 'to offer first fruits' (of agricultural produce, booty from war, etc.), *enarchesthai* 'to perform the preliminary rites of sacrifice', and *eparchesthai* 'to sprinkle the first drops of wine before a libation'. We tentatively restore the first of these and suggest that the *poinikastas* was to give meat to the *andreion* each year when the other members contributed a tithe of the animals from their flocks. The provision may suggest that ten axes of meat represented the average amount (or value) of an individual's first-fruit offering. Beattie 1975: 40–1 and Koerner 1981: 188–9 prefer [*en*]*archesthai* in the sense of 'begin'; the *poinikastas* was required to give *dikaia* just as others did on the day they took office. This seems doubtful: *ai* is not attested in the sense required, 'as when', and the identity of the office would be unstated.

'Yearly obligation (?)' (*to epeniaution*): the word is not otherwise attested, but it is clearly derived from *eniautos* ('year'), and thus probably refers either to an annual obligation or to a yearling animal, presumably for sacrifice. It is worth observing that at Axos (**A1**.12–13) individuals who were given rations and tax exemption were nonetheless required to help pay for the Great Hekatomb (a sacrifice of one hundred animals), and also for 'the sacrifice' (not otherwise identified).

14–15 'The *laksion*': the meaning of this word is unknown (see n.).

16–17 JM–D 120, 146 observe that these lines are inscribed more neatly and deeply than the rest and are perhaps an addendum. They restore [*preig*]*istos* 'the eldest', a possible but by no means certain restoration, whom they identify as the senior member of the *andreion*. Even if the restoration is correct, other senses are possible, e.g. in **G80**.11 'elders' (*preigistoi*) may refer to a group of public officials, perhaps ambassadors or a council of some kind.

DREROS

Site

Dreros is located on the Gulf of Mirabello in northeastern Crete and is the easternmost community on Crete known to have published laws during the Archaic period. The urban center lies on the two peaks (west peak and east peak) and the connecting saddle of the hill Agios Antonios, one of the southern spurs of Mt. Kadiston, overlooking the inland plain of the Gulf of Mirabello to the south.

The town appears to have been extensive; the remains of walls of uncertain date are traceable across much of the 38 ha. of Agios Antonios (Xanthoudides 1918: 28–9; Marinatos 1936: 216–17; Demargne and van Effenterre 1937a: 7). A circuit wall dating to the Byzantine period protected the top of the east peak, the higher of the two.[373] Traces of walls of uncertain date lower down on the east slope of the east peak and the west slopes of the west peak have been identified as the remains of a second, possibly archaic defensive circuit protecting the two peaks and the saddle in between, but both the nature of these walls and their date are far from certain (Frederiksen 2011: 135; cf. Coutsinas 2013: 208–9, 417–18 no. 20).

Settlement on Agios Antonios before the ninth century is not certain. The earliest evidence of human activity on the hill dates to the twelfth century; it includes the earliest burials in the cemetery located at the northern foot of the east peak and some vases, possibly twelfth-century, from the top of the west peak and the saddle.[374]

The center of the town occupies the saddle between the two peaks where Marinatos (1936: 219–83) excavated a hearth temple, often attributed to Apollo Delphinios on the basis of third-century inscriptions (*IC* 1.9.1; Bile 52 no. 48). Demargne and van Effenterre (1937a: 10–15) dated the temple and the plateia, the large open area to the southeast of the temple with banks of steps along its west and south sides that they dubbed the 'agora', to the middle of the eighth century. Hansen and Fischer-Hansen (1994: 62) suggest that the banks of steps were used for political meetings. New excavations, which began in 2009 under the direction

[373] See Coutsinas (2013: 208–9, 417–18 no. 20) who notes (p. 209), following Demargne and van Effenterre (1937a: 7), that the Byzantine walls may rest on earlier foundations.

[374] For the early (possibly votive?) vases from the settlement, see Mulliez 2011; Gaignerot-Driessen 2013: 97–8. For the cemetery, see van Effenterre 2009; Gaignerot-Driessen 2013: 107–11. Gaignerot-Driessen (2013: 111) suggests that the cemetery may have served the early settlement (twelfth to ninth centuries) on Kephali Limnes, located just to the east of the cemetery, because the evidence for a twelfth-century settlement on Agios Antonios is so slight. Cf. Nowicki 2000: 173.

FIG. 20. Plan of Dreros

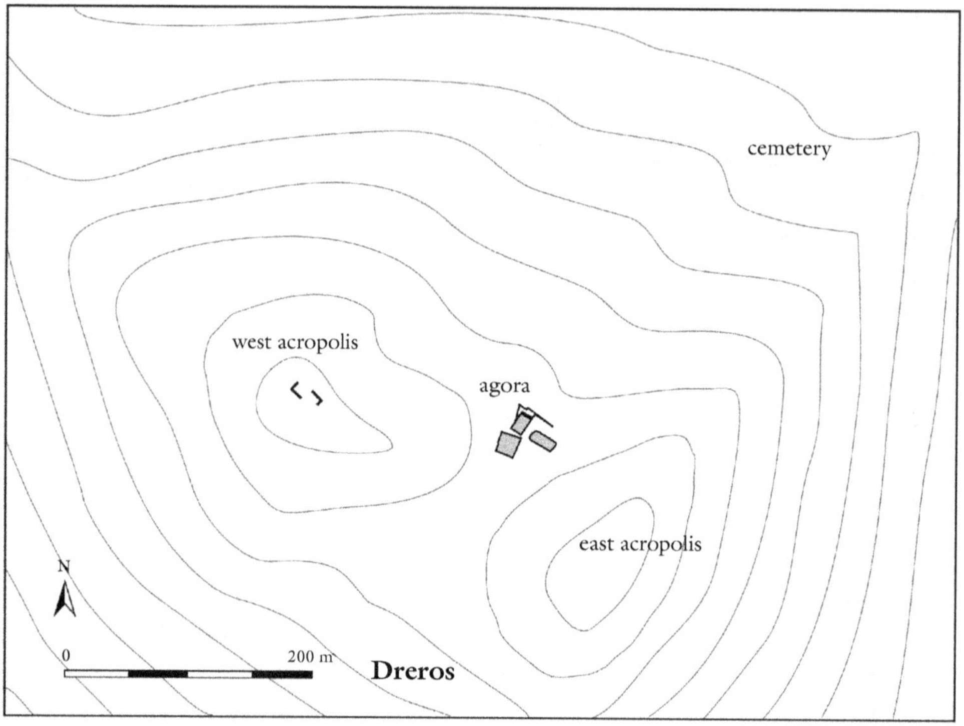

of Vasiliki Zographaki and Alexandre Farnoux, may alter our understanding of the plan, dating, and function of the remains in the saddle.[375]

Xanthoudides excavated what he identified as a monumental temple (24 by 10.7 m.) on the west acropolis.[376] The new excavations have revealed instead a more modest structure (12.6 by 10 m.) built on an artificial terrace at the top of the hill and a second terrace at a lower level to its east. A deposit consisting of blackened earth, animal bones, and fragments of vases and animal figurines (late eighth–seventh century) suggests the antiquity of ritual activity in this area.[377] A better understanding of the chronology, form, and function of the temple and the terraces must await publication of the new excavations.

There is at present very little evidence for the continued occupation of the town during the late Archaic and Classical periods. But the city did revive later on, and the new excavations are contributing significantly to our understanding of the town during the Hellenistic period.

[375] Zographaki and Farnoux 2010. The possibility that the plateia and steps are contemporary with the Hellenistic cistern is of particular relevance to our understanding of the lay-out of the putative civic center of the archaic polis-town.

[376] Xanthoudides 1918: 23–8. Cf. Marinatos (1936: 253–5), who identified the structure as an *andreion*.

[377] The preliminary report dates the deposit to the thirteenth–eighth century (Mulliez 2011), but Kotsonas per ep. informs us that the material from the deposit is probably eighth–seventh century.

ᶦIG. 21. Blocks
ɲped in Cistern
with **Dr3**

Texts

Dr1–7 were all found in 1936, in a Hellenistic-era cistern located alongside the hearth temple to the west and the plateia to the north.[378] Each text was inscribed on a single block, though several of these were or have since been broken. None of the blocks appears to have been dressed as preparation for inscribing, and most of the inscriptions adapt to irregularities in the surface by deviating in various ways from the straight-line neatness of later Cretan texts. The excavator's conclusion, that the inscribed blocks originally formed part of the east wall of the temple, is generally accepted. This wall faced the area where the cistern was later built; it is hoped that the new excavations will clarify the original location of the inscribed blocks and function of the wall from which they came.

[378] The 1936 excavation at Dreros was directed by Pierre Demargne, assisted by Henri van Effenterre, then a student at the French School in Athens. Originally planned to last a month, the excavation was extended when inscriptions began to be found, but Demargne had to attend to prior commitments and so he left van Effenterre in charge. The initial publication by both scholars first described the whole excavation (1937a) and they then published **Dr1** (1937b). The war then intervened and the remaining texts were not published until 1946 by van Effenterre alone (1946a, 1946b), as Demargne had turned his attention to other sites.

The excavation yielded eight separate texts. We include seven of these; the eighth (van Effenterre 1946b), which may have a few Greek words but seems to be written primarily in the language dubbed 'Eteocretan', cannot be understood. Apart from the loss of a few letters at the right or the left, **Dr1–5** are complete. **Dr6–7** appear to be broken at the right and an unknown number of letters have been lost.

Jeffery (1990: 311, 315) tentatively dates all seven to the middle and second half of the seventh century. The letter forms vary somewhat from inscription to inscription and two different methods of inscribing (chisel and punch and hammer) were used. We order our texts according to the arrangement of Duhoux 1982.[379] **Dr1, 3–4, 5** (fragment from left), and **7** (fragment from left) are currently in the Archaeological Collection of Neapolis.

As a group, **1–7** are remarkable in that at least four (**1**, **3–5**), and probably five, of these texts begin with an enactment clause that includes the verb *ewade*, 'it was pleasing [to X]' (i.e., 'X approved' or 'X decided'), and the other two (**6–7**) may have begun in this manner but the opening words of each are now lost. Such explicit enactment clauses are rare in the laws from the other cities. See **Da1**, **G78**, and **Lyktos1A** and **B**.

Dr1 (*SEG* 27.620; Demargne and van Effenterre 1937b; Bile 29–30 no. 2; K 90; VER I.81). Law on the iteration of the *kosmos*. *c.*650. Archaeological Collection of Neapolis (Inv. nos. 907 and 908). FIG. 22

Five lines of text, on a single block of limestone now broken into three pieces (from right A, B, C). Lines 1–3 are inscribed boustrophedon beginning at the right. Line 4 begins at the right, breaking the boustrophedon pattern. A partial fifth line (1a) is inscribed between lines 1 and 2 beginning from the right. This line begins with the word *thios* ('god') and thus is almost certainly an invocation; as such, it ought to come at the beginning. Why it does not and what the rest of the line means have been much debated. Any discussion of the line's position must begin with the nature of the stone's surface (for the meaning, see notes).

The limestone block has an irregular surface. The mason had to take considerable care in fitting his text to it. Line 1 is inscribed on a slightly projecting band of uneven width that extends along the upper edge of the block to the left edge of the stone. It is noticeably indented (0.12 m from the right edge); it curves down to avoid a deep gash along the upper edge of C and then curves up at the far left of C. Line 2 runs from left to right and traces the same course as 1, diverging only at

[379] Duhoux (1982: 28–9) arranges the eight inscriptions into three chronological groups based upon the criteria of inscribing technique (chisel or punch and hammer), use of word division, and other characteristics including letter forms and archaic paragraphing: Group I (*c.*650) = **Dr1–2**; Transitional = **Dr3**; Group II (*c.*600) = **Dr4–7**.

FIG. 22A. **Dr1**, Fragments A and B

FIG. 22B. **Dr1**, Fragment C

the far right where, rather than rising to follow the lower edge of the projecting band (and of line 1), it runs straight to the right edge of A. The ten letters of 1a are inscribed in considerably smaller letters between the lower edge of the projecting band and line 2. Lines 3 and 4 follow the meandering course of 2.

The letters of the four full lines are similar in size, and to the left of line 1a the four lines fill the height of the stone. The mason seems to have calculated the height of the letters by dividing the height of the surface by four. Indentation of the first line of an inscription is rare, but if the mason had begun line 1 at the right edge of the stone, he would have had to use very small letters in order to fit them onto the projecting band, which becomes narrower toward the right edge of the stone. Thus the lengthy indentation very likely stems from a desire to maintain a consistent size of lettering.

As noted above, the mason wrote line 2 from the left just below line 1, but he seems to have followed the lower edge of 1a when he came to it. In view of the mason's tendency to follow the course of the line above in his placement of the next line, this suggests that 2 was completed after 1a had already been inscribed. We believe that the mason omitted 1a when he began to inscribe the text. He caught the omission before he completed 2, and inscribed 1a as close as he could to the start of the text before completing 2, writing it in smaller letters so as not to upset his layout.

We present the Greek text in the order the lines appear on the stone but in our translation we begin with line 1a.

1 ← *ἆδ' ἔϝαδε | πόλι· | ἐπεί κα κοσμήσει, | δέκα ϝετίον τὸν ἀ-*
1a ← *θιός. ολοιον*
2 → *ϝτὸν μὴ κοσμêν· αἰ δὲ κοσμήσιε, ὅπε δικάκσιε | ἀϝτὸν ὀπῆλεν | διπλεῖ | κἀϝτὸν*
3 ← *ἄκρηστον | ἦμεν | ἆς δόοι, | κὄτι κοσμήσιε | μηδὲν | ἤμην. vac.*
4 ← ⧖ *ὀμόται δὲ | κόσμος | κοὶ δάμιοι | κοὶ ἴκατι | οἱ τᾶς πόλ̣[ιο]ς̣.*

1a God. *oloion*?

1–3 Thus has the polis decided: when someone has been *kosmos* the same person is not to be *kosmos* (again) for ten years. But if he should serve as *kosmos*, whenever he should give judgment, he is to owe double, and he is to be without rights as long as he lives, and whatever he should do as *kosmos* is to be void.

4 The oath-swearers (are) the *kosmos* and the *damioi* and the twenty of the polis.

1a *θιός· ολοιον*: Demargne and van Effenterre 1937b: 343 construe this as a single word *θιοσόλοιον* 'cursed' (otherwise unattested), and insert it towards the end of 2: . . . *ὀπῆλεν | διπλεῖ, (ἀϝτὸν) θιοσόλοιον (ἦμεν) | κἀϝτὸν* . . . 'he will owe double, he will be cursed, and he . . .'). Guarducci 1941: 20–3 preferred *θιὸς ὀ λοΐον*, 'God is good!' (*θιὸς ὀ λωΐων* = *θεὸς ἀγαθός*); for *θεὸς ἀγαθός* at the beginning of public inscriptions from Hellenistic Hierapytna and Itanos in east Crete, see e.g. *IC* 3.3.4; 3.4.8; 3.4.9. Buck 1955: 116 suggested *θιὸς ὄλοι ὄν* 'may god destroy him/it', and inserted the phrase in line 2: *διπλεῖ | κἀϝτὸν θιὸς ὄλοι ὄν ἄκρηστον | ἦμεν* 'he shall owe double penalty and himself—god destroy him—be without function'). Pounder 1984: 243–5 followed Buck's reading, but put the imprecation at the beginning of the text.

2 *κοσμήσιε* . . . *δικάκσιε*: much about these forms is uncertain. Both are aor. opt., the latter apparently resulting from attraction to the former. The final vowel is probably short, and so we have followed G's accentuation of a similar form *ϝέρκσιεν* (**G78**.7, see G's n. ad loc.); K, however, makes the forms paroxytone. See further Bile 234–7.

ὅπε 'when': see Bile 363. The *pi* faces left (against the direction of the line); contrast the *pi* in *ὀπῆλεν*, which faces the correct way.

3 *ἦμεν* ... *ἤμην*: for the two forms, see Dialect 20.

δόοι = *ζόοι* (Dialect 11).

4 The 'hourglass' symbol and the break in the boustrophedon pattern mark 4 as a separate though related section. See Introd. 3D2.

ὀμόται is otherwise attested only in the late grammarian Theognostus Can. 45, but cf. ὀμομόταs 'co-swearer' (?) (**G4**.3, **L5**.13), and also perhaps [ὀρ]ϙομόταs (**G8**.*i*, *a–f*, with note). Gallavotti 1977: 135 suggested ὀμοῦται (fut. ind. 3 s), 'he [the *kosmos*] will swear'; *contra* Gagarin 1986: 84 n. 13, and K 337 n. 28.

This is the longest and syntactically the most complex of the laws from Dreros. Apart from 1a (an invocation?), the text presents an enactment clause ('Thus has the polis decided'), a law (1–3), followed by a list of the parties who swear an oath (4). The law prohibits individuals from holding the office of *kosmos* more than once in ten years and specifies the consequences of noncompliance: fines, loss of rights, and annulment of the offender's decisions qua *kosmos*.

Although we do not know the exact composition of the polis at this time (see below on line 4 and Introd. 4A1), a *prima facie* reading of the text suggests that the Drerian community, in some sense, is imposing its authority on an important official in the city, the *kosmos*, a position that was probably held primarily if not exclusively by a member of the elite. However, a recent trend among historians to emphasize the role of elite competition in the early history of the polis has led to the view that the law was the work of elites regulating their own competition for office.[380] We see several difficulties with this view, which, as K notes (1993: 334–5), assumes that an aristocracy had sole control of public affairs while the people ('Volk') had no say until the rise of democracy. It does not explain why the elites would have the law approved by a wider community, why they would display it in public rather than just regulating themselves, or why they would impose such a severe penalty on offenders, especially since any potential violation would almost certainly be perceived and prevented before any violator took office. Thus, we take the law to mean what it appears to mean, that the wider community is regulating its important officials (so K 1993: 335). This suggests that some abuse of the office had recently occurred or been threatened, and because the law first addresses penalties for judgments handed down by the *kosmos*, it seems likely that a primary motive for the law was to curb abuse of judicial authority by the *kosmos* (Gagarin 1986: 84–6; 2008a: 76–9). Others have seen it as limiting the possibilities of using the office as a stepping stone to tyranny (Demargne and van Effenterre 1937b; Guarducci 1941: 20–1; cf. K) or to bolster the power of an individual family (Ehrenberg 1943: 17).

Seelentag (2009a) proposes that the law does not seek to prohibit a recent *kosmos* from holding the office of *kosmos* but rather from issuing judgments in disputes that would be brought to him for judgment because of his prestige

[380] e.g. Osborne 2009: 174–8: 'the purpose [of the Dreros law] . . . was not to control the powers of the élite with regard to the people, nor to restrict the arbitrariness of those with authority, but to control the distribution of powers within the élite. This is élite self-regulation, motivated not by any sense of overwhelming injustice but by a concern over which individuals have power' (176).

(attained when he formerly served as *kosmos*). This is unlikely for several reasons, two in particular. First, *kosmen* in line 1 and everywhere else in our texts (notably in **G14**p–g2) means 'serve as *kosmos*', and it seems impossible that without warning it could take on a different meaning in the middle of a sentence. Second, informal dispute resolution by family members, friends, and others was common in Athens and almost certainly everywhere else (as it continues to be today); it would be pointless (and impossible) to prevent two people from talking about their dispute to a third party, whether or not he was a former *kosmos*, and from listening to any resolution he might propose.[381]

1a 'God': this translates the first four letters of the line (*thios*); the meaning of the rest (*oloion*) is unclear. See n. ad 1a above and the introductory n.

1 'Thus has the polis decided' (lit. 'these things were pleasing (*ewade*) to the polis'); cf. the common Athenian enactment formula, 'it seemed (best) to the demos' (*edoxe tōi dēmōi*). We do not know the process by which the polis demonstrated its approval of the law. A fifth-century decree from Gortyn was approved (the verb, *ewade*, is the same as here) by 'the Gortynians voting' (**G78**.1), the verb used there (*psapidonsi*) indicating voting by 'pebble' or ballot, but the explicit mention of voting there may indicate that this was exceptional and it seems more likely that at this early date the Drerian polis votes by acclamation. In any case, it is extraordinary that what may be the earliest surviving Greek law forcefully asserts the power of civic authority, and that the thrust of the law is to control one of the community's most important officials by limiting office-holding to at most one term every ten years. For the composition of the polis, i.e. assembly (Willetts 1955: 168–9) or a smaller body such as a council (Ehrenberg 1943: 14), see on 4 below ('the twenty of the polis') and Introd. 4A1.

'Has been *kosmos*': the verb *kosmen* ('be *kosmos*', 'hold the office of *kosmos*') is widespread in Cretan laws, as is the noun *kosmos*, which designates the most important official in many, perhaps all, Cretan cities. There is much we do not know about the *kosmos* including how he was chosen and how long his term of office was. The common assumption is one year but we have no solid evidence of this. See Introd. 4C1e.

1–2 It is unclear why the period of ten years was chosen; the interval at Gortyn is just three years for the *kosmos*, five for the *ksenios*, and ten for the *gnomones* (**G14**.p–g2). The fact that an individual (or several individuals if there were several *kosmoi*) was removed from the pool of candidates for ten years may suggest that the pool was larger than we tend to imagine.

2–3 'If he should serve as *kosmos*': the consequences of non-compliance are severe: fines, loss of rights, and nullification of all that he does as *kosmos*. The fines

381 See also Chaniotis in *SEG* 59.1023.

and nullification may only apply to the actions of the *kosmos* while holding the office illegally, not to his previous term in office.

These penalties suggest a particular concern with abuse of the office for personal ends. But since violations of the law would have been immediately evident to anyone who could count to ten, it seems unlikely that violations would have been allowed to occur. And if an individual and his supporters were powerful enough to assume the office in violation of the law, then he would presumably be too powerful to be punished by the community. The publication of the rule limiting office-holding and the prescription of severe penalties for violators, therefore, may have served an 'expressive' or 'symbolic' function in articulating what the community considered acceptable and unacceptable behavior. For the 'expressive' function of even rarely enforced Athenian laws in altering behavior, see Lanni (forthcoming).

2 'Whenever he should give judgment, he is to owe double': reference to the *kosmos* giving judgment suggests that this was a particularly important or prominent function of the office; it may also suggest that the process of judging was particularly prone to abuse. For the *kosmos* as judge, see also **Da1**, **Elt1**, and Introd. 4C1c). It was fairly common in early Greece to impose a fine on officials for not carrying out their duties. For a double fine, see e.g. **G78**.7–8.

3 'He is to be without rights' (*akrēstos*, lit. 'useless'): we cannot be certain of the implications of the term in this context. Suggestions range from the loss of all rights comparable to the extreme form of Athenian *atimia* (Demargne and van Effenterre 1937b: 343–5), to loss of certain civic rights only, e.g. the right to serve again as *kosmos* (Ehrenberg 1943: 16), to public recognition of the *akrēstos* as an object of scorn without (necessarily) any loss of civic rights (Triantaphyllopoulos 1964: 907–8).

'Whatever he should do as *kosmos* is to be void': the expression implies that he exercised functions in addition to judging. To enforce this penalty would require, first, remembering everything the *kosmos* had done—a *mnamon* ('rememberer') would help, if there was one at Dreros (Introd. 4C3)—and then reversing court judgments and other acts that may have occurred as much as nine years earlier. This is another reason for thinking that the penalties are primarily an expression of community sentiment (see above on 2–3).

4 The last line is doubly marked as a separate (though presumably related) provision, by the break in the boustrophedon pattern and by the unusual punctuation mark.

'Oath-swearers': references to oath-taking are common in the laws of Crete, most notably in the case of judges who often swear an oath before deciding a case (Introd. 10D2). Laws usually specify the occasion when an oath is to be sworn and identify the oath-takers; as a rule they do not provide the details of the oath itself (cf. **G51**, **G72**.3.5–9), but the general thrust of the oath can usually be inferred from the context. Here, no context is specified, so we are forced to speculate.

The provision is included as part of the inscription but is also set off from the law proper by punctuation, archaic paragraphing, and the change in syntax to a simple declarative in line 4 ('The oath-swearers (are) . . . '). This suggests that these oaths were sworn when the law was enacted. The swearers presumably promise to uphold the law and its provisions for punishing violators. We would expect the *kosmos* to be one of the oath-swearers on such an occasion; the other two groups presumably represent the community and confirm its support for the law. Demargne and van Effenterre (1937b: 346–7) proposed that the officials whom the law most directly concerned (i.e. the *kosmos* and others) swore to observe the law on the occasion of its enactment and speculated that their successors would do so upon taking office.

The oath-swearing clause suggests that the legislative process at Dreros was seen as a joint action, involving the community as a whole, its chief official, and other representative groups. **Da1**A1–2 suggests a similar procedure: the Dataleis decided and a group consisting of five men from each of the tribes as representatives of the polis promised (the verb probably implies that an oath was sworn) to comply with their decision.

'The *kosmos*': the singular has been variously interpreted as a collective singular referring to a board of *kosmoi* (Demargne and van Effenterre 1937b: 346; Ehrenberg 1943: 17; M&L 2; VER I.81), or as a reference to a *protokosmos* or chairman of the board who took the oath on its behalf (Beattie 1975: 14). However, the term *protokosmos* is only attested in Hellenistic inscriptions from a few Cretan cities (Arkades, Gortyn, Itanos, Lyktos, Milatos, Priansos, Praisos), and the evidence for more than one *kosmos* or specialist *kosmoi* is inconclusive (Introd. 4C1a). Moreover, the contrast with the plural *damioi* that follows suggests that if more than one *kosmos* were present, the plural would have been used. Thus, although we cannot absolutely rule out the presence of more than one *kosmos* at Dreros, we see no reason to interpret *kosmos* here as anything but a single official.

'The *damioi* and the twenty of the polis': neither group is attested elsewhere; their identity and function remain obscure. The original editors suggested that these were the officials with a direct interest in the law, and that they functioned as watchdogs and debt collectors (Demargne and van Effenterre 1937b: 346–7). Later, however, van Effenterre (1985, cf. VER I.308) suggested that the *damioi* were powerful landowners residing in the agricultural hinterland or *damos* (for *damos* in the sense of 'agricultural land', see Chantraine 1980: s.v. δῆμος) and 'the twenty of the polis' were representatives of the urban dwellers (taking polis in the sense of 'urban center'). The swearers, then, were the *kosmos*, potentially rich landowners residing in the country, and a group representing those who resided in the city. We think this unlikely for two reasons.

First, there is very little evidence for dispersed habitation in the agricultural hinterlands of the early archaic communities of Crete and none at all for Dreros. The seventh-century pattern appears instead to favor aggregation (Introd. 2A3b, 2C). A passage in **G72** mentions town houses and country houses (**G72**.4.33–5), but **G72** dates to the fifth century, by which time there is greater evidence for dispersed settlement and intensive agriculture at least in the Western Mesara (Watrous and Hadzi-Vallianou 2004a: 313–14, 318–25). In seventh-century Dreros, however, we should imagine that landowners lived primarily in the urban center, making the distinction between urbanites and country dwellers difficult to accept. Second, *polis* is unlikely to be used in a different sense here and in line 1, where it clearly means 'political community'. Where different senses of *polis* are found in the same law (e.g. **G79**.9–10, 16) the meaning is clear from the context. Most scholars, however, identify 'the twenty of the polis' as a council of some kind (Ehrenberg 1943: 17; J–MD 1970: 129; Beattie 1975: 14) or a committee of the council (Demargne and van Effenterre 1937b: 347) or of the assembly (Willetts 1955: 168). More likely, 'the twenty of the polis' is a representative group selected out of all the members of the political class comparable to the 'five from each tribe' in **Da1** and selected for a similar reason; the ritual of swearing an oath (or pouring a libation at Datala) was important for the entire political community, but it would be impractical for all members to participate directly in the ceremony. Thus a smaller group swore the oath on behalf of all. The identity of the *damioi* remains for us obscure.

Dr2 (van Effenterre 1946a: 588–90, no. 1; Bile 30, no. 3; VER I.66). Enactment of an action initiated by the Prepsidai and the Milatioi. *c.*650–600. Current location unknown.[382] FIG. 23

Two lines inscribed on the two joining fragments of a limestone block. The text began at the right and continued below in boustrophedon from the left.[383] Several letters are missing from the beginning of line 1, and a space above the beginning of the line suggests that it is probably the first line of the text. The *vacat* in line 2 indicates that the end of the text is preserved. Van Effenterre notes the similarity between the letters here and those in **Dr1**.

1 *[ἔϝα]δε· ἆι οἰ Πρεπσίδαι | κοὶ Μιλάτιοι ἆ-* ←
2 *ρκσαν. vac.* →

It was decided (?): as the Prepsidai and the Milatioi initiated.

[382] VER report that the blocks bearing **Dr2** were lost during World War II.

[383] See van Effenterre 1946a: pl. XXX.3. The direction of the text is reversed in his drawing on p. 589; this error is repeated by VER, who think the lines are the end of a text that began on another block (presumably the one above this one).

FIG. 23. **Dr2**
:awing after JP)

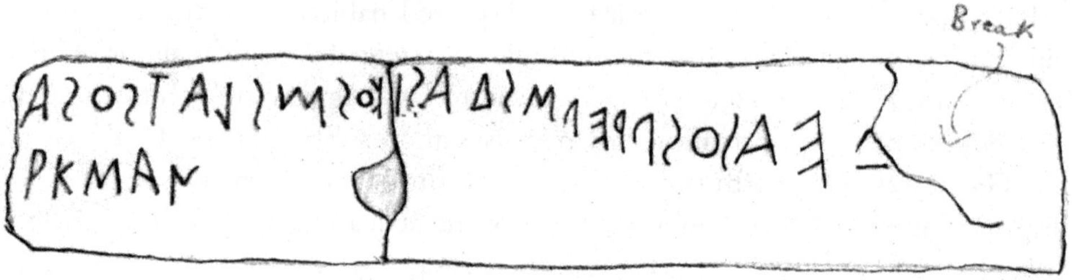

1 [ἔϝα]δε: van Effenterre. The space to the right of the initial *delta* appears to be just right for these three letters. VER tentatively reject both this and simple δέ in favor of the suffix -δε, indicating direction towards); but if the text begins with this line, then ἔϝαδε seems most likely, despite the absence of a dative qualifier. We are maybe meant to understand πόλι with ἔϝαδε (Introd. 10B).

ἆι 'as', the most common sense of this term (Bile 262). The indicative mood of ἆρκσαν rules out the conditional αἰ.

|: The vertical dividing line is recorded in the drawing and visible in the photo in van Effenterre 1946a, but is omitted in the text he publishes and in VER.

1–2 ἆρκσαν: there is no parallel for this use of the verb or for a procedure of initiating a piece of legislation; elsewhere in Cretan laws ἄρκο occurs in the sense of initiating a law suit (ἄρκον τᾶς δίκας, **G42**B4; **72**.11.51) or beginning a fight (ἄρκσει μάκας, **Elt2**.2).

If the text as restored is complete, as seems likely, it immediately raises the question: What was enacted and by whom? Since the text has no meaning without an answer to the first question, this information was probably supplied by some other text, now lost, that would have been displayed above or in the vicinity of this text. The enacting body is most likely the polis, which enacts **Dr1** and **5**. Only this body might not need to be mentioned explicitly in an enactment formula, if it was assumed that any publicly displayed enactment was the work of the polis. Cf. **Dr3**, which in our view is similar in this regard.

1 'The Prepsidai and the Milatioi': Milatos was located on the coast nine km. northwest of Dreros. For the location, see Nowicki 2000: 170–1, who notes the easy communication between Milatos and the Neapolis valley to the south; for its history, see Perlman 2004b: 1178. The Milatioi are mentioned in a (possibly archaic) text embedded in the Hellenistic Drerian oath of the *agelaoi* that describes them as having waged a war for territory against Dreros (*IC* 1.9.1, lines 137–64). During the Archaic period the territory of Milatos most likely shared a border with Dreros. The name Prepsidai is not otherwise attested. The patronymic suffix -*idai* suggests a community that defined itself on the basis of personal affiliation and descent from a common ancestor; it is the only example of such a name from Crete. Faure 1959: 202 identifies the community as a village descended from a single ancestor rather than a state; VER suggest a tribal or familial group.

The location of the group is unknown; one possibility is the settlement on Vrachassi Anavlochos, a high ridge six km. northwest of Dreros (see Nowicki 2000: 171–3).

1–2 'Initiated': there is no parallel in Crete for this use of the verb, which elsewhere is used for initiating a law suit or beginning a fight (see note on 1–2 above), but it would not be difficult to extend this sense to initiating legislation. The two groups were probably political dependencies (so VER) or allies of Dreros; they may have acted singly or together. Beyond this, we can only guess at the procedure involved.

Dr3 (*SEG* 23.530; van Effenterre 1946a: 597–600, no. 3; Bile 30, no. 5; K 92; VER I.68 and II.89). Law concerning the *etaireiai*. *c.*650–600. Archaeological Collection of Neapolis (Inv. no. 906). FIGS. 24, 25, 26

Two lines of text on a single block which was intact at the time of its discovery but was subsequently broken into at least three pieces. The band of uneven width worked with a punch and hammer along the upper edge of the inscribed face was probably associated with the construction of the temple. The right end of the block with the first four letters of line 1 is lost; what survives consists of two joining fragments. The text begins at the lower right and continues above in boustrophedon, a highly unusual order. Line 1 was inscribed on a relatively smooth band along the lower edge of the block. Line 2 was inscribed on a protruding but also relatively smooth surface above this. This surface dips down and interrupts the surface of line 1 about two-thirds of the way toward the left edge. A single letter, or a word-divider, inscribed on this dip appears to belong to line 1 (FIG. 26). The circular and curved letters (*omicron*, heads of *beta* and *rho*, *iota*) were produced with a punch and hammer, the others with a straight chisel.

Van Effenterre first published **Dr3** in 1946, and then published a slightly different text with a substantially different interpretation in 1961. The two texts agree on the last five letters of line 1 (*τô ὐπε-*) and all of line 2. Since then, scholars have adopted one or the other of these versions, and VER include both as separate texts. We have decided to adopt van Effenterre's first version of the text but with a different understanding of what it means (**Dr3**). We then give van Effenterre's second version (**Dr3**A), followed by a new version that combines these two (**Dr3**B).

2 *ρβοίο | μῆνος | ἐν ἰκάδι | ὄρον ἦμεν.* *vac.* →
1 *ἐτ̣αρηιᾶν | ἔϝαδε ὅζ' ἀγ̣έλασι τô ὐπε-* ←

Concerning *etairēiai*, it was decided, as much as for *agelai*, the twentieth of Hyperboios is to be (the) limit.

1 Van Effenterre 1946a: 597 suggested that 3–4 letters may have been lost to the right of the initial *epsilon*. His photograph suggests that enough of the inscribed surface survives to the right of the epsilon that traces of the upper part of a letter would probably have been preserved, but the possibility of missing letters cannot be completely ruled out.

. **Dr3**

FIG. 25. **Dr3**
rawing after JP)

IG. 26. Close-
up of **Dr3** with
(from bottom
ght): *ΖΑΓΕΛΑ*
or *ΖΑ|ΕΛΑ*

ἐτ̣αρηιᾶν | ἔϝαδε ὅζ' ἀγ̣έλασι: in our understanding, ἐτ̣αρηιᾶν is a genitive of reference used at the beginning of a provision to state its subject (see note on **G72**.1.4), ἔϝαδε is used impersonally ('it was decided'), and ὅζ' = ὅσα ('as many as') has the sense of 'just as'. The construction of the dative ἀγ̣έλασι is understood from what follows: 'just as (it is) for the *agelai*, the twentieth of Hyperboios is the limit (for the *etairēiai*)'. Van Effenterre understands ἐτ̣αρηιᾶν as a genitive ('of the *etairēiai*'), but its precise function in the sentence is not clear. He then understands ἔϝαδε as impersonal, as we do, and ὅζ' ἀγ̣έλασι together with what follows: 'for everything that concerns the *agelai*'.

τ̣ The 1946a photograph and drawing show only the vertical stroke, which reaches up to the lower edge of the protruding band above it.

ἐτ̣αρηιᾶν (= ἐταιρηιᾶν) gen. pl., though the form could also be acc. sing. This spelling is otherwise unattested, but cf. the epic variant ἕταρος/ἑτάρη.

ἔϝαδε: most other examples at Dreros are construed with a dative, but there is apparently no dative in **Dr2**.1; we are probably meant to understand the polis as the enacting body. Seelentag 2009b: 152 suggests that πόλι originally stood at the beginning of line 1 because an absolute usage would be without parallel, but **Dr2** provides a parallel, and (as he admits) the separation of ἔϝαδε from its dative complement would be unusual.

ἀγ̣έλασι: although the dotted *gamma*, inscribed on the dip in the surface bearing line 2, was later interpreted as a vertical dividing line (n. ad **Dr3**A.1), the hook at the top of the vertical line is clear (Fig. 26). The letter could also be *pi*. Before this, there is a clear space with room for one letter. It is puzzling that the mason did not inscribe the *gamma* (if that is what it is) in this space rather than in the protruding dip.

1–2 τô ὑπερβοίο μῆνος ἐν ἰκάδι ὅρον ἦμεν: the meaning is unproblematic (lit. 'the limit is to be on the twentieth of Hyperboios'), but there is no indication of what was being limited. Another law before or after this one may have made this clear.

Although **Dr3** was completely preserved at the time of its discovery and the Greek of the main provision is transparent ('the twentieth of Hyperboios is to be the limit'), the sense of the whole law is far from certain.

1 These are the earliest references from Crete to the *hetaireia* and the *agelai* (Introd. 6A and 6B); neither is otherwise attested at Dreros. The provisions for adoption at Gortyn imply that every Gortynian was a member of a *hetaireia* (**G72**.10.37–9). The *agela* ('band' of youths) is attested for Sparta and Crete by later writers; the inscribed 'oath of the 180 *agelaoi*' from Dreros proves the existence there of the institution of the *agela* in the Hellenistic period (*IC* 1.9.1). For the *agelaoi*, see also **Elt2**.7.

1–2 The month name Hyperboios is not otherwise known, but a festival called the Hyperboia is attested on Crete in the Hellenistic period at Hierapytna, Malla, and Priansos. This annual festival appears to have served as the occasion for the renewal of treaties and for the graduation of the *agelaoi* (see Willetts 1962: 239; Trümpy 1997: 191, 227; Sporn 2002: 320). Van Effenterre 1946a identified the twentieth day of Hyperboios as the day of the ceremony when the youths of Dreros were inducted into the *agela*, current members graduated from it, or both;

this is not impossible (though the supporting arguments are based on much later evidence), but it does not explain why the text speaks of a 'limit' rather than specifying 'on the twentieth'.

Dr3A. Law regulating hunting (*SEG* 23.530; van Effenterre 1961: 547–52; K 92; VER II.89)

2 ρβοίο | μῆνος | ἐν ἰκάδι | ὅρον ἦμεν. *vac.* →
1 ἐ̃ | ἀρήιαν | ἔϝαδε ὄζα· *vac.* | ἐλάσι τô ὑπε- ←

In the event that they should hunt it was decided how much (they would hunt). For driving (prey?) the twentieth of Hyperboios is to be the limit.

---

1 The two crucial paleographic changes in the 1961 text are to read the second sign and the eighteenth sign as word-dividers instead of ṭ and γ respectively. The second change is difficult (see above note on **Dr3**.1). Moreover, the gap just before this also suggests word division here, making the word divider redundant. There is no other example in Crete of a dividing line and a gap together in the middle of a text (but cf. **G14**p–g2).

ἐ̃: 'when'; see n. ad **G72**.6.1.

ἀρήιαν: van Effenterre 1961: 547 takes this as an optative (= ἄρειαν, from αἴρω/ἀείρω, in the sense of 'to take up and carry off'), though there is no other example of this form of the optative in archaic and classical Crete (for a full discussion of optative forms, see Bile 233–8). The construction of ἐ̃ with the optative is also unattested. But an optative cannot be entirely ruled out, and there is no evident reason why ἐ̃ could not be construed with an optative. More difficult is the meaning 'hunt', which van Effenterre 1961: 548–9 infers by presuming a method of hunting in which beaters flush game towards the hunters who then 'catch and carry off' the animals. He compares *Odyssey* 21.18, which involves robbery not hunting. K accepts this text but understands the verb to mean 'take up, begin', with a reference to hunting understood from ἐλάσι in the following clause: 'when they should begin (the hunt)'.

ἔϝαδε: see n. ad **Dr3**.1.

ἐλάσι: Van Effenterre takes this as dat. sing. from ἔλασις 'driving', which is not elsewhere used of hunting.

The advantage of **Dr3**A is that the gap in line 1 occurs between clauses, not in the middle of the word *agelasi*, as in **Dr3**.1. The difficulties are first the meanings of *arēian* and *elasi*, neither of which normally has anything to do with hunting, and second the interpretation of the eighteenth sign in line 1 as a word divider (not a *gamma*). The presence of a word divider right after an initial conjunction would also be unusual, as would a word divider together with a gap.

1–2 would regulate hunting at Dreros by prescribing some sort of limit. Although no other Cretan law concerns hunting, we may presume that hunting was common on the island. If we assume that Hyperboios was a month in the autumn the regulation would prescribe an end to the hunting season, presumably to prevent the complete disappearance of game (so van Effenterre 1961: 550–1). But the idea of restricting hunting for this purpose is not only unknown but difficult to imagine in antiquity (K ad loc.).

Dr3B

Another possible version of this law would be to combine parts of **Dr3** and **Dr3**A as follows. This version would have some of the advantages and disadvantages of each.

2 *ρβοίο | μῆνος | ἐν ἰκάδι | ὅρον ἦμεν. vac.* →
1 *ἐ̑ | ἀρήιαν | ἔϜαδε· ὅζ' ἀγ̣έλασι τô ὑπε-* ←

When they hunt it was decided: whatever concerns the *agelai* the twentieth of Hyperboios is to be (the) limit.

Dr4 (van Effenterre 1946a: 600–2, no. 4; Bile 30–1, no. 6; K 93; VER I.27). Law concerning ritual? *c*.650–600. Archaeological Collection of Neapolis (Inv. no. 360). FIGS. 27, 28, 29

Three lines of text on a single block, which is broken in two, with some of the inscribed surface lost at the join. The text appears complete with an enactment clause marking the beginning and a noticeable space below line 3. The mason began all three lines at the right (but the last two letters of 2 curl below and back to the right). The significance of the direction of writing is uncertain. Jeffery (1990: 47–8) suggests that perhaps the mason was left-handed. The mason took care to avoid areas with an irregular surface. He used a punch and hammer throughout; his *gamma*, *lambda*, and *upsilon* are later forms different from those in the other Drerian laws (see FIG. 3: *Γ*2, *Λ*2, *Υ*3). Thus, **Dr4** is probably one of the later laws from Dreros.

1 *ἔϜαδε τοῖ[σ]ι θύστασι·* ←
2 *ὃς μέν κα διδôι μισθόν* ←
3 *λαγκάνεν .Υ̣ΕΙ̣. vac.* ←

The *thystai* decided: whoever gives a wage, is to receive [*c*.5].

---

1 *θύστασι* van Effenterre, K; see Hesychius s.v. *θύστας· ὁ ἱερεὺς παρὰ Κρησί*. Cf. *τοῖς ἰθυντᾶσι* ('redresseurs'): VER from *ἰθύνεν* (Attic *εὐθύνειν*); but the letter they read as *nu* is clearly *san*.

2 *μισθόν* VER; van Effenterre 1946a recorded . *ι̣σο̣* ., suggesting *μ* or *san* before the *ι̣* and *ι* after the *ο̣*, but no trace of an *ι* at the end of the line survives. Duhoux 1982: 29 suggested [*Ϝ*]*ῖσο*[*ν*] (cf. J–MD 1970: 141; K p. 342), but *μ* and *θ* are legible.

3 Following the second *nu* there is a vertical stroke then the left oblique of *Υ̣*. Van Effenterre and JP record the vertical stroke then *Ο̣ΕΗ̣*. These letters appear to be the end of the text as there is a space below line 3 and the final letters of line 2 would prevent 3 from continuing to the left. This appears, then, to be a case of *μέν* solitarium.

FIG. 27. **Dr4**

FIG. 28. **Dr4**
rawing after JP)

FIG. 29. **Dr4**, right

The law concerns the payment of a wage (*misthos*), but uncertainty about the last few letters prevents us from saying more. The particle *men* in the relative clause without an answering *de* is unusual.

1 'The *thystai*': Hesychius (fifth century CE?) identifies *thystas* as a Cretan word for priest; the term is not otherwise attested. As the enactors of this law, it is likely that the *thystai* were a specific group of priests. The term derives from *thyō*, 'to sacrifice', and the law may concern sacrificial procedure (so van Effenterre 1946a; K; VER); but insofar as sacrifice was performed in connection with many if not most cults and public festivals, it is also possible that the *thystai* were associated with a specific cult and that the law concerns some other aspect of that cult (Introd. 9C, 9E).

2 'Wage': the term *misthos* is attested in several other Cretan laws (**A1**.11, **Da1**A11, **G79**.8–9) where it refers to wages paid by a polis to its employees (Perlman 2004a: 112–17). Here, however, it is not the polis but an individual, perhaps one of the *thystai*, who gives the wages.

3 'Is to receive': the object cannot be made out. If the wage was payment for the performance of a sacrifice, it is likely that the person who paid received in return a portion of the meat.

Dr5 (van Effenterre 1946a: 590–7, no. 2; Bile 30, no. 4; K 91; VER I.64). Law concerning the *agretas*? *c.*650–600. Archaeological Collection of Neapolis (fragment from left: Inv. no. 358). FIGS. 30, 31

Two lines of text written boustrophedon from the right on a single limestone block, which was broken in two. The right fragment is lost; we know of no photograph of it. The text begins near the top right corner and continues irregularly to the left, dipping lower to avoid irregularities in the stone; line 2 follows the course traced by 1. The mason used a punch and hammer throughout.

πόλι ἔϜαδε διαλείσασι πυλᾶσι· | ὅστ̣ις προ- ←
πολέϜ̣σ̣ειε μὴ τίν[[τ]]εσθα⟨ι⟩ τὸν ἀγρέταν. vacat →

The polis decided, with the tribes assembled (?): whoever ministers, the *agretas* is not to punish (him).

---

1 διαλείσασι: van Effenterre aor. pass. part. of διειλέω (aor. pass. διάλην)? Van Effenterre transcribes η rather than ει, but notes (p. 592) that ει is possible. We think ει is almost certain: the *H* in line 2 and those in other Drerian inscriptions are different; the feminine participle of διαλῆν should be διαλεῖσα; and the preceding *epsilon* is similarly connected to the letter that follows (*delta*). The meaning of διειλέω, which otherwise occurs only in Plutarch, *Moralia* 1039e in the sense 'unroll', is uncertain, but if διαλείσασι is a form of διειλέω, it should probably be connected with κατειλέω, which occurs several times at Gortyn with the meaning 'assembled' (**G72**.10.35, 11.13, **G80**.14–15). Van Effenterre (p. 592) was reluctant to claim the same meaning for the compound with διά, and

FIG. 30. **Dr5** (drawing after JP)

IG. 31 **Dr5**, left

suggested instead 'consult' (so K), and VER also suggest 'disperse'; but in compound verbs both διά and κατά frequently denote completion of the action of the verb stem (Smyth 1956: §1648). διειλέω, then, could be taken to mean much the same thing as κατειλέω. Cf. Bile 135 n. 245, 197 n. 172 and Genevrois 2012: 286 who question the form, derivation, and meaning. For the construction, see commentary.

Van Effenterre's drawing records what appear to be traces of a letter at the left edge of the stone, but we do not see them and if they are accurately recorded we cannot suggest to what letter(s) they might belong.

2 Ϝ̣ the upper oblique stroke of the *digamma* is legible.

ϙ̣ the right half of the *san* is legible.

1–2 προπολέϜ̣ϙ̣ειε: aor. opt. from προπολεύω, 'attend to' or 'minister to', not otherwise attested on Crete. The word is used of individuals who minister to the gods, e.g. θεαῖς ταθηνηι (?) προπολεύειν (*IK Knidos.* I.131; *SEG* 53.1225, fourth century). It may be worth noting that **G90*** preserves προπο . [—]. The traces of the letter following the *omicron* (the lower part of a vertical stroke) are consistent with *lambda* (as well as other letters). **G9** also has two occurrences of ἀγρῆιον, a cognate of ἀγρέτας (see below).

2 τίν[[τ]]εσθα⟨ι⟩: the mason intended τίνεσθαι 'to punish', but inserted a *tau* where he should not have and inscribed a *tau* rather than an *iota* at the end of the infinitive. The

drawing in van Effenterre suggests that the future infinitive τίσεσθα⟨ι⟩ is possible, but the future infinitive is not used to express the imperative anywhere on Crete (although the future indicative may be used in this way); see Bile 264.

ἀγρέταν may be derived from the ἀγείρω ('gather, cause to assemble') and is attested in the sense of 'military leader' (Aesch. *Persians* 1002 ἀγρέται στρατοῦ; Hesychius s.v. ἀγρέταν· ἡγεμόνα, θεόν; cf. Xen. *LP* 4.3; *Hell.* 3.3.9 for the ἱππαγρέται at Sparta). Van Effenterre suggested that the *agretas* of Dreros was a military or political official, perhaps a herald, and K thinks a military role is most likely, but priest/ess is also possible (Hesychius s.v. ἀγρεταί· παρὰ Κῴοις ἐννέα κόραι κατ' ἐνιαυτὸν αἱρούμεναι πρὸς θεραπείαν τῆς Ἀθηνᾶς; cf. Sokolowsky 1969: no. 156).

If **Dr5** is completely preserved, as we believe it is, it prevents the punishment of someone who serves (a god?) by an official, the *agretas*. But the many difficulties involved in interpreting the text make any reconstruction uncertain.

1 'Tribes' (*pylai*) are otherwise given a formal role in public matters on Crete only in **Da1**A1–2, where the polis, represented by five men from each of the tribes promised its compliance with the agreement enacted by the citizens ('the Dataleis'). The names of two of the tribes of Dreros, Aithaleis and Dymanes, are known from later inscriptions (Aithaleis: Demargne and van Effenterre 1937a: 29–32; *IC* 1.9.1; Dymanes: Marinatos 1936: 280–5). The role of the tribes is uncertain (Introd. 4B3); it appears likely that they are coextensive with the polis but the relationship between the two remains unclear. Elsewhere, a formal role for the *pylai* in the enactment of decrees is attested only at Mylasa, Caria, where three mid-fourth-century decrees were decided by the Mylaseis at a sovereign meeting of the assembly, and ratified by the three tribes (*IK Mylasa* 1–3). In those texts the membership of the three tribes is certainly coextensive with the citizen population of the polis.

1 'With the tribes assembled': if 'assembled' is the correct meaning of *dialeisasi* (see note), the implications of the phrase 'with the tribes assembled' are uncertain. The expression could mean that the tribes assembled and then a separate body, i.e. the polis, decided, and thus that the tribes had only an advisory role; but it is not clear that a dative participial phrase can be construed in this absolute way, which would normally require the genitive. Thus, it is more likely that the participial phrase stands in apposition to *polis* (also in the dative)—'it was pleasing to the polis, that is, to the tribes assembled'—indicating that, at least for the purpose of ratification, the assembled tribes comprised the polis. This may suggest that when the whole polis met, it assembled by tribe, and that the polis was thus roughly equivalent to all those who belonged to one of the tribes.

1–2 'Whoever ministers': if the text is correct, the context is probably that of ministering to a god.

2 'Is not to punish (him)': if correct, compare this provision granting immunity to anyone who 'ministers' with provisions in several Cretan laws that grant

immunity for various actions; the phrase commonly used was *apatos emen* ('is to be without penalty'). See Bile 326.

The *agretas* may be a military, political, or religious official (see note).

Dr6 (van Effenterre 1946a: 603–4, no. 6; Bile 31, no. 8). Law concerning sacrifices. *c.*650–600. Current location unknown. FIGS. 32, 33

Two lines of text on a single block, with another three letters carved in a slight depression at the bottom with an empty space above them. Our text assumes that the original block was broken and that what survives is the left-hand portion. Some of the inscribed surface from the left edge of the extant fragment also appears to have broken off. The upper and lower edges of the inscribed surface are very irregular. The text begins from the right and continues boustrophedon. The letters were inscribed with a punch and hammer; van Effenterre notes their similarity to the letters in **Dr4**.

1 [—] ἔν τε *Πυτίοι* | π̣ε̣ν̣[τε —] ←
2 [—] ἐν 'Αγ[ο]ραίοι | μηρός Ρ̣[—] →
3 [—]*NOI*[— (?)] ←

[—] in the Pythion five (?) [—] in the Agoraion thighs [—]

FIG. 32. **Dr6**

FIG. 33. **Dr6** (drawing after JP)

1 *ἔ̈ν τε*: van Effenterre also suggests [*π*]*έντε*; an infinitive in *-εν* is possible, though unlikely.

|: as in **Dr2**.1, the vertical dividing line is clear in the drawing and photo in van Effenterre but is omitted in the text there; a similar divider in line 2 is printed in his text.

π̣ε̣ν̣[*τε*—]: van Effenterre also suggests *γ̣ε̣ν̣*[—]. He records a vertical stroke following *ν̣* and possibly traces of a letter at the left edge of the inscribed surface.

2 Van Effenterre reads the last letter as *Π*, but both his drawing and his photo indicate the rounded head of *P*.

What survives of this text indicates that it concerns sacrifice, and more specifically is a type of 'sacrificial calendar'; cf. **G3**, which similarly has the form of a list, and Introd. 9A, 10C.

1–2 Pythios and Agoraios are also attested at Dreros in the Hellenistic period, as oath gods (*IC* 1.9.1, lines 17–18, 24), and elsewhere on Crete as epithets of Apollo and Zeus respectively (Sporn 2002: 320, 321), but always together with the name of the god. However, the neuter singular, Pythion, is attested alone as a name for the temple or sanctuary of Apollo Pythios (*IC* 3.4.7, lines 15, 31, third century; *IC* 4.182, line 19, second century). Thus, the text more likely refers to the temples or sanctuaries of the two gods, probably as the locations of sacrifices. No material remains have been associated with a temple or sanctuary of Zeus Agoraios at Dreros, but it was presumably in the vicinity of the agora. See D'Acunto 2002–3: 23–4; 50–3. The temple in the saddle is usually identified as the Delphinion because Apollo Delphinios is mentioned in the Hellenistic inscription commemorating the completion of the cistern, which lies just east of the temple (Demargne and van Effenterre 1937a: 29–32). But some scholars prefer to identify the temple in the saddle as the Pythion and the temple on the west acropolis as the Delphinion. For a detailed review of the identification of the temples and the nature of the cults, see D'Acunto (2002–3), who associates the temple in the saddle with Apollo Delphinios and the temple on the west acropolis with a warrior goddess, possibly Athena Poliouchos.

Dr7 (*SEG* 15.564; van Effenterre 1946a: 602–3, no. 5; Duhoux 1982: 113–18; Bile 31, no. 7; VER II.10). Law concerning oaths. *c*.650–600. Archaeological Museum of Heraklion (fragment from left, Inv. no. ?). FIGS. 34, 35

Three lines of text on a single block, now broken in two pieces, the right one of which was lost shortly after its discovery. Apart from the left-hand piece, we depend for our knowledge of the text on drawings (van Effenterre and JP) and a photograph taken by van Effenterre but published in Duhoux 1982 (pl. 29). The drawings and photograph suggest that some of the inscribed surface is lost along the right edge; furthermore, it is also possible that the block is broken at the right. The boustrophedon text begins at the upper right and follows the irregular surface of the stone.

FIG. 34. **Dr7**

FIG. 35. **Dr7** (drawing after JP)

[—]ς | τ' ὑπ⟨ε⟩ρμηρίδια, ὀμô- ←
νται δ' ἅπερ ἐν ὀρκίοισι, α[—] →
[—] καθαρὸν γένοιτο. *vacat* ←

[—] the femurs (?), they will swear just as in (the) oaths, [if (?) —] it should be pure.

---

1 There is room for 5 letters to the right of the first preserved letter, but we cannot be certain that the stone did not originally extend further to the right.

τ' = τά (τε without καί is not attested in the epichoric inscriptions from Crete).

ὑπ⟨ε⟩ρμηρίδια: attested only on Crete; cf. *SEG* 41.743 (Eleutherna, fourth–third century).

1–2 ὀμôνται: cf. ὀμόσ̣αι VER, but the letters are clear in the photographs in McDonald 1956 (pl. 27a) and Duhoux 1982 (pl. 29).

ἅπερ ἐν ὀρκίοισι: cf. *IC* 3.4.7, lines 10–13, third century, ἐξορκιζόντω αὐτοὺς . . . τοῖς αὐτοῖς ὀρκίοις οἷσπερ ὤμνυον τοὶ ἐπίδαμοι, 'let the officials swear them to the same oaths as the residents swore'.

2 α[—]: possibly α[ἰ] if there is a relatively short space between lines 1 and 2.

2–3 If relatively few letters (4–5?) are missing from the right, one possibility would be α[ἰ τὸ ἱήριον], 'if the sacrificial victim' (cf. *IC* 4.145, line 4, ἱήρια καθαρά̣, fifth–fourth century).

There is no room on the stone as it survives for an enactment clause (cf. **Dr6**); but it may be that a piece of the original block has broken off at the right.

1 'Femurs' (*hypermēridia*): the word is also attested at Eleutherna in a Hellenistic inscription (*SEG* 41.743) that preserves the text of an oath. There the reference occurs before the oath, perhaps in the description of the sacrifice that was to accompany the oath ceremony. Thigh bones were the quintessential sacrificial offering, and the femur is one of the bones most frequently found in sacrificial contexts; see Berthiaume 1982 48–9; Reese 2005.

1–3 The rule that 'they will swear' is apparently premised on the purity of something, most likely the sacrificial offering. Thus understood, the law concerns an oath ceremony, describing the sacrifice that must precede or accompany the oath and emphasizing the requirement to recite the oath faithfully. There is no indication of the occasion or the content of the oath or the identity of the individuals involved.

ELEUTHERNA

Site

The polis-town of ancient Eleutherna was located twenty-five kilometers south-east of Rethymno in the foothills of Mt. Psiloritis (ancient Mt. Ida) at an altitude of almost 400 m. The ancient remains occupy two parallel ridges running roughly north–south, Pyrgi (Prines Hill) to the east and Nisi (Eleutherna Hill) to the west (FIG. 36). Excavations undertaken by The University of Crete at Eleutherna since 1985 have greatly increased our knowledge of its settlement history and topography.[384]

Archaeological remains attest human presence in the area during the Early and Late Bronze Age,[385] but the earliest secure evidence of occupation dates to the early ninth century. Early Iron Age Eleutherna (ninth to seventh centuries) appears to have been settled as several small nuclei, with traces thus far identified on the east slope (Katsivelos) and on top of Pyrgi, the east slope of Nisi (Xeniana), and possibly on top of Nisi.[386] Pyrgi appears to have been the center of the early settlement. A large possibly public building (*c.*5 m by 15 m), dubbed the 'Geometric-Archaic megaron', was located on the east slope of Pyrgi at Katsivelos;[387] a second seventh-century building of comparable size (*c.*6.5 m by 11 m) on top of Pyrgi has been identified as a temple (Kalpaxis 2004: 110–13). Concentrations of votive offerings (terracotta figurines) dating to the eighth and seventh centuries attest the location of a second early sanctuary on Pyrgi and another on Nisi (Stampolidis 2004a: 94; Kalpaxis 2004: 107–11). A significant cemetery was located on the west slope of Pyrgi at Orthi Petra, 20–40 m above the stream Chalopota (Stampolidis 1993, 1994, 1996, 2004b: 117–38; Kotsonas 2008). The area was used as a cemetery from the early ninth century until at least the early sixth. Pottery dating to the period *c.*600–400 found in the upper levels of the cemetery may mark the location of disturbed tombs of the Archaic and Classical periods (Erickson 2010a: 45–6).

[384] For the topography and history of Eleutherna and the archaeological remains of the polis-town, see Stampolidis 2004a.

[385] Stampolidis (2004a: 82–3) suggests the possibility of a settlement there, although no Bronze Age architectural remains have been identified. Kalpaxis (2004: 106–7) reports the discovery of a significant quantity of Bronze Age pottery on Pyrgi, including LM IIIC, but he does not think there was a settlement, citing the small size of the area where LM IIIC sherds were found (30 m.^{2}) and the absence of contemporary tombs in the vicinity. Cf. Nowicki 2000: 192–3 no. 90.

[386] Stampolidis 2004a: 85, 2004b: 117; Kalpaxis 2004: 107–10. Stampolidis proposes that each small nucleus had its own necropolis, although the only early cemetery thus far located is the one at Orthi Petra.

[387] Themelis 2002: 25–31, 2004: 48–9. Ceramic material associated with the foundations dates to the eighth and seventh centuries.

FIG. 36. Plan of Eleutherna

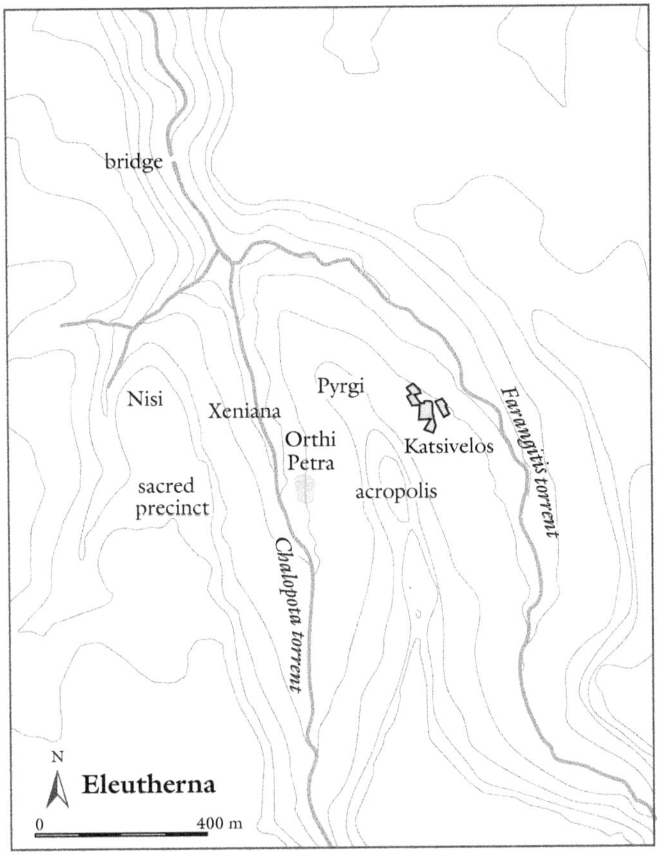

The inscribed blocks, none of them discovered in situ, comprise the only evidence for the presence of monumental structures until the end of the fifth century.[388] At the end of the fifth century (*c*.400?) a large enclosure (*peribolos*) (35 m. by 50 m.) with a monumental gateway was built on Nisi in the location of the earlier sanctuary (Stampolidis 2004a: 94; Kalpaxis 1991, 2004: 107–11). Van Effenterre (1991b: 28–30) identifies the *peribolos* as the sanctuary of Apollo Wilkonios and the meeting place of the Cretan *koinon*, an ephemeral federation of Cretan poleis that is certain to have existed only during the Hellenistic period at a time when Nisi was largely residential (Kalpaxis, Furtwängler, and Schnapp 1994).

The town commanded the coastal plain extending east from Rethymno to the coastal Kouloukounas range. This plain served as a major east–west artery in antiquity as it does today. The Amari valley, a principal north–south route linking the western Mesara and the north coast of Crete, intersects the coastal plain

388 Stampolidis 2004a: 93–4; Kalpaxis 2004: 112–13. Of course, the walls could have been built long before the texts were inscribed on them.

thirteen kilometers due west of the polis-town. Mt. Psiloritis occupied much of the hinterland of Eleutherna and no doubt served as the frontier between Eleutherna and Axos to the east, and the poleis of Phaistos and Gortyn to the south. To the north, Eleutherna may have controlled the territory all the way to the coast (see **Eleutherna1**).

Texts

We include thirteen of the nineteen epichoric inscriptions published in *IC* 2 (**Ele3–6, 8–9, 11, 13–18**) and five inscriptions that were discovered after its publication (**Eleutherna1–5**). We omit *IC* 2.12.1–2, 10, 12, and 19 and a number of very fragmentary texts published after *IC* 2 that are likely laws but which preserve no obviously legal language.[389]

All but one of our inscriptions of known provenance were found either on or in the vicinity of Pyrgi, the eastern ridge and acropolis of Eleutherna, or to the east of Pyrgi at Katsivelos; none was found in its original context.[390] It seems likely that the majority of these texts were originally inscribed on the walls of one or more public buildings, or, in the cases of **Ele18** and **Eleutherna1** and **3** inscribed on stelae and displayed in the vicinity of public buildings located on Pyrgi.

The inscriptions that consist of more than one line are written boustrophedon. The upper edges of seven are preserved (**Ele3–6, 14A, 16Aa, Eleutherna4**). The first lines of four of these begin at the left (**Ele4, 14A, 16Aa, Eleutherna4**).[391] Moreover, all *iotas* face to the right regardless of the direction of the line of text in five (**Ele5, 7, 8, 13, 15A+B.1–4**), suggesting that the masons of Eleutherna not only began writing from the left, but also conceived of writing as a rightward motion. The occurrence of successive lines beginning at the left in several texts (**Ele4, 9, 14, 15, Eleutherna4, 5**) represents the same system of paragraphing as is found elsewhere on Crete. An uninscribed band appears to have been left between the paragraphs in three of these (**Ele14A, 14B, Eleutherna4**).

Word-division is rare. A single vertical line occurs in *IC* 2.12.1, 10, and possibly **Ele18**.4, and two dots, one above the other, are used in **Ele13** and **15** (Introd. 3D1). The use of dots seems to be similar to that of the vertical line in the laws

[389] See *SEG* 39.955, 957; 41.747–52; Kalpaxis 2004: 112 fig. 8; Stampolides and Ikonomaki 2009: 305–10; Tzifopoulos 2009: 106–7, no. 5; Kotsonas forthcoming.

[390] **Ele3–8** were reused in Roman and early Byzantine walls near the church of Agia Irini on the eastern slopes of Pyrgi. **Ele9, 14A, 14B, 15B,** and **18** come from the walls of private homes in the village of Prines. **Eleutherna1** and **3** come from Area E on top of Pyrgi. **Ele16** was reused in a Christian tomb near the chapel of Agia Anna (Pyrgi). **Eleutherna2** is reported to have come from Nisi. **Ele11, 13, 17, Eleutherna4** and **5** appear to be of unknown provenance.

[391] In some cases (**Ele3, 5,** and **6**) the first line is not preserved.

inscribed on the Pythion at Gortyn. More common than word-division is the use of horizontal guidelines (**Ele3–4, 16–18**, and **Eleutherna1–4**).

Establishing a relative chronology for these inscriptions, let alone an absolute date for any of them, is not possible (cf. Ikonomaki 2010: 229–31). Guarducci (1939: 146) saw no reason to consider any of the inscriptions from Eleutherna published in *IC* 2 to be earlier than the sixth century and suggested that some might even belong in the fifth. Jeffery (1990: 314, 316 nos. 26, 27) dated all of them to the period *c*.525–500, identifying the two-bar *epsilon*, which occurs in **Ele3–5, 7, 9, 11, 13–16, 18, Eleutherna1, 3A, 4–5**, as a late archaic shorthand form of the letter. Other notable letter forms in the epichoric inscriptions from Eleutherna are: a straight (rather than a crooked or curvy) *iota* (**Ele16Aa, 18, Eleutherna3A**) and angular forms of *beta*, *theta*, *omicron/omega*, and *rho* that are used in several inscriptions (**Ele3, 14**A1–4, **16Ab, 16Ac, Eleutherna1**) and may be the work of a single mason. The possibly earlier three-bar epsilon is used in just one inscription (*IC* 2.12.1), which uses other forms (curvy *iota* and legless *rho*) unique to this text. References to staters (**Ele13, Eleutherna4**) and triobols (**Ele4**?, **9**), probably referring to coins, support a date no earlier than the late sixth century for these inscriptions (Introd. 7D).

Ele3 (K 109 [no text]; VER I.10). Law concerning *allopoliatai*. Sixth to fifth century. Archaeological Museum of Rethymno (Inv. no. E21)

Seven lines of text inscribed boustrophedon beginning at the left on a limestone block with a preserved upper edge; all other edges are broken. The text begins above line 1 (traces); it continues to the left and the right, but we cannot determine if it continues below line 7. The difficulty in making sense of this inscription suggests that a good deal of text has been lost on each side. For the distinctive hand that forms all letters with straight lines, see also **Ele14**A1–4.

traces	
[—]δοι̣ [τ]οῖς ἀλλοπολ̣[ιάταις —] →	— to the *allopoliatai* —
[—] κ' ὅρκον τιθέμεν τὸν̣ [—]	— the [—] is to make an oath —
[—]οι τὰν ἀρὰν ἰνήμε[ν —]	— the curse is to be included —
[—]πινυμεν μήτε θηρίον̣ [—]	— ? neither a beast —
[—]τα ἄπατον ἦμεν ὀϝτο[—]	— is to be immune —
[—]ν̣. αἰ δὲ μη[τ' ἐ]π̣ι̣βάλοι επο[—]	— but if he neither imposes —
[—]πομε̣[. . . .*c*.7 . . . .] . σ . [—]	

Unless otherwise indicated:

H = Halbherr notebook 4, p. 87; Comparetti and Halbherr 1888: 161–3 no. 2; Halbherr *ap.* Comparetti 1893: 419–21 no. 194.

C = Comparetti and Halbherr 1888: 161–3 no. 2; Comparetti 1893: 419–21 no. 194.

1 ι̣: the bottom stroke is visible. [— προ]δδο̂ι̣ C; [— ἀπ]ο̣δδο̂ι̣ VER.

λ̣: the lower tip of the vertical stroke is visible.

2 ν̣: the right two strokes and lower bit of a third stroke are visible (*san* and *mu* are also possible).

3 [το̂ι δὲ ὅρκ]οι G.

4 [μήτε Ζῆνα σ]πιν ὕμεν (= σφιν ὕειν) 'neither Zeus rain for him' C.

ν̣: the left stroke is visible.

5 [τὸν δ' ὀμόσαν]τα C, but many other restorations are possible.

ὀϝτο[—] = ὁ αὐτός, οὗτος, or οὕτως.

6 ν̣: upper part of oblique stroke; other letters are epigraphically possible (ι, μ, κ, υ), but less likely at the end of a sentence.

[ἐ]π̣ι̣βάλοι: H records a stroke (no longer visible) to the right of what we take to be the upper stroke of an *iota*. He interprets these two strokes as belonging to a single letter (*kappa, nu, upsilon*). μὴ[τ' ἐ]κ̣βάλοι C; μὴ[τ' ἐγ]βάλοι VER; ἐ]ν̣βάλοι *SGDI* 4954. The drawing in Halbherr notebook 4 is not consistent with the upper part of *K* (the tip of the vertical leans towards the right). We suggest the horizontal stroke of *pi*.

επο: could be ἐπ' ὀ[—] or ἐπο[—].

7 πομε̣: possibly [μεμ]πομε̣[νο —] 'plaintiff'? Elsewhere in **Ele3** the vertical and upper oblique strokes of the *epsilon* do not touch as they clearly do here, perhaps, then, ν̣ is also possible, e.g. [ἀ]πομν̣[—].

[—] . σ . [—]: the upper tips of two oblique strokes are visible on either side of *san*; [—]σ̣ο̣ [—] Guarducci 1967: 190.

---

1 *Allopoliatas* is otherwise attested at Lyktos (**Lyktos1A1–2**). G understands it to mean 'citizen (*poliatas*) from elsewhere (*allo-*)', similar to the Athenian metic or resident alien. Van Effenterre and van Effenterre 1985: 186–8 and VER think an *allopoliatas* is an expatriate (e.g. émigré, colonist, exile, or captive seized in war or by pirates), but the use of *poliatas* 'citizen' in **G83** supports G's view. Cf. *eks allopolias* 'from another city?' (**G72**.6.46–50). Perlman 2004a: 126–7 proposes that the term was coined to distinguish this from other categories of non-citizen (Introd. 5A5). Whether these *allopoliatai* were resident in Eleutherna or simply visitors there cannot be determined.

2–3 preserve the terms *orkos* 'oath' and *ara* 'curse'. For oaths in the archaic and classical laws, see Introd. 10D2. C, followed by G, restored line 3 to read 'the curse is to be included [in the oath]'. The link between an oath and a curse is attested in **G72**.2.36–41, where someone who is accused of seizing an adulterer by subterfuge is to swear (presumably that this is not the case) and to invoke a curse against himself.

4 C suggested that line 4 preserves part of the curse referred to in line 3. The construction is consistent with the syntax of curses in Hellenistic civic and treaty oaths, which are expressed as conditions (e.g. *IC* 3.3.5, lines 11–26). The apodosis expresses a wish, e.g. 'If we foreswear, may our land and trees not bear fruit, etc.' Here, line 4 probably begins with the infinitive of an unknown verb and then continues with a new subject, *therion* ('beast'). C understood *therion* to mean

'livestock', but domesticated animals fall well outside the meaning of this term. Perhaps **Ele3** preserves part of the wish that in keeping the oath 'let not a predator (*therion*) attack my livestock'.

5 For legal immunity, see **Ele11**.5.

Ele4 (K 110; VER I.83). Sixth to fifth century. Archaeological Museum of Rethymno (Inv. no. E19)

Six lines of text inscribed on a limestone block. The upper edge of the block may have been re-cut for use in a later structure; all other edges are broken. Lines 1–5 are inscribed boustrophedon beginning at the left between horizontal guidelines. Lines 5 and 6 both begin at the left, indicating that line 6 begins a new unit of text.

[—] μηδὲ δα[μ]οσ̣[ι—]	→	[—] and not public [—]
[—]ον τ̣ὸν ἀϝτὸν μ̣[—]		[—] the same [—]
[—]ι̣ δ' ἐγράπεν τριὸν̣ [—]		[—] he wrote for (?) three [—]
[—]ον μήτε τô κσεν[—]		[—] neither of the foreign(er ?) [—]
[—ἐπ]ι̣δαμῆι. αἰ δέ κα̣ [—]	→	[—] be at home. But if [—]
[———]υς π[———]	→	?

Unless otherwise indicated:

H = Halbherr notebook 4, p. 91; Comparetti and Halbherr 1888: 163 no. 3; Halbherr *ap.* Comparetti 1893: 421–2 no. 195.

C = Comparetti and Halbherr 1888: 163 no. 3; Comparetti 1893: 421–2 no. 195.

1 σ̣: the lower tip of the left stroke is visible. δα[μ]οσ̣[ι]: a form of the adjective δαμόσιος 'public'; the noun δᾶμος (VER) is also possible.

2 μ̣: first three strokes and the upper tip of the fourth (VER I.83). *San* is also possible: ἀϝτόνς (C), ἀϝτόν σ[—] (G).

3 ι̣: a short oblique stroke high in the letter space is visible. H suggests *iota* or *mu*; *iota* is more likely in this position (at the end of a word followed by a word beginning with delta).

[ἅ]ι δ' ἐγράπεν: cf. **G72**.11.19–20 ἅι τάδε τὰ γράμματ'ἔγραπσε. δὲ γράπεν (pres. inf.) is also possible (VER; G notes it).

ν̣: faint trace of the left oblique stroke; perhaps τριὸν̣ [ϝετίον] 'for three years'? C suggests δ̣ and restores τριόδ̣[ελον], for which see **Ele9**.3.

4 τô: τό is also possible.

κσεν[—]: perhaps a form of κσένιος (sc. κόσμος?). See Introd. 4C1b.

5 ι̣: middle oblique stroke is visible at the left edge of the stone (lower oblique of a *kappa* is also possible).

[ἐπ]ι̣δαμῆι: C suggests [ἐ]κ̣δαμῆι 'away from home', but G observes that the spelling ἐγδαμῆι would be more likely and Bile 337 notes that in the Hellenistic period ἀπόδαμος, not ἔγδαμος, served as the antonym of ἐπίδαμος 'at home' (cf. **G72**.8.37–8).

α̣: left oblique stroke is legible.

The archaic paragraphing in line 6 indicates that **Ele4** consists of at least two units of text: lines 1–5 and line 6. It is not possible to determine how much text has been lost, but judging from the difficulty in determining the subject of this enactment the loss is likely to be considerable. G suggests that **Ele4** like **Ele3** concerned foreigners. VER propose instead that **Ele4** concerns iteration, noting some shared language with **G14** ('the same' in line 2 and 'foreign(er)' in line 4), but line 3 has nothing to do with iteration.

Ele5. Sixth to fifth century. Current location unknown

Six (or seven?) lines of text inscribed boustrophedon (lines 2–5) beginning at the left on a limestone block with preserved left, right, and upper edges. Halbherr's drawing (Halbherr notebook 4, p. 89) indicates what appear to be traces of letters in the band along the upper edge of the block, to the immediate right of the *omicron* in line 1, and all along the lower edge of the band between lines 1 and 2. He raises the possibility that a band *c.*0.10 m. along the right edge of the stone may have been left uninscribed.

traces?
[—] . ο[—]
traces
[—]π̣[. .]οιτ̣ο καρπὸν ον[—] → — fruit —
[—]ατ̣ον ᾇιπερ κατ̣α̣γ̣[—] — just as —
[—]ι̣ροις τραποι̣[—]
[— τ]ὰν διπλ̣[οίαν —] — (pay) the two-fold (fine) —

Unless otherwise indicated:

H = Halbherr notebook 4, p. 89; Comparetti and Halbherr 1888: 164 no. 4; Halbherr *ap.* Comparetti 1893: 422–3 no. 196.

C = Comparetti and Halbherr 1888: 164 no. 4; Comparetti 1893: 422–3 no. 196.

2 π̣: all drawings record the left vertical and faintly the upper tip of the right vertical.

τ̣: the drawings of H and G record the vertical and a very short horizontal stroke; the author (possibly De Sanctis) of notebook 54 (Scuola Archeologica Italiana di Atene, undated and without pagination), records only the vertical stroke.

[ἀ]π̣[οδ]οῖτ̣ο? 'sold'.

3 τ̣: H notes that the first τ̣ could also be λ̣.

τ̣α̣γ̣: H records as faint traces.

ᾇιπερ κατ̣α̣γ̣[έγραπται] 'just as recorded'? Cf. *SEG* 41.744, line 23 (sacrificial calendar from Eleutherna, second century BCE) ᾗ καταγ̣[έγραπται]).

4 ι̣: H faintly records the first ι̣.

[κα]ι̣ροῖς: C, but other restorations are possible, e.g. [ἀπετα]ί̣ροις, [ϙο]ί̣ροις.

ι̣: Halbherr notes that the final *iota* is 'multo dubbio'.

τράποι̣: perhaps τρέφοι 'raise, nourish'.

The subject of **Ele5** cannot be determined, but *karpos* (line 2) also occurs in **Ele13**, a law that seems to concern produce that is disputed, perhaps concerning its ownership. In addition, **Ele5** and **Ele13** both refer to 'the two-fold (penalty)' and **Ele5** may preserve part of the phrase 'just as is recorded', comparable to the phrase 'in accordance with what is written' in **Ele13**. The letters in **Ele5** and **13** are the same size, their shapes appear to be similar, and the *iotas* in both face right regardless of the direction of the line. On the basis of these observations, G suggested that **Ele5** and **13** may belong to the same text.

For *karpos*, see Introd. 7A.

Ele6 and 8. Sixth to fifth century. Current location unknown

Two small fragments of limestone blocks that, with a third similar fragment (*IC* 2.12.7), Fabricius 1885: 94 associated on the basis of similarities in the stone (thickness) and the inscription (forms and size of the letters; rightward facing *iotas*). We take no position on this. Each preserves a word or phrase that occurs in other laws; otherwise, too little survives to make any suggestions about their contents.

Ele6

Small fragment of a limestone block with preserved left and upper edges. Halbherr's drawing (notebook 4, p. 89) indicates that the mason left uninscribed bands between lines 1 and 2, lines 4 and 5, and lines 6 and 7. Lines 4 and 5 both read left to right (archaic paragraphing), suggesting that line 5 begins a new section of the text or possibly a new text. G's line numbers are slightly different.

[—]α̣[—]
vacat ?
[—]α̣[—]
[—]τ̣ε̣ι̣α̣ν̣ο̣[—] ←
ι̣υ̣τ̣α̣α̣ [—] →
vacat ?
[—] ἀ̣ποδιδο[—] → — sell (?) give back (?) —
[—]σε̣κεν[—] ←
vacat
[—]σελ̣[—] →

1–4 following Halbherr (notebook 4, p. 89), who records the letters very faintly, noting for line 3 in particular 'tutto dubbio'.

[—]τε̣ιαν ὀ[—]: Comparetti and Halbherr 1888: 164–5 no. 5; Comparetti 1893: 423 no. 197.

5 ἀ̣ποδιδο[—]: see n. ad **G41**.4.7–8.

6 [—]ς ἔ̣κεν [—]: Comparetti and Halbherr 1888: 164–5 no. 5; Comparetti 1893: 423 no. 197.

7 λ̣: upper part of the letter is legible; ϵ is also possible.

Ele8

Small fragment of a limestone block with preserved left and upper edges.

[— μ]αιτυρ[—]	→	— witness —
[—]ο καὶ το[—]	←	— and —
vac.		

Ele9 (VER I.25). Law concerning a cloak maker. Sixth to fifth century. Archaeological Museum of Rethymno (Inv. E203)

Seven lines of text inscribed on a limestone block that was re-cut into the shape of an arch and reused above a door of a house in the village Prines. We follow the line numbering of G. We do not know if the text began above the traces preserved at the top of the block or if it continued below line 6, or how many letters are lost to the right and the left.

traces		
[—] Διοννυσίαν νενομ̣[—]	←	— Dionysian —
[—κ]α̣ὶ Τίμαρκος ἐκόσμιο̣ν̣ [—]	→	— and Timarkos were *kosmoi* —
[—] ϙ̣ισυροποιôι τριόδελον το[—]	→	— (to?) the cloak maker, a triobol —
[—ἠ]μιτυέκτο κριθâ[ν]. αἰ δὲ διαπ[—]	←	— of a *hemiekteon* of barley. But if —
[—]ι ἀμισθεὶ [. . c.5 . . σισ]ύ̣ρ̣αν π[—]	→	— without pay [—] cloak —
[—]αλαϙ̣[. . . . . . . c.16 . . . .] . ι̣[—]	→	

Unless otherwise indicated:
C = Comparetti and Halbherr 1888: 165–70 no. 8; Comparetti 1893: 425–30 no. 200.

1 *Διοννυσίαν* 'Dionysian'; the gen. pl. is also possible. For the spelling (*-νν-*), see Bile 154 n. 334.
μ̣: traces consistent with *μ* are visible at three spots low in the letter space; G noted that *san* is also possible.
Διοννυσίαν νενομ̣[ηίαν] VER 'Dionysian new moon' (i.e. first day of the month Dionysios); they propose an 'interversion' of consonants for later Cretan *νεμονηία* (= Attic *νεομηνία/νουμηνία*). This is perhaps possible, but normal consonantal shift in Crete is the assimilation of consonants, e.g. *νύναμαι* = *δύναμαι* (Dialect 9). As an alternative to restoring *νενομ[ηίαν]*, we suggest e.g. the pf. of *νέμομαι* 'distribute' (*IC* 3.4.10, lines 56, 64–5 *νενωμημένοι εἴησαν*; for the form, see Bile 323) or of *νομίζω*. The month name Dionysios is attested at Praisos (*IC* 3.6.7, third century). 'Dionysian' may stand alone or modify a noun that preceded, perhaps 'priest' or 'sacrifice'.
2–3 Both lines read from the left indicating that 3 begins a new unit of text.
3 *ϙ̣*: all drawings record the lower part of the right oblique stroke.
σισυροποιôι: nom. pl. is also possible.
τριόδελον: Attic *τριώβολον*.

We read no traces following *το* where JP records the tip of a horizontal stroke towards the middle of the letter space at the right edge of the block and G suggests a circular letter. Neither is consistent with the reading *τôι* [*δὲ* ? —-] of VER or with C's suggestion that lines 3–4 wrap around yielding *τô* [*ἡ*]||*μιτυέκτο κτλ*.

4 [*ἡ*]*μιτυέκτο*: gen. sing. = Attic *ἡμιεκτέου*, 'one-half of one-sixth' of a *medimnos*, see Bile 136.

κριθâ[*ν*]: *κριθα*(*ί*) C; *κριθαί* G, JP, VER. The space following the *alpha* is damaged. The earliest drawings (Fabricius 1885: 92; Halbherr notebook 65 p. 75) and autopsy do not confirm the reading of *iota*. We propose restoring *nu* and reading the gen. pl.

5 *ἀμισθεί*: adv., cf. *ἀμίστος* (**A1**.7); see Bile 214.

ụ: the upper tip of the right stroke is visible.

ρ̣: the head of the *rho* is visible (*beta* is also possible).

[*σισ*]*ύ̣ρ̣αν*: the gen. pl. is also possible.

5–6 Both lines read from the left indicating that 6 begins a new unit of text.

6 *σ̣*: all four strokes of *san* are visible, but *mu* is also possible.

The upper part of a vertical stroke is legible to the left of the dotted *iota*.

ι̣: upper stroke is visible.

The use of archaic paragraphing suggests that this text consists of three units: lines 1–2, 3–5, and 6. The three sections may be related (*pace* VER), but we cannot identify any connection between them.

1–2 perhaps preserve parts of one or possibly two temporal expressions: the month Dionysios (see note), and the names of Timarkos and at least one other individual who were *kosmoi* (*ekosmion*). Hellenistic treaties from Crete (e.g. *IC* 1.16.3, lines 1–4; *IC* 1.16.4, lines 4–9) and consular dedications (e.g. *IC* 1.16.29) date their enactment by the name of the month, sometimes with the day of the month specified, and the name (and tribe) of the eponymous *kosmos*. Although it is tempting to interpret lines 1–2 as part of a dating formula of this kind, neither the naming of at least two *kosmoi* nor the accusative case of the adjective *Dionnysian*, which in temporal constructions expresses duration rather than a particular point in time, support this. VER suggest the supplement *Dionnysian nenom*[*eia*], which they take to mean 'on the first day of the month Dionysios', but this is linguistically and syntactically very unlikely. It is not possible to determine whether Timarkos and his colleague(s) were *kosmoi* at the time of the enactment of **Ele9**, as is the case in **G72**.5.5–6 'when the *startos* Aithaleus, Kyllos and his colleagues, were *kosmoi*', or in a prior year.

3–5 concern a specialist craftsman, the *sisyropoios*, a maker of goat's-hair cloaks (*sisyra* line 5). See also **Eleutherna3**A for leather-working at Eleutherna and Chaniotis 1995 for evidence of animal husbandry in the economy of Eleutherna and other communities of interior Crete. References to 'triobol', a 'measure of barley', and 'without pay' suggest that the provision has to do with wages for the *sisyropoios*, but further details elude us. For other laws with provisions concerning wages, see Introd. 7C.

3 'Cloak maker': the noun could also be plural. In either case, the verb is missing and the construction of the two nouns is thus obscure. If as we suggest *sisyropoios* is the indirect and triobol the direct object, the subject of the sentence is missing. For a discussion of the economic implications of this provision, see Introd. 7C and Perlman 2004a: 104–7.

The term triobol could refer to silver bullion or a unit of weight or worth, e.g. '[pay] to the *sisyropoios* a triobol weight or worth of some commodity' (Stefanakis 1999: 249–50), but there is no a priori reason to exclude the possibility that triobol here refers to (probably Aiginetan) coins (VER), which were introduced to Crete before 500 (Introd. 7D).

All editors have construed the letters that follow the term triobol (*to*[—]) as the definite article. If they are right, this weakens the likelihood that the use of triobol here is metrological. With one possible exception (**G63**.2), all other expressions of the weight, volume, or value of a commodity in the epichoric inscriptions of Crete refer to the commodity without the definite article (e.g. **Ele15**.5; **G79**.3–5). On the other hand, *to*- could be the first two letters of a longer word.

4 A *hemiekteon* is a volumetric measure for dry goods, especially grain, equal to slightly under 4.5 liters. The term is not otherwise attested on Crete. VER assert, without discussion, that the cloak-maker received a triobol and the *hemiekteon* of barley was compensation for his assistant (e.g. *miston to hemituekto krithan* 'a wage of a *hemiekteon* of barley'). One *hemiekteon* of barley represented roughly 70% of the daily caloric requirements of an average family, defined as a male head of household, his wife, an elderly woman, and three children (Perlman 2004a: 105). If not compensation, the triobol and the *hemiekteon* of barley might be understood as legal penalties owed to or by the cloak-maker.

5 The circumstances of non-payment (*amisthei*) cannot be determined here. Was non-payment justified, e.g. in the case of poor fabrication or untimely completion (VER), or unjustified and so subject to a penalty? For another case of 'working without pay', see **A1**.6–7.

Ele11 (K 112 [no text]; VER I.14). Sixth to fifth century. Archaeological Museum of Rethymno (Inv. no. E42)

Six lines of text inscribed boustrophedon beginning at the left between incised horizontal guidelines on a rectangular block of limestone. The right, upper, and lower edges appear to be original. The block is broken at the left. The inscribed surface is damaged at the right with the loss of four to six letters at the right in lines 1–4 and one (or none?) in line 5. Only the upper part of the letters in line 6 are preserved, suggesting that the lower parts of the letters were inscribed on the block below. We cannot determine if the text continued onto additional blocks to the left or right, or if it began on a block higher up the wall or continued after line 6.

[—. αἴ τι]ς̣ πέρανδε πλέοι ἢ θιαρ̣ὸς ἢ . [—] →
[—]ος διαλαιη ἐκσενιοϝτιτό[ς —]
[—]οπιος. αἴ τις τôινυ ποινικα[κσίε ? —]
[— τ]ôινυ μὴ δικάζοντας, τὸς ζ[—]
[—] ἀπάτος ἤμεν. αἰ δὲ καρπόσαιτ̣ο [—]
[—7–9—]α̣ν [. .] π̣ [. .] ο̣ [. . .] ντο . [.] . . σ̣ [—]

—. If someone sails abroad, either a *thiaros* or —
— should be away (?) in the sixth year (?) —
—. If someone serves as writer for him —
— those who do not decide the case for him, the —
— are to be immune. But if he should harvest —

---

1 ς̣: the lower tip of the right oblique stroke is legible.
ρ̣: the lower tip of the vertical is legible.
θιαρ̣ός = Attic θεωρός (Dialect 3).
A vertical stroke is preserved at the right edge of the inscribed surface.
2 [— ἢ αλ(λ)]ος 'or otherwise' VER.
διαλαιη (or διαλαι η ?): both the form and the meaning of διαλαιη are obscure. G suggested that the term belongs to the family ἀλάομαι (also ἀλαίνω), 'to wander', 'to be an exile'. If the term is a verbal form (aor. opt.?), the preverb δια- emphasizes the sense of separation (Bile 275). VER assert that the context requires the sense of 'distance' or 'absence', but do not suggest a derivation. Van Effenterre 1946a: 592 associated the term with ἴλλω/ *εἴλω 'assembly/assemble' (see **A1**.8–9; **Dr5**).
ἐκσενιοϝτιτό[ς]: ἐκς ἐνιοϝτιτο[—] G, who suggests that ἐνιοϝτιτός, attested only here and **Ele15**.2, is an adjective meaning 'of/for a year' (cf. Attic ἐνιαύσιος). Bile (per ep.) objects that the change from */au/* to */ou/* is unparalled in Cretan. We adopt G's suggestion but follow VER in preferring the compound ἐκσενιοϝτιτός (ἔκς = ἕξ) 'in the sixth year'. Cf. *IC* 2.12.12, line 2, μὴ ἐκσε[νιοϝτιτο (?) —].
3 VER [ἐκτ]όπιος 'absent' or [ἐντ]όπιος 'at home', but ἐκτόπιος more commonly means 'foreign' and ἐντόπιος 'local'.
αἴ τις: asyndeton suggesting the beginning of a new but related provision.
τôινυ = dat. sing. masc./neuter of the Arcado-Cyprian demonstrative pronoun ὄνυ (Dialect 35). On Crete ὄνυ appears to look back to someone or something previously mentioned like Attic οὗτος, rather than forward like Attic ὅδε. See J-MD 133–4. Alternatively, the use of the dat. may be adverbial, e.g. 'here' or 'thus'.
ποινικα[κσίε?]: we think a verb is more likely here than the noun ποινικαστάς (Beattie 1975: 29); for both see **Da1**. VER restores ποινικά[ζοντας] to achieve symmetry with [τ]ôινυ μὴ δικάζοντας in line 4. Also possible is ποινικάζον/ποινικάκσας '(If someone) serving/ having served as *poinikastas*'.
4 Perhaps τὸς ζ[αμίοντας] 'those who assess a fine', but elsewhere in Crete (**A1**, **G80**) the verb has the form δαμιόο. Whatever it is, the term could be either the subject (with an infinitive) in the apodosis, or the object of the participle δικάζοντας.
5 ἀπάτος: the acc. pl. is attested only here. More common is the impersonal acc. sing. ἄπατον with ἤμεν, 'there is to be immunity'. The recipient(s) of immunity either is not expressed (**G41**.5.4–7; **G72**.4.17; **G77**B4–8) or is indicated in the dative (**Elt1**.4; **G42B**11–14; **G43**Bb1–4; **G46B**7–9; **G72**.1.56–2.2; **G73**A1–3). Ἄπατον appears to be

used personally in **G75C6–7** and impersonally with an acc. pl. in **G80.11–12**. Those receiving immunity here might be those mentioned in line 4, in which case we must presume that relatively few letters are lost at the left edge of the stone.

Uncertainty about the amount of text that is missing impedes our interpretation of **Ele11**. If relatively little has been lost to the right and left, the surviving text probably consists of two provisions: lines 1–3 and 3–5. See note on line 3, *ai tis.*

1–3 We are inclined to agree with VER, who suggest that this provision concerns the legal status of those who have been abroad (line 1) for an extended period of time (line 2). But this view is based on two words in line 2 (those rendered as 'should be away' and 'in the sixth year') that are otherwise unattested and not securely understood, and a third at the beginning of line 3 that is partly restored.

1 At least two different categories of travelers were specified, although only the first survives. *Thiaros* can be the title of local officials, a general term for sightseer, a sacred envoy sent out as an official representative of a city to a distant festival, an oracular consultant, or someone sent abroad to announce the dates of the sacred truce for a festival celebrated at home (Dimitrova 2008: 10–13). This is the sole occurrence of the term in the inscriptions from Crete and one of the earliest occurrences anywhere. The context (sailing abroad) makes it unlikely that the term here refers to a local official of Eleutherna, and we do not know of any Eleuthernian festivals that the *thiaros* might be announcing abroad. Most likely, in our view, the *thiaros* was a sacred envoy sent either to consult an oracle or to represent Eleutherna at a distant festival, though evidence for the participation of the Cretan poleis in international festivals is largely Hellenistic.[392]

2–3 'Should be away' (*dialaiē*): the Greek is more than likely a verb meaning something like 'wander apart'. We prefer to read the compound adjective *ekse-nioutito* 'in the sixth year', rather than the prepositional phrase *eks enioutito* 'from the annual'. If relatively little is missing at the right edge, line 2 may continue the protasis of the condition; and if so, all that survives of the apodosis are the final five letters (-*opios*) of a nominal form (line 3). The form could be either masc. nom. s. or acc. pl. We take it as a nom. s. agreeing with the subject of the protasis, *tis.* Thus, the condition stated, 'If someone sails abroad, either (serving as) a *thiaros* or [—] is away, in the sixth year he is [—]*opios*'. The string of letters -*opios* does not otherwise occur in the inscriptions from Crete and is found only in proper names (personal, month, tribal) in inscriptions from elsewhere. VER suggest restoring *ektopios* meaning 'absent', but see note. In the sixth year the individual's absence

[392] Delphi included Eleutherna in the itinerary of the sacred envoys it sent out to announce the celebration of the Pythia and the Soteria (*SEG* 26.624, col. 3.106, *c.*230–220), and at least one Cretan polis, Elyros, sent its own official delegation of *thearoi* to represent it at Delphi (*IC* 2.13.1A, second century; Perlman 2000b: 17). A Hellenistic agreement from east Crete implies similar embassies sent out from east Cretan poleis to Olympia and to Delphi (*IC* 3.6.7B, lines 12–15).

becomes official. This sounds like a rule establishing the period of time after which the absent individual is presumed dead.

3–6 Two rules, both in the form of conditions, are preserved from the second provision: lines 3–5 and 5–6.

3–5 The first rule appears to offer immunity (line 5) to officials, perhaps judges, perhaps in cases concerning the person who is absent, since 'him' (lines 3 and 4), probably refers to someone previously mentioned.

3 'Serves as writer': the Greek could be either a noun or (as we read) a verb; both are attested in **Da1**, where the writer Spensithios is appointed by the polis to write and remember. **Da1** does not further specify what Spensithios is to write, but as Gagarin 2008a: 120–1 observes, while laws were written, there is no evidence for any other public writing in Crete. It is difficult to imagine, however, what role a writer of laws may have played in rules concerning absent individuals. Perhaps, then, **Ele11** attests the use of writing in judicial procedure, or perhaps the verb (or noun) in **Ele11** subsumes both writing and remembering as does the noun in **Da1**. If so, the writer may be assigned to a legal action concerning the absent individual perhaps as his representative or as a witness of earlier actions.

5 Those (plural) receiving immunity cannot be the singular subject 'someone' (line 3). They may be the ones who do not decide the case or those recorded at the end of line 4, where the only surviving letter may be part of a noun meaning 'those who assess the fine'.

5–6 'If he should harvest': this may concern the right to harvest the produce of property belonging to the absent person, either before or after he has been recognized as officially absent.

Ele13. Law concerning produce (K113). Sixth to fifth century. Archaeological Museum of Rethymno (Inv. no. E59)

Seven lines of text inscribed boustrophedon beginning at the left. The upper and right faces are preserved, but the block is damaged along the upper edge of the inscribed surface. The text must have continued onto a contiguous block (or blocks) to the right. All *iotas* face to the right regardless of the direction of the line; two dots, one above the other, are used for word-division. Both features are also found in **Ele15**. For similarities between **Ele5** and **Ele13**, see comm. ad **Ele5**.

[— δε]κ̣α : [με]δίμνος : κριθ[ᾶν —] →
[— πέ]ντε στατῆρας : ὀπήλ[εν —]
[—] καρπô : τὰν διπλοίαν ὀ[π]ήλε̣[ν]. α̣ἰ δ[έ —]
[— μ]αιτυραμένο : πέροι παρόντο : δ[—]
[— δέ]κα μεδίμνος ἀποτίν̣[ε]ν [—]
[— μέδι]μ⟨ν⟩ον δ' αἰ νικαθείη κατασ̣[τασεῖ —]
[— τ]ὸν καρ̣πὸν κατ' ἆ γέγραπτ[αι —]

— ten? *medimnoi* of barley —
— he is to owe five? staters —
— he is to owe twice (the value of) the produce. But if —
— with (X) being witness and present he should take —
— he is to pay ten? *medimnoi* —
— But if he is convicted, he shall pay a *medimnos* —
— the produce in accordance with what is written —

---

1 κ̣: lower oblique is visible.
3 ε̣: lower tip of the vertical is visible.
α̣: lower portion of the right vertical stroke is visible.
4 μ]αιτυραμένο: the verb 'testify', 'bear witness to' is not otherwise attested in the epichoric inscriptions from Crete, but Bile's attempt (351 n. 105) to avoid a verbal form (μαίτυρα μὲν ο?) yields no sense. The genitive may be absolute, either personal ('with X being a witness'), as we translate above, or impersonal ('testimony being given').
παρόντο: we take this genitive too as absolute, but the construction is not clear.
5 ν̣: upper part of the left oblique stroke is visible.
6 ⟨ν⟩: the mason inscribed *mu*.
σ̣: two right strokes are legible; κατασ̣[τâσαι is also possible. καταδ[ικαδδέτο] or καταδ[ικαδδέθο] G, but the angle formed by the two oblique strokes is too acute for *delta*.
7 καταγέγραπτ[αι] is also possible.

The rule seems to establish penalties for wrongs that involve agricultural produce (*karpos*). The penalties include measures (*medimnos/medimnoi*) of barley (lines 1, 5), weights or units of silver or coin (staters, line 2), and a double fine (*tan diploian*) calculated on the value of the produce (line 3). If the fines in lines 1–2 represent alternative methods of payment ('he shall owe ten? *medimnoi* of barley (or) five? staters') it is worth pointing out that the same ratio of silver to grain (one-half unit of silver (one-half stater) to one unit of grain (*medimnos*) occurs in **Ele9** (one-half *medimnos* of barley or one-quarter stater). If so, a bushel of barley in archaic Eleutherna was worth about 6 gm. of silver (Perlman 2004a: 106–7).

It is not possible to determine the precise nature of the dispute. Possibilities include produce that was wrongfully taken (line 4), damages to crops, or produce that was owed as taxes.

Ele14 (VER I.46). Sixth to fifth century. Frag. A: Archaeological Museum of Rethymno (Inv. no. E167); Frag. B: current location unknown

Two fragments of limestone blocks (A, B) found reused in two private homes in the village of Prines. G suggested that they belong to the same block.

The upper edge of A may be original; all its other sides are broken away, as are all the sides of B.

Ele14A preserves seven lines from two texts (lines 1–4, lines 5–7) inscribed boustrophedon by two masons. An uninscribed band *c.*0.06–0.07 m wide separates the two. The letters in 1–4 resemble those in **Ele3**; the letters in 5–7 resemble those in B.

B preserves six lines from two texts (lines 1–4, lines 5–6); the beginning of the second text is marked by a narrow uninscribed band framed by two horizontal lines and a break in the boustrophedon (FIG. 37).

A

[—]ο̣ραστο[—] →
[—]κ̣εσθῆι [—]
[—]λαιον[—]
[—]ο̣ς ρασι[—]
vacat
[—-π]όλις ἀ̣ . [—] → — polis —
[—κ]όσμο[—] ← — *kosmo*[*s*] —
[—]ο̣[.]σ̣[—]

B

[—]ατοζ[—]
[—]ηδατον . [—] →
[—] ὀϝκ ἔ̈δοκε̣ [—] ← — did not give —
[—]αι τὰ τριημι [—] → — the one and one-half —
vacat
[—-] . ακσιτο[—] →
[—-]ο̣ . . . [—-]

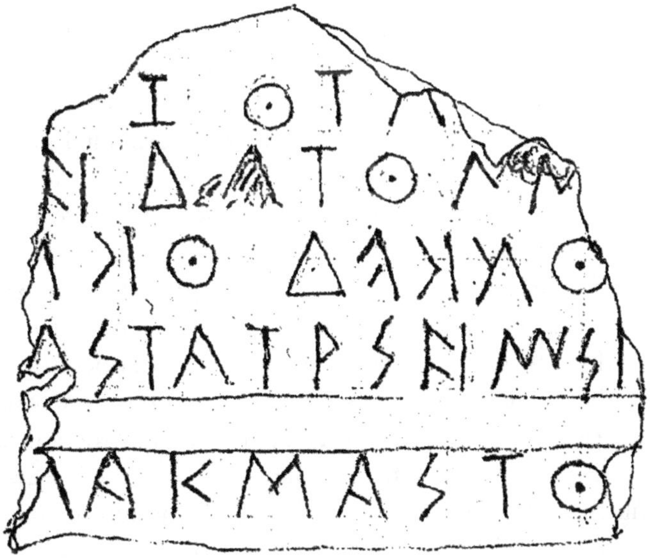

FIG. 37. **Ele14**, Fragment B (drawing after Halbherr, notebook 65: 79)

A

2 ̣κ: the lower oblique stroke is legible.

[—]κ̣εσθῆι: perhaps [ὀρ]κεσθῆι from ὀρκίζω 'be sworn'.

3 [—]λαιον: [ἔ]λαιον G, VER. The Cretan god [Ταλ]λαῖον is also possible.

4 ρασι[—]: G hesitantly suggests ῥᾶσις = ῥῆσις?

5 An oblique stroke and the upper part of a second oblique where it connects with the top of the first are visible at the right edge of the stone; λ, μ, ν, *san* are possible.

7 ο̣: upper curve is visible.

σ̣: upper part is visible.

B

1 The direction of the line is uncertain; ζοτα is also possible, but less likely (cf. the uninscribed space above the break in boustrophedon at line 5).

2 [—]ηδατον: δα̣τομ̣[ενο] G and VER, but drawings, including G's own, record a clear ν. Halbherr's drawing records three strokes to the left of *nu* consistent with ν, μ, or *san* (FIG. 37).

3 ε̣: upper part of the vertical and the upper oblique stroke are visible.

5 An oblique stroke is visible at the left edge of the stone.

6 The upper curve of an *omicron* followed by the upper tips of three letters are visible along the lower edge of the stone in G's drawing.

Ele15 (VER I.46). Sixth to fifth century. Archaeological Museum of Rethymno (A: Inv. no. E54; C: Inv. no. E206); current location of B & D unknown

Four fragments of limestone blocks (A+B, C+D). G suggested associating A+B and C+D on the basis of the size and appearance of the letters. The lower edge of the block with A+B is preserved. C may preserve an original lower edge with the lower parts of the letters in C.5 inscribed on a joining block below. The letters on A+B and C are inscribed between lightly incised horizontal guidelines. All *iotas* face to the right. Two dots, one above the other, are used for word division in A+B.4–5; *vacats* appear to be used as word division in A+B.6 and C.

C+D preserve only one complete word (*apo*, line 4), and so we omit it here.

Frags. A+B. Six lines of text all written left to right except line 2; there are traces of another line (4a) between lines 4 and 5. G suggests that the line had been erased, but in that case the stone would be concave, as it does not appear to be. We suggest instead that the letters of 4a were laid out on the stone with light incising, but for some reason were never fully cut. Alternatively, the entire surface of the stone may have been cut back before **Ele15** was inscribed, leaving traces of an earlier text in the band that was not reinscribed, though in that case we would expect to see traces of the earlier text elsewhere on the stone.

traces
[——————————]σιο κρη[—] →
[— ἐ]ν τôι ἐνιοϜ̣τ̣[ιτοι . . *c*.4 . .]δο . ισθ[—] ←
[—] μολêν : *vacat* →
[—]λαν : ἕλοι : ἀποβαπσάμενον : ἤ ο[—] →
4a [—]ονο[—]ε̣ρε̣γλοϜσαιτονα . μ[—]
5 [—]κσαι : ἤ κâπον : ἤ συκίανς : μὴ κελομ̣[ένο —] →
[—]οντον *vac.* κέρσον *vac.* τ̣ρία Ϝέτια *vac.* κερ[—] →
vacat

— within] the year? —
— go to court.
— he should seize . . . having been immersed? or —
5 — either a garden or fig-trees not being bidden —
— barren land for three years —

---

2 G reads ε̣ at the right edge of the stone.
Ϝ̣: lower two-thirds of both oblique strokes are visible.
τ̣: lower tip of the vertical is visible.
ἐνιοϜτ[ιτος]: 'annual', cf. **Ele11**.2; for the phrase ἐ]ν τοι ἐνιοϜ̣τ̣[ιτοι, cf. ἐν τôι ἐνιαυτôι (**G72**.1.47).
There is the lower tip of a vertical stroke between the *omicron* and the *iota*.
3 [—] μολêν: compounds (e.g. ἀμφιμολêν, ἀπομολêν, ἐπιμολêν) are also possible.
4 ἀποβαπσάμενον: gen. pl. is also possible.
ἤ: the conjunction, as in line 6 (so G), or the adverb ἧ ('when', 'where').
4a γ̣: G records the two oblique strokes.
G records a vertical line between α and μ.
5 μ̣: left oblique stroke is visible.
κελομ̣[ένο] could be restored differently, but the verb appears only in this phrase in the early laws from Crete. See Bile 261.
6 [—]οντον κέρσον: [—]ον τôν κέρσον (gen. pl.) 'of the barren lands', is also possible, although χέρσον seldom appears in the plural.

The direction of writing may indicate four separate provisions: lines 1–3, 4, 5, and 6. It is not clear if they are all connected. The use of *vacats* as word division in 6 rather than two dots in 1–5 suggests that a different mason inscribed this line; on the other hand, 5 ('garden', 'fig trees') and 6 ('barren land') both concern agricultural land and they may be connected.

3 'Go to court' (*molen*). Outside of Gortyn, this only occurs here in our texts.

4 The topic is uncertain. *Bapto* ('dip' or 'immerse') could apply to tempering metal or dying cloth, but no agricultural applications are known. **Ele9** indicates the production of goat's-hair cloaks (*sisyra*) at Eleutherna and these could have been dyed, but there is no obvious connection between textile production and regulations concerning agricultural lands. It is, however, worth noting that the settlement of Eleutherna occupied two long, narrow ridges formed by three

streams of the Mt. Psiloritis watershed that flow between and around the ridges, converging to their north. The slopes of both ridges are extensively terraced and were clearly farmed in antiquity; land farmed at the foot of the slopes may have been subject to flooding. The cognate verb *baptizo*, which is used in the same sense as *bapto* for dipping something into a liquid, also occurs in the sense of 'to flood' (e.g. Aristophanes 13 K.–A.). Perhaps *bapto* in the middle/passive voice as here could mean land immersed in water or 'flooded', although we can cite no parallel for this use.[393] If so, the provision might refer to cultivable land carried off (*eloi*) by the flood-waters.

5 The phrase *me kelomeno* 'not being bidden' is possibly part of a defense against culpability (**G41**.5.7–8; **G72**.6.52).

6 Land that is barren for three years is probably agricultural land that has been left fallow. For fallowing practices in antiquity, including the practice of leaving land uncultivated for three years, see Gallant 1991: 52–6.

Ele16 (K 114 [Aa and Ac], 115 [Ab]; VER II.67 [Aa, Ac], I.26 [Ab]). Sixth to fifth century. Archaeological Museum of Rethymno (Inv. no. E18)

At least four texts (**Aa, Ab, Ac, Ba**) are inscribed by at least three different masons on two adjacent faces (A and B) of a rectangular limestone block from the corner of a wall. **Aa**, **Ab**, and **Ba** are inscribed between horizontal guidelines that are 0.026 m. apart from one another. **Ac** is inscribed in a rasura on A.

The upper and left edges of A are preserved; the block is broken at the bottom and right. The texts are complete at the left; it is not possible to determine how much text has been lost at the right or at the bottom.

The upper, left, and right edges of B are preserved, but it is considerably more weathered than A. **Ba** is complete at the right, but it is not possible to determine if the text of **Ba** is complete at the left or if it continued onto a contiguous block. The mason who inscribed **Ba** appears to have made a conscious decision to align **Ba**1 with **Ab**1. It is, however, clear that **Ba** was not inscribed by the same mason as **Ab**. Not a single word of **Ba** can be retrieved and we omit it here.

Face A. The texts of at least three and possibly four inscriptions are preserved. **Aa** is inscribed at the top of the block, **Ab** at the bottom. The central portion was erased presumably in order to accommodate **Ac**. The size and spacing of the traces of letters from the under-text of **Ac** appear to be similar to the letters in **Aa**. The under-text of **Ac** is possibly a continuation of **Aa** or a fourth text. There is no question that different masons were responsible for inscribing **Aa**, **Ab**, and **Ac**.

[393] For evidence of attempts in antiquity to control the flow of the stream Chalopota, see Stampolidis 2004a: 92–3.

The beginning of **Ab** is preserved, as is perhaps the beginning of **Aa**. The first preserved letters of **Aa** (*omicron*, *san*, and perhaps *tau*) are the same as the first letters of Ab. Both texts may thus have begun with the same construction.

Our lettering system indicates the likely order of inscribing.

Aa2–11 are inscribed boustrophedon beginning at the left. An uninscribed band follows **Aa**11. If the under-text of **Ac** is the continuation of **Aa**, **Aa** consisted of approximately eighteen lines organized into at least two provisions.

Ab consists of seven lines inscribed boustrophedon beginning at the left. **Ac** consists of six lines of text inscribed boustrophedon beginning at the left. Asyndeton at the beginning of both texts indicates the beginning of a new provision.

Aa

ὅστ̣[ις —]		1	Whoever —
[—]ε πλίας ἀ-	←	2–3	— should sell more —
ποδοῖτο [—]			
[—]ν ἄργυρο-		4–5	— the money where —
ν υἶ διαμ . [—]			
[—] κρέεσθαι μὲ-		6–7	— use the pledges —
ν τοῖς ἐνεκ[ύροις —]			
[— κολ?]ύ̣εσθαι δὲ μή.			— but is not to prevent? it.
ἦμεν δὲ τὰ [—]			But the — are to be —
[—]σα πᾶς περ[ὶ]			— all concerning
τἀπρίατα ἐ[—]			the things not purchased —
vacat			

1 τ̣: lower tip of the vertical stroke is visible.
2 πλίας = πλείονας acc. pl.
5 υἶ = οἶ adv. 'whither' or 'where' (Bile 214).
The lower tip of a vertical stroke is visible at the right edge of the stone.
8 υ̣: left oblique stroke is visible.
9 τὰ[ν —] is also possible.
10 ἅπας: G; elsewhere possibly in **A2**.3.
11 τἀπρίατα = τὰ ἀπρίατα; the adjective occurs in archaic poetry in reference to women captured by force (e.g. *Il.* 1.99; *h. Ceres* 132; Pi. Fr. 169a.8). τὰ πριατά (G) is also possible, but the adjective is otherwise unattested.

Ab

ὅστι⟨ς⟩ κι[θ]αριστὰς κ[—]	→	1	Any harpist who —
[—] μὴ ἰν ἀπαμίαι μ-		2–3	— not in the *apamia* nor in the city —
[η]δ' ἰν πόλι πλυριτ[—]			
[—] Ϝικοτῆρας ἔμ-		4–5	— are to be initiated in? —
Ϝεσθαι κε[—]			
[—]οπαιον			
ο̣ς *vac.* μ[—]			
traces			

1 ὅστι⟨ς⟩ VER, suggested already by G, who however reads ὅς τι. We prefer not to clarify an obscure construction by suggesting mason’s error, but there are parallels in the early laws for a conditional indefinite relative clause with ὅστις without κα, but none for ὅς without κα.

κιθαριστάς: acc. pl. is also possible.

2 μ̣: the right oblique and in G’s drawing the upper bit of the connecting stroke are visible; *nu* and *san* (ἀπαμίαις G) are also possible.

2–3 ἀπαμίαι μ̣[η]δ’: the term ἀπαμία (= ἀφαμία) occurs in a later text; it may be associated with ἀφαμιώτας; see commentary below.

3 πλυριτ[—]: VER associate this partially preserved term with πλευρά, ‘side’ or ‘flank’.

4 ϝικοτήρας acc. pl., a *hapax legomenon* of uncertain meaning (Bile 113 n. 162). Perhaps related to ἱκέτης ‘suppliant’ or ‘exile’.

4–5 ἔμϝεσθαι from ἐ(μ)μυέω, ‘to be initiated in’. The final letter in line 4 is clearly *mu*, ruling out (δύ)εσθαι ‘undress’ (Petrulakis 1914: 226) and ἐνν̣|ϝ̣εσθαι from ἕννυμι, ‘to wear’ (VER).

6 οπαιον: either ὀπαιὸν ‘smoke-hole’ (**G46**B2) or ὁ παίον ‘the one who strikes’ (VER) are possible (so G); or perhaps a reference to the *paian* ([τ]ὸ παιὸνο̣ς), though the Attic-Ionic form (with *omicron*) is unexpected.

7 ο̣: the upper right curve of the *omicron* is visible; G reads an oblique stroke and an *iota* to the left of the *mu*.

Ac

ἐνέκυρα μ̣ὴ π̣έρεν ἀ[—]	→	One shall not take security —
[—] . ανοε . . εο[. . c.4–5 . .]ροσο		
. ετεσε[c.2–3]α . αρκο . . εσκ		
[—]α̣ν τὸν ἐνεκύρον ν̣ικη̣-		— of the security —
σ̣θαν̣[—]		
traces		

2–3 All letters as read from G’s drawing.

4 α̣: two oblique strokes are visible; *delta* is possible.

τὸν ἐνεκύρον: the plural is more likely in view of ἐνέκυρα in line 1, but the nom./acc. s. is possible.

ι̣: lower tip of the *iota* is visible.

η̣: could be ε̣.

VER mistakenly insert a *tau* between ἐνεκύρον and ν̣ικη.

5 σ̣: lower part of the right stroke of the *san* is visible.

4–5 νικη̣σ̣θαν̣[—]? The letters yield no recognizable form of νικάω, which in these laws commonly refers to winning (or losing) a case. Probably either our reading is wrong or the mason made a mistake.

Aa and **Ac** appear to concern commercial transactions.

Aa2–3 refer to the sale of goods (*apodoito*); **Aa**4–5 mention money (*argyron* = silver), whether silver bullion or coined silver cannot be determined (Introd. 7D);

Aa6–7 concern the use of goods pledged as security (*kresthai tois enekyrois*); and **Aa**10–11 probably refer to goods that have not been purchased (*ta apriata*), perhaps in the sense of seized.

Ac also refers to goods pledged as security, prohibiting the taking of goods pledged as security (line 1) and perhaps regulating the disposition of goods pledged as security following a decision at law (lines 4–5, n. ad loc.).

Aa and **Ac** may have been inscribed together, and it is possible that **Ac** superseded the part of **Aa** that was erased in order to accommodate it.

Ab appears to be unrelated to **Aa** and **Ac**, since nothing in what survives suggests that it concerns commercial transactions. VER propose that **Ab** preserves the terms of a contract between harpists and Eleutherna. We tentatively propose instead that **Ab** regulates festivals; the provision concerning harpists being but one of several rules.

Ab1 The first provision may concern harpists or someone who engages harpists. It is worth noting that ancient tradition associated Eleutherna with several legendary harpists: Eleuther, the eponymous founder of the polis, Linos, and Ametor. See Perlman 2004a: 112.

2–3 *Apamia* occurs in just one other inscription, a Hellenistic treaty from Crete with a description of the border of the east Cretan polis of Lato (*SEG* 26.1049, 71–2 'straight ahead to the summit of the ancient barren land that borders on the *aphamia* of Exakon'). The term may identify lands farmed by *ap(h)amiotai* ('men without renown' Chantraine s.v.), a Cretan term for a category of dependent people that is not found in the epichoric texts (Athenaeus 6.263f; Hesychius s.v.; see Perlman 2004a: 103). The *aphamia* of Exakon was located in the hinterland of Lato some distance away from its urban center. Here *apamia* is juxtaposed with *polis*, which in this case probably refers to the polis-town of Eleutherna. VER assume that lines 1–3 belong to a single provision and propose that it concerns where a harpist may (not) reside; they also suggest that the partially preserved term *plyrit*[—] refers to the residential area of the polis-town on the slopes of Pyrgi (n. ad loc.). It is quite possible, however, that lines 2–3 belong to a different provision and are not connected with harpists.

4–6 The phrase *wikoteras emwesthai* may mean 'suppliants are to be initiated'; if so, the possible reference to the *paian*, a hymn to Apollo (n. ad loc.), suggests that the focus of these lines may be religious ritual, but this is very uncertain.

4 The term *wikoteras* may be a form of Attic *hiketēs* 'suppliant', though this is quite uncertain. *Hiketēs* was used of (among others) individuals who sought cures

at sanctuaries of Apollo and his son Asklepios (e.g. *IG* IV^{2} 1 121, line 4 and *passim*, from the sanctuary of Apollo and Asklepios at Epidaurus).[394]

6 If a term associated with the *paian* is read here (n. ad loc.), it is worth noting that these hymns to Apollo were sung to the accompaniment of the kithara.

Ele17. Sixth to fifth century. Archaeological Museum of Rethymno (Inv. no. E26)

Eight lines of text inscribed on a fragment of a limestone block that is broken along all edges; 2–7 are inscribed boustrophedon between horizontal guidelines.

[—]ο . [—]	
[—]κνοṿ[—] ←	
[—]οαιλε[—]	
[—]ι ἀπομ[—]	
[—]λοι. αἰ δ̣[ὲ —]	—. But if —
[— τὸ]ν κρόνον [—]	— the time —
[— ἄ]ργυρον δ[—]	— money —
traces	

---

2 ṿ three oblique strokes (*san* and *mu* are also possible).
4 ἀπομ[—]: from ἀπόμνυμι? G.
5 δ̣: both oblique strokes are visible.

If lines 6–7 are part of the same provision, 'the time' may refer to the (re)payment of money (line 7).

Ele18. Sixth to fifth century. Current location unknown

Five lines of text inscribed boustrophedon on a fragment of a limestone stele (0.07 m. thick) that is broken at all edges. The opposite face of the stone is also inscribed in very similar letters that closely resemble those of **Ele18**. G associated another small fragment (*IC* 2.12.18bis) with **Ele18**.

[—]σενε[—] →
[—]κυρα[—]
[—]ηστao[—]
[—]νο . μ[—]
traces

---

2 Perhaps ἐνέκυρα or a form of the verb ἐνεκυράζειν G.
4 A vertical line is visible between *omicron* and *mu*, possibly a rare example from Eleutherna of the use of the vertical line for word division.

---

[394] See Perlman 2004a: 122–3 for Apollo's association with the medicinal plant Styrax at Eleutherna.

Eleutherna1 (*SEG* 41.739; van Effenterre 1991a (VE); VER II.98; Lupu 2005: 323–5). Law concerning the consumption of wine. Late sixth century. Archaeological Museum of Rethymno (Inv. no. E125). Fig. 38

Twelve lines of text inscribed boustrophedon from the left between horizontal guidelines on a small limestone stele broken above and below with preserved right and left edges. An empty space at the top of the stone suggests that line 1 is the beginning of the law.

Fig. 38. **Eleutherna1.**

μὴ ἰνπίνεν· α[.] →
[.] . με δρομέα ⟨ἰ⟩σ̣-
ς Δῖον Ἄκρον σ-
υνινπίνοντα
πίνεν. vacat
ἰαρέα δὲ μὴ αἰ δ-
ιαρόϜϜοι τôι θ-
ιôι αἰ μὴ̣ [υ]ἶ τεκ[ν]-
[ό]Ϝστεν ἀρκαῖ-
ον ἐστι. ὄσστι̣[ς]
[. . 3–4 . .]τῆρας τ . [.]
[. . . 5–6 . . .]μ̣η̣ι̣[. 2–3 .]

lines 1–5: Excessive drinking is prohibited; [—] an adult at Dios Akron may drink his fill in the company of others.

lines 6–10: But a priest may not (drink excessively) if he is sacrificing for the god except where it is traditional to do so (?). Whoever—

---

1 ἰνπίνεν = ἐμπίνειν 'drink one's fill'.

2 The lower part of an oblique stroke is legible at the beginning of the line compatible with α, δ, ε or *san*.

μὲ⟨ν⟩ VE; VER.

ọ: the first three strokes are legible; ν is also possible, and is tempting as it yields δρομέανς acc. pl. But this creates problems with both the toponym in the acc. without a preposition and συνινπίνοντα in the acc. s., although the difference in number between the participle and its antecedent might be possible. The construction of Δῖον Ἄκρον is more difficult; VE suggests δρομέα ⟨ἰ⟩ọ|ς with ⟨ἰ⟩ος/⟨ἰ⟩ς = εἰς. For the geminated form ⟨ἰ⟩ος, cf. διαρόϜϜοι (lines 6–7) and ὅσστι[ς] (line 10); see Dialect 10, 14.

3 Δῖον Ἄκρον: 'divine promontory/peak' or 'Zeus' promontory/peak'. If Δῖος is used here as the adjective of 'Zeus', this is likely the earliest such use.

6 διαρόϜϜοι may be the 3rd sing. opt. of the *hapax legomenon* διϊερεύω 'sacrifice'.

VE prefers punctuating in line 6 after μή followed by the beginning of a condition: ἰαρέα δὲ μή· αἰ δ' | ἰαρόϜϜοι, 'But not a priest; and if he performs cult for the god . . . ' We think the sense is better taking ἰαρέα δὲ μή as the apodosis and αἰ διαρόϜϜοι τôι θιôι as the protasis of a condition.

8 ẹ: right vertical stroke and the lower tip of the left vertical stroke are visible.

αἰ μὴ [υ]ἷ: cf. αἰ μὴ [Ϝ]ί⟨ν⟩ or αἴμ[ατ]ι (VE; VER).

[υ]ἷ: see n. ad **Ele16Aa5**.

8–9 τεκ[νό]Ϝοτεν: VE and VER print τεκṿ[ό]Ϝοτεν and postulate the otherwise unattested verb *τεχνουστέω, meaning 'perform', of which this may be the infinitive.

10 ị: the upper stroke of the *iota* is visible.

11 [—]τῆρας: VE suggests κρατῆρας or ἀρυτῆρας; στατῆρας is also possible.

The upper tip of a vertical stroke and possibly the upper tip of a connecting oblique stroke are visible at the right edge of the stone. Possibly ε.

Eleutherna1 consists of two provisions: 1–5 regulating drinking is fairly straightforward; 6–12, regulating the activities of a priest, is less clear.

1–5 The text begins with a general prohibition of excessive drinking and then apparently specifies an exception to the general rule (lines 1–5): an adult male (*dromeus*) may drink (excessively?) in the company of others at a particular place, Dion Akron ('Zeus's promontory/peak' or 'divine promontory/peak'). VE identifies Dion Akron with a cape on the north coast at the frontier of Eleutherna and Axos that is mentioned by Ptolemy, *Geogr.* II.15.5. The context for communal drinking at a remote location is perhaps more likely to be religious than either a private gathering or civic ceremony. VE suggests that the men were stationed at Dion Akron on guard duty, although it seems unlikely that a community would specifically permit its sentries to drink heavily. The general rule may be intended to restrict the consumption of wine in other contexts such as the symposium and the *andreion*. For a possible reference to drinking in the *andreion*, see **G4**.4. H. and M. van Effenterre 1995: 337 draw attention to a passage from the pseudo-Platonic dialogue *Minos* that attributes to the mythical king of Crete a law (*nomos*) forbidding intoxication when drinking in a communal setting.[395] VER cite *Laws* 666a–b, which is more complex: no wine before age 18, no heavy drinking or intoxication before age 30.

6–10 A *vacat* extending more than half of line 5 marks the end of the first provision. The text continues on the next line, without, however, breaking the boustrophedon pattern. Drinking is not mentioned in 6–10, but it is probably understood as the context for the new provision, which may record a second exception to the general rule against excessive drinking for a priest who is performing cult for the god if he is at a location where it has long been permissible to do so. If we are right in restoring 'there where' (*ui*) in 8 (see note), the second provision, like the first, regulates both the context (not while sacrificing) and the place where drinking is permissible.

8–9 'Traditional to do so (?)': *arkaion* ('old') likely implies 'established' and thus traditional. *Teknowsten* is otherwise unattested but may mean 'to perform'.

10–12 A new sentence begins, possibly a condition with an indefinite relative clause as the protasis. The letters in line 11 could be restored to yield 'staters' (perhaps a reference to the fine imposed on someone who engages in unlawful drinking), 'kraters', or 'ladles' (see note).

Eleutherna 2 (*SEG* 54.839; Tzifopoulos 2004: 155). *c.*500. Archaeological Museum of Rethymno (Inv. no. E67). FIG. 39

Five lines of text inscribed boustrophedon between horizontal guidelines on a limestone block that is broken across the top. The text continued to the left and probably to the right. There is an empty space above line 1, but we cannot determine if there was more text above this or if the inscription continued below.

vacat		
[— ἀ]ντιμολίοι ενα[—]	→	— (if someone?) should dispute about —
[—]ον τὸν μὴ ἐλθόντα [—]		— the one who does not come —
[—]λίοντι οτιμδαπ[—]		
vacat		
[—]μοτονμην[—]	→	
[—]ν *vacat*?		

[395] [Plato] *Minos* 320a: ἐν Κρήτῃ δὲ εἷς οὗτός ἐστι τῶν ἄλλων νόμων, οὓς Μίνως ἔθηκε, μὴ συμπίνειν ἀλλήλοις εἰς μέθην.

FIG. 39
Eleutherna2

3 [—]*λίοντι*: probably a dat. sing. participle or 3rd pers. pl. ind./subj. Possibilities include: [*μο*]*λίοντι* 'litigate', or a compound with *ἀντι-*, *ἀνπι-*, *ἀπο-*; [*κα*]*λίοντι* 'summon'; [*τε*]*λίοντι* 'pay'.

οτιμδαπ: Tzifopoulos: *ὅτιμ⟨ι⟩ δ' ἀπ*[—] 'but for whomever'.

4 Tzifopoulos: *μοτον* could be read as: [—]*μο τὸν* or [—]*μοτον*, restored as [*ἀπό*]*μοτον* 'oath of denial' or [*ἐπό*]*μοτον* 'sworn'.

μην: *μὴ ν*[—] or *μην*[—].

The text apparently consists of two provisions: 1–3 and 4–5. There may have been more above or below or both.

The law may regulate procedure: disputing is certain in line 1; 2 may refer to appearing in court; a form of *kaleo* ('summon') may have stood in 3; and some sort of oath may have been mentioned in 4. For details, see notes.

Eleutherna3 (*SEG* 41.740; van Effenterre 1991c: [VE]). Law concerning leather workers or leather products. Sixth to fifth century. Archaeological Museum of Rethymno (Inv. no. E122). FIGS. 40, 41

Fragment of an opisthographic limestone stele broken on all sides. The well-preserved Face A (FIG. 40) has seven lines of text, the poorly preserved Face B (FIG. 41) has five. Both are inscribed boustrophedon between horizontal guidelines. The letter forms on both faces are similar, and both texts may have been inscribed by the same mason, but we cannot determine if they belong to a single document.

A	[—]λ̣λ̣ . ϵ̣[—]		
	[—]η ἀπο⟨δ̣⟩ο[—]	→	— give back (?) / sell (?) —
	[— τὸ]ν σκυτέα [—]		— leather worker —
	[—]ϵν ὅστις [—]		— whoever —
	[—]τ̣αιπαροπλ̣[—]		
	[— ὅ]σ̣τις ζϵ[—]		— whoever —
	[—]ντρ̣[—]		

FIG. 40. **Eleutherna3A**

1 λ̣λ̣: oblique strokes of the two lambdas are visible; VE records α̣λ̣.

ϵ̣: lower tip of the vertical stroke and the lower oblique stroke are visible.

The lower tip of a vertical stroke is visible between λ̣ and ϵ̣.

2 ⟨δ̣⟩: there is no indication of the bottom stroke of the *delta*, but rather a stroke that resembles the oblique cross-bar of an *alpha*, but *ΗΑΠΟΑΟ* seems an unlikely sequence of letters.

ἀπο⟨δ̣⟩ο[—]: probably from ἀποδίδωμι, possibly with [μ]ή. See on **G41**.4.7–8.

3 σκυτέα: acc. sing., Chaniotis 1995: 51. VE reads σκύτϵα neuter pl. 'leather objects'.

5 τ̣: left portion of the horizontal stroke is visible.

λ̣: right oblique stroke is preserved.

παροπλ̣[—]: VE suggests a reference to armaments (ὅπλα). The only attested compound of ὅπλον with παρ- is παροπλίζω 'disarm'. Or perhaps a form of ὅπλεμα 'debt'.

6 σ̣: left oblique stroke is visible.

ζε[—]: VE suggests ζε[υγ-] 'belt'/'harness' or ζε[ρμ-] = δερμ- 'skin'; the latter is very unlikely, since although *zeta* may appear as *delta* in Cretan (δοός, **G72**.4.49, cf. ζοός, **G13**), the reverse never occurs.

7 ρ̣: upper part of the vertical stroke and the upper part of the head of the *rho* are visible; π is epigraphically possible, but unlikely following τ.

Eleutherna3A seems to concern tanned leather, either tanned leather products or leather workers (n. ad line 3). VE's suggestion that it concerns revenues from the skins of animals killed for sacrifice is less likely. The disposition of such skins is often addressed in laws concerning sacrifice, but in such case the normal term is *derma*, an untanned hide, not *skytos*; see e.g. *SEG* 28.750, a Hellenistic or Roman law from Lissos, Crete. For craft production at Eleutherna, particularly craft production from animal products (cf. **Ele9**), see Chaniotis 1995: 49–51; Perlman 2004a: 103–8.

FIG. 41. **Eleutherna3B**

B [—] . . ο . . [—]
[—]δομεν[—] →
[—] . α[.]μεα[—]
[—] . δομεν[—]
[—] . . ματο[—]

2, 4 Perhaps [ἀπο]δόμεν or a form of the participle.

FIG. 42.
Eleutherna4

Eleutherna4 (*SEG* 23.571; Manganaro 1965: 304; Bile 41, no. 33; VER II.15). *c.*500–450. Archaeological Museum of Rethymno (Inv. no. E183). FIG. 42

Four lines of text with traces of a fifth inscribed on a limestone block with preserved upper, lower, left and possibly right edges. The text continued to the left and right and perhaps below. An uninscribed band between lines 2 and 3 indicates separate provisions, both inscribed boustrophedon between horizontal guidelines. An uninscribed band at the top roughly the same width as the distance between horizontal guidelines (*c.*0.03 m.) may indicate that we have the first line of this text.

vacat		
[—]θαι ἐκ⟨σ⟩ομνύηι ἠ̣[—]	→	— he swears an oath of denial —
[—]τις καταστᾶσαι . [—]		— is to pay —
vacat		
[—]κο . [. . 4–5 . .]αν αἰ μὴ μ[—]		— unless —
[—]α̣ στατῆ[ρανς *c.*2]ε̣σο̣[—]		— staters —
traces		

1 ἐκ⟨σ⟩ομνύηι only here. Elsewhere (Axos, Gortyn) the verb is ἀπόμνυμι.
η̣: lower tip of the right vertical and the lower oblique strokes are visible (*epsilon* is also possible).
2 [—]τις: if not the indefinite pronoun, perhaps an adverb in -ις, e.g. αὖτις (Bile 215–16). The lower tip of a vertical stroke is visible at the left edge of the stone.

3 An oblique stroke consistent with triangular letters and *mu*, *nu*, and *san* is visible to the right of the *omicron*. [—]κοσ̣[—] Manganaro.

4 α̣: traces of the cross-bar are visible; perhaps the end of a numeral, e.g. [τρί]α̣, [δέκ]α̣?

ε̣: upper tip of the vertical and upper oblique strokes are visible.

ο̣: traces of the right half of the curve are visible.

The two provisions appear to concern judicial procedure: an oath of denial; payment of the penalty; and probably staters.

FIG. 43.
Eleutherna5

Eleutherna5 (*SEG* 23.572; Manganaro 1965: 303). Fifth century. Archaeological Museum of Rethymno (Inv. no. E55). FIG. 43

Fragment of a limestone block, broken on all sides, preserving six lines of text. The direction of the writing suggests that several provisions may be represented.

[—] . ονε[—] →
[—]σ̣υνπαρε[—] →
[— ἐ]ν δρόμο Ϝ[—] ← — during a foot race? —
[—]ολυ[—] →
[—]εκα[—] →
[—]σ[—]

1 The lower tip of an oblique stroke is visible to the left of *omicron*.
2 Σ̣: lower part of the right oblique stroke is visible.
3 [ἐ]ν δρόμο Ϝ[—]: possibly [ἐ]νδρομοϜ[—] from ἐνδρομέω 'run into'? The noun is not otherwise attested in our texts.

3 'On the race-track' is also possible (LSJ s.v. δρόμος II), but Tzifopoulos 1998 observes that not only is 'race' the primary meaning of *dromos*, but the more specialized meaning 'foot-race' is associated with Crete in particular.

Site

Ancient Eltynia was located near the modern village of Kounavi about 14 km. SE of Heraklion in the fertile Pediadha plain of north-central Crete. Although a systematic archaeological survey of Kounavi and the surrounding agricultural land has not been conducted and the location of the urban center has not been clearly defined, small-scale excavations in the vicinity of the village and chance finds from the area have revealed artifacts dating from the Protogeometric through the Roman periods. Remains of the Archaic period include a mid sixth-century sculpted grave stele (Lebessi 1976: 175 pl. 42:b), the inscriptions **Elt2** and **Eltynia1** and a dedicatory inscription (*IC* 1.10.1) that was found together with **Elt2**, several uninscribed architectural blocks, and a limestone Doric capital (Xanthoudides 1920). Xanthoudides 1920: 75–7 concluded that the block bearing **Elt2** and the capital came from an archaic Doric temple. **Elt2** contributes further information concerning the ancient town (see below). For a useful account of what is currently known about the ancient settlement, see Kritzas 2010: 3–6.

Texts

Elt2 (K 94; VER II.80). Law concerning assault, *c.*500. Archaeological Museum of Heraklion (Inv. no. 210)

Eleven lines of text inscribed on a very large limestone block (w: 2.40 m.; h: 0.46 m.; th: 0.21 m.), in one piece at the time of its discovery in 1918; the block was sawn in two to facilitate its transport to Heraklion. The nature of the monument from which the block comes (e.g. altar, wall of a building) cannot be determined.[396] The original edges are preserved at the top, bottom, and left; the block is broken at the right. Lines 2–11 are written boustrophedon beginning at the right; line 1, also beginning at the right, is written on a molding along the upper edge. The inscription continued to the right and the left, and perhaps below; it seems likely that a considerable amount of text has been lost at both sides. The upper surface of the block indicates that there was at least one block above, but the molding strongly suggests that the inscription did not start higher up on the monument.

We record the sign ⊙ together with *o*; the former is often (but not always) used as it is at Lyktos for *ō*, a diphthong, a glide, or a contraction.

[396] Comparetti 1927: 246 observes that the relatively small size of the letters (0.02–0.03 m.) suggests that the block was situated at about eye level.

[—]ι[.]ο | αἰ δέ κα | κηρὶ | τρ⊙όσει | ἀποτ[ει]σεῖ | πέντε | δαρκν[άς]· | ← αἰ δὲ κῆ⟨ς⟩ ῥινὸς | αἷμα ῥυῆι [—]

[—] τοῖς Ἐλτυνι⊙ῦσι. | αἴ κ' ἄρκσει μάκας | ἀποτεισεῖ | δέκα δαρκνὰς | ← ὄπε κ' ἄρκσε[ι —]

[—] ἀμερᾶν | ἆι κ' ἀνεείπηι | ὕστερον δὲ μή· | κόσμον δὲ πράδεν | τὰν ἐς → πόλιν | τιμάν. | ὅτερος [—]

[— τ]⊙ν ϝερημενον | ϝ⊙ν ϝειπ⊙ν· | αἰ δέ κ' ἀλεκσόμενος [πα]ίηι | ἄνατον ἦμεν | τôι ἀλεκσο[μένοι —]

[— τιμ]ὰν (?) | κατιστάμεν | τ⊙̀ν τρ⊙⊙σ[άν]τον· | [αἰ] δέ κ' ἀ[ν]ὴρ | τὸν πηΐσκον παίηι | μὴ [—]

[—]ṭον | ἦν ἀνδρηίοι | ἦν ἀγ[έ]λα[ι] | ἤ(ν) συν[β]⊙λήτραι | ἢ 'πὶ κορôι | ἢ 'πὶ [. .]ο[. . . .] | η[—]

[—] αἰ δέ κ' ἀγέ[λ]α[ος] | τὸν πηΐσκον | ὄνη[ται (?)] ἂ ἤγραται | αἰ ἐς καιρ⊙̀ν η[—]

[— τὸνς] | κόσμος | γ[ι]γν⊙́σκεν | ὄμνυντας | τὸν ἐπὶ πόλεος | τὸν τ' ἀ[—]

[— τρο]ό[σε]ι (?) | ἀποτεισεῖ | πέντε δαρκνὰς | ὅ[πε ν]ίν κα παίσει. | α[ἴ] κα ἰ[—]

[—]ι ἢ | παίσει ἀποτει[σ]εῖ | [πέ]ντε δαρκνὰς | ὀθά[κι]ς [κα π]αίσε[ι] | η[—]

[—]ς | πέντε δαρκνὰς | [. . . . 7–8 . . . .]ι δὲ | ὀ παθὸν | πανσα[—]

— but if he should wound with his hand he shall pay five drachmas; and if blood should flow from the nose —

— to the Eltynians. If he should start a fight he shall pay ten drachmas whenever he should start —

— within X] days from when he should proclaim (it), but not later; and a *kosmos* is to exact the fine for the city. Whichever —

— (?). But if he should strike defending himself there is to be no fine for the one defending himself —

— the person wounding is to pay the fine (?); and if a man should strike the *pēiskos*, let (him?) not —

— or in the *andreion*, or in the *agela*, or in the *synbolētra*, or at the dancing ground, or at —

— and if an *agelaos* (?) the *pēiskos* what is written, if timely, —

— the *kosmoi* are to swear an oath and decide, the one for the polis and the one —

— he should wound (?) he shall pay five drachmas whenever he should strike him. If —

— or he should strike, he shall pay five drachmas for each time he should strike —

— five drachmas [. . . . 7–8 . . . .] but the victim all (?) —

---

1 κηρί = χειρί.

κῆ⟨ς⟩ = κα ἐκς (Dialect 14); cf. **G51**.12. Bile 1997: 115 suggests κήρινός.

2 For Ἐλτυνι⊙ῦσι instead of Ἐλτυνιεῦσι, see Bile 111.

Comparetti 1927: 248–9 and others restore an enactment formula: [θιοί· τάδ' ἔϝαδε] τοῖς Ἐλτυνιοῦσι. If this is correct, line 2 might be the beginning of the text (so VER). But the collective ethnic need not belong to an enactment formula (e.g. **Gortyn5**.2–3).

ὅπε usually means 'where' but sometimes means 'when' (better 'whenever'), as it must in **Dr1**.2. Bile 263 argues for the latter, but Bile 1997: 115 retracts this view in favor of 'where' (so too VER). In our view, 'where' makes little sense either here or in line 9. 'Whenever' (i.e. 'no matter when') is preferable; 'wherever' (i.e. 'no matter where') would also be possible (so K), and the sense would be almost the same.

3 ἀμερᾶν was probably preceded by a number, indicating the number of days within which something had to be done.

ἇι: '*depuis que*' (Bile 262).

ἀνεείπηι: for the omission of the *digamma*, see Bile 1997: 115, 120–1. Cf. Ϝειπ⊙ν (line 4).

πράδεν τὰν ἐς πόλιν τιμὰν: this phrase is not otherwise attested. At Gortyn the usual expression is θέμεν (vel sim.) πόλι (**G41**.3.17; **G78**.8; **G79**.15–16 & 21; **G84**.2).

4 [τ]⊙ν (τ̣⊙ν G) Ϝερημενον Ϝ⊙ν Ϝειπ⊙ν. The sense is unclear. If, as seems likely, Ϝειπ⊙ν is a participle and Ϝερημενον comes from ἐρῶ 'speak', then we might translate 'saying that the [. . .] that was mentioned is his own (Ϝ⊙̂ν)'. Along these lines, K translates 'as he expresses his assertion' ('*indem er seine Behauptung ausspricht*'); VER suggest 'declaring his own the one who has been denounced', but this is an unparalleled sense of ἐρῶ. Bile 1997: 116 compares the clause with **G72**.1.19–20.

ἄνατον (from ἀτά) 'without fine' is not otherwise attested; elsewhere immunity is expressed by ἄπατον (e.g. **G41**.5.6; **Ele3**).

5 [τιμ]άν is likely with κατιστάμεν (cf. line 3), but [ἀτ]άν or [διπλεί]άν are possible.

τ⊙̀ν τρ⊙⊙σ[άν]τον: gen. pl. part. with -ο- instead of -⊙- is also possible, but it is hard to imagine what sense it might make.

ἀ[ν]ήρ: ἀν̣ήρ G, K, VER, but no drawing records any trace of the dotted *nu*. There appears to be room for two letters between *alpha* and *eta*, but Halbherr 1910: 64 indicates that the stone immediately to the right of *alpha* may have been damaged leaving space for one letter.

At Gortyn *anēr* almost always designates either a father or a husband (comm. ad **G41**.7.12). Thus, the sense here could be 'if a father strikes his child'.

πηΐσκος (also in 7) is probably a diminutive of παίς, though its precise meaning is obscure.

6 ἦν = ἢ ἐν (cf. **Da1**B9; Bile 93 n. 83).

ἢ(ν). For the 'non-notation de la nasale', see Bile 1997: 117.

συν[β]⊙λήτρα is not otherwise attested and is the only example from Crete of a noun with the rare fem. suffix -τρα denoting place. Most scholars have associated the term with συμβάλλω ('to meet (in combat)/to contribute') and συμβολή ('combat'), suggesting that it means either 'exercise ground' or 'refectory' (place where pot-lucks are held). Bile 179 suggests 'place where contracts are made' (from σύμβολον, 'contract'), but Bile 1997: 116 prefers 'exercise ground'. A connection with συμβουλή 'deliberation' is also possible 'place where deliberation occurs'. See also Mandalaki 2010: 17.

ἢ 'πὶ [. .]ο[. . . .]: ἢ 'πὶ ν̣η̣ο[. . . . .] G, K, VER, but no drawing records traces of letters between *iota* and *omicron*. If ν̣η̣ο- is correct, the term possibly has something to do with youths (*neo-*).

7 ⊙̓νη[. . .]: ⊙̓νη[ται] (?) 'dishonor/blame' (Hesychius s.v. ὄνοται· ἀτιμάζει, μέμφεται). ὀνη[δῆι] C, G, K, VER, Mandalaki 2010: 28–9, who understand this as a shortened form of ὀνειδίζω 'to insult'. Bile 1997: 118 rejects this on linguistic grounds, suggesting instead ὃν η[. . .].

η[—]: ἦμ̣[εν] G.

8 γ[ι]γν όσκεν occurs nowhere else in our inscriptions, though γνόμονας (meaning uncertain) occurs in **G14p–g2**. Both γιγνώσκειν and διαγιγνώσκειν are used in Draco's homicide law in the sense of 'decide'.

τ'ἀ[—]: τ' ἀν̣[—] G, but no other editor records any traces after the *alpha*. Bile 1997: 119 with n. 39 suggests τ' ἄν̣ (= τε ἀνά); Comparetti 1927: 247 suggests τὸν τ' ἀ[νδρηίω καὶ τὸν ἀγελᾶν]. The two appositives might be understood in conjunction with ὄτερος (sc. κόσμος) in line 3 to indicate that there were two *kosmoi* at Eltynia, but this is just a guess. τα[—], the beginning of a longer word, is also possible.

9 [τρο]ό[σε]ι: [τρο]ό[σ]ηι G, but we see no trace of the *eta*; cf. τροὄόσει in line 1.

[ν]ίν: Bile 1997: 119 notes that if correctly restored, this is the only attestation of this Doric pronoun, which elsewhere in our inscriptions is always αὐτόν.

10 ὀθά[κι]ς = ὁσάκις.

11 δαρκνὰς | [7–8]ι: δαρκνὰς | [δο]σε[ί]· | αἰ G, followed by K, VER. We are unable to make out any letters between the word division and the *iota*. Bile 1997: 119 notes that [τει]σε[ί] is also possible. The drawing of Halbherr *ap.* Comparetti 1927 records -ση-.

This is the only early Cretan law concerning assault and personal injury. Like the section of laws on rape and adultery at Gortyn (**G72**.2.2–45), it contains a series of provisions imposing fines in monetary terms for particular situations (lines 1, 2, 9, 10, and 11); here, however, because the text is fragmentary, it is more difficult to discern any organizing principle (but see below on line 5). The rules appear to distinguish between wounding and striking, between instigating a fight and striking in self-defense, among categories of perpetrator and victim, among locations, and possibly between wounding with one's hand and wounding with an object, and among types of wound. Several provisions concern procedure, with the *kosmos* both adjudicating and exacting fines. Finally, a number of words are not found elsewhere on Crete (Bile 1997).

For a recent discussion of **Elt2** in light of the ancient literary record, see Mandalaki 2010.

1–2 'To the Eltynians'. Most scholars conclude that this phrase at the start of 2 is part of an enactment formula ('it was pleasing to the Eltynioi') and that this is the beginning of the text. Line 1, on this view, was mistakenly omitted from somewhere within the text (VER inserts it after line 2), and when the mistake was detected the line was inscribed immediately above line 1 on the molding. See further our n. above.

The significance of the direction of lines 1 and 2 is not clear. If line 1 is the first line of this inscription then the fact that the first two lines read in the same direction should be understood as archaic paragraphing with line 1 recording a separate but related provision. If line 1 was written after line 2, its direction might reflect the fact that writers at Eltynia were conditioned to begin from the right and continued boustrophedon from the left only if the length of the text required it.

1 'With his hand' implies a distinction between injuries caused with one's hand and those caused with a weapon (or other object). Athenian law incorporated the

same principle with its category of 'intentional wounding', which apparently required the use of a weapon (see Lysias 3).

2 'Whenever'. VER and Bile 1997: 115 translate 'where' and argue that the perpetrator is to pay the fine at the place where the fight began. In our view, this makes little sense. We understand this as an indefinite relative clause similar to **Dr1**.2 ('whenever he judges'): the person who starts a fight is culpable regardless of when (or where) the fight takes place. Thus 'wherever' (K) is also possible.

Note that the fine for starting a fight (ten drachmas) is twice as much as the fines in lines 1, 9, 10, and 11.

3 'Proclaim': the verb (*aneipon*) is not otherwise attested in Cretan inscriptions. The provision may limit the number of days that may pass between a proclamation (e.g. alleging a wrong occurred) and some other step in the judicial process.

Fines are also paid to the city at Gortyn (for references, see n.).

'Whichever' (of two). We punctuate this as the beginning of a new sentence (so K, VER), perhaps 'whichever of the two disputants'; but it might also continue the sentence (so Comparetti 1927, G), perhaps with the sense 'whichever *kosmos*'. For two (or more) *kosmoi*, see line 8.

4 The meaning of the words at the beginning of the line is unclear (see n.).

This is the only certain example from the Cretan laws of immunity from prosecution for someone acting in self-defense, though **G41**.2.16–17 may pertain to self-defense against the attack of dogs.

5–7 *Pēiskos* (5, 7), *agelaos* (7), and 'man' (5) probably refer to age divisions, roughly equivalent to child, adolescent, and adult, although *agelaos* ('member of an *agela*') is probably also a civic and social status term. Because 'man' (*aner*) at Gortyn almost always designates a father or husband (comm. ad **G41**.7.12), line 5 might refer to a father striking his child (see below). The term for 'child' (*pēiskos*) is not otherwise attested and its etymology is uncertain (see n.), but all scholars probably rightly understand it to mean 'child'. *Agelaos* occurs in the Hellenistic 'oath of the *agelaoi*' from Dreros (*IC* 1.9.1A, line 11). For recent discussions of the ages these terms designate, see Mandalaki 2010: 14–16; Kennell 2013: 52 and *passim*; Introd. 5A2.

5 The first part of 5 probably makes the individual who wounds another liable for paying the penalty. This suggests some special circumstance concerning the parties or the wrong has been lost, otherwise the rule would seem to be unnecessary (cf. line 9, where the wounder probably also pays).

'A man . . . the child': the same construction occurs in line 7 where 'an *agelaos*' is the perpetrator and 'the *pēiskos*' is again the victim. Bile 1997: 117 n. 21 observes that the use of the definite article with *pēiskos* may be 'generic' (as it is several times in **G72**.2.2–28), but it could also be possessive ('his child') in both places. There may have been a cluster of provisions here concerning injuries caused to a *pēiskos* by different categories of perpetrator.

6 All scholars assume that the five (or possibly six) places linked with 'or' are locations where an assault of some kind is envisaged as occurring. The first three—'men's hall' (*andreion*), *agela*, and *synbolētra*—follow the preposition 'in' (*en*); the latter two—'dancing ground' (*koros*) and another location of which only one letter survives—follow 'at' (*epi*). Because the 'men's hall' was a structure, whereas the 'dancing ground' was probably an open space, the two prepositions might distinguish between places with structures 'in which' and open spaces 'at which' something occurred. If so, *agela* and *synbolētra* may also have been structures.

Andreion (Introd. 6C); for 'in the *andreion*', see **G4** and **A1**.

Agela elsewhere in inscriptions and literary sources concerning Crete designates a cohort of young men or sub-adult boys (Introd. 6B); only here is it a place where they reside or perform an activity closely associated with it (if it occurs in **Dr3**, its sense there is obscure). This double sense can be paralleled, however, in e.g. the term *choros*, which refers both to a group of dancers and to the place where they danced.

Synbolētra is not otherwise attested. Previous scholars have suggested that it means 'exercise ground', 'refectory', or 'place where contracts are made'; it might also mean 'place where deliberation occurs' (see n.).

'Dancing ground' (*koros*) is attested in several interstate agreements that are not included in our texts, first in the mid fifth-century agreement of Knossos, Tylissos, and Argos (M&L 42B 36–8), although in this case it is not clear that the dancing ground here is Cretan, and then in a Hellenistic treaty in a clause inviting the treaty partners to attend one-another's dances and footraces (*IC* 3.4.1, lines 68–73). Pausanias 3.11.9 notes that the Spartans call their agora '*choros*'; the term, then, possibly denotes more generally an area within the polis-town for public gatherings.

7 We suggest restoring *ōnē*[*tai*] 'dishonor/blame' (see n.). If the meaning is 'dishonor', the implications of the term here are unclear. If the meaning is 'blame', the provision possibly concerns an *agelaos* who claims that the *pēiskos* is at fault, possibly to counter an accusation that he has harmed the *pēiskos*.

'What is written' (cf. 'whatever is written', **G75**D4) presumably refers, as elsewhere in early Crete to a law, either this very law or one written somewhere else.

'If timely' is oddly vague if it refers to a procedural time limit, but it is difficult to imagine its referring to anything else. Most scholars restore 'to be' at the end of the line: 'what is written, if timely, is to be' sc. authoritative.

8 This provision specifies at least two *kosmoi*, 'the one for the polis and the one . . .'.[397] Note that in line 3, *kosmos* occurs in the singular, but 'whichever' (of two) at the end of the line may imply there were at least two *kosmoi* at Eltynia.

[397] Comparetti 1927: 252–3 suggests that the *kosmos* for the polis was the chairman of the *kosmoi*, but there is no evidence for this.

Polis here might designate the urban center, which would imply that another *kosmos* was responsible for overseeing rural affairs; but it seems more likely that *polis* designates the city as a political unit, in which case this *kosmos* may judge matters involving citizens with another *kosmos* judging those of foreigners. For the office of 'foreigners' *kosmos*' at Gortyn (e.g. **G78**.4), see Introd. 4C1b.

'To swear an oath and decide'. This expression, with a different verb for 'decide' (*krinen* rather than *gignōsken*), occurs only here and at Gortyn, where it is common in **G72** (Introd. 10D1). Evidently, at Eltynia the *kosmoi* adjudicated disputes as did the *kosmos* at Dreros (**Dr1**) and (perhaps) at Datala (**Da1**B7–11). It is unclear whether the *kosmoi* here decide a matter related to the dispute in line 7, and if so, what matter that might be.

10 'Or he should strike': a verb may have preceded ('If someone [does X] or he should strike...').

Eltynia1 (Kritzas 2010 = Kr). *c.*600–525. Archaeological Museum of Heraklion (Inv. no. 423). FIG. 44

Six lines of text inscribed boustrophedon beginning at the right on a block of conchiferous hard limestone. The block is broken at the right and the left. The upper and lower edges are preserved. The text continued to the right and the left. We cannot determine if line 1 is the first line of the text. There does not appear to be any writing in the wide band below line 6, suggesting that this is probably the final line.

44. Eltynia1

Letter forms (esp. *theta* and *pi*) and phonology (e.g. *zeta* instead of the later double *delta*, see Dialect 11) suggest that this inscription may be slightly earlier than *IC* 1.10.1 and **Elt2** (Ikonomaki 2010; Kr). All *iotas* face left.

[—] . η̣ . ὀ̣νηθ̣ὲν | δικάζεν̣ [—]	←	— has been bought he is to judge —
[— τὰ] π̣οινικήια | τάδε | ἅ κ̣ . [—]		— these writings which —
[—]η | ἅ κα μὴ συνπρασια[—]		— whatever are not —
[—]ι | . απ[. . .]ι̣ς | ἅ κ̣α μὴ αμ[—]		— whatever are not —
[— τ]όδε | ὃ | κατέκσει | [—]		— this which he shall occupy —
[—] . . . ι | δι κα [. . .]αι | παρῆι | τοι[—]		— to whom (?) it belongs —

1 η̣: the bottom horizontal stroke and the lower tips of the verticals are visible.

ο̣, θ̣: the circles are complete, but it is not possible to determine if there are central dots or crossbars.

ν̣: *san* is also possible (δικάζεσ̣[θαι]?).

1–2 δικάζεν̣ [— κατὰ τὰ] π̣οινικήια τάδε Kr; this assumes that only a few letters have been lost at the left edge.

2 π̣: the curved 'head' of the *pi* is visible.

κ̣: the vertical stroke is visible.

A vertical stroke is visible at the right edge of the stone.

3 συνπρασια[—]: Kr suggests that πρασια[—] derives from πέρνημι 'sell', yielding either the phrase σὺν πρασια[—] or an otherwise unattested compound, which could be either a noun συνπρασία 'joint sale' (for the form, cf. παμπρασία 'general sell-off'; ἀπρασία 'no sale'; for the sense, cf. συμπράται 'joint purchasers') or less likely a verb συνπράσια[ν] (= opt. συνπράσεια[ν]; see Bile 234–5, 263), but words connected with 'selling' with the root πρα- only appear late in Cretan inscriptions (Bile 328–9). Another possibility is πρασιά 'garden-plot'.

4 . απ[. . .]ι̣ς: we see no trace of the *iota* that Kr reads to the left of the *alpha*. The string *ΙΑΠ* would be difficult.

The second word division is very faint.

κ̣: the vertical stroke is visible.

5 τ]όδε: τ]ο δὲ and [τ]οδε are also possible.

ὃ | κατέκσει: ὃγ̣ κατέκσει Kr, who reads a dotted *gamma* facing the wrong direction. The assimilation ν > γ at this early date would be unusual (cf. συνπρασια[—] in line 3). We think that what Kr reads as the oblique stroke of the *gamma* is damage to the stone (there is a longer gash in line 4 just to the left of and parallel to the stroke that Kr attributed to the *gamma*). We can see only (part of) a vertical stroke that may belong to a word-division line.

κατέκσει (καθέξει). Kr suggests that the active may have a middle sense 'to have one in his power', and proposes for ὃγ̣ κατέκσει 'the one whom he will possess'. But this seems unlikely, and even if ὃγ̣ is correct, it could refer to a thing or place.

6 κα [. . .]αι: possibly κ' ἀ[λλ]ᾶι or κα with another adverb ending in -αι?

δι κα παρῆι occurs in **G41**.5.4–5, where it refers to the master of an indentured person.

1–3 It is not possible to determine the subject of this law, but the terms 'has been purchased' (line 1) and possibly *synprasia* 'joint sale' (line 3, see n. ad loc.) suggest that it may concern buying and selling (Kr).

2 This is the earliest attestation of *poinikēia*, 'writings' (from *phoinix* in one of its two senses, 'Phoenician' or 'red-purple'), and its only occurrence on Crete. See comm. ad **Da1**A5 (cf. **Ele11**.3). Kr is surely right that *poinikēia* 'writings' is synonymous with *ta egrammena* ('things written'), used elsewhere in Cretan laws to refer to written law (cf. **Elt2**.7 *a ēgratai* and Gagarin 2008a: 110–11). We note that *poinikēia* and related terms occur in texts dating to *c*.600 (**Da1**, **Ele11**, **Eltynia1**), whereas *ta egrammena* and related terms do not appear before the fifth century; but the difficulties in dating, the very small sample, and the possibility of local variation in vocabulary make it unwise to conclude that this was a diachronic development.

5–6 Kr proposes that these lines concern someone who is being held, possibly by force (5), and someone who is indentured or otherwise belongs to another (6). The first proposal seems impossible (see n.) and the second is only one of many possibilities.

Site

Gortyn is situated in south-central Crete, at the northern edge of the Mesara plain, the largest and most fertile plain in Crete. The Mesara stretches west from Gortyn some 20 km. to the coast and about the same distance to the east. A small river, the Mitropolianos (ancient Lethaios), flows down out of the hills north of the city.

In the Catalogue of Ships, Homer describes the Cretan contingent under the leadership of Idomeneus as inhabiting seven cities, including 'walled Gortyn' (*Gortyna teichioessan*, *Iliad* 2.646). If historical, this presumably refers to the hill Agios Ioannis (the so-called acropolis) west of the gorge formed by the Mitropolianos, which shows traces of habitation in late Minoan times continuing into the Sub-Minoan, Protogeometric, and Geometric periods (*c.*1200–700).[398] During the Protogeometric period settlements formed on hilltops to the east of the gorge, Armi and Prophitis Elias. A temple identified with the goddess Athena was built on Agios Ioannis in the eighth or seventh century (Prent 2005: 272), but already in the ninth century and continuing into the eighth, the inhabitants gradually moved down from the hills to the plain below (see Introd. 2A3a, b). No trace of defensive walls has been found in the plain. Perhaps in the second half of the seventh century a temple of Apollo Pythios was built to the south of the modern road (Prent 2005: 274), on which the earliest texts were inscribed (*c.*600–550). The temple's walls are not ideal surfaces for the inscriptions they contain, and it seems clear that the temple was not built with the idea of inscribing laws on it.[399]

The temple of Apollo was used for the display of laws until around the end of the sixth century, when a new public area was created some 500 m. to the north-west, which later became the site of a Roman Odeon. Most of the laws from the Classical period, including the Great Code (**G72**), were displayed in this area.[400] The exact layout of buildings and (presumably) the civic center in the Classical period is difficult to determine because of the many Hellenistic and Roman buildings on the site, but many scholars think that the curved wall with the Great Code would have formed one side of a public building (e.g. Di Vita 2005: 13–21), as would the straight Northern (*murum septemtrionalis*) and Eastern (*murum orientalis*) walls, on which are inscribed **G41–51**.

From the ninth through the sixth centuries Gortyn seems to have expanded its influence over other small communities in the Mesara. To the west Gortyn would

[398] See Coutsinas 2013: 214–15, 424–6 no. 29 for the identification of walls on Agios Ioannis with the defensive walls mentioned in the *Iliad* 2.646.

[399] For a thorough study of the architecture and architectural history of the Pythion, see Ricciardi 1991.

[400] For the location of structures used for the display of public inscriptions in archaic and classical Gortyn, see Perlman 2000a: 60–2; Marginesu 2014.

FIG. 45. Plan of Gortyn

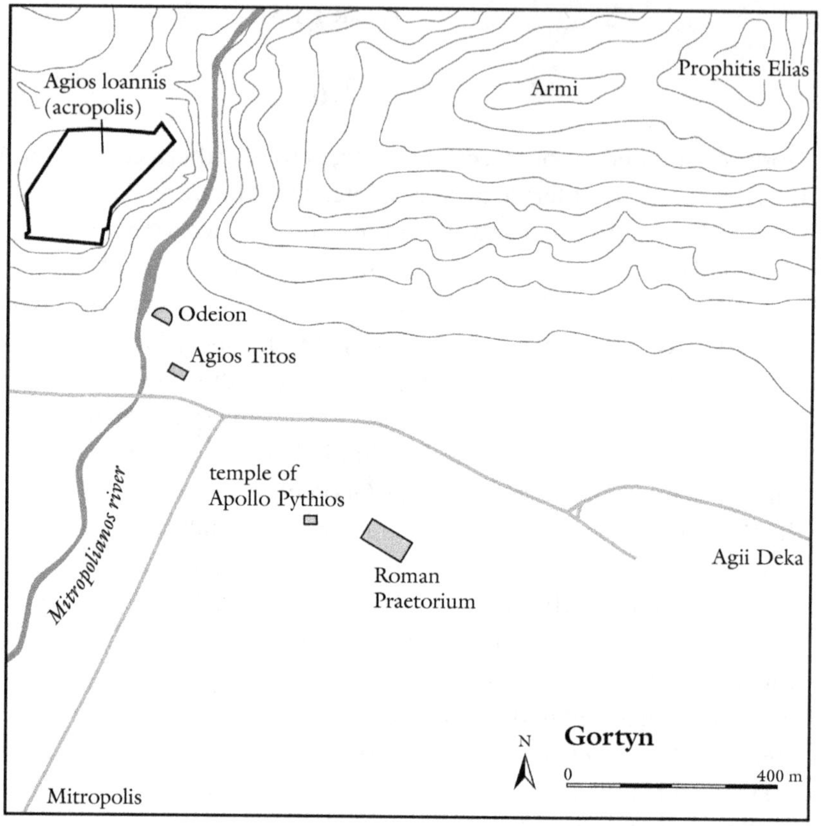

have run up against Phaistos, a far more powerful site in the Minoan period which continued to be inhabited as an independent polis into the Classical period (Phaistos Site). The evidence of Homer, *Odyssey* 3.293–6 (discussed Introd. 2C) implies that Gortyn controlled the southern part of the western Mesara, while Phaistos presumably controlled the northern part. On current evidence, the physical remains of Gortyn suggest that it was the more important city in the Archaic and Classical periods, but it must be noted that archaeologists have not located the civic center of archaic and classical Phaistos and the topography and monuments of the city are largely unknown.[401]

Texts

The inscribed laws from Gortyn, in particular the Great Code (**G72**) provide more evidence for the legal system of this city than we have for any other Greek city besides

[401] For more on the early history of Gortyn as a polis, see Introd. 2C and Perlman 2000a, 2004b: 1161–5.

Athens. The kind of evidence we have from the two cities is largely different—forensic speeches from Athens, the texts of laws from Gortyn—but on many points the two cities can be compared or contrasted. Because many readers of this text will be familiar with Athenian law, we have referred far more often to Athenian practices than to those of any other city. The resulting Atheno-centric bias is perhaps misleading, but seems to us unavoidable. Archaic laws from other Greek cities can be found in Koerner 1993 and van Effenterre and Ruzé 1994–5.

With regard to dotted letters and other details of the Greek texts we generally follow Guarducci unless otherwise indicated.

G1–40 are generally agreed to be the earliest texts from Gortyn. Guarducci (1950: 40) dates them to the mid-seventh to the late sixth centuries, but Jeffery's date (1990: 311–13, 315) of *c.*600–525 is probably more accurate. They were probably all inscribed on the walls of the temple of Apollo Pythios (see above). Undoubtedly the purpose of inscribing them on the temple was in part to invoke the support of the god for this legislation, but the temple may also have been the only public structure at that time with surfaces suitable for inscription. Inscribing the laws on these walls would not only have made them accessible to the local inhabitants but would have advertised them (so to speak) to the inhabitants of other settlements around the plain who might visit the temple.

There were two sorts of surfaces available for inscribing: tall orthostate blocks (about twice as tall as they are wide) placed side by side to form a wall, and short but wide blocks placed end to end; **G8–17** are inscribed on these wide blocks. On the tall blocks the inscribed texts normally begin at the right top and run to the left across several blocks, in some cases returning again from the left (boustrophedon style). Other laws were regularly added on the tall blocks, one below the other, each beginning anew from the right. In most cases, texts inscribed together on the same set of stones appear to treat related subjects. The short blocks only had room for one or two lines of writing, so texts are either a single line, usually right to left, or two lines, with the top line usually running right to left and a second line returning under it, boustrophedon. The texts generally remain within a single row of blocks, whether tall or short, and do not continue on a block below, though **G12** may be an exception (see further on **G12** and **G13**). Very rarely (**G22**, **G23**) we find vertical writing.

Most of these texts are written in large, often rather crude letters. All are fragmentary and rarely do more than a few continuous words survive. Even so, it is evident that these early laws covered a wide range of topics.

All the penalties or fines prescribed in **G1–40** are stated as objects of value—usually some number of cauldrons, but a tripod in **G8** and an obol or metal spit (apparently) in **G25** and **G26**. It is uncertain whether these were to be actual objects or (more likely) they represented units of weight or value (Introd. 7D).

G1 (VER 2.22, K 116). *c.*600–525. Figs. 46, 47

Five lines of text, all running right to left, on six orthostate blocks. We follow G in designating the blocks a–f, corresponding to C's 1–6. Blocks a–c contain five lines, d and f have only four lines, and e has only two lines. There is a large space below the bottom line on all the blocks. Blocks a and b join, as do d and e, and the last two lines on d–f can easily be restored on the assumption that the lacuna between e and f was two letters. We maintain the traditional order of the blocks, noting that blocks d–f have fewer lines and thus probably come after a–c; c could come before a–b, however, and the amount of space separating a–b from c and c from d–f (or a–b from d–f if c came first) is unknown.

FIG. 46. G1 (drawing after Comparetti 1893: 17–18)

The traditional restoration of this text has been influenced by H's drawing (FIG. 46), reproduced in Comparetti 1893 and in G, which shows the six blocks separated in two rows. This led Blass and all editors since to conclude that lines 3 and 4 on blocks d and f and the two lines on block e were continuations of lines 3 and 4 in blocks a–c. However when the six blocks are all aligned in the same row (FIG. 47) it is clear that lines 3 and 4 in d–f are continuations of lines 4 and 5 in a–c.[402]

The resulting arrangement also seems preferable with respect to content.

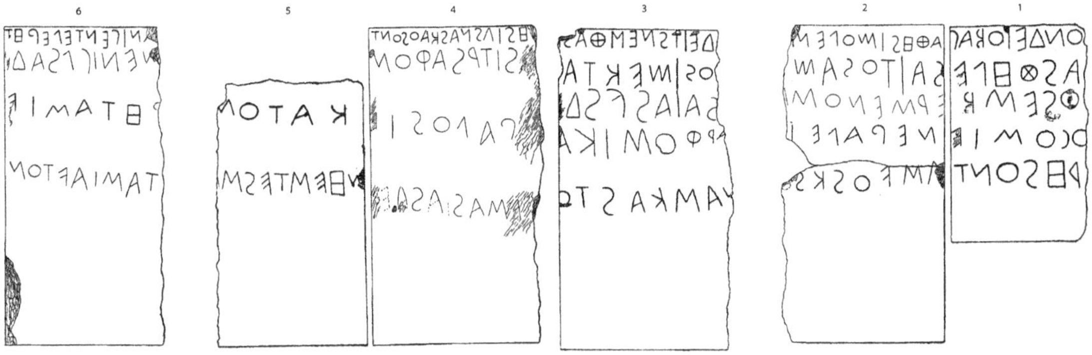

FIG. 47. **G1** (drawing with all blocks on the same line)

1 a–b ← [—]ονδε | ὅκα πάθηι | μολε̂ν | [—]
c [—]δε | τίνεσθαι [—]
d–f [—]ηι | γιναι̂κα ὀίον τ[c.18–20]α̣ν | πέντε λέβητ[ας —]
2 a–b ← [—]αι θήλεια | τôι ἀμ[νôι (?) —]
c [—]οι | μεκτα[—]
d–f [—]ι | τριάϘον[τα c.12]μεν | πλία δ[ὲ μή —]
3 a–b ← [—] ὅϊες κε̋ρσενος | [—]
c [—]ια | αἰ Ϝίδ[ια (?) —]
4 a–b ← [— ἄνθρ (?)]οπος | ἐνέβαλε | [—]
c [—] ἀρϘός | κα[—]
d–f [— ἐμ]βάλοι | ἑκατὸν [λέ]βητας | Ϝ[εκαστ —]
5 a–b ← [—]κ̣ρηιον τα̂ς Ϝοικιό̣[νσας (?) —]
c [—]νας καὶ το[—]
d–f [— καταστ (?)]ᾶ̣σαι· | αἰ δὲ μὴ ἐστείσα̣[ι | ἄ]τας | ἀϜτὸν [—]

1 — of these (?) whatever harm he suffers, let him contend (in court) — pay a fine — a woman, of sheep (?) — five cauldrons —
2 — female, to the lamb (?) — thirty [c.15] but not more —
3 — the sheep and of a male — if personally (?) —

[402] Comparetti first published all six blocks together, concluding that they belonged to the same inscription and that the blocks with two or four lines would come later than those with five lines (1893: 21–2). Blass (# 4962) first printed a continuous text, which is followed by G, who prints drawings of *a–c* and *d–f* on separate pages (1950: 42–3) so that the alignment of the lines of text is not evident. Only when all six blocks are placed on one line is it apparent that it is line 3 (not line 5) that stops before blocks *d–f*.

4 — a person (?) attacked — a leader — should attack, [he is to pay (?)] one hundred cauldrons each (?) —

5 — debts (?) of the female inhabitant (?) — is to pay (?), but if he does not fully pay the fines, he himself —

---

1 τ]ôνδε C.

μολêν is the general verb for 'participate in litigation', whether as plaintiff or defendant.

γιναῖκα = γυναῖκα The vowel shift from *upsilon* to *iota* is unparalleled in Cretan, and so Bile 89 divides the letters -γιν αἴ κα. The word division marker before *gamma*, however, which is clear in FIG. 46 (the stone is lost), makes this explanation impossible, and (in correspondence) Bile now has no solution to offer.

ὀίον: gen. pl. The accent is uncertain; for discussion, see Bile 106–7.

2 ἀμ[μνôι (Att. ἀμνῷ): VER, who cite **G65**.5.

μ' ἔκτα[νεν C. is very unlikely; μὲ κτά[ναι would be better, though the verb is unattested in Cretan inscriptions.

4 ἄνθρ]οπος (if correct) and ἀρϙός could both also be acc. pl. rather than nom. sing.

5 τôν κ]ρηιôν C. For κρῆιος = Att. χρέως ('debt'), cf. **L6**.5 (see Bile 105).

τᾶς ϝοικιό[νσας could also be acc. pl. (τὰς ϝοικιό[νσας).

ἐστείσα[ι from ἐστίνω (ἐκτίνω) 'pay in full'.

There appear to be links among the five texts. Lines 1–2 and 4–5 mention fines; 1, 2, and 4 mention a specific number (of cauldrons in 1 and 4) in ascending order—five, thirty, one hundred; the last of these would be a severe penalty. In addition, 1–3 mention sheep, 1 talks of a woman, 2 of a female, 3 of a male and 5 (probably) of a female inhabitant. Thus, although the five lines were probably five different laws (see below), it seems likely that they were placed together because they address aspects or stages of the same general subject, perhaps damages involving animals and humans.

It is unclear how close in time to one another the five texts were inscribed. At first glance, the lines may appear to have been written in different hands, since several letters are quite obviously written in different forms in different lines. But masons at this time may have been relatively inexperienced and variations in letter forms by the same hand may have been fairly common. In fact, on this and several other early inscriptions there are clear variations in letter forms within the same line, which was presumably inscribed by the same mason. There are different forms of *nu*, for example, in line 1 and also line 2. Thus, we cannot rule out the possibility that the same person wrote all five lines (Perlman 2002: 193–4), and that the five provisions were enacted at about the same time and inscribed together. But since each begins from the right, they were still apparently considered separate provisions.

4 'Leader': cf. **G75**B8, where an *arkos* (= *archōn*?) is the leader of an *andreion*.

G3. Sacrificial calendar. *c.*600–525

Six lines of text on four orthostate blocks. Blocks *b* and *c* join, and the text of *a–c* lines 2–4 can be restored on the assumption of a lacuna of eight letters between *a* and *b*. Block *a* breaks off after line 5, and *d* has only the first two lines, for which reason it is placed after *a–c*. But there are traces of writing below line 2 on *d* and so it is not impossible that *d* might precede *a–c*.

1 a–c ← [— ἰα]ρὰ | τετελημέ[να . . . c. 6 . . .] . υι | τôι [Ϝ]ελκα̣νί[ôι —]
d [—]αι | ἐν τᾶι πένπτα[ι —]
2 a–c ← [—]ν | τέλησν | καὶ αἶγα | ἐν̣ [τᾶι ἕκται (?)] ὄιν̣ θήλε[ι]α̣ν | τôι Ἀπ[έλλονι —]
d [—]εϙ[. .]ς̣ | ταϜῦρος | ἐσ . [—]
3 a–c ← [—] τᾶι Ἥραι | ὄις | θή[λ]ε[ια | τᾶι Δάμ]ατρι | ὄις | ἐπίτεκ[ς —]
4 a–c ← [—] αἰ μὲν δύο | θήλει[αι, οἰ δὲ δύ]ο ἔρσενες | καὶ τρ[άγος (?) —]
5 a–c ← [—]λ̣[. . . .]ιο[. . . . . .]απρ̣οσ̣υναι κα̣[—]
6 b–c ← [—]α̣ ς | οι̣ ὄϜτοι ον̣[—]

1 (These) sacred rites have been performed — in the month Welkanios — on the fifth day —
2 — a grown — and a goat on (the sixth day?), a ewe to Apollo — a bull —
3 — to Hera a ewe, to Demeter a ewe about to give birth —
4 — two females and two males and a goat (?) —
6 — these —

---

1 τετελημέ[να: perf. pass. part. from τελέο.
2 ἐν̣ [τᾶι ἕκται] Blass (# 4963), accepted by G; but other numbers (e.g. ἕπται) are possible.
5 [—]απρ̣οσ̣υναι κα̣: Bile (in correspondence) suggests perhaps αἴ κα, but in that case it is difficult, if not impossible, to see what might be made of]απρ̣οσ̣υν.
6 ὄϜτοι = οὖτοι (cf. **Ele3**.5). The position of the article is irregular and Bile (personal correspondence) wonders if the word division mark before οἰ could be the bottom stroke of a *tau*, yielding τ̣οιοϜτοι. The stone is lost, but the drawing in G (taken from Comparetti 1893: 19-20) clearly shows the divider extending well below the bottom of the line of letters; thus a *tau* seems impossible.

The first four lines contain a list of sacrifices of male and female animals to at least three different gods, on different days of the month. As in **G1**, the lines may appear to be in different hands, but here too it is possible that one person inscribed the whole text (Perlman 2002: 193–4). In any case, these provisions were very likely inscribed together to form a list of sacrifices (cf. **Dr6**). A similar list of sacrifices is found in **G65**, where two gods are named (Zeus and Helios) and other factors are also mentioned (priest, neighbors, additional sacrifices). For more on sacrificial calendars, see Gagarin 2011.

1 The letters of line 1 on block *a* ('sacred rites have been performed') are slightly larger and more deeply incised than in the other lines; this suggested to Comparetti (1893: 21) that these words were a kind of title for this group of provisions. But variations in the size of letters in different lines are not uncommon,

and since all the letters in line 1 appear to be slightly larger than the rest, the variation is probably not significant.

'Have been performed': the perfect participle (*tetelēmena*) seems to indicate that we have a list of completed sacrifices; presumably this was inscribed and displayed in order to serve as a guide for sacrifices in the future. It is also possible that the participle simply means 'perfect' ('perfected'), and that the first words thus prescribe 'perfect victims' for the following sacrifices.

G4 (VER 2.61, K 117). *c.*600–525

Four lines of text, all reading right to left, on two orthostate blocks which join in line 3. Line 1 appears to be the top line, and the space below line 4 is empty.

1 ← [—] *οπερ οἰ ἄλοι | μη πρίασ[θα]ι | μὴ ἀμεϜύσασθαι | ὅζο[ι —]*
2 ← [—]*τυτυι | ἔτι δὲ ϙοῖρο[ι |] τέτορες | καὶ Ϝαρὴν* [—]
3 ← [— *τô*]*ι ὀμομόται | μὴ ἀπ̣ορηθῆμέν | ποκα* [—]
4 ← [—]*τ̣ . . . α̣ηι . . τ̣ .* [. . .] *ἐν ἀνδρήιοι π̣ί*[*νεν* (?) —]

1 — just like the others, not to buy, not to exchange, those (which) —
2 — and four more pigs and a sheep —
3 — for the co-swearer, not to refuse (?) ever (?) —
4 — in the *andreion* to drink (?) —

---

1 *ἀμεϜύσασθαι = ἀμεύσασθαι = ἀμείψασθαι.*
ὅζο[*ι = ὅσοι*; Dialect 13.
2 *τυτυι*: from *τιτύς* 'penalty'? (Bile 89)
3 *ἀπ̣ορηθῆμέν*: a form of *ἀποϜείπεν*, it may mean 'refuse, deny' or 'speak out' (see n. ad **G72**.9.37–8).
ποκα = ποτε (Bile 216); see above Dialect 33.
4 *π̣ί*[*νεν* VER. The restoration is tempting but uncertain.

No connection between the four lines is evident in these scanty remains. It is hard to make much of this text. Line 1 seems to be a commercial regulation; in 2 the animals may be for a sacrifice or a penalty; 3 may be concerned with legal procedure; and 4 may regulate drinking in the *andreion*.

3 *Omomotai* ('co-swearers') occurs only here and in **L5**.13 (without context); cf. *omotai* in **Dr1**.4.

4 This is the earliest mention of the *andreion* on Crete; see also **A1**.8, 15; **Da1**B11; **Elt2**.6; **G75**B7–9; Introd. 6C.

G5 (VER 2.92). *c.*600–525

Only the bottom of this text remains, with two lines of text at the top of one block, a single line at the top of a second block, and on both a large empty space below.

An unknown amount of space separated the two blocks, either of which could have stood first.

1 ← [—]ν̣ς ἑπτὰ | τᾶς Ϝοιϙο̣δ[ομίας —]
2 ← [—]ι̣κα ἀνδάζαθαι ὀτειο[— ῥ]οὰν ῥήκσαιεν̣ ἐ̣κ̣α̣τ̣ὸ̣ν̣ λέβητ̣[ας —]

1 — seven — of the building —
2 — to redistribute to whom (?) — they might break the flow (?), one hundred cauldrons —

---

1 Ϝοιϙο̣δ[ομίας: Bile (p.c.) notes that Ϝοιϙο̣δ[ομήσιος ('act of building') is not impossible. Neither word is attested elsewhere in Crete.

2 ἀνδάζαθαι = ἀναδάσσασθαι.
ῥ]οὰν C, accepted with doubt by VER.

---

2 Blass (#4965) first interpreted *rēksaien* (line 2) as an optative with *roan*, which is used of the flow of a river in **G43**Bb2. But it is not clear just what 'break the flow' might mean here. The heavy fine suggests a serious public harm, perhaps the permanent diversion of a stream rather than a temporary interruption.

G6. *c.* 600–525

Two blocks with two lines of text at the bottom running right to left, with an unknown amount of space between the two. Block A has an additional line above the lines common to both blocks; this line, commonly designated a, is written in very different lettering and is followed by a *vac.*, indicating the end of a (probably unrelated) provision.

a ← [—]ρ̣ομ̣νυ μέγα *vac.*
1 ← [—] | μηδὲ λέβητος [—]ϙον | Ϝοιζηαζε [—]
2 ← [—]ται | πριν[—] το]ῖσι | ναοῖσι | [—]

a — great — *vac.*
1 — nor of a cauldron — to appropriate (?) —
2 — for the temples —

---

a The first letter might be *koppa* rather than *rho*. Neither letter makes a recognizable word but it is tempting to suppose that some form of ὄμνυμι lurks here, (e.g. 'swears a great oath').

1 C, followed by G, takes Ϝοιζηαζε as a form of οἰκεάζειν ('make one's own'), but Bile 146 n. 295 doubts this is phonologically possible.

---

1 This is the only example of 'cauldron' (*lebēs*) in the singular; elsewhere we find only multiples of five (Introd. 7D). Perhaps the law specified something worth one cauldron.

G7. *c.*600–525

A single stone with a few letters visible at the top.

[—λέβ]η[τ]α̣[ς ἑκα]τ̣ὸν τὰ δ' ἀλ[—]

— one hundred cauldrons, and the others (?) —

The supplements, all from C, are very uncertain.

G8–17 are all inscribed on long blocks with either one line (**G8–12**) or two lines (**G13–17**) of writing.

G8 (VER 2.11, K 118). *c.*600–525

Fifteen blocks with a single line of text. The joins between *a–b*, *c–d*, and *e–f* are certain, those between *b–c*, *d–e*, and *g–h* are likely; otherwise the order is uncertain. We follow Blass (#4969) in joining *i* (ϙομόταs |ἐ) directly to *a* (κατὸν | ποι).

i, a–f [— ὀρ]ϙομόταs | ἑκατὸν | ποινᾶs | καταιστάμεν | τρίποδα | ἕνα | δ[ε]κα λεβήτον | ἐπόμοτον | ἤμ[εν —]
g–h [—]ατα | θήλειαν | δυόδεκα̣[Ϝέτια (?)]
k [—]αματίs | ἐ[—]
l [—]ονον | ἀδα̣[—]
m [—]ομεν | παισ̣[ίν (?) —]
n [—]οραι | ἀματο[—]
o [—]αι | ἤ βαλὲν [—]
p [—]ιs | πριγνο̣[—]

i, a–f — oath-swearers, one hundred, as blood-money (he) is to pay one tripod sworn to be (worth?) ten cauldrons —.
g–h [—] female twelve[-year-old (?)] —
m — children (?) —
o — or to throw —

---

i, a–f Blass (#4969), followed by VER, joined ϙομόταs | ἐ on block i with κατὸν | ποι on block a; the join is attractive, but uncertain. It is not accepted by G or K (who only gives the text of a–d).
καταιστάμεν: an archaic form; elsewhere the second *alpha* is elided (Bile 148).
ἐπόμοτον ought to mean 'sworn in accord with' or 'sworn in addition to'; cf. ἐπωμοσμένων in *IC* 4.184B22–3 (perhaps early 2nd century BCE), Bile 352.
g–h δυόδεκα̣[Ϝέτια (Blass, VER) seems likely, but other restorations are possible; see commentary.
k ἐπιπ]αματίs Blass, VER. This is very unlikely, since this would be the only occurrence in Crete of this Doric word for 'heiress' (from πᾶμα, πάματοs, the Doric word for 'property'; cf. ἐπίκληροs). The Cretan word is πατροιôκοs (*passim* in **G72**.7.15–9.24 also also twice in **G44** and perhaps also in **G74**) and it would be very surprising if two words existed for the same institution. Moreover, the occurrence of ἀματο[in n suggests that we may have an entirely different (and unknown) word here.
l π]όνον (= φόνον) 'homicide' VER.
o βαλὲν: the present infinitive (with single *lambda*) is perhaps most likely, but the letters may represent other forms of the verb.
p πρὶ(ν) γνô[ναι 'before he knows' G, VER.

The expression 'is to pay as blood-money (*poinē*)' indicates that this law concerns, and probably sets fixed payments for, homicide (perhaps mentioned in l), perhaps specifically for killing children.

i, a–f Even if the join proposed by Blass is correct, the sense is not clear. One hundred seems an improbably large number of oath-swearers, whatever their capacity, so perhaps the number qualified a noun that is now missing.

g–h Other restorations are possible, e.g. 'twelve pigs', 'twelve *medimnoi*'.

Payment of a tripod may mean an actual tripod, not its equivalent value, since otherwise the law could simply have specified ten cauldrons. The equivalence of a tripod with ten cauldrons is plausible: the prizes in *Iliad* 23 include a tripod worth twelve oxen (702–3) and a cauldron worth one ox (885–6).

Poina should be the blood-price for a homicide (Bile 326), but one tripod, even an expensive one, seems far too small an amount. Possibly this is compensation for an accidental homicide.

The restorations proposed for the remaining lines (see notes above) are very uncertain.

G9 (VER 2.78, K 119). *c.*600–525

Thirteen blocks from a row of stones on one side of the Pythion, all connected (a–n), and fourteen from another side, of which the first eleven (a*–l*) appear to be connected. It appears that all the blocks were inscribed but only a few bits of text are now legible. On both sides all the letters are at the top of the blocks, except for m, where the letters (μὴ ἀϝ̣τ[ὰ] ϝ̣οιζη) are written lower down on the stone; it may be that the original letters at the top of m were erased (none are legible today) and the correct text was written below.

a–m [— τ]ô ἀγρήιο | [—]ι̣ος | ἄγεν | [—] πονό̣σει | ἢ δ̣ίκ[αν] δ[ι]κάζε̣[ν] | ἢ ἀϝ̣τ̣ὸ[ς] κατα [. . .]ηι [—]ελες | ον | ἐλ[ὸ]ν | μη̣ [—] λεν | τ̣ὸ̣ ἀγρήιο | [—]ε πον[.]ιον μὴ ἀϝ̣τ[ὰ] ϝ̣οιζη[—]

m*–o* [—]εσ̣μ[c.3] . ητ̣αι[—] ὄρϙοι | ἢ ἐ[—]ν μολοῖ | ἢ προπον̣[—]

a–m — of the gathering place — is to lead — he should kill, either to judge the case or he himself (is to pay?) — seizing is not to — of the gathering place — says, not these their own (?) —

m*–o* — oath or — should plead or declare beforehand (?) —

---

a–m *πονό̣σει* from *πονόω* (Att. *φονεύω*) is probably aor. subj.

δ̣ίκ[αν] is restored as plural (*δ̣ίκ[ας]*) by G, followed by K, VER.

κατα[βάλ]ηι? C; oddly, G (followed by VER) does not print the last two letters (*ηι*), though they are clearly visible in C's (i.e. H's) drawing, which she reproduces.

[—]*ε πον[ε̂]ι* C (Attic *φωνέω*, 'speak'); G omits the preceding *epsilon*, though it is clearly shown in her drawing. The simple verb is used of statements by litigants, as opposed to *ἀποπονε̂ν*, used of the testimony of witnesses; see **G72**.1.14 and 19 (with notes).

ϝ̣οιζη[—]: see above on **G6**.1

[—]*ὄρϙοι*: more likely dat. sing. than nom. pl.[—]

m*–o* *προπον̣*[—]: a trace of the bottom of a vertical is visible, which we read as *nu*; *mu*, *sigma*, *rho*, and other letters are also possible.

This text may set procedures to be followed in a homicide case, including perhaps a provision that the judge either decide the case or pay a fine himself. It is possible that **G8** and **G9** are complementary in that the first sets fines for homicide and the second specifies procedures.

a–m The *agrēion* or gathering place (mentioned twice) is probably not the same place as the *agora*, which is mentioned in a contemporaneous text (**G13**h–g2) but a separate public area, perhaps for smaller gatherings (so G, citing van Effenterre 1946a: 596). If the context of this law is homicide procedure, the *agrēion* may be where homicide trials were held. Cf. *agretas* in **Dr5**.2.

'Judge the case': in **G72** *dikazein* is regularly used of a judicial ruling that is determined by law, but here (and in **G13**g–h1 and **G21**.7–8) it appears to refer more generally (as in Homer) to judging or deciding by any means. The plural ('cases') could also be restored, but the law is more likely requiring a judge to decide a specific case (or else face a penalty) rather than cases more generally.

m*–o* These lines appear to continue the procedural focus of a–m: *moloi* (*molen*) is the general verb for pleading a case or contending at law, and *propon-* (*proponen*), if that is correct, may be a variant of *proweipen*, which has a judicial sense (e.g. **G72**.2.28).

G10. *c.*600–525

Forty-four blocks with a single line of text running perhaps around all four sides of the Pythion. The large letters (0.17–0.25 m.) occupy nearly the entire space on the blocks. Only a few of the blocks can be joined.

On three blocks (p*–r*) the text is written over an earlier text (**G10a**) in smaller letters; no attempt was made to erase the earlier letters.

We do not give a text for blocks for which no useful text can be restored.

<table>
<tr><td>b</td><td>[— κ]ατισ̣[τα —]</td><td>b</td><td>— pay —</td></tr>
<tr><td>c–e</td><td>[— κατι]σ̣τάντον | καὶ τ̣ôν δενδρέ[ον —]</td><td>c–e</td><td>— let them pay, and for the trees —</td></tr>
<tr><td>f–h</td><td>[—] κατισ[τάντο]ν | πεντήϙοντα λ̣[έβητας —]</td><td>f–h</td><td>— let them pay (?) fifty cauldrons —</td></tr>
<tr><td>i</td><td>[—] ϙόσμο[—]</td><td>i</td><td>— kosmos —</td></tr>
<tr><td>k–l</td><td>[— λέβ]ητας | Ϝέκαστον [—]</td><td>k–l</td><td>— cauldrons each —</td></tr>
<tr><td>m–n</td><td>[— λ]έβητας | Ϝὲκς τον̣[—]</td><td>m–n</td><td>— cauldrons, six —</td></tr>
<tr><td>o–p</td><td>[—] | αἰ κ' ἐσδέκσεται | [—]</td><td>o–p</td><td>— if he should receive —</td></tr>
<tr><td>q–r</td><td>[—] . ον | διπλῆι | παντο[—]</td><td>q–r</td><td>— double —</td></tr>
<tr><td>s–t</td><td>[— Ϝί]κ̣ατι λέβητας | [—]</td><td>s–t</td><td>— twenty cauldrons —</td></tr>
<tr><td>u</td><td>[— κατισ (?)]τ̣άντον | ἐ . [—]</td><td>u</td><td>— let them pay (?) —</td></tr>
<tr><td>v</td><td>[—]ον δ' ἐς πο[—]</td><td>v</td><td></td></tr>
<tr><td>x–y</td><td>[— Γορτ (?)]υνια [—]</td><td>x–y</td><td>— Gortynian (?) —</td></tr>
<tr><td>z</td><td>[—]ν̣οι | κατιστάτο | [—]</td><td>z</td><td>— let him pay —</td></tr>
<tr><td>a*–b*</td><td>[— κατιστάντ (?)]ο̣ν | πε̣ντήϙοντα̣ [—]</td><td>a*–b*</td><td>— let them pay (?) fifty —</td></tr>
</table>

g*	[— δ]άμο [—]	g*	— of the people (?) —
h*	[—]ς | ὄς κ[α —]	h*	— whoever —
k*	[—] | λαγα[—]	k*	— release (?) —
o*	[—]ν ἀϜταν | [—]	o*	— herself (itself?) —
p*	[—]ς λέβητα | τ[—]	p*	— cauldron —
q*	[—]ς δᾶμον | [—]	q*	— the people —

f–h κατισ[τάντō]ν or κατισ[τάμē]ν Blass (# 4968).
v πό[λιν C.
g* δ]αμο C (followed by G), who notes an apparent space after the *omicron*; the noun must thus be a gen. sing.
k* λαγα[—] probably a form of λαγαίω; see Bile 228 (cf. on **G78**.4).
x–y If the proposed supplement is correct, this would be a unique example of either the feminine or the neuter plural of a city collective.

The subject of this text is not clear, but it appears to set fines for several different offenses. Note in particular the occurrence of *damos* ('people') in q* (and g*?) and perhaps also 'Gortynian' in x–y (cf. **G23**.8b). Precisely whom either of these terms would designate at this time is not certain.

G10a. *c*.600–525

Three blocks with one line of small letters over which was written the text of **G10** (see above).

p*	[—]ερετυος | κατὰ τ[—]		
q*	[—]ερμει | μή ποκα δ[—]	q*	— never —
r*	[— θ]ανατοιε[—]	r*	— death (?) —

r* θ]ανατοιε Blass (#4968) wrongly read a *theta* at the end of q* and proposed joining q* and r*.

G11. *c*.600–525

Nine blocks, the last of which (i) is a corner with writing on two contiguous sides.

a–b	[—]ν | μὴ Ϝοιζηα | το[—]	a–b	— not their own (?) —
c–d	[—]μες | μιγέντα | ἐν[—]	c–d	— being mixed —
h–i	[—]λοι | Ϝίκατι λέβητ[ας —]	h–i	— twenty cauldrons —

a–b Ϝοιζηα: see above on **G6**.1.

G12. *c*.600–525

Eighteen blocks with similar handwriting but only two joins. The writing on a–h runs right to left, but left to right on i–s. G. takes this as a single text written boustrophedon on two courses of stone. But the blocks are of different heights (the tops of many are broken) and i–s may be a separate inscription. We may even have more than two texts here. If i–s are separate, the single line of text running left to right would be unique in this period at Gortyn; but since some two-line texts (such as **G13**) apparently begin from the right, it is not impossible that a one-line text might.

a–b	[—] *μὴ σκάπεν* [—]	a–b	— not to dig —
c	[—] *ἀϜτᾶς* [—]	c	— of herself (itself?) —
l–m	[—]*ε ἄγει τὸν* [—]	l–m	— leads the —

G13 (VER I.1, K 120). Judicial procedure. *c.*600–525

Twelve long blocks with two lines of writing on each (K gives only line 2). Only one join is likely. The direction of the writing is unusual: the top line runs left to right and the second line continues boustrophedon to the left. C (followed by G and VER) thus suggests that the first line of the inscription was on a block above these and ran right to left. But many of these blocks have a substantial space above the first line of text, which would be odd if there were a line of text above.

The top line is carved in much larger letters than the bottom line. It appears that the mason did not leave enough room and thus had to make the second line smaller to fit on the stone. Perhaps he did not realize he would reach the end of the available blocks and have to continue with a second line; or (more likely) line 2 may have been added later.

The two lines may be in different hands; in particular the *pi* in k1 is quite different from the *pi*'s in l2, i2, e2 (3x) and c2. But cf. above on **G1** and **G3**.

a1	[— *ἀντί*]*μολος* | *αἰρ*[—]	a1	— opposing litigant —
b1	[— *ἀντ*]*ιμολίαι* | *ἀ*[—]	b1	— litigation —
c1	[—]*ιμεν* | *ἠ*[—]	c1	
d1	[— *μ*]*ολῆι* | *νικα*[—]	d1	— pleads, wins —
e1	[—] | *τôι δὲ ζοô*[*ι* —]	e1	— for the one living —
f1	[— *ἐ*]*νίκασε γα*[—]	f1	— he won —
g–h1	[—]*ζαι* | *ἅ μο*[*λίοντι*] *ἐδίκαζε* | *ἢ μὴ ἐ*[—]	g–h1	— what he judged for the pleader, or that one not —
i1	[—]*λεν* | *ἢ μ*[*ὴ* —]	i1	— or not —
k1	[—]*αν* | *πα*[—]	k1	
l1	[—] *ἢ ἐνικάθη* [—]	l1	— or was defeated —
m1	[—]*λεν* | *καὶ ἐς ἄλος* | *ἀλâι δ*[*ὲ* —]	m1	— and to others, but otherwise —
m2	[—] *θοαίοι καὶ κσανθᾶς* [—]	m2	— should pay a penalty (?), and of the blond —
l2	[—]*ịσοι* | *ϙ' ὅζοι ἐπὶ τ*[—]	l2	— and as many as against —
k2	[— *Ϝοι* (?)]*κίαι ἢ σ*[*τέγαι* (?) —]	k2	— for the household (?) or the house (?) —
i2	[—] . *οι ἀϜτὸς διπλῆι* [—]	i2	— he himself (is to pay?) double —
h–g2	[— *λ*]*άϙοι Ϝαστίαν δίκαν* [*ἐν τᾶι ἀγ*]*ορᾶι καὶ ἀ δίκạ* [—]	h–g2	— he should obtain a citizen's trial in the agora and the trial —

f2	[—]οεσι | ὅ τι τίς κ' ἀγάγη[ι —]	f2 — whatever someone seizes —
e2	[—] . | πόλι πάνσαι πρά[ζεσθαι—]	e2 — exact a penalty (?) for the entire city —
d2	[—]α̣ι τᾶς τιτύϝος [—]	d2 — of the fine —
c2	[—]ειον καὶ παρα̣[—]	c2 — and —
b2	[— α]ἰρεθῆι τôι κσενοδό[ϙοι —]	b2 — [if (?)] he should be taken for (by?) the host —
a2	[— μ]ὴ λύηι. *vac.*	a2 — should not release (him). *vac.*

g, h, i VER are probably correct to reject Blass's (#4976) joining of h and i, accepted by G, K, et al., since the letters in line 1 do not align correctly; but all editors agree that g can be joined with h on the assumption of a lacuna of 6–7 letters between them.

m Blass (#4977) doubted that m, a corner block on which the top line is written on two sides, was part of the same text, but the size of its letters and the placement of its lines on the stone fit well with the others in this text, and so G, VER, and K all include it. The missing second line on one side of m appears to have been chiseled out, perhaps for architectural reasons.

a1 ἀντί]μολος: ἀμπί]μολος ('the object of litigation') is also possible (cf. **G72**.10.27–8).

αἰρ[ει? For the form, see above Dialect 30.

b1 ἀντ]ιμολίαι (dat. sing.) is a *hapax*; see Bile 351.

i1 μο]λῆν?

m1 μο]λῆν?

m2 θοαίοι: perhaps an optative associated with θωή 'penalty'; see Bile 229 n. 306.

l2 ὄζοι: see on **G4**.1

k2 ϝοι]κίαι ἢ σ[τέγαι C, VER; G is perhaps right to be doubtful.

e2 πρά[ζεσθαι C, VER; G is doubtful.

d2 τιτύϝος: gen. sing. of τιτύς (Bile 327).

b2 α]ἰρεθῆι: see above on a1.

a2 The line ends with a vertical rectangle (▯) marking end of the line (and the text) less than half way across the stone.

Despite the fragmentary nature of this text, it yields important information about the city and the judicial process in archaic Gortyn. The fragments of line 1 suggest that we have rules concerning litigation: note *molen* ('contend, litigate, plead in court') and its compounds in a, b, d, g–h, and perhaps at the beginning of i and m, *nikan* ('win, defeat' in court) in d, f, and l, and *dikazen* ('judge', see below) in g–h.

The text is most interesting as an early indication of a growing sense of civic community. In line h–g2, mention of a 'citizen's trial' (*wastian dikan*) suggests that the inhabitants of the town (*asty*) were recognized as a civic group that was apparently treated differently with regard to judicial procedure than were those who lived in other places. The phrase *pansa polis* ('entire city') in e2 also may have a civic sense (see further below on e2), especially in view of the absence of any evidence of farmsteads or villages in the countryside around Gortyn. If everyone lived in the urban center, then there would be little need to use *pansa polis* to designate the 'whole urban area'. Both expressions thus suggest that the inhabitants of Gortyn were already in the sixth century beginning to see themselves as a civic unit, elsewhere referred to as 'the Gortynians' (e.g. **G23**.8b), as distinguished from those from other cities (foreigners).

a1 VER consistently translate *antimolos* 'defendant', but it strictly means 'adversary' and can be used of either litigant (Bile 351). Similarly in g–h1 *molionti* is 'pleader' (not 'plaintiff') and can designate either litigant.

g–h1 For *dikazein* in the general sense of 'judge, decide', see on **G9**a–m.

h–g2 VER (p. 29) insist that *wastian dikan* is 'a citizen's justice' ('droit de l'astos'), not 'trial', but in Athens *dikēn lankhanein* is the standard expression for obtaining a trial (i.e. bringing suit), and in any case, to 'obtain justice' in the *agora* would mean essentially to obtain a trial there; cf., however, **G64**.4. The *agora* is the traditional civic space or meeting place where trials were held (e.g. Homer, *Iliad* 18.497–508). The expression indicates that already in the sixth century those living in the town (*asty*) were recognized as a civic group that apparently received different treatment in the judicial process than foreigners did. Cf. *kseneia dika* ('foreigners' trial') in **G80**.8 and the comm. on the *ksenios* ('foreigners' [official]') in **G14**p–g2. See also Introd. 4C1b, 5A4–5.

f2 The verb 'seize' (*agen*) here, together with *airen* ('take') in b2 (and perhaps a1) raise the possibility that this text has something to do with the issue of illegal seizure, which is the subject of **G72**.1.2–2.2.

e2 The expression *poli pansai* ('to/for the entire city') is striking (cf. 'all Gortyn' in **G64**.2). If we accept VER's suggestion that it was followed by some form of *prazesthai*, it is possible that the law concerns a fine paid to the city ('is to exact [payment] for the city'), but other syntactical constructions are also possible.

We do not know just what is meant by the word *polis* at this time (cf. on **Dr1**) or how it is related to *asty*, but it must indicate a significant degree of communal self-awareness and organization. Scholars debate whether the construction of the temple or the inscribing of laws is the more important step toward the creation of the polis (see Marginesu 2005a: 29–33, with n. 1); both are certainly important, but the presence of this phrase in one of the earliest inscriptions suggests that Gortyn was acting as and calling itself a polis before it began inscribing laws.

G14 (VER 1.82, K 121). Laws concerning officials and non iteration. *c.*600–525

Eighteen blocks with two lines of writing on twelve of them (g–s) and one line on the remaining six (a–f). The writing is boustrophedon with line 1 running right to left as usual. Line 2 ends at the beginning of g with a simple mark of word division. All editors join g–p, with short lacunas between h and i and m and n. Koerner gives only g–p.

a1 [—]η π̣εδαθ[—]
b1 [—]η ἀμύοτον π[—]
c1 [—]α | τ̣αν πσ̣[—]
d1 [—]ι λαγάσαι ὀ ἀ[—]

e1 [—]ς ταν πσάμα̣[—]

f1 [—]ονοαϘοσ̣[—]

g–p1 [—] π̣ε̣ντήϘοντα λέβη[τας Ϝ]εκάστο καταστâσαι. Ϙόσμος ὁ ἐπιστάς | αἰ μὴ ἐστείσαιτο, ἀϜτ̣[ὸν ὁ]π̣ήλεν | καὶ τὸ̣ν̣ τ̣ίταν | αἰ μὴ 'σ̣τείσαιτο τ[—]

q1 [—]σε̣ι̣[—]

r1 [—]μον | τοσ[—]

s1 [—]εν αἶπ̣ερ τô ἀνδ[ρὸς —]

s2 [—] τὸν ἄνηβο̣ν το[—]

r2 [—]τ̣α̣ς δο[—]

q2 [—]κ̣αὶ πσ[—]

p–g2 [—] λέβητας κα[τ]αστậσαι Ϝέκαστον. | τρι[ô]ν̣ ϜετίονJ τὸν ἀϜτὸν μὴ Ϙοσμêν, | δέκα μὲν γνόμονας, | πέντε̣ [δὲ κσ]ενίος | *vac.*

b1 — uninitiated (?) —

d1 — to release —

e1 — the sand (?) —

f1 — *kosmos* (?) —

g–p1 — he is to pay fifty cauldrons in each case. The *kosmos* in charge, if he does not exact payment, is to owe it himself, and the *titas*, if he does not exact payment, —

s1 — in which the man's —

s2 — the boy —

p–g2 — each is to pay — cauldrons. The same person is not to serve as *kosmos* again for three years, as *gnomones* for ten years, and as the foreigners' official for five years. *vac.*

---

b1 ἀμύοτον = (apparently) ἀμύητον, but the vocalic shift is not easy to explain (Bile 98 n. 102).

c1 πσ̣[αμα G (cf. e1).

e1 πσάμα̣[(perhaps also in c1 and q2) is presumably ψάμμη, a rare form of ψάμμος ('sand'). VER suggest that sand may have something to do with initiation (see b1).

f1 [—]ονοα Ϙοσ̣[μο (?).

g–p1 ἐστείσαιτο from ἐστίνω (ἐκτίνω) 'pay in full', and in the middle 'exact full payment'. τ[ὰν διπλέαν Blass, G, VER. Cf. **G78**.7–8 and **G79**.16–20, both of which impose double fines.

q2 πσ[αμα G (cf. e1).

p–g2 κσ]ενίος is written here with an *epsilon* but in **G53**A2–3 it is written with an *eta*, indicating that the lengthening is recent (see Bile 95 on the orthographic problems). The restoration is accepted by all editors. If the word is strictly parallel to γνόμονας, it should be plural, but because every other non-fragmentary occurrence of *ksenios* is singular, we (like G, K, VER) take it as a singular here and assume a change of construction to the nominative.

The restrictions on holding office in p–g2 are often compared to the law from Dreros (**Dr1**), which requires a ten-year interval before one can be *kosmos* again and imposes penalties on the *kosmos* who violates this restriction. Here the requisite interval is only three years and no penalties are stated, but restrictions are also imposed on holding the office of *gnomon* and *ksenios*. The purpose of such restrictions was presumably to ensure greater rotation of office among individuals; rotation among tribes, which would probably impose the same interval for all offices, may have come later (see Introd. 4C1e). Longer waiting periods may be imposed on the lower offices because more candidates would be qualified for these than for the position of *kosmos*.

The rules in g–p1 have drawn less attention. They address the common problem in archaic communities (and later) of enforcing verdicts. The method followed here (and often in other cities)[403] is to hold the officials responsible for collecting the fines and make them pay the fine themselves (or perhaps double the fine) if they do not.

g–p1 'The *kosmos* in charge': the expression may suggest that there were more than one *kosmos* at Gortyn at this time, but the details of how many *kosmoi* there were and how this office was structured remain uncertain. See further below on p–g2 and Introd. 4C1a.

The *titai* are mentioned in **G78**.5–8 and **G79**.16–20; in both texts they collect fines and are responsible for paying the fines if they do not collect them. We don't know what other duties (if any) they may have had. Cf. also **G15**a–b2.

s1 'In which': the antecedent may perhaps be the agora, but this is only one of many possibilities.

p–g2 'The same person': the syntax of this elliptical sentence is not entirely clear. We have given a literal (elliptical) translation above; a fuller version would perhaps be 'the same person is not to serve as *kosmos* again for three years, (the same people are not to serve as) *gnomones* for ten years, and (the same person is not to serve as) the foreigners' official for five years.' G and others understand the infinitive *kosmen* ('to serve as *kosmos*') as governing the other two nouns, with the implication that the *gnomones* and the *ksenios* were also *kosmoi*, but Willetts (1955: 107) doubts that this was the case, and it is certainly easy to supply the sense 'to serve as *gnomones* (or *ksenios*)' instead. Moreover, if all these officials were *kosmoi*, then one might expect them to have the same restrictions on serving again.

Another difficulty is the grouping of a singular *kosmos* and *ksenios* with a plural group of *gnomones*. It is hard to explain the variation except by assuming that there was only one *kosmos* and one *ksenios* but several *gnomones*.

The *gnomones* ('knowers' or 'deciders') are not mentioned elsewhere in Crete, and although they could not have had the same duties as at Athens, where the *gnomones* were inspectors of the sacred olive trees, they are likely to be investigators of some sort. Some think they are identical to the *mnamones* ('rememberers', mentioned in **G72** and elsewhere), but there is no good reason why they would have a different name in this inscription. Ruzé (1988: 85–9) makes the interesting suggestion that they are similar to the early Athenian *thesmothetai*, who

[403] See e.g. VER I.78, Blocks 1–4; VER II.95.11–13, 48–9.

according to *Ath. Pol.* (3.4) wrote down *thesmia* for use in future decisions (on which see Gagarin 2008a: 114–16); but in archaic and classical legislation at Gortyn there is no evidence for or mention of written texts except for laws. On the other hand, since *gignōskein* can mean 'judge', as in **Elt2**.8 (though this sense is much more commonly conveyed by *diagignōskein*), the *gnomones* may possibly have been judges.

The *ksenios* ('official for foreigners') is also mentioned in **G53**A2–3, **G72** 11.16–17, **G79**.15 (= *IC* 4.144), **G89**.7, and **G98**. It is often suggested that he is the same person as the *ksenios kosmos* mentioned in **G30**.4 and **G78**.4, and it does seem unlikely that two officials would exist side-by-side with these nearly identical titles. The most likely explanation is that the official known as the *ksenios* had the rank of *kosmos* (either originally or at a later date), so that he could be known as the *ksenios* or the *ksenios kosmos.* See Introd. 4C1b, where we compare the (*archōn*) *basileus* at Athens. For the duties of the *ksenios* (*kosmos*), see Perlman 2004a: 109–11. For the singular number, see n. above ad loc.

G15 (VER II.23). *c.*600–525

Three blocks with two lines of writing boustrophedon. Blocks *a–b* join; *c* might go either before or after.

a–b1	[— ἀ]τ̣ι̣τάλτας μὲν ἐκσῆσθαι [—]	a–b1	— foster father (?) is to give up (?) —
a–b2	[—] τίνεν καὶ τίτας ὅς κα [—]	a–b2	— to pay, and the *titas* who —
c1	[—] τιτοϝτὸς λ̣[—]	c1	— liable to a fine (?) —
c2	[—]υτος | τον π[—]		

a–b1 ἀ]τ̣ι̣τάλτας must be related to ἀτιτάλλειν, 'to raise' (a child); someone who raises a child may be a foster father, or a relative, or even an official in charge of the education of certain youth.

ἐκσῆσθαι: there is no satisfactory explanation for the form. Bile 152 takes it as the future middle infinitive of ἔχω, but future infinitives are very rare in these laws. Others (see G ad loc.) connect it with ἐξίημι, which seems more likely, but the *eta* cannot be explained in this case.

c1 τιτοϝτός is probably related to τίνειν ('pay a fine') and τίτας (for which see on **G14**g–p1); cf. **G13**d2 and Bile 327.

a–b1 If the two words in this line are understood correctly, this law may have to do with a foster parent giving up a child (for adoption?).

G16 (VER II.24). *c.*600–525

One block with two lines of text boustrophedon. There is nothing above line 1.

1	[—] καὶ ἄι κ' ἀλοτ[ριος —]	1	— and if another's —
2	[—]ο̣ν | ἠ̃ ἐσδυσ[άμενο —]	2	— or undressed —

2 ἐσδυσ[άμενο- is almost certainly from the same verb (Att. ἐκδύω) as ἐδδυσ̣[άμενον] in **G72**.6.46, but the meaning of this term is disputed (see ad loc.).

2 *Esdusameno-* may have the meaning of 'strip off, undress'; if so, the context may be that of ritual initiation. But other meanings and contexts are conceivable; see notes on **G72**.6.46.

G17 (VER II.52). *c*.600–525

One block with two lines of text boustrophedon; the first line runs left to right (cf. **G13**). There is a large space below line 2.

1	[—]α̣ | ὅς κα ἐκς ἔδνο[ν —]	1	— whoever from (?) the bridal gifts —
2	[— τ]ô ἀνδρὸς | κ̣[—]	2	— of the husband —

This is the only mention of bridal gifts (*hedna*, Homeric *eedna*) in Crete; other texts speak of the wife's own property (**G72**.2.45–8, etc.; cf. 'mother's property' in **G20**.4). The law here may be protecting a woman's marriage gifts from appropriation or abuse by others; or it may concern the division of property in a divorce or an inheritance.

G18. *c*.600–525

One block with three lines of text boustrophedon; almost nothing remains of line 1.

2	[— κατασ (?)]τάσηι | αἰ δ̣ὲ [—]	2	— he pays (?); but if —
3	[—]ν τέ[κ]να τ[—]	3	— children —

2 κατασ (?)]τάσηι: the supplement is by no means certain.

G19. *c*.600–525

One block with three lines of text boustrophedon.

1	[—]σθαι | ὅζοι . [—]	1	— as many as —
2	[—]ς̣ δ' ἅτερος | μισ̣[—]	2	— but another —
3	[—] κ' ἐς πυλᾶ̣[ς —]	3	— from the tribe —

1 ὅζοι = ὅσοι; cf. **G4**.1

2 μισ̣[θός C.

3 πυλᾶ̣[ς = φυλῆς.

3 If the supplement is correct, this is one of the earliest mentions of a tribe in Crete; see Introd. 4B3.

G20 (VER II.37, K 122). Law on inheritance? *c*.600–525

Two blocks with four lines of text boustrophedon. The writing continued to the right of A, but the left edge of B appears to mark the end of the lines. The space between the two blocks is unknown.

1 [—]ρμον | κâπον | αἰ δὲ [— Ϝ]ισϜό-
2 μοιρ[ον —]ι | οἰ γνήσιοι | ὀτερο[—]
3 [— ἔρσ]ενα | ἀναιρêσθ[αι . . . θ]ήλε-
4 ια | [—]α | καὶ τὰ ματρôια | [—]

1–2 garden, but if — an equal part — the natural children, the other —
3–4 male is to take up (an inheritance ?) — female — and the maternal estate —

1–2 *Ϝ]ισϜόμοιρ[ον*: could also be *Ϝ]ισϜόμοιρ[ος* (or other forms, including feminine).

3 *ἀναιρêσθαι* ('take up for oneself') is used of receiving an inheritance in **G72**.5.24–5 and may have that meaning here.

The mention of natural children suggests that the context is inheritance where there are both natural and (perhaps) adopted children, a subject also treated in **G72**.10.48–11.10, where *wiswomoiron* ('equal part') designates an adopted son's share of the estate. The garden mentioned in line 1 may be part of the father's estate. The mention of *matroia* in line 4 suggests that already at this time (as in the Code) women had their own property, both males and females could inherit, and adopted sons could inherit something even if there were natural children. Not enough remains here to know what relationship existed between the rules here and those in the Code.

4 The word *matroia* ('maternal estate') occurs only here, in **G72**, and in **Ph1**.4 (without context). Where the context is clear, it is always inheritance. See further on **G72**.4.44.

G21 (VER II.38, K 123). Law on family property. *c.*600–525

The text is inscribed on two orthostate blocks from the front of the Pythion. Most of the text is written on one block, with 1–3 letters at the right inscribed on the joining block that formed the northeast corner of the temple. The corner stone also contains **G22** to the right of **G21** and **G78** around the corner to the right (on the north wall of the Pythion). The writing on **G21** continued to the left on at least one more stone. It appears that the top edge of the original block is preserved, so that the first words of line 1 are probably the beginning of the law (Perlman 2002: 190). Among the early inscriptions from Gortyn (**G1–40**) only here and in **G22** (and perhaps in **G3**) do the first words survive.

Eight lines of writing are visible. Each of the first four runs right to left, indicating that each begins a new provision, but 5–8 continue boustrophedon, indicating that lines 4–8 were a single continuous text. The writing ends well before the bottom of the stone.

1 ← [τὸ]ν | μολ̣[ίοντα —]
2 ← ὄστις | μεζ̣α̣ . [. .] ἴοι | [—]
3 ← τôι ἀνπαντôι μ' ἦμεν ἀνκεμο[λίαν —]
4 ← ὀμοπάτηρ ἄ κ' ἦι καὶ ὀμομάτηρ ἀ[—]
5–6 [— αἰ δὲ κ' ὀ μ]ὲν πατρôια μολῆι, ὀ δ' ἀλâι, αἴ κ' ἀνποτέρος ἴοντι οἰ μαίτυρε[ς —]
7–8 [— δικά]ζε[ν] ἀ⟨Ϝ⟩τὸς ἐπαιρῆι | πέντε λέβητας | καταστâσαι, αἰ δέ κα μολ[ῆι] τ[—]

1 The pleader —
2 Whoever, in the middle (?) —
3 For the adopted son there is not to be a suit against the family (?) —
4 A woman who has the same father and the same mother —
5–6 — if one person contends that it is (part of?) the paternal estate and another (contends) otherwise, if there are witnesses on both sides —
7–8 — (if?) he chooses to judge (?) (the case) himself, the penalty is to be five cauldrons; but if he (the accused?) contends (in court) —

---

1 τὸ]ν | μολ[ίοντα: or perhaps τô]ν | μολ̣[ιομένον ('matters in dispute'). It is unusual for a word-division mark to come between an article and its noun/participle but there is only room on the stone at the right for at most two letters.

2 μέζα̣τ̣[ος] ἴοι C, VER; μεζα̣ [μω]λίοι Blass # 4972 (though he may have meant μ̣[ωλ]ίοι, since there is no trace of the letter before ιοι, but a bit of the bottom of a vertical line is visible after μεζα̣).

3 ἀνπαντôι: cf. ἄνπανσιν (**G72**.10.33).

ἀνκεμο[λίαν Blass: on the model of Homeric ἀγχέμαχος ('fighting at close quarters'), this may designate litigation concerning a close relative (Bile 351).

4 H thought there was a trace of a letter, perhaps *gamma* or *lambda*, before ὁμοπάτηρ (see G ad loc.), but there is no room for a complete letter here, and so whatever scratches are now visible must all be incidental.

6 ἀνποτέρος (= ἀμφοτέρως, 'on both sides'), G, VER, K.

ἴοντι = ἔωσι = ὦσι, present subjunctive of εἰμί.

7 δικά]ζε[ν] (if restored correctly) probably has the general sense of 'judge, decide'; see on **G9**a–m.

ἀ⟨Ϝ⟩τὸς̣: the mason appears to have written a *lambda* by mistake for the second letter.

ἐπαιρῆι: the derivation is uncertain. If from ἐπαίρο (ἐπαείρω), 'rouse up, persuade', it could mean 'if he persuades (others) that he should judge'; or it could be from ἐπαιρέο (ἐφαιρέω), a rare verb that in the middle can mean 'choose' but perhaps is used in the active in this sense. The verb also occurs in **Da1**A8.

These provisions are generally thought to concern the property of an adopted son who dies without leaving a direct descendant (cf. **G72**.11.6–10: 'If the adopted son dies without leaving natural children, the property reverts to the adopter's next-of-kin.'). But we do better to treat it as a set of provisions concerning litigation (aspects of which are mentioned in every line except 2 and 4), with specific regard to litigation concerning an inheritance. These rules would then complement the rules on inheritance (and perhaps also adoption) in **G72**, which say very little about procedure.

1 The words could also be restored as a passive participle in the genitive ('of/concerning things being disputed'). If these are the first words of the inscription, they are likely to give an indication of the subject of the law (see below on **G47**). It is possible that the specific area of pleading was specified in the next few words: e.g. 'the pleader concerning his father's property'.

2 The word most often restored in this line is *mezatos*, allegedly meaning something like 'arbitrator' or 'arbitration' (*mesos* = middle), but the restoration is problematic, and the term is unparalleled.

5–6 This is the earliest mention of witnesses (*maityres*), who appear commonly in the Gortyn laws but otherwise only in **L5**.10.

7–8 There are clear echoes of **G9**a–m, where (apparently) someone is supposed to decide the case himself or pay something. At first glance, the text here seems to mean that someone has to pay a penalty if he decides to judge a case himself; but it is hard to see the purpose of such a rule. Koerner calls the payment a fee (*Gebühr*) rather than a penalty (*Strafe*), but elsewhere *katastasai* always designates the payment of a court-imposed penalty, and in any case, this would not resolve the difficulty. If *dikazen* is correctly restored, the text may mean that if someone chooses to judge the case, a convicted litigant will have to pay five cauldrons, but it may be better to assume that a *mē* ("not") originally stood in the gap before *dikazen*, 'if he chooses not to judge the case himself'.

G22 (VER II.84, K 124). *c.*600–525

The text is written vertically on a tall, narrow strip of the corner stone to the right of **G21** (*q.v.*). The inscription has two lines of text beginning at the bottom left corner and running up, then bending horizontally to the right for perhaps four letters, and then bending downward along the right edge. Thus, the two lines face each other (so to speak) and must each be read from a different angle. As usually restored, the last four letters are missing, and there does not appear to be room for additional text after this. Thus, the text appears to be complete, and all the missing letters can easily be restored.

C suggested that this text might be an amendment to a law now represented by a few traces of an early text that are visible above the text of **G78** (see G's drawing of **G78**), which she numbers 22A (numbering this text 22B). But it is very unlikely that an amendment would be written around the corner from the main law with no evident physical connection to it, and in any case, this text may be able stand on its own (depending on the meaning of *prothesin*).

πρόθεσιν | μήτ' ἀ[πο]δ̣ικάζαι | μήτ̣' ἀπομ̣[όσαι].

There is to be no release from a time limit (?) by means of a court judgment or an oath of denial.

ἀ[πο]δ̣ικάζαι: aorist inf. We retain G's supplement, although this compound occurs only here in Crete (Bile 349) and its sense is uncertain. The gap occurs at a bend in the text, and so its width is not precisely determinable, but it must have been 1–3 letters. Other restorations (e.g. ἀ[ν]-, ἀ[να]-, ἀ[νπι]-, ἀ[υτο]- are thus possible.

The meaning of these lines depends entirely on the sense of the first word, *prothesin*, which scholars have suggested could refer to (1) the 'laying out' (Attic *prothesis*) of a corpse for viewing (VER; Garland 1989: 10–11; Engels 1998: 51), (2) a prescript or rule of law (K), or (3) a time limit (Attic *prothesmia*) for bringing a case or a time-limit in general (G; Frisone 1995: 59–60, 2000: 38–40). We find (3) the least objectionable.

(1) This presumes that there was a law requiring the laying out of a corpse and that a family member might try to avoid this requirement by obtaining a court judgment or by swearing an oath. But it is hard to imagine why the city would require the display of the corpse (as distinct from its burial), why a family member would want to avoid this, or how a judgment or an oath could invalidate the requirement.

(2) This presumes that (like the US Supreme Court) a judge could invalidate a law by a court judgment or by an oath, which seems very unlikely. In addition, it is not clear how the word *prothesis* might come to mean a law or rule.

(3) Some mss. of the *Suda* give *prothesmia*, the term for a time limit for bringing litigation in Athens, as one meaning of *prothesis* (π2443–44); if a time limit was imposed on certain kinds of litigation at Gortyn, a litigant might try to avoid it by obtaining a court ruling or by swearing an oath.

G23 (VER II.25, K 125). *c*.600–525

A single block of stone, broken diagonally, with eight lines of text, the first five lines right to left and the next three boustrophedon. The left edge of the text is partially preserved, indicating that it (like **G21**) consists of four one-line provisions followed by a longer provision in lines 5–8a. The inscription has several peculiarities, however. Line 8 is written in two parts: on the left, 8a runs left to right for about six letters followed by a short gap of about one letter. Then comes the end of 8b running right to left. Below this at the right edge are two letters running right to left followed by a blank space (9), and lower down on the left are traces of three more letters, also running right to left (10). Finally, what is apparently another text (11) runs vertically downwards at the left edge of the stone beginning at the end of line 5.

This unusual arrangement has prompted some rather far-fetched speculation. C suggested that after lines 1–5, 7–8a were written next, followed by either 6 or 11 together with 8b–10. VER suggest that line 4, followed by line 11, may be the beginning of **G22** (also written vertically). But there is no way to position **G23** in such a way that these lines could be near the beginning of **G22**. More likely, 1–8a were inscribed first, with 5–8a stopping short of the left edge because of a flaw in the stone's surface. 8b was then inscribed in the space to the right of 8a, and 11 was squeezed in later along the left edge. 9 and 10 remain a puzzle.

The arrangement may suggest that good space for inscribing on the temple may have been in short supply, so that shorter provisions were being inscribed on empty spaces in longer texts.

1	[—] . ς *Ϝίκα[τι —]*	←	1	— twenty —
2	[— *ἀ]Ϝυτάν*. *vac.*	←	2	— herself *vac* —
3	[—] *τ̣ὸ̣ Ϝοικῆ̣ος* | [—]	←	3	— of the serf —
4	[—]*ν̣ ἐσβολὰν ἤμ[ε]ν* | [—]	←	4	— there is to be a removal (?) —
5	[—]*τ̣εσθαι* | . *οτο* . *σ*[—]	←		
6	[.]*αι τô Ϝô ἀποδόμεν* | [—]	→	6	— to give back his own —
7–8a	[—] *α̣ἰ μὴ ϙ' ὀπυστυῖ μὴ̣ [ἐ]νϜοικε̂ν* . *vac.*		7–8a	— if (they) should not live together in marriage
8b	[—] *τôν Γ̣[ο]ρτυ̣νίον*		8b	— of the Gortynians
9	[—]*τι*			
10	[—]*ιβ*[—]			
11	*ὃς δέ κα̣* [—]		11	Whoever —

3 *Ϝοικῆ̣ος*: genitive of *Ϝοικεύς* (cf. **G72**.2.8 and *passim*).

4 *ἐσβολάν* (= *ἐκβολήν*) could also be *ἐς βολὰν* (i.e. *εἰς βουλήν*); this possibility has generally been rejected (G; Bile 156 n. 356), in part on the ground that the word *boulē* does not otherwise occur at Gortyn before the first century CE (also because one would expect a verb of motion with *ἐς*). However, *τὰν βολάν* occurs in **A9**.13 from the sixth century and the word may now occur in **Gortyn3**.6 (*q.v.*).

6 *κ*]*αι* C, *κ̣αι* VER. The restoration is possible, but there is no trace of a letter on the stone.

7 *ὀπυστυῖ*: C's explanation that this is an adverb related to the verb for marriage (*ὀπυίειν*) has been accepted by most editors since, but more likely it is the dative of *ὀπυστύς*, 'marriage' (so Bile 178).

8a The trace of a letter after [*ἐ*]*νϜοικε̂ν* is usually taken as an *epsilon*; but if this is the end of a sentence, as it appears, no sense can be made of this or any other single letter. Perhaps we have instead the traces of a punctuation mark similar to the ⧗ found in **Dr1** and **G72**.9.24 and 9.43. Or perhaps the text continued somehow on the line below.

8b *τôν Γ̣[ο]ρτυ̣νίον* is usually taken as accusative sing. but the plural is far more common and seems to us more likely here. In the only other use of the singular as a noun (**G63**) it is part of a pair (with 'the Lebenian'). These words may have stood alone, signifying perhaps '[an enactment] of the Gortynians', or may have been preceded by words to the right.

9 VER suggest that these two letters (*τι*) standing alone at the right edge may be the letters missing at the end of line 1 (*Ϝίκα[τι*), but this sort of puzzle seems very unlikely.

Little can be said about the content of this inscription, which is of interest for the peculiar positioning of its texts as much as for their content. The overall subject, if there was one, may have been the marriage (or cohabitation) of a free woman and a serf; cf. **G72**.7.1–10.

3 This is the earliest mention of the serf (*woikeus*) at Gortyn. For discussion of the status and rights of serfs at Gortyn, see Introd. 5A7.

8b This is the earliest certain occurrence of the collective noun 'Gortynians' (but cf. **G10**x–y), an important sign of the growing self-awareness of Gortyn as a political community; see above on **G13**.

G25. c.600–525

Twenty-five small pieces of stone with a few letters each, all found in the vicinity of the Pythion. G collects them under one number, but they may come from several different inscriptions. Most pieces yield no significant sense.

s	[—] ϙοσμ̣[—]	s	— *kosmos* —
u	[— ὀ]δελὸς | θήλεια [—]	u	— obol, female —

u ὀ]δελός = ὀβολός

u For the obol as a monetary unit, see Introd. 7D and the introduction to **G1–40** above; this and the two examples in **G26** are the only occurrences of the word at Gortyn before the fifth century.

G26. c.600–525

Sixteen small pieces of stone with only a few letters or traces visible on each; many may come from the same inscription. Most yield no significant sense. First published by De Sanctis (1907).

a2	[—] . ος | ὀδελὸ . [—]	a2	— obol —
a3	[—]εος | ϙοίρο ὀ . [—]	a3	— of a pig —
b	[— ὀ]δ̣ελὸς	b	— obol —
c	[— δ]εκα	c	—]ten (?) —
d	[—δ?]οδεκα	d	— twelve (?) —
g	[—]π' ὀτερος [—]	g	— whichever —

a3 ϙοίρο | ὀ De Sanctis, G; but there is only a small scratch between the two *omicrons*—quite different from the clear heavy dividing mark earlier in the line.

d δ]όδεκα De Sanctis

g G reads ὀ]πότερος, but Bile maintains (p.c., cf. Bile 205, n. 194) that this is not a Cretan form. Perhaps ἐ]π' ὀτέρος.

Perhaps regulations about sacrificing (thus the pig in a3); or perhaps a series of fines.

a2, b For the obol as a monetary unit, see **G25**.

G27. c.600–525

One block with three lines of writing, all retrograde, probably originally from the Pythion.

1	[—] . ισα . [—]		
2	[—]μενο | υἶ ἰε[—]	2	— where —
3	[—]εμενα νῦν ἐ[—]	3	— now? —

2 υἶ is adverbial; see n. ad **Ele16Aa5**.

3 νῦν (G) is found nowhere else in Crete, but no other reading seems more likely.

G28 (VER II.12). *c*.600–525

One block found (in three pieces) on the acropolis of Gortyn with four lines of writing boustrophedon. The stone is lost and we must rely on the photo and drawing in G. It is possible that we have the beginning of line 1, and perhaps also the end, if it continues boustrophedon in line 2 (but see note below on 1–2), but lines 2–3 must have continued to the right and 3–4 to the left. Line 4 ends 2–3 letters before the right edge, and there is a large space between it and the bottom of the stone.

1	οἵ κα μὴ ἀπο[—]	1	— whoever — not —
2	[—]μοσεν ἒ ὀτρ[—]	2	— swear (?) or —
3	[—]νεν κιτοσ[—]		
4	[—]ν̣ πέρεν. *vac.*	4	— to carry —

1–2 It is tempting to join these lines, producing ἀπόμοσεν, but the singular verb with a plural subject is grammatically impossible, so that one would have to presume scribal error (οἵ for ὅς). 3–4 must have continued to the left, and 1–2 almost certainly did too.

2–3 Similarly, it is tempting to join these to produce ὀτρ[ύ]νεν ('rouse up'), but there is no room on the stone in either line for an *upsilon*, and it seems unlikely that a single letter would have been written to the right. The verb is unattested in Cretan laws, moreover, and it is hard to imagine what sense it might have here.

VER suggest that both edges of the stone are nearly the original edges and that the text is thus almost complete except perhaps for some text above. They restore it as follows: οἵ κα μὴ ἀπόμοσεν ἒ ὀτρ[ύ]νεν κῖτος [ἐ]κ̣πέρεν, which they translate: 'those who do not swear their innocence or who push, may they go to the devil' (lit. 'the monster is to carry them off'). The law, they suggest, targets those who would push stones down the slope of the steep hill. Aside from the questionable sense of such a law, their suggestion is grammatically impossible (see on 1–2 above) and epigraphically very unlikely: (1) although 1–2 fit together smoothly, putting together 2 and 3 or 3 and 4 would in each case require an additional letter at the end of one line or beginning of the next, so that the column edge would have been noticeably uneven; and (2) the traces visible at the beginning of line 4 cannot fit a *kappa* as it is written in this inscription (lines 1 and 3). VER also make the unlikely assumptions that *kitos* is a Cretan form of *kētos* ('whale'), which is phonologically difficult, and that the impossible grammar is the work of a foreign worker who did not know Greek well; but it is inconceivable that a person with limited Greek would be allowed to compose or inscribe an official text concerning a communal and probably sacred space. In short, VER's suggestion is impossible; we reproduce it only as a potential stimulus for new ideas.

G29. *c.*600–525

A fragment with a few letters visible from three lines; only one word can be restored with some likelihood.

3	[— ϙ]όσμοι κ̣[—]	— to the *kosmos* (or *kosmoi*) ? —

3 ϙ]όσμοι: G. If the restoration is secure, this could be either dative singular or nominative plural. But the reading could also be, e.g., [—]ος μοικ̣[ιον —].

G30 (VER II.68, K 126). *c.*600–525

One block with four lines of text found built into a stable in the nearby town of Agii Deka. The text certainly continued to the left and right and perhaps above and below as well.

1	[—]ν μηταυ̣ιον τρίπεδο̣ν [—]	1	— three-footed —
2	[—]αριον ἐπιστάμην μεδι[μνο—]	2	— to impose (a fine?) [of X ?] *medimnoi* —
3	[— καταστ]τᾶσαι ὄτοι κα καταθίοντ[ι —]	3	— to pay (a penalty) to the one who has indentured —
4	[—] κσένιον ϙόσμο[ν —]	4	— the *kosmos* for foreigners —

1 μηταυ̣ιον: The fifth letter could also be a *lambda* but probably not a *rho*, as VER claim (see G). The word is unknown, nor can we make sense by dividing it.
3 ὄτοι: We would expect the form ὄζοι, as in **G4**.1, **G13**l2, **G19**.1.
4 κσένιον ϙόσμο[ν: probably acc. sing., though the gen. pl. cannot be excluded.

Although several expressions in this text are interesting, we cannot determine the subject.

1 The three-footed object (*tripedon*) is apparently not a tripod (*tripodos*, cf. **G8**).
2 A *medimnos* is a dry measure of grain a bit larger than a bushel.
3 This is the earliest mention of the practice of pledging or mortgaging a person (sometimes oneself), which is a common subject in later laws at Gortyn (e.g. **G41**.5–6, **G47**).
4 The *ksenios kosmos* may be the same official as the simple *ksenios*; see comm. on **G14**p–g2.

G40. *c.*600–525

A tiny fragment with two lines of text.

1	[—]ις δέκα [—]	— ten —

G41–140

These texts are generally dated to the fifth century, though **62–4** may be from the late sixth. Jeffery (1990: 315) follows G in tentatively dividing the texts into four groups, and suggests dates for them as follows: **62–4** *c.*525–500?, **41–61** and **65–71** *c.*500–450?, **72** (the Code) mid-fifth century, and **73–140** *c.*450–400. But even the relative datings are uncertain.

Most of these inscriptions (including the Code) were found (and may have originally stood) in the area of the later Roman Odeion. Some were inscribed on the walls of buildings; others may have been free-standing.

G41–51

These texts are inscribed on stones that were discovered built into two walls, usually designated Northern (*murum septemtrionalis*) and Eastern (*murum orientalis*), that formed part of a rectilinear Hellenistic building. The stones were placed in random order, with no regard to the texts inscribed on them (see drawing in Guarducci 1950: p. 88). We do not know where these laws were displayed in the Classical period. Several of the blocks show traces of earlier writing that appears to have been lightly erased, but no continuous sense can be made of these letters (see **G48**).

The texts are generally longer and most are shaped into columns that are considerably narrower than the long lines of most earlier inscriptions. Several texts have more than one column. The writing runs boustrophedon from the top; the first line may begin in either direction (cf. **G43**Ba and Bb), though most often it begins from the right. Fines are regularly expressed in staters (= two drachmas) and drachmas (= six obols).

In general these texts are written in smaller, neater letters and straighter lines than **G1–40**. Sometimes faint ruling lines are visible. The letter shapes are similar to **G1–40**, except that *zeta* is missing, *koppa* occurs only once (**G64**), and *eta* is used in **G41–58**, but not consistently.[404] Dividing lines between words are gone, except for **G62**, where the line has become two small circles, one above the other. Elsewhere, gaps between words sometimes indicate the ends of sentences.

G41 (VER II.65, K 127–128). 'Little Code'. *c.*500–450?

Sometimes called the 'Little Code', this is the longest of the surviving fifth-century texts after the Great Code (**G72**). Three adjacent blocks from the North wall are preserved. They contain about 17 lines of text from each of seven columns. It is generally accepted that we have the bottom of each column. Not only do most columns run to the bottom of the stone, but the surest sign that these are column bottoms is that in most cases (5 out of 7) the last line ends with a complete word (only about one-third of the other lines end thus). Masons were often reluctant to divide a word between the bottom of one column and the top of the next. The end of column 7 (for the text, see below) is especially notable since the bottom line ends in mid sentence with the word *kai* ('and') about six letters

[404] See G. p. 87 for a list of the places where an *epsilon* is used rather than an *eta*.

before the end of the line, leaving a relatively large gap. The top of the next column no longer survives, but we may assume that the first word (or the phrase of which it was part) was too long to fit in this gap at the bottom of column 7; note also the end of column 3 (with the note on 3.17). The same principle is found in **G72** (see head note there).

An unknown amount of text is missing above these lines. If as much is missing as is preserved, then the columns would each have about two-thirds as many lines as in the Great Code (whose lines are on average about one-third longer than those of **G41**). Since a few letters are visible to the right of column 1, and column 7 ends in the middle of a sentence, there must have been at least one more column on either side, perhaps more. All in all, then, the Little Code may have had one-quarter to one-half as much text as the Great Code (or more), an impressive document in its own right.

The preserved columns treat injuries to animals (1–3) and other transactions involving animals (3), the fugitive serf (4), litigation involving an indentured servant (5–6), and purchase (7). It is not clear whether these subjects were thought of as loosely related—many, at least, concern persons or things owned or controlled by someone else—but as in the Great Code, the connections among different provisions were probably fairly loose.

For a more detailed study of the organization of provisions in this inscription, including the use of asyndeton and gaps, see Gagarin 2008a: 128–34. K treats this text in two parts, first columns 1–4.1–5 (#127), then the rest of column 4 and columns 5–7 (#128).

1—ANIMALS INJURING ANIMALS

[— ἐπὶ τô]-
ι ἀ̣δικ̣ηθέντι ἤμην
[αἴ] κα λῆι τὸ Ϝ̣[ὸν] αὐτ-
ô δόμην τὸ δὲ κήνο ἔ-
κ̣εν. αἴ κά Ϝοι μὴ λ̣ῆ̣ι
δέκσαθθαι, τὸ ἀπλὸ-
ν τεισῆται. vac. αἰ δέ
κα μὴ ἐπιδίηται τὸ π-
αροθὲν ἢ μὴ ἐπελεύ-
σει τὸ τετνακὸς ἢ μὴ
δείκσει ἆι ἔγ⟦ι⟧ρ⟨α⟩τται,
μὲ ἔνδικον ἤ⟨μ⟩ην. vac. αἰ
δέ κα σῦς καρταῖπο-
ς παρόσει ἢ κατασκέ-
νηι, τόν τε σῦν ἐπὶ τôι
πάσσται ἤμην ὂ κ᾽ ἦι τ-
ὸ καρταῖπος καὶ το

→

— It is to be in the hands of the injured party if he wishes to give his own and take that of the other party. If he does not wish to take it for himself, he will be paid the simple value. *vac.* And if he does not lead his wounded animal (to the offending animal's owner), or does not bring his dead animal, or does not display it as is written, there is not to be a legal action. *vac.* And if a pig wounds or kills an ox, the pig shall be in the hands of the owner of the ox, and the —

6–7 ἀπλόν = ἀπλόον. At Gortyn this word is normally written with double *omicron* (three times in this inscription) and G (followed by VER, K) assumes a mason's error and supplies a second *omicron*; but Bile 199 considers the variation acceptable, and the single *omicron* also occurs in 5.2–3 below (also 'corrected' by G and others).

8–9 παροθέν: 'maimed, wounded' (Att. πηρόω).

9–10 ἐπελεύσει: aorist subj. of ἐπελεύθω, a verb found only at Gortyn and only in the future or aorist (Bile 281, etc.). It means 'bring something/someone (acc.) for presentation to someone (dative)' (cf. Hesychius' gloss ἐπελεύσω · οἴσω), and is used (in **G41**.1.9–10, 2.15, 7.3–4) of presenting a dead animal in order to receive compensation and (in **G72**.3.45, 3.52, 3.53, 4.7–8, 4.10, 4.15–16) of presenting a baby born out of wedlock to its father or father's master. The contrast here with ἐπιδίηται, used when the animal is able to walk by itself, is clear. Note that ἐπελεύσει is an aorist subjunctive here, but a future indicative in **G72**.4.15–16 (Bile 232 n. 311).

11 ἔγ⟦ι⟧ρ⟨α⟩τται: the mason mistakenly omitted the *alpha* and squeezed in an *iota* that does not belong.

12 ἤ⟨μ⟩ην: the mason mistakenly omitted the *mu*.

14–15 κατασκένηι (which occurs only here) is a variant of Att. κατακτείνω; see Bile 278 n. 77. Like παρόσει it is an aor. subj.

Column 1 addresses three aspects, separated by gaps in the text, of the general subject of one animal killed or injured by another: (1) the compensation to be received by the victim's owner; (2) the proper procedure for demonstrating the injury or death to the owner of the offending animal; and (3) compensation for the owner of an ox that is injured by a pig. Rules (1) and (2) are clear and reasonable; they give the person whose animal is injured certain rights and responsibilities, as well as two options for receiving compensation. The specification in (3) of an ox injured by a pig may suggest that (1) and (2) also applied to specific kinds of animals; or (1) and (2) may apply to animals in general while (3) concerns an exceptional situation (see below).

1 *Epi* with the dative, 'in the hands of' (also below, col. 7.12), is fairly common in the Code; see on **G72**.4.37 and for a full discussion, Gagarin 2008b: 10–16.

4 'That of the other party' may designate the actual animal that caused the injury or may mean an animal equivalent to the one injured.

7–11 In order to confirm the nature and extent of the animal's injuries, three possible acts are envisaged: leading a wounded animal to the person, carrying or bringing the dead animal, perhaps in a wagon, or displaying it, presumably by summoning the person to come and view the corpse, which may not be easily transportable. The rules for summoning someone in such cases are given in the next column (2.6–12).

8 'If he does not lead': the verb *epidiomai* occurs only in this inscription, where it appears seven times. Here the sense is clearly to 'lead' an animal. For a full discussion, see Bile 2000 (and for Maffi's very different interpretation, see the comm. ad 4.6–7 below).

11 'As is written' (and similar expressions) are the common form of cross-reference in the fifth-century laws at Gortyn. Gagarin (2008a: 142–3) argues that

such cross-referencing indicates that legislators had a sense that their laws formed a unified whole. Here, the cross-reference implies that specific rules for bringing the injured animal or showing it to the person responsible can be found in an earlier part of this inscription, perhaps in the top part of column 1 that is now lost.

12 The expression 'there is (is not) to be legal action' ((*me*) *endikon ēmēn*) also occurs below (col. 3.3–4) and is common in fifth-century laws from Gortyn. It points up the procedural orientation of many of these laws.

12–17 The specification here of a pig wounding or killing an ox, together with the mention of other kinds of animals in columns 2–3, suggests that the provisions in lines 1–12 either applied to another specific kind of animal (perhaps an ox wounding or killing another ox), or perhaps applied to any case where the animals in question were the same species. Here the two animals are of unequal value, so there cannot be an equal exchange.

2—ANIMALS INJURING ANIMALS (CONT.)

[—]ϵ[. . .] →
ται, τὸ ϜίσϜον κατασ-
τασεῖ. vac. ἵππον δ̣ὲ κ̣' [ἠ]μ̣-
ί[ο]νον κ' ὄνον τὸ μὲν
νυνατὸν ἐπιδίεθαι
ᾶι ἔγραπται· αἰ δέ κα
τετνάκηι ἢ μὴ νυν-
ατὸν ἦι ⟦η⟧ ἐπιδίεθθαι,
καλῆν ἀντὶ μαιτύρ̣-
ον δυôν ἐν ταῖς πέν-
τε ᾶι δείκσει ὀπῆ κ'
ἦι, κ' ὀρκιότερον ἤμη-
ν αὐτὸν καὶ τὸνς μα-
ίτυρανς αἰ ἐπεδίετ-
ο ἢ ἐπήλευσε ἢ ἐκάλη
δεικσίον. vac. κύνανς
ἀπαμπαιόμενο[—]

— he shall pay an equal amount. *vac.* If possible, a horse or a mule or an ass is to be led (to the offending animal's owner) as is written. But if it is dead or cannot be led, then (the injured animal's owner) is to summon (the other) in the presence of two witnesses within five days in order to display it, wherever it is; and the summoner and his witnesses are to be the ones who swear as to whether he led or brought it or summoned him so as to display it. *vac.* Someone who wards off the attack of dogs —

5 *νυνατόν* = Att. *δυνατόν* (Dialect 9).

11 *ᾶι* indicates purpose (Bile 262), a meaning found only here; elsewhere (e.g. in line 6 above) it commonly means 'as', but see on **G42**B2.

16 *δεικσίον*: the future participle is very rare in Cretan texts—only here and possibly in **Elt2**.4, in both cases expressing purpose (Bile 273 n. 48).

17 *ἀπαμπαιόμενο[ς* (or *ἀπαμπαιόμενο[ν*) = *ἀπαναπαιόμενος* 'warding off with blows'.

Column 2 primarily addresses procedures for demonstrating the nature and extent of injuries to a horse, mule, or ass. Injuries to these animals were probably the subject of the partially preserved provision that ends in line 3. At the end of the column the subject changes to attacks by dogs. Columns 1–2 together show that the legislator spelled out the rules about injuries to animals by animals in at least four categories (perhaps more) depending on what kind of animals are involved: oxen?, pig and ox, horses/mules/asses, dogs.

5, 8, 14–15 For *epidiomai* ('lead'), see above on 1.8.

6 'as is written' probably refers to the same rules as the same expression in 1.11.

6–12 The standard rules for summoning someone at Gortyn include the requirement of a certain number of witnesses (sometimes qualified as adult or free), and a time limit, as here.

12 For *orkioteron* ('the one who swears'), see on **G72**.2.15. Witnesses (with others) are also said to be *orkioteros* in **G72**.3.49–50, 4.6–7; cf. **G42**B5–6, and **G45**B3–4. See further Gagarin 2010b: 130–2.

16–17 By putting the word 'dogs' first, the legislator highlights a new subject. Dogs commonly attack in groups, and the plural suggests that a group attack is his concern here.

3—TRANSACTIONS INVOLVING ANIMALS

→

[— αἰ μὲν κ' ἀμπό]-
τεροι ἔπον[ται] οἰ ἀλ-
οῖοι μ[ὴ] ἔνδικον ἤμ-
ην, αἰ δέ κα μ[ὴ] ἀμπότ-
εροι ὀ [c.5]ẹνος τὰ-
ν ἀπλόον ṭị[μὰ]ν κατα-
στασ[εῖ]. vac. αἴ κα τετ-
ράπος ἢ ὄνν[ι]θα παρ-
καταθ̣[ε]μένοι ἢ κρη-
σάμενος ἢ [ἀλ]λᾶι δε-
κσάμẹ[νο]ς μὴ νυνατ-
ὸς εἴη αὐṭ[ὸν ἀ]ποδόμ-
ην, τὸ ἀ[πλ]όον κατασ-
τασεῖ. αἰ δ[έ κ' ἐ]πὶ τᾶι
δίκαι [μο]λ̣ίον ἐκσαν-
νήσεται, δι[πλ]εῖ κατ-
αστᾶσ[αι κ]αὶ θέμημ πόλι

—(If both) the different ones are following, there is to be no legal action; but if both are not, he (the attacking dog's owner?) shall pay the simple value. *vac.* If someone has used or for some other reason received an animal or bird and is not able to give it back to the person who entrusted it to him, he shall pay the simple value. But if while contending in court he denies (having received it?), he shall pay double and is to give to the city —

Column 3 straddles two separate blocks with a small space between them, so that letters are missing from the middle of all the lines.

1 [*αἰ μὲν κ' ἀμπό*]*τεροι* is restored by all editors.

6 *ἀπλόον*: see above on 1.6–7.

7–14 Although the general sense of this sentence is clear, the translation poses difficulties; Metzger 1973: 97–9 has a good discussion. We understand *tetrapos* and *onnitha* as objects of the dat. participle *parakatathemenoi* ('to the one who entrusted'), which is the indirect object of *apodomēn*.

7–8 τετράπος: neuter acc. sing. (Bile 184), as is ὄνν[ι]θα (= ὄρνιθα).

8–9 παρκαταθ[ε]μένοι: cf. Attic παρακαταθήκη, the act of entrusting something or someone to the care of another; VER suggest that the loan may be for breeding purposes.

15–16 ἐκσαννήσεται = ἐξαρνήσεται (subjunctive); cf. **G72**.3.6; *IC* 4.141.12; Bile 121, 232.

17 θέμηµ (θέμην): aorist infinitive of τίθημι.

The last eleven letters of this line are noticeably smaller than the others in this column, resulting in a line of 19 letters vs. 15–16 for the rest of the column. It appears that the mason wanted to squeeze in the full word *poli* at the end of the column.

Column 3 has two parts: the first seems to continue the subject of attacks, presumably by animals and perhaps by dogs (see above 2.16–17), but in line 7 the subject changes to transactions involving animals, which may be continued at the beginning of column 4.

1–7 The sense of this sentence is uncertain. Most editors assume that relatively few lines are missing from the top of column 3 (VER actually supply the three lines preceding 3.1), and that the subject continues to be dogs, as in 2.16–17, specifically dogs hunting (*hepomai* 'follow' can be used of dogs chasing their prey). This is perhaps not impossible, but we urge caution. First, 2.16–17 seem to concern a person who is defending himself (or another person or animal) against an attack by dogs, and it seems unlikely that this would often happen during a hunt. Second, all the columns were very likely the same length, and the gaps between some other columns (e.g. 3 and 4) are very likely longer than three lines. Third, it is hard to see how it could matter in a hunt if both dogs are following (the prey?). Perhaps the provision refers to an attack by two dogs belonging to different owners, one of which is injured as a result; the other owner is not liable for the injuries if the two dogs attacked together, but he is liable if his dog alone attacks and the other is somehow injured. One must bear in mind, however, that as preserved, these lines make no mention of dogs, and the subject may be something quite different.

2–3 *Aloioi* 'otherwise, different': it is not at all clear in what sense the two are different (different owners? different kinds of dogs? different kinds of animals?).

7–17 Whatever we make of 1–7, 7–17 certainly present a new subject marked off by a gap and asyndeton (see Introd. 3D3–4), though the general subject of litigation involving animals continues. The first provision (7–14) is relatively clear: whoever fails to return someone else's animal or bird must pay a fine. 14–17 then impose a double penalty on someone who denies something in court: he probably denies having received the animal. Cf. **G47**.26–31, where, after the death or disappearance of a slave, the person responsible must pay the simple value; but if the case goes to court and he is convicted, then he must pay double. Here nothing is said of a conviction, but it is surely implicit that a double penalty is only assessed after a conviction.

4—THE FUGITIVE SERF

[—]π̣ερο̣ν̣σ̣[—]
δ̣οντι τετραπλεῖ. *vac.*
ὄτι δέ κά τις αὐτὸν
ἀποδôι σομελές, τὸ ἀ-
πλόον καταστασεῖ. *vac.*
τὸν δὲ Ϝοικέα τὸν ἐπ-
ιδιόμενον μὴ ἀποδό-
θθαι μήτε ναεύοντα
μήτ' ἦ κ' ἀπέλθηι τô ἐν-
ιαυτô. αἰ δέ κα κοσμί-
οντος ἦι ὀ ἐπιδιόμε-
νος, μὴ ἀποδόθαι ἆς κ-
α κοσμῆι μηδ' ἦ κ' ἀπέ-
λθηι τô ἐνιαυτô. αἰ δ-
έ κα πρὸ τô κρόνο ἀπο-
δôται, νικήθθο· ἀμπὶ
δὲ τὸν κρόνον ὀμνύ-
[ντα κρίνεν τὸν δικαστάν]

→

— [give back?] fourfold. *vac.* But for whatever someone returns safe and sound, he shall pay the simple value. *vac.* The fugitive serf is not to be sold when he has taken refuge in a temple nor during the year when he has run away. If the fugitive belongs to someone who is *kosmos*, he is not to be sold while he is *kosmos* nor during the year when he has run away. But if he is sold before this time, let [the one who sells him] be convicted. Concerning the time, after swearing an oath [the judge is to decide] —

---

1 No convincing restoration has been suggested for these letters.

1–2 ἀπο]δ̣οντι ?

9–10 ἦ (often ἦ κα) is the common conjunction 'when'; see Willetts on **G72**.6.1. The sense here is clearly 'for one year after he has run away'.

(18) The supplement, which is a common expression in **G72** and elsewhere (e.g. 5.8–10 below), is widely accepted.

1–5 These lines may continue the subject of animals on loan begun in 3.7 (K), but this is quite uncertain, and they may more likely be the conclusion of a different subject; or they may perhaps be connected with what follows.

2 Cohen 1983: 66–7 (cited by K) suggests that the distinction here between a fourfold fine and the simple fine may result from the same assumptions as are found in Exodus 22 (where the fines are fivefold and double), namely that when an animal is returned, it might have found its way into a neighbor's flock by mistake, whereas once the animal (in Exodus) is slaughtered and sold, it was clearly stolen intentionally and thus deserves the higher penalty.

6–17 The subject of these provisions, the *woikeus* ('serf'), is placed at the beginning of the sentence to indicate the subject matter (cf. **G47**.1). Whatever the meaning of *epidiomenon* (see below), the serf is envisaged as taking refuge in a temple, from where he is not to be returned (or sold—see on 7–8 below). This clearly implies that a serf not taking refuge in a temple could be returned. For the difficult question of what difference (if any) there is between a serf and a slave (*dolos*), see Introd. 5A7 and more fully Gagarin 2010a.

6–7 *Epidiomenon*: the participle is generally translated 'fleeing, fugitive', but Lévy 1997: 32–3 suggests it designates a serf 'poursuivi en justice'—the serf is being pursued because he owes money, and the law gives him a year to earn the money to pay his debt before he can be sold in order to pay it. Bile 2000: esp. 170–3 insists that it should have the sense of 'lead' that it has in columns 1–2. She suggests that the serf is taking refuge in the temple because he has stolen property from his master (could he be leading off one of the master's animals?), and that although (in her view) serfs are not normally sold, here the sale (if that is the meaning of *apodoththai*—see below) is intended to provide compensation for the master for what the serf has taken. Thus the serf is protected from his master and the master is compensated for his loss. Maffi (2003b: 41–55), following a suggestion by Blass, argues improbably that *epidiomenon* means 'being healed' (*curato*), here from wounds inflicted by the master.

Certainly it is difficult to reconcile the meaning 'fugitive' with the clear meaning 'lead' that *epidiomai* has in columns 1 and 2. But it is a mystery why a serf who was leading something (perhaps his animal, since serfs could own livestock—see **G72**.4.35–6) would want to take refuge in a temple. And if the verb is passive here ('a serf being led'), the mystery remains. It seems that we must have an idiomatic use of the verb that would have been evident to Gortynian readers, in which case 'fugitive' is perhaps more likely than other suggestions.

If this is the meaning, however, it is still not easy to understand the passage. If the serf seeks refuge to avoid being sold, as may be implied, he may be hoping that his master, perhaps burdened by financial difficulties, will sell a different slave instead. If so, this would seem to suggest that serfs, like slaves, could be sold apart from land (cf. Introd. 5A7, with n. 223). But much remains uncertain both about this passage and about the condition of serfs in general.

7–8 *Apodoththai* (also in 12, 15–16): for the double *theta*, see Dialect 11. *Apodidōmi* in the middle normally means 'sell', whereas the active means 'give back' (e.g. in line 4 above). Here the verb in each case could be middle—'(one) is not to sell'—or passive—the serf 'is not to be sold' or 'is not to be given back'. But 'sell' is the more likely meaning (whether middle or passive). The time interval, up to a year, would be intended to allow the serf's master time to persuade the serf to return to his service; if he could not, then the serf would be sold. Whether other serfs could be sold or only fugitive serfs, is uncertain; see further Gagarin 2010a: 25–6.

8–9 The two conditions are perhaps more likely meant to be combined—he is protected for one year while he is taking refuge—rather than alternatives—he is protected either when he has taken refuge (for however long) or for one year (whether or not he is taking refuge). Cf. **G72**.1.39–49, where a slave (*dolos*) taking refuge in a temple need not be given back to his true master for one year.

10–14 For a similar provision protecting a *kosmos* while he is in office but not thereafter, see **G72**.1.51–5.

12–14 If the serf belongs to a *kosmos*, he is not to be returned while his owner is *kosmos* and not for a year. Maffi (2003b) argues that these conditions are sequential—that is, not while he is *kosmos* and not for a year after the end of his term. But the Greek, which says 'the year when [i.e. from when] he has run away', clearly implies that the year is counted from the time the serf became a fugitive. Thus the conditions are probably alternatives: not while he is *kosmos* and not for one year from the time the serf ran off, whichever is longer. This would seem to imply that the term of a *kosmos* could be longer than a year; but the owner might not become *kosmos* until after the slave has run away and taken refuge in a temple, in which case the immunity would last until the end of his (one-year) term.

5—LITIGATION INVOLVING AN INDENTURED PERSON

[—]ι . ιọα . [. .]ν. α[ἰ δέ] →
κα μὴ ὀμόσει, τὸ ἁπλ-
ὸν καταστασεῖ. *vac.*
αἰ δέ κα κελομένο ὅ-
ι κα παρῆι Ϝεργάδδ-
ηται ἢ πέρηι, ἄπατον
ἤμην. αἰ δὲ πονίοι μ-
ὴ κελομένο, τὸν δικ-
ασστὰν ὀμνύντα κ-
ρίνεν, αἰ μὲ ἀποπον-
ίοι μαίτυρς. *vac.* *ἀλλό-*
τριον δ' αἴ τί κ' ἀδικ-
έσει ὁ κατακείμεν-
ος, αὐτὸν ἀτῆθαι. αἰ
δέ κα μὲ ἔκηι ὅπο κατα-
στασεῖ, ὁ νικάσανς
κ' ὁ καταθέμενος[—]

—And if he does not swear, he shall pay the simple fine. *vac.* And if on the orders of the one to whom he belongs (i.e. his temporary master) he (the indentured person) has done or taken something, he is not liable. But if (the temporary master) should affirm that he did not so order, the judge is to swear an oath and decide, unless a witness testifies. *vac.* And if the indentured person wrongs another, then he himself is to be liable. And if he does not have the means to pay, the person who won his case and the temporary master [will arrange for payment?]
—

2–3 *ἁπλόν*: for the single *omicron*, see on 1.6–7 above.

4–5 *κελομένο ὅι κα παρῆι*: *ὁι* is the dative relative pronoun (*ᾧ*) with the verb *παρῆι* ('belong to'), and the entire clause is then the subject of the genitive (absolute) participle *κελομένο*.

8–9 *δικασστάν*: The double *san* also occurs in **G42**B12.

15 *ὅπο*: see on **G72**.5.23.

Columns 5–6 address litigation involving an indentured person—that is, a free man who is temporarily under the control of another person in order to work off a debt (Introd. 5A6). The indentured man is free in some respects (see 6.7–8 below) but not in others. He is liable for wrongs he does on his own but not if he acts on his temporary master's orders. But it seems that if the wrong is especially serious (lines 11–17), he is liable regardless. Column 6 addresses cases where the indentured man is the victim. These rules should be compared to those regarding the indentured slave in **G47**.

1–3 The preceding text (now lost) very likely allowed one party to swear an exculpatory oath: if he does not swear it, he must pay the fine; cf. the similar provision in **G47**.23–6. The provision that follows (5.4–11) almost certainly concerns an indentured man, and since the word *katakeimenos* first occurs in 13–14, the provision that ends in lines 1–3 must have had something to do with the indentured man; otherwise the subject of lines 4–11 would be unclear.

VER think the rules in column 5 may also apply to the *woikeus*, who was the subject of column 4, but similar rules concerning an indentured *dolos* are given in **G47**, and these rules (not those here on column 5) must also have applied to a *woikeus*, since like a *dolos* but unlike a free man, he would also have a permanent master (his owner) as well as a temporary master to whom he has been given by his owner in order to pay off a debt.

7–11 The distinction between *ponen*, 'affirm', used of the statements by litigants, and *apoponen*, 'testify', used of testimony by witnesses, is consistently maintained at Gortyn. See note on **G72**.1.14.

10–11 In Gortynian law witnesses could be formal—called to observe a legal act and if necessary to testify about the act later in court (as in 2.6–16 above)—or accidental—called to testify in court about something they happened to have observed. Some have thought that all witnesses at Gortyn were formal, but here the witness must be accidental (since a master would surely not summon a formal witness to observe his giving an order to the indentured person to do something wrong). See Gagarin 1989: esp. 35–7.

11–17 It is not certain how the wrong addressed in these lines differs from the wrong in the preceding provision, but it seems that the wrong here is more serious. Perhaps 4–11 addressed crimes against property whereas 11–17 concern crimes against a person.

13–17 *Katakeimenos, katathemenos*: lit. 'the one who lies under (an obligation)', 'the one who has put (someone) under (an obligation) to himself'. These are the standard terms for the indentured person and the person to whom he is indentured for a specific period of time (see Bile 330). The terms can also apply to a slave temporarily put in the service of another person in order to pay a debt (see **G47**; **G72**.10.25–32), in which case one must distinguish between the temporary master and the permanent master who has temporarily indentured the slave and thus does not have control over him. See Bile 344–5. *Katatithēmi* can also be used of someone who receives a piece of land as security (e.g. **G43**Ba4–5).

14–17 If the indentured person is convicted but cannot pay the fine, his temporary master will probably arrange to pay it (or perhaps stand surety for it) and then arrange for the indentured person to pay the fine later or remain indentured for a longer time.

6—LITIGATION INVOLVING AN INDENTURED PERSON (CONT.)

[—]ε̣ι̣ο[c.4 πλί] ←
οδ δὲ μή. *vac.* αἰ δέ τις
τ]ὸν κατακείμεν-
ον ἀδικήσει, ὀ κατ-
αθέμενος μολησε-
ῖ καὶ πρακσῆται τ-
ὰς τιμὰνς ᾶι ἐλευθέ-
ρο, κ' ὅτι κ' ἐσπράκσ-
εται τὰνν ἡμίναν ἔ-
κεν τὸν κατακείμ-
ενον, τὰν δὲ τὸν κατ-
αθέμενον. αἰ δέ κ' ὁ κα-
ταθέμενος μὴ λῆι
μολῆν, ἤ κ' ἀποδôι τὸ ὀ-
πήλομα αὐτὸς μολή-
το. αἰ δέ τί κ' ὁ κατακεί-
[μενος—]

— but not (more). *vac.* But if someone wrongs the indentured person, the temporary master shall bring suit and shall exact the penalties as for a free person, and whatever penalty he exacts, the indentured person is to have one half and the temporary master the other (half); and if the temporary master does not wish to bring suit, let him (the indentured person) bring suit himself when he has discharged his debt; and if the indentured person —

1–2 πλί]οδ δὲ μή ('but not more') C, a common expression in **G72** (1.38, etc.).

2–4 The conditional clause is missing the particle κα (Attic ἄν) that regularly accompanies the subjunctive in conditional clauses; perhaps a scribal error. Cf. **G43**Ba8–9.

7–8 ᾶι ἐλευθέρο: 'in the (same) way as (Attic ᾗ) in the case of a free person'—a recognition of the person's underlying status as free.

9–11 τάνν . . . τάν: for the variation, see Dialect 10, 11.

These provisions address procedural issues that would arise if the indentured person is injured. The temporary master is granted the right to bring suit if he wishes and to keep half of the fine. Otherwise, the indentured person can bring suit himself when his indentureship is completed; cf. the arrangement postponing transactions involving a *kosmos* until his term in office is ended (4.10–14 above).

16–17 The missing text at the end of this column may have contained further specifics concerning the outcome of the later suit by the indentured person himself, perhaps something to the effect that any fine levied at this later date is to be retroactive (as in **G72**.1.53–5).

7—PURCHASE

[—]ν[c.9]ṭαι κ- →
ρήματα ἐπὶ ṿαὸν ἐπι-
διόμεν[ον] ἢ ἐπελεύσ-
αντα ἢ θ̣[c.6]στα[.]
[.]λο[c.2–3]α[c.2–3] πεπᾶθ̣αι
τοῦτον [c.5]ια[. .]

— having led or brought property to a temple or —

— to have acquired him (?) —

. π̣ε[c.3] . α̣ι̣ [τὸ]μ πριάμ-
ενον̣ [τοῖς μεμπ]ο̣[μέ]-
[νοις τôν] κρημάτον τὰν
ἄταν κατ[ι]σ̣στά[μ]η̣ν ἆ-
[ι] Ϝεκάστο ἔγραττται· κ-
αὶ τὸν ἄνδρ' αὐτὸν ἐπὶ
τοῖς [μ]εμπομένοις τ-
ôν κρημάτον ἤμην̣, αἴ κ-
α μὴ περαιόσει ᾗ κα πρία-
ται ἐν ταῖς τριάκοντ' ἀμέ-
ραις. αἰ δέ κα συνγνôντι τ-
âν δέκ' ἀμερâν μὴ περαιόσ̣-
[η]ν, ἀνδοκὰν δὲ καὶ [—]

— the buyer is to pay the fine to those who lay claim to (?) the property, as it is written in each case; and the man himself is to be in the hands of those who have a claim on the property (?) if he does not terminate (the purchase) within thirty days after he buys (it). But if they agree within ten days not to terminate it, — the security and —

2–4 ἐπιδιόμεν[ον] ἤ ἐπελεύσαντα: the same verbs are paired in columns 1 and 2; see on 1.9–10.

5 πεπâθαι: perfect infinitive from *πάομαι 'acquire'.

6 τοῦτον: could also be τουτôν.

8–9 [τοῖς μεμπ]ο̣[μένοις τôν]: C's supplement (μεμπ]ο̣[μένοις = Att. μέμφομαι), based on 13–14, is accepted by G, K, and VER, despite the fact that only a trace of one letter (*omicron*) is visible. We print it with serious reservations.

15–19 περαιόσει . . . περαιόσ̣[η]ν at Gortyn this verb, probably related to Attic περαίνω ('bring to an end'), is found only here (twice) and in **G72**.7.11–12, where the context is also that of purchasing; see Bile 278. For the meaning here, see below on 15.

17–19 The mason has squeezed the lines together at the bottom of this column, resulting in two extra lines. It may be that he was nearing the end of this set of laws and hoped to avoid beginning another column. On the other hand, there is a large space after *kai* ('and') at the end of this column. It seems that when he finally realized that he could not squeeze in another line, he followed his regular practice (see above in the heading to **G41**) of ending a column with a complete word, even if that meant leaving a longer than usual gap (cf. column 2).

19 ἀνδοκάν is generally taken as = ἀναδοχήν 'surety'; see further **G72**.9.24–40, where this noun and the related verb ἀναδέχομαι are discussed (notes on 9.24–5).

The better preserved part of this passage (lines 7–18) concerns a purchase, though there is much disagreement about just what it means (see below). Lines 5–6 probably belong to the same provision, but 2–3 probably address a different subject.

1–4 In our translation of this fragmentary sentence, we have made property (*krēmata*) the direct object of the two participles, but it is possible that the construction was quite different. In view of the strong echoes of columns 1 and 2, it is likely that whatever is being led or brought to the temple has been damaged and that the law specifies a procedural step required in order to assert a claim for damages. It is not clear, however, what kind of property (or whatever) is in question. *Epidiomenon* ('leading') implies an animate object, but the law has already addressed the matter of injured animals. Perhaps the subject is an injured slave, though it is unlikely that *krēmata* would have been used just to designate slaves (since other, more precise words were available). This passage could also concern animals not covered in columns 1–2, but in that case it is odd that these regulations were not placed closer to those earlier ones. If the property is a slave, the temple might offer him some refuge. But all this is uncertain.

5–6 Use of the verb *pepasthai*, 'acquire', indicates a broader context than simply purchase; it likely includes inheritance and perhaps gift.

7–18 This passage is usually interpreted together with a short provision in the Code (**G72**.7.10–15) where the verb *peraiosei* (see below on 15) also occurs. That provision addresses the specific issue of liability for a slave who does some wrong around the time that he is sold; it gives the buyer of a slave sixty days to terminate the agreement if the slave has wronged someone. As most scholars understand it, this passage here allows thirty days to cancel the sale of a slave. The passage in the Code is thus seen as a revision of the rule here (e.g. Davies 1996: 46–7). If this is true, the provision would be important for those who follow Pringsheim in the view that a sale in Greece was concluded at the time of the transfer of property and the (simultaneous) payment of the purchase price, and thus it was not possible that a sale might only be concluded some time after the transfer of property (Pringsheim 1950: 451–3).

A different interpretation has been proposed by Jakab 1989 (followed by Kristensen 2004: 76–7), who proposes that *peraiosei* means 'transfer, deliver' (*herausgeben*, sc. the property), a sense that may be possible here, but is very unlikely in **G72**.7.11–12 (see n. ad loc.). Assuming a close connection between the provision in the Code and this passage, Jakab suggests that an animal belonging to a slave has injured someone else's animal; the injured animal's owner demands compensation; someone then buys the slave together with his property, including the offending animal; the buyer can then either pay the damages or deliver the offending animal to the claimant, and if he does not, the claimant takes possession of the slave. Thus, in her view, this is a law about responsibility for the damage, not a law about sale. Though this is perhaps not impossible, there are serious obstacles to this view (see Maffi 1990).

Maffi himself has recently proposed a different interpretation (Maffi p.c.), that the property in question is an estate whose owner has recently died, but who agreed to a sale of some of the estate, including a slave, before he died. The purchaser wants to make certain that those who inherit the estate (*tois mempomenois ton krematon*) will conclude (*peraiosei*) the sale fairly quickly (within thirty days). The slave has committed some offense and the offended party has claimed compensation from the heirs to the estate; thus the buyer is required to pay the fine before the sale can be concluded. In some ways this is an attractive interpretation, but it rests on many assumptions that are purely speculative, and the sense 'conclude' for *peraiosei*, though possible here, seems very difficult, if not impossible, in **G72**.7.10–15.

In our view, the passage has nothing to do with the sale of a slave (see below on line 12), and thus it has no connection with **G72**.7.10–15. Rather, the law may concern the purchase of property which is claimed by someone other than the seller; the buyer is apparently penalized and the seller must put himself in the hands of the true owners if he does not terminate the sale; or they can agree to go ahead with the sale, with the sale price presumably going to the true owner. But even if this suggestion is correct (and we claim no certainty), many questions remain.

7–11 The buyer is to pay a fine concerning some property, presumably property that he has bought. If C's suggested restoration of 8–9 is correct (see above), the fine is paid to those who have a claim to or are bringing suit concerning the property. This would suggest that someone has bought property belonging to someone else, a situation also envisioned in **G72**.6.2–46 (where the seller of the property is heavily penalized). Perhaps this represents an earlier stage in the law in which the buyer is also penalized.

8–9 *Memphomai* ('blame'), in a legal context means 'complain, accuse', and the participle thus designates 'plaintiff' (see also line 13 below; **G72**.9.54; **G78**.8; and **G82**.8–9). Here (if the restoration is correct) it seems to mean 'those who lay claim to'; it is not clear whether they have actually brought suit. But there is considerable doubt about the restoration.

10–11 'As it is written in each case' may refer to the different ways of acquiring property or (more likely) different sorts of property.

12 Most editors, undoubtedly influenced by **G72**.7.10–15, take 'the man' here to refer to a slave who has been purchased. But the use of *aner* to mean 'a slave' instead of the normal *antropos* (e.g. **G72**.10.25) would be unprecedented. *Aner* occurs sixteen times in **G72**, always in the context of a family (slave or free), where it designates a husband or (less often) a father. The same meaning is very likely in **G17**.2 (in **G14**s1 there is no context). Outside Gortyn *aner* occurs only in **Elt2**.5, where a law regulating fighting specifies punishment 'if a man strikes the child'. It thus seems impossible that *ton andra* here could designate a slave. The syntax and structure of the sentence, moreover, suggest that *andra* is the unexpressed subject of *peraiosei* in the conditional clause that follows ('if he does not terminate . . .'). In short, nothing in this column indicates that it treats the purchase of a slave. It thus seems much more likely that the *aner* is the seller (less likely the buyer), who himself will be 'in the hands of' the true owner if he does not terminate the sale within thirty days or reach some other agreement about the sale.

12–13 *Epi* with the dative, 'in the hands of', does not usually indicate ownership but rather temporary control. In **G72**.6.46–51 a person who is ransomed is 'in the hands of' his ransomer until he has reimbursed him for the ransom money. See further on **G72**.4.37, and for a full discussion, Gagarin 2008b: 10–16.

'Those who have a claim': the normal meaning of *tois mempomenois* would be 'the plaintiffs' (e.g. **G72**.9.54), but it is not clear here whether a suit has been filed.

15 'Terminate': *peraiosei* (see above, note on 15–19) means 'bring to an end', and thus could either designate the completion of a sale or (much more likely in this context) its termination. For the views of Jakab and Maffi, see on 7–18 above.

15–17 If the buyer has thirty days to terminate the purchase 'after he buys' the property, it would seem reasonable that any claims on the property should be made before this time limit, but nothing is said of this in the preserved text.

17 The subject of 'they agree' (*syngnonti*) is probably not the buyer and the seller, because they arranged the purchase in the first place and so must have agreed. The subject must, therefore, be those who claim the property together with the buyer or the seller (or both).

19 *Andokan* is usually understood to mean 'security', though it is unclear what the role of security might be in the transaction; perhaps the buyer had provided security instead of the purchase price. Maffi 1983: 150–1 makes the interesting proposal that *andokan* means 'admission, confession'; he connects it with *syngnonti* (line 17), which he understands as 'admit', not 'agree', as most scholars take it. On this view, however, it is hard to find a suitable meaning for *peraiosei.*

G42 (VER II.5, K 129). Procedural rules in a boundary dispute. *c.*500–450?

One block with parts of two columns of text; both columns continue a text that originally began on a stone above. No coherent sense can be obtained from Column A (on the right side). It probably has parts of three texts: 3–4 letters are preserved from lines 1–7, but only 6–7 produce a significant word. Below these after an empty space of about four lines are six lines of writing with 5–6 letters preserved from each; 8–10 run boustrophedon beginning from the left, but then 11 runs left to right (like 10) with 12–13 continuing boustrophedon. Moreover, in 8–10 the letters are about the same size as 1–7, but in 11–13 they are significantly smaller. Clearly the mason was squeezing this third text into the remaining space, though he managed to leave a small space at the end before the bottom of the stone.

Column B, on the left, has fourteen complete lines, written boustrophedon beginning from the right. There is a space at the left edge marking the edge of the column. A space at the bottom indicates the end of this text, and the last line ends well before the left edge of the column, leaving a space of about four letters. The last three words of line 3 (*αἰ πονίοι πεντεκαίδεκ'*) are written in a shallow indentation, where some earlier letters have apparently been erased.

Several words from lines 13–14 are repeated in **Gortyn1**; see that text for discussion of the overlap.

VER and K give only Column B.

A [—] δίκα- ←
ς μολ[—]
vac.
αἴ κα δ[—]
[—] ἀταθῆι
ὅτι κατ[—]
κηρίθε[κν —]
[—]μενον
ἐπικατα[—]

6–7 — of a case, pleads (?) —
vac.

8 If—
9–10 — is fined (*or* should pledge?)

11 skillful (or worked by hand?) —

B

. σ̣ο̣ν̣τ̣ι [c.4]ο̣[c.4]ο ἐν ταῖς πεντεκαί- →
δεκ' ἀμέραις ᾇι ἀκριᾶι ἀτέρα γᾶ πορ-
τὶ τὰ μολιόμενα. αἰ πονίοι πεντεκαίδεκ'
ἀμέρανς ἀμπεληλεύθεν ὁ ἄρκον τᾶς
δίκας, ὀρκιότερον ἤμην τὸν δικαστ-
ὰν καὶ τὸμ μνάμονα. αἰ δέ κα μὲ ὀμόσ-
οντι κελομένο, κατὰ τὰ αὐτὰ πράδε-
θαι τô μὲ ὀμόσαντος ᾇπερ αἴ κα μὴ λ-
ῆι δικάκσαι. *vac.* αἰ δαμόσιόν τι κολύσ-
αι ἢ θάνατος οἶος διακολυσεῖ, μηδατ-
έρ⟨ο⟩νς ταύταις καταβλάπεθαι. *vac.*
τôι δ-
ὲ τᾶν ἑταιρηιᾶν δικασστᾶι κ' ὅς κα τ-
ôν ἐνεκύρον δικάδηι, αἰ αὐταμέριν δι-
κάκσαι ἢ ἐς τὰν αὔριον ἄπατον ἤμην.
vac.

— (he is to judge?) in fifteen days where the other's land ends with reference to the pleadings. If the initiator of the suit should affirm that fifteen days have passed, the judge and the rememberer are the ones who swear. And if they do not swear after a summons, the same penalty is to be imposed on the one who does not swear as if he were unwilling to judge. *vac.* If a public matter should prevent it or a death of some sort prevents it, neither of them is to be hurt by these. *vac.* But for the judge of the *etaireiai* and whoever judges in cases of pledges, if they judge on the same day or the next, there is to be immunity.

A 6–7 [ὁ ἄρκον τᾶς] δίκας C; cf. col. B4–5.
ἀταθῆι: could also be κ]αταθῆι.
11 κηρίθε[κνος] = χειροτεκνικός (with metathesis of the aspiration, Bile 139); also in **G75**B4–5. If masculine, the meaning would probably be 'skillful'; if neuter, 'worked by hand'.

B 1 [κελ]ο[μέ]νο: VER (cf. line B7).
2 ᾇι: the usual meaning is 'as' (see on **G41**.2.11), but in this passage (not mentioned by Bile 262) it seems it must mean 'where' (so K, VER).
ἀκριᾶι: the only occurrence of this verb (ἀκριάω), which must be related to ἄκρος 'farthest'.
7 κελομένο: the middle used in an active sense (cf. **G72**.9.53): 'he (the plaintiff) having summoned (them)'.
9–10 κολύσαι ... διακολυσεῖ: the combination of an aorist optative and a future indicative is very curious, and the difference in meaning (if any) between the two words is unclear.

B This law specifies certain duties of judicial officials in a case involving a property boundary, together with penalties if they do not carry out their duties. Certain exemptions are provided, however.

1–3 'With reference to the pleadings': This expression occurs only here outside **G72**, where it occurs in 5.44, 6.54–5, and 11.30–1; in each case it qualifies the prescription that the judge should 'swear an oath and decide' (*omnynta krinen*). A similar prescription almost certainly preceded the preserved text: first, it is hard to imagine any other action occurring 'with reference to the pleadings' (for the meaning of this expression, see comm. ad **G72**.5.44), and second, this entire law provides rules for those who judge cases and the reference in 7–9 to 'the same penalty as if he were unwilling to judge' implies that a rule requiring someone to judge preceded. True, the separation of the prescription that the judge decide from the phrase in question at the end of the sentence would be somewhat awkward but perfectly comprehensible. We conclude that the law directed the judge to decide where a piece of land ends with reference to the pleadings within fifteen days.

There is no obvious way to restore the opening words of line 1 to achieve this sense. C suggested *dikaddeto*, but H saw traces of another *omicron* in the middle of the line, which would preclude this (see G's note). But the verb may have come in the preceding line. VER's suggestion, [*kel*]*o*[*men*]*o* ('being summoned') is unlikely, since judges are not summoned to give judgment.

3 'Should affirm': for the use of *ponen*, see note on **G41**.5.7–11.

4–5 The 'initiator of the suit' is also mentioned in **G72**.11.51, another passage where the judge and the rememberer are paired. The plaintiff can complain if his case drags on, but the judge and the rememberer can swear an oath to the contrary and thus have the upper hand. It is not clear why the judge might need fifteen days to decide after listening to the pleadings, but perhaps he might wish to inspect the land in question or talk to neighbors.

5–6 For *orkioteron* ('the one who swears'), see on **G72**.2.15.

6 The 'rememberer' (*mnamon*) at this time is an official who assists judges and other officials. He attended trials and other proceedings and could later testify about what he remembered (see further on **G72**.9.24–37 and Introd. 4C3.).

6–9 For the imposition of penalties on officials in connection with litigation see e.g. **G14**g–p1. The cross-reference ('the same as') to penalties for those unwilling to judge implies that these rules were written elsewhere—either earlier in this same inscription or in another one, such as perhaps **G9**a–m.

9–11 'Neither of them' probably refers to the judge and the rememberer; but cf. **G82**.1–3, where special circumstances also prevent punishment.

11–14 There were several kinds of specialized judges at Gortyn (e.g. orphan-judges in **G72**.12.7). Judges of the *hetaireiai* and of pledges are not mentioned elsewhere; we do not know whether they were specialists who only judged these types of cases or whether the provision applies to ordinary judges when they were judging these types of cases.

13 'Security' or 'pledges' (*enekura*) of all sorts were widely used all over Greece. Cases involving security might most likely arise when someone was accused of defaulting on an obligation for which he had provided security (see comm. ad **G43Ba7–8**).

G43 (VER I.47, II.70, K 130–3). Various laws. *c.*500–450? FIG. 48

A single block with two columns of text, each divided into two separate texts. The four texts are separated from one another by clear vertical and horizontal spaces, and all four may be complete (see FIG. 48). Column B on the left is approximately twice as wide as column A. The writing runs right up to the edge on each side, and there is a small space above the two columns. The writing in **Bb** begins at the left; the other three begin at the right, as is normal. A few traces of earlier letters are visible in the empty horizontal spaces in both columns, indicating that the stone had been erased and was being reused.

At the bottom, **Bb** ends 4–5 lines before the edge of the stone, but the last line of Ab goes right to the bottom edge and most of the word at the end of Ab12 (which may be the last word of **Ab**) must have been inscribed on the stone below,

FIG. 48. G43 (drawing after Comparetti 1893: 293–4)

even though the last two preserved lines of **Ab** (11–12) are a letter longer than the rest of the lines in A, and the last five lines appear to be squeezed together more closely than the rest. It seems that the mason was trying to finish **Ab** on this one stone but ran out of room and had to continue on the stone below (or possibly to the right). This suggests that column B was inscribed first, and later **Aa** and **Ab** were inscribed in the narrower space remaining, but could not quite fit on the stone. With some hesitation, we have taken up this suggestion and present the texts in that order, column B first, rather than the traditional order beginning with column A.

VER treat **Ba** as a separate text (I.47), but then they print it together with the other three in II.70; K treats the four as separate texts. See also Davies 1996: 50–3. We will first discuss each text on its own and then consider possible relationships among the four.

Ba—PUBLIC LAND

θιοί. τὰν ἐ[ν] Κησκόραι καὶ
τὰν ἐμ Πάλαι πυταλιὰν ἔ⟦ϵ⟧-
δοκαν ἁ πόλις πυτεῦσαι. α-
ἴ τις ταύταν πρίαιτο ἢ κα-
ταθε[ῖ]το, μὴ κατέκεθαι τô-
ι πριαμένοι τὰ[ν ὀ]νὰν μηδ-
ὲ [τὰ]ν κα[τά]θεσιν. μηδ' ἐνεκ-
υράδδεν αἰ μὴ ἐπι[μ]ετρ[ῆι] τὰ-
ν ἐπικαρπίαν. vac.

←

Gods. The polis have given the farmland at Keskora and Pala for growing. If someone should buy it or give a mortgage on it, the purchase is not to be valid for the purchaser nor the mortgage (for the mortgager). And a person cannot accept a pledge unless he calculates the revenue (it will produce).

---

5 *κατέκεθαι* (*κατέχεσθαι*): 'prevail, be valid'.

7–8 *ἐνεκυράδδεν* = Att. *ἐνεχυράζειν*.

8–9 For the absence of *κα*, see above on **G41**.6.2–4.

9 As in **Aa**9 (see note), faint traces of letters are visible in the rest of this line and below it; C tried to restore these lines so as to continue the sense of **Ba**, but G argues that (as in **Aa**9) these belonged to an earlier inscription that was erased. Here too the sense is complete as it is.

The first sentence states that the polis has made land that is presumably public available for growing. This is commonly taken to mean that the land is now owned by the recipients, though it cannot be sold or mortgaged; but the root sense of *pytalion* is 'grow, produce' (*phyō*), and it seems more likely that this designates land that a person may use for growing but does not own. In this case, the city is protecting its own interest by further prohibiting the grower from selling or obtaining a mortgage on the land, though he is allowed to obtain a loan based on the revenue the land will produce. (Koerner 1987 examines this together with regulations from other cities concerning the distribution of land, and concludes that Greek cities employed various means to protect the land of new property owners.)

1 'Gods': the invocation here and at the beginning of **Bb** may suggest that these two texts were inscribed first.

1–2 The locations of Keskora (Keschora?) and Pala (Phala?) are unknown. But cf. on **G64**.5 for public land at Gortyn.

2–3 The use of a plural verb (*edokan*) with the singular noun *polis* indicates that the polis is here thought of as a collective entity: 'the members of the polis have given'; cf. *IC* 4.146.6.

3–7 The prohibition on selling or mortgaging this land implies that ordinarily land could be sold or mortgaged.

4–5 The basic meaning of the verb *katatithesthai* (middle) is 'put someone under an obligation to oneself' (see above on **G41**.5.13–17). Here, applied to land, it means 'accept a piece of land as a mortgage', that is lend someone money with the land as security. If the landowner does not repay the loan, he will lose the land.

7–9 Cataudella 1976 argues that this last clause is part of the preceding sentence, and that the conditional clause at the end thus qualifies the whole sentence (beginning in line 3), so that a purchase or a mortgage would be valid as long as one calculates the amount of revenue the land will produce. But this would make little sense, at least for purchase, and VER and K both reject it, probably correctly.

7–8 *Enekyrazo* means to receive a pledge or security (*enekyron*, see on **G42**B13 above) from someone. It also occurs in **Aa**2–3 and **Ab**3 below and in **G45**A5–6, **G81**.14, **G85**.2–3 and **Axos1**.7–8 (see Bile 330). It is not found in **G72**. It appears to differ from *katatithesthai* (see above on 4–5) in being used of short-term loans for which something (but not usually land) is given as security. Here the sense is that a person cannot obtain a loan secured by the produce he plans to harvest without first calculating the revenue the harvest will bring.

8–9 'The revenue': the Greek is *epikarpia*, which we distinguish from *karpos*, 'produce'; see further on **G72**.7.32–3.

Bb—A RIVER'S WATER

θιοί. τô ποταμô αἴ κα κατὰ τὸ
μέττον τὰν ῥοὰν θιθῆι ῥῆν [κ-]
ατὰ τὸ Ϝὸν αὐτô, θιθεμένοι ἄ-
πατον ἦμην. τὰν δὲ ῥοὰν λείπ̣-
εν ὅττον κατέκει ἀ ἐπ' ἀγορâ-
ι δέπυρα ἢ πλίον, μεîον δὲ μή.

→

Gods. If someone diverts the river's water at its middle point to flow over one's own land, he is not to be penalized for the diversion. But he is to leave the flow as large as the bridge by the agora contains or more, but not less.

2 *θιθῆι* = *τιθῆι*. The change from active to middle (line 3) does not appear significant.
5 *ὅττον* = *ὅσσον/ὅσον* (Dialect 13).
κατέκει 'encompasses': here active (cf. Ba5).
6 *δέπυρα* = *ζέφυρα* (Dialect 11).

This is the least problematic of the four texts of **G43**. The river is probably the modern Mitropolianos which ran through Gortyn. Water regulation was naturally important in the dry climate of Crete; two later laws (**G52**, **G73**) also treat the subject.

1–2 'At its middle point' probably refers to the middle part of the river between its source in the hills around the acropolis and the center of town (so G, followed by K and VER). In order to irrigate their fields people would naturally want to take water from a relatively high point in its course.

5–6 The location of the bridge in the agora is unknown.

Aa—A THRESHING FLOOR AS SECURITY

αἴ κ' ἄλος ἀδ-	←	If someone has
ίκος ἐνεκ[υρ-]		unjustly taken thresh-
[άκ]σανς μὴ κ-		ing floors as a pledge
αρπόσετ̣[αι, τ-]		and does not harvest
ἀς τιμὰνς τô-		(thresh?) the produce,
ν ἐνεκύρον κ-		he shall pay the value
αταστασεῖ ᾇι		of the pledged prod-
ϝεκάστο ἔγρ-		ucts as is written for
ατται.		each case.

1 ἄλος: All editors take this as Att. ἅλως (acc. pl.), 'threshing floors'; Bile (p.c.), however, suggests it may instead = ἄλλος, 'another' (for the variation between single and double consonants, see Dialect 11). But it is hard to see any reason to write αἴ κ' ἄλος instead of αἴ κέ τις. See further comment below.

2–3 ἐνεκ[υράκ]σανς: see above, note on **Ba**7–8.

3–4 καρπόσετ̣[αι: (Blass #5000) is aor. subj. The drawings of C and H (reproduced in G) show the trace of an oblique stroke at the end of the line, more suitable to a *mu*, *nu*, or *san* than a *tau*, but VER and K follow G in adopting Blass's reading.

9 A few faint traces of letters are visible in the rest of this line and below it, but G argues that these belonged to an earlier inscription that was erased, and nothing more is needed here to complete the sense. Cf. note on **Ba**9.

The meaning of this provision remains uncertain. It appears that one person lends another money (seed grain?) with a threshing floor pledged as security; but if the lender refuses to thresh his produce (presumably paying for the use of the threshing floor), then he must pay the borrower the value of the produce he does not thresh there. But all this is not easily obtained from the Greek.

1 'Threshing floors' (*alōs*): this is the traditional interpretation of *alos*. Bile (see note above) interprets it as *alos* ('another'); but it is hard to see why a legislator would begin a provision with 'if another' rather than the more normal 'if someone'. 'Threshing floors' is also supported by the verb 'harvest' in 3–4 (see below). On the other hand, the plural is puzzling, as few if any landowners would have had more than one threshing floor. Therefore, 'threshing floors' are sometimes understood as the product of threshing, namely grain, which may seem to be

more suitable as security (G, VER, K), though the use of *alōs* for threshed products is rare and late (see LSJ s.v.).

1–2 The word order implies that 'unjustly' (*adikos*) goes with the verb *enekyraksei*, 'obtained as a pledge'. Strictly speaking, this means that only someone who both obtains the pledge unjustly and fails to harvest produce is penalized; a person could, in other words, unjustly obtain the pledge without penalty as long as he harvested the produce. Another possibility is to take 'unjustly' with 'fails to harvest', though this is not the natural way to read the sentence. In this case, the law is targeting only the crime of failing to harvest 'unjustly'. But it is then hard to see the force of 'unjustly' (could he fail to harvest justly?).

Just how someone may have obtained something as a pledge unjustly is not certain, but since the same expression occurs in **Ab2** below, it must have been evident that one could do so.

2–3 *Enekyrazo* means to receive a pledge or security; see above on **Ba7–8**.

3–4 *Karposetai* (also in **Ele11**.5, without context) normally means 'harvest', but if the context is threshing floors (see above on line 1), it may imply 'harvest and thresh'.

4–7 Presumably the fine is paid to the debtor.

5–6 'The pledged products': this seems more likely to mean the product of threshing (see above on 1) than the threshing floors.

7–9 'As is written for each case' may refer to an official list of values for different sorts of produce. See Introd. 7A.

Ab—MISTREATMENT OF SLAVES

α[ἴ] κα δô λον ἤ
δόλαν ἀδίκος
ἐνεκυράκσει
ἤ ἐδύσει ἤ ἀπ[ολ]-
ύσεται, ἐκς ἠμ-
ίνας καταστα-
σεῖ ἔ ἆι τôι ἐλ-
ευθέροι ἔγρα-
πται, τὰ δὲ τρί-
τρα τâ[ς] Ϝῆμα-
ς καὶ τâς ἀνπιδή-
μας ἆιπερ [τ]ôι ἐ-
[λευθέροι (?)].

←

If someone unjustly obtains a male or female slave as a pledge or strips him/her (of clothing) or removes (his/her footwear?), he shall pay half as much as is written for a free person and triple the value of the clothing and footwear, just as (is written?) for a free person (?).

3–5 *ἐνεκυράκσει ἤ ἐδύσει ἤ ἀπ[ολ]ύσεται*: The three verbs are all aorist subjunctives and indicate three separate acts (so K). G and VER take the second and third verbs as dependent on the first: 'if someone wrongly obtains and either strips or takes'; this is tempting, but very difficult syntactically.

7 ἒ: Att. ἢ, used in comparisons; for the variation between ἒ and ἢ (in lines 1 and 4), see above Introd. to **G41–51**, with n. 404.

11–12 ἀνπιδήμα occurs only at Gortyn (here, **G72**.5.40 and **G75**B3–4); it is always paired with Ϝῆμα (Att. εἷμα)). It is probably derived from ἀμφί + δέμας, lit. 'around the body'. For the meaning, see below on 11–12.

12 ἅιπερ [τ]ôι ἐ[λευθέροι Blass #5000, followed by G, K, VER. But ἅιπερ [ἰ]ôι ἐ[γραπται 'as is written for him' (C) seems also possible (for ἰôι, see **G72**.8.8).

This provision is aimed at preventing abuse of a slave who is either received as security, again perhaps for a debt, or stripped of clothing or shoes. Someone who abuses a slave in these ways must pay half the amount as is specified for abusing a free person, but three times the value of anything taken from him, the last of these being the same value as in the case of a free person.

2 'Unjustly' raises some of the same difficulties as in the preceding law; see on **Aa**1–2. Here it must modify the first verb, 'obtain as a pledge', but probably does not modify 'strips' and 'removes', which would be illegal acts regardless.

9–10 Scholars disagree about whether *ta tritra* means 'one-third' (G et al.), 'triple' (K et al.), or even two-thirds (VER II p. 48). Elsewhere the word only occurs in **G72**.1.37, where 'triple' makes the best sense; here either one-third or triple is possible, but 'one-third' seems unlikely, since this would allow someone to steal clothes from a slave and if caught, pay much less than the value of the stolen clothes, thus making a profit from the crime.

11–12 *Anpidēma*, lit. 'around the body' occurs only at Gortyn (see note above). It is translated 'jewelry' by G, VER, and K, though it strikes some commentators as odd that a slave would have jewelry. We follow Bile 189 n. 157, who translates 'footwear' (as in LSJ), comparing Attic *hypodēma*. VER suggest that 'jewelry' might refer to a slave's chains, but it is hard to see why someone would steal the chains from a slave (and we have no evidence that slaves were normally chained).

12 The supplement *eleutheroi* ('for a free person') is widely accepted and seems very likely (but not certain). The words 'is written' may also have followed. If *eleutheroi* is correct, however, the expression *aiper toi eleutheroi* ('just as for the free person') should not be translated in the same way as the earlier expression 'half as much as is written for a free person' (5–8). The syntax here is different: there is no comparative (*e*) to suggest a difference, and *aiper* ('just as') in fact implies similarity (cf. **G72**.10.50).

Although the substantive relationship among the four texts is problematic, there are certainly verbal links among them. **Ba** and **Bb** both begin with the invocation *thioi* ('gods') followed by a noun that conveys the subject of the provision, which in both cases is a public resource (public land, a river). **Aa** and **Ab** both begin with nearly identical language, differing only in what was obtained by pledge, they impose fines relative to the value of an object, and refer to something written elsewhere. And **Ba**, **Aa**, and **Ab**, all regulate pledges. VER treat **Aa** and **Ab** as a pair, both concerned with ownership by pledge and the resulting damages, but they treat **Ba** and **Bb** separately from them and from one another. K treats all four texts separately, while acknowledging that the first two have some relationship. Davies (1996: 50–3) concedes that the two texts in each column might somehow belong together, but argues that the four are more likely to be separate enactments that were inscribed together, and that the similarity in subject matter of the first two texts is mere chance. G speculates that the two texts in A might be *additamenta*, or texts added on to texts now lost to the right of A, which seems to us less likely.

We have suggested a connection between **Ba** and **Aa**, but since each text is short and self-contained and addresses one specific situation, it is possible that each was a response to a specific issue for which the legislator found a remedy. These four laws would then be an example of Hölkeskamp's theory (1999) that all early legislation consisted of one-off enactments addressing specific issues (see also Davies 1996). But by creating verbal connections among the four, the legislator also suggested that there were more substantive connections among them, which would account for their being inscribed together.

On the other hand, the verbal similarities, especially between the texts in column A, are also curiously misleading. Despite similar wording, for instance, the syntax in **Aa**1–4 and **Ab**1–5 are quite different ('If someone, having obtained [participle] as a pledge, fails [subjunctive]...' vs. 'If someone obtains [subjunctive] as a pledge or...'). The fine in **Aa** is the full value, 'as is written' [specification], whereas in **Ab** it is half as much 'as is written for a free person' [comparison]. These echoes cannot be accidental; perhaps someone wanted to make the four texts appear more closely related than they actually are.

G44 (VER II.50, K 134). Marriage of an heiress. *c.*500–450?

One block from the north wall; only scattered letters are visible.

2	[—]ν τὰν ἠ[βιονσαν (?)]	←	2	— the girl [past puberty (?)] —
3	[—] πάντον ἄλλο̣ν [—]		3	— of all others —
4	[— ὀπ]υ̣ιέθ̣[ο —]		4	— let her be married —
6	[—] ὀπυιέθ̣[ο —]		6	— let her be married —
7	[—] ἀμπὶ τα[.]δ̣[. . . .]ολια[—]		7	— concerning —
9	[— π]ατροιοκο[.]ο[—]		9	— heiress —
11	[— π]ατροιôκον δ[—]		11	— heiress —
12	[—] . τηι μὴ εἴη [—]		12	— should not be —
13	[— ἀ]δ̣ε̣λ̣π̣ι̣[. .]ο δ' ἐς τô αὐτô π̣α̣[τρὸς —]		13	— brother (?) from the same father —

2 τὰν ἠ[βίονσαν: G, VER; cf. **G72**.7.41–2, 53.

4 ὀπ]υ̣ιέθ̣[ο here and in line 6 could also be ὀπ]υ̣ιέθ̣[αι.

7 *τὰ[ν] ạ̓[νκεμ]ολία[ν*, G, VER. If this supplement is correct, it would mean 'concerning family litigation' (see on **G21**.3 above), which is consistent with the general sense of the other lines; but the partial *delta* G records in this line (and quite visible in her drawing) does not allow it. If this letter was *alpha*, moreover, then *ạ̓[ντιμ]ολία[ν*, 'litigation' (cf. **G13**b1), seems more likely.

13 There is room for two letters in the lacuna; VER suggest *ἀ]δ̣ε̣λπ̣ι̣[δί]ο* (?) ('nephew'). But this word occurs nowhere else in Cretan texts, and 'nephew from the same father' makes little sense. The expression 'brother from the same father', which also occurs in **G51**.12–13 and **G72**.8.41–2 (also in connection with an heiress), would make better sense, though it is more difficult to restore this word.

Despite the condition of the text, the occurrence of the words *patroiokos* 'heiress' (i.e. a girl without brothers whose father dies) and *opuiethai* 'marry' (twice each) confirms that the subject is the marriage of an heiress, which is treated at length in the slightly later **G72**.7.15–9.1. We cannot say whether the provisions here represent an earlier version of a regulation found there, or whether they treat an aspect of the subject not treated there.

G45 (VER II.69, K 135). Procedural rules about pledges. *c.*500–450?

A single long block from the north wall with two columns of writing. The text originally extended above and to either side of the stone, and perhaps below as well. About twice as much is preserved of B (on the left) as of A; B is also in better condition.

K gives only column B.

A			A	
1	[— *αἰ δ]έ κ̣α τôν κνη-*	←	1–2	— If he should obtain some of the (?) or —
2	*νίον [λ]ạ́κηι ἢ* [—]			
5	[—] *τὸν ἐνεκυρạ́-*		5–6	— the one who accepted a pledge —
6	*κσαντα . . . ι*[—]			
7	[—] *κ̣' ἔτι στέρεθα[ι* —]		7	— still deprived of —

B			B	
1	[—] . *ας̣ ἐς πόλ̣ιν η . . ε . . γαν*	→	1–2	— to the polis — having been (?) *vac.* If someone —
2	[.]*ανκε ἐγρυμμέν[α]* *vac.* *αἴ τις* [—]			
3	[— *ᾶι*] *ἔγραται Fεκάστο, ὀρκιότε-*		3–4	— as is written for each case, the one who accepted a pledge is to be the one who swears —
4	*ρον ἤμην τὸν ἐνεκυράκσαντ̣[α* —]			
5	[—]*α.* *vac.* *αἰ δὲ μὴ ὀμόσαιεν πὰρ τô-*		5–6	*vac.* And if they should not swear in front of the judge, both the one who accepted a pledge [and —] are to lose the case —
6	*ι δικαστᾶι, νικῆθαι τόν τ' ἐνε[κυράκσαντα* —]			
7	[—] . *ρόματος δ' ἐνεκυράδεν ὀ*[—]		7	— to accept a pledge —

The *editio princeps* (Comparetti 1916–20: 193–6) is worth consulting.

A 1–2 *κνηνίον*: no plausible meaning (or emendation) has been suggested for this word, which occurs nowhere else.

B 2 *ἐγρυμμέν[α]*: *ἐγρυμμέν[αν* C, who understands it as modifying *γᾶν* in B1; he cites Hesychius (s.v. *γρυπάνιον*) in support of his understanding that the participle is from *γρύπτω*, 'become bent', and that it refers to an earthquake. For G, however, this is very uncertain.

4 In view of the plural *ὀμόσαιεν* in line 5, line 4 may have continued with *καί* followed by another person.

6 *νικῆθαι*: pres. pass. inf. (Bile 243).

τὸν τ' ἐνε[κυράκσαντα: the restoration of this or some other form of the verb (Attic *ἐνεχυράζω*) here is very likely in view of the fact that it occurs in three other places in this text (A5–6, B4, B7).

7 [—].*ρόματος*: G's drawing shows a *γ*, which could be supplemented *ἀγρόματος* (something to do with hunting), but she cites Halbherr's observation that *ạ* (*ἀρόματος*) is also possible.

These lines regulate litigation somehow involving pledges or security (for *enekyraden*, see above on **G43**Ba7–8). Otherwise the sense is unclear, in part because we do not know the meaning of *knēnion* (A1–2) or *egrummena* (B2).

B 3–6 For *orkioteron* ('is the one who swears'), see on **G72**.2.15. Lines 5–6 may refer to the oath sworn by the person who accepted a pledge in 3–4. In this case, at least, if the person who has preference in the oath does not swear, he will lose the case. The plural verb *omosaien* in 5 suggests that there were at least two oath-swearers, and the connective *te* in line 6 indicates that more than one person would lose the case if the oath was not sworn. A possible scenario is that someone who accepted a pledge as security is now suing to gain ownership of the property that was pledged because (he alleges) the conditions of the agreement have not been fulfilled. As a first step he, together with a witness, are required to swear that he did receive such a pledge; otherwise he cannot proceed with the case. But this still leaves uncertain who else might lose the case together with the person who took a pledge.

G46 (VER II.85, K 136–7). Transport of a corpse. *c.*500–450?

A block from the north wall with two columns of text. B on the left is complete on both sides, but only a few letters are preserved from column A, of which only the left side is preserved; it must have continued on a block to the right. The writing almost certainly began above and continued below as well, and there may have been other columns to the right and left. An unusual border, about the size of a line of writing, was later chiseled into the stone along the top, bottom, and left edge, and a little bit of the right edge at the top. K treats B1–5 and 6–14 as separate laws.

A

[—] κ' ὅρ[κ]ο
ἀντὶ μ[αιτύρον (?) —]
[—] ἢ αὐτ-
ὸν θεμ̣[—]

A

9–10 — an oath before witnesses (?) —

11–12 — or himself —

B

ρος ἐκσôσαι ἢ διαϜά-
κσαι ἢ ὀπαῖον δόμα-
τος δέκα στατῆραν-
ς καταστασεῖ αἰ ἀ-
ποπονίο⟨ι⟩ μαίτυρς. *vac.*
αἰ μὴ εἴη δαμοσία ὀ-
δός, δι' ἀλλότριον κο-
ρίον νέκυν πέρονσ-
ι ἄπατον ἤμην· αἰ δὲ
κολύοι τις, δέκα σ-
τατῆρανς καταστα-
σεῖ· αἰ δ' ἰάττας ὀδô
διαπέροιεν οἱ καδ-
[εσταὶ —]

B

1–5 — (If someone?) should push out or break through (?) — or the smoke-hole of a house, he shall pay ten staters, if a witness should testify. *vac.*

6–14 If there should not be a public road, there is to be immunity for those who carry a corpse through another person's land; and if anyone should prevent it, he shall pay ten staters. But if there is a road and the relatives should carry (a corpse) through —

A 10 ἀντὶ μ[αιτύρον: G.

12 θεμ̣[—]: Bile 349, with n. 95, says that the Cretan dialect abandoned the Homeric word θέμις, but she cites a gloss of Hesychius θεμισσέτω· μαστιγούτω, νομοτεθείτω. This suggests a possible restoration θεμ̣[ίδεν, he himself 'is to enact a law', though it is hard to suggest an appropriate context for such a phrase, and μ̣ could also be *nu* or *san*.

B 1–2 G suggests that ἐκσôσαι and διαϜάκσαι are aorist optatives (from ἐξωθεῖν and *διαγνύναι respectively), presumably in a conditional clause (G).

7–8 κορίον = χώριον.

12 ἰάττας = Att. οὔσης (Bile 243).

13–14 καδ[εσταὶ: Brause.

B consists of two separate but perhaps related provisions separated by a gap at the end of line 5 and asyndeton at the beginning of 6. 6–14 establishes a public right-of-way for carrying a corpse for burial through someone else's property if no road leads there. The sense of 1–5 is unclear. On the assumption that the two provisions are connected, G (followed by VER) suggests that 1–5 may have authorized passage across a neighbor's roof, though any damage would have to be paid for. But it is hard to see any reason for establishing a right-of-way across a neighbor's roof. Further discussion in Frisone 2000: 25–30.

1–2 It appears from the second 'or' (ē̄) that the preceding text contained another direct object for the two verbs; this might have clarified the meanings of the verbs.

4–5 For *apoponioi*, see note on **G72**.1.14. This is likely to be an accidental (not formal) witness; see above on **G41**.5.10–11.

6–14 This provision raises questions about archaic and classical burials at Gortyn, where archaeologists have not yet discovered any burials from this period.[405] This provision may help explain why, for it indicates that at least some burials took place in rural areas, probably in a communal burial ground, since, as Erickson observes (2010a: 254), 'If the inhabitants of the Gortynian countryside buried on their estates, they would not have needed to cross a neighbor's land to convey the corpse to a public road. Thus, the state's role in guaranteeing access to public roads implies the existence of formal burial grounds.' Since we have very little evidence for habitation outside the urban area of Gortyn, there may also have been very few roads; thus most of these burial grounds would not have been served by any road, and access across someone's property was required. For discussion, see Marginesu 2005b: 68–9, and see Introd. 2A1 for more on Cretan burial practices.

6–9 As long as there is no public access, the property owner must allow a funeral processions to cross his land. Reluctance to do so may have been caused by fears of pollution (Frisone 1995: 60–2), but it may more likely have been a normal reaction to groups of other people crossing through one's fields.

6–7 *Damosia odos*: this, the only evidence we have for public roads in Gortyn, is an important indication of the level of organization of the community (*damos*). No archaeological evidence for roads in the country around Gortyn has been found from this period, but presumably there were roads to neighboring communities and there may have been roads to shrines in the countryside. But most of the *chora* must have consisted of fields with simple footpaths made over time by the owners of the land.

13–14 The *kadestai* may be the relatives, who have an obligation to do something (here to bury the deceased); see on **G72**.2.18 and Introd. 5C3.

G47 (VER II.26, K 138). Litigation involving indentured slaves. *c.*500–450?

A stone from the east wall with one and one-half columns of neatly inscribed, well-preserved, continuous text. There is a narrow margin between the right edge of column A and the edge of the stone; on the narrower column B, the writing runs right up to the left edge of the stone but is complete there. A small rectangle, three lines high and about 2–3 letters wide, is cut out of the top right corner of the stone. Traces of older writing can be seen on the blank surfaces of the stone below this text.

[405] *IC* 4.71 (fifth century), with the single name 'Sotimos', was found near a grave site but its original location may have been elsewhere (see G. ad loc.). *IC* 4.348, a stele with a funeral scene and the letters *Zeus* and *ele*…, is dated by G. to the late fourth or early third centuries.

Most scholars think more text is missing at the beginning (see below on line 1), but we think the text is complete, with at most a letter or two missing at the beginning. First, the text makes good sense as it is, with no need for further provisions. And second, the physical layout of the text indicates that it is probably complete. Because the text in B follows directly from A, there cannot have been additional text on the stone above. And the careful way in which A and B are positioned—with a very small space between the right edge of column A and the edge of the stone, and the width of B adjusted to fit on the one stone—makes it unlikely that there was originally another column (or more) to the right.

A

[?] *κατακείμενος αἰ κ' ἀδική-* ←
σει δôλος ἢ δόλα, ὅτι μέν κ[α κα]-
[τα]θ̣εμένο κελομένο ἁμάρτη-
ι τôι καταθεμένοι τὰν δίκαν
ἤμην, ὅτι δὲ κ' αὐτὸς πρὸ Ϝιαυτ-
ô τôι ἀρκαίοι πάσται τὰν δίκ-
αν ἤμην τôι δὲ καταθεμένοι μ-
ή. αἰ δέ κα νικαθῆι ὀ καθένς, ἀπ-
οδότο τôι καταθεμένοι ὅτι κ'
ὀπήληι. vac. αἰ δέ κα τὸν κατακεί-
μενον ἀδικήσει ἄλλος, αἰ μέν
κ' ἀνπότεροι μολίοντες νικά-
σοντι, τὰν ἠμίναν Ϝεκάτερο-
ς ἐκσίοντι· αἰ δέ κ' ὀ ἄτερος μ-
ὴ λῆι, ὀ ἄτερος μολίον αἴ κα νι-
κάσει αὐτὸς ἐκσεῖ. αἰ δέ κ' ἀ-
πόληται ὀ κατακείμενος, δικ-
ακσάτο ὀμόσαι τὸν καταθέμε-
νον μήτ' αὐτὸν αἴτιον ἔμην μήτ-
ε σὺν ἄλλοι, μήτ' ἐπ' ἄλλοι Ϝισάμη-
ν. αἰ δέ κ' ἀποθάνηι, δεικσάτο

B

ἀντὶ μαιτύρον δυôν. ←
αἰ δέ κα μὴ ὀμόσει ᾆι ἔ-
γραται ἢ μὴ δείκσει, τ-
ὰν ἀπλόον τιμὰν κατα-
στασεῖ. αἰ δέ κ' αὐτὸν αἰ-
τιῆται ναὶ ἀποδόθαι ἢ
ἀποκρύπσαι, αἴ κα νικ-
αθεῖ, τὰν ἀπλόον τ-
ιμὰν διπλεῖ κατα-
στασεῖ. αἰ δέ κα ναεύ-
ηι, ἐμπανία δεικσάτ-
ο.

(A) If an indentured male or female slave wrongs (someone), in that he does wrong on the orders of his current master, the case is to be brought against the current master, but in that he himself (does wrong) on his own, the case is to be brought against his old master and not his current master. And if the one who indentured him (his old master) loses the case, he is to give to the current master what he owes. *vac.* But if someone else wrongs the indentured (slave), if both (masters) bring suit and win, they shall each have half (of the penalty). And if one of them does not wish (to bring suit), if the other brings suit and wins, he shall have (the penalty) himself. And if the indentured (slave) disappears, let (the judge) rule that the current master is to swear that he is not to blame himself nor with someone else nor does he know (that the slave is) with someone else. And if (the slave) dies, let (the current master) show (him to the old master) (B) before two witnesses. And if he does not swear as is written or does not show him, he shall pay the simple value (of the slave). And if (the old master) accuses him (the current master) in fact of selling or hiding away (the slave), if he (the accused) loses the case, he shall pay double the simple value. And if (the slave) takes refuge in a temple, he is to show him clearly (to the old master).

1 θιοί]?
8–9 ἀποδότο: for the active meaning 'give back', see comm. ad **G41**.4.7–8.
10 An inscribed sign (ᛘ) fills this gap; cf. **G72**.9.24.
11–13 ἀδικήσει . . . νικάσοντι: both aor. subj.
14 ἑκσίοντι: 3rd pl. fut. ind. (Dialect 5, 7, 24) from ἔκο (ἔχω).
20–1 Ϝισάμην: inf. from ἴσαμι, a Doric form of οἶδα.
32 ἐμπανία: masc. acc. sing. (= ἐμφανῆ).

The provisions as they stand are a complete text: the first half (1–16) gives rules for litigation involving an indentured slave who in effect has two masters, his old master (*o arkaios pastas*) and the master to whom he is temporarily indentured (Introd. 5A6). The second half (16–33) then regulates situations in which the temporary master loses possession of the indentured slave either because the slave disappears or dies or takes refuge in a temple, or because the temporary master sells or hides him from his old master. This pattern of organization—the main rules followed by several rules addressing additional contingencies—is similar to that in **G72**.1.2–2.2 and elsewhere at Gortyn.

1–16 These rules are very similar in both content and structure to those regarding the indentured free person in columns 5–6 of **G41**; for the terminology of indentureship, see the notes to **G41**.5.13–17. In both places the law addresses first wrongs done by the indentured person and then wrongs done to him. In both, the current, temporary master is responsible for any actions he ordered, but not for those he did not order, for which here the slave's old master is liable, not the slave himself.[406] If the indentured slave is injured, either the old master or the temporary master, or both, may bring suit; in **G41** the free person's temporary master may choose whether or not to bring suit. In both texts, the rules appear both fair and reasonable.

1 G (followed by K, VER) assumes that the first word *katakeimenos* ('indentured') is the end of a sentence that originally began on a stone to the right, but it is not easy to imagine what such a sentence might have said or why it would end in the nominative participle. It is thus more likely that the inscription is complete as it is—so Halbherr 1901b: 294 ('un capitolo intero'). The first sentence can be satisfactorily understood as we have it, if we assume that *katakeimenos* was taken out of the conditional clause and put first in the sentence in order to make the topic of this law clear at the beginning. This feature is found elsewhere at Gortyn (e.g. **G43**Bb and **G72**.2.11, 3.37, 4.8–9, 8.30), and is evidently intended to help readers immediately see the subject of the law. Even if *katakeimenos* were the last word of a preceding sentence, it would have to be understood with *dolos/dola*.

[406] In Greek law generally, liability for the actions of a slave rests with his master (for Athens, see Hyperides 3 (*Athenogenes*) 22), but there may be exceptions at Gortyn; see Gagarin 2010a: 29–30.

If the text is complete, what originally stood in the space before *katakeimenos*? We suggest three possibilities. (1) Nothing may have stood there, though indentation of the first line would be unparalleled at Gortyn. (2) The article (*o*) may have preceded the participle, though this would still leave a somewhat smaller indentation. (3) Perhaps most likely, the word *thioi* ('gods') may have stood first as it does in several other laws (e.g. **G43Ba, Bb**; **G72**). *Thioi* would require space for four letters, whereas only three are missing from lines 2 and 3. But *ΘΙΟΙ* would take about as much space as these missing letters—in **G64** the word *thioi* at the beginning takes up exactly the same amount of space as the three letters in line 2 of that text (*NMA*)—and a slight protrusion to the right in the first line, such as occurs in **G72**.1.1 (also *thioi*), would not be impossible.

16–33 There is nothing like these rules in what survives of **G41**, but similar provisions may originally have stood in parts of that inscription that are now lost.

16–31 The law requires that the temporary master be allowed to swear an exculpatory oath (16–21), but then it also allows a suit to be brought if there is an accusation (presumably by the old master) that the temporary master sold or hid the slave away. This indicates that here, at least, an exculpatory oath would not be automatically decisive, but a suit could still be brought against someone even after he had sworn the oath. By setting the penalty for not swearing—in effect for admitting guilt—as the simple value but making it double if someone denies the accusation and is then convicted in court, the law exerts some pressure on those who are guilty to admit their crime.

16–21 This is the only example at Gortyn outside the Code (see on **G72**.3.5–9) where a exculpatory oath is required of a defendant.

G48. *c.*500–450?

Under this number G collects the traces of earlier letters that can be seen on several of the blocks from the east wall, including **G47**. From all these, only two significant words can be read.

A [—] θιοί [—]	→	A — gods —
C [—] πέρηι [—]	→	C — carries —

A The letters forming the word 'gods' are at the bottom of the stone in the middle with writing above it and on both sides. The word could possibly be at the beginning of a new text that was continued on the stone below, but the letters might also belong to other words.

G51 (VER II.13, K 139). Swearing oaths. *c.*500–450?

This inscription, on a block from the east wall, preserves most of a column of writing. The top line is probably not the first line of text (see note on line 1), which may have begun above or in a column to the right, but the bottom line may be the end of it, since there is a small space below it. On the right one or two letters are missing from most lines and on the left about 8–9 letters were probably written on a separate block. Whether the text extended in one or more columns to the right or left is uncertain. G and others note that the writing and layout of this text resemble that of **G42**; it is possible that the two were originally part of a single set of procedural laws.

θιôι, ὀμνύμην δὲ δικάκ̣[σαι τὸν Ζῆ-] ←
[να καὶ τὸν (?)] Ἀπέλλονα καὶ τὰν Ἀθαν̣-
αίαν καὶ τὸν Ἕρμαον, οτ̣[........]
[... μηδένα] ἄλλον θιὸν ὀνυμαινέτ̣-
ο. τô δεκαστατῆρο καὶ πλί̣[ονος ....]
[........]εν κ' υἰῦνς οἵ κ' ἡβίοντι
καὶ πολιατεύοντι καὶ τ[ούτον υἰῦ-]
[νς οἵ κ' ἡβίο (?)]ντι ὀμνύμην πάντανς
[Ϝ]ιναυτôι Ϝέκαστον ἐπαριό[μενον ἦ μὰν]
[κακίστοι (?)] ὀλέτροι ἐκσόλλυθαι. τὸ[ν-]
[ς] μαίτυρανς αὐτὸν Ϝέκασ[τον καὶ τὸ-]
[νς ἀδελπι (?)]όνς οἵ κ' ἠβίοντι κῆς τô α[ὐ-]
[τ]ô πατρὸς ἴοντι κ' ἀδαιτηὶ [........]
[........]ρονς αὐτὸν Ϝέκαστο[ν —]

— to the god, and (the judge) is to rule that (a litigant) swear [by Zeus (?) and] Apollo and Athena and Hermes [*c*.11] let him [not] swear by any other god. In a matter of ten staters or more [*c*.14], and the sons who are past puberty and are active as citizens and [their sons who are past puberty] (?) are all to swear, each invoking a curse on himself to die [the worst (?)] death (if he perjures himself). The witnesses, each one himself, and [the brothers (?)] who are of age and are from the same father, and without division [*c*.20] each himself—

---

1 θιοι could be dative singular or nominative plural, but G argues, correctly we think, that the presence of a connecting particle (*de*) after the next word means that it is part of the preceding clause, not the common invocation 'gods'.

ὀμνύμην δὲ δικάκ̣[σαι: the first infinitive is dependent on the second (cf. **G72**.3.6–7). VER translate 'pour juger, (il faut) jurer'; but this sense cannot be obtained from the Greek.

1–2 τὸν Ζῆνα: the restoration was first suggested by Brause 1914: 105. Given the prominence of Zeus on Crete and the difficulty of fitting a longer name into the space available, the restoration is likely, but not certain. G notes that an oath to Zeus, Apollo, and Athena is mentioned in a Hellenistic inscription from Ceos, but this is no reason to add Zeus here.

5–6 πλί̣[ονος καὶ αὐτὸν ὀμνύμ]εν: Brause 1914: 107; this is rejected by G (who restores only μ]ὲν in line 6) on the ground that the infinitive should end in -μην (as in line 8). But VER rightly note that *epsilon* and *eta* are often interchanged at this time.

7–8 καὶ τ[ούτον υἰῦνς οἵ κ' ἡβίο]ντι G, K, VER; the visible letters are written in a space that was erased; so too, presumably, were the missing letters in each line.

9 Parallels (e.g. **G72**.2.40 and others cited by G) confirm the supplements proposed for this line, but κακίστοι (10) remains uncertain.

Ϝ]ιναυτôι = Ϝιν αυτôι; cf. **G72**.2.40.

12 ἀδελπι]όνς = Att. ἀδελφούς. G, followed by VER, K, writes ἀδευπι]όνς, but although the word is sometimes spelled with an *upsilon* (**G72**.5.18), the *lambda* spelling is more common (Bile 120).

κῆς = καὶ ἐκς (Dialect 14).

13 ἀδαιτηί: ‘without division’? The precise sense is uncertain: G understands ‘without distinction’, VER suggest it refers either to an undivided inheritance (cf. K: ‘ungetrennt’), or means ‘without exception’ (which is how they translate it).

The law specifies the gods one must swear by (1–5), the identity of the swearers and the content of their oath (5–10), and the identity of witnesses, who may also have been required to swear oaths (10–14). All those mentioned are close relatives (sons, grandsons, brothers), suggesting that the law concerns a dispute over the division of the estate (see **G72**.4.23–48). The dire nature of the oath to be sworn suggests a very serious matter, though this seems at odds with the limitation to cases where the penalty might be as small as ten staters.

1 The connecting particle (*de*) implies that a clause preceded the preserved text and that the first word is thus not the invocation ‘gods’. An initial clause might provide a context for the rules that follow.

1–3 As restored, the list of authorized gods does not include Artemis, to whom a woman must swear in a divorce case in the roughly contemporary **G72**.3.7–8, or several of the gods to whom sacrifices are given in **G3** and **G65**. It is possible that some god other than Zeus should be supplied in the lacuna in 1–2, but it would not be so easy to fit a longer name in the available space.

6 ‘Past puberty’ (also in 8): the provisions in the Code concerning heiresses seem to require that *ēbionti* designate someone past puberty but perhaps not yet at the age of majority, and scholars generally accept this conclusion (for references, see commentary on **G72**.7.29–30); but this sense is difficult here because of the implication that one could fulfill one’s civic duties but not be an adult. Nonetheless, we think this is what it must mean. VER and K both translate the term here as ‘adult’ (*majeurs*, *erwachsen*).

7 ‘Active as citizens’ (*poliateuonti*): see on **G72**.9.33.

G52 (VER II.90, K 140). Law about water. *c.*500–450?

Part of a stone with remnants of two columns of text. The shape and size of the letters and columns resemble **G46**. More remains of the left column than the right; the latter apparently contains two provisions separated by a horizontal gap of about one line. Text is missing on all four sides; G’s restorations assume that 6–8 letters are missing from the left of column B. The three texts may all be related.

A	A
3 [— δια]ρύ-	3–4 — flows —
4 ηι	
vac.	
5 αἰ [—]	
6 [— δι’ ἀλλότρ (?)]ιον	6–7 — through another’s land (?) —
7 κορί[ον —]	

B

[— αἰ δέ] κ'ἀμ[ελ]ία λα-
γαίηι, πέντ[ε δαρκνὰς]
[ἀποτει]σῆται κατ'
ἀμέραν ὀτ̣τ̣[άκιν κα]
[λαγαίη]ι. αἰ δὲ κ' ὀκ-
ετô ἰόντος [c.5–6]
[c.7–8]τ̣ος ἀνάγ-
εν δι[—]

B

1–6 — [If someone] negligently (?) releases (water?), he shall pay five [drachmas (?)] per day as often as he should [release it (?)]. But if, when there is a conduit [c.5–6]

7–8 [c.7–8] bring back —

A6–7 For the restoration cf. **G46**B7–8.

B1 αἰ δέ] κ' ἀμ[ελ]ία: G.

2–5: G's restorations are based in large part on **G73**A4–6.

4 ὀττάκιν = ὁσάκις (Bile 215, 263).

5–6 ὀκετô = ὀχετοῦ.

Water is the subject of the first part of A, probably of B, and perhaps of the second part of A as well. B may concern captured water which is inadvertently released onto a neighbor's property. The use and misuse of water was naturally a concern at Gortyn (see **G43**Bb; **G73**A), as it was elsewhere (for Athens, see e.g. Dem. 55).

G53. *c*.500–450?

One block with three columns of text very close to one another. About five letters are visible per line in the right column (A) and only one per line in C on the left. Originally there was more writing on all four sides.

A

[—] ἐπικα[—]
[— κ]σήνιο-
ς παν[—]
[—]τ̣ι κόσ-
μος ἠ[—]

A

2–3 — foreigners' —

4–5 — *kosmos* —

B

[—]όμην δὲ τ̣ὰ θῖνα̣ ἇ-
ιπερ πρόθα. *vac.*
αἴ κα πρὸ ν̣εμήιο ἠ
πιλ̣όσ[ι]ος̣ ἄλλη δ'ἐπ-
ερ κ' οἰ ἄλλοι νέμον̣-
τ̣[ι —]

B

1–2 — sacred things, just as before. *vac.*

3–6 If before the distribution (?) or compression of wool (someone distributes?) differently from the way in which the others distribute —

B2 πρόθα = Att. πρόσθεν; for the variation πρόθθα, see Dialect 11.

3 G suggests that νεμήιο may be a noun (genitive singular) from the verb νέμω 'distribute'; see Bile 323.

4 πιλόσιος gen. of πίλωσις = πίλησις ('compression', used, among other things, of compressing wool).

A2–3 For *ksēnios* 'foreigners'' (official?), see above on **G14p–g2**. *Ksēnios* almost certainly does not go together with *kosmos* in 4–5, since too many letters must have intervened (even if column A was not as wide as B). But *kosmos* may either have originally stood before *ksēnios* in line 2 or *ksēnios* alone may mean *ksenios kosmos* (see **G14p–g2**, with comm.).

B contains two laws (separated by a gap of about four letters and asyndeton); the first has something to do with sacred matters, the second probably with wool. Neither preserves enough text for us to know what its purpose is.

4 Wool was commonly pressed or compressed to make it into a kind of felt cloth. G takes 'differently' (*allē*) in the sense of 'from a different place'.

G54. *c.*500–450?

A small block with the remains of two columns; no sense can be recovered from the right column.

B

1	[—]ọαιεν	1–2	— or from —
2	ἢ ἐς στα[—]		
3	[—]οιεν ἢ ἐ-	3–4	— or from —
4	ς κραυρ[—]		
5	[—]ιοντα ἐ-	5–6	— hundred —
6	κατὸν [—]		

---

1 The first letter could also be a *gamma*.

4 κραυρ[could be the noun κραῦρα (a fever in pigs and cattle), or the adjective κραῦρος ('brittle'). C, assuming the former, suggested ἀποθάν]οιεν in line 3.

G55 (VER II.21, K 141). *c.*500–450?

A damaged block with the left side of one column of text.

4	[—]ν κα γέν-	4–5	becomes [— if —]
5	ηται . ι[—]		
6	[— ὀμοσά]το μὴ μ-	6–7	[— let him swear (?)] that verily he is not —
7	ὰν ἤμην [—]		
8	[— δ]όλο ἐνε-	8–9	— of a wounded slave (?) —
9	ρημμέν[—]		
10	[— π]άσσṭạṿ	10–11	— master, verily not to —
11	μ̣ὴ μὰν το[—]		

---

6 ὀμοσά]το (C) is likely but not certain.

8–9 ἐνερημμέν[possibly = ἐνερηγμέν[ο (from ἐνρήγνυμι), 'broken' (Bechtel 1923: 708).

The Greek expression *mē man* ('verily not') in 6–7 and 11 indicates that these are the words of an oath, perhaps something to do with a master's treatment of his slave.

G56. *c.*500–450?

A small block with scattered remains of eight lines.

2 [—] τοῖλ λε . [—]	2 — to those —
4 [—] ἔγρα (?)]ττaι. *vac.*	4 — (as is) written (?). *vac.*
5 [—] ἡβ̣ιοντ[—]	5 — is of age —
6 [— ἐπ]ιβάλῃι [—]	6 — claims [an heiress (?)] —
7 [— ἔγρ (?)]ατται ἰ[—]	7 — [as is] written (?) —

2 The surviving trace of the letter after *epsilon* could be an *alpha* or *san*, but not an *iota*, thus precluding the restoration τοῖλ λε[ίονσι.

The words in lines 5–6 suggest that this law may have concerned the marriage of an heiress (so C, G; cf. **G72**.7.15–9.24). But *epibalēi* (line 6) might also refer simply to claiming an inheritance.

G57 (K 142). *c.*500–450?

A small fragment with remains of ten lines.

[—]ντες λ̣[—]	
[—]α διπλῆι κ[—]	— double —
[—]αι τôι ἐλε[υθέροι (?) —]	— for the free person (?) —
[— στατ]ῆρανς οἰ δὲ [—]	— staters, but the —
[— ἀπ]οδόμενοι [—]	— selling —
[—] ἄτας το λ[—]	— fines —
[—]σται ἀποδ[—]	— sell (?) —
[—]ι̣ ἀποδοντο [—]	— they sell —
[—] ἀ̣ντιμολος̣ [—]	— litigant(s) —
[—] ὀς ὀδ[—]	

2 κ[αταστασεῖ C.
3 [— ἠ] ἆι τôι ἐλε[υθέροι ἔγραπται: Blass (#5001), comparing **G43Ab**7–9.
5 ἀπ]οδόμενοι (nom. pl.) could also be ἀπ]οδομένοι (dative sing.).

G58 (VER I.15, K 143). *c.*500–450?

A small piece of stone with six lines of text from the left side of a column. There is a small space between the left edge of the column and the edge of the stone, and a smaller space at the top, perhaps indicating the top of the column (but not the beginning of the text).

δείκσοντι αἰγ[—]	1	they show —
[ὀμ (?)]οσαντας δέκα σ-	2–3	— [swearing (?)] ten staters —
τατῆρας τᾶς [—]		
[—]ν τοῖλ Λατοσίοι-	4–5	— is to assign to the Latosians —
ς καταδόμην κα[—]		
[—]αναι. [α]ἰ δὲ μὴ ἐσκ[—]	6	— but if not —

2 ὀμ (?)]όσαντας (Baunack and Baunack) is possible, but not certain.

4–5 The Latosians were apparently a group of people who had settled in Gortyn; see note on **G78**.2.

G59 (VER I.3). *c*.500–450? FIG. 49

Seven lines with 1–6 letters each are visible in the drawing of this small fragment; the stone is now lost.

G59,
awing
'ernier
-6: 18,
; right
awing
ter G)

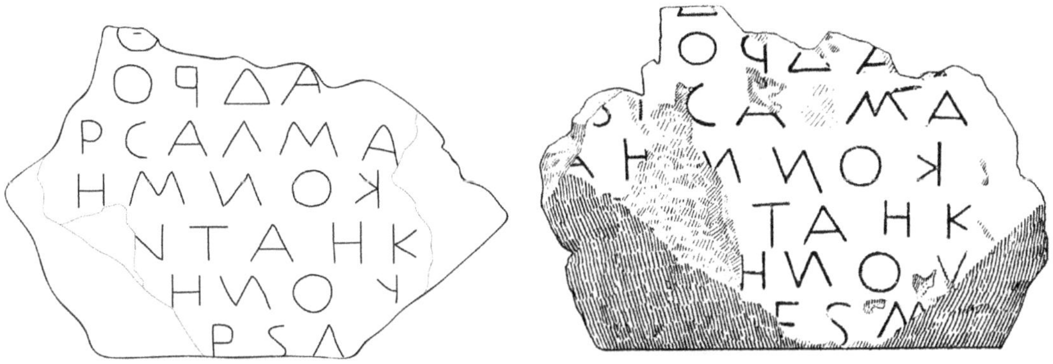

2 [—]α δρο[μεὺς —] 2 — adult —
3 [—]ι πά[ν]σα[ι —] 3 — for the whole —
4 [—]κονς ἤ α̣[—]
5 [—]ντα ἤ κ[—]

3 πόλ]ι | πά[ν]σα[ι: VER, based on the drawing in G, which she says is Pernier's (1925–6: 18, no. 8), though her drawing is significantly different. Both words conflict with Pernier's drawing, though his drawing, which shows ρπαγσα, cannot be correct; moreover, the word-division mark VER restore is not found in any other fifth-century text at Gortyn. It is not clear that anyone has seen the stone since. G herself prints no text for this line.

3 If VER's restoration is correct—they call it 'not impossible', but there are significant difficulties with it (see above note)—mention of 'the whole city' (*poli pansai*, cf. **G13**e2) would be significant.

G60. *c*.500–450?

A small, more or less rectangular block with three lines of text.

1 [—]οι ἆι ἔγρα[πται —] 1 — as is written —
2 [—]τος κρηιο[—]
3 [—]ι̣ Ϝεκάσστ[—] 3 — each —

G61. *c.*500–450?

A large block with parts of five lines visible in the upper right-hand corner and large spaces to the left and below; the lines represent the lower left corner of a column of text.

[—]τοδενα̣[—]		
[— κατισ (?)]τάμην	2–3	— to pay (?) and —
καὶ κο[—]		
[—]αν τὰν	4–5	— [he will pay (?)] the fine —
ἄταν κ[αταστασεῖ (?)]		
vac.		*vac.*

G62–4 are probably the oldest texts in the group **G41–71** (see above). **G63** and **G64** are written in long lines on blocks that in their original state were perhaps two meters or more long; **G62** may originally have been similar, though only a small piece has survived. There is no sign in any of the three inscriptions that the text was formed into columns or that gaps were used to separate provisions.

G62 (VER II.3, K 144). Law concerning status? *c.*525–500?

A single block, discovered near Mitropolis, about 0.5 m. wide and 0.660 m. tall with nine lines of text that continued to the left on the same stone and to the right on a separate stone, and probably began above and continued below too. In five places word-division is indicated, not by vertical lines as in **G1–40**, but by a pair of small circles, one above the other (Introd. 3D1)—a practice found in other archaic laws such as a sixth-century law from Chios (M&L 8; VER I.62; K 61).

[—]νασ[—]	
[—] οἰ Γο[ρτύνιοι (?) —]	— the Gortynians (?) —
[— ἐλε]Ϝθερο . [—]	— free —
[— αἰ δ]ε̣ τις δολ[ο —]	— but if someone a slave —
[— κοσ]μίον ⁚ ἒ ἄ[λλος (?) —]	— being *kosmos*, or another (?) —
[— λ]αγαῖεν ἀ[—]	— they should release —
[—] τὰ θῖνα ⁚ ε . [—]	— divine matters —
[—]ι ⁚ αἰ δὲ μὲ λε̣[ίοι (?) —]	— but if he should not wish (?) —
[—]οι ⁚ πίνεν ⁚ τ[—]	— to drink —

1–9 The restorations are taken from Halbherr 1897: 166–7.
8 λε̣[ίοι: λε̣[ίοντι (pl.) is also possible.

Despite its scantiness, this fragment is of interest not only for the plausible restoration of 'the Gortynians' in line 2 (cf. **G23** and perhaps **G10x–y**), but also for the apparent occurrence of 'free' and 'slave' in 3–4, which led H (followed by G and, uncertainly, by VER) to think the subject may be manumission, an action not otherwise mentioned in Cretan inscriptions until the Hellenistic period (cf. *IC* 4.231–6). More likely, we think, is a connection with the first column of the Code, which not only concerns free and slave but also uses the same verb *lagaien*, 'release' (in **G72**.1.6, etc.), as here (line 6). Moreover, the words in line 5 (assuming they are correctly restored) echo the wording of **G72**.1.51–3—'if a *kosmos* seizes (someone) or another (seizes someone) belonging to a *kosmos*' (*ai de ka kosmion agei e kosmiontos allos*). We must bear in mind, however, that the lines in this text may originally have been quite long, so that words that happen to be positioned one above the other on the stone, could have been separated by a large amount of intervening text.

7 For *thina*, see on **G72**.10.42–4; Introd. 9A.

G63 (VER I.59). Gortyn and Leben. *c*.525–500?

One long block of stone with five lines of writing and part of a sixth. A rectangular border chiseled into the stone (probably so that it could be reused in a later building) has removed some of the original writing. There appears to be a small space above line 1, suggesting that this may have been the first line of the inscription. The stone is lost and is only known from a photograph by H (reproduced in G).

[—]ν̣ανα . . π̣έρεν ε̣κ̣ορμιοκεσλυ[. . .]α[—]
[—]γ [κρι]θᾶν μεδίμνονς δυόδεκα [—]
[— ὀ Λεβεναῖος (?) κ]ατὰ τô Γορτυνίο κ̣ατὰ δὲ τô Λεβενα[ίο] ὀ̣ Γ[ορτύνιος (?) —]
[—]ιο[. .] τôι Λεβεναίοι κ̣αρτερὸς μαῖ̣τ̣[υς —]
[— ἄ (?)]ρτον̣ κατ' ἀμέραν πέντε στατêραν̣[s] αἰ [—]
[—]γα[.]ν̣ο̣[—]

— to carry —
— twelve medimnoi of barley —
— [the Lebenian (?)] against the Gortynian and against the Lebenian [the Gortynian (?)] —
— for the Lebenian the witness [is to (?)] prevail —
— bread (?), five staters per day if —

1 π̣έρεν = Att. φέρειν. The remaining letters are a puzzle; it is tempting to see κ̣ορμιο as some form of κόσμος, but this variant is not otherwise found at Gortyn before the third century BCE (*IC* 4.165, 171).

2 τᾶ]γ G; but as Perlman notes (2004a: 105, with n. 54) this would be the only example of the article with a genitive in expressions of weight, volume, or value in archaic Crete.

3 G's restorations are very plausible.

4 κ̣αρτερός: for the comparative, see on κάρτονανς, **G72**.1.16.

5 ἄ]ρτον̣ G; VER are doubtful.

στατêραν̣[s κ]αὶ [—] G, VER, but there does not appear to be enough space in the gap for a *kappa*.

This fragment is evidently from an agreement between Gortyn and Leben, on the south coast of Crete, which served as a port for Gortyn. The agreement may concern transportation between the two places (cf. line 1, 'carry'). It is uncertain how independent Leben was from Gortyn at this time, but this text appears to treat the two on equal terms. See Perlman 2004b: 1174.

3–4 The agreement apparently regulates litigation involving a Lebenian and a Gortynian, and under some conditions (now lost) gives priority to a witness testifying on behalf of a Lebenian. This may be a concession on the part of Gortyn, made in exchange for other benefits.

5 As G notes, the five staters per day may be a fine or a payment for services.

G64 (VER I.8). Decree honoring Dionysios. *c.*525–500?

Two long blocks with six lines of text. Line 6 ends half way across the stone, marking the end of the text, which starts at the beginning of line 1 with an invocation to the gods. The text is complete on the left; on the right, five letters or more have been lost where the stone is damaged, but a few letters are visible to the right of this in lines 1–3. The text must then have continued on a block to the right, but perhaps for no great distance, if 'all Gortyn and those living in Aulon' (2–3) are the subject of the verb 'gave' (1).

θιοί. θυκἀγαθᾶι. δοριὰν ἔδοκ̣αν Διονυσ[ίοι τô]ι Κο[—]
[—]ολε[5–6 ἐ]Ϝεργεσίας ἕνεκα Γόρτυνς ἐπίπανσα
ϙ' οἰ ἐν ἈϜλôνι Ϝοικίοντες ἀτέλειαν [πάντον ἀ]Ϝτô[ι —]
[— Ϝα]στίαν δίκαν καὶ Ϝοικίαν ἐν ἈϜλôνι ἐ-
νδος Πύργο καὶ Ϝοικόπεδον ἔκσοι γᾶν κ[—]
[—]κον κ̣αὶ γ[υν]ασίο. vac.

1–3 Gods. With good fortune. All Gortyn and those living in Aulon gave as a gift to Dionysios the son of (?) Ko[—] because of his good work exemption from taxation [in all matters?] for himself—

4–5 — a citizen's justice and a house in Aulon inside of Pyrgos and a plot other than (agricultural?) lands —

6 — and of the gymnasium. *vac.*

---

1 *θυκ(αι)* = Att. *τύχη* (with metathesis of the aspiration, Bile 139); cf. note on **G42A11** *κηρίθε[κνος*.

τô]ι Κο[: the name could be a patronymic or an ethnic designation.

2 *ἀρετᾶς ἐμ π]ολέ[μοι καὶ ἐ]Ϝεργεσίας*: C's supplement is followed by all later editors, but it is quite uncertain, especially as we do not know how much text is missing at the end of line 1 and beginning of 2.

3 *ἐ]Ϝεργεσίας* = *εὐεργεσίας*.

C, followed by G, VER, writes *ἀ]Ϝτô[ι καὶ ἐσγόνοις* (Att. *ἐκγόνοις*); but *ἐσγόνος* does not occur elsewhere in Crete before the Hellenistic period. We suggest instead *ἀ]Ϝτô[ι καὶ γενιᾶι*, which occurs in **Da1**A3. The supplement is by no means certain, however, and the text may not have mentioned Dionysius' descendants.

4 *ϝοικίαν*: usually translated 'house', but Brixhe 1999: 88 suggests here it means 'lot for a house'—i.e. a piece of land on which Dionysius can build a house.

4–5 *ἔνδος*: 'de accentu nihil constat', G.

5 *ἔκσοι* (Att. *ἔξω*) is usually taken to mean 'outside' but it can also mean 'except for, other than' (see e.g. Herodotus 5.46 and refs. in LSJ *s.v.* III). See commentary below.

γᾶν: with G, VER we read this as a genitive plural with *ἔκσοι*, though it could also be an accusative in apposition to *ϝοικόπεδον*. Brixhe 1999: 112 cites **G42**B2, where *ga* is private land, and **G43**Ba, where the city has given land for planting.

6 *τει*]*κôν* C, rejected by G, VER. Note that there must be at least 25–30 letters missing between the end of line 5 and the beginning of line 6, so that it is very unlikely that *γ*[*υν*]*ασίο* goes with *ἔκσοι*, as Ferruti 2004 seems to think.

This decree conferring honors on a certain Dionysios is interesting in several respects. It is comparable in some ways to the honors conferred on Spensithios and his descendants (**Da1**), but at least in the preserved text, Dionysios (unlike Spensithios) has no reciprocal obligations to the city but is simply being rewarded for past actions. We know nothing of the good work (*ewergesia*) that prompted these honors, but it appears that Dionysios is not a native Gortynian, since he is being given certain citizen rights (line 4).

It is notable that the honors are awarded by 'all Gortyn and those living in Aulon'. This is the only occurrence of the toponym 'Gortyn'; whether it differs from 'the Gortynians', and if so how, is unclear. The qualification 'all' must be for emphasis, since 'Gortyn' alone would presumably designate the whole city (i.e. all free adult males), perhaps added to show the honoree that the decree was approved unanimously; cf. 'the whole city' (*pansai poli*) in **G13**e2 (and see on 4 below). As for 'those living in Aulon', Perlman (1996: 266–8) suggests that 'Aulon, like Rhitten [see on **G80**], was a dependent polis of Gortyn', though it is unclear why they would be jointly conferring honors on Dionysios. G suggests that Aulon was a district within Gortyn and compares Athenian decrees that mention the Athenians together with an individual deme of Athens. But if this were the case, there would be little reason to give Dionysios a place to build a house in Pyrgos (see below on 4–5).

1–3 Despite the wide separation, the expression 'all Gortyn and those living in Aulon' in the nominative case in lines 2–3 is very likely the subject of 'gave' in line 1. Or, if they are the subject of another verb that originally intervened, it very likely was something like 'voted' that in some way confirmed the gift.

2 All previous editors restore the beginning of this line on the basis of three letters to read 'because of his valor in war and his good deeds'. This is not impossible, but we consider it too speculative to put in the text.

3 The text is usually restored at the end of the line to read 'for himself and his descendants' (see note); the same expression occurs in a similar context in **Da1**A3.

4 The expression *wastian dikan* occurs in **G13**h–g2, where we translate it 'a citizen's trial'. Here the context is apparently more general, and so 'a citizen's

justice' is more appropriate, though the 'justice' envisaged for Dionysios would probably involve primarily access to the same judicial process as citizens have—i.e. to a citizen's trial.

4–5 VER argue that *pyrgos* is a 'fortress', but it is more likely the name of a place, as there is no sign of a fortified area in Gortyn at this time and it seems unlikely that a fortress (lit. a 'tower') would contain a house within it (Ferruti 2004: 285 n. 10). We do not know its location.

5 The expression *eksoi gan* is usually taken to mean 'outside (private) lands', on the assumption that the city's land that it is giving Dionysios is beyond the land owned by individuals; but there is no evidence for such a meaning of *ga*. Thus we take *oikopedon* to be a plot either attached to the house in Aulon or elsewhere in the city, perhaps to be used for building a house.

6 Ferruti 2004 examines the evidence for gymnasiums in Greece at this time and concludes that this was probably an open space marked out for exercise without significant buildings. Dionysios is probably being given the right to exercise there.

G65. Regulations for sacrifices. *c.*500–450?

A tall stone, discovered near Mitropolis, with fourteen lines of writing; the top and left edge of the text are preserved, but an unknown amount of writing is missing to the right and below. The single word invocation in line 1 runs left to right and the text then begins again from the left in line 2, continuing boustrophedon thereafter. First published by Halbherr 1897: 162–6.

[θι]οί. vac. —	1	Gods. *vac.*
τ̣ôι Ζενὶ τôι [—]	2	To Zeus the —
[—] οῖ̈ις θέλεια	3–4	— a white female sheep, and —
λευκά, τὸ δὲ κό[—]		
[—] ἀμμνά, τὰ⟦τα⟧ν δ-	5–6	— a ewe lamb, and let the priest [take (?)] the cow hide —
ὲ βοῖ̈αν ὀ ἰαρε[ὺς —]		
[—] κριὸν· τôι Ἀλί-	7–8	— a ram. To Helios a male sheep —
οι οῖ̈ιν ἔ̈ρσεν[α —]		
[—]α τὰ δὲ παρθύμ̣-	9–10	— the additional sacrifices, as neighbors (?) —
ατ' ᾶ̈ι περιϝοι[—]		
[—]τε τρίινς κ' ἀμ-	11–12	— three and a ewe lamb, but of the others —
ν̣άν, τôν δ' ἄ̈λλο[ν —]		
[—] μεδιμνιαία[ν	13–14	— that holds a medimnos, and of cheese —
καὶ τυρô ἐμιπ̣[—]		

3 *οῖ̈ις θέλεια*: the same expression in **G3**.3 but with a single *iota*; cf. *οῖ̈ιν ἔ̈ρσενα* in line 8.

4 *κό[διον*: H, who cites a gloss in Hesychius: *κώδιον· σκῦλον ἢ δέρμα προβάτου χωρὶς σώματος*. *Probata* refers to sheep and goats, and we would expect a sheep's hide to be mentioned here (cf. *boian* in line 6). Alternatively, H suggests *κο[λοβόν* ('maimed') followed by a prohibition against sacrificing imperfect victims.

5 ἀμμνά: for the double consonant (cf. ἀμνάν in 11–12), see Bile 158.
6 H's proposed supplement ἰαρε[ὺς λαβέτο is deemed very likely by G, but other verbs or more complex constructions are possible.
9–10 The text is very uncertain: τὰ δὲ could be τάδε, αἶ could be αἰ, and περιϜοι[could be a form of περίϜοι[κος, or the verb περιϜοι[κὲν, or two words—περὶ Ϝοὶ[κειôν. Bile (p.c.) observes that Cretan uses *amphi* instead of *peri* for 'around', but *peri* might nevertheless mean 'around' as a preverb in *perioikoi*.
11 τρίινς: masc. acc. pl. of τρέες; Bile 217.
14 The last letter could also be an *omicron*.

The text is a list of animals to be sacrificed to Zeus, Helios, and probably other gods. It should be compared to **G3**. No dates are mentioned here, however, though these could have come elsewhere in the inscription. And a priest is assigned some part of the sacrifice, apparently a hide (5–6), and perhaps also the commodities in 13–14, which were not normally part of a sacrifice.

1 The letters in this line are slightly smaller than in the rest of the text and also appear to be less strictly linear than the remaining lines, suggesting that the mason may have had to work around rough spots on the stone. It is also possible this invocation was inscribed after the rest of the text.

2 An epithet for Zeus probably followed.

3 A female sheep is sacrificed to Hera in **G3**.3; perhaps here too.

4 For possible restorations of the end of this line, see note above.

7 G (following H) suggests the ram may have been sacrificed to Hermes.

10 Larsen 1936: 12–13 sees a reference to *perioeci* ('those living around', i.e. a subordinate population living on the land akin to the helots in Sparta), but the letters are open to other restorations (see above); see Guarducci 1936: 358 n. 4.

G66. *c.*500–450?

A tiny piece of stone with parts of five lines.

3 [— Ποτε]ι̣δάονι [—]	3 — to Poseidon —

If correctly supplemented, this would be the first mention of Poseidon at Gortyn, though he is mentioned in **A5+6**.

G67. *c.*500–450?

A rectangular stele broken off diagonally at the top. Parts of five lines of writing (and traces of a sixth above line 1) are visible; the stone is empty below line 5.

1 [—]οιοδ̣[—]	
2 [—] . . κειτ[—]	
3 [—]αι ταν δε[—]	
4 [—]κας τὰ το[—]	
5 [— γ]υναικός [—]	— of a woman —

G68. *c.*500–450?

A small piece with about five letters from each of three lines.

1 [—]ι Γορτυ̣[ν —]	— Gortyn[—]
2 [—]θαι με[—]	
3 [—]ιε τὸνς [—]	

1 ο]ἰ Γορτύ̣[νιοι? Cf. **G62**.2.

1. 'The Gortynians' is a possible restoration.

G69. *c.*500–450?

Parts of four lines on a small block.

2 [—] δένδρ[ε]α τ[—]	2 — trees —
3 [—] ἀλλαι . [—]	3 — otherwise (?) —
4 [— τὰ]ν̣ δαῖσ[ιν —]	4 — the division (of property) —

G72–140

These texts are generally dated to the second half of the fifth century (see Introd. to **G41–140**). They are distinguished from **G41–71** by the lettering, including the fact that *eta*, and *koppa* are no longer used. Bile (2012: 9) suggests that the reduced number of letters represents a conscious archaizing, intended to suggest that these laws are infused with ancient values. But the change from **G41–71** is minimal, for *koppa* occurs only once in that group (in one of the earliest laws) and *epsilon* replaces *eta* in a number of texts (see above on **G41–71**).[407] If archaizing was the goal, moreover, one would expect to find *eta* and *koppa*, as well as *zeta*, which are all used in **G1–40**. Thus, it seems more likely that the Code and later inscriptions continue a trend toward simplification of the alphabet that is evident much earlier at Gortyn (21 letters in **G1–40**, 20 in **G41–71**, and 18 in **G72–140**).

G72. (Willetts 1967) The Gortyn Code. *c.*450?

The Gortyn Code[408] is inscribed in twelve columns boustrophedon with the top line of each column reading right to left on a slightly curved wall, which was probably constructed in order to display this law and others (see below); contrast the earliest texts which certainly, and the 'Little Code' (**G41**) which probably, were inscribed on walls that were already part of a building. It is often thought that the wall with this inscription formed part of an enclosed building because there is an open space

[407] Cf. Jeffery 1990: 28 n. 2.

[408] **G72** is not a 'code' in the modern sense of a complete, systematically organized text of all the laws of a single legal system, but it is commonly—and appropriately—called a code in the sense of a large collection of laws covering a range of different topics (see van Effenterre and van Effenterre 2000).

or 'window' at the top of column 12. But there may originally have been a stone in this space, with or without text. G plausibly suggests that the wall was part of a roofed portico, in part because the good condition of the letters suggests the inscription was sheltered. The wall currently stands on site in a covered portico.

One block of the Code from the top of column 11 was discovered by Thenon in 1857, who purchased it for the Louvre, where it can now be seen (Thenon 1863). A second, damaged block with the tops of columns 8–10 was discovered in 1879 by Haussoullier built into a house in Agii Deka (Haussoullier 1880, see G p. 126, with photo p. 138); it is currently in the Heraklion Museum and a replica has been inserted in the inscribed wall at the site. And a broken stone with the bottom line and a half of column 11 was read by Halbherr, discovered in 1900 (see G p. 149; we can find no other information about this stone).

The more than thirty stones that make up the Code also contain pairs of letters of a later date representing numbers that recorded the position of each stone in the inscription so that they could be correctly reassembled in the Roman period (perhaps in the late first century BCE). Willetts 1967: 35 has a convenient chart of these numbers, but note the corrections of Keyser 1987.

Several other inscribed blocks found in the vicinity (**G51**, **G73**, **G75**, **G76**, **G77**, *IC* 4.144, *IC* 4.152) have the same slight curvature as **G72**; four of these blocks (**G73**, **G75**, **G76**, **G77**) also have similar writing as **G72**, and where enough is preserved, we can see that they are organized in columns of roughly similar width. One of these (**G73**, *q.v.*), moreover, also has an identification number (number 43) similar to those in **G72**. This indicates that the wall which currently contains only **G72** originally extended for some distance further to the left and contained much other legislation besides **G72**. G (*IC* 4, p. 124) estimates that either approximately eight or approximately 20 columns of text may have intervened between **G72** and **G73**.

Because of its length, we present the text in sections. These largely follow the divisions noted in Gagarin 1982, which are based primarily on asyndeton,[409] though we have combined some of the shorter sections and divided some of the longer ones. For each section we give the number or numbers for the treatment of the text in VER and K. Both of these often divide their presentations of the Code differently and sometimes group together different parts of the Code that in their view treat the same subject. This method has the advantage of making it easier to study several provisions concerning a specific matter all together, but we do not follow this practice because it obscures the organization given to the Code by the Gortynian legislator or legislators.

The main visual indication of the organization of the Code is the frequent presence of blank spaces (*vac.*) between sentences. These usually occupy

409 Asyndeton is when a new sentence begins without a connecting particle; see Introd. 3D3.

about the same amount of space as a single letter, sometimes a bit more; we note any gaps that are significantly longer. Some of these gaps still show traces of red paint (as do some of the letters); with one exception (5.17), we do not note these because it is very likely that designs painted in red originally filled all the gaps, but that most of the paint has worn off. Thus a gap with a painted sign has no more significance than an unpainted gap, since the latter was almost certainly painted originally. On the other hand, we do note the few signs that are carved in stone.

The tendency to end a column with a complete word, which we noted in **G41**, is evident here, where in 9 of the first 11 columns the mason ends the last line with a complete word, even if this means leaving a significant space at the end of the line (see e.g. **G72**.7.55). The two columns which end in the middle of a word (4 and 6) both end a little above the bottom of the stone. The mason may have thought he could squeeze one more line below and so did not bother to break off after the last complete word in the bottom line, but then decided that there was not enough space for another line after all.

Many difficult questions arise concerning the origin and enactment of these laws, for which no certain answers can be given. Are they all earlier laws that were later brought together and 'published' as a single document? We know that topics such as the heiress were treated in earlier texts (**G44**) but there is no evidence that any earlier law was copied directly into the Code. Undoubtedly, the Code drew on earlier laws and customs, such as the priority of direct descendants in inheritance, but it is more likely that the many details concerning inheritance and other subjects, some of them addressing very unlikely circumstances, were elaborated as part of a single later enactment. Bile is quite certain that the Code is 'the expression of a complex social crisis' (2012: 15); this is not impossible, but it is just as easily understood as a legal reform, collecting and synthesizing previous legislation, which includes some changes from existing rules but also much continuity.

Davies (1996: 54) suggests that **G72** and other inscriptions with more than one law (such as **G41**) represent the work of a group of magistrates during their term of office;[410] but the enormous range of texts, with the large majority having just one law, a few having two to four laws, one with perhaps ten or twelve, and then the Code indicates that the larger texts must have been the result of a conscious act of legislation. Furthermore, the skillful organization of certain sections of the Code, such as 1.2–2.2 on ownership and 10.33–11.23 on adoption, point, in our

[410] 'Each of them . . . is the document issued by (let us say) the relevant magistrates at the end of their period of office setting out the changes in the law which they proposed/instigated/proclaimed/approved during their period of office'.

view, to a single legislator as the primary author of the Code (see further Gagarin 2008a: 145–75).

The edition of Willetts 1967, with introduction, translation, and commentary, is very useful, especially on matters of dialect (on which we therefore provide less information for **G72**). Willetts' view that the society regulated by the Code can be placed in a quasi-Marxist evolutionary schema is now universally rejected (see Wolff 1968; Meyer-Laurin 1969), but his vast knowledge of Crete and Cretan society make his conclusions always worth consideration.[411]

The following subjects are treated in the Code:

1.1–2.2—Ownership of Persons
2.2–45—Sexual Offenses
2.45–3.16—Divorce
3.17–40—Disposition of Property after the Death of a Spouse
3.40–4—Separation of Serfs
3.44–4.23—Children Born to Unmarried Women
4.23–48—Distribution of an Estate
4.48–5.9—Gifts to a Daughter
5.9–54—Inheritance and the Division of the Estate
6.1–2—Gifts to a Daughter
6.2–46—Misuse of Others' Property
6.46–55—Ransom
6.55–7.10—Children of Mixed Marriages
7.10–15—Liability for Wrongs Done by a Slave
7.15–8.20—Marriage of an Heiress
8.20–36—Married or Widowed Heiresses
8.36–9.1—More on Heiresses
9.1–24—Management of an Heiress's Property
9.24–40—Litigation Concerning Property of the Deceased
9.40–3—Liability of a Son
9.43–10.1—Commercial Ventures Abroad
10.1–25—Gifts to Women
10.25–32—Acquisition of Slaves
10.33–11.23—Adoption
11.24–5—Amendment to 1.1–2.2 on Seizure before Trial
11.26–31—The Judicial Decision
11.31–45—Supplement to 9.24–40 on Obligations of the Deceased
11.46–55—Amendment to 2.45–3.16 on Divorce

[411] Our comments about dialectal forms or Attic equivalents of words will be less extensive in **G72** than for other laws, because Willetts' commentary is in general good on these matters.

12.1–5—Amendment to 10.14–25 on Gifts to Women
12.6–19—Amendment to 8.42–53 on Heiresses who are Children

1.1–2.2—OWNERSHIP OF PERSONS (VER II.6, K 163, BLASS #4991)

This large section of laws regulates claims concerning ownership of a person in cases where there is a dispute about whether the person is slave or free, or to whom a slave belongs. There is a short (and controversial) addendum to this section in 11.24–5. There may perhaps have been earlier legislation on this topic at Gortyn; see on **G13**f2.

θιοί ←
ὄς κ' ἐλευθέροι ἒ δόλοι μέλλει ἀν- ←
πιμολὲν, πρὸ δίκας μὲ ἄγεν. αἰ δ-
έ κ' ἄγει, καταδικακσάτο τô ἐλευθέρ-
ο δέκα στατêρανς, τô δόλο πέντ-
ε ὄτι ἄγει καὶ δικακσάτο λαγάσαι
ἐν ταῖς τρισὶ ἀμέραις. αἰ [δέ] κα
μὲ [λαγ]άσει, καταδικαδδέτο τô μὲν
ἐλευθέρο στατêρα, τô δόλο [δα]ρκν-
ὰν τᾶ̣ς̣ ἀμέρας Ϝεκάστας, πρίν κα λα-
γάσει· τô δὲ κρόνο τὸν δι[κ]αστ-
ὰν ὀμνύντα κρίνεν. *vac.* αἰ δ' ἀννίοιτο
μὲ ἄγεν, τὸν δικαστὰν ὀμνύντ-
α κρ[ί]νεν αἰ μὲ ἀποπονίοι μαῖτυς.
αἰ δέ κα μολêι ὁ μὲν ἐλεύθερον
ὀ δ[ὲ δ]ôλον, κάρτονανς ἔμεν *vac.*
[ὄτερο]ί κ' ἐλεύθερον ἀποπονίον-
τι. αἰ δέ κ' ἀνπὶ δόλοι μολίοντι
πονίοντες Ϝὸν Ϝεκάτερος ἔμ-
εν, αἰ μέν κα μαῖτυς ἀποπονêι, κ-
ατὰ τὸν μαίτυρα δικάδδεν, αἰ
δέ κ' ἒ ἀνποτέροις ἀποπονίοντι
ἒ μεδατέροι, τὸν δικαστὰν ὀ-
μνύντα κρίνεν. ἐ̂ δέ κα νικαθêι ὀ
ἔκον, τὸμ μὲν ἐλεύθερον λαγ-
άσαι τâν πέ[ν]τ' ἀμερâν, τὸν δὲ δô-
λο[ν] ἐς κêρανς ἀποδόμεν. αἰ δέ
κα μὲ λαγάσει ἒ μὲ ἀποδôι, δικακ-
σάτο νικêν τô μὲν ἐλευθέρο
πεντέκοντα στατêρανς καὶ σ-
τατêρα τâς ἀμέρας Ϝεκάστ-
ας, πρίν κα λαγάσει, τô δὲ δόλο
δέκα στατêρανς καὶ δαρκνὰν
τâς ἀμέρας Ϝεκάστας, πρίν κ' ἀ-

Gods.
Whoever is going to dispute concerning a free person or a slave is not to seize him before trial. If he does seize him, let (the judge) rule that he pay ten staters for a free person and five for a slave because he seized him, and let him rule that he release him within three days. And if he does not release him, let him rule that he pay a stater for a free person and a drachma for a slave for each day until he releases him. And the judge is to swear an oath and decide about the amount of time. *vac.* If he should deny he seized him, the judge is to swear an oath and decide, unless a witness should testify. If one party contends that he is a free person and the other that he is a slave, whichever ones testify that he is a free person are to prevail. And if they contend about a slave, each affirming that he is his, if a witness testifies, (the judge) is to rule according to the witness; but if they testify either for both sides or for neither, the judge is to swear an oath and decide. When the person in possession (of the disputed person) loses the case, he is to release the free person within five days and return the slave into the hands (of the proper owner). And if he does not release or return him, let (the judge) rule that (the successful party) win, in the case of a free person fifty staters and a stater for each day until he releases him, and in the case of a slave ten staters and a drachma for each day until he returns him into the hands (of the proper

ποδôι ἐς κἒρανς. ἒ δέ κα καταδι-
κάκσει ὀ δικαστάς, ἐνιαυτôι π-
ράδδεθθαι τὰ τρίτρα ἒ μεῖον,
πλίον δὲ μέ· τô δὲ κρόνο τὸν δι-
καστὰν ὀμνύντα κρίνεν. αἰ δέ
κα ναεύει ὀ δôλος ὄ κα νικαθê-
ι, καλίον ἀντὶ μαιτύρον δυôν δ-
ρομέον ἐλευθέρον ἀποδεικσάτ-
ο ἐπὶ τôι ναôι ὄπε κα ναεύει ἒ α-
ὐτὸς ἒ ἄλος πρὸ τούτο· αἰ δέ
κα μὲ καλêι ἒ μὲ δείκσει, κατισ-
[τάτ]ο τὰ ἐγ[ρα]μένα. αἰ δέ κα μεδ'
αὐτὸν ἀποδôι ἐν τôι ἐνιαυτôι,
τὰνς ἀπλόονς τ[ι]μὰνς ἐπικατ-
αστασεῖ. *vac.* αἰ δέ κ' ἀποθάνει μ-
ολιομένας τâδ δί[κ]ạς, τὰν ἀπλ-
όον τιμὰν κατ⟨α⟩στασεῖ. *vac.* αἰ δ-
έ κα κοσ[μ]ίον ἄγει ἒ κοσμίοντο-
ς ἄλλος, ἒ κ' ἀποστâι, μολêν, καἴ κ-
α νικαθêι, κατιστάμεν ἀπ[ὸ ἆ]ς
[ἀμέρα]ς ἄγαγε τὰ ἐγραμένα. *vac.*
[τ]ọ̀ν δὲ νενικαμένọν κα[ὶ τὸν κα]-
Col. 2
τακείμενον ἄγοντι ἄπατον
ἔμεν. *vac.*

owner). And when the judge has ruled, after a year (the winner) is to exact a triple fine or less, but not more. And the judge is to swear an oath and decide about the amount of time. And if the slave concerning whom (a litigant) has lost the case takes refuge in a temple, (the loser) will summon (the winner) in the presence of two free adult witnesses, and either he himself or another for him will point him out at the temple where he is taking refuge. But if he does not summon him or point him out, let him pay what is written; and if he should not give him back even in a year, he will pay the simple fines. *vac.* And if he (the disputed person?) dies while the case is being tried, he will pay the simple value. *vac.* If a *kosmos* seizes (someone) or another (seizes someone) belonging to a *kosmos*, it will be tried after he leaves office, and if the person in possession loses, he is to pay what is written from the day (he seized him). *vac.* There is to be immunity for one who seizes a person (**Col. 2**) who has lost a case or has indentured himself. *vac.*

---

1 The initial *theta* of θιοί is one letter space to the right of the rest of the column, an additional sign that this is an extra-textual invocation.

4–5 τô ἐλευθέρο: 'The genitive is often used loosely, especially at the beginning of a construction, to state the subject of a remark', Smyth 1956: §1381, who classifies this as a 'genitive of connection'; W sometimes calls it a 'genitive of reference'. It is very common in the Code and other laws.

6 ὄτι ἄγει: following Blass and others, W, VER, read ὄτι (= οὖτινος, see Dialect 18) ἄγει and translate 'for a slave of whomsoever he does seize'. We follow G, K in reading ὄτι.

12 ἀννίοιτο: pres. opt. 3rd. sing. (from Att. ἀρνέομαι, see Dialect 3, 9).

14 ἀποπονίοι: whenever the context is explicit, as here, *apoponen* always refers to the testimony of a witness, and this is also almost certainly its meaning in all other cases. The simple verb, *ponen*, is used of litigants (1.19 below, etc.).

16 κάρτονανς: lit. 'stronger', a comparative form (cf. καρτερός, 4.24–5 below); see Bile 181, 287, and Dialect 4.

There is a gap of about two letters at the end of the line even though there is no break in the sense. The mason may have mistakenly thought the sentence ended here and inserted a *vac.*

17 C, G say there is only room to restore [ὄττο]ί ('those who'). After examining the stone, we conclude that there is probably room for five letters, though it would be a tight fit, and thus, following Blass, W, and VER, we restore [ὄτερο]ί ('whichever of two parties'),

which makes better sense (see W ad loc.). The width of letters at Gortyn generally varies widely depending on the specific letter, but there is also some variation in the width of the same letters in different places and the spacing between them.

19 πονίοντες: the simple verb *ponen* refers to assertions made by litigants; see on *apoponen* (1.14).

Ϝόν is the possessive pronoun, = Att. ὅν (ἑόν); see W.

24 ἒ: 'when'; see on 6.1 below.

36 ἐνιαυτôι: 'in one year'. With most editors we understand this as one year after the judge's ruling. VER argue that it means 'at the end of the current year', but this would mean a different fine for the same offense depending on when during the year the case was tried.

40–1 ὃ κα νικαθêι: 'with regard to whom he has been defeated'—for the genitive, see on 1.4 above. Cf. **G80**.9 (αἰ δέ κα ν[ικ]αθ̣êι τôν ἐνεκύρον).

43 After ναôι the rough surface of the stone causes a gap in the text of approximately two letters here and also in line 44 (after πρ).

κατ⟨α⟩ατασεî: the mason mistakenly wrote *iota* instead of *alpha*.

52–3 ἒ κοσμίοντος ἄλλος: lit. 'or another person (seizes) a *kosmos*' (slave)'. This use of the genitive *kosmiontos*—'of a *kosmos*' = 'someone of (or belonging to) a *kosmos*—is not uncommon in the Code; cf. *apetairo* (2.5), *dolo* (2.27).

This initial section is commonly analyzed as concerned with status disputes, on the one hand, and ownership disputes on the other (e.g. Thür 2002), but it is more important to note that the legislator treats these as the same type of dispute, subject to the same procedural rules. The section is thus aimed at clarifying the procedures for resolving disputes where a claim to ownership is disputed, regardless whether a dispute over status is also involved. The first, and therefore probably most important, rule is that no action to remove the person from his current owner is to be taken before a trial.

The section is clearly and coherently organized to deal with several different aspects of these disputes (Gagarin 2008a: 159–62). It begins with the rule that one should not use force (or 'self-help') before taking a dispute to court, and provides penalties for violating this rule. It then provides procedural rules for deciding the dispute over status or ownership and for enforcing the decision. Finally, it addresses several special situations, including two exemptions to the prohibition of seizure.

The decision to put this section first on the wall must mark its importance. The subject is not directly related to the central concerns of the Code (family, property, inheritance), but considerations of ownership (and status) have relevance for many different parts of the Code, and the procedures set forth in this section provide a kind of model that could be used in many different sorts of cases. Thus, although the opening sentence, strictly speaking, prohibits self-help by means of force only in cases of disputed ownership of persons, it may have been intended to apply implicitly to all disputes at Gortyn (with the exceptions noted in 1.56–2.2). A general prohibition of this sort would also be implicit in the act of writing such an extensive piece of legislation, which in itself would convey the message that members of the community were expected to submit their disputes to the judicial process that is elaborated in these laws rather than resorting to self-help.

2 The simple duality free/slave (*eleutheros/doulos*) is fundamental at Gortyn and this entire section is structured in these terms. Two more status categories will be introduced in 2.2–7, *woikeus* ('serf') and *apetairos* (lit. 'out of the *hetaireia*'). The *apetairos* is commonly agreed to be free, though he is contrasted with the *eleutheros* in 2.2–5 (see further on 2.5). Some critics think the *woikeus* was a descendant of the native inhabitants who remained on the land in a servile status, rather like the Spartan helots, and who formed a status category distinct from *doloi* (*douloi*), who were chattel slaves (cf. Maffi 2003a: 175–6), but there is no good evidence for this. Some, however, think *woikeus* is essentially synonymous with *dolos*. The rules in this section imply that the only status that would be disputed, and thus the only status that was legally significant, was *eleutheros* or *dolos*, though this does not mean *dolos* and *woikeus* are synonymous. For further discussion, see Introd. 5A7; Gagarin 2010a.

2–3 Rosén 1982 argues that the first sentence should be understood 'whoever is going to contend *against* a free person or a slave is not to seize him before trial'. For criticism of Rosén's views, see Maffi 1983: 3–99 (also Maffi 1997c: 17–20), and Gagarin 1988, 1995. Rosén's argument is marred by his tendency to assimilate Gortynian procedures to those known from Athens. Van Effenterre at first (1983) accepted Rosén's view but he later returned to the traditional view (VER II.6, p. 47). For an Athenian case where a person's status as free or slave is disputed, see Lysias 23.9–11.

4 'Let (the judge) rule': the Code maintains a consistent distinction between a ruling prescribed by law (*dikadden*, or here *katadikadden*) and a decision arrived at by the judge himself (*krinen*), where he is required to swear an oath before deciding. *Katadikadden* (1.4, 1.8, 1.35–6) differs from the simple verb *dikadden* in that it is always used of a ruling that states a punishment specified by law. See below 11.26–31 with notes; Introd. 10D1; Gagarin 2010b.

4–6 The fines specified here are twice as much for a free person as for a slave, and the same proportion (with some variations) is generally found elsewhere in the Code.

8–10 A stater is worth two drachmas.

11–12 'The judge is to swear an oath and decide': according to the rule in 11.26–31 below, this is the default method of judging, to be used whenever the law does not specify in writing that the judge must rule in a certain way.

14 'Unless a witness should testify' implies that if there is a witness, the judge should rule according to the witness (as in 1.18–24 below). The witness would probably testify that he saw the accused seize the person, though he might testify that the person allegedly seized came of his own volition. This kind of 'accidental'

witness, who just happens to have knowledge of the case, should be distinguished from a 'formal' witness, who is present by request at a significant event and can later testify to that event in court. The law usually attaches certain requirements to formal witnesses, that they must be a certain number, age, or status (or some combination of these), but this is not so for accidental witnesses. See further Introd. 10D3; Gagarin 1989, 2010b.

15–49 This long section provides for the trial of the original dispute over ownership (15–24), specifies a course of action if the current possessor loses the case (24–39), and adds an exemption from punishment for one year if the slave in question takes refuge in a temple (39–49).

15–24 Like others before him, Maffi 1997c: 21–4 observes similarities between the procedure in these lines and the Athenian *diadikasia*, a special procedure used primarily in inheritance disputes where there are several claimants, rather than a plaintiff and defendant. Koerner argues that the process in 15–18 is a *diadikasia* but that in 18–24 is delictual. But there is no indication in any of the laws at Gortyn that the Gortynians recognized such a distinction, and the procedural terminology used here is exactly the same as that used elsewhere in the Code for delictual disputes between two parties; see Thür 2003: 85–91, and the further remarks in Maffi 2011.

15–18 'Whichever ones' (for the reading, see above). Since *apoponen* refers to the testimony of witnesses (n. ad 1.14), 'whichever ones' must mean 'whichever witnesses'. The law thus asserts the important principle that in a dispute over whether someone is free or slave, the law favors free status. A simple assertion of free status is not sufficient, however; witnesses must also testify to this point and they may not be automatically decisive (see next note). Athenian law seems to have followed the same principle, judging from Lysias 23.9–11. Some editors (VER, K) introduce the idea of an oath here and liken this case to those where someone is *orkioteros*, but as Martini observes (1999: 388 with n. 23), there is no mention (or even hint) of an oath here.

16 'Are to prevail': lit. 'are to be stronger'. Most editors (G, W, K, VER) understand *kartonans* to mean that these witnesses will prevail—i.e. will win the case—(though G translates 'potiores'). But if this was the legislator's intent, he could easily have made this clear by writing, e.g. 'if one party contends that he is free and a witness testifies, the judge is to rule according to the witness'; or 'the party contending that he is free is to win the case, if a witness testifies'. The plural 'witnesses', moreover, implies that there might be several witnesses on each side, in which case the law would have to specify whether a single witness declaring the person free would prevail over several witnesses on the other side, or whether an equal or greater number was needed (so Maffi 1983: 79). It seems likely, therefore, that the expression means that the testimony of any witness testifying that the person is

free, should be given more weight than opposing testimony but would not automatically prevail (see Gagarin 1989: 39–40).

23 'Or for neither': i.e. there is no witness for either side.

24–35 The daily fines for non-compliance are referred to as 'astreintes' in French law. Pelloso 2009–10: 101 compares 'contempt of court' in common law; his long article reviews much of the earlier scholarship on this section.

35–8 *Ta tritra* (37) also occurs in **G43Ab**9–10, where we argue that it most likely means 'triple'. The same is true here: most editors (see above), perhaps influenced by the addition of 'or less', think the fine is reduced to one-third (or perhaps two-thirds) after a year; but this would encourage someone who was delinquent not to pay the fine until a year had passed. In view of the evident difficulty so many cities faced in enforcing verdicts at this time, this seems unlikely. Thus, *ta tritra* more likely means that the fines are tripled, but the recipient may, if he wishes, accept less than this.

39–49 In cases where a slave who is to be returned to the true owner takes refuge in a temple, the law balances the interest of the (illegitimate) possessor, who for a year is not liable for the slave's act as long as he follows proper procedure, and the true owner's legitimate claim to have his slave or receive adequate compensation. But if the slave is still not returned to the owner after a year, then he must be paid 'the simple values' (see below). Cf. the rule in **G41**.4.6–10, where the fugitive serf who takes refuge in a temple does not have to be returned within a year.

41–2 The requirement that formal witnesses (see above on 1.14) must be two in number, free, and adult (*dromeus*) is imposed in two other laws concerning family property (**G72**.3.17–24, 5.53–4). In cases where there is no such restriction, it is possible that women, children, and even perhaps those who were not free could testify (so Maffi 2003a: 163–7, though he rejects the possibility of slave witnesses).

45–6 'What is written' is the common way of cross-referencing at Gortyn in the fifth century. Rarely is there any explicit indication where these other rules are written, but in many cases (as here) the reference is easy to determine. Here 'what is written' clearly refers to the fine for not returning a slave in 1.27–35. The provisions in 39–46 allow someone to avoid a fine if the slave has taken refuge in a temple, but he must demonstrate this.

46–9 The relation of this sentence to what precedes is complex: 24–39 require the losing party in a suit to return a slave or release a free person and sets fines for not doing so, fines that triple after one year; 39–46 exempt the losing party in case the slave in question takes refuge in a temple, provided this asylum is properly demonstrated; 46–9 then reveal that this exemption only lasts for one year; after that, if the slave is not returned, the losing party must pay 'the simple fines'. The plural here designates the initial fine of ten staters plus the drachma per day specified in 1.32–4, and the fines are simple, not triple (as in 35–8 after a year-long delay) because the year-long delay is allowed when the slave cannot be returned because he has taken refuge in a temple.

49–2.2 The *vac.* in 49 marks the beginning of the last part of this section, which contains three provisions addressing special situations: where a disputed person dies during the trial (49–51), where one of the litigants is *kosmos* (51–5), and where seizure may be made with impunity (1.56–2.2).

49–51 The meaning of this highly elliptical provision depends on who is the unexpressed subject of 'he dies'. We agree with most editors (including G, K, VER) in understanding the clause as a continuation of 39–49, with the subject being the slave who is the subject of the dispute. W argues that the subject is rather 'the defeated party', and that his heirs would then pay the simple fine, without any additional fines for delay; but it goes without saying that the heirs are responsible for the debts of the deceased and would take the place of a litigant who died during the trial.

51–5 As in **G41**.4.10–14, the law sensibly protects a *kosmos* from becoming involved in litigation over a private matter while he is *kosmos*; but once his term has ended, any fines he must pay or receive are calculated retroactively from the time of the offense.[412]

52–3 'Or another (seizes someone) belonging to a *kosmos*' (lit. 'of a *kosmos*'). Though elliptical, the Greek is clear (see note above). The provision applies to any suit involving illegal seizure in which a *kosmos* is either plaintiff or defendant (so G, K, VER, and most others). Maffi 1983: 79–80 argues that this interpretation would result in an imbalance between the first alternative, which would apply to a *kosmos* who seizes either a free person or someone else's slave, whereas the second would apply only to the seizure of the slave of a *kosmos* (seizing a free person 'of a *kosmos*' makes no sense). He therefore understands the expression to mean 'or another on behalf of a *kosmos*' (so too Bücheler–Zitelmann; Kohler–Ziebarth). But since the purpose of the provision is evidently to free a *kosmos* from involvement in a legal affair while he is *kosmos*, then the imbalance is irrelevant, since the same reasoning would not hold for cases involving someone acting on behalf of a *kosmos*. Maffi later (2003b: 37–41) adds a second argument, that the majority interpretation would leave the *kosmos* with less protection than an ordinary citizen if someone seized a slave of his. But we must assume that the first procedure stipulated in this section—that someone who seizes another before trial must immediately give him up—is still in effect (if it is not, then Maffi's interpretation

[412] In Clinton v. Jones, 520 U.S. 681 (1997), the U.S. Supreme Court decided to allow a civil suit to be brought against then President Clinton by Paula Jones, following the principle that a sitting President has no immunity from civil suits against him for acts committed before taking office and unrelated to the office. The Court might have done better to follow the Gortynian example, since the ensuing impeachment significantly distracted the President and Congress from the nation's more pressing needs.

would give the *kosmos* free rein to seize other people's slaves and keep them during his term of office); it is only the second procedure—the determination of whose slave it is—that would be delayed until after the *kosmos*'s term in office. Maffi's view is rejected by Thür (2003: 89, with n. 110) and Chaniotis (*SEG* 53.941).

56–2.2 Two exceptions to the prohibition on seizure are when the seized person has lost a judgment (in any case, not just a case of illegal seizure—Maffi 1983: 81–3) or he is a free person pledged into temporary servitude (not a slave, who would have a permanent master). The first exception probably allows seizure only by the person who won the judgment and only in case the losing party does not fulfill the terms of the judgment; he would probably be seized and held for ransom until he pays, though Kristensen 2004: 76 suggests that he would become a *katakeimenos*. The second exception probably allows only the person to whom the seized person is pledged to seize him.

56–2.1 For the *katakeimenos*—lit. 'one who has put himself (or has been put) under the control of another'—see **G41**.5–6 with notes.

2.2–45—SEXUAL OFFENSES (VER II.81, K 164)

This section addresses four kinds of sexual offenses ranging from rape to adultery. This is the only part of the Code that contains a gradation of successive offenses and their punishments of the sort that are common in many premodern law codes.

αἴ κα τὸν ἐλεύθερον ἒ τὰν ἐλευθέραν κάρτει οἴπει, ἑκατὸν στατε̂ρανς καταστασεῖ· αἰ δέ κ' ἀπεταίρο, δέκα· αἰ δέ κ' ὀ δôλος τὸν ἐλεύθερον ἒ τὰν ἐλευθέραν, διπλεῖ καταστασεῖ· αἰ δέ κ' ἐλεύθερος Ϝοικέα ἒ Ϝοικέαν, πέντε δαρκνάνς· αἰ δέ κα Ϝοικεὺς Ϝοικέα ἒ Ϝοικέαν, π[έν]τε στατε̂ρανς. vac. *ἐνδοθιδίαν δόλαν αἰ κάρτει δαμάσαιτο, δύο στατε̂ρανς καταστασεῖ· αἰ δέ κα δεδαμν[α]μέναν, πεδ' ἀμέραν, [ὀ]δελόν, αἰ δέ κ' ἐν νυττί, δύ' ὀδελόνς· ὀρκιοτέραν δ' ἔμεν τὰν δόλαν.* vac. *αἴ κα τὰν ἐλευθέραν ἐπιπερε̂ται οἴπεν ἀκεύοντος καδεστâ, δέκα στατε̂ρανς καταστασεῖ αἰ ἀποπονίοι μαῖτυς.* vac. *αἴ κα τὰν ἐλευθέραν μοικίον αἰλεθε̂ι ἐν πατρὸς ἒ ἐν ἀδελπιô ἒ ἐν τô ἀνδρός, ἑκατὸν στατε̂ρανς καταστασεῖ· αἰ δέ κ' ἐ-*

If someone rapes a free man or woman, he will pay a hundred staters. If (someone rapes) an *apetairos*, (he will pay) ten. If a slave (rapes) a free man or woman, he will pay double. If a free man (rapes) a male or female serf, (he will pay) five drachmas. And if a serf (rapes) a male or female serf, five staters. *vac.* If someone should subdue by force a household slave woman, he will pay two staters; but if she has already had intercourse, (he will pay) one obol during the day, but if at night, two obols. And the slave woman is to be the one who swears. *vac.* If someone attempts to have intercourse with a free woman while a relative is watching over her, he will pay ten staters, if a witness should testify. *vac.* If someone is caught committing adultery with a free woman in her father's or brother's or husband's house, he will pay a hundred ν ἄλο, πεντέκοντα· αἰ δέ κα τὰν τô ἀπεταίρο, δέκα· αἰ δέ κ' ὁ δôλος τὰν ἐλευθέραν, διπλεῖ καταστασεῖ· *vac.* αἰ δέ κα δôλος δόλο, πέντε. προϝειπάτο δὲ ἀντὶ μαιτύρον τριôν τοῖς καδεσταῖς τô ἐναιλεθέντος ἀλλύεθθαι ἐν ταῖς πέντ' ἀμέραις· *vac.* τô δὲ δόλο τôι πάσται ἀντὶ μαιτύρον δυôν. *vac.* αἰ δέ κα μὲ ἀλλύσεται, ἐπὶ τοῖς ἑλόνσι ἔμεν κρêθθαι ὄπαι κα λείοντι. *vac.* αἰ δέ κα πονêι δολόσαθθαι, ὀμόσαι τὸν ἑλόντα τô πεντεκονταστατέρο καὶ πλίονος πέντον αὐτὸν ϝὶν αὐτôι ϝέκαστον ἐπαριόμενον, τô δ' ἀπεταίρο τρίτον ạὐτὸν, τô δὲ ϝοικέος τὸν πάσταν ἄτερον αὐτὸν μοικίοντ' ἑλέν, δολόσαθθαι δὲ μέ. *vac.*

staters. And if in someone else's house, fifty. And if (he is caught committing adultery) with the woman of an *apetairos*, (he will pay) ten. And if a slave with a free woman, (he will pay) double. *vac.* And if a slave with a slave's (woman), five (staters). Let (the captor) declare before three witnesses to the relatives of the one who is caught that he is to be ransomed within five days; *vac.* and to the master of a slave before two witnesses; *vac.* and if he is not ransomed, he is to be in the hands of his captors to be treated as they wish. *vac.* But if he affirms that he was tricked, the captor is to swear, in a case of fifty staters or more, with four others, each calling down curses upon himself, and for an *apetairos* with two others, and for a serf the master and one other (are to swear) that he took him in adultery, not by trickery. *vac.*

---

5 ἀπεταίρο: '[someone] of an *apetairos*'; so G, K and others. For this elliptical use of the genitive, see above on 1.52–3, and below note on 24–5. Because in all the other provisions on rape (2–10) both male and female victims are explicitly mentioned, the ellipsis probably does not restrict the class of victims to dependents (i.e. women and children) but includes adult male *apetairoi*. W and VER understand *apetairo* as a genitive of connection ('as regards'—Smyth 1956: §1381, 'of the matter or person involved'—Willetts), which is possible here, but not in 1.52–3 (*kosmiontos*) or 2.27 (*dolo*).

14–15 νυττί: Att. νυκτί (Dialect 9).

15 ὀρκιοτέραν: the original function of the ending -τερος was to mark opposition, not comparison. Sommerstein 2013: 65 n. 22 compares Homeric θηλυτέρη, which means not 'more female' but 'female' as opposed to male (see Chantraine 1948: 257, with further examples). Thus ὀρκιότερος does not mean that both parties swear oaths but the oath of one carries more weight than the oath of the other (so Bile 287); rather, the person who is ὀρκιότερος is allowed to swear and his or her oath will be decisive.

17–18 ἐπιπερêται οἶπεν ἀκεύοντος καδεστâ: G, W, VER, et al. correctly understand ἐπιπερêται as Att. ἐπιπειρâται ('attempt'); ἀκεύοντος probably means 'watching over' (in line with the Hesychian gloss ἀκεύει· τηρεῖ). Maffi 1984–5 reads ἐπιπέρεται and takes this as Att. ἐπιφέρηται ('respond') and ἀκεύοντος as Att. ἀκούοντος ('listening to'), meaning 'if someone responds (in court) that he had intercourse when a relative listened (i.e. agreed)'—i.e. the seducer claims he is acting with the complicity of the woman's relatives. Among the many obstacles to this interpretation is the fact that it is highly doubtful that *epipheromai* in the middle can mean 'respond', let alone 'respond in court', for which several other terms are consistently used in the Code, including compounds of *molen* (see further Gagarin 1989: 41–3, esp. n. 26; Maffi 1997a: 24–9 and Maffi p.c.). *Epipherō* (active) is sometimes used of presenting something in court (Maffi p.c.), but always with a direct object. Link 2004b proposes that the genitive absolute *ἀκεύοντος καδεστᾶ* be understood as the subject: 'if someone attempts to coerce a free woman while he, as her *kadestas* is protecting her' (p. 175); but this use of the genitive absolute is impossible.

21 *αἰλεθεῖ* = Attic *αἱρηθῇ* (subj.); see Dialect 30.

24–5 *τὰν τô ἀπεταίρο*: Bile (2012: 43 n. 133) suggests that this periphrasis results from the absence of a feminine form of *apetairos* (a compound noun). But cf. *δόλο*, '[a woman] of a slave' in 27 and see above on *ἀπεταίρο* (5).

30–1 *ἀλλύεθθαι* = *ἀναλύεσθαι* (also in **G72**.2.34, 6.49–50, 10.26–7); see Dialect 12.

40 *Ϝὶν αὐτôι*: 'himself' (reflexive); see Dialect 17.

These provisions establish fines for specific instances of rape and adultery. Many potential cases are not mentioned, such as the rape of an *apetairos* by a slave (or vice versa). Presumably the judge used the fines that are specified as a guide for cases that are not mentioned. That fines were more severe in general for offenses against a free person than for offenses against a slave is implied by **G41**.6.4–8

2–10 The provisions on rape all explicitly (or implicitly in the case of the *apetairos*) include male as well as female victims. The victims of the other sorts of violations are only female.

2–7 In the first two provisions, where the object of rape is first a free person and then an *apetairos*, we must understand the unexpressed subject of *kartei oipei* to be a free person. When the subject changes to a *dolos* in 5–7, it is expressed.

2 For the *eleutheros*, see above on 1.2. The four categories in this section (*eleutheros*, *apetairos*, *woikeus*, *dolos*) do not invalidate the basic duality of free/slave (*eleutheros*/*doulos*) established there.

Normally (e.g. in col. 1), the masculine *eleutheros* would comprehend both males and females, but sometimes (not surprisingly in connection with sexual offenses, but in other cases too) each gender is specified individually.

3 *Kartei oipen* = 'to have intercourse by force'. The difference between this and *kartei damazen* ('subdue by force') in 11–16 may be that the latter refers to the owner who pressures a slave to have intercourse, though he does not necessarily use physical force. Davies (1996: 40) considers it a fault that the difference between these acts is not defined, but like much else in the Code, the specific application of the two expressions was probably clear to readers at the time even if it is obscure to us. Expressions relating to sexual conduct are particularly likely to develop localized (and often euphemistic, as here) variants.

5 An *apetairos* (Attic *aphetairos*) is literally a person apart from a *hetaireia*, a civic group open to most (but apparently not all) free male Gortynians (see further on 10.38; Introd. 6A). In the classical period *apetairos* occurs only in this section of

the Code and in **G84**.6 (without context). An *apetairos* is probably a free person, since in 27–45 below there are references to a master for a *dolos* and a *woikeus* but not for an *apetairos*. He is evidently not a full citizen (*poliatas*), but since we know next to nothing about the rights or obligations of citizens at Gortyn, this tells us little. Willetts 1967: 12–13 reviews various theories concerning who might have belonged to this class (for one suggestion, see below on 5.27).

5–16 The laws regulating crimes against serfs and slaves raise many difficult questions: Do they apply to all such offenses against a slave or a serf, or do certain offenses not count, such as those by the slave's or serf's master or by slaves or serfs belonging to the same master? Does the master or the slave/serf prosecute or defend the case? Who pays the fine and who receives it? For a full discussion, see Gagarin 2010a. Here we note only that as these statutes are written, they seem to imply that the slave/serf is the offender or the victim in each case.

7 'Double' is understood by all commentators to mean double the fine of a free person raping a free person, or two hundred staters; but Brixhe (cited by Bile p.c.) takes it as meaning double the fine mentioned in the immediately preceding clause, or twenty staters. On the one hand, two hundred staters might be more than a slave could be expected to pay or than a master should have to pay for an offense committed by his slave, though we do not know whether the slave or his master would be expected to pay these fines; on the other hand, one might expect a slave to be punished more severely than a free man for such a crime. Syntactically, either interpretation is possible. But because a *woikeus* pays double what a free man pays for the rape of a *woikeus* (2.7–10), the traditional view is probably correct.

8 The 'serf' (*woikeus*) is clearly not a free person, since he has a master, but there is much debate about just what this category was and what difference, if any, there was between a *dolos* and a *woikeus* (cf. on 1.2 above). In this section, in particular, the terms appear to be legally interchangeable, but that would not mean they are synonyms. See further Introd. 5A7 and Gagarin 2010a.

11–16 It is quite remarkable that so much space (7 of the 14 lines about rape) is devoted to the rape of a household slave woman (*endothidian*), though we must note that the fine for a virgin victim (two staters = four drachmas) is less than for the rape of a male or female *woikeus* (or presumably an ordinary *dolos* of either sex). Domestic female servants, whether slave or free, are commonly subject to sexual advances on the part of their masters, but rarely are they given special protection, as here. If the provision was intended to apply to the woman's master, it would be truly extraordinary, but it seems more likely that it was intended to apply only to others, and that the slave woman was protected so that her master could exercise his right to use her as he wished, whether that right was established in law or in custom. We may perhaps see here a Gortynian version of the *droit de seigneur*.

11–12 For *kartei damasaito*, lit. 'subdue by force', see on 3 above.

15 *Orkioteros* ('the one who swears') occurs twice more in the Code (3.49–50, 4.6–7) and also in **G41**.2.12, **G42**B5, and **G45**B3–4. In the first three of these, witnesses and litigants together are allowed to swear. This may suggest that all witnesses may have sworn oaths. See Introd. 10D2, 10D3, and the discussion in Gagarin 2010b. The household slave woman is probably allowed to swear that she was a virgin before being raped (the question of whether she was raped would still have to be decided in court). The other facts she might swear to are whether or not she was raped and whether it was day or night; but it is hard to see why a slave woman would be allowed to swear decisively that she was raped when none of the other victims of sexual assault are given a similar opportunity, and the issue of night or day is likely to have been evident, not a matter of dispute. In any case, it is striking that a slave woman is given preference over her free assailant in swearing an oath.

16–20 It is not clear why attempted seduction is included in this group of offenses. Attempted acts are only rarely regulated in Greek law (or in any legal system). The only example at Athens might be the law against 'intentional wounding', if this in fact means 'wounding with intent to kill', i.e. attempted homicide; but even in this case an actual offense (wounding) must have occurred. Because the crime is only attempted intercourse, the fine is only one tenth as much as for adultery or rape. The woman in question is probably unmarried; it is possible that she is an 'heiress' and thus in need of special protection (see Gagarin 1989: 41–3; also Bile 2012: 23), but the law does not specify this. The requirement that a witness testify suggests that false accusations of attempted seduction may have been a concern.

17–18 'While a relative is watching over her': this seems to suggest that any free woman being visited by a male non-relative would have a chaperone, but this practice may have been common only with unmarried women. Some scholars maintain that an institution of guardianship equivalent to the Athenian *kyrieia*, in which virtually every woman has a *kyrios* ('guardian') who handles her affairs, also existed at Gortyn, but neither here nor anywhere else at Gortyn do we find the language of guardianship; see further Gagarin 2008b and Introd. 5B.

18 *kadesta*: Bile 333–4 and others have argued that the *epiballontes* (see on 5.22–5) are the paternal relatives, and that *kadestai* are therefore maternal relatives. Sealey (1994: 58) argues, more plausibly in our view, that the two groups are 'relatives regarded from different aspects': *epiballontes* are relatives with a claim to something by virtue of being relatives, whereas *kadestai* have obligations with respect to their relatives. See further Introd. 5C3. *Kadestai* are also mentioned in **G72**.3.50–1, 7.44, 8.14 below and **G46**B13–14.

20–44 The laws on adultery at Gortyn, unlike those of most other ancient societies (including Athens), do not punish a woman caught in adultery. Lacey (1968: 215, followed by Bile 2012: 44, 51) suggests that the placement of the section on divorce immediately after the laws on adultery may indicate that adultery was the primary reason for divorce, and thus that divorce would be the expected response to adultery.

20–4 The inclusion of the father's or brother's house together with the husband's indicates that 'adultery' here includes intercourse with an unmarried daughter or sister, not just with a married woman, but it is doubtful whether this sheds light on the much debated nature of *moicheia* in Athens (see Cantarella 2005: 76–7).

27–8 The fact that a slave is fined for committing adultery with '(the woman) of a slave' implies that slaves could marry and such marriages had some of the same protections as free marriages. See further Gagarin 2010a.

28–36 Although there is much we don't know about the Athenian laws on adultery, the normal treatment of adulterers at Athens appears to have been similar: they could be held for ransom (though the ransom amount may have been negotiated rather than specified by law, as here) or treated however their captor wished short of death.

34–5 'In the hands of': see on 4.37, and for temporary servitude 6.49–51.

36–45 On the possibility of entrapment in Athenian law, cf. Dem. 59.64–6; Lysias 1.37–42.

37 'Is to swear'. This is one of four decisive oaths in the Code (the others are at 3.5–9, 9.38–9, 9.54; cf. **G42**B5; **G47**.16–26). By swearing, the accused will clear himself of the charge of entrapment; if he does not swear, he will in effect admit the charge. See further Gagarin 2010b.

2.45–3.16—DIVORCE (VER II.30, K 165–6)

This section addresses the division of property between spouses in a divorce; additional rules concerning the woman's oath are given in 11.46–55. Note also the rules for the divorce of serf couples (3.40–4), and for children born after a divorce (3.44–4.17). Some of the issues in this section are treated more fully in Gagarin 2008b.

K treats this passage as three separate texts: 2.45–3.1 (no. 165), 3.1–9, and 3.9–16 (both no. 166).

*αἴ κ᾽ ἀνὲρ [κ]ạὶ γυ̣-
νὰ διακρ[ί]νον[τ]αι, τὰ Ϝὰ α-
ὐτᾶς ἔκεν, ἄτι ἔκονσ᾽ ε̂̓ιε π-
ὰρ τὸν ἄνδρα, καὶ τô καρπô τ-
ὰνν ἐμίναν, αἴ κ᾽ ε̂̓ι ἐς τôν Ϝô-
ν αὐτᾶς κρεμάτον, κο̂̓τι
κ̣᾽ ἐνυπά̣νει τὰν [ἐμίνα]ν ἄτι
κ᾽ ε̂̓ι, καὶ πέντε στατε̂ρανς αἴ κ᾽ ὀ ἀ-
νὲρ αἴτιος ε̂̓ι τᾶς κ̣ε̣[ρ]εύσι-*

If a husband and wife are divorced, she is to have her own things, whatever she had when she came to her husband, and half of the produce, if there is any from her own property, and half of what she has woven, whatever it is, and five staters if the husband is responsible for the separation; but if the husband affirms that

ος· α[ἰ] δ̣ὲ πονίοι ὀ ἀ̣ν̣ὲρ [αἴτι]-
[ος μὲ ἔ]μεν, τὸν δικαστὰν
Col. 3
ὀμνύντα κρίνεν. αἰ δέ τι ἄλλ-
ο πέροι τô ἀνδρός, πέντε στ-
ατêρανς καταστασεῖ κὄτι
κα πέρει αὐτόν, κὄτι κα παρ-
έλει ἀποδότο αὐτόν. ὂν δέ κ'
ἐκσαννέσεται, δικάκσαι τ-
ὰν γυναῖκ' ἀπομόσαι τὰν Ἄρ-
τεμιν πὰρ Ἀμυκλαῖον πὰρ τὰν
Τοκσίαν. ὄτι δέ τίς κ' ἀπομο-
σάνσαι παρέλει, πέντε στατ-
êρανς καταστασεῖ καὶ τὸ κρ-
έος αὐτόν. vac. *αἰ δέ κ' ἀλλόττρι-*
ος συνεσάδδει, δέκα στ[ατ]ê-
ρανς καταστασεῖ, τô δὲ κρέ-
ιος διπλεῖ ὄτι κ' ὀ δικαστὰς
ὀμόσει συνεσσάκσαι. vac

he is not responsible, the judge (**Col. 3**) is to swear an oath and decide. But if she should take away something else of her husband's, she will pay five staters and (return) the object that she carries away, and let her give back whatever she has stolen. But with regard to things she denies, (the judge) is to rule that the woman is to take an oath of denial by Artemis, before (the statue of) the Archeress at Amyklaion. And whatever anyone may steal from her after she has sworn an oath of denial, he will pay five staters and the thing itself. *vac.* And if some other person helps her remove (something), he will pay ten staters and twice the value of whatever the judge swears he helped remove. *vac.*

46–7 *διακρίνονται*: the verb only occurs here in archaic and classical Crete. It apparently has the same meaning as the simple verb *κρίνεται* (3.41, 11.46). The form here is probably middle, 'separate themselves from one another' (cf. *κριθêι* in 3.41), perhaps because it includes the possibility of separation by death (Bile p.c.).

46 *τὰ Ϝὰ αὐτᾶς*: the reflexive pronoun (also *τôν Ϝôν αὐτᾶς κρεμάτον*, 49–50); see Dialect 17.

47 *ἄτι*: Att. *ἄτινα* (see Dialect 18).

ἐ̂ιε: imperfect of *εἶμι*.

49 *ἐμίναν*: Att. *ἥμισυ*; see Dialect 32.

53–4 *κερεύσιος*: *χηρεύω* and related words normally refer to widowhood, but here it must refer to divorce, as also in 3.44–4.17 below.

3.2–5 *πέροι* (*φέροι*) indicates that the issue here is movable items. The difference between this and *παρέλει* (*παραιρέω*) in 4–5 is not clear. Maffi 1988 takes *κρέος* in 11–12 to be a debt (but see our note on 11–12): *παρέλει* in 10 would then designate the act of removing a debt. But it is not clear what this might mean or how it might be accomplished. W, K and others more plausibly take *παρέλει* as an act of secretly 'filching' something before or during the divorce, as opposed to openly carrying off something. See also Brixhe 1999: 79 n. 14.

6 *ἐκσαννέσεται*: see on **G41**.3.15–16.

11–12 *τὸ κρέος αὐτόν*: we follow most editors (but see Maffi 1988) in translating 'the thing itself', but since *kreos* may also mean 'value' (as in 14–15), the implication is probably that either the object itself can be returned or something of equal value. Contrast *auton*, 'the thing', in 3.4 and 5.

13 *συνεσάδδει* (and 16 *συνεσσάκσαι*) are compounds of *σάττω* ('pack, provide') and mean 'remove together with (someone)'.

16 Because there is a space of about half a letter at the end of this line, recent editors (G, W, VER, K) mark a *vac*. But the space at the end of, e.g., 3.14, where no gap is intended, is just as large.

This section addresses the division of the property in a divorce. It says nothing about the grounds for divorce, but it appears that divorce could be initiated by either spouse. The Code also says nothing about children in a divorce, probably because they automatically remained with their father, though he may have been able to relinquish his right to them, as when a child is born after the divorce (3.44–52). The law also says nothing about the husband's property, but presumably he kept it. And in view of the Code's concern for a woman's property against misuse by her male relatives (6.9–31), we may probably assume that a woman was able to bring action against her husband if he took her property in a divorce.

The rules here imply that upon marriage a woman normally moved to her husband's house, bringing with her her own property, which she had either received as inheritance or as a gift from her father. Many scholars speak of this property as a dowry, but this term is never used at Gortyn. Instead, a father's gift is treated like her share of the inheritance (see on 4.48–5.1). and a husband's or son's gift (see 10.14–17, 12.1–5) obviously cannot be a dowry but must become the woman's own property. The property is fully hers, so that in a divorce, she gets to keep it.

Potential litigation is envisioned at three points: whether the husband is to blame for the divorce (2.54–3.1); whether a woman took her husband's property (3.5–9); and what is the value of anything a third party helps the woman remove (3.12–16); presumably one could also contest whether the third party did in fact help her. In the first two instances, at least, the dispute must be between the husband and wife, and these two must have been the opposing litigants in court. This would be impossible in a system in which (as in Athens) a woman had to be represented in court by a male guardian (*kyrios*). The fact that the woman herself swears an oath (3.5–9) also shows conclusively that Gortynian women could participate fully in litigation.

45–52 The law first establishes precisely what property the wife can keep; by implication, everything else is to go to the husband. The wording makes clear that she possesses her own property, and the fact that her property may yield produce (*karpos*) indicates that some of it may be land (but see below on 48–50).

47 The simple verb *eken* ('have') always designates the ownership of property in what appears to be a fairly strong sense including possession and perhaps management (Gagarin 2008b: 7); but in 1.24–5 *o ekon* is an owner whose ownership has been rejected by the court.

48–50 The natural sense of *karpos* is 'produce, fruit of the land'; those who deny that women could own land must assume a more general meaning such as 'profit'

(Brixhe 1999: 101–2, relying on a third-century BCE text). But *karpos* must have its normal meaning 'produce' in 5.39–40, and there is no good reason to deny this sense here or to deny that women could own land at Gortyn, although perhaps landownership among women was not common (note 'if there is any' in 49). See Maffi 1997b: 441.

50 *Kremata* ('things, property') here must include land, and the word may in fact normally designate real property, which was primarily land, as opposed to movable property (*epipolaia kremata*, 5.41), though there are some passages where it almost certainly includes both real and personal property (see esp. on 4.37–8, 12.2; Introd. 7A).

52–3.1 Responsibility for a divorce might often be disputed, and in most cases the judge must have had to decide simply on the basis of each party's account.

1–9 It is clear from this passage that any litigation would have been between the husband and his wife; she would not, as in Athens, need the help of a male relative.

5–9 Disputes might concern whether the wife took something or whether it was hers. It is remarkable that the wife alone is allowed to swear the decisive oath; presumably if she swore the oath, she kept what she had taken, but if she refused to swear, she had to return it to her husband and pay a fine of five staters. For other decisive oaths at Gortyn, see on 2.37 above, and for additional procedural rules concerning the woman's oath, see below 11.46–55.

7–8 For Amyklaion, see Introd. 2C. A temple of Artemis was located near the coast west of Gortyn, near modern-day Kalamaki (Shaw 2006: 134–5). If this is the Amyklaion referred to here, then a woman would have had to travel *c.*20 km. in order to swear this oath, rather a long way for what may have been a relatively small amount of property. This may have been intended to ensure that she would not swear unless the property was truly hers.

15–16 It is unusual for the judge to swear to the amount that has been removed. Normally the law would simply say, 'twice the value of whatever he helped remove'.

3.17–40—DISPOSITION OF PROPERTY AFTER THE DEATH OF A SPOUSE (VER II.32–3, K 167)

This section is not concerned with the regular process of inheritance (see 4.23–6.2 below) but only with the surviving spouse's interest in the deceased spouse's property.

VER treat 3.17–37 (II.32) separately from 3.37–40 (II.33).

αἰ ἀνὲρ ἀποθάνοι τέκνα κατ- αλιπόν, αἴ κα λε̂ι ἀ γυνά, τὰ Ϝὰ αὐτᾶς ἔκονσαν ὀπυίεθθα- ι κἄτι κ' ὀ ἀνὲδ δο̂ι κατὰ τὰ ἐγ- ραμμένα ἀντὶ μαιτύρον τρ-	If a man should die leaving children, if his wife wishes, she is to marry, keeping her own things and whatever her husband gives her according to what is written in the presence of three adult free witnesses;

ιôν δρομέον ἐλευθέρον· αἰ
δέ τι τôν τέκνον πέροι, ἔνδι-
κον ἔμεν. *vac.* αἰ δέ κα ἄτεκνον
καταλίπει, τά τε Fὰ αὐτâς ἔκε-
ν κὄτι κ' ẹ̄[νυ]πάνẹι [τ]ạ̀ν ἐμίν-
αν καὶ̣ [τ]ô καρπ[ô] ṭô ἔνδ[ο]θεν π-
εδὰ τôν ἐπιβαλλόντ[ον] μοῖρα-
ν λακὲṇ καἴ τί κ' ὀ ἀνὲδ δôι ậι ἔγ-
ρατται· αἰ δέ τι ἄλλο πέροι, ἔν-
δικον ἔμεν. *vac.* αἰ δὲ γυνὰ ἄτεκ-
νος ἀποθάνοι, *vac.* τά τε Fὰ
αὐτâς τοῖς ἐπιβάλλονσι ἀπ-
οδόμεν κὄτι ἐνύπανε τὰν ἐ-
μίναν καὶ τô καρπô, αἴ κ' ἐ̂ι, ἐς
τôν Fôν αὐτâς, τὰν ἐμίνα-
ν. κόμιστρα αἴ κα λε̂ι δόμεν
ἀνὲρ ἐ̂ γυνά, ἐ̂ Fε̂μα ἐ̂ δυόδεκ-
α στατε̂ρανς ἐ̂ δυόδεκα στατ-
έρον κρέος, πλίον δὲ μέ. *vac.*

but if she should take away anything of the children's, it is a matter for trial. *vac.* If he leaves her childless, she is to have her own things, and half of whatever she has woven, and she is to get a share of the produce of the house along with the heirs, and if her husband gives her anything as is written; but if she should take away anything else, it is a matter for trial. *vac.* And if a wife should die childless, *vac.* (her husband) is to return her own property to her heirs and half of whatever she has woven and half of the produce, if there is any, from her own things. If the husband or wife wish to give something for burial (?), (it should be) either clothing or twelve staters or (something) of the value of twelve staters, but not more. *vac.*

20 κἄτι: see on 2.47.
26 ὄτι: Att. οὗτινος (Dialect 18).
κὄτι̣: There appears to be a space after the *tau*, perhaps caused by some surface defect, but the top of the *iota* following this is quite clear.
32 There is a clear gap for no apparent reason after ἀποθάνοι at the end of a conditional clause but in the middle of a sentence. Presumably this is a mason's error.
37 κόμιστρα occurs nowhere else in Cretan inscriptions. Elsewhere, it seems to mean payment for services rendered, perhaps to recover something (e.g. Aesch. *Ag.* 965); it may be derived from κομίζω 'carry, convey'. The word is taken out of the conditional clause and put first, marking the subject matter of this provision, which is introduced with asyndeton but no gap.
38 Fε̂μα: this is the accusative form of a neuter noun (= Att. εἷμα, εἵματος), but elsewhere (5.40 below; **G43Ab**10–11; **G75**B3) we find the genitive Fέμας, as if Fε̂μα were feminine.

As in a divorce, the death of a spouse requires a separation of the husband's property from the wife's. The law's treatment of the two estates is essentially equal, the main difference being that the man's property is taken for granted whereas the woman's is specified in detail. But just as his property passes directly to his children upon his death, or to his other heirs if he dies childless, her property, which includes property she brought to the marriage and what she acquired while married, would similarly go to her children upon her death, or her other heirs if she dies childless. The relevant rules of inheritance are in 5.9–28; cf. 4.23–48. The restrictions on gifts (cf. 4.48–5.1) and *komistra* (3.37–40) are probably intended mainly to preserve as much of the estate as possible for the heirs.

This section first provides for the husband's death in two parts, when he has children and when he does not, the only difference being that in the first case things the widow has woven and produce from her property all go to the children. It then provides for the death of a wife without children. If a wife dies leaving children, her property will go to them (4.43–6, 6.31–46), and (it goes without saying) the husband will keep his property and may remarry.

20–1 'Whatever her husband gives her according to what is written': cf. 10.14–17 below, where (assuming the supplement is correct; see note ad loc.) the gift is limited to one hundred staters.

21–2 Cf. 'two free adult witnesses' in 1.41–2 (with comm.).

23 'Anything of the children's': primarily their inheritance from their father.

23–4 'It is a matter for trial' (*endikon emen*) is a common expression in the Code (but not in other Gortyn laws). It can be used personally (with a dative, e.g. 7.14–15) or impersonally, as here. When used of something that happened before (i.e. before the Code became law), it is always negative—that is, it indicates the non-retroactivity of a provision. The law apparently envisions the children (or a relative on their behalf) suing their mother to recover the property she had wrongly taken.

24–31 The law here specifies what property a widow without children is to have but otherwise says nothing about what she is to do. In Athens she would return to her family (father or brother) together with her dowry, but since at Gortyn she has her own property, she may have been able to live on her own if she so desired.

27 'The produce of the house': Brixhe 1999: 103 notes the common opposition between property inside the house, overseen by women, and outside property (primarily land and livestock) managed by men. Here 'the produce of the house' is presumably different from 'the produce from her own things' in 35–6 below (so VER). For *karpos* ('produce'), see on 2.48–50.

28, 33 The *epiballontes* are lit. 'those who have a claim' (see note on 5.22–5). It is only found in **G72**, where it is used of two groups: heirs, who have a claim on the estate (as here), and prospective grooms or claimants, who have a claim to marriage with an heiress (7.28–9, etc.). For the difference between the *epiballontes* and the *kadestai*, see on 2.18 above.

37–40 are marked off by asyndeton (but no gap) and could be considered a separate section, but (like others) we think it likely that it also regulates matters after the death of a spouse and so we present it as a continuation of the same subject.

37 'Something for burial': the meaning of *komistra* is debated. After reviewing the evidence, W translates 'porterage', that is, a payment intended to help the wife take away her possessions after her husband's death. But since a wife can give *komistra* to her husband, who will not be moving, this seems unlikely. We follow VER, who more plausibly connect it with the verb *komizein* in the sense of 'carry

off a corpse for burial' and understand it to refer to 'funeral expenses', which either spouse may contribute, if they so wish. Maffi too connects the payment with the deceased's funeral (1997a: 63–4), but sees it as intended to help clothe the corpse. Perhaps the term denotes specifically a cloth (sometimes a cloak) used to wrap the body.

3.40–4—SEPARATION OF SERFS (VER II.31, K 167)

After treating the dissolution of a marriage of free persons by divorce or death, the Code now very briefly regulates both sorts of dissolution of the marriage of a serf couple.

αἴ κ-
α Ϝοικέος Ϝοικέα κριθêι δοô
ἒ ἀποθανόντος, τὰ Ϝὰ αὐτâ-
ς ἔκεν· ἄλλο δ' αἴ τι πέροι, ἔνδ-
ικον ἔμεν. *vac.*

If a serf woman is separated from her serf husband either while he is living or by his death, she is to have her own things, but if she should carry away anything else, it is a matter for trial. *vac.*

---

41 *κριθêι*: There is no apparent difference in meaning between *κρίνω* here and in 11.46 (divorce of a free couple) and *διακρίνω* in 2.46.

The regulations regarding serf separations are a simplified version of those for free persons in 2.45–3.16 and 3.17–31. Many scholars assume that serf 'unions' were not true marriages (Bile 2002: 124–5, with n. 31). But the similarity in language (see n. ad 41 below) indicates that the legislator saw both unions as essentially the same (the same verb is used for marrying; see n. ad 4.4). A serf woman can also, like a free woman, 'have her own things', though these probably do not include land, which would explain why there is no mention of produce from their property. It is possible that some rules for serf marriages were given in an earlier inscription (**G23**), but too little of this text survives to know what these might have been. Some scholars (e.g. Maffi 2012: 100–1; see now Lewis 2013: 404–5) argue that this rule is meant to apply primarily to slave couples who originally had different masters, and that since the slave's property (like the Roman *peculium*) basically belongs to his master, the main purpose of the law is to allow the slave woman's original master to reclaim her and her property after a divorce. If this were the law's purpose, it is strange that it does not specify the master's claim but instead leaves it to the divorced slave woman to claim 'her own property' so that her master can recover it. It would make more sense to allow the master to take his property, especially since in cases where the couple had children, who would presumably remain with the husband, the wife would have good reason not to take 'her own property' with her, if that meant that it would belong to her master; instead she would leave it with her former husband for the benefit of her children.

The fact that the rules for divorce here and the rules governing children born out of wedlock in 3.44–4.23 specify *woikeis*, not *doloi*, may suggest that the *woikeus* was more commonly envisaged as living in a family group (but see 2.27–8, which implies that *doloi* could be married). It is also implied below (4.31–7) that *woikeis* could reside in houses by themselves and own livestock. This suggests that a *woikeus* may have been primarily engaged in agricultural work and often lived on the land. It is possible that *woikeis* originally had a greater degree of independence, but when chattel slaves (*doloi*) were introduced at a later period (perhaps in the late sixth century), *woikeis* were assimilated into the same status category as *doloi* for legal purposes. *Dolos* became the general term for this category in legislation, but *woikeus* continued to be used in legal rules that were originally formulated (perhaps orally) for their special circumstances. But any such historical reconstruction remains speculative; see Introd. 5A7.

41 'Is separated': the verb is *krinen*, also used in 11.46 (of free persons divorcing); in the section on divorce of free couples (2.45–3.16), the compound *diakrinen* is used.

43–4 'A matter for trial': W expresses the view of most scholars when he writes, 'no doubt her master would be involved in the legal proceedings'. This could only happen when the two serfs have different masters, and it is not impossible that this section applies only to such cases (cf. the rules in 3.52–4.8). Masters do sometimes litigate on behalf of slaves in cases involving free opponents (e.g. **G47**). Here, however, since some serf couples must have had the same master, who could not be instructed to litigate against himself, it is more likely that the two serfs would resolve their differences through litigation on their own. See further Gagarin 2010a.

3.44–4.23—CHILDREN BORN TO UNMARRIED WOMEN (VER II.34–5, K 168)

These regulations concern children born after divorce or born to a serf out of wedlock; they give the right to the child to the husband (of a free woman) or the husband's master (of a serf).

VER treat 3.44–52 together with 4.8–17 as one text (II.34) and 3.52–4.8 together with 4.18–23 as another (II.35). K treats this whole section as one (168).

αἰ τέκοι γυνὰ κ-
ε[ρ]ε[ύο]νσα̣, ἐπελεῦσαι τôι ἀ-
νδρὶ ἐπὶ στέγαν ἀντὶ μαιτ-
ύρον τριôν. αἰ δὲ μὲ δέκσαι-
το, ἐπὶ τâι ματρὶ ἔμεν τὸ τέκ-
νον ἒ τράπεν ἒ ἀποθέμεν· ὀρκ-
ιοτέροδ δ' ἔμεν τὸς καδεστ-
ὰνς καὶ τὸς μαίτυρανς, αἰ
ἐπέλευσαν. *vac.* αἰ δὲ Ϝοικέα τέ-
κοι κερεύονσα, ἐπελεῦσαι

If a divorced woman should bear a child, (she) is to bring it to her (former) husband at his house before three witnesses; and if he should not accept it, it is to be in the hands of the mother either to rear or to expose the child; and the relatives and witnesses are to be the ones who swear, whether they brought it. *vac.* If a divorced serf woman should bear a child, (she) is to bring it to the τôι πάσται τô ἀνδρός, ὃς ὄπυιε, ἀντὶ μαιτύρον δ̣[υ]ôν.

Col. 4

vac.

αἰ δέ κα μὲ δέκσεται, ἐπὶ τôι πάσται ἔμεν τὸ τέκνον τôι τâς Fοικέας. αἰ δὲ τôι αὐτôι αὖτιν ὀπυίοιτο πρὸ τô ἐνιαυτô, τὸ παιδίον ἐπὶ τôι πάσται ἔμεν τôι τô Fοικέος. κὀρκιότερον ἔμεν τὸν ἐπελεύσαντα καὶ τὸς μαίτυρανς. *vac.* γυνὰ κερεύονσ' αἰ ἀποβάλοι παιδίον πρὶν ἐπελεῦσαι κατ̣ὰ τὰ ἐγραμμένα, ἐλευθέρο μὲν καταστασεῖ πεντέκοντα στατêρανς, δόλο πέντε καὶ Fίκατι, αἴ κα νικαθêι. δι δέ κα μὲ 'ἴ[ε] τ̣ις 'τέγα ὀπυῖ ἐπελευσεῖ, ἒ αὐτὸν μὲ ὀρêι, αἰ [[αι]] ἀποθείε τὸ παιδίον, ἄπατον ἔμεν. *vac.* αἰ κύσαιτο καὶ τέκοι Fοικέα μὲ ὀπυιομένα, ἐπὶ τôι τô πατρὸς πάσται ἔμεν τὸ τέκνον· αἰ δ' ὀ πατὲρ μὲ δόοι, ἐπὶ τοῖς τôν ἀδελπιôν πάσταις ἔμεν. *vac.*

master of her husband, who married (her), in the presence of two witnesses. (**Col. 4**) And if he does not accept it, the child is to be in the hands of the master of the serf woman. And if she should marry the same man again within a year, the child is to be in the hands of the male serf's master. The person who brought (the child) and the witnesses are the ones who swear. *vac.* If a woman separated (by divorce) should dispose of her child before bringing it in accordance with what is written, (she) will pay fifty staters for a free (child), twenty-five for a slave, if she is convicted. And if there should not be a house to which (she) will bring it or (she) does not see him (there), if (she) should expose the child, there is to be immunity. *vac.* If an unmarried serf woman should be pregnant and give birth, the child is to be in the hands of the master of her father; but if the father is not alive, it is to be in the hands of the masters of her brothers. *vac.*

45, etc. ἐπελεῦσαι (from ἐπελεύθω) means 'bring something/someone for presentation to someone'; see on **G41**.1.9–10, where we note that in 15–16 ἐπελευσεῖ is future indicative. See further on 7–8 below.

4.3–4 αὖτιν: Att. αὖθις.

9 ἀποβάλοι is probably equivalent to ἀποτίθημι (in 3.49 and 4.16–17), as G, W, and VER maintain, but it may also include other means of disposing of a child (such as giving it to someone else).

14–16 The syntax is difficult. Lit. 'For whom (δι) there is no house to which she can bring it, or she does not see him . . .'.

14–15 μὲ 'ἴ[ε] is elided from μὲ εἴ[ε]; see W ad loc. The stone is now damaged so that the last ε has disappeared.

18 The line begins one letter from the edge of the column and so like all other editors we mark a *vac.* But the surface is damaged in this space, which coincides with the edge of a stone, and if this damage occurred before the text was inscribed, it may have been the reason for leaving a space, not the desire to leave a gap.

Children were essential to the (patrilineal) continuation of the family and estate at Gortyn, just as at Athens and elsewhere. Thus, children were under the control of their father (4.23–5) and normally remained with him after a divorce. So too did a child born after a divorce—presumably soon enough after a divorce that the former husband could be assumed to be its father, unless the father did not want it. One reason for rejecting such a child might be its poor health; with limited resources it was too costly to raise weak or sickly children. Or if the husband did not remarry and had few servants, he might not want the burden of raising it. Or he might have doubts about the child's paternity, if his wife had been suspected of adultery. In any case, the child was brought to the father, and only if he did not want it, could the mother choose whether to keep it or expose it.

45 Here and in 3.53, 4.10, and 4.15–16 the verb *epeleusai* or *epeleusei* ('is to bring, will bring') has no subject expressed, but in our view, the text clearly implies—most clearly in 4.10 (see note below)—that the mother is normally the one who brings the child, though nothing prevents others from accompanying her or sometimes acting on her behalf. Most scholars, however, assume a woman would not have this task, and so W takes the subject here to be the *kadestai* who are allowed to swear in 49–52, and in 3.53 G, K, and VER understand the subject as the master of the serf woman (W adds the possibility that it is a relative of the serf woman). In all such cases, however, one would expect such a change of subject to be made explicit.

47–9 If the ex-husband does not want the child, it is to be 'in the hands of the mother' whether to raise it or expose it. Bile (2012: 51–2) assumes that her male relatives would make the decision, but there is no good reason not to take the text at face value. The legislator could easily have written 'in the hands of her relatives'.

48 For *epi* with the dative ('in the hands of'), see on 4.37.

49–50 For *orkioteros*, see above on 2.15; cf. below 4.6–7.

50–1 For the *kadestai* as relatives with a duty, see above on 2.18. Here they may have acted as witnesses or they may have accompanied and lent support to the mother.

52 'They brought': The plural may designate the mother together with her witnesses.

52–4.8 The rules for serfs are similar to those for free couples, though there is an added provision regulating the possibility that the couple will remarry within a year. (If a free couple remarried, the question of the baby's future would not arise.) The rules only matter for serf couples belonging to different masters; if both have the same master, he decides the child's fate whether the serfs remarry or not. There is much we do not know about marriages between serfs with different masters, but any child born in wedlock probably belonged to the husband's master. It is uncertain what obligations the wife had to her own master in such situations; he may sometimes have sold her to her husband's master, but this cannot always have happened or there would be no need for this law.

54 For *pastas*, see Maffi 1997b: 443–5. Since the master owns the serf child's father, he is the one to decide on the fate of any child who is born. Among other

things, he would have to consider whether arrangements could be made for the baby's upbringing; since the primary duty of the serf husband would normally be to tend to the land, he might often be unable to raise a child alone.

54 'Her husband' (*to andros*): use of the regular term for the husband (*aner*) of a serf woman surprises some (e.g. Bile 2012: 53 n. 172) who think serf couples were not truly married.

4.3–6 The provision that the baby goes to its father's master if the couple remarries implies that in a significant number of cases the father's master would refuse the baby when the couple was separated (see preceding note). When the two are reunited, however, there would be no reason for him not to want to have the baby. Remarriage of a free couple would pose no problem, and thus is not addressed in the law.

4 The verb *opuien* is used for marriage, whether the two parties are serfs or free persons; cf. the note on 3.40–4 above. The middle (*opuiesthai*) is used for the woman and means 'get married', as here, or 'be married', as in 4.19, etc.

6–7 For *orkioteros*, see above on 2.15.

7–8 'The person who brought (the child)': in our view, it is normally the mother who brings the child, but because in some cases it might be someone else, the masculine participle *ton epeleusanta* ('whoever brings (it)') is used. Cf. 'they brought' in 3.52.

10 'Before bringing it': just like the English, the Greek (*prin epeleusai*) implies continuity of subject, i.e. the woman.

8–14 G, W, K, and others take *gyna* ('wife, woman') to mean all women, free and serf, who would have free and slave children respectively. VER and others, however, argue that the distinction between *gyna*, 'free woman', (3.44) and *woikea*, 'serf woman', (3.52) has been so clearly established that *gyna* here designates only a free woman, who could have either free or slave children with a slave (6.55–7.4). Since the rules for free and serf mothers are essentially the same, however (*mutatis mutandis*), we would expect them to face the same penalty (adjusted to status) for violating these rules. Bile notes (2012: 60 n. 195) in addition that if the child of a free woman and a slave were free (because the couple was living in her house), it would make no sense for the slave to have the opportunity to keep a free baby born after their separation.

There is no reason why *gyna* here cannot mean a woman in general, free or serf (note that *aner* is used of the serf husband in 3.54). When first used in 3.44, *gyna* is understood to be a free woman because laws normally apply to free persons unless they are somehow qualified. But after a serf woman in a similar situation has been discussed (3.52–4.8), then it is natural to understand *gyna* as referring to both free and serf women.

12 '(She) will pay': as with *epeleusei* (see note on 3.45 above), the subject of *katastasei* is naturally the same as the subject of the conditional clause, namely the woman.

14–17 can only apply to a free divorced woman, whose husband has lost his property or left town; the master of a serf woman's former husband could not have lost his property (or else the husband would belong to another master). If the woman cannot find her former husband, she is reasonably allowed to act without his permission.

The woman is the natural subject of *orei* ('see') and *apotheie* ('expose') as well as *epeleusei*, though no subject is expressed for any of these verbs (see above on 3.45).

18–23 The Code does not envision a free woman having children out of wedlock, but it may not have been uncommon for an unmarried serf woman to become pregnant, perhaps with her master's child (as happens often in slave societies).

21–3 The plural 'masters' has caused difficulties. Maffi correctly notes (1997b: 444 n. 12) that the law does not speak of multiple masters of the same serf, but of different masters for different brothers. This implies that it was common for a master to sell some or all of the sons of his serfs. But there is no mention of the 'law of primogeniture' (*droit de l'aînesse*) that Maffi evokes to argue that the child would go to the master of the eldest brother. The law could easily have specified such an arrangement, but instead it says 'masters'. This implies that all of the brothers' masters would share ownership of the baby and decide its fate together. In practice they may have normally arranged for one of them to have the baby, perhaps by purchasing it from his brothers. Bile 2002: 127–8 suggests translating the plural as a singular ('the master of her brothers'), but her arguments for this are not convincing.

4.23–48—DISTRIBUTION OF AN ESTATE (VER II.49, K 169)

The basic inheritance rules in the Code are divided into three parts. Here the law specifies the division of the estate of each parent when there are surviving children including at least one son. The next section (4.48–5.9) digresses a bit to regulate gifts to daughters while the father is alive, but this has implications for inheritance too. Then, in 5.9–6.2 come the rules for estates when there are no surviving children, followed by rules for settling disputes about the division of the property. These rules are followed, after several sections on other subjects, by an extensive set of rules for cases where only a daughter (the 'heiress') or daughters survive (7.15–9.24).

VER group 4.23–4.48 and 5.1–9 together with 5.28–54 (II.49). K puts all three sections on inheritance together (4.23–6.2).

τὸν πατέρα τôν
τέκνον καὶ τôν κρεμάτον κ-
αρτερὸν ἔμεν τâδ δαίσιος

The father is to have control of the children and of his property with respect to its division, and the mother (is to have

καὶ τὰν ματέρα τôν Fôν αὐ-
τᾶς κρεμάτον. ἆς κα δόοντι,
μὲ ἐπάνανκον ἔμεν δατê-
θθαι· αἰ δέ τις ἀταθείε, ἀποδ-
άτταθθαι τôι ἀταμένοι ἆ-
ι ἔγραπται. ἐ̂ δέ κ' ἀποθάνει τις,
'τέγανς μὲν τὰνς ἐν πόλι κἄ-
τι κ' ἐν ταῖς 'τέγαις ἐνêι αἶ-
ς κα μὲ Fοικεὺς ἐνFοικêι ἐπ-
ὶ κόραι Fοικίον καὶ τὰ πρόβατα κα-
ὶ καρταίποδα ἅ κα μὲ Fοικέος ἐ̂ι,
ἐπὶ τοῖς υἰάσι ἔμεν, τὰ δ' ἄλ-
λα κρέματα πάντα δατêθθα-
ι καλôς, καὶ λανκάνεν τὸς μ-
ὲν υἰύνς, ὀπόττοι κ' ἴοντι, δύ-
ο μοίρανς Fέκαστον, τὰδ δ-
ὲ θυγατέρανς, ὀπότται κ' ἴον-
τι, μίαν μοῖραν Fεκάσταν. δ̣-
ατêθ[θ]αι δὲ καὶ τὰ ματρôια, ἐ̂
κ' ἀποθά̣[νε]ι, ἆιπερ τὰ [πατρô]ι'
ἔγ[ραπ]ṭαι. αἰ δὲ κρέματα μὲ εἴ-
ε, στέγα δέ, λακὲν τὰθ θ[υ]γατέ-
ρας ἆι ἔγραπται. *vac.*

control) of her own property (with respect to its division). As long as they are alive there is to be no need to make a division; but if one (of the heirs) should be fined, a distribution is to be made to the person fined, as is written. And when one (of the parents) dies, the houses in the city and whatever is inside the houses, those in which a serf who lives in the country is not residing, and the livestock, small and large, that are not those of a serf, are to be in the hands of the sons; and all the rest of the property is to be fairly divided, and the sons, however many there are, are to receive two shares each, and the daughters, however many there are, (are to receive) one share each. The maternal estate too is to be divided, when she dies, in the same way as is written for the paternal estate. And if there should be no property but (only) a house, the daughters are to receive their share as is written. *vac.*

23–7 The syntax is difficult, particularly as regards the unusual position of τᾶδ δαίσιος. καρτερὸν must govern τέκνον (since there is no question of a division of the children), and we believe it also governs κρεμάτον. τᾶδ δαίσιος then focuses or specifies the meaning of τôν κρεμάτον:[413] the father 'is to be in control of his property with respect to its division'. Kristensen (1994: 22), followed by Maffi (2003a: 187–8), argues, probably correctly, that τᾶδ δαίσιος is also meant to be understood with the second half of the sentence (as is καρτερὸν ἔμεν), so that the mother too has control of her own property and its division.

27 ἆς = ἕως (Bile 90). Note the asyndeton marking the separation of a general rule from specific rules that are only loosely connected with it.

δόοντι = ζῶσι (ζόωσι), subj.

28–30 δατêθθαι . . . ἀποδάτταθθαι: the first verb designates only the division of property; the second designates its actual distribution to the heirs.

34–5 ἐπὶ κόραι (= ἐπὶ χώρᾳ): VER consider this expression (read by all previous editors) superfluous ('une lapalissade'), because a serf who lives in the country necessarily does not live in a house in the city. They read the Greek as ἐπικόραι (= Att. ἐπικουρίαι, 'for assistance') and translate 'where a serf does not live, who has come to live there for (i.e.

[413] See Smyth 1956: §§1380–1 on the 'genitive of connection'.

to perform) a service' ('où n'habite pas un serf venu habiter pour un service'). But this reading is even more problematic (see Maffi 1997b: 439–41; Lévy 1997: 36; Brixhe 1999: 90), and so the traditional understanding is probably correct, even if the expression is not strictly necessary.

36 The mason mistakenly added an extra diagonal stroke in front of the *alpha* following *kartaipoda*.

48 The *vac.* in this line is only about half a letter wide and might have been caused by roughness in the surface of the stone. In any case asyndeton marks the end of a section.

This section first prepares for the division of the parents' property by separating the mother's property from the father's and putting each in charge of their own. If necessary, they may distribute some of it while still alive (23–31). Then come rules concerning the distribution of the property among the children after death (31–48); the division of property by the parents must presumably be made in accordance with these general rules. The rules give priority to the father and sons but do not neglect the mother's property or the daughters' share of the estate. With certain qualifications, houses in the city with their contents and livestock are to 'be in the hands of' the sons (see below on 37). The rest of the property is divided among all the children, the sons' shares being twice as large as the daughters'. If however, the estate consists only of a house, the daughters are to have a share of this.

23–7 That the father has control of the children—perhaps primarily in the sense of control of their property (see next note)—and of the division of his own property is hardly surprising; unlike in Athens, however, the mother also controls the division of her own property.

23–5 The nature of the father's control over the children is unclear. There is no reason to think that this implies the same sort of total control as the traditional Roman *patria potestas*; more likely it designates only his control of their property, which is the subject of the rest of the sentence.

24–5 'Have control of' (*karteron emen*), lit. 'be stronger than, superior to'. This expression occurs four more times in the Code (6.33; 6.45–6; 8.43; 8.48–9), always in connection with property that is part of an estate and always of control that is temporary: in 6.33, 6.45–6, and 8.43 the property is explicitly labeled someone else's, and in 8.48–9 the property does not at the time belong to the heiress, though she may receive some or all of it later. Here in 4.24–5 the mother and father do own their own property, but the law apparently considers their ownership as temporary, extending only until their death. See further Gagarin 2008b: 7–10.

25 'With respect to its division': the law specifies control over the division of property because that is the focus of the provisions that follow (4.23–48). Most scholars agree that *karteron emen tad daisios* must also be understood with the elliptical second half of the sentence: (lit. 'and the mother of her own property'). Kristensen (1994: 22) and Maffi (2003a: 187–8) further argue that by referring

specifically to the division of the property, this part of the law implies that the mother does not control her property in other respects (her husband does). But (a) the same reasoning ought then to apply to the first half of the sentence, but no one thinks the father was not in control of his own property as well as its division, and (b) if the law gave control of a woman's property to her husband, it would make little sense to give the mother herself control over its division. It is far more likely that both husband and wife are given control of the division of their own property, because division is the specific issue in this section; that they also both control their own property is not explicitly mentioned here because it is not relevant to the issue of division or inheritance.

27–9 There is some ambiguity about when a division would take place. On the one hand, it need not happen while the parents are alive, but on the other hand, once dead, a parent obviously will not have control over the division. This suggests that the legislator has in mind two stages of division: first each parent decides how his or her estate will be divided among the children (consistent with the rules in 31–48), and then at a later stage, often after death, the estate is distributed according to the division the parent had made. Part of the estate could also be distributed before death if necessary to pay a fine (29–31). It could probably also be distributed for some other reason, since the expression 'there is no need to make a division' is not a prohibition against making one. One reason for dividing the estate earlier would be so that a father could give a gift to his daughter when she gets married (4.48–5.9); since the gift cannot exceed the amount of her inheritance (4.48–51), he would need to calculate the division of his estate beforehand to know how much he could give her.

30–1 'As is written' refers to the rules concerning the division of the inheritance set forth in 31–48 below. From one perspective it would have made more sense to put these rules first, but the legislator is following a chronological order here and so places the division of property before death ahead of its *post mortem* distribution.

31 'When someone (*tis*) dies': this could apply to either parent, but it probably is directed at the father's death, since division of the mother's property is addressed in 43–6.

31–7 This provision probably assumes that the sons will continue to live in the family's houses after they marry and that daughters will live with their husbands or one of their brothers until they get married. It also assumes that sons will be in charge of the family's livestock. Similar assumptions probably existed everywhere in Greece (and are common in exogamous agricultural societies everywhere). Note that in some cases a man may not have a house (4.14–16).

32–5 'The houses in the city and whatever is inside the houses, those in which a serf who lives in the country is not residing'. There are two ways to read this. (a) The phrase 'inside the houses' may mean 'inside these houses' (i.e. in the city houses), in which case the qualification 'those in which a serf who lives in the country is not residing' applies to both the city houses and their furnishings. (b) 'The houses in the city' may be a separate provision and implicitly include the furnishings of these houses; 'whatever is inside the houses' then refers to other houses as specified by the expression that follows, the country houses in which no serf is residing. The difficulty with (a) is that the qualification about 'serfs who live in the country' is very odd: if they live in the country' they should not be living in a city house. Maffi (1997a: 67–8) argues that although domestic servants would normally be living in the city houses, 'a serf who lives in the country' may designate a country serf who is probably brought into the city in order to live in an extra house that is not being used at the time. But if a *woikeus* was in some sense attached to the land, it is unclear why he would be brought to live in the city. VER propose a variant on this view (see note on 34–5 above). The difficulty with (b) is that the sons would apparently receive the contents of the houses in the country (where no serf was living) but not the country houses themselves. In a long, complicated explanation, W seems to argue that on this interpretation the sons would also get the country houses in which no serf is living, but it does not seem possible to get this from the Greek. Of course, the sons might get these houses in the second round of inheritance, which they would share with the daughters, but this would depend on the number of sons and daughters, the number of houses, and the other items in the estate. We leave the question open.

35–6 'The livestock, small and large, that are not those of a serf'. W (ad loc.) explains the *probata* as the small cattle, sheep, and goats, who 'walk in front' of the herd; the *kartaipoda* are then the larger cattle. Two questions. First, which livestock would the sons get? VER and Maffi (1997a: 68) take them to be livestock living in the city with the serf. Although we know nothing about residence patterns in Gortyn at this time, it is hard to imagine that the polis (4.32) or 'urban area' would provide grazing for a significant number of livestock. It is possible, however, that a country serf who came into the city to live would bring with him a few animals for milk and meat, who could graze on a small patch of land next to the house. But the law seems to mean that the sons get all the livestock except that owned by a serf, and most of these would probably be in the country. Second, does the serf own the livestock? Serfs could own property in some sense (3.40–4), but serfs also belonged to a master and thus must have been included (along with *doloi*) in the total estate that was divided among all the children. Any cattle that a serf 'owned' presumably were inherited along with the serf himself by one of the children in the distribution of 'all the rest of the property'. And yet the law distinguishes cattle belonging to a serf from cattle belonging to his master, implying that in some sense the serf owns his cattle, even if he himself is owned by someone.

37 'In the hands of' (*epi* plus the dative) is elsewhere used to specify that an adulterer is 'in the power of' his captor to do as he wishes (2.34–5), that a person who has been ransomed is 'in the power of' his ransomer until he repays the ransom money (6.49–50), or that the decision to raise or expose a baby is to be 'in the hands of' the husband or the master of a serf (several times in 3.44–4.23). In none of these cases does it indicate ownership, though the master of a serf does own the baby. Here it is assumed by all scholars that the expression indicates ownership, since the items mentioned are part of an estate to be inherited. But in 5.32–3 (see below) the expression clearly designates only temporary possession of the property. Thus the sons' control of the city houses and livestock is qualified: they are given only the right to live in the houses and to manage the livestock. This might often amount to the same thing as ownership, but it may be that if, say, a son sold any of this property, the proceeds would be divided among all the children according to the proportions established in 37–43. See further, Gagarin 2008b: 10–16.

37–43 With the exception of the city houses and livestock specified in 31–7, all the property, including city houses in which a country serf is living and livestock owned by a serf, is divided among the sons and daughters according to a strict ratio of 2:1.

37–8 'All the rest of the property' would include country houses together with their furnishings, slaves and serfs, livestock, and land. Those who think land at Gortyn was inalienable (e.g. Brixhe 1999: 108–15) argue that because land is not explicitly mentioned here, it is excluded from 'all the rest of the property', but there are no grounds for this view. Daughters, of course, would inherit their share of the land. VER insist that the Greek (*ta d' alla kremata panta*) cannot mean 'all the rest of the property' as all editors translate but (lit.) 'all the rest, that is the *kremata*' (i.e. the land). But although *kremata* often designates land (see above on 2.50), it is probably used inconsistently in the Code (as G and others have noted). But the city houses, their contents, and the livestock, cannot be all the property of the deceased, and a fair division of what remains must include more than land. See Introd. 7A.

40–3 'Two shares each' and 'one share each' mean that if, for example, there are two sons and one daughter, each son will receive ²⁄₅ of the estate and the daughter will receive ¹⁄₅. The sons' 2:1 advantage over the daughters may seem unfair to our eyes but daughters in Gortyn fare better than those in classical Athens, who receive no share of the estate. According to Ephorus (*FGrH* 70F149.81–2 = Strabo 10.4.20), in Crete 'a girl's dowry, if she has brothers, is half as much as her brother's share'.

43–6 It appears from 6.31–46 that the children do not fully own their mother's property immediately, but that their father controls it as long as he obeys the rules stated there and does not remarry. Probably the children assume full ownership when he dies.

44 The word for 'maternal estate' (*matroia*) occurs several times in the Code (6.34, 6.45, 11.44–5), and in **G20**.4 and **Ph1**.3. Very likely it was a Gortynian coinage on the model of *patroia*, 'paternal estate' (4.45, 11.43–4), which occurs already in Homer (so Bile 284, with n. 109). If Gortynian women could own property in a more complete or direct way than women in cities outside of Crete, as it appears they could, it would make sense that *matroia* was coined in Crete and not elsewhere.

46–7 'If there should be no property (*kremata*) but a house': *kremata* here must include land, probably together with livestock, but not personal property. It is inconceivable that someone could have a house and no personal property, but a family without land could still have a house in the city.

47–8 'The daughters are to receive their share': most likely, the house would be sold so that each heir could receive a share, the daughters half as much as the sons 'as is written'.

4.48–5.9—GIFTS TO A DAUGHTER (VER II.53, 49, K 169)

This section allows a father to give a daughter a gift at her marriage but apparently puts certain restrictions on it; it also contains an important dating formula.

αἰ δέ κα λε̂-
ι ὁ πατὲρ δοὸς ἰὸν δόμεν τâ-
ι ὀπυιομέναι, δότο κατὰ τ-
ὰ ἐγραμμένα, πλίονα δὲ μέ. *vac.*
ὀτείαι δὲ πρόθθ' ἔδοκε ἒ ἐπέσ-
πενσε, ταῦτ' ἔκεν, ἄλλα δὲ μὲ
ἔτι τộν π[α]τρόι[ο]ν [κ]ρ̣έ[ματ']
Col. 5
ἀπολαν[κά]νεν. γυνὰ ὀ[τ]εία κ-
ρέματα μὲ ἔκει ἒ [πα]τρὸδ δό-
ντος ἒ ἀ̣[δ]ελπιô ἒ ἐπισπέν-
σαντος ἒ ἀπολα[κ]όνσα â-
ι ὄκ' ὁ Αἰθ[α]λεὺς 'ταρτὸς ἐκόσ-
μιον οἰ σὺν Κύ[λ]λ̣οι, ταύτ-
ας μὲν ἀ̣π̣ολανκάνεν, ταῖ-
δ δὲ πρόθθα μὲ ἔ[ν]δικον ἔμ-
εν. *vac.*

If her father while he is alive wishes to give to (his daughter) who is getting married, let him give according to what is written, but not more. *vac.* And any (daughter) to whom he gave or promised before is to have these things, but from the paternal estate she is not (**Col. 5**) to receive (as inheritance) any other property. Any woman who does not have property, either as a gift from her father or brother, or as a promise, or as her share (of the inheritance), as (was written?) when the *startos* Aithaleus, Kyllos and his colleagues, were *kosmoi*, they are to have their share; but for those before this time it is not a matter for trial. *vac.*

---

49 ἰόν = ἐών (ὤν).

52 ὀτείαι: Att. ὁποίαι—dative sing. (cf. ὀτεία, nom. sing., in 5.1).

54 The bottom line of column 4 is badly damaged; some have seen an intentional erasure (see G ad loc.), but more likely it is simply damage that occurred later.

π[α]τρόι[ο]ν: cf. πατρôια in 4.45 and 11.43–4.

5.1 ἀπολαν[κά]νεν: the compound verb occurs five other times in the Code (5.4; 5.7; 6.6; 6.9; 7.34), with essentially the same meaning as λανκάνεν, which occurs four times (3.29; 4.39; 4.47; 10.51–2), namely 'to receive' a share of an estate as an inheritance. Cf. also διαλανκάνεν, 'receive a share of a divided estate' (5.50; 8.4–5; 24–5; 45–6).

ὀ[τ]εία: see above on 4.52.

4–5 ἆι ὄκ': G and others take both conjunctions (for ὄκα, see Dialect 33) as expressing time and translate something like 'as of when'. But notwithstanding a possible parallel in Apollonius of Rhodes, W notes that every other occurrence of ἆι in the Code (and indeed at Gortyn except for **G41**.2.11, where it expresses purpose) is followed by some expression for writing and means 'as is written' (see also Bile 262). He translates 'as (enacted) when', as do VER, K.

5 (σ)'ταρτός (Att. στρατός) also occurs in **G80**.7 (cf. **G80**.4–5, σταρταγέταν) and has been restored in *IC*4.142.2.

This short section contains important regulations concerning women, marriage, and property at Gortyn, but several uncertainties in the interpretation of the text render any conclusions we reach tentative.

48–50 A father's gift to his daughter resembles a dowry, in that it conveys family property to a daughter who is getting married, and Sealey 1994: 80 (also Maffi 2012) sees this gift as equivalent to the dowry at Athens ('a mere difference in wording'); but the Athenian dowry was a financial arrangement between the bride's father (or other relative) and her future husband, who had complete control of the dowry and only returned it to the father in case of divorce. Here the gift belongs to the bride (see above on 2.45–3.16) and is essentially an advance on her inheritance (Bile 2012: 16). Bridal gifts (*edna*), which in Homer are given by the husband to his wife's father, are mentioned without context in an early fragment (**G17**.1), but we have no idea what these were or how they functioned.

50–1 'According to what is written, but not more': This may mean 'according to the rules for inheritance' just above (in 31–48), or it may refer to later rules about gifts, if these can be restored in 10.4–17 (with the amendment in 12.1–5). In the first case, the law would allow the father, in essence, to give his daughter her share of the inheritance at the time of her marriage rather than waiting for his death; in the second case, the marriage gift would be separate from her inheritance. In favor of the first view is 6.1–2, 'When (a father) gives to a daughter, (it is done) in the same way (*kata ta auta*)'. It seems that 'in the same way' can only refer to the regulations immediately preceding (in 5.28–54), which concern the division of the estate after a parent's death.

52–5.7 The law first limits what a daughter may receive from her father to the amount of her inheritance (4.52–5.1); it then specifies that a daughter who has not previously received anything must receive her share of the inheritance when her father dies (5.1–7). Thus, a daughter must receive her specified share of the estate, either as a gift or as inheritance. Technically, it might be possible to argue that a daughter who had received a small gift from her father should receive no more when he dies according to 4.52–5.1, and would also not be eligible for compensation according to 5.1–7, because she had already received something. But this seems to go against the clear intent of the law.

4.52–5.1 One issue that might arise is whether a daughter who had received a marriage gift equal to her share of the inheritance could later receive an additional gift if before her father's death one or more of her siblings died without leaving children. Clearly, if all her brothers died without issue, she would be an 'heiress' and would be treated differently (see 8.20–30), but if, for example, one of her two brothers died, her share of the inheritance would now be larger. Is she now entitled to an additional gift? A similar situation might arise if the father subsequently received an inheritance or otherwise significantly increased the size of his estate. The difficulty of redividing and redistributing an estate, perhaps several times, might make it difficult for fathers to adjust the amount of their gift in such circumstances, but additional gifts in such situations would probably not be prohibited by this law.

52–3 'Promise': *epispenden* means literally 'pour a libation over' and refers to a promise reinforced by this ritual ceremony (W ad loc.; Bile 354–6), as in **Da1**A1. As used at Gortyn, however, there is no hint of a ritual context. This promise is often compared to the Roman *sponsio*, but the Roman promise was probably more formal than the Gortynian equivalent. Since a daughter would receive her inheritance upon her father's death, there would normally be no point in a father promising a gift to his daughter at his death. So this provision may envision a father giving his daughter a small gift at her marriage and adding a promise that she will have the remainder of her share upon his death; this might be desirable for property that was not easily divisible among the children, such as a house. Or a father might promise a gift at a specific time in the future, for example in a year's time or after the birth of a child, but die before giving it. Maffi 1997a: 115 suggests that a father might promise his daughter something after his death as a means of specifying which parts of his property she will inherit, rather than leaving it to the heirs when they divide the estate, but the Code has already put the father in control of dividing his property (4.23–5), so that in most cases he would have determined the specific share of his estate that each heir would receive before his death.

52 'Before' (*proththa*): in the Code *proththa* usually occurs in the context of retroactivity (but cf. 7.13), so 'before' might mean 'before this law (was enacted)', or perhaps before some other date. However, this provision does not seem to concern retroactivity, which elsewhere is always addressed in the same words: 'for previous matters there is to be no legal action' (see below 5.7–9). Thus *proththa* here probably means 'before the father's death' (so Gagarin 1994: 64–6; Maffi 1997a: 45). Link 2003b is correct that, strictly speaking, it is redundant to specify

before the father's death here because 48–51 has just specified that these gifts are given while the father is alive. But 4.52–5.1 are addressing the matter of inheritance, and from this perspective the law specifies gifts given 'before', i.e. before the estate is distributed to the heirs, even though this specification is not strictly necessary.

5.1–7 There is asyndeton (Introd. 3D3) at the beginning of this sentence, but it is closely connected with the rules in 4.48–5.1.

4–6 The date of the enactment of the Code is placed here, in the first provision in which the question of retroactivity is raised, and only here. In none of the provisions that precede would this date be important, and once the date is given here, there is no need to repeat it in any of the later provisions concerning retroactivity. The date here thus stands as the date for the entire code. No other law at Gortyn has a date, but there is a date in an early law from Eleutherna (**Ele9** = VER I.25), where in line 3 we find the words '[?] and Timarkos were *kosmoi*'.

Many scholars (e.g. VER; Maffi 1997a: 46) assume that the date when Kyllos and his colleagues were *kosmoi* was sometime before the enactment of the Code. On this view, girls whose father died before Kyllos and left them no gift or inheritance will receive nothing, but girls whose father died after Kyllos but before enactment of the Code and who left them no gift or inheritance would receive their share of his estate retroactively. There are several objections to this view. First, the other four examples of non-retroactivity in the Code (see below on 7–9) all assume that the two significant time periods are before and after the Code. There seems no reason why there should be a difference here. Second, if the reference to Kyllos does not establish a date for the enactment of the Code, then the Code would be undated, posing significant difficulties in applying the later retroactivity provisions. Third, administering the provision in 5.1–7 could be quite difficult if there was a considerable time between Kyllos being *kosmos* and the enactment of the Code, as there probably was (since there would be little reason to specify a point of retroactivity only shortly before the enactment of the Code). If Kyllos was *kosmos* two or more years earlier, then after the Code was enacted, daughters who wished to claim their share of the inheritance because their father had given them nothing would have to establish that he died before the time of Kyllos. And if the estate had already been distributed to the other heirs, as is likely, it would now have to be redistributed; this could be especially difficult if parts of it had been sold in the meanwhile. We therefore follow G, K, and others in taking the date to refer to the time of enactment of the Code. Daughters whose fathers had died before the Code and had inherited nothing (presumably allowed under previous law) would not be able to claim any inheritance retroactively.

5–6: The expression 'when the *startos* Aithaleus, Kyllos and his colleagues, were *kosmoi*' seems to imply that the office of *kosmos* rotated among different *startoi*, which may be sub-units of tribes, and that at this time Kyllos and others were members of this 'troop' and held the office of *kosmos* as a group. Presumably a group from another troop took over the following year.

5 *Aithaleis* in the plural (*Aithaleis*) occurs in four later inscriptions. In *IC* 4.142.2, it is restored (together with *startos*) and the context is unclear; in *IC* 4.167.3, 184.1, and 259.1 it occurs in the phrase *tōn Aithaleōn kosmiontōn* ('when the Aithaleis were acting as *kosmos*').

Startos: G translates '*gens*', and W ad loc. and p. 11 (cf. 1955: 28–9) also argues for the general meaning 'clan'; but many scholars retain the military sense that *stratos* ('army') has in Attic (see G on **G80**.4). VER explain it as 'the part of the tribe that can be mobilized—i.e. those of military age'. See further Introd. 4B3.

6 'Kyllos and his colleagues': lit. 'those with Kyllos'; the expression implies at least two others but otherwise gives no indication of the total number.

7–9 It is very likely (though not certain) that the provision for non-retroactivity applies only to the immediately preceding provision (5.1–7) and not to the provisions that precede this. In general, the exact application of a provision on retroactivity may be unclear, as (e.g.) in Draco's homicide law (*IG* I^3 104.19–20), but here the asyndeton in 5.1 indicates that 1–7 are thought of as a separate piece of legislation from what precedes, and suggests that the non-retroactivity provision is most likely confined to this sentence. One reason for non-retroactivity is that (as noted above) once the estate had been divided among the children, it would have been difficult to redistribute it, especially if the original distribution took place many years earlier; thus, the law quite reasonably prohibits suits that might require such a redistribution.

This is the first of five sections in the Code where a rule is specified as not being retroactive (also 6.9–25; 9.7–17; 11.19–23; 12.1–5). All except 11.19–23 concern the property of women. Gagarin 1994 argues (primarily against W) that for the most part the Code treats women more favorably than did earlier legislation, about which we know nothing more than what we learn from these laws. Maffi 2003a: 183–7 concludes that some women may have fared better under the Code, others worse, and Link 2003b: 9 argues that the Code focuses on specific situations and is not concerned with the overall economic position of women. In our view, 6.9–25 and 9.7–17 clearly benefit women by protecting their property from possible misuse by male relatives. 5.7–9 also very likely benefit women, since 5.1–7 implies that before the Code a daughter could receive none of her father's estate, whereas the new rule prevents this. And even if the non-retroactivity provision also applies to 4.48–51, although some daughters may previously have received more than is allowed in this new law, it seems very unlikely that before this law the number who were receiving gifts that were larger than their inheritance was larger than those receiving smaller gifts or no gift at all. Thus this provision in 5.7–9 too almost certainly benefited women. Finally, the effect of the non-retroactive clause in 12.1–5 is uncertain, since the rules in 10.14–25 that are amended by this clause may or may not have benefited mothers and wives who received gifts. In sum, two of the four clauses specifying non-retroactivity in matters concerning women relate to new rules that are clearly beneficial, one relates to rules that are very probably beneficial, and in the fourth case we cannot tell whether or not the new rule benefited women. Overall, then, the Code almost certainly improved the condition of women. See further Gagarin 2008b.

8–9 'It is not a matter for trial': the expression clearly implies that after this time a woman who did not receive her share could bring suit, presumably against her own children who would be in line to inherit all her deceased husband's property, another indication that women participated directly in litigation at Gortyn (see above 3.1–9).

5.9–54—INHERITANCE AND THE DIVISION OF THE ESTATE (VER II.48, 49, K 169)

This section first (5.9–28) addresses the order of inheritance when there are no direct descendants, extending the group of heirs beyond the immediate family; it then regulates the process of dividing the estate among several heirs (5.28–54). The next section makes a small procedural point about gifts to daughters (6.1–2). VER discuss these three parts in different places.

ἒ κ' ἀποθάνει ἀνὲρ ἒ γυν- ά, αἰ μέν κ' ἒι τέκṇα ἒ ἐς τέ- κνον τέκṇα ἒ ἐς τούτον τέ- κνα, τούτος ἔκε[ν] τὰ κρέμα- τα. *vac.* αἰ δέ κạ μέτις ἒι τούτο- ν, ἀ⟦α⟧δελπιοὶ δὲ τô ἀποθανόν- τος κὲκς ἀδε[λ]πιôν τέκν- α ἒ ἐς τούτον τέκνα, τούτ- ος ἔκεν τὰ κρέματα. αἰ δέ κα μέτις ἒι τούτον, ἀδευπιαὶ δ- ὲ τô ἀποθανόντος κὲς ταυτ- âν τέκνα ἒ ἐς τôν τέκνον τέ- κνα, τούτος ἔκεν τὰ κρέμα- τα. *vac.* αἰ δέ κα μέτις ἒι τούτον, οἷς κ' ἐπιβάλλει ὄπο κ' ἒι τὰ κρ- έματạ τούτος ἀναιλêθθα- ι. *vac.* αἰ δὲ μὲ εἶεν ἐπιβάλλοντε- ς, τâς Ϝοικίας οἵτινές κ' ἴοντι ὀ κλâρος, τούτονς ἔ- κεν τὰ κρέματα. *vac.* αἰ δέ κ' οἰ ἐπιβάλλοντες οἰ μὲν λεί- οντι δατêθθαι τὰ κρέματ- α, οἰ δὲ μέ, δικάκσαι τὸν δι- καστὰν ἐπὶ τοῖλ λείονσι δ-

When a man or a woman dies, if there are children, or children of children, or children of children of children, these are to have the property. *vac.* But if there is none of these but brothers of the deceased and children of brothers or children of these, these are to have the property. And if there is none of these but sisters of the deceased and sisters' children or children of these, these are to have the property. *vac.* And if there is none of these, those to whom it falls are to take up the property whatever the source. *vac.* And if there should be no claimants, those of the household who are the *klaros* are to have the property. *vac.* And if some of the claimants wish to divide the property while others do not, the judge is to rule that all the property is to be in the hands of those who wish

ατε̂θθαι ἔμεν τὰ κρέματα π-
άντα πρίν κα δάττονται.
αἰ δέ κα δικάκσαντος τô δ-
ικαστâ κάρτει ἐνσείει ἒ ἄ-
γει ἒ πέρει, δέκα στατε̂ραν-
ς καταστασεῖ καὶ τô κρέι-
ος διπλεῖ. *vac.* τνατôν δὲ καὶ καρ-
πô καὶ Ϝέμας κἀνπιδέμας κ-
ἐπιπολαίον κρεμάτον αἴ κα μ-
ὲ λείοντι δατέ̣θ̣[θαι, τὸ]ν̣ δ̣-
[ικαστ]ὰν ὀμνύντα κρîνα-
ι πορτὶ τὰ μολιόμενα. *vac.* [α]ἰ [δ]-
έ κα κρέματα δατιόμενοι
μὲ συνγιγνόσκοντι ἀν-
πὶ τὰν δαῖσιν, ὀνε̂ν τὰ κρέμ-
ατα· κὄς κα πλεîστον διδ-
ôι ἀποδόμενοι τâν τιμâν
δια[λ]ακόντον τὰν ἐπαβο-
λὰν Ϝέκαστος. *vac.* δατιομέ-
νοιδ δὲ κρέματα μαίτυρα-
νς παρέμεν δρομέανς ἐλε-
υθέρονς τρίινς ἒ πλίανς.

to divide it until they divide it. And if, after the judge has ruled, someone enters by force or leads away or carries off (something), he will pay ten staters and double the value (of what he took). *vac.* As for the mortal possessions and produce and clothing and footwear and movable property, if they do not wish to divide (these), the judge is to swear an oath and decide with reference to the pleadings. *vac.* And if, when dividing the property, they cannot agree about the division, the property is to be sold; and when they have sold it to the person who gives the most, let them each receive their shares of the proceeds. *vac.* And when they are dividing the property, three or more adult free witnesses are to be present.

---

9 ἒ: 'when'; see W's very thorough note on 6.1.

10 ἐς = ἐκς (ἐκ); see Dialect 14.

17 The gap in this line is indicated by a *palmula* painted between two letters which have no gap between them, but where, on the analogy of 5.13, 5.22, and 5.25, a gap ought to be. The mason apparently forgot to leave a space and later went back and painted a *palmula* to indicate where it should have been. This should caution us against drawing hard and fast conclusions from the distribution of gaps; if this *palmula* had rubbed off as many other painted signs have, we would not know that a gap was supposed to be here.

18 ἀδευπιαί (ἀδελπιαί): for the variation, see Dialect 3; Bile 120. Cf. Ϝευμέναν (Ϝελμέναν) in **G80**.14–15.

23–6 οἶς κ' ἐπιβάλλει . . . ἐπιβάλλοντες: the structure of the provisions here and the use of ἐπιβάλλοντες in 25–6 indicate that οἶς κ' ἐπιβάλλει must be equivalent to οἰ ἐπιβάλλοντες (so e.g. W ad loc.); but as van Effenterre notes (1982: 460), this raises the question, how a passive construction ('those on whom it is imposed') can be equivalent to an active one ('those who impose on'). If we understand the relative clause to mean 'those to whom it falls' and the participle phrase to mean 'those who fall on (i.e. lay claim to)', then the expressions both mean 'those who have a claim'. Here the expression is used for the more distant relatives but it can designate any claimant. Cf. *ta epibalonta* 'things that are claimed' (**A9**.9–10).

23 ὄπο = ὀπόθεν; see W ad loc. with references.

24–5 ἀναιλêθθαι (ἀναιρεῖσθαι), 'take up'; see Dialect 30. Cantarella (Di Vita and Cantarella 1978: 434), Avramovic (1990: 369), and others think it significant that this verb (also in 7.10, 10.44, 11.4, 11.34, and without context in **A10B2–3** and **Ph1**.6) is used for more distant relatives whereas ἔκεν ('have') is used of direct descendants. But in 25–8 below, ἔκεν is used of the *klaros*, an even more distant group, and in 11.34 ἀναιλêθαι is used of heirs in general, who in most cases would be direct descendants. Thus, no significance is apparent in this variation; *anairesthai*, however, is limited to inheritance whereas *eken* is more general.

26–7 τᾶς Ϝοικίας οἵτινές κ' ἴοντι ὀ κλᾶρος: for the syntax and other difficult questions about this clause, see commentary below.

31 δικάκσαι: for the form, see Dialect 15.

34 Previous editors record a *vac.* at the end of this line, but there is at most space for half a letter and the ends of lines in the Code often have such variation. If the mason had wanted to record a gap, he would have had to do so at the beginning of the next line.

36 ἐνσείει (Att. εἰσίῃ): pres. subj. (Dialect 14).

39 τνατôν: for the form, see Dialect 5; for the genitives, see n. ad 1.4.

41 ἐπιπολαίον κρεμάτον, 'movable property' (Att. ἔπιπλα).

44 There is room for a gap of one letter after *moliomena*, but the stone is damaged so that it is impossible to be certain whether the empty space was intended to be a gap.

47 ὀνêν: the active voice meaning 'sell' is uniquely Cretan (Attic would use πωλεῖν); but the middle (ὀνêθθαι), as in Attic, means 'buy' (e.g. 6.4 below).

50–1 ἐπαβολάν: the noun is probably related to ἐπιβάλλω, but no one has satisfactorily explained why the third letter is *alpha*; Bile 323 notes that the word means 'share of the money' rather than 'share of the property' (which is *moira*).

54 τρίινς: masc. acc. pl., cf. **G65**.11 note.

9–28 This section first lists those who may inherit in five groups in order of priority: one group can only inherit if there are no living members of the groups ahead of it. The section thus extends the number of potential heirs well beyond the immediate family, perhaps even to a person's serfs (see on 5.25–8).

9–13 The first group are the direct descendants. The fact that the rules are the same for the estates of women implies that females are included along with males in the same 2:1 ratio that was established in 4.39–43. On the other hand, brothers of the deceased have priority over sisters. Grandchildren or great-grandchildren probably inherited only if their parent had died. It seems more likely that inheritance was *per stirpes* than *per capita*, so that a single son of a deceased daughter would receive her single share not the double share of a son.

13–17 There is no apparent significance in the variation (also in 17–22) between 'and' and 'or' ('brothers of the deceased *and* brothers' children *or* children of these').

22–5 'Those to whom it falls' (*ois k' epiballei*): most agree that this group, more commonly called the *epiballontes* ('claimants' or 'heirs'; see n. ad 23–6 above and comm. ad 3.28), are relatives outside the circle of the first three groups. Maffi

(1997a: 58–9) argues that these are not parents or grandchildren of brothers and sisters, but cousins, but it seems more likely that this is a catch-all phrase and that many relatives (though perhaps not parents) could arguably include themselves in this group. Bile argues (1988: 333–4) that the *epiballontes* are only paternal relatives, but all we can say with certainty is that they are more distant relatives than those already mentioned, namely the direct descendants of the deceased or of the deceased's brother or sister. It seems likely, however, that the next set of heirs would come from the same or later generations, namely cousins and cousins' descendants, and since both males and females seem to be equally involved in inheritance up to this point, it seems to us unlikely that the *epiballontes* would be restricted to one side of the family. But this is not impossible.

For the distinction between the *epiballontes* and the *kadestai*, see on 2.18 above.

23 'Whatever the source' (lit. 'from wherever it is'): the subject of this clause is disputed and the reference is obscure. Maffi (1997a: 59), following Bücheler-Zitelmann, K, and VER, takes the subject to be the next group of claimants: 'whatever their provenance', that is, from whichever side of the family they come. But the singular verb 'is' (*ei*) would be very difficult to construe with 'those to whom it falls' as the subject. Thus, we follow Blass and G (so also Bile 2002: 122, with n. 23) in understanding *kremata* ('property') as the subject: that is, 'from whatever place' or 'wherever it happens to be'. This is unlikely to mean from the mother or from the father, since from the beginning it is clear that all the rules in this section apply to both the mother's and the father's property (lines 9–10). The clause may refer to whether the property is in the city or not (see 4.31–48), or to whether it was inherited or acquired by other means. This addition may have been suggested by the change in verb to *anaileththai* ('take up'), or the fact that the object *kremata* is put ahead of the verb and its subject; but this would not mean that a different kind of inheritance is involved.

25–8 'Those of the household who are the *klaros*': the composition of this fifth group has provoked the most controversy. The main difficulties are first, does *woikia* mean 'household' or 'family', and does it qualify the preceding 'claimants' ('no claimants from the family') or the clause that follows, as we translate? Second, who or what was the *klaros*? Below we conclude that *woikia* means 'household'—that is, those living in or around the house and attached to it (including serfs)—and that it goes with the clause that follows. For further discussion, see Gagarin 2010a: 26–9.

26 'Of the household/family': G and others understand this as qualifying 'claimants', but since the fourth group ('those to whom it falls') presumably includes all the remaining family members, the qualification would be superfluous. See Brixhe 1999: 109. We therefore understand it with the clause that follows: 'those of the household who are the *klaros*'.

27 More difficult is the question, who was the *klaros*? In this context it must designate a person or persons, not a piece of land (as its Attic equivalent, *klēros*, often does), and in the absence of any family heirs, 'those of the household who are the *klaros*' can only be the serfs, who lived on and worked the land belonging to the estate. This was the view of several older scholars, including Comparetti (1893: 193), though he would (perhaps correctly) restrict the *klaros* to a small, select group among all the serfs. The idea that serfs could inherit their owner's estate (and would necessarily be free of any ownership) is unacceptable to many scholars (e.g. Maffi 1997a: 59–61), but in very rare cases where a person died without heirs, serfs would have no master but would presumably continue to work the land to which they had traditionally been attached. Thus, they would be the de facto owners of the land, and the law simply recognizes and ratifies this situation, making them the legal owners. It probably also makes them free persons, since they have no master, and Dareste et al. 1891–1904: I.422 make the plausible suggestion that they would now be *apetairoi*. The startling nature of this result may account for the legislator's writing the full expression, 'those of the *woikia* who are the *klaros*' rather than more simply 'those who are the *klaros*' or 'those of the *woikia*', both of which would designate the same group.

28–54 The rules in 4.23–48 specified that after sons received certain items, the estate was to be divided among all the children. The process of division, however, could lead to disputes about just how to make a fair division. Disputes might concern, first, whether to divide property or hold it jointly, and second, how to make an equal division into the required number of shares. For example, if one piece of land with two or three serfs was inherited by two sons and a daughter, should the land in fact be divided into three pieces—two larger pieces for the sons and a smaller one for the daughter, adjusted perhaps depending on who inherited a serf—or should the heirs hold it jointly? In many cases joint ownership would clearly have been preferable to division. If the heirs could not agree, however, then the property could be sold and the proceeds divided among them.

This passage gives rules for handling such situations. The heirs can evidently own property together without dividing it. But the law favors division if any of them so wish; presumably, division was considered preferable to conflict among joint owners. First (28–39), the property (*kremata*, see next note) is put in the hands of those who wish to divide it until it is divided; at this point removal of anything is prohibited. This provision covers all the property, including land, houses, secured loans, and all the items mentioned in the next provision. Second (39–44), however, disputes may arise over some of the smaller items, which the heirs may not wish to divide. These are more personal items—clothing, a personal slave, furniture—that one of the heirs may feel a particular attachment to. The judge decides these sorts of disputes. Third (44–51), during the division process if the heirs cannot agree, the property is to be sold and the proceeds divided among the heirs. Finally (51–4), the required witnesses are specified.

30–1 Property (*kremata*) here and in 45–52 refers to everything the deceased owned, almost certainly including land (see comm. ad 2.48–50 above and 39–44 below).

32–3 'In the hands of': see on 4.37. Control of the property is explicitly made temporary.

37–9 'He will pay ten staters and double the value': the same expression is in 3.13–15.

39–44 The specification of items that the heirs may not wish to divide clearly implies that the other parts of the property (*kremata*), including the real property, would still be divided. If real property were indivisible, as some think (Introd. 7B), then this provision would amount to allowing virtually all the property to remain undivided, and in many cases this would make it highly impractical, if not impossible, to observe the rule that the property is to be divided with sons inheriting two shares and daughters one (4.37–43).

39–41 The heirs may not wish to divide these items, probably because one heir may wish to have one or more of them in their entirety. For instance, if a man dies, a son might reasonably wish to have all his clothing; or the heirs might want to divide the land but have all the animals go to the heir who will get the best land for grazing.

39 'Mortal possessions' (*tnaton*): most scholars take this as designating livestock, but VER take it to include slaves as well. Maffi (1997a: 72) translates 'mortal things' (*cose mortali*), which includes slaves and animals. It is even possible that this also included produce (but not land, cf. **G76**B8–9). Slaves must have been an important part of some estates and it is easy to imagine disputes among the heirs about how to divide them.

39–40 For *karpos* as 'produce', see on 2.48–50.

40 'Footwear': the word *ampidema* is more often translated 'jewelry', but in **G43Ab**11–12 (see comm.) it probably means 'footwear'. We keep this translation here, but it is possible that the word could have both meanings.

44 'With reference to the pleadings' (*porti ta moliomena*): This expression also occurs in 6.54–5 and 11.30–1; in each case it qualifies the prescription that the judge should 'swear an oath and decide' (*omnynta krinen*). *Pace* Maffi (2007: 204; 2011: 155 n. 4) it cannot simply refer to the initial claims and counter-claims of the parties but must refer to all the arguments presented by all parties to the dispute, which might be more than two. In the kind of case described here, disputes could be quite complex, and a judge would have an impossible task if all he could consider were the initial claims of the parties. See below on 11.30–1 and further Gagarin 2010b: 136–7.

44–51 If the heirs cannot agree on how to divide any of the property, such as a plot of land, it will be sold and the proceeds will be divided.

48–9 The property is auctioned off to the highest bidder.

52–4 For the requirement that witnesses be free and adult, see on 1.41–2.

6.1–2—GIFTS TO A DAUGHTER (VER II.53, K 169)

Gifts to a daughter are essentially her inheritance and must follow the same rules concerning the division of the estate.

θυγατρὶ ἐ̂ διδôι, κατὰ τὰ αὐτ-
ά. vac.

When (a father) gives to a daughter, (it is to be done) in the same way. *vac.*

6.1 ἐ̂: 'when'; see W's very thorough note ad loc.

This rule concerning gifts to a daughter (4.48–5.1) is probably put right after the rules for inheritance because these gifts often constituted the daughter's share of the inheritance. The highly elliptical sentence must refer to the rules for the division of an estate before death in 5.28–54. A man would have to calculate the division in order to know how much he could give his daughter. If there was disagreement among the heirs about this division, he might have to sell something. Thus, the process of determining the amount of a gift to a daughter must follow the same procedural rules as the division of the estate.

6.2–46—MISUSE OF OTHERS' PROPERTY (VER II.54, K 170)

This section prohibits someone from selling, pledging as security, or promising property that belongs to a relative, and prescribes consequences for doing so.

ἆς κ' ὀ πατὲδ δόει, τôν τô π-
ατρὸς κρεμάτον πὰρ υἰέος
μὲ ὀνêθθαι μεδὲ καταθίθ-
εθθαι, ἄτι δέ κ' αὐτὸς πάσετ-
αι ἒ ἀπολάκει ἀποδιδόθθο,
αἴ κα λêι· μεδὲ τὸν πατέρα τὰ τô-
ν τέκνον ἄτι κ' αὐτοὶ πάσον-
ται ἒ ἀπολάκοντι. vac. μεδὲ τὰ τ-
âς γυναικὸς τὸν ἄνδρα ἀπο-
δόθαι μεδ' ἐπισπένσαι, μεδ'
υἰὺν τὰ τâς ματρός. vac. αἰ δ-
έ τις πρίαιτο ἒ καταθεῖτο ἒ ἐ-
πισπένσαιτο, ἀλλâι δ' ἔγρατ-
[τα]ι, âι τάδε τὰ γράμματα ἔγ-
[ρ]ạ[τται, τὰ] μ[ὲ]ṿ
κρέματα ἐπὶ τâι ματρὶ ἔμ-
εν κ' ἐπὶ τâι γυναικί, ὀ δ' ἀπο-
δόμενος ἒ καταθὲνς ἒ ἐπι-

As long as the father is living, no one is to buy any of the father's property from a son or accept it as security, but whatever (the son) himself has acquired or inherited, let him sell it, if he wishes; nor is the father (to sell or pledge as security) his children's property, whatever they themselves have acquired or inherited. *vac.* And the husband is not to sell or promise his wife's property, nor the son his mother's. *vac.* And if anyone should buy it or accept it as security or as a promise, and it is written otherwise than these writings are written, the property is to be in the hands of the mother or the wife, and the one who sold it or gave it as security or

σπένσανς τôι πριαμένοι
ἒ καταθεμένοι ἒ ἐπισπεν-
σαμένοι διπλεῖ καταστα-
σεῖ καἴ τί κ' ἄλλ' ἄτας ἐ͂ι, τὸ ἀπ-
λόον· τôν δὲ πρόθθα μὲ ἔν-
δικον ἔμεν. *vac.* αἰ δέ κ' ὁ ἀντίμ-
ολος ἀπομολêι ἀνπὶ τὸ κρ-
έος ὄι κ' ἀνπιμολίοντι μ-
ὲ ἔμεν τâς ματ[ρ]ὸς ἒ τâ-
ς γυναικός, μολὲν ὄπε κ' ἐπ-
ιβάλλει, πὰρ τôι δικαστâι
ἒ Ϝεκάστο ἔγραπται. *vac.* αἰ δέ κ' ἀ-
ποθάνει μάτερ τέκνα καταλιπό-
νσα, τὸν πατέρα καρτερὸν ἔμεν
τôν ματροίον, ἀποδόθαι δὲ μὲ
μεδὲ καταθέμεν, αἴ κα μὲ τὰ τέκ-
να ἐπαινέσει δρομέες ἰόντες.
[α]ἰ δέ τις ἀλλâι πρίαιτο ἒ κατα-
θεῖτο, τὰ μὲν κρέματα ἐπὶ τοῖ-
ς τέκνοις ἔμεν, τôι δὲ πριαμ-
ένοι ἒ καταθεμένοι τὸν ἀποδ-
όμενον ἒ τὸν καταθέντα τὰν
διπλείαν καταστâσαι τâς τ-
ιμâς, καἴ τί κ' ἄλλ' ἄτας ἐ͂ι, τὸ ἀ-
πλόον. αἰ δέ κ' ἄλλαν ὀπυίει, τὰ τ-
έκνα [τô]ν [μ]ạτροίον καρτερὸν-
⟨ς⟩ ἔμεν. *vac.*

promised it will pay double to the person who bought it or accepted it as security or as a promise, and if there is any other damage, (he will pay) the simple value; but for earlier matters it is not a matter for trial. *vac.* If the opposing litigant contends (in court) that the item about which they are contending is not the mother's or wife's, the matter is to be tried where it belongs, before the judge where it is written in each case. *vac.* If a mother dies leaving children, the father is to have control of the maternal estate, but he is not to sell it or use it as security unless the children approve and are adults; but if someone should otherwise buy it or accept it as security, the property is to be in the hands of the children and the one who sold it or gave it as security is to pay double the value to the one who bought it or took it as security, and if there is any other damage, (he will pay) the simple value. And, if he should marry another woman, the children are to have control of the maternal estate. *vac.*

---

2 ἆς, δόει: see on 4.27 above.

4 ὀνêθθαι: see on 5.47 above.

5 ἄτι: see on 2.47 above, Dialect 18.

6 ἀποδιδόθθο: for the meaning, see above on **G41**.4.7–8; for the variation between double *theta* and single *theta* (in 6.10–11), see Dialect 11.

7–9 Like VER, we follow W in putting a full stop after ἀπολάκοντι (9); G, K, and others put a comma there, but the *vac.* in line 9 makes it difficult (though not impossible) to construe the clauses before and after it so closely together. With a full stop one needs to supply the verbs from 4–5 (in their active rather than middle forms) in 7–9. This sort of ellipsis is not uncommon in the Code.

12–31 The wording is very similar to that in 9.7–24. The main differences are the omission of promising in 9.7–24, the simplification of ἀλλâι δ' ἔγραπται, etc. to ἀλλâι (see next note), the addition of αἴ κα νικαθêι in 9.13, the addition of ἐπικαταστασεῖ in 9.15 (implied but unexpressed in 6.23–4), the addition of ἆι τάδε τὰ γράμματα ἔγραπται in 9.15–16, the switch to the optative ἀπομολίοι in 9.18–19 (a relatively minor change), and the puzzling addition of what seems to be an extra stage in the procedure in 9.21–3 (ὁ δικαστὰς ὀμνὺς κρινέτο· αἰ δὲ νικάσαι μὲ τâς πατροιόκο ἔμεν).

14–16 ἀλλᾶι δ' ἔγρατ[τα]ι, ᾶι τάδε τὰ γράμματα ἔγ[ρ]α[τται]: lit. 'and it is written otherwise as these writings are written'. A shorter expression, ἀλλᾶι δ' ἔγραττι 'and it is written differently') in 8.54, means essentially the same thing; and the same idea is expressed with the simple ἀλλᾶι in 37–8 below and in 9.8. It is hard to see what purpose, if any, the clause beginning with ᾶι has. W and others take ᾶι in a temporal sense: 'when' or 'since', and explains 'and it is written otherwise since the inscription of this law'. But this implies that the legislator is prohibiting someone from following a later amendment to the law, which seems impossible, and in his translation W sticks with the more traditional 'and it is written otherwise in these writings'. Similarly, Bile calls ᾶι a 'polyvalent' conjunction (1988: 262), here meaning 'since' (*depuis*). But it is better to understand ᾶι τάδε τὰ γράμματα ἔγραττι as an expanded form of the common expression ᾶι ἔγραττι, 'as is written'. Maffi (1997a: 108–10, and p.c.) understands it to imply that there are ways a man could sell or promise his wife's property legally, and suspects he could do so in order to pay her debts; this is not impossible.

16 The writing in this line stops at the edge of the stone in the middle of the column. It would normally continue on the new stone to the right, but this stone has a projection along the top edge which prevented the mason from writing on it.

26 ἀπομολῆι: the meaning of the compound verb (only here and in 9.18–19) is not clear; it may signify a suit that responds to an earlier accusation (Bile 274: 'un procédé de renouvellement'), presumably denying the charge.

29–30 ὅπε κ' ἐπιβάλλει: lit. 'wherever it falls'.

31–43 The wording here is a shorter version of 9–24 above.

35–6 τὰ τέκνα . . . δρομέες ἰόντες: the shift from masculine to neuter is natural and easy, there probably being no neuter form of *dromeus*. Very probably there was also no feminine form, so that as it regularly does, the masculine plural here stands for both genders.

42 There is an apparent erasure between the *alpha* and the *san* of *tas*, suggesting that the mason made a mistake and then cut out the faulty letter before proceeding.

45–6 καρτερὸν⟨ς⟩: the mason mistakenly wrote *nu* instead of *san*.

This section protects the property of one family member from abuse by another. It begins (2–9) by prohibiting misuse by a son of his father's property before his death, and by a father of property that already belongs to his children; 9–12 then prohibit similar misuse by a husband of his wife's or mother's property or by a son of his mother's. Sanctions are then prescribed (12–31) for violations, but these only apply to the rule in 9–12. The final part of this section (31–46) then addresses the related matter of a husband's control of his deceased wife's property. It appears, then, that three sets of rules that may originally have been separate are here combined: 2–9, 9–31, and 31–46.

2–14 Three types of financial transactions are mentioned, (a) buying and selling (*oneththai*, see n. ad 5.47), (b) pledging and accepting security (*katathitheththai*, see below on 4–5), and (c) promising or accepting a promise (*epispendo*, see below on 11). In the first set of rules (2–9), (a) and (b) are specified; in the second (9–12), (a) and (c) are specified; and in the provisions for sanctions (12–31), all three are specified; and finally in 31–44, which like 2–9 concern a father and his children's property, (a) and (b) are specified. Since there is no apparent reason why in some of these cases only two of the three actions should be mentioned, and since there is little discernible difference between pledging as security and promising (see below on 11), we should probably assume that all three are prohibited in each case. If the provisions were drafted at different times, and perhaps by different legislators, this might explain the variation in wording.

4–5 'Accept as security' (*katathitheththai*): *katatithēmi* in the active means to pledge something or someone as security for a loan. If land is pledged, this is similar to obtaining a mortgage on it; if a person (free or slave) is pledged, this is essentially an indentureship (for which see **G41** cols. 5–6 for an indentured free person, and **G47** for an indentured slave). In the middle (as here) the verb means to accept someone or something as security. The *katathens* (19) is the person who pledges something, i.e. the debtor; if he pledges himself, he becomes a *katakeimenos* (as in **G41** cols. 5–6).

6 *Apolankanen* (lit. 'receive as a share'): the verb is always used of inheritance. Here it must refer to a distribution of the father's estate before his death (see n. ad 5.1 above). It cannot designate the share of the mother's estate which a son has inherited while the father is still living, since this is addressed in 31–46 below.

9–12 By prohibiting male relatives from selling or promising a woman's property, the law implies that the woman herself could sell or promise her own property; see Gagarin 2008b: 12, 18–19. No mention is made of protecting a daughter's or a sister's property, probably because these were less subject to misuse.

11 'To promise' (*epispensai*): up to this point, *epispendo* has only been used of promising property to a daughter in connection with her marriage (4.52–3, 5.3–4), and W argues (p. 21) that the verb is only used in this 'technical sense' of a promise made in connection with marriage. Such a view would have the curious consequence that a man who wanted to give his daughter at her marriage more than the amount allowed in 4.48–51 would be able to promise that amount from his wife's property, let this be discovered, and then pay the 'penalty' of giving his daughter twice as much as he had promised. Moreover, his wife could probably promise (or give) the property herself if she wished. Rather, the clear thrust of this whole section seems to be to prevent one family member from using the property of other family members to satisfy their own obligations (Maffi 1997a: 115–16). Thus, *epispensai* here most likely refers to using a wife or daughter's property to guarantee a future payment, probably to cover one's own debt. See Bile 354–6.

12–31 This section sets out the consequences of violating the prohibition against misuse of a wife's or mother's property in 9–12; they do not mention misuse of a father's or child's property described in lines 2–9. Maffi 1997a: 42 suggests that no sanctions are given for the first two cases because the property in question is entirely within the family so that any compensation can be arranged within the family, whereas the property of a wife or mother comes originally from another family. But it seems unlikely that misuse of a father's or child's property could always be dealt with within the family, especially since a child's property may have come from its mother and thus from outside the family. More likely, the legislator assumed that rules in 12–31 would also apply to misuse of a father's or child's property. But the absence of explicit rules for these cases may be a sign of poor organization in this section.

These provisions are very similar to those concerning the property of an 'heiress' in 9.7–24; see note above on 12–31 for variations in the Greek text; these mostly serve to clarify the sense and make it more specific. For substantive differences, see on 9.7–24. An abbreviated version of these rules governs the mismanagement of the property of a deceased wife in 6.31–43.

12–16 Maffi (p.c.) understands the prohibition against acting 'otherwise' than the law as implying that some types of sale (etc.) were allowed by law, namely (by analogy with 9.1–24) a sale to pay the woman's debts. In our view, the woman could sell (etc.) her property herself, to pay debts or for any other reason.

13–14 Three offenses are mentioned here, though only two were explicitly prohibited in 9–12; see above on 2–14.

16–18 The fact that the law puts a mother or wife in charge of her own property if her son or husband abuses it, suggests that the male relative was previously in charge of it. Some women must thus have allowed their husband or son to oversee the day-to-day management of some of the property; indeed, this may even have been the norm. Presumably, a woman could reclaim management of her property from her husband or son whenever she wished.

17–18 'In the hands of the mother or the wife': for the meaning of *epi* with the dative, see on 4.37. Maffi (1997a: 107) translates 'the property will be the mother's or the wife's', i.e. it will belong to her; this implies that the husband or son will continue to manage the property, though Maffi is not clear on this point. But *epi* with the dative in other cases refers to having charge of a person or property, not (permanent) ownership, which is indicated by *eken* or a possessive genitive (cf. 28–9 below). Moreover, returning ownership of the property to the woman would only be relevant after a sale; if a husband unlawfully pledged or promised the property, it would still belong to the wife and it would make no sense to require that it now be hers. And if the husband did sell his wife's property unlawfully, it seems unlikely that the law would allow him to continue managing it after his misuse was discovered.

23 The reference of 'other damage' is unclear. It may refer to additional damages or losses incurred by the third party (who buys or accepts a promise or pledge of security), but more likely it refers to damage to the property, for which compensation would be paid to the woman who owns it.

24–5 The fact that rules protecting a woman's property from misuse by male relatives are non-retroactive implies that before the Code, women's property did not have such protection, and that the rules in this section were thus enacted to protect the woman's property. For retroactivity in the Code, see further on 5.7–9.

25–9 There is much disagreement about the precise nature of the litigation envisioned here. Three parties have an interest in it: the male relative, the female relative, and a third party (the buyer or receiver of a pledge or promise). It is fairly certain that the male relative is the defendant; he faces the possibility of a substantial fine for misusing his wife's or mother's property, and so he must be claiming that the property did not belong to her; presumably he claims it is his own, and thus that the sale, pledge, or promise was legal. The plaintiff, then, must be either the woman or the third party, and the woman is the more likely candidate. First, the third party would be far less likely to know that the defendant did not own the property. Second, he would have no reason to bring suit since he has benefited, not suffered, from the misuse. He might possibly try to learn that the property does not belong to the seller so that he could sue and receive double compensation (but give up the property), but this seems a far less likely scenario than one in which the wife or mother sues to regain control of her property. She would know for certain that the property was hers and would have every reason to bring suit to recover it, and she would deserve compensation for damages to the property if there were any. Maffi argues (1997a: 110–13, at 112) that if the woman wants her property returned, she would bring suit against the purchaser, but this would be an odd suit, in which the defendant would be better off if he lost, since he would then receive double the value of the property. He would also (on Maffi's interpretation) receive compensation for damage to the property, which surely ought to go to the woman. It is far more likely, therefore, that the woman brings suit against her male relative. The law does not specify what happens if she wins, but presumably the buyer would have no objection to returning the property, since he will then receive double compensation, and the property will then be controlled by the woman. Suits between husband and wife or mother and son would be impossible in Athenian law, but were allowed in Gortyn, as we see in the regulations concerning divorce in 2.45–3.16. See further Gagarin 2008b: 13–14.

25–6 Both *antimolos* ('litigant', lit. 'opposing pleader') and *apomolen* ('contend in court') occur in the Code only here and in the nearly identical expression in 9.18–19. The verb may also occur in **G81**.5–6. *Antimolos* is often translated 'defendant' (W, VER), and in this case it is in fact the defendant, but the word can refer to either litigant; so Maffi 1997a: 113.

29–31 Some lawsuits at Gortyn were heard by different judges depending on the nature of the case. 'Orphan-judges' (*orpanodikastai*) are mentioned in 12.6–19, and in **G42**B11–14 'the *dikastas* of the *etaireiai* and whoever judges in cases of pledges'. Here different judges may have handled cases of sale, promise, and pledge (so W and others). The rules referred to must have been written elsewhere than in the Code.

31–46 After a mother with children dies, her husband takes control of her property, although her children will eventually inherit it. The children apparently gain full control of the property only after their father's death, or if he misuses it or remarries. The restrictions on the father's control of the property are similar to those in effect when the mother was alive (see n. ad 6.2–14); the same penalty is specified in both cases.

33 'Have control of' (*karteron emen*, also in 45–6): see on 4.23–7. The difference between this and 'in the hands of' in 38–9 is not clear, but the former seems to indicate a greater degree of control.

37–43 The rules here are the same as one part of those in 6.12–31 and 9.1–24; there the rules are also said not to be retroactive, and the alleged violator is allowed to argue that the property does not belong to the woman in question. Both qualifications are probably meant to be understood here too.

44–6 A man who remarries and perhaps has children with his new wife should not control his former wife's property, because he might try to use it for the benefit of his new family; but it is surprising that the children, who might be quite young, are put in control of it without any age limit. Presumably a male relative would act as guardian in such circumstances, and the legislator apparently saw no need to mention this. Cf. the similar provision for the underage heiress in 8.47–50.

6.46–55—RANSOM (VER I.13, K 171)

Someone who asks to be ransomed must repay his ransomer; until he does, he is in the ransomer's hands.

αἰ κ' ἐδδυσ̣[άμενον] πέ-
ρα̣[νδε] ἐκς ἀλλοπολίας ὑπ' ἀν-
άνκας ἐκόμενος κελομ̣ένο τι-
ς λύσεται, ἐπὶ τôι ἀλλυσαμέν-
οι ἔμεν πρίν κ' ἀποδôι τὸ ἐπιβά-
λλον. αἰ δέ κα μὲ ὀμολογίοντ-
ι ἀμπὶ τὰν πλεθὺν ἒ μὲ κελομέ-
[ν]ο αὐτô λύσαθθαι, τὸν δικασ-
τὰν ὀμνύντα κρίνεν πορτὶ τὰ
μολιόμενα.

If someone, bound by necessity, ransoms someone who has gone abroad from another city at his request, he is to be in the hands of the ransomer until he pays back his obligation. But if they do not agree about the amount or (he claims) that it was not at his request that he ransomed him, the judge is to swear an oath and decide, with reference to the pleadings.

46 ἐδδυσ̣[άμενον] G, W, K; Metzger (1973: 50 n. 130) and VER supply a nominative participle (ἐδδυσ̣[άμενος]), but they must then translate λύσεται (subj.) as a passive—'if someone who has gone abroad (or has been stripped—see next note) is ransomed'—but λύσεται must be an aorist middle; even if it could be passive, the separation of *tis* from ἐδδυσ̣[άμενος] would be very awkward. With ἐδδυσ̣[άμενον] λύσεται has its normal sense: 'if someone ransoms a person who . . .'.

ἐδδυσ̣[άμενον]: elsewhere at Gortyn (e.g. **G43Ab4**) the verb (Attic ἐκδύω) means 'undress, strip'. VER argue that it designates a young man who has undressed and put down his arms in an initiation ceremony ('sans vêtements et sans armes'), but this makes little sense here. Possibly it means 'stripped of his arms', i.e. taken prisoner, but it may be better to understand another sense of Attic *ekduō* (though always in the active), 'get out of, escape' (LSJ s.v. III), and translate 'someone who has gone away' (so G, W, K).

46–7 πέρα̣[νδε]: for discussion, see W, who compares **Ele11**.1 and a fifth-century treaty between Knossos, Tylissos, and Argos (M&L 42).

47–8 ὐπ' ἀνάνκας: 'by necessity', as in **A9**.5 (cf. 8.33 below). Martínez-Fernández 1983 argues that ἀνάνκα here is equivalent to the Attic ἀναγκαιότης, 'kinship ties' (also suggested by G, W; cf. Bile 332, with n. 56). We prefer to translate 'by necessity', understanding that the necessity to ransom another person might often be a tie of kinship, but 'because of kinship' might better represent the law's meaning.

48 κελομ̣ένο: cf. **G41**.5.7–8, αἰ δὲ πονίοι μὴ κελομένο ('if he should affirm that it was not done at his request').

49–50 ἀλλυσαμένοι (ἀναλυσαμένοι): see n. ad 2.30–1.

50–1 τὸ ἐπιβάλλον: intransitive, 'something that imposes itself'—i.e. an obligation; see on 5.23–6.

53 αὐτô: W, K, VER correctly read this as a genitive, providing a subject for κελομένο; G, followed by Metzger (1973: 50), reads an accusative ending in *lambda* by assimilation, but they must then assume that the mason omitted a *lambda* by mistake (αὐτὸλ (λ)ύσαθθαι).

The construction of 46–9 is disputed (see notes above), in part because of damage to the stones that join at the end of line 46 and beginning of 47, but the general sense is not in doubt (see W): someone who asks to be ransomed is obliged to repay the ransom amount and is in the power of the ransomer until he does. Disputes over the amount that was paid or whether the ransom was requested are decided by a judge. The rule is reasonable and is paralleled at Athens (Dem. 53.11). The provision may be concerned primarily with the ransom of merchants captured by pirates, who were a constant danger at sea, but it would not exclude prisoners of war and others held for ransom abroad. Metzger's discussion (1973: 50–51) is clear and straightforward.

47 The precise meaning of *allopolia* ('another city') is unclear; it may mean something like 'in another city without rights' (VER). Cf. Perlman's discussion (2004a: esp. 124–7) of *allopoliatas* ('foreigner') at Eleutherna (**Ele3**.1) and Lyktos (**Lyktos1A**1–2).

49 'In the hands of': see on 4.37. As in 2.34–5 with regard to the captured adulterer, the control is expected to be temporary. The law assumes that the prisoner (or adulterer) is unable to pay for his release, and it probably envisions a temporary indentureship (cf. **G41**.5–6) that will allow him to work until his obligation is paid.

54–5 'With reference to the pleadings': see above on 5.44.

6.55–7.10—CHILDREN OF MIXED MARRIAGES (VER II.36, K 172)

The status of the children of a slave and a free woman depends on where they reside.

τô ἐλευθέρο τον
δ̣ε[*c.*8 αἴ κ' ὁ δôλος]
Col. 7
ἐπὶ τὰν ἐλευθέραν ἐλθὸν ὀπυίει,
ἐλεύθερ' ἔμεν τὰ τέκνα. *vac.* αἰ δέ κ'
ἀ ἐλευθέρα ἐπὶ τὸν δôλον, δôλ' ἔμ-
εν τὰ τέκνα. *vac.* αἰ δέ κ' ἐς τâς αὐτ-
âς ματρὸς ἐλεύθερα καὶ δôλα
τέκνα γένεται, ἐ̂ κ' ἀποθάνει ἀ
μάτερ, αἴ κ' ἐ̂ι κρέματα, τὸνς ἐλε-
υθέρονς ἔκεν. αἰ δ' ἐλευθέροι
μὲ ἐκσεῖεν, τὸνσς ἐπιβάλλον-
τανς ἀναιλêθαι. *vac.*

— of the free man [*c.*7 If the slave] (**Col.** 7) goes to a free woman and marries her, their children are to be free; *vac.* but if the free woman (goes to) the slave, their children are to be slaves. *vac.* And if free and slave children are born from the same mother, when the mother dies, if there is property, the free children are to have it; but if there should be no free children, her relatives are to inherit it. *vac.*

---

55 The letters οελευθερο are written in a depression that may be an erasure. They include two unusual letter shapes, a *lambda* with a horizontal (not angled) top bar and an *upsilon* with a slight tail. Both forms are more common in some of the addenda (e.g. 11.13–14), which may indicate that this string of letters was a later correction. On the other hand, the depression may be just a worn spot on the stone, and the form of the *upsilon*, at least, is paralleled in 6.53 (*lysaththai*). If the letters are a later correction, then the initial *tau*, which is not written in the erasure, may have filled a blank space that was originally a gap at the end of the previous section. VER (II.16) put τô ἐλευθέρο τὸν δε at the end of col. 11.

55–7.1 The bigger question is whether τô ἐλευθέρο τὸν δ̣ε (or τόνδε/τôνδε, see next note) goes with what precedes it or is connected to the provisions in 7.1–10 (and if so, how). In either case, some amount of text must be missing before the beginning of col. 7.

55–6 τονδ̣ε[could be read as τὸν δέ (or τôν δέ) or as τόνδε (or τôνδε), or δε could be the first letters of a noun, adjective, or participle. Each solution has difficulties. If we read the article and δέ, it is hard to see what *de* might be connecting; the demonstrative pronoun ('this person' or 'of these people') has no evident point of reference; and no word beginning with δε- seems to fit the sense (*dendreon*? *deuteron*? *dedaismenon*?).

56 δ̣ε: the initial letter could be α, but it is very hard to make the second letter anything but an *epsilon*, and the sequence *TONAE* seems impossible. No other letters are visible in the bottom line, and so the text probably continued on the stone below, which is no longer preserved, as it does at the bottom of column 11.

[αἴ κ' ὁ δôλος] (proposed by C) is required by the alternative given in 7.2–4, and is accepted by all editors.

2 There is clearly a space between τέκνα and αἰ δέ, but this could be due to the roughness of the stone at this point.

9 ἐκσεῖεν: in Attic this verb (ἔξεστι) is always impersonal, but here the prefix seems to have its full force: 'are (born) *from* (her)'; see W ad loc.

τόνσς: for the double consonant, see Dialect 10.

9–10 ἐπιβάλλονταυς: for the meaning, see above on 5.23–6.

10 ἀναιλêθαι: for the form, see Dialect 30; for the meaning, see on 5.24–5.

The provisions regulating the marriage of a free woman and a slave (presumably including *woikeis* together with *doloi*) are extraordinary and point to the relatively greater rights of slaves (and women) at Gortyn than elsewhere in Greece. Mixed marriages are also regulated in the Laws of Hammurabi 175–6, where the children are to be free and rules are given for the division of property when one spouse dies. In Roman Law the *Senatusconsultus Claudianum* (Gaius *Inst.* 1.160) condemned a free woman who cohabited with a slave to slavery herself, but this was later considered overly harsh and the law was repealed. Some text is missing between 6.55 and 7.1 (see notes above) and this section may originally have begun with provisions concerning marriage between a free man and a slave woman.

We can only guess at the circumstances under which a free woman (or a free man) would marry a slave. The family may have been impoverished, her father and brothers may all be indentured, or perhaps a slave or a serf had accumulated some wealth. Bile (2012: 59–60) suggests that economic circumstances played a part: a rich woman (or her rich family) would accept a slave into their house, whereas a poor woman would have to go to the slave's house. But other factors must also have been involved.

6.55–7.1 Apparently, the words 'of the free person' begin a new provision (see below on 6.55), marked by asyndeton (Introd. 3D3). An unknown amount of text is then missing before the beginning of column 7, including at least the words 'if the slave' (see below on 6.56). Since provisions that follow concern marriages between free women and slave men, it is natural to ask whether marriages between free men and slave women were not also allowed, and if so, whether this subject was addressed here in the missing text? The mason may have originally omitted these provisions by mistake and later tried to correct the error by erasing a few letters (n. ad 55 above), adding the omitted text in the erasure, and continuing on the stone below. VER argue that marriages were allowed between free women and slave men, but not between slave women and free men, because war, shipwrecks, and the like left more free women than men available for marriage. Some of these, including some poor heiresses who could not find a husband among free men (8.19–20), had to resort to marrying slaves. However, other societies have faced similar shortages of men but have not resorted to this remedy.

55 'Of the free man': C understood this phrase as going with 'with reference to the pleadings' in 54–5, but if the judge were instructed to decide (on oath) 'with reference to the pleadings of the free man' (i.e. of the ransomer), his decision would not be freely arrived at, as it must be when the 'swear and decide' method is specified. 'Of the free man' must, therefore, go with what follows and we must presume that some amount of text, perhaps several lines, is missing from the bottom of column 6 and the top of column 7 in addition to the words 'if the slave', which must be supplied before 7.1 in any case.

56 The supplement *ai k'o dolos*, 'if a slave', is required by the phrasing that follows and is accepted by all editors. W (followed by VER; Bile 2002) argues that 'since legal marriage did not exist between slaves . . . *dolos* in this section is likely to mean "serf"'. But marriage between *doloi* is implied in 2.27–8, and there is no reason for the legislator to write *dolos* if he meant only *woikeus*. It is likely that *dolos* here includes *woikeus* (so Brixhe 1999: 96), because surely a woman who could marry a *dolos* could also marry a *woikeus*. See further Gagarin 2010a: 23–4.

7.1 'Goes to a free woman': this expression almost certainly means that the slave goes to live in the woman's house (and similarly when the woman goes to the slave in 3–4). Bile 2002, however, argues that the expression does not indicate residence but a change of *woikia*, a kind of inheritance group, but this conclusion rests on a series of unlikely premises drawn from different parts of the Code. Maffi (1997a: 149) supposes that the woman must be all alone, and thus an heiress whom no free man will marry; but Bile notes (2012: 59 n. 190) that such an heiress would be poor (or else someone would marry her) and thus would not have a house.

'And marries her': the same verb for 'marry' (*opuien*) as is used for free couples and slave couples (see above 5A7 with n. 222).

2 The fact that the children's status is determined (apparently) by the place of residence probably reflects practical considerations. If a male slave goes to live with a free woman, she probably has her own house and is fairly well off, whether or not she is an heiress. The slave may or may not be one of those from her own household, and it may have been common in such situations to set the slave free (or to ask a relative to set the slave free), so that in most cases the children would then be free anyway. If, on the other hand, a woman goes to live with a slave (whether or not he belongs to her family), she is probably less well off, and she may be acting without the approval of her family. A child brought up in such circumstances would probably be treated like a slave in any case and thus could be assumed to be slave.

4–10 Both free and slave children would be born if a woman lived in both her house and her husband's, either in the same marriage or in two different mixed marriages. Slave children do not inherit property from a free mother because then her property would pass from her family's estate into the estate of the slave's master (Maffi 1997a: 151).

6–7 'When the mother dies': if marriages between free men and slave women were also regulated either by law (see above on 6.55–7.1) or by custom, the couple very probably lived in the free man's house and their children were probably all free and would inherit. Thus, there is no need to specify what happens when a free man dies.

7.10–15—LIABILITY FOR WRONGS DONE BY A SLAVE (VER II.66, K 173)

The buyer of a slave is liable for the slave's previous acts unless he terminates the purchase within sixty days.

α[ἴ] κ' ἐκς ἀγ- *ορᾶς πρ[ι]ạ́μενος δôλον μὲ π-* *εραιόσει τᾶν Ϝεκσέκοντ' ἀμ-* *ερᾶν, αἴ τινά κα πρόθ' ἀδικέ-* *κει ἒ ὕστερον, τôι πεπαμέν-* *οι ἔνδικον ἔμεν. vac.*	If someone has bought a slave from the agora and has not terminated (the purchase) within sixty days, if (the slave) has done wrong to anyone before or after (the purchase), litigation is to be conducted against the one who has acquired him. *vac.*

11–12 *περαιόσει* ('terminate'?) occurs only here and twice in **G41**.7; see n. ad **G41**.7.15–19. The alternative meaning 'deliver' (sc. the purchase price) would imply that a buyer has sixty days in which to pay for a slave after he buys him, but besides the fact that this sort of credit arrangement would be unparalleled, this meaning makes the text incomprehensible: if someone buys a slave but does not conclude the purchase in sixty days, 'the one who has acquired (the slave)' is liable for the slave's wrongdoing. But the purchaser cannot have acquired the slave, since he has not completed the purchase, and no one else is mentioned.

13 *τινά* is more likely to be acc. sing. after a transitive *ἀδικέκει* (C, K) than n. pl. (i.e. adverbial) with the intransitive verb ('does wrong in any way', W, VER); G is undecided.

15 The gap at the end of this section is 3 letters wide, one of the widest that does not occur at the end of a line.

This provision gives the buyer the right to return a slave he has bought within sixty days; it is usually contrasted with **G41**.7.7–18, which supposedly allows one to terminate a contract within thirty days (e.g. W ad loc.). In our view, however, **G41**.7.7–18 is not about sale; see our discussion ad loc. The provision here concerns only the question of liability for a wrong committed by a slave who is sold. If the buyer terminates the sale within sixty days, the seller will be liable; after that date the buyer is liable. This rule should be compared to the provisions about liability for an indentured man who does wrong in **G41** columns 5–6, and **G47**. For the interpretation of Jakab 1989, see above on **G41**.7.7–18.

7.15–8.20—MARRIAGE OF AN HEIRESS (VER II.51, K 174)

7.15–9.24 provide rules for the marriage of a an 'heiress', a girl who has no brothers when her father dies (8.40–2) and is thus his only direct heir. Nothing is said about a girl whose mother dies leaving an only daughter. Presumably, the girl inherits all her property but is not required to marry until her father dies, by which time he may have remarried and produced a male child.

We divide these rules into four sections for convenience; VER and K treat all four as a single section.

τὰμ πα[τ]ροι[ô]κοṿ ὀπυίεθαι ἀδελπιôι τô πατρὸς τôν ἰόντον τôι πρειγ[ί]στοι. αἰ δέ κα πλίες πατροιôκοι ἴοντι κἀδελπι[ο]ὶ τô πατρός, [τ]ôι ἐπιπρειγίστοι ὀπυίεθαι. αἰ δέ κα μὲ ἴοντι ἀδελπιοὶ τô π[α]τρός, υἰέεδ δὲ ἐκς ἀδελπιôν, ὀπυίεθαι ἰôι τôι ἐ̣ς τô πρειγίστο. αἰ δέ κα πλίες ἴοντι πατροιôκοι κυἰέες ἐκς ἀδελπιôν, ἄλλοι ὀπυίεθαι τôι ἐπὶ τôι ἐς τô πρειγ[ί]στο. μίαν δ' ἔκεν πατροι[ô]κον τὸν ἐπιβάλλοντα, πλίαδ δὲ [μ]έ. *vac.* ἆδ δέ κ' ἄνορος ἐ͂ι ὁ ἐπιβάλλον ὀπυίεν ἐ͂ ἁ πατροιôκος, [σ]τέγαν μέν, αἴ κ' ἐ͂ι, ἔκεν τὰν πατροιôκον, τâδ δ' ἐπικαρπίας παντὸς τὰν ἐμίναν ἀπολανκάνεν τὸν ἐπιβάλλοντα ὀπυίεν. *vac.* αἰ δέ κ' ἀπόδρομος ἰὸν ὁ ἐπιβάλλον ὀπυίεν ἐβίον ἐβίονσαν μὲ λêι ὀπυίεν, ἐπὶ τâι πατροιόκοι ἔμεν τὰ κρέματα πάντα καὶ τὸν καρπὸν, πρείν κ' ὀπυίει. *vac.* αἰ δέ κα δρομεὺς ἰὸν ὁ ἐπιβάλλον ἐβίονσαν λείονσαν ὀπυίεθαι μὲ λêι ὀπυίεν, μολὲν τὸς καδεστὰνς τὸς τâς πατροιόκο, ὁ δὲ δικαστ̣ὰ̣[ς] δικ[α]κ̣σ̣[ά]το ὀπυίεν ἐν τοῖς δ[υ]οîς μενσί. αἰ δέ κα μὲ ὀπυίει ἆι ἔγραται, τὰ κρέματα πάντ' ἔκονσαν, αἴ κ' ἐ͂ι ἄλλος, τôι ἐπιβάλλοντι· *vac.* αἰ δ' ἐπιβάλλον μὲ εἴε, τâς πυλâς τôν αἰτιόντον ὄτιμί κα λêι ὀπυίεθαι. *vac.* αἰ δέ κα τôι ἐπιβάλλοντι ἐβίονσα μὲ λêι ὀπυίεθαι ἐ͂ ἄνορος ἐ͂ι ὁ ἐπιβ-

The heiress is to marry her father's brother, the oldest of those living. And if there are more heiresses and father's brothers, they are to marry the next oldest (in turn). But if there are no father's brothers (available) but sons of the brothers, she is to marry the son of the oldest brother. And if there are more heiresses and brothers' sons, each heiress is to marry another son, the one after the son of the oldest. And the claimant is to have one heiress and not more. *vac.* As long as the claimant to marry (her) or the heiress is prepubescent, if there is a house, the heiress is to have it, and the claimant to marry is to receive half of all the revenue (from the estate). *vac.* And if the claimant to marry her is a minor and should not wish to marry (the heiress) although both are past puberty, all the property and the produce are to be in the hands of the heiress until he marries (her). *vac.* And if the claimant is an adult and the heiress is past puberty and is willing to marry him, but he should not wish to marry her, the relatives of the heiress are to bring suit in the matter, and the judge is to rule that he is to marry (her) within two months. And if he does not marry her as is written, she is to have all the property and if there is another, (she is to marry) this claimant. *vac.* And if there is no claimant, she is to marry whomever she wishes of those of the tribe who ask (her). *vac.* And if the heiress is past puberty but does not wish to marry the claimant, or the claimant has not reached puberty and

ἀλ[λ]ον [κα]ὶ μ[ὲ λêι μέν]εν
Col. 8
ἀ πατροιôκος, στέγαμ μέν,
αἴ κ' ἔ̂ι ἐν πόλι, τὰμ πατροιôκο-
ν ἔκεν κἄτι κ' ἐνêι ἐν τâι στέγ-
αι, τôν δ' ἄλλον τὰν ἐμί⟨ν⟩αν δ-
ιαλακόνσαν ἄλλοι ὀπυίεθ-
αι τâς πυλâς τôν αἰτιόντον
ὅτιμί κα λêι. *vac.* ἀποδατêθαι δ-
ὲ τôν κρεμάτον ἰôι. *vac.* αἰ δὲ μὲ
εἶεν ἐπιβάλλοντες τâι π- ⟦αιπ⟧
ατροιόκοι ἆ[ι ἔ]γραπται, τὰ κρ-
έματα πάντ' ἔκ[ον]σαν τâς πυ-
λâς ὀπυίεθ[α]ι ὅτιμί κα λêι.
vac. αἰ δὲ τâς πυλ[â]ς μέτι⟨ς⟩ λε-
ίοι ὀ[π]υίεν, τὸς καδεστὰνς
τὸς τâς πατροιόκο Ϝεί̣π̣αι κ-
ατὰ [τὰν πυλ]ὰν ὅτι οὐ λ̣[êι ὀ]πυ-
ίεν τις· καὶ μὲν τίς κ̣' [ὀ]πυίει, ἐ-
ν ταῖς τριάκοντα ἔ̂ κα Ϝείπον-
τι· αἰ δὲ μ‹έ›, ἄλλοι ὀπυίεθαι ὅτι-
μί κα νύναται. *vac.*

she does not wish to wait, (**Col. 8**) the heiress is to have the house, if there is one in the city, and whatever is in the house, and she is to receive half of the remaining (estate) and is to marry another from the tribe, whomever she wishes of those who ask. *vac.* But a share of the property is to be given to him (the rejected claimant). *vac.* And if there are no claimants for the heiress as is written, she is to have all of the property and is to marry whomever she wishes from the tribe. *vac.* And if no one from the tribe should wish to marry her, the relatives of the heiress are to proclaim throughout the tribe: 'Does no one wish to marry (her)?' And if anyone should marry her, (it should be) within thirty days from when they made the proclamation. And if not, she is to marry someone else, whomever she can. *vac.*

15–16: πα[τ]ροι[ô]κον: lit. 'one who has (*eken*) the paternal estate' (*patroia*, 4.45, 11.43–4). Its formation implies that the 'heiress' at Gortyn owns the estate (see on 2.47 above)—a significant difference from Attic *epiklēros* ('one who is over [attached to] the estate').

16 ὀπυίεθαι in the middle is used for a woman, 'get (or be) married to', with a dative object; the active (with accusative) is used for a man. Cf. οἴπεν, 'have sexual intercourse with', in 2.3, etc.

18–20 πρειγ[ί]στοι (πρεσβυτάτῳ, Dialect 34) is the 'oldest', ἐπιπρειγίστοι the 'next oldest'; the latter occurs only here, but its meaning is not in doubt.

22 υἰέεδ (υἰέες): for the assimilation (cf. πλίαδ in 7.29), see Dialect 9.

22–3 ἐκς . . . ẹ̀ς: see Dialect 14.

23 ἰôι τôι: lit. 'him, the one' (see n. ad 8.8 below). G (following Maas 1931) considers ἰôι a mason's error, wrongly comparing παι in 8.9, which can be explained as dittography.

28–9 τὸν ἐπιβάλλοντα: see on 5.23–6. Here the claim is to the hand of an heiress, not to an estate, as the addition of ὀπυίεν in 30, etc. makes clear.

29 ἆδ (ἆς) = ἕως (cf. 4.27).

29–30 ἄνορος (ἄωρος) and ἄνεβος (11.19) are apparent synonyms (Bile 343) for someone not yet at the age of puberty; cf. ἀπόδρομος (35–6) for someone past puberty but still a minor (not yet a *dromeus*).

37 ἐβίον: from Att. ἡβάω, Dialect 2, 19. The participle indicates a stage after puberty but before adulthood.

40 πρείν = πρίν.

55 The writing ends about four letters before the end of the line, in keeping with the mason's desire not to split words between columns (see head note to **G72**). Here the article could have been inscribed at the end of 7.55 but the mason chose to keep it with the noun in 8.1.

8.4 ἐμί⟨ν⟩αν: the mason mistakenly wrote *san* instead of *nu*

8 ἰôι: Probably a form of the third-person pronoun related to the Homeric form ἑοῖ (so G, following Maas 1931: 266, and VER); W (note on 7.23, following Buck 1955: 94) takes it as a form of the numeral ἰός ('one').

9 ⟦αιπ⟧: A mason's error (dittography).

13 μέτι⟨ς⟩: The mason mistakenly wrote a *mu* instead of a *san*.

18 ἐ̂: 'when' (see on 6.1).

This section gives the basic rules for an unmarried heiress, specifying whom she should marry and what happens to the estate if she or the designated husband is underage, and then addressing a variety of circumstances in which one of them does not wish to marry. First priority among the claimants is given to her father's brothers and nephews, who are the only named claimants. Next come members of the tribe (*pyla* = Attic *phylē*), and if none of these wishes to marry her, she is to marry anyone she can. VER (II, pp. 194, 196) review the diverse opinions of scholars about the social structure revealed by these provisions. In the end they understand the rules in 7.15–9.24 as a realistic attempt to both protect heiresses and give them considerable freedom, while still ensuring the continuity of the family. In practice, although the law directs the heiress and the specified claimant to marry and gives each one-half of her father's estate, she can choose someone else (though the first claimant keeps half the estate, 7.52–8.8), and he too can refuse but must then give up his half of the estate (7.40–50). Other practical considerations were probably the size of the estate—a rich heiress would be more attractive to potential claimants—and the marital situation of the claimant, who may be reluctant to divorce his current wife.

Similar laws are found in Athens and other Greek cities, and in other ancient cultures, notably the Old Testament. The *patroiokos* is the Cretan counterpart to the Athenian *epiklēros*, but she actually owns the property whereas the Athenian heiress is only thought of as conveying the estate to her (male) children (cf. n. ad 15–16 above).

15–16 *Tam patroiokon*: the noun is put at the beginning in order to indicate the subject of the following sections; cf. **G47**.1. 'Heiress' is a more appropriate translation of *patroiokos* than of the Attic equivalent (*epiklēros*), since an heiress at Gortyn does, in fact, inherit part or all of the estate. However, the Greek term does not imply, as the English does, that the estate she inherits is large. The heiress is defined below as a girl who has no brothers when her father dies (8.40–2).

18–21 Beginning in 7.29, the rules about dividing the estate assume a single heiress. Presumably if there was more than one, each would have a proportionate share.

21–2 Since a claimant can refuse marriage by giving up his share of the estate (7.40–50), 'if there are no father's brothers' means if none exists who is willing to marry her.

26–7 'The one after the son of the oldest': this may mean the next son of the oldest brother or the son of the next oldest brother.

27–9 This provision has been understood as prohibiting an earlier practice of polygamy (G, W), of which there is no other trace, or as prohibiting a claimant from marrying another heiress if the first one he married dies (C), but it is probably aimed primarily at the possibility of a divorce. If the heiress and the claimant are divorced, he is not to marry another heiress either because he has not proven himself a good husband, or to prevent him from marrying one heiress, receiving some of her father's property, and then divorcing her and marrying her sister in order to control even more of the family's estate.

28–29 For the meaning of *ton epiballonta* ('the claimant'), see above on 3.28.

29–8.12 The law never specifies how the estate is divided when the heiress marries a claimant, but presumably each receives half the estate. Only when there is no claimant—that is, no relative willing to marry her—does the heiress get the whole estate (8.8–12)

The age terminology is fairly clear (Introd. 5A2). *Anoros* (and *anebos* in 11.19) is one who has not yet reached the age of puberty and thus is too young to marry. In 12.17–19 the marriage age for an heiress is given as twelve. *Apodromos* (35–6) is a 'minor' (not yet a *dromeus*); we do not know the exact age of majority at Gortyn, but it was probably about the same as in Athens, namely eighteen. *Ebion*, *ebionsa* (37, etc.) designate someone 'past puberty'. And *orima*, 'of marriageable age' (8.39), appears to be equivalent to *ebionsa*; see W 10–11; Bile 343–4.

29–35 If either the claimant or the heiress is underage (see preceding note), they must wait to marry. Meanwhile, the heiress is to have the house, presumably so that she can continue to live there (with her mother, see 8.50–1), and the claimant receives half the revenue. The other half is managed by her paternal relatives (8.45–6).

31–2 Here, the underage heiress gets simply 'the house, if there is one', whereas in 8.1–5, an older heiress who does not wish to marry is to have 'the house, if there is one in the city, and also whatever might be in that house'. The additional details are appropriate to that situation, where the division of the estate is permanent; here, on the other hand, the situation is temporary and the law therefore specifies only what the heiress needs—a place to live—until she is married.

32–3 We distinguish the 'revenue' (*epikarpia*), the total value of all that the land produces, from the 'produce' (*karpos*), which is the produce itself. Besides here, the former term occurs only in **G43Ba9** and in two other passages in **G72** concerning the heiress (8.45, 12.15–16). It appears to be used to designate the total amount of revenue from the land on a continuing basis. Here the claimant will receive half the revenue on a continuing basis. In 8.45 the paternal relatives will receive the same amount. And in 12.16 the relatives are to administer the revenue as best they can. In other cases of division of property, someone may get the produce, sometimes with the qualification 'if there is any' (2.48, 3.35). In these cases the produce appears to be distributed as a one-time occurrence, for example in a divorce.

35–40 The wording implies that the claimant, though past puberty, wants to postpone the marriage, but by giving the heiress interim possession of the estate and its produce, the law also seems to envision the possibility that he will not wish to marry even when he is adult.

40–50 A claimant can refuse to marry the heiress as long as he is willing to give up his claim to a share of the estate. The judge's action will then serve as a formal act confirming the refusal and leaving the heiress free to marry the next claimant in line. This suggests that the order of priority may often have been violated, perhaps for good reason. For example, the heiress's oldest uncle may be quite old or may have a family of his own, and his son or younger brother may be a more suitable claimant.

44 The *kadestai* are probably relatives with an obligation to do something (see on 2.18 above).

47–8 'As is written' probably refers to the rules in 15–29 above specifying the priority of claimants, not rules elsewhere concerning marriage procedures.

48–9 'She is to have all the property': this means that the unwilling claimant gets none of the estate, but if the heiress marries another claimant, he probably gets half the estate.

50 'If there is no claimant' (also in 8.8–10): *sc.* none who is willing to marry her (see on 21–2 above).

7.52–8.8 The heiress too is free to refuse marriage with the claimant, but he will take half of the estate, exclusive of the house and its contents, which she keeps.

7–8 The rather elliptical language—'a share of the property is to be given to him'—probably means that the rejected claimant receives the other half of the estate.

14 On the *kadestai*, see on 7.44 above.

17–18 Again a reasonable time limit is imposed, after which the heiress can seek a husband outside the tribe.

8.20–36—MARRIED OR WIDOWED HEIRESSES (VER II.51, K 174)

Special rules are needed for heiresses who are already married or who become widows.

αἰ δέ κα πατρὸ-
ς δόντος ἒ ἀδελπιô πατροιô-
κος γένεται, αἰ λείοντος ὀπ-
υίεν δι ἔδοκαν μὲ λείοι ὀπυ-
ίεθαι, αἴ κ' ἐστετέκνοται, δια-

And if someone becomes an heiress after her father or brother has given her (in marriage), if the one to whom they gave her wishes to be married (to her) but she does not wish to be married (to him), if she

λακόνσαν τôν κρεμάτον ᾇι ἔ-
γραπται [ἄλλ]οι ὀπυιέθ[ο τᾶ]ς̣ π̣-
υλᾶ[ς]. *vac.* αἰ δὲ τέκνα μὲ εἴε, πάντ'
ἔκονσαν τôι ἐπιβάλλοντι ὀπυ-
ίεθαι, αἴ κ' ἐ̂ι, αἰ δὲ μέ, ᾇι ἔγραττ-
αι. ἀνὲρ αἰ ἀποθάνοι πατροι-
όκοι τέκνα καταλιπόν, αἴ κα λε̂ι,
ὀπυιέθο τᾶς πυλᾶς ὅτιμί κα ν-
ύναται, ἀνάνκαι δὲ μέ. αἰ δὲ τέ-
κνα μὲ καταλίποι ὁ ἀποθανόν,
ὀπυίεθαι τôι ἐπιβάλλοντι ᾇ-
ι ἔγραπται. *vac.*

has borne children, let her take a share of the estate as is written and marry another of the tribe. *vac.* But if there are no children, she is to have all (the property) and marry the claimant, if there is one, but if not, (she is to marry) as is written. If a husband should die leaving children to an heiress, if she wishes, let her marry whomever she can from the tribe, but not under compulsion. But if the deceased should not leave children, she is to marry the claimant as is written. *vac.*

---

24 ἐστετέκνοται (ἐκτετέκνωται): perfect subjunctive.

24–5 διαλακόνσαν: 'receive a share of a divided estate'; see n. ad 5.1.

30 It appears that the mason mistakenly repeated a letter in ἀνέρ, but because the stone is now damaged, it is impossible to tell whether he wrote *AANEP* or *ANNEP*.

The rules in 7.15–8.20 presume an unmarried heiress who in some cases is only a child. This section concerns married heiresses—when a man dies leaving no sons but a daughter who is already married—and heiresses who become widows. Rules are first given for a married heiress with children, then for one without children, and then for a widowed heiress when there are children and when there are not.

8.20–30 In a most interesting article, Maffi 1987 has challenged the traditional view that these lines concern married heiresses. He argues that the language of the passage, especially the genitive absolute clause 'after her father or brother has given her' (20–1), implies not marriage but a betrothal, in which the woman's father or brother, as a precaution against his unexpected death, has given her to one of his relatives to be her future husband. Thus, the woman is not married but still single (or perhaps divorced or widowed). Maffi further argues that *opuien* in 22–4, which we have translated 'be married to' would more naturally be understood to mean 'marry' rather than 'remain married to', and this too implies that the couple are not yet married. Maffi's article generated several rebuttals (notably, Link 1994b, 1997; Karabélias 2004) and further responses by Maffi (1995), all summarized in Maffi 2003a: 204–12, where the whole debate is reviewed.

Maffi's important observations have forced scholars to reconsider the passage, but in the end, his proposed interpretation raises more problems than the traditional view. His strongest argument is that elsewhere in the Code *opuien* is always transitive. However, in the middle used of a woman it can also refer to the state of being married (most clearly in 4.19), and thus it is not impossible that it is here used intransitively. Second, although betrothal (*engyē*) is a formal institution in Athens, there is no evidence of betrothal as a formal act at Gortyn, and it seems conspicuously absent from situations in which we would expect a couple to be formally betrothed, such as in 7.29–35. Third, the Code gives detailed and specific rules directing the heiress to marry a close relative if possible, and it seems very unlikely that these could be overridden by a father or brother simply by betrothing the woman to someone outside the family. Finally, the law gives two rules, if the woman has borne children and if she has not. This is what we would expect in the case of a married woman, but it is very odd for a woman who is only betrothed. Maffi must resort to suggesting that the woman was previously married, is widowed or divorced, and is now betrothed to another, but surely such cases would be extremely rare. It is hard to imagine why the law would address such situations but (on Maffi's view) would say nothing about cases where the woman was previously married and is still married, which must have been far more common. We thus follow the traditional view, according to which the law first (7.15–8.20) addresses the subject of unmarried heiresses—the most urgent, and probably the most common cases—then sets rules for heiresses who are already married, dividing these naturally into those with and without children, and finally considers married heiresses who lose their husbands, again dividing these into those with and without children.

22–3 It is hard to explain why the legislator adds the qualification that the husband (or husband-to-be) wishes to stay married to (or to marry) the heiress, since the heiress who does not wish to be married will apparently do as she wishes regardless of his desire (Maffi 2003a: 207–8). We might also expect a rule to follow specifying what happens if the man does not wish to be married.

25–6 'As is written' probably refers to rules written elsewhere than in the Code. These may have specified that the heiress gets the house and its contents and half of the estate; the other half would be for the children, who would probably remain with their father. She would then hope to bear more children with her new husband, who would be more closely related to her father's family.

30–6 Following 8.20–30, which regulate cases where the woman was married before she became an heiress, these lines regulate cases where an heiress is widowed after marrying as directed (in 7.15–8.20). If she has children, she is free to remarry or not, but if she is childless, she is obligated to marry the next designated relative so as to produce a suitable heir to the estate.

33 An heiress who is widowed but has children is under no compulsion to remarry. The decision is entirely her own, and there is no hint of any *kyrios* who might play a role in getting her married or managing her property if she decides to remain unmarried.

8.36–9.1—MORE ON HEIRESSES (VER II.51, K 174)

These rules regulate special situations concerning heiresses and define an heiress.

αἰ δ' ὀ ἐπιβάλλον τ-
ὰν πατροιôκον ὀπυίεν μὲ ἐπ-
ίδαμος εἴε, ἀ δὲ πατροιôκος
ὀρίμα εἴε, τôι ἐπιβάλλοντι ὀ-
πυίεθαι ᾇι ἔγραπται. πατροιô-
κον δ' ἔμεν, αἴ κα πατὲρ μὲ ἐ͂ι ἒ ἀ-
δελπιὸς ἐς τô αὐ[τô] πατρός. τôν
δὲ κρεμάτο[ν κα]ρτερὸνς ἔμεν τ-
ᾶς Ϝεργασία[ς τὸς] πάτροανς,
[τ]ᾳ̂[δ] ⟨δ'⟩ ἐ̣π̣ι̣[καρ]πίας διαλ[αν]κ̣[ά]ν̣-
εν τὰν ἐμίναν, ᾶ͂ς κ' ἄ[ν]ορ̣[ο]ς ἐ͂ι.
vac. αἰ δ' ἀν[ό]ροι ἰάτται μὲ εἴε ἐπ-
ιβάλλον, τὰν πατροιộκον καρ-
τερὰν ἔμ̣εν τôν τε κρεμάτον κ-
αὶ τô καρπô. κᾶ͂ς κ' ἄν[ο]ρος ἐ͂ι τ-
ράπεθαι [π]ạρ τᾶι ματρί· αἰ δὲ μ-
άτερ μὲ εἴε, πὰρ τοῖς [μ]άτροσι
τράπεθα[ι. vac.] αἰ δέ τις ὀπυίοι τὰ-
ν πατροιôκον, ἀλλᾶι δ' [ἔγ]ραπται,
πε̣ύθε̣ν̣ [πορ]τ̣ὶ κ̣ό̣σ̣μ̣ο̣ν̣
Col. 9
τὸνς ἐπιβạ́[λλοντανς. vac.]

And if the claimant to marry an heiress is not living in the city, and the heiress is of age, she is to marry the (next) claimant as is written. Someone is an heiress if she does not have a father or a brother from the same father. The paternal relatives are to have control of the property with respect to its management and are to receive half the revenue while she is underage. *vac.* And if there is no claimant for the heiress who is underage, she is to have control of the property and its produce. And as long as she is underage, she is to be raised by her mother; and if her mother is not alive, she is to be raised by her maternal relatives. *vac.* And if anyone marries the heiress and it is written otherwise, the claimants are to inform (**Col. 9**) the *kosmos. vac.*

---

39 *ὀρίμα* ('of age') is the opposite of *ἄνορος* (46, 47, 50); see on 7.29–30.

40 A vertical line is carved on the stone between *ἔγραπται* and *πατροιôκον*. This may have been made later, or it may be another means of indicating that the mason mistakenly omitted a gap between these sentences, as apparently in 5.17; cf. also 4.36.

42–6 The sentence consists of an infinitive (*emen*) with its subject in the accusative (*tos patroans*) followed by a connective (*de*) and a second infinitive (*dialankanen*). No subject is expressed for this second infinitive, but its subject would normally be understood to be the same as the subject of the first infinitive, which is how we have translated it; the qualification *as k' anoros ei* is singular and must thus refer to the heiress; very likely it qualifies both infinitives.

42–4 *τôν δὲ κρεμάτο[ν κα]ρτερὸνς ἔμεν τᾶς Ϝεργασία[ς]*: the construction and word order is exactly the same as in 4.24–5 (*τôν κρεμάτον καρτερὸν ἔμεν τᾶδ δαίσιος*), and the genitive here similarly makes the general idea of control more specific: 'with respect to its management'.

42–3 *τôν κρεμάτον* is placed at the beginning of the sentence to indicate the new topic.

44 *[τὸς] πάτροανς*: commonly translated 'paternal uncles' (W, VER, K), but it is better to follow G, who takes the term as designating the paternal uncles or, if there are no uncles, then other paternal relatives. Thus we translate 'paternal relatives' (cf. 'maternal relatives' in 52).

45 *[τ]ᾳ̂[δ]⟨δ'⟩* W, VER; G, K omit the second *delta* but a connective seems necessary. See W (app. crit. *ad loc.*) for other suggestions

47 ἰάττᾳι = Att. οὔσῃ (Bile 243).

52 τοῖς [μ]άτροσι: see above on 44 ([τὸς] πάτροανς).

55 πεύθεν is an active form of πυνθάνομαι and means 'inform' (Bile 248, 349 n. 97).

9.1 For the state of the text here, see below n. ad 9.1–10. The restoration of this line is accepted by all scholars.

This section addresses cases in which the claimant is abroad, the heiress is underage, or she marries illegally. It also defines an heiress as a surviving daughter with no brothers. The provisions give even an underage heiress a fairly large role in determining her future husband and managing her inherited property, though this latter freedom is restricted by an amendment to the Code (12.6–19).

36–8 *Me epidamos* implies that the claimant is living in some other city, most likely as a merchant or a mercenary; he is not just absent temporarily.

39 'The (next) claimant': the Greek has only 'the claimant' (*toi epiballonti*), but all editors understand this to be the next claimant in line; strictly speaking, it could mean that she must marry the absent claimant (and join him abroad?), but this would not be in keeping with the flexible nature of these provisions concerning the heiress.

40–2 It may seem odd to us that this definition is not placed at the beginning of the provisions concerning the heiress, but the legislator could assume that readers knew in general what an heiress was and did not need a precise definition. Indeed, it may be more surprising that a fairly precise legal definition of the term is provided—the only such definition in the Code (but cf. the precision about who could be adopted in 11.18–19).

41–2 The specification, 'brother from the same father', would exclude a maternal half-brother; it probably does not exclude an adopted brother, who would share the inheritance with the daughters (see on 10.52–11.1), who would thus not be 'heiresses' (Maffi 1997a: 79–80 n. 68). It is probably understood that if a daughter had a brother who was now dead but had sons of his own, she would not be an heiress, since the sons would inherit his share of the estate directly (5.9–13) and the daughter would only have her normal share of the estate according to 4.39–43; but see Maffi 1997a: 88.

42–4 'Have control of the property with respect to its management (*tas wergasias*)': this must be a limited control, probably over the 'working' of the estate (Bile 319 n. 8) in contrast to *karterons emen* in general (see on 4.24–5), which may designate broader financial management, such the ability to buy and sell land, livestock, slaves, etc. Or perhaps *wergasia* refers primarily to the management of land (so Bile 319 n. 8). In any case, the assignment of management to the paternal relatives indicates that there was no general institution of 'guardianship' at Gortyn like the Athenian *kyrieia*, or else there would be no need to assign a manager for the heiress's property in this case; see further on 47–50 below.

44 We do not know exactly which paternal relatives were included among *tos patroans*, but this group must normally have included most, if not all, the claimants for the hand of an heiress (7.15–29), that is, her paternal uncles and cousins. Since multiple managers of the estate might be impractical, the law may have been interpreted to mean that the relative with the first claim to the heiress, the oldest paternal uncle, would be the chief manager. In some cases he would also be the one who eventually married the heiress. Maffi (1997a: 100) assumes on the basis of 12.9–17 that the paternal relatives are not the claimants to marry the heiress, and thus must be the father's cousins or perhaps their sons. But there is no good reason why the legislator would want a more distant relative to manage the property, and if he did, he would surely have made this more explicit. See further on 12.13, where it is important to note that the singular *ton patroa* is used.

45–50 It is not clear that there is any difference in this section between *epikarpia* ('revenue') and *karpos* ('produce'), though elsewhere the two seem to be different (see on 7.32–3).

45–6 Lit. 'and (X) is/are to receive half the revenue while Y is underage': no subject is specified for either verb. Most commentators (G, W, K, VER) take the heiress as the subject of both ('and she is to receive . . . while she is'); half the revenue would presumably be intended for her support. Zitelmann (Bücheler–Zitelmann 1885: 159–60), however, correctly understands that the subject of the infinitive 'receive' is the same as that of the preceding infinitive, 'to have control' (see above n. ad 42–6); he compares 7.29–35. Maffi 1997a: 100–2, on the other hand, argues that since the heiress will continue to receive her share of the revenue when she is no longer underage, the clause 'while Y is underage' refers not to her but to the claimant. But the claimant is not mentioned in this section, and he is thus very unlikely to be the subject of 'is'; nor can paternal relatives (in the plural) be the subject. Thus the paternal relatives are to receive half the revenue while the heiress is underage and they are managing the estate. The relatives would presumably use the other half to provide for the needs of the underage heiress.

47–50 In the absence of a claimant, and thus of a paternal relative (since any claimant would be a paternal relative; see above on 44), the legislator puts the heiress herself in charge of the property. But someone must soon have realized that a very small child might become an heiress, and an amendment in 12.6–19 assigns other relatives, including maternal relatives, to manage the property until she is married. This provision is further evidence for the absence of a *kyrieia* at Gortyn (so Link 2004a, *contra* Maffi 2003a: 193–5). It is inconceivable that a legislator could have thought, even for a moment, to put an underage heiress in control of her property and its produce if it were the norm at Gortyn (as at Athens) that all the property of a woman was administered by a male guardian.

50–3 The specification that the underage heiress is to be raised by her mother is sometimes taken to apply only to cases where there is no claimant, but it seems very unlikely that a young heiress (who might even still be a baby) would be taken from her mother and raised by other relatives (Maffi 1997a: 102–3). Thus we understand this provision as applying to all underage heiresses. Maffi thinks that the mother would take the heiress and return to her family's house after her husband's death, but there is no reason why the heiress and her mother could not continue to live in the same house, with the same household servants and perhaps other relatives, after their father/husband died. We must not import assumptions from classical Athens, where it would be more difficult for a widow to live on her own.

51–3 Since there is no claimant and thus no paternal relatives, it makes sense to let the heiress be raised by her mother's relatives if her mother is no longer alive.

53–9.1 If the heiress married someone outside the group of claimants, or if she married someone within that group who was not clearly first in the legal order, the other claimants are to inform the *kosmos*, though we are not told what he would do in that case.

9.1–24—MANAGEMENT OF AN HEIRESS'S PROPERTY (VER II.51, K 174)

An heiress's property may be sold or mortgaged in order to pay debts, but any action beyond the amount necessary for this purpose is prohibited.

αἴ κ' ὀ-
πέλο[ν ἄργυρον πα]τροιôκον κα-
ταλίπει, ἒ αὐ[τὰν ἒ διὰ τὸν]ς̣ π-
άτροαν[ς καὶ τ]ὸ̣νς μάτροαν-
ς καταθέμεν ἒ̣ [ἀποδ]όθαι τô ὀπ-
λέματος̣ [καὶ] δ̣ικαίαν ἔμεν τ-
ὰν ὀνὰν καὶ τὰν κα̣[τάθε]σιν. αἰ
δ' ἀλλᾶ[ι πρί]αιτό τις κρέματα ἒ
καταθεῖτο τôν τᾶς πα[τρ]ο̣ιόκο, τ-
ὰ μὲν [κρ]έ̣ματα ἐπὶ τᾶι πατροιόκ-
οι ἔμεν, ὀ δ' ἀποδόμενος ἒ κατ-
αθὲνς τôι πριαμένοι ἒ καταθε-
μένοι, αἴ κα νικαθε̂ι, διπλεῖ κα-
ταστασεῖ καἴ τί κ' ἄλλ' ἄτας ἐ̂ι, τ-
ὸ ἀπλόον ἐπικαταστασεῖ. *vac.* ἆ-
ι τ̣ά̣δε τὰ γ[ράμμ]ατ̣[α ἔγραπται, τ]-
ô[ν δ]ὲ̣ πρόθα μ[ὲ ἔ]ν̣δικον ἔμεν.
vac. αἰ δ' ὀ ἀντίμολος ἀπομ[ολ]ίο-
ι ἀ[νπ]ὶ τὸ κρέος ὀ̂ι κ' ἀνπιμολί-
οντι μὲ τᾶς πατροιόκο ἔ̣[μ]εν,
ὀ δ[ικ]αστὰς ὀμνὺς κρινέτο· αἰ

If someone owing money (dies and) leaves an heiress, either herself or through her paternal and maternal relatives she is to mortgage or sell (property) in the amount of the debt, and the purchase and mortgage are to be legal. And if anyone should otherwise buy or give a mortgage on the property of an heiress, the property will be in the hands of the heiress, and the seller or mortgagor, if he is convicted, will pay double to the buyer or mortgagee, and if there is any other damage, he will pay in addition the simple value. *vac.* (It will be) as these words have been written, but for earlier matters it is not a matter for trial. *vac.* If the opposing litigant should (contend) in court that the item about which they are contending is not the heiress's, the judge is to swear an oath and decide. And if he should win his case that it is not the

*δὲ νικάσαι μὲ τᾶς πατρ[οι]όκ-
ο ἔμ̣ε̣ν, μολε̂ν ὄπε κ' ἐπιβάλλει, ἐ̂
Ϝεκάστο ἔγραπται.* ⧗

heiress's, the matter is to be tried where it belongs, where it is written for each case. *vac.*

1–10 A large piece is missing from the top of column 9, leaving gaps in the first ten lines. Several small fragments found nearby have been fitted into the space, and there is now general agreement about the placement of these pieces. G's restorations of the text of these lines, including the *vac.* in 9.1 (see the preceding section), have been accepted by all editors since.

3–5 *πάτροαν[ς καὶ τ]ὸ̣νς μάτροανς*: see above on 8.44.

7–24 The wording is very similar to that in 6.12–31; see our note there for the main differences. The effects of these changes are discussed in the comments below.

15 Editors print a comma after *ἐπικαταστασεῖ*, but the distinct gap after it (*c.*1½ letters) indicates that stronger punctuation is needed. It is not difficult to understand what follows as a new sentence (cf. **G80**.12 with note), as Maffi does in his translation (1997a: 169; cf. 107), though he prints a comma in the facing Greek text.

18–19 *ἀπομ[ολ]ίοι*: only here and in 6.25; for the sense, see note ad loc.

23 *ὄπε κ' ἐπιβάλλει*: lit. 'wherever it falls'; see on 6.29–30, and cf. 5.23–6.

24 There is a trace of an engraved sign (a double ax?) in the gap, but it is far fainter than the similar sign in 9.43, which is carved to the same depth as the text. Since the stone appears quite smooth at 9.24, it is possible that the mason either forgot to carve the sign outlined by this trace, or for some reason decided not to. There is a similar sign in **Dr1**.

The rules prohibiting someone from buying or using as security an heiress's estate (except as necessary to pay debts incurred previously by her father) bear many similarities to, and are in part identical with, those which prohibit men from wrongly managing the property of their wives or mothers (6.9–31), and husbands from wrongly managing the property of their deceased wives (6.34–43). In all three passages there is a prohibition on selling or mortgaging a woman's property (except under special circumstances in the case of an heiress); if such a sale or other action occurs, the property is to be in the hands of the woman who owns it, and the violator is to pay double the value of the property to the buyer or mortgager, and if there is any other damage, he is to pay the simple value.

1–15 Cf. 9.24–40, where an heir is obliged to pay the debts of an estate.

3–5 'Either herself or' (*e autan e*): the law is clear: the heiress may act by herself if she wishes. Maffi 2003a: 192 (cf. 1997a: 106) argues that *e autan* 'does not entirely exclude the intervention of a *kyrios*', but in fact it does. A *kyrios* would necessarily be one of the heiress's relatives, and it would make no sense to say that she could act either on her own, that is, with her *kyrios* (who is a relative), or through relatives. Moreover, if an heiress had a guardian, it is hard to imagine why she would be allowed to act through other relatives if she wished. In fact, *e autan* is as clear and explicit a statement as one could expect to find in a set of laws that a woman could act on her own and that there was thus no *kyrieia* at Gortyn. (We could hardly expect to find a provision stating that 'there is no *kyrieia* at Gortyn'.) The older the heiress the more likely she would be to act on her own, but there is no sign of a precise rule about this (*pace* Maffi, who argues that the heiress would act on her own if she was past puberty but through relatives if she was not).

'Paternal and maternal relatives': for the identity of these, see above on 8.44.

7–24 These provisions are very similar to those in 6.12–31; for differences in wording, see our note there. The effect of most of these changes is to simplify and clarify the law here: in line 8 a complex and unclear expression is simplified to one word, 'otherwise' (*allai*); in 13 the clause 'if he is convicted' is added to make explicit what was only implicit in the earlier passage, and in 15 'he will pay in addition' is added for similar effect; in 15–16 another clause is added—'(It will be) as these words have been written'—presumably for clarity, though it is not really necessary; and finally there is a puzzling addition in 18–24, on which see below.

Substantive differences also exist between the two passages, as Maffi (p.c.) observes. 6.12–31 follow an absolute prohibition that men may not alienate the property of their female relatives (6.9–12), whereas here the prohibition against alienating an heiress's property applies only when the proceeds are not used to pay debts owed by the father's (or brother's) estate. In 6.12–31 it is implied that women may alienate their own property, whereas here the heiress is also (implicitly) prohibited from alienating the property of the estate. The reason for the difference is that although the law speaks of the heiress's property (line 9), she does not yet fully own any of the estate, since it will later be divided between her and her husband. The rules here do not fit the situation quite as well as they do in 6.12–31; it may be that the rules were more or less copied here without all the adjustments in wording that were needed.

7–15 Strictly speaking, the prohibition here applies to the heiress as well, but because the remedy for a violation involves putting the property in the hands of the heiress, the prohibition clearly envisages violators being relatives, not the heiress herself.

8 'Otherwise': that is, without using the proceeds to pay debts of the estate.

15–17 The provision of non-retroactivity implies that before the Code an heiress's property did not have this protection; cf. on 6.24–5.

18–24 Maffi (p.c.) argues that the heiress's *kyrios* alienated the property, and that this would lead to a legal case in which the heiress, with the support of relatives, was opposed to the *kyrios*. Maffi also argues that in this case the *kyrios* has not sold the property in question but has transferred it to the creditor as payment for his own personal debt, claiming that the property is his own. This scenario is not implausible, though in our view the violator is just a relative, not the *kyrios*, and the specification of 'buying or giving a mortgage on' the property in 7–9 carries over implicitly into the rules here. There is no reason why the property could not have been sold to a third party and the proceeds used to pay a personal debt (or for any other reason).

The procedure here has become more complicated in comparison with the rules for similar litigation in 6.29–31. There, 'the matter is to be tried where it belongs, before the judge where it is written in each case'; here it appears that the case is to be judged first ('the judge is to swear an oath and decide'), and then 'if he should win his case', there will be further litigation. But if the judge decides that the property does not belong to the heiress, then what issue remains to be decided in the court 'where it belongs'? Perhaps the judge first decided that the property did not belong to the heiress, and then had to decide whose property it was; but a two-part trial seems needlessly complex.

18 'Opposing litigant' (*antimolos*): so Maffi 1997a: 169; see above on 6.25–6.

23–4 As in 6.29–31, the law here may imply that there were different courts for property that had been sold and property that had been mortgaged.

9.24–40—LITIGATION CONCERNING PROPERTY OF THE DECEASED (VER II.45, K 175)

This section provides rules for suits involving a deceased person's creditors or debtors.

αἰ ἀν[δ]εκσ-
άμ̣[ε]νος ἒ νενικαμένο[ς ἒ ἐν]κ̣-
οιοτὰνς ὀπέλον̣ ἒ διαβαλόμε-
νος ἒ διαϝειπάμενος ἀποθά-
νοι ἒ τούτοι ἄλλος, ἐπιμολ-
ὲν̣ν̣ ἰ̓ô πρὸ τô ἐνιαυτô· ὀ δὲ δικα-
στὰς δικαδδέτο πορτὶ τὰ ἀ̣ποπ-
ονιόμενα. αἰ μέν κα νίκας ἐπι-
μολε̂ι, ὀ δικαστὰς κὀ μνάμον,
αἴ κα δόει καὶ πολιατεύει, οἴδε μ-
αίτυρες οἰ ἐπιβάλλοντες, ἀνδοκ-
âδ ⟨δ⟩ὲ κἐνκοιοτâν καὶ διαβολâς κ-
αὶ διρέσιος μαίτυρες οἰ ἐπιβ-
άλλοντες ἀποπονιόντον. ἐ͂ δέ κ' ἀ-
ποϝείποντι, δικαδδέτο ὀμόσ-
α⟨ν⟩τα αὐτὸν καὶ τὸνς μαίτυρ-
ανς νικε̂ν τὸ ἀπλόον. vac.

If someone should die who has undertaken an obligation, or has lost a suit, or owes (money) that he pledged (?), or has initiated litigation, or has agreed (to pay), or if another (has an obligation) to the deceased, litigation is to be brought concerning the matter within a year; and let the judge rule according to the testimonies. If someone brings suit concerning a case he won, (let) the judge and the rememberer, if he is alive and active in civic life, (testify), these being the appropriate witnesses; but in cases of security or money owed or litigation initiated or an agreement, let the appropriate witnesses testify. And when they have spoken, let (the judge) rule that when he (the plaintiff) and the witnesses have sworn, he is to win the simple amount. *vac.*

24–5 *ἀν[δ]εκσάμ̣[ε]νος*: probably = Attic *ἀναδεξάμενος* (*ἀναδέχομαι*) in the sense of 'undertake an obligation'. The verb also occurs at 9.41, but nowhere else in Cretan laws.

25–6 *ἐν]κ̣οιοτὰνς ὀπέλον̣*: 'owing money that is pledged'. We can only guess at the meaning and construction of *enkoiotans*, which occurs only here and in 35 below. Bile 330 (following Maffi 1983: 129–34) argues that it is either an agent noun in the nominative indicating a type of debtor or an adjective modifying an implied accusative noun, such as *darknans*). But in view of *κένκοιοτᾶν* in 35, it is most likely a plural noun in the accusative indicating a type of debt.

26–7 *διαβαλόμενος*: 'has initiated litigation' (only here in Cretan laws). *διαβάλλομαι* can mean 'have a disagreement with', 'accuse', 'slander'. Maffi 1983: 134–8 argues that this must mean 'accusing someone in absentia', but there is no reason for the law to regulate such a specific (and presumably quite rare) type of case.

27 *διαϝειπάμενος*: 'has agreed (to pay)'. W cites the use of *διεῖπον* (in the middle) in two passages in Aristotle (*Oeconomicus* 1351b5; *Ethica Eudemia* 1243a31). *διαϝείπομαι* occurs only here in Crete, but *διαβειπάμε[νος* in *IC* 4.141.11 is probably the same word with a phonetic shift (cf. *Βίδαν* in **G80**.2 vs. *ϝίδαι* in *IC* 4.146.6; Bile 118).

28–9 *ἐπιμολένν*: 'litigation is be brought'; cf. Attic *ἐπιδικάζειν*. For the spelling see Dialect 10.

29 *ἰô*: as in 7.23 and 8.8, we take this as a demonstrative pronoun; W again takes it as the numeral 'one' qualifying *πρὸ τô ἐνιαυτô*, but this expression needs no qualification (cf. 4.4–5); see further n. ad 8.8. The genitive indicates the subject of the litigation ('about that matter', so G, Bile 288); cf. *νίκας* in 31 below.

30–1 *δικαδδέτο πορτὶ τὰ ἀποπονιόμενα* (also in 9.50–1) *apoponen* refers specifically to the testimony of witnesses, as in 37 below (cf. n. ad 1.14).

33 *οἵδε* G, VER is preferable to *οἰ δέ* (W, K). The latter ('and the appropriate witnesses') would add other appropriate witnesses to the judge and the *mnamon*; but these are the only witnesses needed in order to establish the court judgment from an earlier case. Thus we prefer to read *οἵδε*; 'these (sc. the judge and the rememberer), (as) the appropriate witnesses'. In Greek the verb 'let them testify' is postponed until the end of the sentence, after the other witnesses are named. In any case, *de* should not be omitted (as in Maffi 1983: 147, n. 6).

34 *οἰ ἐπιβάλλοντες*: for W these are the heirs ('and the heirs as witnesses'); but the heirs are litigants in these cases, not witnesses. The sense is 'those who impose themselves' in each particular situation, i.e. 'who are appropriate' ('ad quos pertineat', G); see on 5.23–6.

34–6 The four nouns in the genitive (see note on 29 above) each correspond to a verb in 24–7.

34–5 *ἀνδοκᾶδ* (*ἀνδοκᾶς*): Dialect 9. The noun also occurs in **G41**.7.19, probably as an accusative singular, but the context is too fragmentary to shed light on the sense.

35 ⟨δ⟩ἐ: the mason mistakenly omitted a *delta* here.

36 *διρέσιος*: This must be the noun corresponding to *διαϝειπάμενος*, but the word is otherwise unknown. Some editors (G, K) think it is a mason's error for *διαρρέσιος*, but the mason rarely omits two different letters for no apparent reason.

37–8 *ἀποϝείποντι*: in the Code this verb only occurs here and (in the middle) in 11.11–12, where the context makes clear that it means 'renounce' an adoption. In **G73**A4 (in the active) it apparently means 'refuse' or 'deny permission'; cf. **G4**.3 *ἀ̣πορηθῆμέν* (though the sense there is unclear), **A1**1a3, and *IC* 1.28.1A1. Early commentators adopted this sense here, as does Maffi 1983: 157–61, who argues that the procedure changes from a ruling determined by witnesses (in 29–31) to one determined by oaths (in 37–40). But if this were the meaning, we would expect the law to say 'if they refuse to speak' rather than 'when'. Moreover, if the witnesses refuse to testify, it makes little sense to require the judge to rule that they (and the litigant) swear an oath and win the suit, since they would probably also refuse to swear. In Homer *apoeipō* can also mean 'speak out, declare', and this sense is far more likely here (so G, W, K, VER).

38–9 ὀμόσα⟨ν⟩τα: the mason mistakenly wrote *san* instead of *nu*

Notwithstanding our uncertainty about the precise meaning of most of the terms in 24–7, the general sense of this section is clear: it addresses situations in which a person dies under obligation to someone or with someone under obligation to him; litigation concerning such obligations must be brought (by or against his heirs) within a year. The judge must rule according to the appropriate witnesses, who are specified, and when the plaintiff and his witnesses have sworn, the judge is to award the simple amount.

24–7 Most editors (e.g. K, whose discussion p. 538 is good) agree that all the verbs in these lines involve the deceased having been, actually or potentially, under an obligation to someone or someone being under an obligation to him, but lacking a general concept of obligation the legislator has to name each type of obligation individually. As VER note, the terms were undoubtedly known to the Gortynians at the time but only one is clear today: *nenikamenos* is someone who has lost a lawsuit. We think the obligations listed should be broadly interpreted, because the legislator probably intended to establish the procedure for cases concerning any obligation that might commonly arise. Cf. Maffi 1983: 121–42, who argues for more technical (and limited) meanings for the terms, and the response to Maffi by van Effenterre 1984: esp. 48–9.

24–5 *Andeksamenos* probably refers to pledging one's property as security, not pledging oneself, for which, as Maffi notes (1983: 148–52), *katakeimenos* would be used. Maffi argues, however, that *andeksamenos* means 'confess, admit', sc. to owing money, but if the confession was made in court, this situation would be redundant with *nenikamenos*, and if made out of court, the legislator would write 'if someone owes money', not 'if someone admits'. Cf. Bile 330–1.

25–6 *Enkoiotans opelon* ('owing money that is pledged') may refer to someone who stood surety for a debt that is now in default, leaving him to pay the debt himself.

26–7 *Diabalomenos* ('having brought an accusation') may refer to litigation brought by or against the deceased that had not yet been concluded. This situation stands out from the rest, in all of which a debt was owed either by or to the deceased, and the current suit is intended to force payment of the debt; in this case the current suit would be intended to bring the earlier suit to conclusion.

27 *Diaweipamenos*: 'having made an agreement', perhaps to buy something.

28–9 *Epimolenn* ('bring litigation against someone') indicates that a new suit would be brought by or against the heirs of the deceased. Maffi (1983: 126) argues that *epimolen* has a more technical sense, 'to reopen a case' left unfinished at the death of the deceased, but this would imply that the heirs could only collect a debt owed their father or be obliged for his debts if litigation had begun before his death, which seems very unlikely. See Bile 279 n. 82.

29–31 'Let the judge rule according to the testimonies (*porti ta apoponiomena*)': *dikadden* indicates that the judge's ruling is directed by law; see below 11.26–31, where the expression is 'according to witnesses' (*kata maityrans*). Contrast the alternative procedure where the judge decides freely *porti ta moliomena* ('according to the pleadings').

In practical terms, this means that in order to collect a debt owed by or to the deceased one must provide witnesses. Provisions like this made it necessary to be accompanied by witnesses during any financial transaction.

31–7 The appropriate witnesses in most cases would be the formal witnesses who were present when the obligation was incurred. If the current suit concerns a judgment in an earlier suit, then the court officials who presided at that trial, the judge and the rememberer, would testify.

32 For the rememberer (*mnamon*) in Crete, see Introd. 4C3. He is included as a witness here, since one of his duties was to be present at and remember proceedings in court.

33 'If he is alive and active in civic life'. The qualification probably does not apply to the judge too (as W thinks), though this is not impossible syntactically. The judge's testimony would probably be considered essential, and so he would be called even if he was no longer active in civic life; the rememberer's testimony, on the other hand, would be supplementary, though he would presumably testify alone if the judge was not able to. The requirement that the rememberer be alive is obviously unnecessary; the requirement that he be 'active in civic life' (*poliateuen*) may be meant to exclude someone who is indentured. Lévy 1997: 26 takes *poliateuen* to mean 'be present in the country', but in **G51**.7 the verb seems to designate those who not only have reached adulthood but also participate in public life, and this sense seems more likely here. VER suggest that in some cases the rememberer might be a public slave, but even if he was (and there is no evidence for public slaves in Crete at this time), he would still be allowed to testify, since slaves can testify in other matters (e.g. 2.25–6).

37–40 The procedure apparently is that the plaintiff presents his claim, supported by the testimony of his witnesses; the judge then rules that when they (the plaintiff and his witnesses) have sworn, the plaintiff will receive the amount of the original debt. This procedure would work a bit differently if the earlier litigation had only been initiated, if that is the correct meaning of *diabalomenos* (see above on 26–7). In that case, it is likely that after witnesses had testified about the earlier (incomplete) litigation, the judge could try the original case and render a decision.

37–8 'And when they have spoken': some scholars take *apoweiponti* to mean 'they refuse to speak': 'if the witnesses refuse to testify, then the litigant must swear an oath'. But although the verb could mean this, the context makes this meaning very unlikely here. See n. ad 37–8 above.

38–40 'When he and the witnesses have sworn'. The pronoun 'he' (*auton*) designates the plaintiff, who is the unexpressed subject of the infinitive *niken* ('win'). It is unclear how significant these oaths are. The plaintiff's oath appears to be a special oath not normally sworn by plaintiffs; if so, this is the closest example at Gortyn to an accusatory oath, in which an accuser only has to swear an oath in order to win his case. It is possible that witnesses regularly swore oaths at Gortyn, but this is not certain, except in cases where a witness is said to be *orkioteros* (e.g. 3.49–50, 4.6–7). Here the oath might be an additional requirement, perhaps imposed by the legislator in order to add certainty to a case where one of the original parties has died.

40 'The simple amount': the amount of the original obligation. There is no increase in the penalty because of the lapse in time, since it was unavoidable.

9.40–3—LIABILITY OF A SON (VER II.45, K 176)

Law concerning obligations incurred by a son.

υἰὺς α-	If a son has undertaken an obligation
ἴ κ' ἀνδέκσεται, ἆς κ' ὀ πατὲ‹δ› δόει,	while his father is living, (only) he (the
αὐτὸν ἀτε͂θαι καὶ τὰ κρέματα	son) and any property he has acquired is
ἄτι κα πέπαται ⧗	to be subject to a penalty. *vac.*

41 ἀνδέκσεται: See n. ad 9.24–5.

42 ἀτε͂θαι (ἀτάομαι): the verb can mean 'incur a penalty' by losing a case (4.29; 4.30; 10. 21) or 'be subject to / liable for a penalty' (11.42; **G41**.5.14); here both senses are probably at work.

43 πέπαται: in 6.5–9 *paomai* is paired with *apolankano*, the latter specifying inheritance and the former acquisition by other means (cf. 7.14–15). Here inheritance is not in question.

For the incised sign, see n. ad 9.24.

This provision protects the father from liabilities incurred by his son, and allows the son to pledge any property he may have as security while his father is alive without putting his father's estate at risk. The law also prevents a son from using his father's property (i.e. his future inheritance) as security for a current obligation and warns a creditor not to accept such security, since he will not be able to seize it if the son defaults on his obligations. This rule must be distinguished from that in 4.29–31, which allows a son who has been fined by a court to receive some of his share of the estate to pay the fine; this rule probably applies to fines for wrong-doing (such as rape), not to debts willingly incurred.

41 As in 9.24–5, we understand *anadekomai* as the pledging of property as security, as against Maffi (see above on 9.24–5), who argues that it designates a

legal confession or admission and sees the purpose of the law as preventing collusion between the son and others outside the family in order to gain control of the father's estate. But if this were the law's purpose, a son who wished to engage in such collusion could probably get around the restriction simply by agreeing to lose a court case and then obtaining his share of the estate to pay the fine (see 4.29–31). But most sons were probably much more readily tempted to gain some current benefit by pledging a future inheritance than to collude with others outside the family, which might subject them to trial, conviction, and punishment. G. and others have accepted a suggestion of Dareste et al. 1891.1: 479 n. 2, that *an(a)dekomai* here may be taken as a general term implicitly including all five situations mentioned in 9.24–40. But only the pledging of property as security is relevant to the son's situation envisaged here.

9.43–10.1—COMMERCIAL VENTURES ABROAD (VER II.76, K 177)

Fulfillment of contracts for foreign commercial ventures.

αἴ τίς κα πέραι συναλ[λάκ]σει, ἒ ἐς πέρ[α]ν ἐπιθέντι μὲ ἀποδιδôι, αἰ μέν κ' ἀποπονίοντι μαίτυρες ἐβίοντες τô ἑκατονστατέρο καὶ πλίονος τρέες, τô μείονος μέττ' ἐς τὸ δεκαστάτερον δύ̣ο, τô μείονος ἔ̣ν⟨δ⟩, δικαδδέτο πορτ̣ὶ τὰ ἀποπο[ν]ιόμενα. αἰ δὲ μαίτυρε[ς] μὲ ἀ̣[π]οπ̣ονίοιεν, ἒ κ' ἔ[λ]θει ὀ συναλλάκσανς, ὄτερόν κ[α] κέλε[τ]αι ὀ μενπόμενος, ἒ ἀπομόσαι ἒ σὺν

Col. 10

σ[—]

If someone makes an agreement for a venture abroad, when he does not pay back a contributor to the foreign venture, if witnesses who are of age testify — three in a case of a hundred staters or more, two in a case worth less down to ten staters, one for a case worth less — let (the judge) rule with regard to the testimony. But if witnesses do not testify, when the person who made the agreement comes (back), whichever the plaintiff requests, [the judge should rule] either that he deny on oath or with **(Col. 10)** —

43–4 *πέραι . . . ἐς πέραν*: we probably have two forms of the noun *πέρα*, which is connected with *perande* (6.46–47), 'abroad' (so G, VER, K). W (following C) translates 'mercantile venture'; the qualification in 52–3 ('when the person who made the agreement comes [back]') makes clear that the other party was far away, namely abroad. For *ἐς*, see Dialect 14.

44 The lettering in this line spans a horizontal division between two blocks of stone, which in their reassembled state are not precisely aligned; cf. 10.26.

46–7 *ἐβίοντες*: see above on 7.37.

48–9 *μέττ' ἐς* = *μέστ' ἐς* (Homeric *μέσφα*), 'until'; cf. W *ad loc.*, Bile 298.

50 *ἔν⟨δ⟩* (*ἔνς* = *εἶς*); the mason wrote *ἔνα*, but the nominative is needed.

50–1 *πορτ̣ὶ τὰ ἀποπο[ν]ιόμενα*: see on 30–1 above.

54 *μενπόμενος* (*μεμφόμενος*): the plaintiff (lit. 'the one who blames'), as elsewhere (see comm. ad **G41**.7.8–9). It cannot refer to the defendant, as Martini 1999: 390–3 claims.

10.1 Only the first letter is visible. It is always read as *san*, though it could also be *mu*, perhaps some form of *maitys*, if Maffi's suggestion is correct (see below on 9.54–10.1). Much of the text in 10.1–15 is missing; if our proposed reconstruction of 10.4–13 is correct (see below), then this section here must have ended by the end of 10.3. Quite possibly it ended in 10.1.

This provision is intended to ensure that an investor in a commercial venture abroad is repaid. Normally the witnesses who were present when the agreement was made will confirm it, and the judge is bound by their testimony (43–51); but if witnesses are not available to testify, then the plaintiff can ask the judge to require an oath of denial from the accused or can choose some other method of judgment, now lost. No other law at Gortyn (nor to our knowledge anywhere else in Greece) allows a plaintiff to choose the means of deciding a case. It may be intended to compensate for some disadvantage on the plaintiff's part, perhaps the continued absence abroad of the defendant and perhaps of the witnesses too. The law tries to make it easy for the plaintiff to recover his investment.

43–4 VER suggest that *perai* means 'beyond the city's borders' and argue that the agreement concerns export. This is possible, but we think it better to leave open other possibilities, such as an agreement with a foreign investor or even (as C suggests) to set up a pirating venture.

9.52–10.1 'Comes (back)' (*elthei*): the verb simply means 'comes', but in this context the sense is 'returns'. The plaintiff presumably resides in Gortyn. As Martini notes (1999: 392), this case is too complex to fit the rule in 11.26–31; it does not invalidate that rule, but supplements it so that if there are no witnesses, the plaintiff does not necessarily lose (as e.g. in 9.24–40), but has other means of winning a conviction. See Gagarin 2010b: 132–3.

9.53–10.1 The plaintiff can propose whichever of two (*oteron*) procedures he wishes; the second is now lost. Martini suggests (1999: 393) that the alternative is that the defendant pays the simple fine, though the plaintiff presumably would first have to persuade the judge that he is guilty. And since this process is envisioned for cases where there are no witnesses (51–2), it is hard to imagine what other means of deciding the case might be available (arbitration?). Maffi 2011: 159 suggests that the plaintiff might propose to swear an oath himself rather than requiring an oath of denial from the defendant. This is possible: although most oaths sworn by litigants at Gortyn are oaths of denial, in **G76**B5–7, if a judge has to pay for purification after a death because the heirs do not pay, he can swear an oath and collect double from them, and in **G77**B11 someone can collect whatever value they swear to. Thus, the alternative in 10.1 may be that the plaintiff swear an oath, perhaps with witnesses present (see n. ad 10.1) and win the case.

Cf. **Da1**B7–11, where a litigant can apparently choose the venue.

10.1–25—GIFTS TO WOMEN (VER II.53, II.45, K 167, 178)

Regulations concerning gifts to mothers and probably also to wives. An amendment in 12.1–5 addresses the question of retroactivity with regard to these gifts.

[—]τ
αν[. . . . . c.20 . . . .]
[. . . . . c.18 . . . .] αἴ κα
λε̣̂[ι] ἐκα[τὸν στατε̂ρανς ἒ ἐκ]-
[ατὸν στατέρον κ]ρέος ἒ [με]ι̣̂-
[ον πλ]ίον δ̣[ὲ] μέ. αἰ [δὲ πλία δο]-
ίε, [δύο (?) στα]τε̂ρα[ν]ς κ[αταστα]-
[σεῖ vac. (?)] α̣ἰ δέ κα μ̣εῖο[ν . . . c.6 . . .]
[. . c.4 . . πεντέκον]τα στατ[έρο]ν
κρέος, α̣ἰ δ' οἰ [. . . . . . c.12 . . . . . .]
[. . . . . . c.13 . . . . . .]με[. ἀ]ποδόν-
τανς τὸ[ν ἄργυρον . . . . c.8 . . . .]
[. . . . . c.17 . . . .] ματρὶ
δ' υἰὺ̣ν [ἒ ἄνδρα γυναικὶ δόμεν ἐ]-
κατὸν στατε̂ρα[νς] ἒ̣ μεῖον, π-
λίον δὲ μέ. αἰ δὲ πλία δοίε, αἴ
κα λείοντ' οἰ ἐπιβάλλοντες, τ-
ὸν ἄργυρον ἀποδόντες τὰ κρ-
έματ' ἐκόντον. vac. αἰ δέ τις ὀπέ-
λον ἄργυρον ἒ ἀταμένος ἒ μ-
ολιομένας δίκας δοίε, αἰ
μὲ εἴε τὰ λοιπὰ ἄκσια τᾶς ἄ-
τας, μεδὲν ἐς κρέος ἔμεν τὰν
δόσιν. ←

[—] if he wishes, one hundred [staters or] something worth [one hundred staters], or less but not more. But if [he should give more], he will pay [two (?)] staters. [*vac.* (?)] And if [he should give something] worth less than [fifty (?)] staters, and if the [—]

[—] giving back the money [—]

A son [may give] his mother [or a husband his wife (?)] one hundred staters or less, but not more. And if he should give more, if the claimants to the estate wish, let them give her the money and have the property.

vac. And if someone who owes money or has been fined or is engaged in a suit gives a gift, if the remainder of the property is not equal to the fine, the gift is to be invalid. *vac.*

4–15 The heavily supplemented text in these lines is derived in part from several small fragments of stone that were found in the vicinity of the Code, the properties and lettering of which closely resemble those of the Code. Since **G73**, **G75**, **G76**, and **G77** also resemble the Code in these respects but are almost certainly separate texts, we cannot be certain whether these fragments come from the Code or from another text on the same wall. G. prints the fragments as **G74**a–c, and no recent editor includes them here. But H suggested that the fragments be assembled in this way, and C suggested most of the additional supplements printed above (see G, pp. 148, 173). We accept some of these supplements but not the one in line 4 (see below). We stress that any restoration of this passage is highly speculative.

4 C suggested the supplement *θυγατρὶ πατέρα δόμεν*, but gifts from a father to a daughter have already been regulated in 4.48–5.9, and the limit of one hundred staters would be in direct conflict with the rule given there. See comment below. Gifts from a brother to a sister are not mentioned elsewhere in this connection, so perhaps we should supplement the line *ἀδευπιᾶι ἀδελπιὸν δόμεν*.

8 As restored above, there is only space for three letters before στα]τερα[ν]ς, leaving δύο as the only likely supplement; if δοίε was omitted, there would be space for 8–10 letters (but cf. 17).

8–9 If κ[αταστασεῖ is correct, there appears to be space for 1–2 letters after it, making a *vac.* likely.

9–10 μ̣εῖο[ν δοίε ἒ πεντέκον]τα? Other numerals are possible here, but of these, in the Code only this figure designates a number of staters (30 and 60 each designate a number of days).

13 τὸ[ν ἄργυρον: G compares 18–19 below.

15 ἒ ἄνδρα γυναικὶ δόμεν ἒ]: suggested by Baunack and Baunack 1885 (cf. 12.1–5) and accepted by most scholars.

25 There is an inscribed sign here, generally called a *ligo*, in the shape of a mattock ().

We have included in this section (lines 4–13) some text not usually included here, where the large block that formed the top of column 10 is missing. Our text is based on several small fragments found nearby (see above n. ad 4–15).

4–9 These lines are sometimes restored as regulating gifts from a father to daughter, but these have already been regulated in 4.48–51, where a father is allowed to give his daughter a gift upon her marriage 'according to what is written'. But 4.51–5.1 then add that if a daughter has received or been promised such a gift, she cannot receive anything more as her inheritance. Since girls from wealthy families must have expected to receive a far larger inheritance than one hundred staters, imposing such a limit here would be a very severe restriction and would seem to go against the sense of 4.48–5.1, that fathers could, in effect, give their daughters the amount of their inheritance at the time of their marriage (but then, of course, they would not get anything more as their inheritance). If the lines do not concern gifts from a father, and if gifts from husband to wife are correctly restored in line 15, then we suggest that gifts from brother to sister may have been regulated here. No other mention is made of such gifts, though in some circumstances a brother would give his sister away in marriage (8.21), and thus might give her a gift in connection with this event.

9–14 Another provision, perhaps separated by a gap, may prescribe a course of action for gifts of less than fifty staters, though several more letters probably need to be added to lines 9–10 to make these long enough.

14–25 An amendment (12.1–5) states that any gifts made according to earlier rules are not to be contested. These rules here, then, are new, and since they allow the relatives to contest gifts larger than one hundred staters, it seems likely that the earlier rules allowed gifts larger than this amount. It is not impossible that the earlier rules allowed only smaller gifts, perhaps fifty staters or less, to be made to these women, and that some relatives would want to contest even these gifts on the grounds that they were not protected by the current rules, but this seems less likely.

14–17 This rule may be referred to in 3.20–2: 'whatever a husband gives (to his wife) according to what is written'. The mention of heirs (*epiballontes*) in 17–20 has led most scholars to assume that these gifts would be made on the approach of death, since neither a mother nor a wife is in line to inherit (see Maffi 1997a: 53). This may have been common in the case of husbands giving to wives, but sons would probably not expect to die before their mothers except in rare cases.

17–20 If the gift exceeds one hundred staters, the heirs may, if they wish, give the money to the mother or wife in question, and then have the rest of the property. This probably means that if they do not wish to give the designated amount, they may give only one hundred staters. The money would come from the deceased's estate. Maffi 1997a: 53–4 argues that the heirs could, if they wished, give the wife or mother nothing, but this seems less likely.

20–5 The rule against giving away so much property that not enough is left to satisfy creditors, actual or potential, would guard against a person giving away money so as to put it out of the reach of the creditors.

21–2 *Moliomenas dikas*: lit. 'while a suit is being litigated'.

24 'Is to be invalid': lit. 'is to be nothing with respect to value (*kreos*)'. Maffi 1988: 284–6 takes *meden es kreos emen* (here and in 30–1 below) to mean that the gift will not result in an obligation toward the creditor,[414] but it is unclear to us just how this sense can be extracted from the Greek and, more important, why a legislator would allow someone to escape from a debt by giving away all or most of his estate. Gortynian legislators use other terms for 'debt, obligation' (Bile 318, 330–1), and the traditional interpretation of this expression, shared by all other editors, makes good sense here and in 30–1 below.

10.25–32—ACQUISITION OF SLAVES (VER II.6, K 179)

This section prohibits the purchase of a slave who is already or may become obligated to someone else.

ἄντρο[π]ον μὲ ὀνêθαι κατακείμενον πρίν κ' ἀλλύσεται ὀ καταθένς, μεδ' ἀμπίμολον, μεδὲ δέκσαθαι μεδ' ἐπισπένσαθαι μεδὲ καταθέθαι. αἰ δέ τις τούτον τι Ϝέρκσαι, μεδὲν ἐς κρέος ἔμεν, αἰ ἀποπονίοιεν δύο μαίτυρε⟨ς⟩. *vac.*

No one is to buy an indentured person until the one who indentured him obtains his release, nor one who is the subject of litigation, nor is anyone to accept him (as payment) nor accept a promise (to deliver him) nor take him in indentureship. And if anyone should do any of these things, it is to be invalid, if two witnesses should testify. *vac.*

[414] Such a gift 'will not result in an obligation toward the one who would be harmed by the act; thus, the rights acquired by such an act could not be opposed by someone who would be harmed by it' (non darà luogo a un debito a carico di colui che sarebbe danneggiato dal negozio stesso; di conseguenza il diritto acquistato mediante tale negozio non sarà opponibile a colui che ne sarebbe danneggiato).

26 The lettering in this line spans a horizontal division between two blocks of stone which are now not precisely aligned; cf. 9.44.

26–7 *ἀλλύσεται* = *ἀναλύσηται* (aor. subj.); see n. ad 2.30–1 above.

30 *Fέρκσαι*: third person sing. aorist optative of *Fέρδω* (*ἔρδω*) = 'to do'.

32 Regarding the mason's error, see n. ad 11.24.

The gap here is much larger (eight or nine letters) than any other gap thus far; see further in our note on Addenda below.

This section prohibits the purchase or other transactions involving a slave who is indentured or is the subject of litigation (see below on 27–8), and thus may potentially become indentured (if his owner loses the case). The slave's owner who indentured him (*o katathens*), presumably to satisfy a debt, must first obtain a release (*allysetai*) from his creditor, to whom the slave is indentured.

25–6 'Person': *antropos* alone may mean 'slave', as it often does in Attic. Otherwise, no word for 'slave' appears in this section (cf. **G**47.1–3, where *katakeimenos* is followed by *dolos* and *dola*), but the 'indentured person' must be a slave because once he is released from his indentureship, he may be purchased.

27–8 *Ampimolon*, 'the one concerning whom there is litigation' (Bile 351). The litigation may concern the person's status (slave or free) or ownership, as provided for in 1.2–2.2 above, or it might concern a slave accused of rape or adultery, as in 2.2–45.

29–32 The person to whom the slave is indentured would want to invalidate any transaction that deprived him of the slave's services. As W notes, the two witnesses probably testify either that the slave is currently indentured or that he is the subject of litigation; see further Gagarin 1989: 46–7.

30–1 'It is to be invalid' (*meden es kreos emen*): see above on 10.24.

ADDENDA

Scholars agree that the Code ends with several addenda and that these begin at 11.24. The primary marker of these addenda is a large gap at the end of a line: 11.23, 11.25, 11.45, and apparently 11.55 (see n. ad loc.). After these gaps, the writing may begin again in the same direction or may continue in the reverse, maintaining the boustrophedon order. To our knowledge, no scholar thus far has treated 10.33–11.23 as one of these addenda; but the writing in 10.32 ends just past the middle of the line, leaving a gap that is far larger than any of those that precede it (see above, n. ad 10.32), but is similar to the gaps that mark addenda. The conclusion is unavoidable that this section on adoption was also a later addition to the main body of the Code. It is true that 10.33 begins from the right, thus preserving the boustrophedon order of writing, but 11.46 also begins a new amendment and continues the boustrophedon order. It is also true that most of the other addenda (five out of six) modify or supplement legislation in the main body of the Code, whereas 10.33–11.23 addresses a new subject, adoption. But 11.26–31 are not an amendment either; they establish a general rule for judicial decisions that is relevant to the entire Code.

Since C most scholars have agreed that the additional provisions in 11.24–12.19 were carved by a different hand. Davies 1996: 37 calls attention particularly to the *lambdas* and *thetas* in this part of the Code. But although the top bars on some *lambdas* (e.g. in 12.11) are horizontal (Γ), others (e.g. in 11.31–45) are oblique (↾), as in the rest of the Code. Moreover, although the interior crosses of all the *thetas* from 11.14 to the end are upright (⊕), before this some *thetas* are upright while others are tilted (⊗); these variations tend to come in groups—e.g. the first ten *thetas* on column 2 are tilted, but the next seven and the first ones on column 3 are upright (the *theta* at the end of 2.30 is unclear). Other letters, moreover, show some variation, such as *upsilon*, which is sometimes shaped like a V (with straight sides) and sometimes looks more like a *Y* (with curved sides and a tail), and *gamma* also shows variation within the same provision (see further the note on ἄργυρον in 11.31 below). It seems, then, that unless many different masons inscribed different parts of the Code, most of these variations may not indicate different hands but rather the same sort of variations in a mason's hand that we noted earlier (see on **G1**). Even by the time of the Code, masons at Gortyn had not developed such consistent lettering that firm conclusions about different hands can be drawn on the basis of letter forms. On the other hand, there are other indications that column 12, and perhaps also 11.46–55, may have been carved by a different hand: the letters throughout are not as deeply incised, and the lettering in general is not as neat as in the rest of the Code (compare e.g. the size of the *iotas* in 12.5–6). But these characteristics may also be due to other factors, such as the quality of the stone. In sum, distinguishing hands in the Code and other laws (see e.g. on **G1**), is no easy matter; our judgment on these amendments is *non liquet*.

10.33–11.23—ADOPTION (VER II.40, K 180)

This section specifies the procedure for adoption and for renouncing an adoption and the share of the estate an adopted son will inherit under various circumstances.

ἄνπανσιν ἔμεν ὄπο κά τιλ λ-
ἐι. ἀμπαίνεθαι δὲ κατ' ἀγορὰν
καταϜελμένον τôμ πολιατâ-
ν ἀπὸ τô λάο ὁ ἀπαγορεύοντι.
vac. ὁ δ' ἀμπανάμενος δότο τâ-
ι ἐταιρείαι τâι Ϝâι αὐτô ἰαρε-
îον καὶ πρόκοον Ϝοίνο. *vac.* καὶ
μέν κ' ἀνέλεται πάντα τὰ κρέ-
ματα καὶ μὲ συννêι γνέσια τ-

There is to be adoption from wherever one wishes. The adoption is to be presented in the agora when the citizens are gathered, from the stone from which people speak. *vac.* Let the adopter give to his own *etaireia* a sacrificial animal and a jug of wine. *vac.* And if (the adoptee) inherits all the property and there are not natural ἔκνα, τέλλεμ μὲν τὰ θῖνα καὶ τὰ ἀντρόπινα τὰ τô ἀνπαναμέ-νο κἀναιλêθαι ᾆιπερ τοῖς γ-νεσίοις ἔγρατται. αἰ̣ [δ]ἐ̣ κα μὲ λêι τέλλεν ᾆι ἔγρατται, τὰ κ[ρ]έ-ματα τὸνς ἐπιβάλλοντανς ἔκε-ν. αἰ δέ κ' ἐ̃ι γνέσ[ι]α τέκνα τôι ἀν-παναμένοι, πεδὰ μὲν τôν ἐρσ-ένον τὸν ἀμπαντόν, ᾆιπερ αἰ θ-έλ̣[ε]ιαι, ἀπὸ τôν ἀδελπιôν λανκά-νοντι, αἰ δέ κ' ἔρσενες μὲ ἴον-τι, θέλειαι δέ, ϝισϝόμοιρον ἔ-

Col. 11

[μεν] τὸν ἀνπαντὸν· καὶ μὲ ἐ-πάνανκον ἔμεν τέλλεν τ[ὰ τ]-[ô ἀν]παναμένο καὶ τὰ κρέμα-τ' ἀναιλ⟨ê⟩θαι ἅτι κα κατα[λίπε]-[ι ὀ ἀ]ν̣πανάμενος· πλίυι δὲ τὸν̣ ἀνπαντὸμ μὲ ἐπικορέν. *vac.* [αἰ δ'] [ἀπο]θάνοι ὀ ἀνπαντὸς γν̣έσια τέκνα μὲ καταλιπόν, πὰρ τὸ[νς τ]-[ô ἀν]παναμένο ἐπιβάλλονταν-ς ἀνκορὲν τὰ κρέματα. αἰ δ[έ κα] [λêι] ὀ ἀνπανάμενος, ἀποϝειπ-άθθο κατ' ἀγορὰν ἀπὸ τô λά[ο ὀ] [ἀπα]γορεύοντι καταϝελμέν-ον τôν πολιατâν· ἀνθέμε̣[ν δὲ] [δέκ]α̣ [σ]τατêρανς ἐδ δικαστ-έριον, ὀ δὲ μνάμον ὀ τô κσεν-ίο ἀποδότο τôι ἀπορρεθέντι. γυνὰ δὲ μὲ ἀμπαινέθθο μεδ' ἄνεβος. *vac.* κρέθαι δὲ τοῖδδε ᾆ-ι τάδε τὰ γράμματ' ἔγραπσε, τôν δὲ πρόθθα ὅπαι τις ἔκει ἒ ἀ-μπαντύι ἒ πὰρ ἀμπαντô μὲ ἔτ' ἔ-νδικον ἔμεν. *vac.*

children, he is to fulfill the adopter's divine and human obligations and is to inherit just as is written for the natural children. But if he does not wish to fulfill (the obligations) as is written, those in line of succession are to have the property. But if the adopter has natural children, with the male (heirs) the adoptee will receive a share in the same way as the daughters from their brothers, and if there are no males, but females, an equal share **(Col. 11)** is for the adoptee; and it is not necessary to fulfill the adopter's obligations and receive whatever property the adopter leaves; but the adoptee is not to receive more. *vac.* And if the adoptee should die without leaving natural children, the property is to revert to the heirs of the adopter. And if the adopter wishes, let him renounce (the adoption) in the agora from the stone from which people speak, when the citizens are gathered. And he is to deposit ten staters at the court, and let the rememberer (*mnamon*) for the foreigners' official give it to the renounced person. And let not a woman adopt, nor a child before puberty. *vac.* These rules are to be followed from the time he wrote these writings, but in earlier matters, in whatever way someone has (property), either as the result of an adoption or from an adoptee, it is no longer a matter for trial. *vac.*

---

33 ἄνπανσιν: this and related terms for 'adoption' occur only in this section of the Code and in **G21**.3. The root meaning of ἀμπαίνεθαι (= ἀναφαίνεσθαι, Dialect 5, 12) is 'show, declare', referring to the public ritual of declaring someone an adopted son.

ὄπο: see on 5.23 above.

τιλ = τις by assimilation; Dialect 9.

35 καταϝελμένον: for the form (from Attic κατείλω), see note on **G80**.14–15.

40 ἀνέλεται (ἀναιρέω): aor. subj.; see Bile 270–1, cf. 273–4.

42–3 *τὰ θῖνα καὶ τὰ ἀντρόπινα*: the same pair (with *θιήια* instead of *θῖνα*) is found three times in the agreement with Spensithios (**Da1**A4, 6–7, B2–3).

47 *τὸνς ἐπιβάλλονταvς*: 'those who have a claim' (see n. ad 5.23–6 above), *sc.* after the adopted son.

49 *πεδά* = *μετά* (Dialect 50).

11.4 *ἀναιλ⟨ἐ⟩θαι*: the mason mistakenly wrote *iota* instead of *epsilon*.

ἅτι (*ἅτινα*): see n. ad 2.47.

5 *πλίυι*: This adverbial form is found only here; it must be equivalent to the more common *πλίον* (Bile 214).

6 *ἐπικορέν*: In Attic, *ἐπιχωρεῖν* usually means 'yield, agree to, concede', though it can have a more literal sense of 'go toward' either in the sense 'join with' (Thuc. 4.107) or 'go against' (Xen. *An.* 1.2.17). Here it is usually understood to mean 'move into', i.e. receive an inheritance; but see further on 5–6 below.

10 *ἀνκορῆν* (*ἀναχωρεῖν*): 'go back to'.

14 *ἀνθέμẹ[ν* = *ἀναθεῖναι*; see Dialect 12, 20.

17 *ἀπορρεθέντι*: aor. pass. participle of *ἀποϝεῖπον*.

21–2 *ἀμπαντύι*: dative sing. from **ἀμπαντύν* or *-ύς* (?) 'the state of being adopted'. Maffi (1997a: 84) argues that because the noun for 'adoption' is *anpansis*, *ampantui* is the dative of *ampantos*, 'adoptee'. But the dative of *ampantos* is *ampantoi* (**G21**.3), and there is no difficulty in understanding *anpansis* as designating the process of adopting whereas *ampantui* designates the resulting state or condition of being adopted ('l'état dû à l'adoption', Bile 335).

The law first states the procedure for adopting someone (10.33–9), then the rules for inheritance by the adoptee when the deceased does or does not have natural children (10.39–11.6). The rules imply an entirely oral process; there is no hint of testamentary adoption, as at Athens. The fact that nearly half of this section concerns inheritance and no other substantive aspect of adoption is regulated indicates that the main purpose of adoption in Gortyn (as elsewhere in Greece) was to provide an heir. But since the adopter at Gortyn may also have natural children (10.48–11.1), he may have adopted at an earlier age than in Athens, where a man normally adopted late in life. The provision for renouncing an adoption (11.10–17) may have been enacted primarily for men who later had a natural son and thus no longer needed an adopted son for an heir.

Davies 1996: 40 singles out the exemplary organization of this section: 'This really is codification: a general principle is enunciated, whether enabling or prohibitory (here enabling), a cross-reference to existing law is inserted, and the likely circumstances arising from its application are envisaged and systematically provided for—altogether a model of a modern major general law.' We agree that the section is well organized, but on the other hand, the wording of some of the individual provisions is far from clear or systematic (see below on 10.39–11.6).

33 *Anpansin* is put first in the sentence to indicate the topic addressed in this section; cf. 7.15–16.

33–4 The rule allowing adoption from any source whatsoever may mean only that one can adopt someone from another tribe, but it may also allow adoption of a foreigner or a slave. Maffi 1997a: 75–6 rejects this possibility, since this would mean that a slave or foreigner could become a citizen by adoption without a vote of the assembly, which he thinks was impossible. But the little we know about citizenship at Gortyn (see on **G13**, **G51**.6–7) gives us no reason to assume that this should be impossible, and the citizens who are gathered in the agora to witness an adoption may at the same time have been asked to approve the adoption (see further on 34–6).

34–6 The gathering of citizens (*poliatai*) in the agora (also in 11.13–14) implies a kind of assembly meeting. The law does not mention a vote, but it seems more likely that a large gathering of citizens would be asked to approve the adoption than simply observe it. Cf. 'the Gortynians voting' (**G78**.1) and 'all Gortyn' (**G64**.2).

38 *etaireia*: At Gortyn this term occurs only here and in **G42**B12, where 'the judge of the *etaireiai*' is mentioned. It also occurs in a late-fourth-century law from Axos (*SEG* 23.566, 17) and perhaps at Dreros (**Dr2**), and is probably the root of *apetairos* (see on 2.5 above). The law here implies that all citizens belong to a *hetaireia* (Maffi 2003a: 163); see further Introd. 6A.

39 A 'jug' (*prokoos* = Attic *prochous*) is a liquid measure for wine or must (fermenting grape juice); the word also occurs in **G79**.4–5 (= *IC* 4.144.4, which specifies 100 *prokooi* of must), **G79**.7, and **Da1**A12 (where 50 *prokooi* of must are part of the stipend for Spensithios). We do not know how large it was, but even the largest pitcher of wine would not go very far in serving a *hetaireia*, unless this was a very small group. It seems more likely, therefore, that the wine was primarily for the ritual pouring of libations along with the sacrifice of the animal the adopter supplied.

39–11.6 The rules concerning inheritance by an adopted son are odd and unclear in several places. The first rule (39–48) would be clearer if it were more logically organized so that it read, 'if there are not natural children, the adopted son may, if he wishes, inherit and fulfill, . . . but if he does not wish . . .'. In 48–52 'with the male (heirs) the adoptee will receive a share in the same way as the daughters from their brothers' is unclear in several respects: does the adopted son receive the same share as a daughter or a different share in the same way (whatever that is)? Does 'with the male (heirs)' mean that he receives the same share as they do, or does it refer to possession of a city house, etc. (see 4.31–7), or something else? When there are no natural sons, does an 'equal share' (10.52–11.1) mean equal to a son's or to a daughter's? And what does 'more' mean in 11.5–6?

42–4 The 'divine and human' obligations include the funeral rites and subsequent tending of the deceased's tomb, on the one hand, and the payment of debts and fulfillment of other contractual obligations on the other.

45–8 It may seem odd that an adopted son is given the choice not to receive his adopted father's estate, since this might result in the property passing out of the family to quite distant relatives (Maffi 1997a: 78); but this would presumably happen only if the estate was small or was burdened by large debts, in which case there would be less concern to keep it within the family. Nothing is said about the fate of an adoptee who renounces his adopter's estate, but he probably returned to his natural father (where he may have been able to claim a larger estate).

47 'Those in line of succession': here the *epiballontes* ('those with a claim') must be the more distant relatives, who would inherit in the absence of any children (5.13–25).

48–11.1 Since the main purpose of adoption appears to be to provide an heir, it is unlikely that the adopter already had a son when he adopted; thus these natural sons were presumably born after the adoption. A man may have adopted when he had only female children, in which case it is possible that (as sometimes in Athens) the adoptee would be the one who by law was entitled to the hand of one of the daughters.

50 'In the same way as' (*aiper*) probably means that the adoptee receives the same share as a daughter, namely a half-share compared to that of a son (4.39–43); but see above on 10.39–11.6. It is not clear why the adoptee or the daughters (or both) receive the share from the brothers; probably the brothers took all the property after their father's death and then distributed shares to their sisters and adopted brother, if there was one.

53 'An equal share' (*wiswomoiron*): also in **G20**.1–2, but without context. It apparently means equal to each daughter's share, but if 48–52 already assigns the adoptee the same share as a daughter, then this rule would be superfluous. *Wiswomoiron* could perhaps mean equal to a son's share, but it seems odd to say that he should receive a share equal to that of a nonexistent son. A better alternative may be that *wiswomoiron* means equal to the shares of all the daughters together, which would be half the estate. But much is uncertain here.

1–5 If the adoptee refuses his share of the estate and the obligations that go with it when there are natural children, he probably returns to his natural family, perhaps because a larger share awaits him there.

5–6 'The adoptee is not to receive more'. If this means that he is not to have more than what is prescribed in 10.39–11.1 (so W, who translates 'he is not to take possession of more [than the females]'), then the restriction is superfluous (so K), since it goes without saying that he should receive no more than the share specified by law. Similarly, if it means that the adoptee who refuses his share of the estate is not to receive anything more than he received during his adopted father's life, namely his personal property, but this too, it would seem, goes without saying. It is best, then, to understand this clause as prohibiting the adoptee who refuses a share of his adopter's estate from receiving a larger share if he returns to his natural father. The law would then be intended to remove one strong motive adopted sons might have to refuse a share of their adopted father's estate.

Maffi 1997a: 81 argues that because this prohibition is unnecessary, *epikoren* (see above, n. ad 11.6) does not mean 'receive' but has its more common (Attic) sense 'concede'. The provision would then prohibit the adoptee from 'conceding' (i.e. giving) one of the adopter's daughters a larger amount than she is supposed to receive when she is married (see 5.1–9). But there would be no reason to use 'concede' instead of 'give' (which is everywhere else used of gifts), especially when no gifts of any sort have been mentioned thus far in this section.

6–10 Athenian law may have had the same rule that only the natural son of an adopted son can inherit (Dem. 46.14), but interpretation of this law is controversial (Harrison 1968: 85–7).

10–17 The adopter may renounce the adoption by a public process similar to that for adopting (10.33–9). He probably would do this only if natural sons had been born after the adoption. The adoptee is not given the right to object, but the adopter presumably felt an obligation to provide for the adoptee beyond the ten staters specified and would probably not renounce him unless he had a family to return to.

14–17 The ten staters are not given to the adoptee directly but to the rememberer (*mnamon*). This would be a means of 'recording' the renunciation in the rememberer's memory so that he could testify to it later, if necessary.

15–16 This is the only mention of a court (*dikasterion*) at Gortyn; we do not know where it was located or whether it was a building or just a demarcated open area.

16–17 The foreigners' official (*ksenios*) may be the same as the foreigners' *kosmos*, see above on **G14**p–g2 and Introd. 4C1b.

18–19 *Ampaineththo* is usually taken as a middle form: 'let no woman or child adopt'; but it could also be passive ('let no woman or child be adopted'), and Maffi (2003a: 202–4) argues for this sense here. He reasons that it would be unnecessary to prohibit a woman or child from adopting since neither would have been allowed to participate in an assembly meeting where adoptions took place. Moreover, a child not yet at the age of puberty could not even contemplate adoption, and a woman, if unmarried, would aim first to be married and have natural children, and if married, would leave adoption to her husband. Without subscribing to either of these explanations, we would allow that it may have been common custom, and thus taken for granted by the law, that only adult males could adopt. On the other hand, a widow with property who had no children might wish to adopt a son, and a man might wish to arrange for his only child (perhaps one who is quite sickly) to adopt a son in order to keep his estate out of the hands of distant relatives. We thus favor the traditional view, which would prohibit these sorts of manipulations of the prescribed lines of inheritance. If this is the sense, the adoption of women and children would not be prohibited, though the former might be quite rare. Another point in favor of this interpretation is that the term for woman, *gyna*, implies an adult woman usually in her role as wife and/or mother; if the law were to prohibit the adoption of a female, some other expression that left open the age of the adopted daughter would likely be used. Note, moreover, that in Athens a woman could apparently be adopted in a will (examples in Rubinstein 1993: 20), and although all the adoptees in Athens for whom we have information are adults, Moschion in Menander's *Samia* was adopted as a child (references in Rubinstein 1993: 22).

Whichever sense we give the law, the vast majority of adoptions at Gortyn (as at Athens) probably involved an adult male adopting another adult male.

19 'Child': *anebos* designates a child up to the age of puberty; see above on 7.29–30.

19–23 This is the only case of non-retroactivity that does not involve the property of women; see above on 5.7–9.

20 'He wrote' (*egrapse*): elsewhere the verb is always passive: 'is written'; this may indicate that this section had a different author than other parts of the Code.

21–3 'Either as the result of an adoption or from an adoptee': the exclusion of retroactivity is directed primarily at the rules concerning inheritance in 10.39–11.6. The legislator's intent was to disallow any suits regarding the amount of inheritance received in the past by an adopted son or by his natural son from him. For Maffi's interpretation ('either against the adoptee or on the part of the adoptee'), see above, n. ad 21–2.

11.24–5—AMENDMENT TO 1.1–2.2 ON SEIZURE BEFORE TRIAL (VER II.6, K 163)

A provision allowing an illegally seized person to find refuge.

ἄντροπον ὅ⟨ν⟩ κ' ἄγει πρὸ δίκας	One is always to receive a person whom
αἰεὶ ἐπιδέκεθαι. *vac.*	someone seizes before trial. *vac.*

24 ὅ⟨ν⟩: The text on the stone (ὅς) cannot be correct (see below) and so we assume that the mason mistakenly wrote M (*san*) for N (*nu*) just as he did in 8.4 and 9.39; cf. the reverse error, N for M, in 10.32 and 11.52.

ἄγει πρὸ δίκας: the strong echo of 1.3–4 indicates that this amendment applies to the seizure of a person whose status is in dispute, not to any seizure.

25 ἐπιδέκεθαι = Att. ἐπιδέχεσθαι.

The sense of this provision is largely agreed on: it allows anyone to receive a person who has been seized illegally (1.2–3). The person must come to him, however; one is not allowed to seize a person held illegally by another (as one can by the Athenian procedure of *aphairesis*), but must take the wrongdoer to court, as provided for in 1.3–14. How this sense can be derived from the text, however, is debated. The preserved text (with *os* not *on*) is usually taken to mean: 'anyone may at any time receive a person, if any person seize him before trial' (W); but this sense cannot be obtained from the Greek, which would mean literally 'one is always (or 'at any time') to receive a person who seizes (someone) before trial', or (taking *antropon* as part of the relative clause) 'whoever seizes a person before trial is always to receive (him?)'. Maffi (1983: 101–12, esp. 108–12) rightly objects to the common translation, but in our view his solution is no better, namely to understand *epidekethai* as 'assume legal responsibility'. The law's intent, he thinks, was to force someone who seizes illegally always to respond to litigation brought against him, no matter how much time had passed. In other words, the process established in 1.3–14 cannot be annulled by the passage of time. VER accept Maffi's arguments and translate 'whoever seizes a person before trial will be responsible in all circumstances'. Ingenious as this interpretation may be, there is no parallel for such a sense of *epidekethai* ('accept, receive'), and nothing in the law on column 1 suggests that someone who seizes illegally might gain possession of the seized person by the passage of time. Nor is there any hint of a statute of limitations in the Gortyn laws.

The sense that Willetts and others desire requires that one emend the text, as we have done, to read *on* (acc.) instead of *os* (nom.): 'a person *whom* someone seizes before trial, one is always to receive (him)'.

25 For the sense of *epidekethai* cf. **Lyktos1A**1–2, 'whoever receives (*deksetai*) a foreigner'.

11.26–31—THE JUDICIAL DECISION (VER II.4, K 181)

A general rule about judicial decisions.

τὸν δικαστάν, ὅτι μὲν κατὰ μαίτυρανς ἔγραπται δικάδδ- εν ἒ ἀπόμοτον, δικάδδεν ἆι ἔ- γραπται, τôν δ' ἀλλôν ὀμνύντ- α κρίνεν πορτὶ τὰ μολιόμεν- α. *vac.*	Whenever it is written that the judge is to rule according to witnesses or an oath of denial, he is to rule as is written, but in the other cases he is to swear an oath and decide with reference to the pleadings. *vac.*

28 ἀπόμοτον: cf. ἀπομόσαι in 3.7, 3.9–10, 9.54.

This short provision formulates the general rule governing the two methods of judicial decision prescribed in the Code: the first method is followed only when the law explicitly (in writing) directs a judge to give a prescribed ruling in the case (*dikadden*), in accordance with either the testimony of a witness or an oath sworn by the accused; in such cases the judge simply carries out the procedure specified by the law and decides the case automatically. The second method, followed in all other cases, is that the judge swears an oath and decides himself (*krinen*) on the basis of the pleadings. These pleadings (*ta moliomena*) would include any witness testimony or other evidence the litigants have presented (as in 1.21–4 when witnesses testify for both sides). For more on this provision and the cases discussed below, see Introd. 10D and Gagarin 2010b. In the Code, the second method is explicitly specified in eight cases (1.12; 1.14; 1.24; 1.39; 3.1; 5.43–4; 6.54; 9.21); in two of these (5.43–4; 6.54) the judge is told to decide 'according to the pleadings', and this must be implicit in the other six cases. The first method is explicitly specified in only four or perhaps five cases, but several others should be included in this group, including three cases where a litigant or witness is said to be 'the one who swears' (*orkioteros*, 2.15–16; 3.49–50; 4.6–7). In addition, in seven cases (1.4; 1.6; 1.8; 1.28–36; 5.31–5; 7.45–6; 9.38) where the verb used is *dikadden* or *katadikadden*, the judge is not instructed to impose an oath or rule according to witnesses, but his ruling is nonetheless automatic. In most provisions, however, nothing is said about how the dispute is to be judged; in these the second method (swear and decide freely) would have to be used, making this method the more common one.

The distinction between the two verbs, *dikadden* (and its compounds) and *krinen*—which we translate 'rule' and 'decide'—is maintained consistently throughout the Code and in some of the other fifth-century laws from Gortyn (e.g. **G41**.5.8–10), but in earlier laws at Gortyn and in laws from other Cretan cities *dikadden* appears to designate judging in general (see comm. ad **G9**a–m); the whole issue is well treated by Talamanca 1979, who rejects attempts by Wolff 1946 and Thür 1970 to understand early Greek judicial decisions more narrowly. More recently, Maffi (2003a: 213–20; 2007: 201–22) has argued that the law did not necessarily determine which method would be used in judging a case, since in cases where the law prescribed that the judge rule according to an oath or a witness, if the party concerned did not swear the oath or present the witness, then the judge would have to decide on his own, and that when the judge is directed to swear and decide, or when this is the default method, one party may propose a decisive proof and the judge may accept it, thereby converting the judgment into an automatic ruling. Close examination of specific passages shows that Maffi's conclusion may be true in a few cases, but it cannot be the general rule (see Gagarin 2010b).

We may perhaps infer from the fact that the law gives such precise directions for judging that judges at Gortyn were not professional judges, and that the legislator is trying to clarify the rules and in some cases give precise guidance to judges. If the office of *dikastas* rotated, perhaps annually, new judges might often be unfamiliar with these rules. On the other hand, scattered references to judges having specialized jurisdictions (e.g. 6.29–31: 'the matter is to be tried where it belongs, before the *dikastas* where it is written in each case') suggest that judges developed special expertise in some areas. So perhaps this addendum is addressing a different concern, that some judges with long experience may have been judging cases in whatever way they wished, ignoring the directions set forth in the laws.

26 *Ton dikastan*: the words are taken out of the subordinate clause that follows and put first in order to indicate the topic addressed here; cf. 7.15–16, etc.

30–1 'With reference to the pleadings' (*porti ta moliomena*): *ta moliomena* must be the entire case presented by each side; see above on 5.44 and Gagarin 2010b: 136–7.

11.31–45—SUPPLEMENT TO 9.24–40 ON OBLIGATIONS OF THE DECEASED (VER II.45, K 175)

A provision allowing the heirs to pay the deceased's obligations or give up the estate.

αἴ κ' ἀποθάνει ἄργυρον
ὀπέλον ἒ νενικαμένος, αἰ μέ-
ν κα λείοντι οἷς κ' ἐπιβάλλει
ἀναιλêθαι τὰ κρέματα τὰν ἄ-
ταν ὑπερκατιστάμεν καὶ τὸ
ἀργύριον οἷς κ' ὀπέλει, ἐκόντ-
ον τὰ κρέματα· αἰ δέ κα μὲ λεί-
οντι, τὰ μὲν κρέματα ἐπὶ τοῖ-
ς νικάσανσι ἔμεν ἒ οἷς κ' ὀ-
πέλει τὸ ἀρ⟨γ⟩ύριον, ἄλλαν δὲ
μεδεμίαν ἄταν ἔμεν τοῖ-
ς ἐπιβάλλονσι. ἀṭέθαι δὲ ὐ-
πὲρ μ[ὲ]ν τô [πα]τρὸς τὰ πατρô-
ια, ὐπὲ⟨δ⟩ δὲ τâς ματρὸς τὰ μα-
τρôια. *vac.*

If a person should die owing money or having lost a suit, if those to whom it falls to receive the property should wish to pay the fine or the money on his behalf to those to whom he owed it, let them have the property; but if they do not wish to, the property is to be in the hands of those who won the suit or those to whom he owed the money, and there will be no other fine for those in line of succession. And the paternal property is to be liable for fines for the father's (obligations), the maternal property for the mother's. *vac.*

---

31 This provision begins on the same line as the preceding one ends, separated only by a gap (with asyndeton). This may indicate that these two supplementary provisions were inscribed at the same time.

ἄργυρον and ἀργύριον (36, 40) are used interchangeably in the Code. Note that the *gamma* here is drawn with a full down stroke (Λ); in 36 it is drawn with only a slight down stroke so that if the context did not dictate otherwise, it could be mistaken for a *lambda* (compare the *lambda* in *anailethai* in 34 just above it); in 40, the *gamma* is mistakenly written as an *alpha*.

34 ἀναιλêθαι: for the distinction between this verb and ἔκεν, see n. ad 5.24–5 above.

44 ὐπτὲ⟨δ⟩ δέ: the mason only inscribed a single *delta*.

This section supplements 9.24–40, which regulates disputes that might arise after the death of a person who has certain outstanding obligations. When there is no dispute about the obligations, the heirs may either pay the creditors and claim the estate, or forfeit their claim on the estate, which then will go to the creditors. The choice presumably will depend largely on whether the estate is large enough to cover all the obligations. Maffi 1983: 127 argues that the heirs had to make their choice as soon as the estate holder had died, leaving them exposed to the risk that future litigation might reveal additional obligations, but nothing in this section would prevent the heirs from waiting as long as a year (see 9.28–9) until all potential obligations had been revealed. This provision could thus apply both to obligations that are not disputed and to those that are disputed but then validated in a trial (as per 9.24–40).

31–2 In 9.24–7 five different ways of incurring an obligation are listed, including losing a suit. All of these except losing a suit are here included in a single expression, 'owing money'; and 'losing a suit' usually means owing money because almost all penalties at Gortyn are fines. This generalization may represent a more advanced stage of thinking about legislation.

38–9 For *epi* with the dative ('in the hands of'), see on 4.37. This may imply that the property is in the hands of the creditors, but if the heirs wish to pay the debts at a later time, they can then reclaim the property; cf. 6.46–55, where the person held for ransom is 'in the hands' of his ransomer until he repays the ransom money.

42–5 This provision is intended to ensure that one spouse's property is not used to pay the obligations of the other. The separation of maternal and paternal estates (for *matroia*, see above on 4.44) is further confirmation that women at Gortyn owned property in their own right.

11.46–55—AMENDMENT TO 2.45–3.16 ON DIVORCE (VER II.16, K 166)

Procedural rules governing a woman's swearing an oath of denial.

γυνὰ ἀνδρὸς ἄ κα κρίνεται,
ὀ δικαστὰς ὄρκον αἴ κα δικάκ-
σει, ἐν ταῖς Ϝίκατι ἀμέραις ἀ-
πομοσάτο παριόντος τô δικα-
στâ ὄτι κ' ἐπικαλêι. προϜẹιπάτ-
ο δὲ ὀ ἄρκον τâ⟨δ⟩ δίκας τâι γυνα-
ικὶ καὶ τôι δικα⟨σ⟩τâι καὶ [τ]ôι
μṿạ́μονι προτέταρτον ἀντὶ μ-
ạίṭụρọς π̣ẹṿṭεκαιδεκαδρόμο
ἒ πρείγονος. *vac.*

If the judge rules that a woman being divorced from her husband (swear) an oath, let her swear the oath of denial regarding what he charged within twenty days with the judge present. And let the initiator of the suit declare to the woman and the judge and the rememberer on the fourth day before (the oath) in front of a witness who has been adult for fifteen years or more. *vac.*

---

46 *κρίνεται*: in 2.46 the verb is *διακρίνονται*, but see n. ad 3.41.

50 *ὄτι*: accusative of respect (so G, K); as in 1.6 above (see n. ad loc.). W, VER read the genitive *ὅτι* in both passages.

51 *τâ⟨δ⟩ δίκας*: the mason only inscribed a single *delta*.

52 *δικα⟨σ⟩τâι*: the mason wrote *nu* instead of *san*.

53 *προτέταρτον*: the same word is at **G81**.9 (cf. Bile 216).

54–5 The first of these two lines is written partly on the stone below (as also in column 8); the second is then written entirely on this lower stone. Evidently the mason did not wish to start a new column, which suggests that at the time when this provision was inscribed, the provisions on column 12 were not yet planned.

The stone containing these lines was discovered in 1900 according to G (p. 124, cf. 126, 149) but she gives no further information about it; we have no information about its current location.

55 πρείγονος = πρεσβυτέρου; Dialect 34.

VER take the words that are inscribed in the erasure in 6.55–6 (τô ἐλευθέρο τὸν δε[—]) and place them at the end of col. 11 without explanation.

In 3.5–9, when a woman in a divorce denies a charge that she took property not belonging to her, the judge must allow her to swear an oath of denial. There the place for swearing is specified; here other conditions are given.

46–50 The word order in Greek is highly convoluted, and an English translation can only reproduce part of the effect: 'a woman who is (being) separated from her husband, if a judge rules that an oath (be sworn), within twenty days let her swear, with the judge present, whatever he (the husband) charged'.

48 That the oath should be sworn within twenty days seems reasonable and is consistent with other time limits in the Code (e.g. thirty days in 8.17–18).

50–1 *Proweipato* ('declare, declare beforehand'): Maffi (1997a: 33–4; 2007: 207–11) suggests that *proweipato* might be an 'atto formale' that is similar to the *proklēsis eis horkon* ('challenge to swear an oath') in Athenian law. In his view, the judge imposes an oath on the ex-wife but the ex-husband determines the content of the oath. But the content of the oath of denial is necessarily determined by the initial accusation that the wife took property that was not hers. She must swear either that she did not take the property she is accused of taking or that it is hers. In his declaration, the husband could only specify exactly which property he accuses her of taking, and he must have done this when he first made his accusation. Thus, the declaration here may be a formal act, but its purpose must be to remind everyone of the charge in preparation for the oath-swearing.

51 'The initiator of the suit' (cf. on **G42**B4–5) would normally be the husband.

52–3 As the professional 'rememberer', the *mnamon*'s presence would be important if questions later arose regarding the precise charge.

53 *Protetarton* ('on the fourth day before', i.e. three days before as the Greeks reckoned). Maffi (1997a: 33–4; 2007: 207) argues that this means three days before the judge directs the woman to swear an oath, but the amendment presumes that the judge has already so ruled. Most other scholars understand the time as three days before the woman swears the oath, which is far more likely. One reason for repeating the charge at this time might be to give the woman time to reconsider whether she was willing to swear the oath, especially if this required her to travel some distance in order to do so (see above on 3.7–8). But there may also have been some ritual significance in the ceremony.

53–5 *Pentekaidekadromo* ('adult for fifteen years') occurs only here in Greek (Bile 344). No good explanation has been offered why the witness in this case must be this old.

12.1–5—AMENDMENT TO 10.14–25 ON GIFTS TO WOMEN (VER II.53, K 167)

This provision specifies the non-retroactivity of gifts to a mother or wife.

The text in column 12 begins at the top of a block that is one row of blocks lower than the tops of the other columns (at the same level as 11.16). There is currently nothing above it. Some scholars have suggested that a stone with the original beginning of the column would have stood above it, but it is more likely that 12.1 is the original beginning of the column. The Roman-era marking to the side of the column indicates that this was the first block of text in column 12 (see G, p. 149); the text makes good sense as it stands; and 12.1–5 appear to be a complete provision. To be sure, the reassembly of the Code in the Roman era might have occurred after a stone containing text was lost from the top of column 12, and this lost stone might have contained a complete section of text; but this alternative seems unlikely. The space above 12.1 may originally have been occupied by a window or some other architectural feature.

μα̣τρὶ υἰὺ[[ι]]ς ε̈ ἀ[ν]ẹ̀ρ γυναικὶ	If a son gave property to his mother or a
κρέματα αἰ ἔ̈δοκε ᾶ̂ι ἔ̈γρατ-	husband to his wife as was written before
το πρὸ τôνδε τôν γραμμάτον,	these writings, it is not a matter for trial;
μὲ ἔ̈νδικον ἔ̈μεν· τὸ δ' ὔ̈στε-	but for the future one is to give as is
ρον διδόμεν ᾶ̂ι ἔ̈γρατται. vac.	written. *vac.*

---

1 *ματρὶ υἰὺς ε̈ ἀ[ν]ẹ̀ρ γυναικί*: note the chiasmus.

This provision establishes that the rules in 10.14–25 limiting gifts to a mother or wife to 100 staters are not to be applied retroactively. Gifts from fathers to daughters are the subject of 4.48–5.9. The earlier rules referred to here may have allowed larger gifts, in which case these women would be worse off under these new laws (see comm. ad 10.14–25). On non-retroactivity in the Code, see comm. ad 5.7–9.

2 'Property' (*kremata*): if *kremata* designated only land, this law would not apply to someone who gave more than 100 staters to his mother or wife in any other form (money, jewelry, slaves, etc.) except land. This seems highly unlikely, and we should almost certainly understand *kremata* here as designating property of all sorts.

2–3 'as was written before these writings': i.e. as was prescribed in an earlier law (which is no longer preserved).

12.6–19—AMENDMENT TO 8.42–53 ON HEIRESSES WHO ARE CHILDREN (VER II.51, K 174)

These rules assign an administrator for the property of a pre-pubescent heiress for whom there are no claimants. They also set a minimum age for the heiress to marry.

ταῖς πατροιόκοις αἴ κα μὲ
ἴοντι ὀρπανοδικασταί, ἆ-
ς κ' ἀνόροι ἴοντι, κρέθαι κατὰ
τὰ ἐγραμμένα. *vac.* ὀπε[. .] δέ κα
πατρ[οι]ôκος μὲ ἰόντος ἐπι-
βάλλοντος μεδ' ὀρπανοδικ-
αστâν πὰρ τâι ματρὶ τράπε-
ται, τὸν πάτροα καὶ τὸμ μάτ-
ροα τὸνς ἐγραμμένονς τ-
ὰ κρέματα καὶ τὰν ἐπικαρπί-
αν ἀρτύεν ὅπαι κα ν⟨ύν⟩ανται κά-
λλιστα, πρίν κ' ὀπυίεται. ὀπυί-
εθαι δὲ δυοδεκαϝετία ἒ πρεί-
γονα. *vac.*

If there are no orphan-judges, one is to treat heiresses, as long as they have not reached puberty, according to what is written. *vac.* And whatever heiress, in the absence of claimants or orphan-judges, is raised by her mother, the paternal and maternal relative who are specified in writing are to administer her property and its revenue in the best way they can until she marries. And she is to marry at the age of twelve or older. *vac.*

9 ὀπε[ία] G. W (followed by VER) dismisses a deep cut in the stone here, reasoning that the mason skipped over a fault; but the cut extends to line 10, where two letters are missing (πατρ[οι]ôκος). Thus the cut must postdate the inscription of the text. G's suggested supplement—ὀπε[ία] = Att. ὁποία, cf. ὀτεία, 4.52, 5.1)—is very plausible (Bile 205–6 n. 195).

13 τὸν πάτροα: see n. ad 8.44.

16 ἀρτύεν: 'administer'. This is the only occurrence of this verb in Cretan inscriptions, but W refers to the same use of the word in Tegean (in *IG* 5(2).3.27); see also Bile 278, with n. 75. ν⟨ύν⟩ανται: the mason mistakenly omitted *upsilon* and *nu*

18–19 πρείγονα = πρεσβυτέρα; Dialect 34.

The earlier rules (8.42–53) state that when an heiress is too young to marry, her paternal uncles are to administer the property and she is to have half the revenue (42–6), but if there is no claimant, the young heiress herself is to administer the property (47–53). This amendment reaffirms the first of these rules but appoints administrators for an heiress for whom there are no claimants. This revision is clearly necessary, since the heiress might be only a baby and would obviously be unable to manage the property. The rules imply that if there were orphan-judges, they would administer the property but if not, a paternal and a maternal relative are to administer it.

6 As in 7.15–16 (see above), the noun 'heiresses' is put first in the Greek sentence to indicate the subject matter of this section.

7 We know nothing about these orphan-judges; they are only mentioned here and it is odd that they (apparently) may or may not exist.

13–14 The law appoints a paternal and maternal relative uniquely in this case where there is no claimant, since the absence of a claimant may mean that no paternal relative exists (though there may be one who declined to marry the heiress).

14 'Who are specified in writing': every other mention of writing in the Gortyn laws refers, as far as we can tell, to the text of a law; thus, this expression may refer to rules that were written elsewhere specifying which relatives these are. If the law were referring to instructions left by the heiress's father before he died, this would cause problems if the father died suddenly without leaving instructions.

15–16 For *epikarpia*, see on 7.32–3 above.

16 It is not clear what difference if any there is between 'administering' the property (*artunen*) and 'having control of the property with respect to its management (*ergasia*)' in 8.42–4.

17–19 We do not know if the specification of twelve as the minimum age for marriage conforms to existing practice or represents a change from previous practice.

G73 (VER II.91, K 145–6). Rules concerning neighbors. *c*.450–400

Parts of two columns of text with ten lines each are preserved on a large rectangular block. The right-hand column (A) is broken off on the right; B has only a few letters from the right edge of each line. If the generally accepted restorations are correct and each line of A is missing 7–8 letters, then the column would have been exactly as wide as the columns of **G72** (21–3 letters). The text appears to have begun on stones above and continued below the surviving text.

This inscription has virtually identical lettering to that in **G72** and the stone has a similar curvature. Moreover, it has a number (43) inscribed between the columns in letters dating from the Roman era, just as the columns of the Code do. Thus this text must come from another multi-column inscription on the same wall as the Code, but separate from it (since the Code is complete with a clear beginning and end). G calculates from the inscribed number that this text would have been separated from the end of the Code by either eight or twenty columns. See also Di Vita 2005: 35.

VER treat A as one text, but K separates A1–6 (K 145) from A7–10 (K 146).

A

[c.2 αἴ τίς] κα διαρύει ὕδορ ἐ-
ς τô γείτονος, προ[Ϝείπαντ-
ι ἄπατον] ἔμεν αἰ μὲ διαρεῖ.
αἰ δ' ἀποϜείπαντος [διαρύοι, δ-
αρκνὰν κα]ταστασεῖ κατ' ἀμέ-
ραν ὀττάκιν κα δι[αρύει vac.
[c.6 πο]ρτὶ στέγαι μὲ πορ-
τέμεν αἰ μὲ δέκα πο[c.2]
[c.4 μέτε] ἰπνιôνα μέτε κο-
πρίο̣ν̣α̣ μ̣έ̣τε̣ ρ̣[—]

A

If someone leads water across from his
neighbor's (property), if he asks
before, he is [not to be liable] unless it
flows across (his neighbor's field?).
But if [he leads it across] when he says
no, he shall pay [a drachma (?)] per
day as long as he leads it across. *vac.*
There is not to be next to a house,
unless ten feet (?), [*c*.4 neither] nor
ashes, nor manure, nor —

B

[—] ἐπὶ να-
ὸν ἐπ[—]
[—]παν ν-
αευτ[—]
[—]ι τᾶ-
ς τιμ̣[ᾶς
[— αἰ δέ κ]α μ-
ὲ ἒι [—]

B

2–3 — at a temple —

4–5 — take refuge in a temple (?) —

6–7 — of the value —

8–9 — but if there is not —

A1–2 ἐς τô γείτονος: 'from his neighbor's (property)' (Dialect 14). Manganaro (1974: 54) takes ἐς as εἰς, arguing that we must understand στέγαν—'to his neighbor's [house]'. But the parallels he cites from **G72** either mention *stega* explicitly (3.46, 4.32) or are the common Greek construction, *en* with the genitive (= 'in X's [house]'); nothing supports the use of *eis* with the genitive to mean 'to X's house'.

2–3 προ[Ϝείπαντα is also possible, but *apaton emen* is more commonly constructed with a dative (e.g. **G72**.1.56–2.2).

3 ἄπατον: ἔνδικον Manganaro, who translates 'let him be punished', though elsewhere the expression means 'it is a matter for adjudication'; see below on A1–6

4–5 [δαρκνάν]: G, who notes that στατêρα is also possible.

6–10 Manganaro, citing parallels from urban regulations elsewhere in Greece, restores these lines as follows: δι[αρύει· λά/κκον δὲ πο]ρτὶ στέγαι μὲ πορ/τέμεν αἰ μὲ δέκα πο[δôν, μέτε/Ϝοικοδομεν(?)] ἰπνιôνα μέτε κο/πριôνα μέτε ῥ[ῖνα (?). See commentary below.

6 ὀττάκιν = ὁσάκις (Bile 215, 263).

G and others restore a *vac.* at the end of the line, but this is not certain.

7–8 πορτέμεν (= Attic προσεῖναι): Dialect 4, 20.

8 πό[δας or πο[δôν is likely.

B4–5 G suggests that ναευτ- may be a form of ναεύειν.

A1–6 We follow G's text and translation: this provision regulates water flowing through neighboring fields. Manganaro 1974: 53–4 doubts the law would incorporate such an abrupt transition from a rural to an urban regulation (in 7–10) and suggests that 1–4 should be understood to mean 'if someone discharges water toward (the house) of his neighbor, even if he has notified him, he is to be punished whenever (the water) does not flow away'. VER and K reject Manganaro's interpretation, which seems impossible to derive from the Greek.

1 Since the space at the beginning of this line was probably larger than the restored letters, G suggests that the first words (*ai tis*) were preceded by a gap. This is plausible, but far from certain.

3 'Unless it flows across'. This may mean that if the water flows across his neighbor's property, a person may not take it from his neighbor but should instead take it from below his neighbor's property. Or it may prohibit taking water from a neighbor's property and letting it flow across one's own property to

another person's land. Water, of course, was (and still is) in short supply in the area; for other laws regulating water use, see **G43Bb** and **G52**.

7–10 This provision apparently regulates the disposal of ash, manure, and at least one other product, requiring them to be a certain distance from a house. Manure would certainly have been used for fertilizer, and ash may have also been so used. Its connection to what precedes is that it concerns relations between neighbors. Manganaro 1974 restores the text to mean, 'A cistern (?) may not be closer to a house than ten feet, nor can one build a kiln ('fornace') or a garbage dump or a canal (?)'. Again, VER and K stick to the traditional text.

B4–5 For taking refuge in a temple, see **G41**.4.6–17; **G72**.1.39–49.

G74. *c*.450–400

Under this number G assembles a dozen very small fragments with lettering very similar to that of the Code. We believe that *a–c* come from the Code; see n. ad **G72**.10.4–15. Of the other fragments, only one may yield a significant word.

d 2 [—]ανεα[—]
3 [—]ιναιο[—]
4 [—]σαπ[—]
5 [—]σαντ[—]
6 [— πατρ]οιοκ[ο—] — heiress — (?)

G75. Giving and receiving security (VER II.46, K 155 [= G81], 147–9). *c*.450–400.

Parts of four columns of text on two adjoining blocks; the writing originally extended on all four sides. The columns have the same width as those of **G72** and (probably) **G73** and the stones have the same slight curvature; thus **G75** probably formed part of the same wall as these two. K treats the columns as four separate texts, except that for A he gives the text of **G81**.

Column A has been restored from **G81**.4–14, with which it is almost identical. For our notes and commentary, see **G81**.

A

κα̣λ̣[ὲν δ' ἀντὶ μαιτύρον δυ-]
[ôν πρότριτον τὸν] ἐνεκυρ-
άκσαντα μ̣[ετρεσιόμενον · α-]
[ἰ δέ κα μὲ εἴει] καλίοντι ἆ-
ι ἔγραπται, α[ὐτὸς μετρέθο τ-]
[ε καὶ προπονέτ]ο προτέταρτ-
ον ἀντὶ μαιτύ[ρον δυôν παρέ-]
[μεν ἐνς ἀγορ]άν. ὀμνύμεν δὲ
ἐ̑ μὰν τοῦτο μ[έν ἐστι ἀβλοπί-]

A

[He] is to summon before two witnesses three days in advance the person who received a pledge (of security), so that he can measure that indeed this (the property). And if he does not come after he summons him as is written, let him measure it himself and declare to him four days in advance before two witnesses that he should be present in the agora. And he is to swear that indeed this

[αι δικαίος πρὶν] μολέθαι τ-
[ὰν δίκαν —]

(the property) is (as claimed) without fault and lawfully before the case is tried.

B

[— ὄ]π̣λ̣α ἀνδρὸς
ἐλευθέρο ὄττ' ἐνς πόλεμον̣
ἴσκει, πλὰν Ϝέμας κ' ἀντιδέ-
μας, ἰστός, ἔρια κερίθεκν-
α, Ϝεργαλεῖα σιδάρια, ἄρατ-
ρον, δυγὸν βοôν, κάπετον, μ-
ύλανς, ὄνον ἀλέταν, ἐ⟨κ⟩ς ἀν-
δρείο ὄτ⟨τ⟩' ὀ ἀρκὸς παρέκει
κατ' ἀνδρεῖον, εὐνὰ ἀνδρὸς
καὶ γυναικό̣[ς], ἐ̣[λε]υ̣θέρο ὀ[—]

B

— the arms of a free man which he has for war, except for a cloak and footwear, a loom, wool that has been worked (i.e. woolen cloth), iron tools, a plow, a team of oxen, a pot (?), lower millstones, upper grinding stone, from the *andreion* whatever the leader provides for the *andreion*, the bed of a husband and wife, a free man's —

C

[c.9]δυ[c.9]
ν̣α̣ Ϝέκ̣αστος [c.10]
. τ̣ι̣[c.7] *vac.* αἴ κά τις πρ-
εῖγυς ἔι ἒ ἄλ[ος μ]ὲ νυνατὸ-
ς ἔι ἔρπεν [ἒ κ]α δέει ἐνεκυρ-
άδδεν, ἄλλον π[ρὸ] τούτο ἐνεκ-
[υ]ράδδοντ[α] ἄ̣πατον ἔμεν. ὀ-
νυμαινέτο δὲ [τ]ὸ̣ ὄνυμα [. .]
[. .]ο επατ[. .] μ̣αίτυρος ὄτι-
μ̣ι̣ κενθ[. .]ι[—]

C

— each one — *vac.* If someone is old or for some other reason unable to come where he ought to receive security, another person who receives the security on his behalf is not to be liable. But let him name the name [of the agent (?)] witness to whom —

D

[—]ατιμ̣[—]
[—] ἐσπράτται ἒ δικασ-
τâι κ' ὄς κα μαίτυραν[ς —]
[—] κ' ὄττον ἔγραπται ἀ-
μολεὶ πράδεθαι κο . [—]
[—]αστομ[—]

D

2–3 — to the *esprattes* or the judge and the one who — witnesses —
4–5 and whatever is written is to be collected without a trial —

A is supplemented largely on the basis of a very similar text in **G81**.4–16, where most of our notes on the passage can be found.

2–3 ἐνεκυράκσαντα: the equivalent text in **G81**.5–6 is different; see n. ad loc.

8 [ἐνς]: there does not appear to be enough room in the missing part of the text for ἐνσς, which we find in **G81**.11. For variation, see n. ad **G81**.4–14.

B 2 ὄττ' = ὅσα.

3–4 πλὰν Ϝέμας κ' ἀντιδέμας: the two genitives are constructed with πλάν; none of the other nouns are genitive, so presumably only these two items are excluded from the list.

4–5 κερίθεκνα: see on **G42**A11.

5–6 ἄρατρον = ἄροτρον (Bile 81 n. 21).

6 δυγόν = ζυγόν; in the fifth century *zeta* appears in Crete as a single or double *delta* (Dialect 11; Bile 144).

κάπετον: meaning unknown. Hesychius has a gloss *καπέτις* = *χοῖνιξ* (a dry measure of about a liter); if this is relevant, a *κάπετος* may be a container.

7 *ἐ⟨κ⟩ς*: the mason mistakenly inscribed *pi* instead of *kappa*.

8 *ὄτ⟨τ⟩'*: the mason mistakenly inscribed only a single *tau*.

9 *εὐνά*: the nominative (so too perhaps *ἰστός* in B4) is out of place in the list of accusatives, but see G on B4.

C 3–4 *πρεῖγυς* = *πρέσβυς* (Dialect 34).

4 *ἄλος* = *ἄλλως*.

4–5 *νυνατός* = *δυνατός* (Dialect 9)

7 *ἄπατον ἔμεν*: here constructed personally, but more often impersonally with a dative (e.g. **G72**.1.56–2.2)

D 4 *ὄττον* = *ὅσον*; cf. B2, above.

It is not clear whether there is any connection among the subjects of the four columns. A apparently establishes procedures concerning the pledging of land as security; B is a list of items; C allows another person to receive security on someone's behalf if he is unable to receive it himself; and D specifies legal procedure, including the collection of payment in some cases. Scholars have been tempted to assume that all four have something to do with security, but this seems unlikely for B and only one of many possibilities for A.

Col. A allows a person who has received a pledge to measure something, probably a piece of land. The owner of the land may have pledged the produce as security. The rules provide for the usual summonses and witnesses.

Except for the participle *enekyraksanta* in 2–3, the text of A is the same as **G81**.4–16; our notes and commentary can be found there.

2–3 'The person who took security' (*ton enekyraksanta*): for the meaning, see on **G43Ba**7–8. The word order strongly suggests that this is the direct object of the infinitive *kalen*; this verb must have an object, and it is hard to see how it could have preceded the text we have. The subject of *kalen*, on the other hand, could easily have been evident from what preceded.

Since *enekyradden* apparently is not used of pledging land, this law probably concerns a pledge of produce, such as is regulated in **G43Ba**7–9.

B is commonly assumed to be a list of items that are considered basic necessities and thus cannot be used as security. The difficulty with this is that two items mentioned, clothing and footwear (*emas*, *ampidemas*), are exceptions to whatever rule governs the list, and thus they could be seized (see comm. ad 3 below); but it would seem that if anything were exempted from seizure, clothing and footwear ought to be. We conclude, therefore, that the list has some other purpose; it may even be a list of items which could be seized (except for clothing and footwear).

Understanding is complicated by variation and uncertainty about the case of all the nouns. Without the preceding context, we cannot say if *opla* is nom. or acc.; *wemas* and *ampidemas* are gen. with *plan*; *istos* is often taken as acc. but (as

G. notes) it must be nom.; *eria*, *wergaleia*, *sidaria*, and *aratron* can be nom. or acc.; *mylans* and *onon* are acc. (for the variation between pl. and sing., see G); *otti* is either nom. or acc.; and finally *euna* is nom. Following strict syntactical rules, there is no way to account for all this variation, so we have to assume that nom. and acc. are used interchangeably in a list.

1 Van Effenterre speculates (1993a: 7–10) that arms for use in war would have been provided by the city and were thus, in essence, the city's property, which would explain why they could not be seized.

2 G maintains that the specification of a free man here (and in B10) implies that the items that are not so qualified would be those of all inhabitants, free and non-free.

3 All recent editors follow Halbherr (1897: 223), for whom the only possible explanation is that in line 3 *plan* ('except for') is 'not exclusive but additional'; in other words, arms are to be excluded 'and also (*plan*) the wardrobe, etc'. This sense, however, is not only unparalleled but is the exact opposite of the preposition's normal meaning. The Greek must mean that a person's cloak and footwear are excluded from the list (whatever the list is for). Only Dareste, et al. (1891–1904, II: 328) give this phrase its true meaning; they understand the provision to mean that one cannot seize arms or a loom, wool, etc., but one can seize a person's cloak and finery, if they are pledged. This is possible, but it seems far more likely that a cloak and footwear (for the meaning of *ampidema*, see on 3–4 below) would be exempt from seizure as essential to a person's survival than that the other items are exempt.

3–4 For 'footwear' (*ampidema*), see on **G43Ab**11–12; **G72**.5.40.

6 'Team of oxen': if B were a list of items exempt from seizure, it seems odd that a team of oxen, not one ox, is exempt.

7–9 On any interpretation of this list, the supplies given to the *andreion* seem out of place in a list of things that otherwise belong to individuals or families.

8 'Leader' (*arkos*): i.e. of the *andreion*. Davies 2005: 166 takes him to be the 'head of household', but this would make little sense here, since presumably more than one head of household provided supplies to the *andreion*. This is the only mention of a leader for the *andreion*, though *arkos* occurs in **G1**.4 without context. See further Introd. 6C.

C 7–8 This could mean that the agent should give his name to the person giving the security, but more likely, the incapacitated person is required to declare the name of his agent in the presence of a witness.

D 2 Officials called *esprattai* are mentioned in **G87** (where they may have a *mnamon*), **G91**, and in a later text from Gortyn (*IC* 4.160). We do not know their duties, but their name suggests they may be 'exactors' or 'collectors' (of fines, debts, etc.); they have been likened to the Athenian *praktores* (G on **G87**).

G76. (VER II.86, K 150–1). *c.*450–400

A block broken in the middle with nine lines of writing from two columns. The few letters that remain from column A on the right yield no significant meaning. B is probably missing only 5 or 6 letters to the left. The space at the top of the stone shows that we have the top of each column, but the text originally continued below. The stone has the same slight curvature as **G72** and thus perhaps was originally in the same wall, though the columns here appear slightly wider (22–25 letters).

K treats B1–7 and 7–9 as separate texts. See also Frisone 1995: 62–5; 2000: 31–43.

A

[—]αι, α-
ἰ δὲ [—]
[—]ρατ-
ος[—]
[—]ọδὸ-
ς ἐ[—]
[—]δι
αλ[—]

A

5–6 — road —

B

θανάτοι· αἴ κ' οἰ ἐπιβάλλ[οντες]
[καθαίρ]εν μὲ λείοντι, δικάκσα-
ι τὸν δικαστὰν καθαίρε[ν . . . . .]
[. . . . .]νσι. αἰ δέ κα μὲ καθαίρει
ᾇι ἔγραπται, αὐτὸν καθα[ίρεν κ' ὅ-]
[τι κ' ἀν]αισιμόσει [ὀ]μόσαντα
διπλεῖ πρ̣[άδ]δεθαι. vac. αἰ κ[. . . . .]
[. . . . .]ας Ϝεργάδ[δε]ται ἀθάν-
ατα κρέματ̣[α ἒ δ]ένδρεα ἒ κ[—]

B

— for the death; if the claimants do not wish to purify (the corpse?), the judge is to rule that [they are (?)] to purify (it) [*c.*13] And if he does not purify it as is written, (the judge) himself is to purify it, and whatever he spends, after swearing an oath he is to collect double. *vac.* If [*c.*12] he works immortal things, or trees, or —

A 5–6 G suggests a possible connection with **G46**B6–14.

B 1 It is generally assumed that *θανάτοι* completes a clause from the bottom of column A, but it is not impossible that it belongs to the conditional clause that follows but was put first in order to indicate the general subject (see on e.g. **G47**.1; **G72**.7.15–16); if so, one might translate, 'if in a death the claimants do not wish . . .'

οἰ ἐπιβάλλ[οντες: here the heirs; see on **G72**.5.23–6.

6 *ἀν]αισιμόσει*: an Ionic verb, not found in Attic but common in Herodotus.

7–8 VER suggest *αἴ κ[α τᾶς Ϝοικί]ας*, but this may be slightly too short (9 letters vs. 11 in 1–2 and 5–6).

1–7 There was a similar law in Athens (cited in Dem. 43.57–8), directing the demarch in each deme to order the relatives to bury a corpse that no one has taken up for burial and allowing the demarch to collect double his expenditures if he has to undertake the burial and purification himself. G also refers to **G22**, but on our reading this law does not concern burial.

5 'As is written' may refer to lines 3–4, where the judge probably directed the person to purify the corpse in a certain way or place.

8–9 'Immortal things' may refer to all non-living possessions, land, houses, furniture, etc.; cf. *tnatōn* (**G72**.5.39), probably of flocks and slaves and perhaps also produce.

G77. Public distribution of produce (VER I.49, K 152). *c*.450–400

One long block with twelve lines of writing from three columns. The middle column (B) is complete but the first three and the last lines are damaged; only a few isolated letters remain from A (on the right), and C preserves only a few letters from the right edge of eight lines. The stone has the same slight curvature as **G72** and columns of similar width; thus it probably formed part of the same wall. The writing originally began above and continued at left, right, and below. K gives only column B.

B

[—]οισοσκο[*c*.13]
[*c*.10 δύ]ο, διεροσύκο-
ν δύο, γλεύκιος τ[ρίι]νς· ὅδ [δέ]
κ̣α μὲ ὅλαν ἐ̣κς ἐμίνας. *vac.* αἰ
εὕροιεν οἱ καρποδαῖσται κα-
ρπὸν ἀποκεκλεμμένον ἒ μὲ
δεδαισμένον, τόν τε καρπὸν
πέρονσι ἄπατον ἔμεν, κ' ἐπεστ-
εῖσαι τὸ ἀπλόον καὶ τὰ ἐπιτίμ-
ια ἆι ἔγραπται. *vac.* καρπô ὅτί κα
κατομόσοντι, ἄργυρο[ν ἐ]σπρ-
[α]δ̣[*c*.12]ο̣ν̣α̣τ̣[—]

B

— two, fresh figs two, must three. Whoever does not (give?) all, (let him give?) half. *vac.* If the produce-distributors should find that produce has been stolen or has not been distributed, they are to be immune from prosecution if they take the produce (themselves), and (those responsible) are to pay the simple value and the additional penalties, as is written. *vac.* Whatever produce (the produce-distributors) swear to, they are to collect it in silver —

C

τα [—]
[— ε]ὕρον-
τι οἱ κα̣[ρποδαῖσται (?) —]
[—]γεν ὅτ-
τα δατιο[—]
[—]ι ἒ ἀνε-
υρόντε̣[ς —]
[— ἆι ἔγ]ραπτ-
[αι (?) —]

C

2–3 — the pr[oduce-distributors] (?) find —

4–5 — whatever they distribute (?) —

6–7 — or discovering —

8–9 — as is written (?). —

B 2–3 διεροσύκον: only here, but the compound is straightforward.
4 ὅλαν: adverbial; see G.
8–9 ἐπεστεῖσαι: from ἐπεστίνω (ἐπεκτίνω), only here (Bile 327–8).

B 2–12 These provisions apparently regulate the public distribution of produce at Gortyn. Many scholars (see VER for references) have connected this with a system of communal meals (*syssitia*), which is attested for some other Cretan cities by later historians,[415] but is not mentioned in Cretan inscriptions of any period.[416] On the other hand, figs and must, together with barley, are listed in **G79** as payment for workers, and it is possible that the collection regulated by this law was intended for that purpose. This text implies that the inhabitants (presumably only those with land) had an obligation to contribute a fixed share, or half a share if a full share was too much, perhaps because of a poor harvest. The officials in charge of the distribution (*karpodaistai*) were allowed to seize produce and fine those who did not contribute.

2–3 The numbers presumably refer to standard measures. The first *duo* (line 2) went with an earlier noun which, if this text is connected with **G79**, may have been barley.

3 Must is 'the juice of freshly pressed grapes before or during fermentation' (*OED*).

C The text and translation assume that the subject is the same as in column B, which is far from certain.

G78. Protection for certain inhabitants. (VER I.16, K 153). *c*.450–400

Eight lines of text are inscribed at the bottom of a long block from the northeast corner of the Pythion, which also contains, to the left and around the corner, **G22** together with a few letters from the right edge of **G21** (see discussion ad loc.). **G78** was written in the empty space below an earlier text, a few letters of which are still visible. At some point the top half of the stone containing this earlier text was apparently erased. The stone preserves the top and bottom edges of our text; the writing begins from the left and continues boustrophedon. On the left, line 1 is complete but 1–3 letters are missing from 2–7; on the right, about 9–12 letters are probably missing from each line. Line 8 ends a few letters before the left edge of the stone and the last few letters of it are widely spaced out, as if the mason was trying to fill out the line. Older drawings show a horizontal trace line below line 8, though this is very hard to see today. Nonetheless, line 8 is almost certainly the last line of the text.

G78, **G79**, and **G89** are the only inscriptions from the Classical period that were displayed on or near the Pythion. The *ksenios* (or *ksenios kosmos*) is involved in all three. Perhaps many of the foreigners in Gortyn resided in the vicinity of the

[415] For the report of Dosiadas (Athenaeus 143a–d) on Lyktos, see Introd. 6C.

[416] A possible equivalent, σίτησις, is found in a third-century BCE text from Malla (*IC* 1.19.3A38); see Bile 344 n. 84.

Pythion, and these laws were thus placed there in order to be more accessible to them. See on **G79**.12–21.

θιοί. τάδ' ἔϝαδε τοῖς Γορτυνίοις πσαπίδονσ̣[ι vac.*] τôν ἀπελευ[σαμένον (?) —]*
[— κ]α λêι καταϝοικίδεθαι Λατόσιον ἐπὶ τâι ϝίσϝαι [κ]-
[αὶ τ]âι ὀμοίαι, καὶ μέτινα τοῦτον μέτε καταδολό[θαι μέτε —]
[— αἰ καταδολ (?)]οῖτο, τὸν κσένιον κόσμον μὲ λαγαῖεν. αἰ δὲ [. . .]
[.]οιεν, ἐκατὸν στατêρανς ϝέκαστον τὸνς τίτανς [—]
[— τὰν δ]ιπλείαν τôν κρεμάτον ἐστείσαντανς ἀποδόμ[ε]-
[ν]. αἰ δ' οἰ τίται μὲ ϝέρκσιεν âι ἔγραται, τὰν διπλείαν ἄ[ταν —]
[— τôι μ]εμπομένοι ἀποδόμεν καὶ τâι πόλι θέμεν.

1 Gods. These things pleased the Gortynians voting. *vac.*
1–3 Of those who left (?) [— whoever] wishes is to settle as a Latosian on equal and similar terms, and no one is to enslave (him) [or —].
4–6 [— If anyone should enslave (?) him], the foreigners' *kosmos* is not to release (him). And if anyone should [*c*.9], the *titai* [—] one hundred staters each [—] are to exact double the value of the goods and give this back (to the victim).
7–8 And if the *titai* should not act as is written, (they?) are (to give?) the double amount [—] to the victim and deposit (the fine) with the polis.

The restorations of some scholars assume that about 9–12 letters are missing from the right edge of each line, but we may be missing more than that. Thus, we are more cautious in our restoration of 1–2, 3–4, 5–6, and 7–8.
1 There is just room to restore a *vac.* in the space here between the enactment clause and the substance of the agreement, which begins with asyndeton. There is a very similar *vac.* in the first line of **G80**.
1–2 *ἀπελευ[σαμένον*: VER; *ἀπελευ[θέρον* C, G, K; see our discussion below.
2 *Λατόσιον*: G, K take this as a place in Gortyn where Latosians (see **G58**.4–5) settled, but this is difficult without a preposition; an adjective (Comparetti 1893: 78; VER) modifying the subject of the infinitive is more likely.
3 *καταδολό[θαι μέτε συλêν*: G, K, VER, who also restore *[συλί]οιεν* in 4–5.
4–5 *[συλί]οιεν* (see above) is perhaps likely, because a verb is needed whose root is only 3–4 letters long; this may also make *μέτε συλêν* more likely in 3, but we hesitate to restore *συλêν* ('plunder') because it only occurs once elsewhere in our texts (**L5**).
5–6 *[ἐσπράδδεθαι]* (G, K, VER) is one of several possibilities.
6 *ἐστείσαντανς* from *ἐστίνω* (*ἐκτίνω*) 'pay in full'; see n. ad **G79**.15–16.
7 *ϝέρκσιεν*: aorist optative (Bile 234–7); for the length of the final vowel and the accent, see n. ad **Dr1**.2.
7–8 *ἄ[ταν τούτονς τôι μ]εμπομένοι*: VER; *ἄ[ταν ϝέκαστον αὐτôν τôι μ]εμπομένοι* C, G, K. Both restorations are probably too short, but the sense of VER's restoration is more appropriate. *ϝέκαστον* in line 5 offers no support for the traditional restoration (*pace* Comparetti 1893: 78). It is reasonable to make each wrongdoer pay double, but not to make each *titas* pay double if one wrongdoer does not pay up.
8 *μ]εμπομένοι*: see comm. ad **G41**.7.8–9.

Most scholars have understood this decree as granting certain rights to freed slaves (see below on 1–2), but as we understand it (following VER), it allows for the return of a group of people who have left the city, having perhaps been exiled or enslaved, and offers them protection from enslavement or robbery.

1 'These things pleased the Gortynians voting'. This is the only enactment clause at Gortyn before the Hellenistic period; cf. *IC* 4.162 (third century), but an enactment formula begins **Da1**, **Dr1**, **Dr4**, **Dr5**, **Lyktos1A** and **1B**, and perhaps **Elt2**. The mention of voting may indicate that this was not the usual procedure for making decisions at Gortyn. We do not know exactly who comprised 'the Gortynians' or how they voted, but the language suggests an assembly open to most or all free adult males (Introd. 4B1). If the group in question (see on 1–2) had previously been exiled for political reasons, it may have been especially important that the whole city formally ratify the arrangement for their return and to record this ratification in writing.

1–2 'Of those who left' (*ton apeleu*[*samenon*]): although the traditional supplement *apeleu*[*theron*] ('of the freedmen') is accepted by most scholars, including Chaniotis (1996: 162 n. 1039), Perlman (2004a: 109–12), and Zelnick-Abramovitz (2005: 113–4), it is probably wrong. *Apeleutheros* is not found in Crete before the second century BCE at the earliest and it is always attached to an individual freed person's name, usually on a grave marker. For *apeleu[samenon]*, see **G41**.4.9, 13–14, where it is used (probably) of a serf (*woikeus*) who has left his master. On this reading, the city is offering protection to a group of people, perhaps slaves, who either left Gortyn and now wish to return or who have left another city and have come to Gortyn. This group is given the status of Latosians, who appear to be another group of non-Gortynians living in the city, and their mistreatment would naturally be a matter for the *ksenios kosmos* ('foreigners' *kosmos*'). VER compare **Lyktos1A**, which in their view concerns the return of emigrants.

2 The Latosians are also mentioned in **G58**.4–5 (without context). G suggests that they were foreigners who settled at Gortyn (see also Perlman 2004a: 109 n. 77) as workers under conditions that are partly specified in **G79** (cf. *IC* 4.144). G takes *Latosion* here as indicating the specific place where they settled ('those who settled in Latosion').

4–8 Cf. **G79**.12–21 (with commentary), where the *ksenios* and the *titai* also collect fines for the city.

4 The *ksenios kosmos* is only mentioned here and in **G30**.4 (without context); he may be the same person as the *ksenios*, mentioned in several texts (see above on **G14p–g2**), including **G79**.15.

'Is not to release him': sc. to the person trying to enslave him. *Lagaien* occurs six times in **G72**.1, where it must mean 'release, dismiss', and some editors concluded that the *ksenios kosmos* is not to release the person after he has been enslaved. Wolff 1946: 64 n. 144 suggests that the law directs the *kosmos* not to interfere with those who are trying to free the person. But the clear sense of the decree is that the *kosmos* must not allow the person to be enslaved; the person is considered to be under the protection of the *ksenios kosmos*, who is not to give him up to anyone trying to enslave him.

5 For the *titai*, see **G14g–p1**.

5–7 The hundred-stater fine probably goes to the city; the victims are compensated with double the value of their (plundered ?) property.

G79. Wages for workers (VER I.30, K 154). *c*.450–400

A tall block from the Pythion with the bottom of a column of text that ends well before the bottom of the stone. The stone is broken above, its right side has been chipped away, destroying 4–8 letters per line, and its left edge was apparently trimmed after the text was inscribed, removing 1–3 letters from the left edge of the text.

[*c*.7] . ο κριθ[ᾶν *c*.5] →
[*c*.5]κια κυ[*c*.9]
[. σύ]κον ἑκατὸν μ[εδίμν-]
[ονς κα]ὶ γλεύκιος προκό̣[ο]-
[νς ἑ]κατὸν καὶ τὰν π[*c*.3]
[*c*.2]ν̣[.]αλκίαν ἒ ἄλλαν Ϝ̣[ισ-]
[Ϝό]μετρον τô προκ[όο. Ϝερ-]
[γάδδ]εθαι δὲ ἐπὶ τôι μ[ι-]
[σ]τôι αὐτôι πάν[τ]α̣ [τοîς]
[ἐμ πόλι Ϝ]οικίονσι το⟨î⟩ς [τ']
[ἐλ]ευθέροις καὶ το[îς δόλ-]
[οις. αἰ δ]ὲ μὲ λείοιεν Ϝερ[γά-]
[δδε]θαι, δέκα στατê[ρ]α[νς]
[τô πα]θέματος Ϝεκάστ[ο]
[τ]ὸ̣ν κσένιο[ν ἐ]στει[σάμ-]
[ενον] πόλι θέμεν. αἰ δ[ὲ μ-]
[ὲ] 'σ̣τείσαιεν [τ]ὰν [ἀπλόον ἄ-]
[ταν (?), πράδ]δεθαι τ̣ὰν διπ[λεί-]
[αν] αὐτôν Ϝέκαστ̣ο̣[ν *c*.6]
[*c*.2]μ[. . . τ]ὸνς τίτανς ἐσ̣[τ-]
[εί]σανταν[ς] τ[âι πόλι θέμεν.]

of barley

of figs one hundred [*medimnoi*, and] of must one hundred *prokooi*, and [*c*.13] or another measure equal to a *prokoos*. And all the work is to be done for this exact wage by those who live in the city, both free men and slaves. And if they should not wish to work, the foreigners' official is to exact payment from them of ten staters for each offense and deposit it with the city. And if they should not pay the simple fine (?), each of them will be fined the double amount; [but if they do not pay?] the *titai* are to pay (the fine) and deposit it with the city.

---

3 σύ]κον: G notes that διεροσύ]κον is also possible here (cf. **G77B2–3**).

7–15 are supplemented with the help of *IC* 4.144.8–14, which are identical.

το⟨î⟩ς: the mason mistakenly omitted the *iota*.

15 κσένιο[ν: this official may or may not be the *ksenios kosmos*; see on **G14p–g2**.

15–16 ἐ]στει[σάμενον from ἐστίνω (ἐκτίνω); in the active (below, line 21; **G78**.6) it means 'pay in full', in the middle 'exact full payment'.

19–20 [καὶ αἰ] μ[ή, τ]ὸνς VER. This supplement is probably wrong, because the gap between μ and ο in line 20 has room for 3–5 letters; but it may accurately represent the sense needed.

This is the end of a decree apparently setting forth rules for work to be done by a group of people, including slaves and free men, who are working for the city. The specification that the group be living in the city and the involvement of the *ksenios* (*kosmos* ?) suggest that these are foreign workers (see van Effenterre 1979). The amounts of produce listed in lines 3–5 may be payments for work done. See also Perlman 2004a: 110–11, 115–17.

1–5 **G77**B2–4 speaks of collecting fresh figs and must. Here it is possible that the figs in question were fresh (the qualification would have occupied line 2, which is now missing), and barley might have been part of the list in **G77** (see comm. ad loc.).

7–15 These lines are repeated in *IC* 4.144.8–14, from which several of the supplements here are taken. The first parts of the two texts differ; on their relation, see Perlman 2004a: 115–16.

9–10 'Those who live in the city': *polis* here probably designates the urban center as opposed to the countryside or *kora* (for the contrast, see **G72**.4.32–5), not the entire territory of the political unit; so Perlman 2004a: 116–17.

12–21 The language about fines and payment to the city recalls **G78**.4–8, where the *ksenios kosmos* and the *titai* are also involved in collecting fines. Since both texts were inscribed on the Pythion, they may both concern the same group of people who settled somewhere near this temple.

15 The *ksenios* here is probably the *ksenios kosmos* in **G78**.4; see comm. ad **G14**p–g2. In **G89**.7 *ksenios* may or may not have originally been *ksenios kosmos.*

G80. Agreement with Rhitten (VER I.7). *c.*450–400

This text was written on two long adjacent blocks; it is complete on either side and at the top but it continued on a stone (or stones) below (though perhaps for only another line or two). It was published with a photograph by Halbherr (1897: 204–11), but since then the left-hand stone has been lost.

θιοί. ἐπὶ τοῖδε [ʼΡ]ι[ττέν]ι[οι Γ]ορ[τυνίοις αὐτ]όνο̣μ[ο]ι κ' αὐτόδικοι τὰ θ[ύ-]
ματα παρέκοντες ἐς Β̣ίδαν τρ̣ί[τ]οι [Ϝέ]τει τριακατίο̣ς ⟨σ⟩[τ]ατε̂ρανς καὶ πεν-
τέκοντα. στέγαν δ' ἄν κα Ϝοικοδομέσ[ει c.6]ς ἒ δένδρεα πυτεύσει, τὸν
Ϝοικοδομέσαντα καὶ πυτεύσαντ[α] καὶ πρίαθαι κ' ἀποδόθαι. vac. τὸν δὲ σταρτ-
αγέταν καὶ τὸν κοσμίοντα ὅς κ' ἄγε[ι] ʼΡ[ι]τ̣τ̣ενάδε κοσμε̂ν πεδὰ τô ʼΡιττενίο
κόσμο τὸν μὲ πειθόμενον τô 'πορ̣ί̣μ[ο, δ]αμιόμεν δὲ δαρκνὰν καὶ κατακρέθαι πεδ-
ά τε τô σταρτô καὶ πεδὰ τôν ʼΡιττενίον· πλ[ίο]ν δὲ μὲ δαμιόμεν· αἰ δὲ πλίον δαμιόσ-
αι ἒ μὲ κατακρέσαιτο, κσενείαι δίκα[ι δι]κάδδεθαι. ἐνεκυραστὰν δὲ μὲ παρέρπε-
ν Γορτύνιον ἐς τô ʼΡιττενίο. αἰ δέ κα ν[ικ]αθ̣ε̂ι τôν ἐνεκύρον, διπλεῖ καταστâσ-
αι τὰν ἀπλόον τιμὰν ἆι ἐν τâι 'πόραι ἔ[γρα]τται, πράδδεν δὲ τὸν ʼΡιττένιον κόσμ-
ον. αἰ δέ κα μὲ πράδδοντι, τὸνς πρειγ[ίσ]τονς τούτονς πράδδοντας ἄπατον
ἔμεν. vac. τὰ ἐγραμμέν', ἄλλα δὲ μέ. vac. ὅτι δέ [κα αὖ]τ[ι]ς ἀνπιπαίσοντι τὸ κοινὸν οἰ ʼΡι-
ττένιοι πορτὶ τὸνς Γορτυνίον[ς προκαλε̂]ν̣ τ̣ὸν κάρυκα ʼΡιττενάδε ἐν ταῖδ ⟨δ⟩έ-
κα παρέμεν ἒ αὐτὸνς ἒ ἄλλονς π[ρ]ὸ̣ [τούτον ἀπ]οκρίνεθθαι κατ' ἀγορὰν Ϝευμέν-
αν τâς α[ἰ]τίας ἆς κ' αἰτι[ά]σ[ονται, τὰν δ]ὲ κρίσιν ἔ[με]ν ἆ̣ιπερ ταῖς ἀ[—]

1–3 Gods. On the following terms, the Rhittenians are to have their own laws and their own judicial system independent of the Gortynians, furnishing every third year 350 staters for (sacrifices on) Ida.

3–4 And a house which (someone) builds [*c*.6] or plants trees, the builder or planter (is allowed) to buy and sell. *vac.*

4–8 The company commander (*startagetas*) and the person serving as *kosmos* who goes to Rhitten are to serve as *kosmoi*, together with the Rhittenian *kosmos*, regarding the person who does not obey the office of *ephor* (?); and he is to levy a fine of one drachma (on him) and is to use the money with the *startos* and with the Rhittenians; but they are not to fine him more. And if he should fine him more or should not use (the fine) (correctly), he is to be tried in a foreigners' trial.

8–12 A Gortynian is not to go and take security from a Rhittenian. And if he is convicted in a case involving security, he is to pay double the simple value, as is written in the *ephors'* place (?), and the Rhittenian *kosmos* is to exact payment. And if they do not exact payment, there is to be immunity for the elders who exact it from them. *vac.*

12 The things that are written (are valid), but other things are not. *vac.*

12–15 And whatever matter the Rhittenians as a community again fight about with the Gortynians, the herald is to summon (?) (the Gortynians), either they themselves or others on their behalf, to Rhitten in ten (days) to be present in the agora with the people gathered to answer the charge of which they are accused; and the decision will be made in the same way as —

---

1 *τοῖδε* = *τοῖσδε*; Dialect 11.

G puts a *vac.* after *αὐτόδικοι*, perhaps misled by H's drawing (which she reproduces). Halbherr's own text (1897: 206) had no gap, and a gap here would be very unlikely. On the stone (and in H's photo) there is a space slightly less than the width of a letter.

2 *Β̣ίδαν*: as G notes, *ϝ̣ίδαν* is also possible (cf. *IC* 4.146.6); both are Cretan forms of *ἴδα*, Mt. Ida, where Zeus was worshipped.

⟨*σ*⟩[*τ*]*ατέρανς*: the mason mistakenly omitted the initial *sigma*.

3 *δένδρεα*: Wilamowitz (*apud* G) suggested *δένδρε' ἅ*, which would provide a clear construction for *πυτεύσει*, but none of the supplements yet proposed for the gap in this line would provide a normal syntax on either reading. As Halbherr notes (1897: 207), one would expect to find a subject in the gap, perhaps *τις*, but [*ει . . τι*]*ς* is too short to fill the gap of about six letters in all, and [*ει Γορτύνιο*]*ς* would be quite a bit too long.

4–5 For *σταρταγέταν* (and *σταρτô* in line 7), see on **G72**.5.5.

5 *ἄγε*[*ι*] is here used intransitively, 'goes' (H, G). VER translate 'le commandant et le kosme en fonction pour Rhitten', but as in line 13, *'Ρ*[*ι*]*τ̣τ̣ενάδε* here clearly implies motion to a place. Maffi (p.c.) suggests that the verb should be understood to mean 'conduct a military campaign' (together with the Rhittenians). Even if the verb could be understood in this way (which is doubtful), it would require (as Maffi notes) a full stop after *κόσμο* (line 6) and a new sentence beginning *τὸν μὲ πειθόμενον*. This would result, however, in an inexplicable asyndeton, unless one assumed an unparalleled postponement of the connecting particle *δέ*.

It is unclear precisely what *κοσμêν* (lit. 'serve as *kosmos*') could mean if *τὸν μὲ πειθόμενον* were a direct object; thus it is preferable to take this expression as an accusative of respect. This provision, then, is intended only for situations of extreme disobedience.

6 *πειθόμενον*: for *πείθεσθαι* with the genitive, see LSJ *s.v.* BI.3.

πορ̣ί̣μ[ο is very difficult (cf. on 10 below). We follow G in interpreting it as *'πορ̣ί̣μ[ο* (= *ἐφορίμου*), the office of ephor. Bile 171, n. 70 objects that this office is otherwise unknown in Crete, though it is well established in Sparta and other Doric cities. But G cites an early inscription from Prinias (*IC* 1.28.1), which may have been ancient Rhitten (but see Prinias Site), where we have the letters *εφορος*, and also ... *ορος* (*ἐφ*]*ορος*?). Bile doubts this evidence and interprets the letters as the gen. of *φοριμον* 'tax' ('taxe', also unattested). VER read '*πορ̣ί̣σμ[ο* which they interpret as *ephorismos* 'boundary', though it is not clear how this (hypothetical) word could have this sense or what not obeying a boundary might mean (were Gortynians and Rhittenians forbidden to set foot on each other's territory?); in any case there is not room on the stone for this restoration. Others (including H at first) read *πολ̣ε̣μ[ο* ('obey during war'), but the traces on the stone are against this (see G ad loc.). All in all, G's suggestion seems to us the least difficult.

δ]*αμιόμεν* (*ζαμιόμεν*) and *κατακρέθαι* (*καταχρῆσθαι*): both infinitives are usually translated with plural subjects (the company commander and the Gortynian and Rhittenian *kosmoi*), but since the verbs in 7–8 are singular (see note below) the subjects here are probably singular, most likely the Rhittenian *kosmos*.

6–7 *πεδά* (*μετά*): we keep the normal meaning, 'with' (i.e. 'in consultation with'), but it may mean 'for' (i.e. 'for the benefit of', VER); in either case, questions arise (see below comm. ad 6–8).

7–8 *δαμιόσαι* ... *κατακρέσαιτο*: Bile 271 correctly translates both verbs as 3rd pers. singular (aor. opt.), but on p. 241 n. 336, she mistakenly calls the first an aorist infinitive.

8 *κσενείαι*: the lengthened ending (normally *κσενι*-) is unique; see Bile 95.

ἐνεκυραστάν: agent noun, 'taker of security (*ἐνεκύρος*)'.

9 *ἐς*: G understands this as *εἰς*, but followed by a genitive, it must be *ἐκ* (Dialect 14): 'security-taker *from* a Rhittenian'.

10 *ἐν τᾶι 'πόραι* has given rise to various interpretations, none of them satisfactory (cf. on 6 *πορ̣ί̣μ[ο* above). G understands *'πόραι* as *ἐφόραι*: the rules were written 'in the *ephors'* place' (*in ephororum sede*); this is perhaps least unsatisfactory. Bile 171 n. 70 (see above, n. ad 6) takes *φόραι* as 'tax' ('impôt'), here presumably a written list of taxes. VER write *ἐν τᾶι* (*ἐ*)*π' ὄραι* (*ἐν τῇ ἐπ' οὔρᾳ*, lit. 'on the one in back', i.e. 'on the backside [of the stele]?'); but they also suggest *'πόρ*(*ι*)*αι* (= *ἐφορίᾳ*, 'frontier') and translate 'on the border stele' ('sur la stèle (?) frontalière'). Neither solution is plausible. Perhaps *Pora* (or *Phora*) was a place name.

11 The switch to the plural is awkward, but may mean that *kosmos* in 10–11 designates the collective group of *kosmoi* (G).

πρειγ[*ίσ*]*τονς* = *πρεσβυτάτους* (Dialect 34).

11–12 *ἄπατον ἔμεν*: here apparently used impersonally with an accusative; the dative is more common (see n. ad **Ele**11.5).

12 *ἀντιπαίσοντι*: *ἀμφιπαίεν* should mean 'strike all around', as in an inscription from Epidaurus (*IG* IV^2 1 121, line 92), or 'come to blows concerning' something, but it is usually understood (G, LSJ supplement) metaphorically as equivalent to *ἀμφισβητεῖν*, 'dispute'. But the law may be concerned with actual physical violence.

12–13 *τὸ κοινὸν οἰ 'Ριττένιοι*: the two nouns are probably in apposition ('the Rhittenians as a community') and *τὸ κοινὸν* may also go with *τὸνς Γορτυνίονς*: 'The Rhittenians and the Gortynians as communities'.

13 *προκαλε̂]ṿ* H. G thinks this is too long for the space (we disagree) and suggests *ἀγγέλε]ν*. In neither case is the object of the verb stated, but it must be the Gortynians, who are summoned to come to Rhitten. VER leave the gap blank and translate, 'the herald will present himself in Rhitten' ('le héraut se présentera à Rhittèn'); but this seems very unlikely.

13–14 ⟨δ⟩*έκα*: the mason mistakenly omitted the *delta*.

14–15 *Ϝευμέναν* (*Ϝελμέναν*): perf. pass. part. of *Ϝειλέω* (Attic *εἴλω*); see above, note on **G72**.5.18, and Bile 223. The verb is most likely a genitive absolute with an unexpressed subject. Cf. *κατ' ἀγορὰν καταϜελμένον το̂μ πολιατα̂ν* ('in the agora when the citizens are gathered') in **G72**.10.34–5 and 11.12–14.

The text lays out an agreement between Gortyn and the community of Rhitten, commonly located near modern Prinias (e.g. van Effenterre 1993b: 14–15); but see Perlman 1996: 262–76; 2004b: 1186; Rizza 2008: 303–5. The agreement is apparently a response to complaints, primarily by Rhittenians against Gortynians, concerning the buying and selling of houses and orchards in the other city, relations between officials in the two cities (perhaps involving military forces), the taking of security from Rhittenians by Gortynians, and possibly physical violence (see n. ad 12 above). At the end the agreement also establishes a procedure for resolving future disputes between the two cities, some of whose details may have been spelled out in what followed. The text is syntactically difficult in several places (see notes above), perhaps indicating that the agreement was drafted by someone with relatively little legislative experience.

1 'Their own laws and their own judicial system': the same expression is found in a decree from the 2nd c. BCE, *IC* 4.184.5 (Chaniotis 1996: no. 69).

2–3 350 staters is a substantial sum; it may have been paid partly or entirely with sacrificial animals.

3–4 'Buy and sell': surely this must mean that the builder or planter, whether Gortynian or Rhittenian, can sell the house he builds or the trees he plants. It is possible, however, that he does not own the land on which he builds or plants, and thus cannot sell that; this would not mean that land at either Gortyn or Rhitten was inalienable, only that those from one city cannot own land in the other. In this case, the land may belong to the city (see Introd. 7B).

4–6 If our interpretation of the sentence is correct (see n. ad 5 above), the Gortynian leadership would probably only intervene in Rhittenian affairs in this manner if someone was so disobedient as to threaten insurrection.

4–5 The pairing of the *startagetas* ('leader of the *startos*') and the *kosmos* is particularly interesting in light of the dating formula in **G72**.5.5–6 ('when the *startos* Aithaleus, Kyllos and his colleagues, were *kosmos*'). The *startagetas* would appear to be the leader of the *startos* to which the *kosmos* belongs; in working together (with the Rhittenian *kosmos*) they may handle military and civilian matters respectively.

5–6 The fact that Rhitten too has a *kosmos* (also in 10–11) indicates that it is a polis in its own right, though it may be under the influence of Gortyn; see Perlman 2004b: 1186.

6–8 'He is to levy, etc.': the Greek indicates that one person acts here but does not specify which one; the Rhittenian *kosmos* is the most likely (see notes above).

6 A drachma is a very small fine for an official, suggesting that the office of *ephor* (if that is the correct sense—see note above) was relatively unimportant. This raises several questions to which we have no answers: why does the treaty devote so much attention to this matter? Why should three of the highest officials concern themselves with the matter? Why is such a small fine divided between two large groups?

8 'In a foreigners' trial' (or 'according to the justice for foreigners'; see **G13**h–g2, cf. **G64**.4.): here the two amount to the same thing. The defendant in this trial is presumably the Gortynian official, probably the *kosmos*, who is authorized to levy a fine of one drachma (line 6) but levies a higher fine or misuses the proceeds. The plaintiff would probably be the Rhittenian who is fined too much or is deprived of the proper share of the fine.

8–12 The prohibition against Gortynians taking security from a Rhittenian may be intended to protect the latter against the sort of treatment envisaged in **G81**.16–22, where a creditor enters a house and takes something as security. Or, since houses were probably one of the main forms of security, this clause may imply that Gortynians were not allowed to acquire real property from a Rhittenian, though they could themselves build and then dispose of a house (lines 3–4).

8 'Take security from': we understand *enekyrastas* as 'a person who takes security (from another)', not 'one who seizes a debtor' (Bile 330).

10 'In the *ephors*' place (?)' (*en tai 'porai*): the sense is uncertain (see note above), but it must refer to an earlier document written somewhere that addressed the valuation of things (perhaps produce) used as security. **G75** or **G81** are possible candidates; neither prescribes a fine of 'double the simple value' or prescribes the method of payment, but such a provision may have once stood in either or both laws where the text is now missing.

11 'The elders': the text suggests that the elders (*tons preigistons*) are a defined group, possibly a council of some sort, though their function here (exacting payment) may rather suggest a smaller group with specific administrative duties. This term does not occur again in this sense until the Hellenistic period, but cf. *pre(i)sgeia* in **Pr7**D1, D3.

12 'The things that are written (are valid), but other things are not', i.e. only written laws are valid. The clause is highly elliptical and the sense is not immediately evident. G understands the words as we do, not as a specific reference to the

rules that immediately precede (H). By declaring that the written laws of each city are to be valid (and only these), the sentence, marked off by gaps and asyndeton before and after it, forms a transition from rules that address grievances that apparently provoked this agreement to rules for resolving future conflicts. Maffi (p.c.), like H, takes the clause as referring to the words of this text only, its purpose being to prohibit any changes to the agreement.

12–15 This provision addresses possible future strife: the Gortynians will be required to appear at a public meeting in the Rhittenian agora to answer charges brought by the Rhittenian community. This is a significant concession to Rhitten, and is in keeping with the tenor of the rest of the agreement, which offers Rhittenians protections against their stronger neighbor.

12 'Again' suggests that this agreement was connected with the resolution of a previous dispute between the two communities, perhaps one in which Gortynians were the aggressors.

'Fight about' (*anpipaisonti*): the verb is usually understood metaphorically ('dispute'), but it may have a stronger sense suggesting physical violence (see note above). It almost certainly does not imply full-scale war. More likely a few individuals from the two cities had come to blows during a dispute.

13 '[The Gortynians]': no object of the verb 'summon' (if this is the correct supplement) is expressed, but the summons was probably issued to all the Gortynians, though very likely only a few representatives went 'on their behalf'.

14–15 'With the people gathered': lit. 'in the agora assembled' (*kat' agoran weumenan*). The expression is puzzling: it cannot mean that the agora is somehow assembled,[417] but is probably an abbreviated version of an expression found twice in a section on adoption in **G72** (10.34–5, 11.12–14), *kat' agoran katawelmenon tom poliatan*, or 'in the agora when the citizens are gathered'. Leaving aside for now questions about citizenship (see Introd. 5A4), the provision in **G72** requires adoption to take place (and in 11.12–14 to be renounced, if one wishes) in the presence of the citizens assembled in the agora. The same idea is almost certainly present here, and so we have translated the expression 'in the agora with the people gathered', leaving the identity of those who gathered vague.

G81. Land pledged as security (VER II.47, K 155). *c.*450–400

A single block probably containing one full column of text. We have the bottom of the column and may have the top; the right edge is complete; only 2–3 letters are missing on the left. The text probably began above or more likely, if we have the top of the column, in a column on the right (see below, n. ad 1–4); it must also have continued in a new column on the left (see below, n. ad 24).

[417] The verb *Ϝευμέναν* (*Ϝελμέναν*) could be accusative singular, but is much more likely to be a genitive used absolutely with an unexpressed subject.

δενδρέον καὶ Ϝοικίας ὅ[κ’ ὀμό-]
[σον]τι τôν ὀμόρον ἐννέα οἱ
ἐπάνκιστα πεπαμένοι, μ̣[ο-]
[λêν, κ]αλêν δ’ ἀντὶ μαιτύρο-
ν δυôν πρότριτον τὸν ἀπ̣[c.3]
[c.2]σ̣αντα μετρε̣σιόμενο-
ν· αἰ δέ κα μὲ εἴει καλίον[τι ᾶ̣ι]
[ἔγρ]αται, αὐτὸς μετρέθο τε
καὶ προπονέτο προτέταρ[τον]
[ἀν]τὶ μαιτύρον δυôν παρέμε-
ν ἐνσς ἀγοράν. ὀμνύμε̣[ν δ-]
[ὲ ἐ̃] μ̣ὰν τοῦτο μέν ἐστι ἀβλο-
πίαι δικαίος πρὶν μολέθ[αι]
[τὰν] δίκαν, ὃ δ’ ἐνεκύρακσαν
μὲ ἔμεν· νικêν δ’ ὅτερά κ’ οἱ π̣[λί-]
[ες ὀ]μόσοντι. *vac.* κ’ αἴ κ’ ἐς στέγα-
ς ἐνεκυράκσοντι, πονίον[τι μ-]
[ὲ ’νϜ]οικêν ὃ ἐνεκύρακσαν συν-
εκσομόσαθθαι τôν ὀμό[ρον]
[τô]ν̣ ἐννέα τρίινς, οἷς κα προ-
Ϝείπει, μὲ ἐνϜοικêν ὃ ἐνεκύ̣[ρα-]
[κσ]α[ν. α]ἰ̣ δέ τίς κα τôν ὀμόρ-
ον *vac.*

— of trees and a house, when nine of the neighbors who possess the nearest land swear, (he) is to bring the case (?) and summon before two witnesses three days in advance the one who [*c.*12], so that he can measure (the property). And if he does not come after he summons him as is written, let him measure it himself and declare to him four days in advance before two witnesses that he should be present in the agora. And he is to swear that indeed this (the property) is (as claimed) without fault and lawfully before the case is tried, and the person from whom they received security (is to swear) that it is not. And whichever the majority swear, (that side) is to win. *vac.* And if they take something as security from a house, if the person from whom they received security asserts that he does not live in (the house), three of the nine neighbors whom he notified earlier are to swear with him that the one from whom they received security does not live in (the house). But if one of the neighbors *vac.*

1–4 With the restorations in 1–2 and 3–4, this could be understood as a complete sentence; other restorations are possible, however, and we think it more likely (see below on 1–4) that the surviving text continues a sentence that began above or to the right.

1 δενδρέον καὶ Ϝοικίας: if this is the beginning of the sentence, these may be genitives of 'connection' ('often used loosely, especially at the beginning of a construction, to state the subject of a remark', Smyth 1956: §1381); cf. Blass #4986 ('in Sachen von Bäumen').

Ϝοικίας: the usual translation is 'house' (G, K, VER) but elsewhere, including 16–17 below, *stega* is used for 'house'. Brixhe 1999: 89, therefore, suggests it should be taken with τôν ὀμόρον ἐννέα, 'nine of the neighbors belonging to the *woikia*', which (comparing **G72**.5.26–7) they take to be a 'sociopolitical unit (?)', which has been referred to in the previous part of this law. But in that case the *woikia* would be a very large unit indeed, since it would have included others besides the nine who owned the nearest properties. The sense of *woikia* may likely have been clarified by what preceded it, but lacking this information, we keep the traditional interpretation.

1–2 ὅ[κ’ ὀμόσον]τι, Blass, G (ὅκα = ὅτε, Bile 216); ὁ[μόσον]τι, H. Either supplement is possible; they would give lines 1–2 together 43 or 41 letters respectively; other pairs of lines have from 40 letters (11–12) to 44 (7–8).

3–4 μ̣[ολêν G; the restoration is very likely. Lines 3–4 together would then have 40 letters. One could also put a full stop after μολêν and then add a *vac.*, but the two infinitives should probably be more closely joined. One could also write μ[ολέτο (cf. **G41**.6.15–16), but the switch to an infinitive (καλêν) immediately afterwards would be awkward.

4–14 = **G75A**. Except for the participle in 5–6 (see next note), the only variations in the two texts are between single and double consonants in ἔγραται and ἐνσς (cf. n. ad 13 μολέθ[αι).

5–6 ἀπ̣[.....]σ̣αντα: we cannot restore ἐνεκυράκσαντα from **G75A**2–3. G suggests ἀπ̣[ομολέ]σ̣αντα, but it is not clear what this would mean (see below on 5–6). Perhaps ἀπ̣[οδείκ]σ̣αντα, 'having displayed' (cf. **G72**.1.42–3).

7 εἴει: pres. subj. of εἶμι (Bile 226).

7–8 'as is written': i.e. 'before two witnesses three days in advance' (4–5).

9 προτέταρ[τον: also in **G72**.11.53.

12 ἐ̃] μ̣άν: the substance of the oath follows; cf. **G55**, where the expression (twice) is negative.

τουτο is (a) genitive (τούτο) 'of this person', 'his' (so K) or (b) nominative (τοῦτο) 'this'. Either would be ambiguous: (a) does 'his' refer to the one who swears or someone else? (b) if we translate 'this is (the case)' (VER: 'cela est fait') does this mean 'this is the land', 'this is the measurement' or something else? See comm. ad 11–15.

13 μολέθ[αι: G and others print μολέθ[θαι, claiming this is necessary *spatii causa*; but since either is possible (at the end of line 11 two letters are missing, at the end of 9 three letters), we prefer to keep the same spelling as in **G75A**10.

14 ἐνεκύρακσαν: for the sense, see comment below.

ὁ̃ ἐνεκύρακσαν (also in 18, 21–2) is the person 'from whom they received a pledge' (ὁ̃ is genitive)—i.e. the debtor. It cannot be 'the person who took it as pledge' (Davies 1996: 48), which would be ὁ ἐνεκυράκσας; and the sense 'part of the pledge which one took' (VER), with the relative being genitive by attraction, is possible here but not possible in 18 or 21–2. The phrase may have developed a technical aspect since it recurs in exactly the same form three times, and the verb is plural even where (as here) the creditor is probably one person.

14–15 ὁ̃ δ' ἐνεκύρακσαν μὲ ἔμεν either (a) continues the oath that begins in line 12, 'and that it is not (the property of) the person from whom they received a pledge' (VER, following G), or (b) specifies a counter-oath: 'and the person from whom they received a pledge (is to swear) that it is not' (K). Note that the syntax switches from the indicative (*esti*) to the infinitive (*emen*). See further commentary on 11–15.

16–22 The dative πονίοντι goes with συνεκσομόσαθθαι: lit. three of the nine neighbors 'are to swear, together with the one who says'. *Ponen* indicates that the subject is a litigant (see n. ad **G41**.5.7–11), who must be the debtor; ὁ̃ ἐνεκύρακσαν then may function effectively as the subject of πονίοντι as well as of μὲ 'νϜοικε̃ν.

22 [ν. α]: G (followed by K, VER) posits a gap between the missing letters ([ν. *vac.* α]) though no previous editor had done so. Measurement of the letters on the stone shows that there would have been at most less than half of a letter-space between *nu* and *alpha*, not enough to mark a *vac.* The top of a letter (*alpha*) is visible in G's drawing (p. 189) but is not now visible on the stone; if it is accurate, there would be no space between the two letters.

23 The last two letters of ὀμόρον are written in line 24 but nothing more. The mason apparently wanted to complete the word before starting a new column.

The law apparently concerns two different situations alluded to in the opening words 'of trees and a house', both involving property pledged as security. The first (1–16) is whether land pledged as security is what is claimed (regarding size and quality), the second (16–23), whether movable property taken as security in fact belongs to the debtor. The first part may concern security in the form of produce from land, not the land itself; cf. VER, who propose as one of several possibilities that a harvest is being measured, and Maffi, who now proposes (p.c.) that the produce is being measured. If there were fixed values for different kinds of produce, it would be necessary to measure and perhaps assess the quality of the land in order to determine the value of the security. The second part (16ff.) concerns security in the form of household goods.

The almost verbatim repetition of lines 4–15 in **G75**A raises the question of the relationship between the two texts (cf. **G42/Gortyn1**, and **G79**/*IC* 4.144). It is generally assumed (e.g. Davies 1996: 47–50) that the same law was written twice, but the significant variation between **G75**A2–3—'the person who received a pledge' (as security)—and **G81**.5–6—perhaps 'the person who responded to the charge' or 'who pointed out (the property)'—suggests that we have two different laws with situations that are similar enough that the same procedural rules could apply in both (cf. **G72**.6.12–31 and 9.7–24). In **G75**A a creditor who accepted a pledge of land as security is summoned, probably by the debtor, to measure the land. In **G81** it is probably the debtor who is summoned. This suggests that the two texts may be part of the same law involving a pledge of land as security but address different stages of the transaction. The lettering of the two inscriptions is quite similar, and the columns of both appear to be the same width. Moreover, **G85** and **G86** have similar lettering (their column widths cannot be determined), and some of the same vocabulary, leading Blass (# 4992) to suggest that they also belong with **G75**. It is possible, then, that all four texts were originally part of the same inscription, and that the law required the same procedure at different stages of litigation.

1–16 Interpretation of these lines raises many problems. A major difficulty is the uncertainty of the text in 5–6 (see below). Other uncertainties are in 3–7: who is bringing the suit and summoning someone to measure, and what is the suit about, and in 11–15: do we have one oath or two, who swears the oath or oaths, and what is the content of the oath(s). In the comments below, we conclude that a creditor brings suit against a debtor, perhaps for non-payment, and summons him to measure a piece of land that he has pledged or intends to pledge. Oaths are sworn and then the nine neighbors add their oaths on one side or the other and the majority wins.

1–4 Even if the surviving text is a complete sentence (see above, n. ad 1), it was probably preceded by some text that made clear the subject of the infinitive *molen* 'is to plead' (if that is the correct restoration). The subject of the next infinitive, *kalen* ('is to summon'), is very likely the same, in which case the suit is to be brought by someone who wishes to have a piece of property measured, most likely because it has been offered as security; see further below on 3–16.

1 'Of trees and a house': no land is mentioned, but since neither trees nor a house are easily measured, most likely the measuring mentioned in 6–7 concerns the land on which these (or at least the trees) are located.

1–2 Some scholars (e.g. VER; Meister 1908: 570–3) have been particularly interested in the many oaths mentioned in this text. It seems reasonable to require the nine closest neighbors to swear, whether as witnesses in court or extra-judicially, in cases concerning the size, ownership, or inhabitants of a piece of property. But this is our only text from Gortyn that speaks of neighbors swearing, and the only instance in Greek law where a majority of oath-swearers wins a case. Thür (2009: 493) takes the method of counting oath-swearers in this text (which he mistakenly cites as *IC* 4.48) as characteristic of judicial procedure at Gortyn, but one instance hardly qualifies as characteristic. See further below on 2–4 and 15–16, and Gagarin 2010b: 139–40.

2–4 These neighbors presumably know the most about the property in dispute. Thus, they are not true 'oath-helpers', who in some legal systems swear in support of a person without necessarily having any knowledge of the facts, as Meister 1908 argues (see Gagarin 1989, esp. 51–2). The subject of their oath is unclear: they may swear to the size of the property or its ownership (or both), or they may swear a preliminary oath, pledging to swear truly at the trial itself (in lines 15–16).

3–7 Someone is instructed to bring suit and issue a summons to measure something, almost certainly a piece of land. The summons is clearly part of the suit and leads to an oath or oaths (11–15) that will decide the outcome of the suit (15–16). In **G75**A, the person summoned is the creditor ([*ton*] *enekyrak-santa*), and the summoner is thus very likely the debtor, who pledged or offered to pledge a piece of property (see on **G75**A2–3); the debtor probably summons the creditor to measure the property that he accepted as security and agree that it is adequate. In **G81**, the person summoned must be different (see on 5–6), but otherwise the wording in lines 4–13 is identical; thus, the procedure here is the same as in **G75**A. This does not necessarily mean that the parties to the suit or the matter at issue are the same. In **G75** the summons may not be part of a suit, since it is not easy to imagine a debtor bringing suit against the creditor. However, mention of 'the person from whom they recieved security' in **G81**.14 indicates that the suit involves a matter for which security was given, and thus probably a creditor and a debtor. A possible scenario is that a creditor brings suit against a debtor for non-payment and wants to measure the land that has been offered as security in order to determine its value before taking all or part of it in payment of the debt. If the debtor answers the summons, they measure the land together; if not, the creditor measures it himself and then summons the debtor in front of witnesses to be present in the agora (lines 7–11), which is presumably where the oath or oaths are sworn (11–15).

5–6 The gap in the text must be filled by a different expression than *enekyraksanta* ('creditor'), which is the reading in **G75**A2–3. G suggests *ap[omole]santa*, which in its only other occurrences (**G72**.6.26 = 9.18–19) apparently means 'respond to an accusation'. More likely, perhaps, is *ap[odeik]santa*, 'display' (cf. **G72**.1.42–3), referring to a debtor who has pointed out property he wishes to use as security.

11–15 'He is to swear' raises three main questions. (a) Who swears? (b) What is sworn? and (c) Do we have one oath in two parts (X swears A and not B) or two opposed oaths (X swears A and Y swears not-A)? We begin with the last of these questions.

(c) 'And the person from whom they received security (is to swear) that it is not' (*o d' enekyraksan me emen*): this could also mean 'and that it is not the person's from whom they took security'. Two factors support the first interpretation: first, the sentence that follows (15–16) specifies that the side with the majority of oath-swearers wins the case; this indicates that oaths must be sworn on both sides. Second, the switch from an indicative (*esti*) in the first oath to an infinitive (*emen*) in the second would be very awkward if both were part of the same oath.

(a) 'The person from whom they received security' (*o enekyraksan*) must be the debtor (see above, n. ad 14), who swears the second, counter-oath. Since no third party has been mentioned, the first oath must therefore be sworn by the creditor.

(b) The content of the oath is *touto esti*, and since *touto* may be nominative or genitive, this could mean 'this is' or [it] 'is his'. We think the nominative more likely: the creditor swears that 'this is', probably meaning that the property which has just been measured is the size that was stated. If *touto* were genitive, then the oath would concern ownership, and the ownership in question would have to be the debtor's. But it is hard to imagine any reason why the creditor would swear to own property that the debtor had pledged (or why in that case the land would need to be measured). Nor is there any reason why the creditor would swear that the land is the debtor's (if 'his' could refer to him, which is unlikely), or why, if he did, the debtor would swear that it was not his own.

We thus conclude that the probable meaning is that the person who brought suit and summoned and measured 'is to swear that indeed this (the property) is (as claimed) without fault and lawfully before the case is tried, and the person from whom they took security (is to swear) that it is not'. The issue then is whether the property in its entirety is the right size to satisfy the debt or is too large to be seized in satisfaction of the entire debt but ought instead to be divided so that part of it can satisfy the debt.

13–14 The words 'before the case is tried' are probably part of the content of the oath, not an indication of when the oath is to be sworn.

14 'The person from whom they received security': for the verb *enekyrazo*, see above on **G43**Ba7–8. The security that is pledged may be trees or a house, though in 16–22 it apparently is something taken out of a house.

15–16 To achieve a majority, supporters must also swear oaths. And since nothing is said about who these supporters are, we are probably to assume that they are the nine neighbors, who were mentioned in 2–3, and who are mentioned again in 19–20. This is the only example of opposing oaths at Gortyn. VER and others (whom they cite) are concerned that the consequence of swearing opposing oaths would be that one of the two sides would necessarily swear a false oath. Their solution is to understand the restored *omosonti* in 1–2 as a subjunctive indicating action of a 'timeless' nature ('intemporelle'): the neighbors indicate their willingness to swear on one side or the other but at the trial only those in the majority are asked to swear. In our view, this is a desperate solution to a non-existent problem. Athenians at the time had no problem requiring litigants on both sides to swear oaths even though one was bound to lose. VER seem to assume that the Gortynians were mired in a primitive fear of divine wrath in which perjury is inconceivable, but the laws give no support to such a view.

16–22 The law now turns to a new situation involving security for a debt: the creditors take something from a house as security, but the debtor (for 'the person from whom they received security' see n. ad 14 above) claims he does not live in the house (and thus presumably he does not own the property that was taken). It appears that the creditor, perhaps with others (since the verb in 'received as security' is plural), is seizing additional security (cf. the seizures in Dem. 47). The three oath-swearers (out of nine neighbors) then affirm what is said by someone, expressed by a dative participle *ponionti*, 'for the person who asserts', in 17).

20–1 'Whom he notified earlier': the debtor is apparently supposed to notify three neighbors if he is not living in the house; probably he is renting it to someone else.

G82. Arbitration (VER II.8, K 156). *c.*450–400

Two blocks of stone each with ten lines of writing from the same column of text; there is a small space between the two where one or more letters are now missing. About one letter is missing from the left edge of the column, but the right edge is preserved and to its right a few letters are visible from the preceding column. The text originally began above and continued below.

[—]ν θύκοι τ̣ο[ῖς ἐπιτρ]απόνσ[ι] [ἒ] ὄι κ' ἐπιτρ[άποντ]ι, μεδατέρο-νς καταβλά[πεθ]αι. ἒ δέ κα πα̣[ρ]-[ί]οντι καὶ καθ[. .]ος γένοντ-αι, ἐδδικακσ̣άτο ἐν ταῖς τρ[ι]-[σ]ὶ ἀμέραις. αἰ [δέ] κα μὲ ἐδδι-κάκσει, αὐ[τὸν] ἀτέθαι ὄ κ' ἐπ[ιτ]-[ρά]ποντι τὸ κρέ[ιο]ς ὑπὸ τôι με-μπομένο[ι. αἰ] δέ κ' ἀμπότε̣[ροι] [μολι (?)]ό̣μενοι ἐ[πιτρ]άποντι, ὐ[—]

[If something] should happen to those who have referred (their case) or to the one to whom they referred it, neither is to suffer a loss. But when they are present and are [*c*.7], let him give a final decision in three days. And if he does not decide, he himself is to pay to the plaintiff the value of the suit they referred to him. And if both refer the case to arbitration while they are engaged in litigation (?) —

1 θύκοι = τύχοι.

1–2 ἐπιτρ]απόνσ[ι . . . ἐπιτρ[άποντ]ι: the verb (the standard verb for referring a dispute for arbitration) is securely restored from the fortunate survival of each half separately.

3–4 πα̣[ρί]οντι = πάρωσι.

4 Many restorations have been suggested to fill this gap of 2 letters but none is convincing (see G).

5 ἐδδικακσ̣άτο (ἐκ-δικάδδεν): see Bile 275.

8 κρέ[ιο]ς = χρήεος, gen. sing. of χρέος; cf. **G72**.3.14–15, 5.38–9, where in both cases the fine is double the value.

8–9 ὑπὸ τôι μεμπομένο[ι: for ὁ μεμπόμενος, see n. ad **G41**.7.8–9. The construction, ὑπό with dative, is unique in Crete; it is explained by Bile 310 as a dative of agent: 'he is to be penalized by the plaintiff'.

10 μολι]ό̣μενοι is suggested but not adopted by G.

This is the only text that deals with arbitration at Gortyn (for the doubtful allusion in **G21**.2, see our comm. ad loc.). Arbitration was common in Athens, and also in Ptolemaic Egypt. This text apparently concerns voluntary (or private) arbitration, where the two parties agree to go to an arbitrator, but the fine levied against a non-performing arbitrator suggests that he was a public official. We do not know if the parties had a choice of arbitrators.

2–3 'Neither is to suffer a loss': the same wording is found at **G42**B9–11.

5 'Give a final decision' (*eddikadden*, also in 6–7), signifying a definitive judgment (Bile 275), occurs nowhere else. It cannot have the strict sense of 'rule' specified in **G72**.11.26–31 because the law does not prescribe a specific outcome (and no single outcome could cover all cases of arbitration). The distinction made in **G72**.11.26–31 does not hold in most texts besides the Code; see Gagarin 2010b: 142–3.

6–9 Punishing an arbitrator who does not make a decision is unknown in Athens, and is an example of the fairly harsh attitude toward officials in Cretan laws.

8–9 'The plaintiff' (*o mempomenos*, see note above): i.e. the plaintiff in the original suit that has now been referred to arbitration.

G83. Procedural regulations (VER II.7, K 157). *c*.450–400

A fragment of a column of text missing 2–3 letters from the right edge and about four letters from the left. The text continued above and below.

[*c*.16] α̣ς πολῖτ̣[α-
[ι] πσιναυτοῖς. *vac.* [. . .]ο̣ι̣δ̣[*c*.4]
[αἰ δέ] κ' ὀ πευσθὲνς συνκατί̣[ει],
[αὐτ]ὸς δικαδδέθο ἆι πε[υσθε̂]-
[ι, οἰ δὲ] ναόσαντες̣ ἆι ἔγρατι[αι ἀ]-
[πο]δ̣όντον τ̣ὸν ν̣ι̣καθέντ[α ἐς κ]-
[ε̂ραν]ς. *vac.* αἰ δέ κ' ὀ πεύσανς ν[ικα]-
[θε̂]ι, αὐτὸς κατιστάτο ὅτ̣τ[ον]
[ἔγρα]τται. *vac.* ὂδ δέ κα πευ[σθ]-
[ὲν]ς μὲ παργένεται, ἐπιτα[κσ]-
[άθ]θ̣ο κ' ἐσπρακσάντον ὅτ̣[το]-
[ν . . . . . .]ο ειτε [. . . . .]ο[—]

citizens for themselves. *vac.* [*c*.10] but if the accused returns with (someone), he himself is to be judged on the matter concerning which he is accused, and let those who took him to a temple (for refuge) as is written deliver him, if he loses the case, into the hands (of the accuser?). *vac.* But if the accuser loses the case, he himself is to pay as much as is written. *vac.* Whoever is accused and does not appear is to be constrained and let them fine (him) as much as —

---

2 *πσιναυτοῖς* = *σφεαυτοῖς*.

3 *πευσθένς*: aorist passive participle of *πεύθω* 'inform against' (cf. **G72**.8.55); *πεύσανς* (line 7) is the active participle.

συνκατί̣[ει: this likely means that he returns from taking refuge in a temple. It might, however, mean 'returns from exile (with someone)', a sense made famous in Aristophanes' *Frogs* 1152–69.

5 *ναόσαντες* (*ναόω*), 'take someone to a temple for refuge', is the transitive form of *ναεύω*, 'take refuge in a temple' (Bile 359–60). It occurs only here and in a third-century text from Malla (*IC* 1.19.1, line 24).

9. *ὂδ δέ* = *ὃς δέ* (often written *ὀδδέ*).

The context for these procedural regulations is not entirely clear. They are sometimes associated with debt-bondage (G) and with some sort of self-help; but several peculiarities should guide our understanding. First, plaintiff and defendant are 'the informer' and 'the one informed against'; this may suggest a serious crime against the state, such as treason. Second, the accused is accompanied by others (3), perhaps those who took him to a temple for refuge (5). Third, the verb 'returns' (3) may imply a return from refuge in a temple or perhaps from exile. Fourth, only here is an accused who does not appear in court to be constrained (lit. 'put under orders') as well as fined. All this may suggest a political conflict: an informer, an accused with supporters, refuge in a temple, possible exile and return. If the accused is convicted, he is delivered into the hands of (probably) his accuser, which may mean enslavement, a severe punishment. On the other hand, if he is acquitted, the informant is penalized.

7–9 This is the only Cretan law that obliges a losing plaintiff to pay a fine himself. For fines for losing plaintiffs in Athenian law, see Harrison 1971: 179–85.

G84. (VER II.20, K 158). *c.*450–400

A single block with seven lines of writing; an unknown amount of text is missing on both sides, above and below .

[— στατêρ]ανς ἒ μεῖον, [π]λ̣ίον δ[ὲ μέ —]	— staters (?) or less, but not more —
[—]ι θ̣έντον πόλι καὶ καρ[—]	— let them pay to the city and —
[—]ο̣τάνς, δαμιόντο[ν .]ν̣[—]	— let them penalize —
[—]τα. *vac.* ὀ δ' ἐπόττας δαμ[ι —]	— *vac.* And the overseer will penalize (?) —
[— τ]ὸμ μὲ πειθόμενον το[—]	— the person who does not obey —
[—] καὶ τὸν ἀπέταιρον [—]	— and the *apetairos* —
[— ὀδε]λὸν κατ' ἀμέραν ἒ τριο[—]	— obol per day or three- —

1 στατêρ]ανς: δαρκν]άνς is also possible
4 Traces of a painted *folium* are visible in the blank space; see introduction to **G72**.
5 τ]ὸμ μὲ πειθόμενον: or τ]ôμ μὲ πειθομένον (gen. pl.).
6 τὸν ἀπέταιρον: or τôν ἀπεταίρον.
7 ὀδε]λόν = ὀβολόν.

4 In this context, the overseer (*epottas*) appears to be a public official.
6 For the *apetairos* (only here and in **G72**), see on **G72**.2.5.

G85. (K 159) *c.*450–400

One block with part of one column of text. The left edge is preserved but an unknown amount of text is missing to the right, and also above and below.

[— ἄντ]ροπον ἐνεκυρ-	2–3 a person, for the one who
άκσοντι ἒ κα[—]	receives security or
[—]ά̣θ̣ο αἴ κα λêι	4–5 if he wishes, with witnesses
σὺν μαίτυρο̣[ι —]	
[— ἐνεκ]ύ̣ρακσαν μὲ πρ-	6–7 they have received a pledge,
ὶν μολέθαι τὰ̣[ν δίκαν —]	not before the case (?) is tried
[—]ασος καὶ τοικ-	8–9 and he destroys little walls.
ία κ' ἀνέλ[ει] ἐν̣ [—]	

7 τὰ̣[ν δίκαν C: the same expression in **G75**A10–11 = **G81**.13–14. But other restorations are possible.
8 καί: could also be καἰ ('and if').

For the possibility that **G85** and **G86** are part of the same inscription as **G75** and **G81**, see above on **G81**. Vocabulary similar to that of **G81** includes 'receives a pledge' (2–3, 6) and 'before the case is tried' (6–7).

G86. (K 160) *c.*450–400

Two adjoining fragments, one with just a few letters. The right edge of the column is preserved in lines 4–6.

[—] δ̣ὲ καὶ τὸ[νς]
[ὀμ]όρονς οἵ κ[α —]
[— ἐγ]ραμένα να[όσ]-
αṿτες αὐτὸṿ [—]
[—]νς τὸνς ἐγραμμ-
ένοṿς. ὃδ δέ κα̣ κατ[—]
[—]ον ἐσπραδε[—]

1–2 — and the neighbors who —
3–4 — what is written, having taken him to a temple (for refuge) —
5–6 — those that have been written. And whoever —
7 — exact a penalty —

3–4 ἐγ]ραμένα να[όσ]αṿτες: The traditional restoration of these lines (G and others) is ἐγ]ραμέναν ἀ[τάσ]αντες, but there is only room for two letters at the end of line 3; it would also introduce the feminine passive participle ἐγραμέναν, which is not impossible though it is hard to think of an appropriate noun for it, and an active form of ἀτάομαι, which is not attested anywhere in Greek. Our proposed supplement fits the remaining space, and results in the common neuter passive participle ἐγραμένα, and an active participle ναόσαντες attested in **G83**.5.

5–6 ἐγραμμένοṿς: The perfect participle of this verb almost always appears as a neuter 'things that are written' (see preceding note); possible antecedents for the masculine are ὀμόρονς or μαιτύρανς.

For the possible connection of this text with **G75** and **G81**, see above on **G85**. Vocabulary similar to that of **G81** includes 'neighbors' (1–2), 'take to a temple (for refuge)' (3–4, but see note above), and (less significant) 'written' (3, 5–6).

G87. Debt collection (K 161) *c.*450–400

One large block divided roughly in half by a horizontal line of dots. The writing is only on the upper half with clear margins above and below, but letters are missing from both edges. Some of the language is that of a law, but see on line 2 below.

[—]ο[.]ο τôν ἐσπραττâν [—]
[—]αδδόμεθα αὐτ[. .]αν[—]
[—] τονδε τοκαν[. . .]δ[—]
[—]οο[. . .] ἐπιβάλλει ϝεκ[—]
[—]εν [τ]ὰṿ π̣λεθὺν [—]
[—] τροπὰν δέκσεται [—]
[—] παριόντον τôν ἐσπρατ τ[âν καὶ τô]
[μνάμ]ονος τô τôν ἐσπραττâν. *vac.* ἀ̣π[—]
[—] αὐτê κ' ὁ κâρυκς ἀνπεραν [—]
[—]δδικάκσει τὰν πλεθὺν το[—]
[— ἄν]α̣ιτον δ' ἔμεν τοῖς ἐσπράτ̣[ταις]
[ἐσπρ]άδονσι ὀπυî κα μέτε ἀποδο[—]
[—]ο. *vac.*

— of the *esprattai* —
— we collect debts (?) —
— then (?) —
— he imposes on each (?) —
— the amount —
— he receives sustenance —
7–8 — with the *esprattai* and the rememberer (?) of the *esprattai* present. *vac.* —
9 — there the herald —
10 — he shall rule [that he pay (?)] the amount —
11–12 — there is to be no fine (?) for the *esprattai* when they are collecting debts where [the debtor (?)] does not pay —

2 ἐσπρ]αδδόμεθα or δικ]αδδόμεθα, G.

3 Perhaps τόκα (τότε, Dialect 33), G.

4 ἐπιβάλλει ϝεκ[—]: cf. ϝε]κάστο ἐπιβάλλει, **G88**.5–6.
6 τροπάν = τροφάν
7–8 τôν ἐσπρατ[ᾶν καὶ τô μνάμ]ονος τô τôν ἐσπραττᾶν G: the restoration is very plausible, but not certain.
11 ἄν]α̣ιτον: G takes this as a variant of ἄνατον, which occurs only in **Elt2**.4 (see n. ad loc.); this is possible but very uncertain.
12 ὀπυῖ: cf. **G72**.4.15.

1, 7–8 For the *esprattai* ('collectors'), see on **G75**D2
2 Any restoration must result in a first-person-plural verb, which would be very unusual in a law or decree; but lines 10–12 in particular read like a law.
7–8 'Rememberer': for the *mnamon*, see on **G42**B6. Assuming the restoration is correct, this is the only mention of a *mnamon* of the *esprattai* at Gortyn; but cf. 'the *mnamon* of the *ksenios*' in **G72**.11.16–17, and **Da1**B1–4, where the *poinikastas*, who is also charged with remembering, is closely tied to the *kosmos*.

G88. *c*.450–400

A small stone with six lines of writing from one column; the right edge is preserved; there is a substantial empty space at the bottom. The stone was found by Haussoullier in 1879 along with a piece of G72 (Haussoullier 1880) and disappeared soon after.

[—] ἐδδίεται τὸμ μὲ πρ[—]	1–2	— leads out the one who does not —
[—]μεμ μὲ δ-ικάδδεθ[αι —]	3–4	— is not to decide —
[— ϝε]κάστο ἐπ-ιβάλλει. *vac.*	5–6	— he imposes on each. *vac.*

---

1 ἐδδίεται = ἐσδίεται (ἐκδίεται); see on ἐπιδίηται (**G41**.1.8).

G89. *c*.450–400

A single block with parts of 12 lines of writing, found not far from the Pythion (see **G79** headnote).

2 [— δ]εκσάμενον̣ δ[—]	— having received —
[—]δεν ἒ ὀ τᾶς θα[—]	
[—]α̣ς ἒ μὲ δέκσαι[το —]	— or he should not receive —
[— α]ἰ μὲ θάνατος̣ [—]	— unless death [prevents it (?)] —
[—]οντι ϝεκαστο [—]	— each —
[—]ς καἴ κ' ὀ τô κσε[νίο —]	— and if the — of the foreigners' —
[—]α̣ καταστασ[—]	— shall pay —
[—] στατêρανς ο̣[—]	— staters —
[— ἐπ]ε[λ]εύσαντα̣ [—]	— bringing to —

---

7 τô κσε[νίο; perhaps τô κσε[νίο κόσμο.

G90. *c*.450–400

A broken block of stone with two columns of writing that are partly obliterated by three or four later inscriptions (*IC* 4.209) written over the earlier text, which was erased. The left edge of A (on the right) and the right edge of B are intact.

A	A
πραδο[—]	
[—]ε̣ Ϝέρον-	2–3 — they do —
τι κατα̣[—]	
[—]ι τὸνς	4–5 — the witnesses —
μαίτυ[ρανς —]	
[—]ν νικά-	6–7 — he wins —
σει ἀρ[—]	
[—]ν τινα	8–9 — and he should have some —
δ̣' ἔκοι ἐ[—]	
B	**B**
[—]μ̣[*c*.8] προ-	1–2 — tell beforehand —
Ϝει[π —]	
[—]ς Ϝε-	3–4 — each —
κασ̣[τ —]	
[—] κ' ἐκ-	5–6 — swear an oath of denial (?) —
σομ̣[—]	
11 [—] ὀμο-	11–12 — neighbor —
ρο[—]	
[—] . ατ-	13–14 — is written (?) —
ον [ἔγρ]ατται ὀ[—]	
[—]οντι ἒ κα̣ρτα-	15–16 — either an ox or other —
ῖπος ἒ ἄλλο [—]	
[— σὺ (?)]μ μαί[τ]υρ-	17–18 — with (?) two witnesses —
σι [δ]υοῖς [—]	

A 2–3 Ϝέροντι from Ϝἔρδω (G, Bile 137).
B 5–6 G prints ἐκσομ̣[οσ (ἐξόμνυμι), which is possible, but the last letter could also be a *nu* or a *san*.

G91. Land used as security (VER II.71, K 162) *c*.450–400

Another block with later writing (*IC* 4.208) obliterating most of the earlier text. Parts of five lines from the right edge of a column are visible (and traces of a sixth above these).

[— Ϝ]εργασίας, αἶπσα [δ]ὲ Ϝερ-γακσάμενος ὁ καταθὲν[ς —]	1–2 — of land management (?), and having quickly done the work, the person who gave it as security —
[— ἐ]πὶ τούτοι ἔμεν τὸν κα[ρ]π̣ὸ-ν. *vac.* ὅτι δὲ κ[αὶ] ἐσπραṭτ̣ạ[ι]ṣ [—]	3–4 — the produce is to be under his control. *vac.* And whatever for the *esprattai* too —
[—] ḳε ὁ γρ[*c*.5]οσ[*c*.3–4] ἐνεκυρα[—]	5 — pledge —

4 ἐσπραṭτạ[ι]ṣ VER; ἐσπραṭτạ[ι G.

These appear to be rules for cultivating land that is being used as security.

2 For the meaning of *katathens*, see on **G72**.6.4–5.

3 For *epi* with the dative meaning 'in the hands of', i.e. under the control of, see on **G72**.6.17–18.

4 For the *esprattai* ('collectors'), see on **G75**D2.

G92. *c*.450–400

A small fragment with parts of nine lines.

2	[—]οποσ̣[—]	— as many as (?) —
3	[— π]ροϜε[ιπ —]	— tell beforehand —
4	[— Ϝ]οικιον̣ [—]	— dwelling —
6	[— Ϝοικοδο (?)]μ̣ε̂σαι [—]	— build a house (?) —
7	[— πρ]οϜειπαν̣[—]	— tell beforehand (?) —
8	[— ἔ]γραττ̣ạ[ι —]	— is written —
9	[—]οτερο[—]	— whichever (?) —

7 ἀπ]οϜειπαν̣[—] is also possible.

G93. *c*.450–400

A small fragment whose text has been erased at the lower right.

1	[—]ν̣αν κρεμ̣α[τ —]	— possessions —
2	[—]ασοι ε̃ δακ[—]	
3	[— ἀμέ (?)]ραις. αἰ δέ κα [—]	— days (?). But if —
4	[—]ται προϜει̣π̣[—]	— tell beforehand —
5	[— αἰ δ]ẹ́ κ' ἀποϜειπ[—]	— but if he denies (?) —
6	[— μα]ίτυρε[ς —]	— witnesses —

These appear to be procedural regulations.

G94. *c*.450–400

Much of this small stone has been erased, leaving only four lines of writing at the bottom.

1	[—] κ' ὁ ἀποδιδο[—]	— the one who gives back —
2	[—] οἰ ὀνιόμε[νοι —]	— those who buy —
3	[— Ϝ]είπει πρὶν . [—]	— declare before —
4	[—]ι ὅτι κρ[—]	

G95. *c.*450–400

A small stone with five lines of writing.

2	[—] ἄγεν καὶ τὸ ἀργύρ̣[ιον —]	— to bring, and the money —
3	[—] κ' ἀνατρεκιδδέτο ὀ[—]	?
4	[—]ạρκος πρὸ ἐπιδομα[—]	— build upon (?) beforehand —

3 For no apparent reason, there is a space of about a letter between the *epsilon* and the *tau* at the end of ἀνατρεκιδδέτο.

4 ἐπιδομα[—]: the verb is unknown in Crete but may be related to Attic ἐπιδωμάω.

3 The meaning of this verb is unknown; see Bile 145 n. 288.

G96. *c.*450–400

A small stone with parts of eleven lines of writing.

3	[— ϝερ]γασία [—]	— [field (?)]work —
4	[— ἀπολ]είποντα [—]	— leaving behind (?) —
9	[— ϝε (?)]ἴπατο [—]	— said (?) —
10	[— ἀ]πέλιπε [—]	— left behind —

4 ἀπολ]είποντα: G (cf. 10), but ϝ]είποντα or a compound is also possible; cf. 9 (the verb has both a first and second aorist).

G97. *c.*450–400

A small stone with parts of six lines of writing.

5	[—] προτέτ[αρτον —]	— on the fourth day before —
6	[—] στέγα [—]	— house —

G98. *c.*450–400

A small stone with traces of eleven lines of writing.

2	[—]ειασι τô κσε[νίο —]	2 — the foreigners' —
7	[— ἄλλ (?)]ον̣ πρὸ το[ύτο (?) —]	7 — another (?) for him (?) —

G99. *c.*450–400

A small stone with a few letters from four lines.

2	[—] πλία δ[ὲ μέ —]	— but not more (?) —

G100. *c.*450–400

A tiny stone with a few letters from four lines.

2	[—]ον πλὰν τ[—]	— except —
3	[—] κοῖλον ạ̓[—]	— hollow —

3 G suggests this may be the name of a place ('the hollows'), and compares *IC* 4.182.10.

G101. *c*.450–400

A tiny stone with parts of three lines.

1	[—] μ̣ὲ ϝισάμ̣[εν (?) —]	— not to know (?) —
2	[— ὀμν]ὺς κριν[έτο —]	— let (the judge) swear an oath and decide —
3	[—] τôι πρι[αμένοι (?) —]	— to the buyer (?) —

1]ṿε G.
ϝισάμ̣[εν: G compares ϝισάμην (**G47**.20–1).
2 For this variation of the more common formulation—accusative participle with infinitive (*omnynta krinen*)—cf. **G72**.9.21.

G102. *c*.450–400

A small stone with parts of eight lines, with a space below the bottom line.

1	[—]τον περ[—]	
2	[—] ἐκς ἀγορ̣[âς —]	2 — from the agora —
3	[—] τίτας [—]	3 — *titai* (?) —
5	[— μα]ίτυρ̣ι̣ π[—]	5 — to the witness —
7	[—] ἐ̣νεκυ[ρ —]	7 — pledge —

2 ἐκς ἀγορ̣[âς: G suggests ἐκσαγοṿ[τ —]; only a short bit from the bottom of a vertical stroke of the seventh letter is visible.
3 Could also be [—]τι τâς.

G104. *c*.450–400

A small stone with parts of eight lines, with a space below the bottom line.

1	[— τâ]ς πυλậ[ς —]	— of the tribe —
3	[— κο]σμι[ον —]	— being *kosmos* (?) —

G106. *c*.450–400

A small block with the right edge of six lines of writing.

1	[—]ιαι̣	1–2 — houses —
2	στέγα[ι —]	
3	[—] αἴ κ' ο-	3–4 — if the claimants (?) —
4	ἰ ἐπι[βάλλοντες (?) —]	
5	[— δι]κάκσ-	5–6 — the judge (?) is to rule —
6	αι̣ τὸ[ν δικαστὰν (?) —]	

All the supplements are G's.

5–6 This is the same formula as in **G72** (e.g. 5.31), where the judge is required by law to give a certain ruling. Without a context, we cannot know whether the verb has the same sense here or is used more generally ('decide the case').

G107. *c*.450–400

A small block with the right edge of four lines of writing and slight traces of another column to the right.

1 ν τίτ̣αν ὀ [—]	1 — *titas* (?) —
2 [—]ιοτôν πα-	2–3 — being present —
3 ριόντον [—]	

---

1 Could also be [—]ντι τ̣αν ὀ [—]. For the *titas*, see on **G14g–p1**.

G110. *c*.450–400

A small block with traces of three lines from the left edge of a column on the right (A) and of two lines from the right edge of another column on the left (B).

A	
2 [— π]ατ̣έ-	— father —
3 ρα̣ [—]	
B	
1 καλêν̣ [—]	— to summon —

G112. *c*.450–400

One block with a few letters from nine lines of a column at the left side; the left edge has been chipped off, destroying about one letter per line in lines 1–4.

1 [— τ]έκν[α]	1–2 — male children (?) —
2 [ἔ]ρσεν̣[α —]	
3 [— τâ]ς Ϝο[ι-]	3–4 — of the house (?) —
4 [κ]ίας̣ [—]	

G136. *c*.450–400

A small block with parts of three lines of writing.

1 [—]ι ἆι ἔγρα[τται —]	— as is written —
3 [—] Ϝεκα̣στ[—]	— each —

Gortyn1–7

These texts have all been published since Guarducci's 1950 edition. All seven texts are inscribed boustrophedon.

FIG. 50.
Gortyn 1

Gortyn1 (*SEG* 23.585, Davaras 1960: 457–8, Bile no. 40, VER II.5). Archaeological Museum of Heraklion (Inv. no 289). Fifth century? FIG. 50

A block of stone with fragments of four lines found at Mitropolis. The words in lines 1–3 also occur in **G42**B13–14. The left edge of the text is preserved, but if lines 1–3 are an exact copy of **G42**B13–14, then about fourteen letters per line are missing on the right, Originally there was additional text above and below. The script appears to date to the fifth century.

1	[— ἐνεκ]ύρον δι[κά]δ[ηι —]	→	1	— whoever judges in cases of pledges —
2	[— α]ὔριον ἄπατ-			
3	ον ἤμ̣ην. *vac.* α[—]		2–3	— the next day there is to be immunity. *vac.* —
4	[—]τ̣ρα . [. .]ονς[—]			

4 After the *alpha* there are traces of an *epsilon* or perhaps a *digamma*, and then room for one or two letters.

The text in lines 1–3 replicates parts of **G42**B13–14, though the lines here would have been shorter. The relationship between the two texts is not certain. **G42**B14 ends with the words *apaton emen* followed by a space of about four letters, apparently marking the end of the inscription. The same words in **Gortyn1** are followed by a gap and then more text. Thus, if **Gortyn1** was a copy of **G42**B, it included (copies of?) other laws too. Alternatively, and perhaps more likely (see on **G81**), **Gortyn1** may be a different law which happens to contain a similar provision for immunity if someone judges on the same day or the next.

Gortyn2–7, together with a one-word dedication not included here (see Bile no. 14 = Magnelli 2008: no. 1) and some twenty-five later texts and fragments, were all published, several for the first time, in Magnelli 2008 (= M). **Gortyn2–7**

are written boustrophedon and are probably from the fifth century. They are all currently in the storeroom of the Italian School in Agii Deka.

Because they are not well known, we supply more epigraphical information for these texts than for other similar fragments from Gortyn.

Gortyn2 (*SEG* 58.979, Magnelli 2008: no. 2). Fifth century? Italian School, Agii Deka (Inv. no. GO 6171). FIG. 51

A small fragment, 0.065 x 0.22 m, with parts of three lines found near Mitropolis.

FIG. 51. GORTYN2

[—]τ̣ει[—] →
[—]κ̣ατακρέ[θ(θ)αι —] — use —
[—]ν̣ δ̣ε τ̣[—]

1 The bottom tip of a vertical stroke of the initial letter is visible.

2 κατακρέ[θαι = καταχρῆσθαι, 'use' (completely or for a purpose); cf. **G80**.6, where the verb refers to using a fine for a specified purpose. The second *alpha* is clear (pace M). The infinitive (suggested by M) is only one possibility; in **G80**.8 the form is κατακρέσαιτο.

3 The *nu* could also be a *mu*; the *delta* could also be an *alpha*; the top horizontal stroke of the fourth letter is clear; this rules out M's suggestion πλίο]ν δὲ [μή.

2 In **G80**.4–8 *katakrethai* refers to using a fine for certain purposes; it may have the same sense here.

Gortyn3 (*SEG* 49.1221, Magnelli 2008: no. 3). Fifth century? Italian School, Agii Deka (Inv. no. GO 6613). FIG. 52

[—]δ̣ . [—] ←
[—]λοντο[—]
[—]δ̣ερ̣ . . . [—]
[—] . ε̣ . τ̣αιδ[—]

[—]ιεν̣ται[—]	
[—]μ̣ βολᾶι[—]	— council (?) —
[—]ρηιοσ[—]	
[—]δ̣εκ̣οδι[—]	
[— τὰ]ἐγραμ[(μ)ένα —]	— written —
[—]νος̣ μ[—]	
[—]ρ̣αι[—]	

Fig. 52. **Gortyn3**

1 Traces could be *delta* or *alpha*.

3 The lower left corner of a *delta* or possibly an *alpha* is visible for the first letter.

4 There are traces of a letter before *epsilon*, possibly an *omicron*. The stone is damaged after the *epsilon*; there may not be room for a letter there. Only the bottom of the vertical stroke of the next letter is visible; it could be *tau* or *rho*.

M mistakenly reads *Τ̣ΑΔΙ*[—], but *Τ̣ΑΙΔ*[—] is certain (see Fig. 52). Perhaps τ̣ᾶι δ[—].

5 ιεσται M; he suggests πλ]ίες τᾶι. But the third letter is almost certainly a *nu*; perhaps -ίενται (or -ι ἐν τᾶι?).

6 The first letter is either *mu* or *nu*; phonologically either is possible (see Bile 126). συ]μ- (συ]ν-) or ἐ]μ- (ἐ]ν-) are the likely supplements (see below).

M adds *epsilon* (undotted!) after the final *iota*, but there is no trace of any letter on the stone or in his photograph.

7 [—]ρηιοσ[—]: after the *san* M reads an *iota*, but no traces of any letter are visible; a *vacat* is possible. M suggests reading ἀνδ]ρήιο σί[τησιν, but the first word could also be ἀγ]ρήιο (cf. **G9***b*) or a subjunctive verb form (cf. παρῆι in **G41**.5.5, καθαίρει in **G76**B4) followed by ὅς or ὁ σ[—].

8 The third letter is very difficult, but the upper oblique of a *kappa* may be visible. There is no trace of and not enough room for *nu*, read (undotted) by M, who suggests restoring (ἐσ)πρά]δεν ('exact payment'). With *kappa* we may have αἰ] δέ κ' ὁ δι[καστὰς vel sim.

9 τὰ] ἐγραμ[(μ)ένα M.

11 Initial *rho* is likely but not certain.

M speculates that this may be a fragment of a law regulating contributions to the *andreion* to be used for the *sitēsis*, or common meal; but he recognizes the hypothetical nature of his restorations and in our view there is good reason to question all of them (see e.g. above, notes on 6, 7).

6 The letters could represent a form of *symbola* or *symbolaion* (M), perhaps referring either (if the former) to contributions to a common meal (M) or (if the latter) to an agreement. But they are probably better read as *em* (or less likely *sym*) *bolai* ('in the council'). M objects that *bola* is not securely attested at Gortyn before the first century, but it may occur at **G23**.4, it is certain at Axos in the sixth century (**A9**.13), and it appears in a mid-fifth-century treaty between Knossos and Tylissos, from Argos (*IC* 1.8.4, line 45); see Introd. 4B2. Thus, there is more contemporary support for *em bolai* than for either *symbola* or *symbolaion*, which are not attested anywhere in Crete (note, however, *synbolētra* in **Elt2**.6, meaning uncertain).

7 M suggests that there is a reference here to the *andrēion* (men's club, cf. **G4**.4, **G75**B7–9); this is possible, but other restorations are possible, including *agrēion* (gathering place, cf. **G9**a–m). He also suggests that a form of *sitēsis* be restored, though this term occurs nowhere else in inscriptions from this period.

Gortyn4 (*SEG* 49.1222, 58.980, Magnelli 2008: no. 4). Fifth century? Italian School, Agii Deka (Inv. no. GO 6614). Fig. 53

Previously published in Magnelli 1999: 149–54. The stone, 0.23 x 0.215 m, was found near Mitropolis; it is broken on the right, but the join is clean and most of the preserved letters are clear.

FIG. 53.
GORTYN4

[— δ]υοδε̣[κα —]	→	— twelve (?) —
[—]α̣τοπορ[—]		
[—]πονιο[—]		— says (?) —
[—]α̣ μή· αἰ δ[έ —]		— not; but if —
[— κ]α̣[τ]ιστα[—]		— pay —

---

1 [— δ]υοδε̣[κα M. The trace of a bottom horizontal stroke, possibly an *epsilon*, is visible after the *delta*. The number could be δύο, followed by either δέ or a noun (δύ' ὀδελόνς); but δυόδεκα seems more likely.

2 The bottom tip of a diagonal stroke is visible before the *tau*, possibly *kappa* or *alpha*. M suggests that we should restore either τô πορ[ίμο (cf. **G80**.6, where the sense is uncertain) or πορ[τί preceded by, e.g., δικαδδέ]το, as in **G72**.9.30. πορ[τί is far more likely, and if the first visible letter is *alpha*, then perhaps we should restore δικακσ]άτο πορ[τί.

2–3 M suggests connecting these lines: δικαδδέ]το πορ[τὶ τὰ || ἀπο]πονιό[μενα. This is attractive, but it would mean that only 3–4 letters are missing on the left, and this would make it very difficult to restore 4–5, since the shortest likely supplement, νικαθε͂ι, would be too long.

3]πονιο[Some form of *ponen* or *apoponen*, referring to the statements of litigants or witnesses respectively, is almost certain; see notes on **G72**.1.14 and 19.

4 The lower part of a diagonal stroke before *mu* is clear, very likely an *alpha* (read by M 2008 but not by M 1999).

5 The triangular top of a letter (*alpha* or *delta*?) is visible at the beginning of the line, followed by a space where no traces remain. This would be consistent with some form of the verb κατίστημι, which is the likely restoration in any case. κ]ạ[τ]ιστά[το (M) or κ]ạ[τ]ιστά[ντον are possible.

These meager remains may perhaps contain procedural regulations—payment of a certain amount (twelve), ruling according to the testimony, payment again. M (comparing **G72**.9.49–51) suggests that we may have part of a commercial law, but all the terminology here is common and could occur in many different kinds of laws.

Gortyn5 (*SEG* 58.981, Magnelli 2008: no. 5). Fifth century? Italian School, Agii Deka (Inv. no. GO 354). Fig. 54

A rather long block of stone, 0.26 x 0.505 m, with letters comparable to **G63** and **G64** (so M). The right edge of the stone is the right edge of the writing, which originally began above and continued to the left and perhaps below. M gives no information where it was found.

[—ἐπισ]πένσαιτο ἀν̣ε̣[—]	←	should accept as a promise
[—] . αι τοῖς Γορτ-		2–3 to the Gortynians
υνί[οις —]		
[—]α[—]		
[—]ι[—]		
[—]ο[—]		

---

1 The first nine letters are clear, but after the second *alpha*, traces of letters are faint. M reads Α̣ΥΕ̣[, but there does not appear to be room for *lambda* followed by *upsilon*. Comparing the *nu* at the beginning of this line, we think Ν̣Ε̣[is more likely. αν̣ε̣[would allow ἀνέρ or some form of ἀνελε͂ν as possible supplements.

2 The trace of the top of a curved stroke (*iota*, *omicron*, *pi*?) may be visible before the *alpha*.

---

1 *Epispendo* occurs six times in **G72** (*epispensaito* in **G72**.6.13–14) with reference to promising property to guarantee a future obligation (see on **G72**.6.11). The simple verb *spendo* is also possible here, though it occurs only once (in the active) with reference to the city of Datala making a promise to Spensithios (**Da1**A1). M suggests it may be followed by some form of the verb *allyomai*, but the letters he reads are doubtful (see above, n. ad 1).

2 'The Gortynians' are mentioned in several inscriptions (**G23**; **G62**; **G78**; **G80**; **G10**?) and in the singular in **G63**.3; see Introd. 4B1.

FIG. 54.
GORTYN5

Gortyn6 (*SEG* 58.982, Magnelli 2008: no. 6). Fifth century? Italian School, Agii Deka (Inv. no. GO 6357). FIG. 55

A small diamond-shaped fragment, 0.375 x 0.36 m, with clear letters, found near Mitropolis.

[—]σ[—] →	
[—]γαι[—]	— land (?) —
[—] . ὄτι α[—]	— that (?) —
[—]κρεθ[αι —]	— use —
[—] . ικα[—]	
[—]ο[—]	

2 There is a fairly large space before the *gamma*. M sees the tip of the top stroke of a letter, which he thinks is probably an *iota* or *upsilon*; he suggests reading τᾶι γᾶι. We cannot see any such stroke. There may be a *vacat* here, though there are fairly large spaces between letters elsewhere on the stone (e.g. between *iota* and *kappa* in line 5).

3 There appears to be a long vertical stroke just at the edge of the stone before the *omicron*, but whether or not this is part of a letter is unclear. The most likely letter is *eta*, but the *epsilon* in line 4 indicates that *eta* is not used at this time. The stroke may thus be a dividing line, in which case a *vacat* is unlikely in line 2, since *vacat* and dividing lines are not otherwise found on the same inscription, at least not at Gortyn.

ὄτι as a conjunction is usually followed by a particle (κε, δέ, μέν); the only other example where it is followed by a word beginning with *alpha* is ὄτι ἄγει (**G72**.1.6), and some form

FIG. 55.
GORTYN6

of ἄγω is certainly possible here (M), but many other words are also possible, as is the relative pronoun ὅτι.

4 κρεθ[(θ)αι, M (cf. **G72**.2.35, 11.19, 12.8), but the tip of a diagonal stroke, consistent with *alpha*, may be visible after the *theta*. κατακρέθαι (cf. **G80**.6, 8; **Gortyn2**.2) is also possible; for the compound, see on **Gortyn2**.2.

5 The top bit of a diagonal stroke is visible for the first letter, consistent with *delta* or *alpha*; either would leave room for many possible restorations.

If we read *gai* with or without an article in line 2 (cf. **G42**B2; **G64**.5), then this text has something to do with land, though not necessarily with disputes concerning the distribution or allotment of plots of land (M).

Gortyn7 (*SEG* 49.1223, Magnelli 2008: no. 7). Fifth century? Italian School, Agii Deka (Inv. no. GO 6569). FIG. 56

First published in Magnelli 1999: 154–60 and (more briefly) in Magnelli 2001: 626–7 (*SEG* 51.1136, where the earlier publication is not noted). A block, 0.22 x 0.35 m, with six lines of writing that probably continued in all directions. Found in a wall of the Praetorium baths.

[—]ενα[—] ←

[— τ]ομ πριαμε̣[νον —] — the buyer(s) —

[— κα]ταθέμενος̣ [—]	— the one(s) who accept(s) as security —
[—κ]αρπομε̣νοε[—]	— produce (?) —
[—]εο̣ ἒ μάν α[—]	— verily (?) —
[—]τ̣ορο[—]	

G. 56. Gortyn7

1 M reads εμα̣, but both the *nu* and the *alpha* are quite clear.

2 There are faint traces of the vertical stroke and the bottom horizontal stroke of the *epsilon*.

3 M reads the last letter as a *nu*, but *san* is equally possible.

4 [— τô κ]αρπô μὲν ὀ ε[—] M who, perhaps correctly, prefers this reading to [—κ]αρπομένο ε[—] (from καρπόομαι, 'enjoy the produce of'), which is not attested in Crete. The stone is damaged at the sixth letter and there is only a slight trace (if that) of the top bar of the *epsilon*.

5 The second letter is an *omicron* or perhaps a *theta*, although traces of a crossbar (if any) are very faint. In either case, although εμαν could be an aorist first person singular verb ending, such a form is highly unlikely in a legal text, and another suggestion of M — that the middle letters represent ἒ μάν (= ἦ μάν, cf. **G51**.9; **G75**A9 = **G81**.12)—seems more likely.

6 The end of a horizontal mark is visible at the top of the line to the left of the first *omicron*, though it may be a mark of later damage to the stone rather than a letter. If it is a *tau*, we may perhaps restore τετόρον ('four', cf. τέτορες in **G4**.2). If it is not a letter, then M's

suggestion ἄν]ορο[ς is possible but so are other restorations, e.g. ὀμόρον (**G81**.2), κορôι (**Elt2**.6), μόρο (**Da1**A14), etc.

M suggests reading *anoros* ('underage') in line 6 and compares the regulations concerning an underage heiress in **G72**.8.36–9.24. But other restorations are possible (see above, n. ad 6), and all we can say is that the law seems to concern produce.

Site

The Early Iron Age town of Knossos was located in the vicinity of the Bronze-Age palace and appears to have been continuously inhabited as a strongly nucleated settlement from prehistoric times until *c.*600 (Introd. 2A3). There is a gap in the material record, however, during the period *c.*600–525; whether this gap is real, and what its implications might be if it is, remain uncertain (Introd. 2C).

Very little is known about the late archaic and classical polis-town. The civic center is suspected to have been in the vicinity of the Roman Civil Basilica, *c.*0.5 km. to the northwest of the Bronze-Age palace, where architectural blocks bearing the dipinti text of a third-century law were found (*IC* 1.8.5). Three early sanctuaries have been excavated: a fifth-century (and earlier?) sanctuary (of the goddess Rhea?) above the ruins of the South Propylaion of the Bronze Age Palace (Evans 1928: 3–5; Coldstream 2000: 284–8; cf. Prent 2005: 261, B.18); the sanctuary and temple of Demeter south of the Bronze Age Palace on Lower Gypsadhes Hill (Coldstream 1973a); and a late archaic sanctuary and shrine (of Glaukos?) west of the Bronze Age palace (Callaghan 1978). Deposits of archaic (excluding the *c.*600–525 gap) and classical material, but no architecture, have been found in the Stratigraphical Museum excavations (Warren 1984–5), above the Unexplored Mansion (Sackett 1992: 6–8), to the southwest of the Minoan Palace (Coldstream and Macdonald 1997), and on both sides of the Royal Road (Coldstream 1973b). The very rich cemeteries appear to have been abandoned *c.*630 (Coldstream and Huxley 1999: 294–6). Kotsonas 2002 discusses the mortuary evidence from Knossos within the context of a broader, central Cretan pattern of late seventh-century abandonment of cemeteries (Introd. 2A1). For an overview of the archaic and classical remains of the urban center, see Hood and Smyth 1981; Coldstream and Macdonald 1997; Coldstream 1999, 2000. For a brief discussion of the territory of Knossos, see Perlman 2004b: 1169–70.

Text

In addition to **K2**, several fragments of epichoric inscriptions, too small to determine if they record laws, come from the area of the town (Jeffery 1949: 35–7; *SEG* 27.629; and at least one unpublished fragment). All are inscribed on fragments of limestone blocks that probably come from the walls of buildings and date to the late sixth century at the earliest. For the fifth-century agreement of Knossos, Tylissos, and Argos (M&L 42), which we do not include, see Preface n. 2 and Introd. 7E2.

FIG. 57. Plan of Knossos

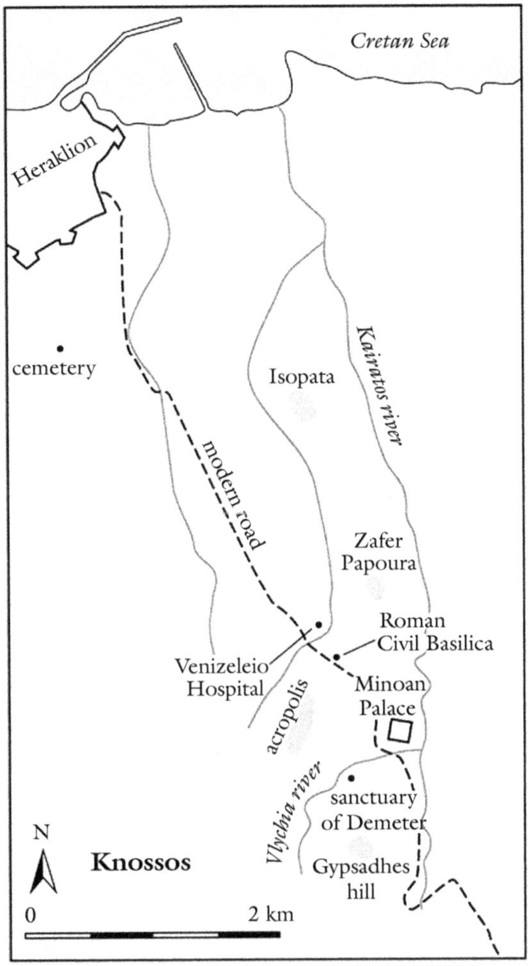

K2 (VER II.39). *c.* 500? Current location unknown

Three lines of text inscribed boustrophedon from the right on a limestone block. The block appears to be complete; the text continued onto contiguous blocks to the right and left. We cannot determine if the text began above this block or continued below it.

[— δα]ρκμὰς | κατισ[τα —]	←	— pay [X-number of] drachmas —
[— αἰ δέ κα] μὴ ’στείσο[ντι —]		— [and if]they do not pay the fine —
[— δαρ]κμὰς | κατι[στα—]		— pay [X-number of] drachmas —

1 κατισ[τα —]: from καθίστημι. If the subject is the same as the subject of ’στείσο[ντι] (line 2), then either 3rd pl. imp. κατισ[τάντο] or the inf. κατισ[τάμεν].

2 ’στείσο[ντι] = ἐκτείσωσι (see Dialect 22).

Site

Ancient Lyktos[418] was located at the far northeast of the 'High-Pediadha', a fertile upland region (250–1000 m. alt.) of hills, plains, and valleys extending south from the lowland coastal strip between Knossos in the west and Malia in the east (Panagiotakis 2003). The urban center of Lyktos is thought to have occupied the summit of a ridge on the northwestern shoulder of the Lasithi massif (Perlman 2004b: 1175–7), although the meager archaeological traces of an early town found there prompted van Effenterre and Gondicas 1999 to conclude that the archaic and classical polis was not organized around a single nucleated settlement but was made up of a number of small villages. The earliest evidence for occupation on the ridge appears to date to the late Geometric or early Archaic period. Buildings of the late seventh or early sixth century and the period *c.*450–400 have been excavated on the ridge (Platon 1957: 336; Alexiou 1971: 496–7), and a seventh-century cemetery has been excavated below near the modern village of Lyttos (formerly Xidas) (French 1993: 72; Rethemiotakis 1986).

In contrast to the meager archaeological evidence for the archaic and classical polis-town, the literary traditions concerning early Lyktos are abundant. In Greek epic, Lyktos was the home of Koiranos, the charioteer of Meriones (*Iliad* 17. 611), and was associated with the cave where Rhea took Zeus to conceal him from his father (Hesiod, *Theog.* 477–84). Later tradition, first attested in Ephorus and Aristotle, maintained that the Spartans had colonized Lyktos.[419] According to Spartan tradition, Lycurgus modeled his reforms after the laws of Minos, which were still used by the Lyktian descendants of the pre-Spartan inhabitants of the region (Perlman 1992). Strabo 10.4.7, C476 recorded that Lyktos and Gortyn for a time superseded Knossos as the foremost cities of Crete. If this is true, a likely time for the emergence of Lyktos as a leading power on the island is the sixth century.

The territory of Lyktos probably extended north to the coast. Sometime after *c.*183 BCE Lyktos and the coastal polis of Chersonesos united politically; the members of the conjoined state were thereafter referred to in official documents as 'the polis of those who inhabit Lyttos-by-the-sea and the polis of those who inhabit upper Lyttos'.[420] Viviers 1994: 252–3 understood the reference to 'those (who come) from above' in **L1** as evidence that the coastal and upland communities were linked far earlier. The border of Lyktian territory to the mountainous south is less

[418] Lyktos is the earlier spelling; in later literary and epigraphic texts the spelling is Lyttos (see Kaczynska 2001). We use Lyttos in referring to the modern village and Lyktos in referring to the ancient polis. The name means 'high place'.

[419] Ephorus *FGrH* 70 frags. 147–9; Aristot. *Pol.* 1271b28–30; on these traditions, see Malkin 1994: 73–83.

[420] e.g. *IC* 1.19.3A8–10; on the conjoined state, see Chaniotis 1996: 430–2.

certain. The highlands to the south and southeast must have served as summer pasture for Lyktian livestock (cf. **Lyktos1B**). The nature of Lyktian interest in the important sanctuaries of Zeus in the Psychro cave at the southwest of the Lasithi plateau and of Hermes and Aphrodite at Kato Syme Viannou high up on the southward-facing slope of the Lasithi massif is uncertain.[421] The claim of the fourth-century geographer Ps.-Skylax 47 that Lyktos extended 'on both sides' has been understood to mean that its territory extended from the north coast to the south coast (Viviers 1994: 252–9). If so, by the fourth century Lyktos had absorbed several ancient communities, including that of the Dataleis, that lay to its south (see **Lyktos1B** and Datala Site).[422]

Texts

We include six of the seven epichoric inscriptions that appear in *IC* 1[423] and one later discovery (**Lyktos1**).[424] Three of these seven inscriptions are part of the epigraphic collection of the Archaeological Museum of Heraklion (**L2**, **L4**, **Lyktos1**). For the rest, whose location is unknown, our texts are based on Guarducci, who autopsied **L2**, **L3**, and **L6**, and on the unpublished notebooks of Halbherr and De Sanctis, compiled during the period 1884–1913. We include below the facsimile drawings from these notebooks when they differ from the drawings of Guarducci.

L1–6 were found in or near the modern village of Lyttos, located a short distance to the southwest of the presumptive polis-town; several had been reused in the walls of village houses (**L1**, **L5**, **L6**). **L1–3** and **5–6** are likely to have come originally from walls rather than free-standing monuments. The blocks bearing **L3** (A and B) and **L4** are both inscribed on two contiguous faces. **L3** is probably a corner block from a wall. The side of **L4** with the as yet unpublished text (see below) appears to have had a molding along its upper edge. **Lyktos1A** and **1B** are inscribed on an ionic capital, perhaps from a small free-standing votive monument. The letter forms of **L4** and **Lyktos1A** and **1B** and the masonry work on both blocks (the upper surfaces in particular) are very similar.

All of the inscriptions included here use a vertical line for word-division, suggesting a date for them no later than the early fifth century (Introd. 3D1). Jeffery 1990: 314 dates **L1** to *c.*550–525 and the others to *c.*500.

The masons of Lyktos used four signs for o: a circle, a circle with a central dot, two concentric circles, and two concentric circles with a central dot. Bile 96 n. 95

[421] Prent 2005: 169–70, 572–6, 609–10; Erickson 2002. Kritzas 2000 suggests that Lyktos controlled the sanctuary at Kato Syme Viannou during the Hellenistic period.

[422] Viviers 1994 identifies the ancient settlement at Aphrati as Datala and dates the absorption of the Dataleis to the sixth century. Erickson 2002 prefers the fourth century.

[423] We omit *IC* 1.18.7, no single word of which is discernible.

[424] We know of one epichoric inscription from Lyktos that remains unpublished (Archaeological Museum of Heraklion, Inv. no. 409). It is inscribed on the same block as **L4**. See ad loc.

concludes that these seem interchangeable, but in most cases the latter two appear to represent ō, a diphthong, a glide (e.g. before *digamma*), or a contraction. We therefore transcribe these with ⊙ and interpret the letter as ō. Also of note is the sign Ξ (for Phoenician *samekh*?) in **L4**.

L1 (VER I.45). *c*.550–525. Current location unknown. FIG. 58

Three lines of text inscribed between horizontal guidelines on a limestone block. Lines 1–2 begin at right, the only certain example of archaic paragraphing at Lyktos.[425] The text continued to the right and the left, and perhaps also above and below.

FIG. 58. L1 (drawing after Halbherr 1884a: 78)

[—] . . ϵς̣| γ[*c*.3] ὄζοι ἄν⊙θϵν | γα[—]	←	— those from above —
[—]ϵ [π]ρ⊙Ϝϵι[π]έμϵν | ἢ αὐτô̂ν | ἢ [—]	←	— declare, either of them or —
[— αἰ δέ (?)] κ̣' ἀ̣μϵύσονται | ἀμπότϵρο[ι —]	→	— if (?)] both exchange —

Unless otherwise indicated:

H= Halbherr 1884a: 78; Comparetti and Halbherr 1888: 171–2; Halbherr *ap.* Comparetti 1893: 431–2.

1 G records a vertical stroke followed by an oblique stroke to the right of the *epsilon*; H records only the vertical.

ϵς̣| γ: the drawings of G and Jeffery 1990: pl. 60.15 record a vertical stroke that extends almost all the way up to the horizontal guideline, unlike the *taus* in lines 2 and 3. H's drawings record only the lower portion of the vertical. G (followed by VER) reads the stroke as a *tau* and must therefore read the next letter as *alpha* (ϵστα), though there is no sign of a crossbar.

γα[—]: possibly a form of γâ, perhaps as part of a compound. VER suggest γά[πϵδον], citing **G64** Ϝοικόπϵδον ἐκσοι γâν.

ὄζοι = ὄσοι (see Dialect 13).

2 αὐτô̂ν: G's drawing records *omicron* (αὐτόν); despite the awkward construction, H's drawings with -⊙̂- are based on autopsy and so we prefer it here.

[π]ρ⊙Ϝϵι[π]έμϵν: The sense of 'beforehand' (προ) may or may not be present; e.g. **G72**.2.28; **G72**.11.50 (with comm.).

3 κ̣: all previous editors record ν̣, but the drawings record only the upper oblique stroke, so *kappa*, *mu*, and *upsilon* are also possible.

[425] Also found, it appears, in *IC* 1.18.7 (see Spratt 1865: ii plate I:12).

ἀμεύσονται = ἀμείψωνται.
ἀμποτέρο[νς] ‘if they exchange both’ is also possible, if less likely.

VER suggest that the law concerns disputes over land: land (*ga*?, line 1), declaration (2), and exchange (3), but too little survives for certainty.

1 Viviers 1994: 253–4 argues that ‘those from above’ implies the existence of ‘those from below’. He identifies the former as the residents of the upland nucleated settlement of Lyktos and the latter as the residents of Chersonesos (see above, Site).

3 The term ‘exchange’ occurs in our texts only here and in **G4**, where it is an alternative to purchase; see further Introd. 7B.

L2 (K 95, VER I.11). *c.*500. Archaeological Museum of Heraklion (Inv. no. 41)

Eight lines of text inscribed boustrophedon beginning at the right on a limestone block that was re-used in a wall of unknown date near the church of Agios Georgios atop the ridge of ancient Lyktos. It was broken on all edges when first recorded by Halbherr; it is now also broken in two fragments, with the loss of a few letters in the break.

[—] . οιη | ἀ̣[—] ←	
[—]σοιτο | η . ο[—]	
[—]ι ἢ ϙοσμιο[—]	— or (?) serving as *kosmos* —
[—]ι | παριοντο[—]	— are present —
[—] πολιατᾶν | η[—]	— of the citizens —
[—] δ’ ἀλᾶι θεῖε[ν (?) —]	— they should put (?) elsewhere —
[—]ιον | μὴ πημ[—]	
[—]α δ’ ἀλᾶι θε̣[ῖεν (?) —]	— they should put (?) elsewhere —

Unless otherwise indicated:

H = Comparetti and Halbherr 1888: 171–2 no. 1; Halbherr *ap.* Comparetti 1893: 433 no. 202;

C = Comparetti and Halbherr 1888: 171–2 no. 1; Comparetti 1893: 433 no. 202.

2 The second *omicron*, the lower tip of a vertical stroke that G records as word-division (but H records a τ̣) and the *eta* are lost in the break.

H records the lower tips of two oblique strokes between *eta* and *omicron*; G records an *alpha* in her drawing, but not in her text. Based on H’s drawing *alpha*, *gamma*, and *delta* are possible (*lambda*, contra H and G, is not likely).

3 H, noting the traces of two vertical lines, one between *iota* and *eta* and a second between *eta* and *koppa*, suggested that the first was a word-division and the second was a defect in the surface of the stone. Both appear to be defects. The texts of G and VER do not record either.

[—]ι ἢ: a word ending in -ιη is possible.

ϙοσμιο[—]: a form of the participle κοσμίον. Cf. **Lyktos1A5**; **G72**.1.51.

4–5 παριόντο[ν τ|ôν] πολιατâν C (cf. **G72**.10.35–6, 11.13–14); but it is not possible to determine how many letters are lost or even if these two terms belong to the same provision.

5 πολιατâν: πολιάταν is also possible. VER suggest [ἀλλο]πολιάταν. See **Lyktos1A1–2**.

6 The first *iota* is lost in the break.

7 The first *mu* is lost in the break.

C suggests μὴ 'πήμ[ην —] (= μὴ ἐπεῖναι) or μὴ πημ[αιν—].

8 -αι of ἀλâι is lost in the break.

L3 (K 96). *c*.500. Current location unknown. FIG. 59

Seven lines of text inscribed boustrophedon on two contiguous faces of a limestone block from the corner of a building (cf. **L4**). The corner edge is preserved; the lines wrap around at the corner on both faces (A3–4, B2–3) rather than continuing across both faces as they appear to do in **L4**. The upper edge of the block is broken; there is an uninscribed band below the final line on both faces, below which the lower edges may be preserved. We cannot determine how much text has been lost above or to the left or right. G identifies as 'A' the face with the preserved right edge (= B in Fig. 59). We follow Halbherr (Fig. 59) in identifying the face with the preserved left edge as 'A'. The final four letters on A (νιπα) yield no sense as a word ending (n. ad loc.), making it likely that this line continued on B (perhaps much further up). What survives on A may or may not be part of the same law as B.

A [—]ημεδ̣[.]	←		
. τον ἀλλ̣[ο —]		2	— the other —
[—] . τὸν Ἑρμ̣-		3–4	— Hermes or —
ε̣̂ν̣ ἢ ἐν . [—]			
[—]αντ̣ατε[.]			
[.]α[. .]ι | [—]			
[—] . νιπα[—]			
vacat			
B [—]ιοσιτεη[—]	←		
[— τôι δ]ικαστâ-		2–3	— to the judge for the —
ι ἰς τὰν | α[—]			
[—] . ασι . αια			
ια | η . ουο[—]			
[—]αιτο | ε			
. ι | τοι . ο . [—]			
vacat			

Doublet 1889 was the first to record **L3**. Comparetti 1893: 438 no. 204 bases his drawing on Doublet's. H = Halbherr 1913: 51.

FIG. 59. **L3** (drawing after Halbherr 1913: 51)

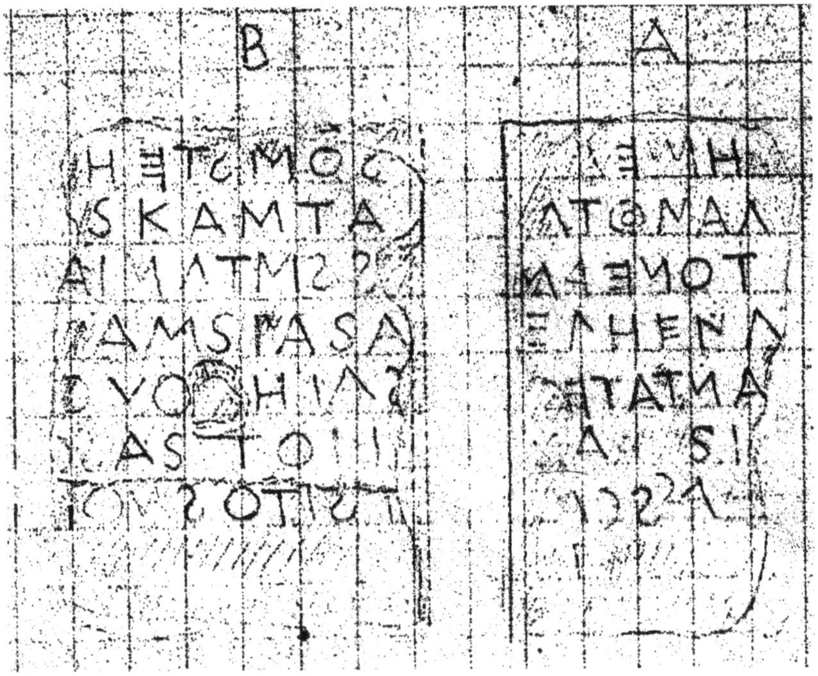

A

1 δ̣: Doublet 1889 and H appear to be certain of the right oblique of the *delta*, recording the other two strokes more faintly. There would be room for one more letter before the corner edge of the block.

2 H records the two oblique strokes of a triangular letter to the right of *tau*; G records a vertical word-division line.

λ̣: G records the lower tip of the left oblique stroke.

3 G records an oblique stroke to the right of *tau*.

μ̣: H and G record the first three strokes; *nu* and *san* are also possible.

3–4 [ν]α̣ τὸν Ἐρμ̣|ε̣̂ν̣ (?): the acc. of Hermes is spelled Ἐρμαον in **G51** and Ἐρμῆν in an agreement between Olous and Rhodes (*SEG* 23.547, late third century). For Ἐρμε͂ν, see *Kerameikos* III.C 9 (curse tablet, *c*.350).

4 ε̣: H and G record the three horizontal strokes; *eta* is also possible.

ν̣: H and G record the first two strokes; *lambda* is also possible; *gamma* (G) is unlikely.

H and G record two oblique strokes at the right edge of the block. G suggests *nu*, but the two oblique strokes do not resemble those of the other *nus*. *Alpha*, *delta*, or *gamma* are more likely.

5 τ̣: H; G records *rho*. We prefer *tau* because neither the string -αυρα- nor -ρατ- occurs epigraphically as part of a word and the particle ῥά for ἄρα does not occur in Crete.

6 α[..]ι: αοι G, but there appears to be room for two letters between *alpha* and *iota* in the drawings of G and H.

7 There is room for one letter before *nu*. H records no traces in the space; G records strokes that resemble a much later *pi*.

[—] . νιπα[—]: apart from the personal name Ἐνίπας, which is fairly common in Crete (*LGPN* I s.v.), we see no way to make sense of the string of letters without some following text.

B

2 There appears to be room for an additional letter at the right edge of the block, but a form of the noun δικαστάς or a compound e.g. ὀρπανοδικασταί (**G72**.12.7, 11–12), seems likely. Perhaps the damage depicted in the drawings of H and G was ancient and the space was left uninscribed.

2–3 [τôι δ]ικαστâι: [οἰ δ]ικασταί is also possible, but all other examples of δικαστάς (all from Gortyn) are singular; the plural occurs in ὀρπανοδικασταί (**G72**.12.7, 11–12).

4 H records a faint oblique stroke at the left edge; G records a small circle that is not consistent with a letter, and the lower part of a vertical stroke.

ασι . αια: in the space H records a vertical stroke and a short oblique stroke that almost meets the top of the vertical consistent with *lambda*; G records the vertical stroke and a second short vertical stroke to its right high in the letter space, but represents only the vertical stroke (as word-division) in her text.

5 η . ουο: H's drawing appears to represent a damaged area after the *eta*; G indicates that there was a letter in the space. In either case, the string of letters -ουο- is difficult.

6 Before the *alpha* H records traces of a circular letter and an *iota* facing the wrong direction.

7 H and G record the lower part of a vertical stroke at the right edge; G reads *tau*.

H records a very faint *nu* between the *iota* and the *omicron*; G reads *tau*.

H and G record a vertical stroke at the left edge.

The possible reference to Hermes (A3–4) may be connected with the sanctuary of Hermes and Aphrodite at Kato Syme Viannou; see above Site.

L4 (K 97). *c*.500. Archaeological Museum of Heraklion (Inv. no. 409). FIG. 60

Nine lines of text inscribed boustrophedon beginning at the left on a limestone block. Seven lines of a second, as yet unpublished, text are preserved on the contiguous face to the left of **L4**. It appears that the texts inscribed on the two faces belong to the same inscription, with the lines running across both faces.

The block was reused in a modern windmill near the ruins of ancient Lyktos, where the unpublished inscription was hidden from sight and unknown until the block was removed and brought to the Archaeological Museum of Heraklion in 1991. Before its reuse a decorative molding along the top of the face with the unpublished inscription was trimmed back. This molding does not appear to have continued onto the face with **L4**, suggesting that the face with the unpublished text was the 'front' of the block. There is an uninscribed space above the first line of **L4**; the right edge of **L4** is worked with a pointed chisel. The decorative molding and the treatment of the upper surface of the block suggest that it was

FIG. 60. L4, left (drawing after De Sanctis 1908–10: 56); right (drawing after Halbherr 1913: 16 no. 47)

originally part of a rather elaborate monument of some kind. The block bearing **Lyktos1** appears to have had a similar history.

The block is preserved at the top and broken at the bottom and at the left of the 'front' face, with an unknown number of letters lost below and at the left. The beginning of line 1 was inscribed on the molding of the 'front' and lost when the molding was trimmed back. A few letters (*c*.2–4) in every line are lost at the corner. **L4** appears to preserve the right edge of the text.

[*c*.2–4]⊙ι | ϙό̔ρ⊙- ι. | ὅ̈Ξοι [*c*.2–4]	→	1–2	— to a young man (?). As many as —
[*c*.2–4]ι̣. | ὀ ἀποδ- όμενο[ς *c*.2–4]		3–4	— the seller —
[*c*.2–4]ιοι | ὀ Λύ- κτιος | [*c*.2–4]		5–6	— the Lyktian —
[*c*.2–4]δ⊙ι. | ⊙̂νυ μὲν | αἰ ἀπ̣[*c*.2–4]		7–8	— In this way, if (?) —
[*c*.2–4]ι ἆ̣ ἤ̈γρατα̣- [ι —].		9–10	— what is written —

1 [τ]⊙̂ι is one of many possible restorations.

1–2 ϙό̔ρ⊙ι = *κούρῳ*. A second possibility is ϙ⊙ρ⊙ι = *χώροι/χώρῳ*. G prefers ϙοροί (*χοροί*), but the spelling with -⊙- appears to rule this out. See comm.

2 ὅΞοι = ὅζοι (ὅσοι); see Brixhe 1982: 213, who interprets Ξ as a Phoenician *samekh* used to represent the sound *dz* (see also Bile 145–6 n. 292). G interprets the letter as a *xi*.

3 ι̣: the tip of the upper loop is legible.

7 ⊙̂νυ = ὧδε: the form is Arcado-Cyprian; see Dialect 35; Bile 204–5. For the pronoun τôνυ, see also **Da1A8**, 10; **Ele11**.3, 4; **Lyktos1B** *passim*.

8 π̣: there appear to be two parallel curved lines. π̣ο̣ is possible, but the two lines are very close together. De Sanctis records only the *pi*; Halbherr 1913 records the left portion of ⊙; G records *pi* and the left portion of *omicron*.

9 α̣: the left oblique is faintly preserved.

η̣: the upper horizontal stroke is legible.

α̣: the left oblique is preserved. For the spelling ἤγραται, see **Elt2**.7.

1–2 ‘Young man’: the Greek word *qōrōi* could be the dative singular of either of two terms: ‘young man’ (*kouros*) or ‘place’/‘land’ (*chōros*). Neither is otherwise attested in the epichoric inscriptions from Crete, though a feminine form of the second (*chōra*) occurs in **G72**.4.34–5 in the sense of ‘country’ (as opposed to ‘city’). The term *koros* (‘dance’/‘dancer’/‘dancing ground’), which appears to be ruled out by the spelling (see note), occurs in **Elt2**.6, where it clearly refers to a place.

5–6 ‘The Lyktian’: this is one of the few occurrences of the ethnic in the singular in the epichoric laws from Crete (Introd. 4B1, with n. 167). It could be used here either to modify a noun (e.g. *o Lyktios* [*kosmos*], cf. **G80**.5–6) or on its own. All other examples of the use of the ethnic on its own occur in interstate agreements (**G63**, **G78**, and **G80**.9). It is uncertain if this use of the ethnic carries the political significance of ‘citizen’ or if it refers more generally to a member of the community without any implications concerning that individual’s civic status.

L5 (K 98). *c.*500. Current location unknown. FIG. 61

Twenty lines of text inscribed boustrophedon beginning at the right on a limestone block that was probably re-cut for use in a wall in a home in the village of Lyttos. It is not possible to determine how much text has been lost from the right, left, top, or bottom.

Some drawings of the inscription (e.g. Spratt 1865 II: 418 Tab. 1.11; Halbherr 1884b: 5 no. 2; Halbherr 1913: 49; Haussoullier 1885: 4–6 no. 6) record considerably fewer letters than do Halbherr’s later drawings that he made from a squeeze (Comparetti and Halbherr 1888: 172–4 no. 2; Halbherr *ap.* Comparetti 1893: 434–7 no. 203).

[—] . . ας κα διδ⊙[—]	←	— gives —
[—]μεν πεντήκο[ντα —]		— fifty —
[—]αι σὺν τôι ἀδε[—]		— with the —
[—] σὺν τοῖς ἰνε[—]		— with the —
[— π]αρέκσοντι | ὀ[—]		— they shall furnish —
[—]ς | ἐπάγεσθ[αι —]		— to introduce —
[—] ⟦μ̣ι̣ο̣ . .⟧ ⋈ ὀσ[—]		
[—]οντι | τρ[ί]ινς [—]		— three —

[—]ιʘ. | αἰ δέ κα πα[—]
[— τὸνς τ]όκα μαιτύρα̣[νς —]
[—]α̣μενος | τὸν ὀ[—]
[—] . | ὀτέρο | κυ[—]
[— ὀ]μ̣ʘμότας η . [—]
[—]ς τô Ϝοικέος̣ [—]
[—] σ̣υλέν | καὶ ὁ β̣ι̣[—]
[—]νεος | τοκ' ἐπυ[—]
[—]ι θυρὶς ἠγε̣τα̣[—]
[— δι]καίʘυς ἠμε[ν —]
[—]σθαι | σ̣[—]
[—]μεν δε . ο . ε . [—]

—. But if —
— [the] witnesses at the time —
— the —
— of whichever —
— the co-swearer —
— of the serf —
— to plunder and the —
— at the time —
— window frame (?) —
— are to be lawful —

FIG. 61. L5 (drawing after Halbherr 1913: 49)

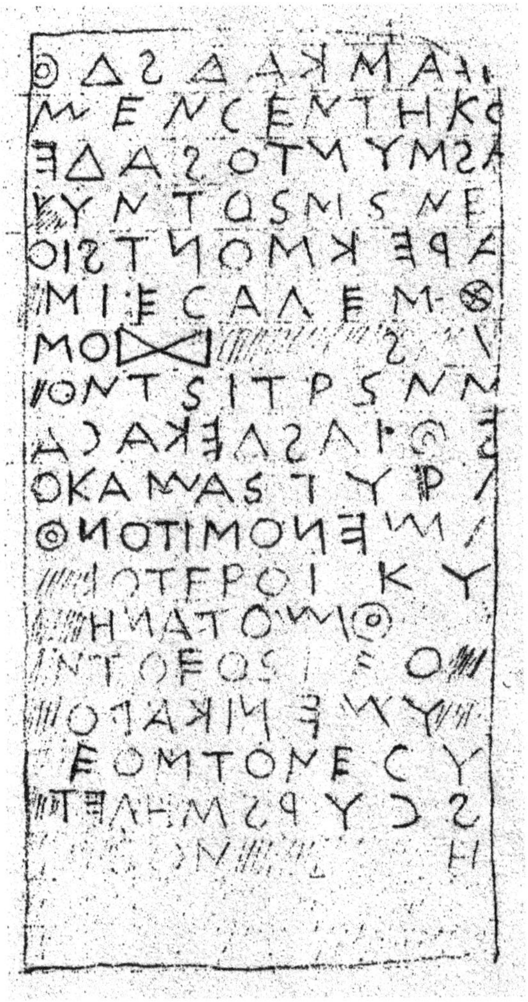

Unless otherwise indicated:

H = Comparetti and Halbherr 1888: 172–4 no. 2; Halbherr *ap.* Comparetti 1893: 434–7 no. 203; Halbherr 1913: 49 no. 20.

C = Comparetti and Halbherr 1888: 172–4 no. 2; Comparetti 1893: 434–7 no. 203.

1 Halbherr *ap.* Comparetti 1893 records the lower tips of two vertical strokes before the initial *alpha*; (σ)τας Haussoullier 1885, but according to C the squeeze does not confirm the *tau*.

3 ἀδε[—]: ἀδε[λπιôι] C.

4 τοîς ἰνε[—]: τοîσιν ἐ[—] C, τοîσι νε[—] G. Possibly ἰνε[κυράσταις] or ἰνε[κυράκσαις] 'guarantors'. For the spelling with *iota*, cf. **Axos1**.7–8 ἰνεκυράκ̣[σει].

7 [[μ̣ι̣ο̣ . .]]: drawings of Halbherr *ap.* Comparetti 1893 and G; possibly [—]μιου̣ς C.

For ⋈, see **Dr1** and **G72**.9.43.

8 τρ[ί]ιυς: see n. ad **G65**.11.

10 α̣: H records the left oblique stroke.

[τὸνς τ]όκα μαιτύρα̣[νς]: the singular is also possible.

11 α̣: H and G record the left oblique stroke.

12 Halbherr *ap.* Comparetti 1893 and G record an oblique stroke before the first word-division line; all drawings suggest there may be room for a letter after the second word-division line.

13 Halbherr *ap.* Comparetti 1893 records an oblique stroke to the left of *eta*; G suggests *nu* or *san*, but other letters are possible.

14 ς̣: H and G record the left oblique stroke.

15 σ̣: Halbherr *ap.* Comparetti 1893 and G record the left oblique stroke.

β̣ι̣: Halbherr *ap.* Comparetti 1893 and G record both letters faintly.

16 [—]νεος |: H's later drawings (see above) and G's show the *nu* and the word-division.

17 ε̣: Halbherr 1913.

α̣: Halbherr *ap.* Comparetti 1893 records the right oblique stroke. A passive verb is likely with θυρίς, possibly ἤγετ' ἀ[—].

19 υ̣: Halbherr *ap.* Comparetti 1893 and G record three oblique strokes consistent with *nu*, *san*, or possibly *mu*; νυντ[—] Haussoullier 1885; σὺν τ[—] C.

The law includes procedural language—'witnesses' (line 10), 'co-swearer' (13), and perhaps 'introduce' [a case] (6)—but we cannot determine its subject. References to 'plunder' (15) and 'window frame' (17) suggest that the law may possibly concern the theft of property, possibly involving a serf (14) in circumstances that would make this lawful (18). For the removal of valuable wooden frames from doors and windows, see Thucydides 2.14.

L6 (K 99). *c.*500. Current location unknown. FIG. 62

Ten lines of text (and traces of an eleventh above line 1) inscribed boustrophedon beginning at the left on a block of limestone that was reused in the doorway of a house in the village of Lyttos. The drawings of Halbherr, unlike that of G, indicate that the inscribed surface of the left third of the roughly rectangular block was illegible (either damaged or covered, e.g. with plaster). The text appears to have continued to the right and left, and perhaps also below.

G. 62. L6, right (drawing after Halbherr 1913: 0); left (drawing after Halbherr 1913: 69)

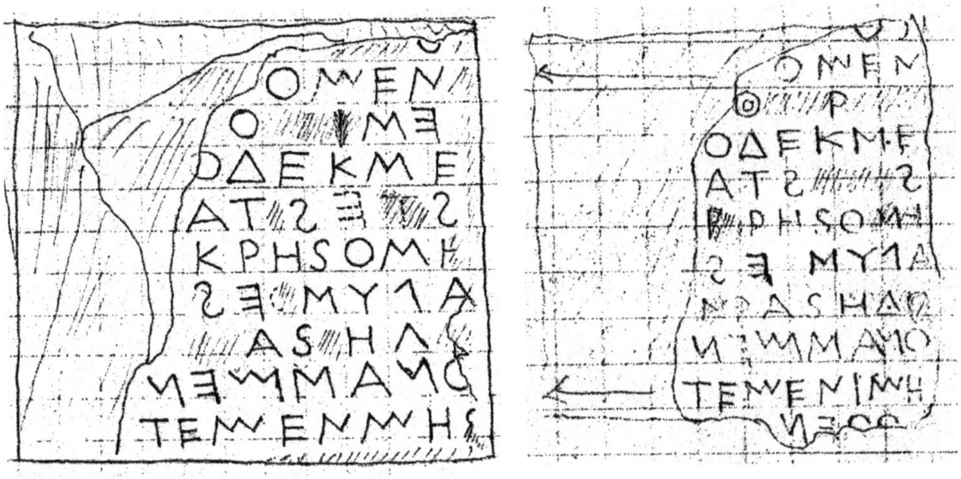

[—]ομεν . [—] →	
[—]ες | ṭο[—]	
[—]ο δὲ κσε[ν —]	— foreign (?) —
[—]ινει | τα[—]	
[—] κρῆιος ῃ[—]	— of the value (?) —
[—. αἰ δέ κ (?)]α λύσει [—]	—. But if (?)] he releases —
[—]ạν | ἇι ἤγ[ραπται — (?)]	— as is written (?) —
[—]ονας μὲν | [—]	
[—]τεμεν | μη . [—]	
[—]ọịẹν[—]	

Unless otherwise indicated, H = Halbherr 1913: 50 (H 50) or 69 (H 69).

H records traces of letters above line 1.

1 H 69 records faintly an oblique stroke after *nu*.

2 ṭ: G records the *tau*; H 69 has a blank space.

3 ὁ δὲ κσέ[νιος] or [τ]ô δὲ κσε[νίο]. Other possibilities include [—]ο δέκσε[ται] = δέξηται.

4 [—]ινει | τα[—] G; [—]ιτειτα[—] H 69.

5 κρῆιος: at Gortyn κρέος means 'thing' or 'value' (see n. ad **G72**.3.11–12), but it might mean something else here. Bile 318 asserts without argument that here only it means 'debt'.

ῃ: H 69 records the left vertical and the left bit of the horizontal stroke; G records the vertical stroke.

6 H 69 records the faint outline of the left portion of a circular letter between *san* and *epsilon*.

[— κ]α λύσει: [κατ]αλύσει is also possible.

7 ạν |: G's drawing records the left oblique of a triangular letter followed by *nu* and a word-division line; H 50 records strokes consistent with *nu*.

8 [—]*ονας*: *ὀ̣νᾶς* ('of the purchase') G. Other possibilities include [*μνάμ*]*ονας* or [*γνόμ*]*ονας*. Both occur otherwise only at Gortyn, the former only in the singular (**G42**B6; **G72**.9.32, 11.16–17); for the latter, see **G14**p–g2.

G records a vertical stroke (word-division?) at the left edge of the stone.

9 H 69 does not record the word-division line.

H 69 and G record a curved stroke (*iota*?) high in the letter space at the right edge of the block.

10 *ο̣ι̣ε̣ν*: H 50, G.

Lyktos1A and 1B (H. and M. van Effenterre 1985 [HMVE], *SEG* 35.991, K 87, 88, Bile 12, VER I.12). Laws concerning the treatment of foreigners (A) and the boundaries of pasture lands (B). *c.*500. Archaeological Museum of Heraklion (Inv. no. 425). FIGS. 63, 64, 65, 66, 67

Eleven lines of text on side **A** and fourteen on side **B**, both inscribed boustrophedon, beginning at the left on **A** and at the right on **B**. We do not know which text was inscribed first. The two texts are inscribed on the two long sides of an archaic ionic limestone capital (h: 0.303 m; w: 0.525 m; th: 0.0355 m), possibly votive in nature (Fig. 63.).[426] The capital does not appear to have been completed when the two faces were cut back for inscribing and the volutes completely removed.[427] The texts are complete at the top and on one side (the right side of **A**, the left side of **B**); one or possibly two lines may have been lost at the bottom of each.[428]

The two texts may have been inscribed at the same time (the letter forms are similar), but they are clearly separate: both begin with an enactment formula and they treat very different subjects.[429]

[426] The late sixth-century ionic votive capital from Paros with the elegiac distich commemorating Archilochus inscribed in the fourth century on its abacus provides a parallel. See Clay 2004: 28–9, 104 no. 1, plate 1.

[427] The collar between the column shaft and the capital appears to have been cut back only as far so as not to damage the column shaft, suggesting that after inscribing the capital remained in position atop a (presumably short) column. At a later date, what remained of the convex surface of the collar was cut back further, removing roughly half of the text from the center of **A**9–11 and **B**9–14. At the same time the block may have been trimmed at the bottom and left of **A** (right of **B**), removing all of the baluster together with several letters along the left edge of **A** (right edge of **B**). See Fig. 64. Cf. HMVE, who suggest that the use of the block as a column capital was secondary. This seems very unlikely.

[428] HMVE 158 estimate that 0.05 m may have been lost along the left edge of **A** (right edge of **B**).

[429] The two texts begin with lines running in the opposite direction. This might indicate that the mason regarded them as in some sense belonging together, so that the start of the second text continued the boustrophedon pattern from the final line of the first, but because the final lines are not preserved, this is just speculation.

Fig. 63. Capital

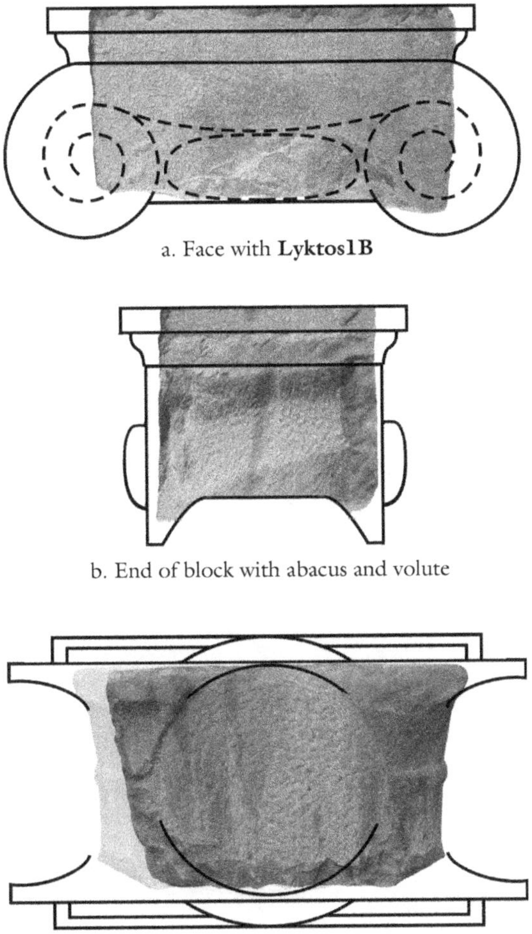

a. Face with **Lyktos1B**

b. End of block with abacus and volute

c. Bottom of block

A

[Θιοί. ἔϜ]αδε | Λυκτίοισι· | ἀλο- →
πολιάταν | ὅστις κα δέκσ[εται .]
[c.3–4]ε̣ν, | αἰ μὴ ὀσ⊙Ϝ̣υτός τε | καρτε-
ῖ | καὶ τὸνς Ἰτανίονς. | αἰ δέ κα [. . . .]
[. .]α̣ι | ἢ κοσμί⊙ν | ἢ ἀπόκοσμο[ς .]
[2–3]ρ̣ Ϝ⊙λᾶς | Ϝαδᾶς | ἐκατὸν λέβητ[ας . .]
[. . .]ει | ἑκάστ⊙ | ὅσος κα δέκσεται. | τ[c.3]
[c.5] δὲ | οἰ ἐσζικαι⊙τῆρες | ἐπ' ὅ τε [2–3]
[2–3]σεται. | αἰ̣ [5–6]ν̣ι̣⊙νται | πι̣[. . . . .]
[. . . . .]ρϜ⊙ιο̣[9–10]σ̣αμεν[1–2]
[2–3]κοσ[14–15]τ̣α̣ι̣ | τ̣[—]

1–4 [Gods.] The Lyktians decided. Whoever receives a foreigner is to [*c*.6–7], except insofar as he himself controls (them) and the Itanians.

4–7 But if [*c*.8] (he?), either a *kosmos* or an *apokosmos*, [*c*.3–4] of enactment of (the) council (?), 100 cauldrons [*c*.5] for each one as many as he receives.

7–9 [*c*.9] and the *eszikaiōteres* (are to) until [*c*.9–11].

9–11 If they [—].

FIG. 64. Phases of Use

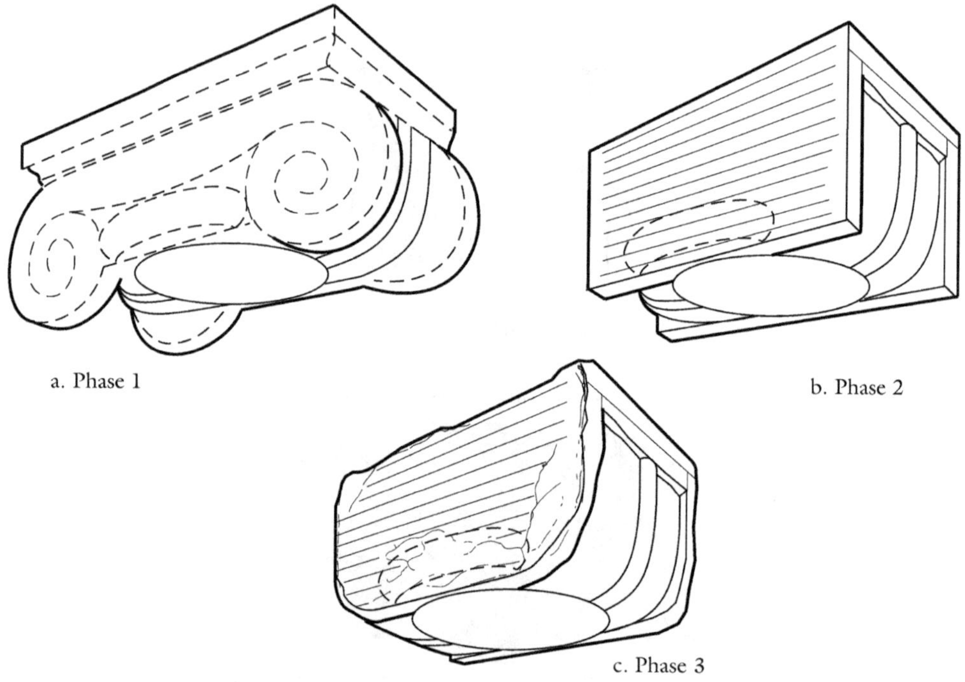

FIG. 65. Lyktos 1A

Chadwick (1987: 330) translates:[430] 'In the name of the gods. It was decreed by the Lyktians that anyone receiving an alien should be prosecuted, except for such number as he arrests and for the Itanians. But if either a magistrate or a non-magistrate should make the arrest, on account of the decree of the council he (i.e. the person receiving the alien) shall pay one hundred cauldrons for each person to the number that he receives. These the exactors, until such time as he ceases, except if they remit the penalty, shall swear before the overseer to pay . . .'

1–2 *ἀλοπολιάταν*: only here and (partly restored) in **Ele3**.1.

3 *ε̣*: the lower part of the vertical stroke and connecting bit of the lower horizontal are visible.

[*c*.3–4]*ε̣ν*: HMVE 173 propose many possible restorations, [*τράπ*]*εν*, [*μὴ συλ*]*ε̂ν*, [*λαγαί*]*εν*, [*ἐκσάγ*]*εν*, [*ἐκσέλ*]*εν*, [*φεύγ*]*εν*, [*ἔνδικον ἤμ*]*εν*, [*πράδδ*]*εν*, [*δαμιôμ*]*εν*, [*δικάδδ*]*εν*, several of which are too long for the available space. Chadwick 1987: 330 suggests [*Ϝέρ(ρ)*]*εν* 'to be prosecuted' (cf. *IvO* 2 *Ϝάρρεν*).

Ϝ̣: the upper horizontal and upper tip of the vertical stroke are visible.

ὀσ⊙Ϝ̣υτός = *ὄσω* (*ἀ*)*Ϝτός* (Bile 32); cf. Chadwick 1987: 330–1.

3–4 *καρτεῖ*: 'has control (over)'. Cf. *καρτερὸν ἔμεν* at Gortyn (**G72**.4.24–5, with further refs. in the comm. ad loc.).

4–5 Uncertainty about the restoration here is compounded by a similar uncertainty in 6–7 (see below). Here, either the ***kosmos*** and ***apokosmos*** are the subject of the missing verb, in which case [*δεκσετ*]*α̣ι* is likely, or the subject is understood from line 2 ('whoever receives') with the ***kosmos*** and ***apokosmos*** being the subject of the protasis that follows, in which case a different verb is almost certain, probably a more serious infraction leading to a more severe punishment. In the first case, the missing verb in 6–7 must specify paying (a fine); in the second case, it must specify exacting it.

5–6 [2–3]*ρ̣ Ϝ⊙λâς Ϝαδâς*: the genitive most likely depends on a preposition ending in *rho*. Chadwick (see above) suggests [*ὑπέ*]*ρ̣* 'on account of' (LSJ s.v. *ὑπέρ* AII4); [*πά*]*ρ̣* 'issuing from' (LSJ s.v. *παρά* AII2) is possible, although perhaps a letter too short.

6 *ρ̣*: the letter appears to be a *rho*, preserved in its entirety. HMVE read ϙ, arguing that the shape of the head does not appear to be as angular as the heads of the other *rhos*; but there is no significant difference in this respect between this *rho* and those in lines 3 and 8 (see FIG. 66). HMVE suggest [*ἐ*]ϙ*Ϝ⊙λâς* (= *ἐξουλῆς*) 'ejectment', but there are strong linguistic arguments against this (see Chadwick 1987: 331–2).

Ϝ⊙λâς = Attic *βουλῆς*? *β* for *Ϝ* occurs in **G80**.2 and is common in later inscriptions from Crete (Bile 118–19); but *Ϝ* for *β* is not otherwise securely attested on the island. For another possible example, see n. ad **Da1**B8.

---

430 We include Chadwick's translation here because his important 1987 study is not readily available.

FIG. 66. **Lyktos1A3**–8. (Comparison of *rhos*)

For *bola* without the article, see Introd. 4B2 (esp. n. 196)

ϝαδâς: gen. s. of *ϝαδά 'enactment' (ἀνδάνω); cf. ἅδος 'decree' (*Syll.*[3] 45.19; *IG* XII 8.263, line 8).

6–7 [*c*.5]ει: [τείσ]ει HMVE, but τίνω (uncompounded) is rare and is attested only in the middle in Crete (Bile 327–8). If a verb meaning 'pay' is required (see above on 4–5), [ἀποτείσ]ει may be possible, but [πράκσ]ει ('exact') is perhaps more likely.

7–8 τ[*c*.8]: the word-division to the left of the *tau* in line 7 and the δέ at the right edge of line 8 indicate that a single word at the start of a new sentence is lost. HMVE suggest a form of τηρεύω ('ensure') or τιτύϝω ('fine'). Chadwick 1987: 332 suggests τ[ούτο(ν)ς] (*sc*. λέβητας).

8 ἐσζικαιΘτῆρες: nom. pl. of the otherwise unattested *ἐκδικαιωτήρ. See Bile 144 n. 287.

8–9 Chadwick 1987: 333 (followed by VER) suggests ἐπ' ὅ τε [κα παύ]σεται; also possible are ἐπ' ὅτε [κα μὴ δέκ]σεται (HMVE) or ἐπ' ὅτε [κα πράκ]σεται.

9 αι̣: the left part of the upper loop of *iota* is visible.

ν̣ι̣: the upper part of the right oblique of *nu* is visible (*kappa* and *mu* are also possible); the left part of the upper curve of *iota* is visible.

αι̣ [5–6]ν̣ι̣ῶνται: either [κα 3–4] or [δε κα 1–2] are possible. HMVE suggest αἰ [δέ κ' ἀν]ν̣ι̣ῶνται = ἀρνῶνται 'but if they deny' (VER [ἀ]ν̣ι̣ῶνται). Chadwick 1987: 333 suggests αἴ [κα μὴ ἀ]νίονται 'except if they (the exactors) remit (the penalty)'.

πι̣: the lower curve of *iota* is visible.

10 ο̣: the upper part of a curve is visible (⊙ or *iota* are also possible).

[—]ρϝΘιο̣[—]: Chadwick 1987: 333 suggests [ἐπιϝ]όρϝοι = ἐπίουρος 'overseer'; VER suggest 'supervisors of the hinterland' (*epi* + *oureia*). Chadwick (330) restores lines 9–10: π[αρ' [ἐπιϝό]ρϝοι ὀ[μίονται | ἀπο]δόμεν. The verb [ἀπο]δόμεν (δ̣ο̣μεν HMVE) is not possible epigraphically.

σ̣: the intersection of the two oblique strokes at left is visible.

σ̣αμεν: HMVE read δ̣ο̣μεν.

11 ṭạị: the right tip of the horizontal stroke of *tau*, the apex of *alpha*, and the upper loop of *iota* are visible.

ṭ[—]: the left part of the horizontal stroke is visible.

Interpretation of this law is hindered by uncertainties about the restoration of missing text and the understanding of rare words. Clearly it concerns the 'reception' of 'citizens of another polis' (*alopoliatai*), but it is not clear what sort of reception is at issue (private hosting, temporary residence, or permanent settlement) or even whether the law prohibited the reception of these foreigners (as most scholars think) or permitted or perhaps even protected it.

1 'The Lyktians decided': cf. **G78**.1, **Da1**.1, and see Introd. 4B1. Together with **Lyktos1B** and **Da1**, this may be the earliest example of an enactment formula with the collective ethnic from Crete. Lyktos and Datala were likely neighbors, and Datala may have been a dependent polis of Lyktos when these laws were enacted (see above, Lyktos. Site).

1–4 The first uncertainty is that the main verb stating the consequence of receiving a foreigner is missing (see n. ad 3). There is general agreement that the consequence is negative: Chadwick 1987 suggested 'is to be prosecuted', VER '(the host) is to expel'.

The general rule against receiving foreigners is apparently followed by two exceptions: 'except insofar as he himself controls (them) and the Itanians'. Since the word for 'foreigners' is literally 'citizen of another polis', those over whom someone has control and Itanians should refer to citizens rather than to slaves or other non-citizens (for the significance of the collective use of ethnics such as 'Itanians', see Introd. 4B1). The possibilities include soldiers captured in war (HMVE) and indentured free men (for the latter, see Introd. 5A6). Faure's suggestion (1993: 69–70) that the Itanians in question were residents of a village near Lyktos is possible if the community was a dependent polis of Lyktos with its own citizen class, but we think it more likely that the reference is to citizens of the polis of Itanos located on the east coast of Crete. In either case, the Itanians and Lyktians may have been bound by treaty or alliance obligations that took precedence over the general prohibition of this law.

4–7 Several factors obscure the meaning of this provision. The main uncertainties are that the verb in the conditional clause is missing and it is uncertain whether its subject is the same as that of the previous sentence ('whoever') or is the *kosmos* and *apokosmos*, and that the main verb is missing. Other uncertainties are the text and meaning of the preposition preceding 'of enactment of (the) council (?)' and the identity of the *apokosmos*.

The main line of interpretation (following HMVE) is that the *kosmos* and *apokosmos* are the subject of the conditional clause and that this provision prescribes a more severe penalty if these high officials receive a foreigner. On this view, we should restore the verb in the conditional clause as 'receive' and that of the main clause as '(he) is to pay'. Thus, 1–4 provide that if someone receives a foreigner he is punished in some way, and 4–7 add that if the violator is a high official the penalty is 100 cauldrons for each foreigner he receives, a heavy fine. The alternative is that the subject of the conditional clause continues to be the violator in 1–4 and that 4–7 treat a new violation or a more specific form of the violation; the *kosmos* and *apokosmos* would then be the officials in charge of punishing the violator and the main verb would be something like 'exact a penalty' of 100 cauldrons. A (less likely) variation of this view is that the conditional clause repeats the same verb, 'if he receives' (a foreigner), and adds a separate consequence; perhaps 1–4 specified that the violator undergo a trial and 4–7 specified the fine.

The identity of the *apokosmos* remains uncertain. The word occurs otherwise only once in a similar phrase in a Hellenistic? inscription from Axos: 'if someone now serving as *kosmos* or an *apokosmos*' (*SEG* 23.566, lines 13–14). Here too the context suggests the performance of an official public act. Bile 274 understands *apokosmos* as '*kosmos*-elect' by analogy with *apodromos*, a '*dromos* (adult) about to be' (see **G72**.7.35–6). The other main view is that the *apokosmos* is an ex-*kosmos* (HMVE, K, VER); cf. 'non-*kosmos*' (Chadwick 1987: 331), *kosmos* discharged for malfeasance in office (Papakonstantinou 1996).

Finally, our reading at the beginning of line 6 (see n. ad loc.) differs from that of HMVE. Following Chadwick 1987 we understand a reference to an enactment of the council authorizing the action of the main verb (either payment or exacting of a fine by the *kosmos* and the *apokosmos*), whereas HMVE understand a reference to a law of 'ejectment' (*exoulēs*), either this very law (**Lyktos 1**A) or some other enactment. The process of ejectment is known only at Athens, where it is used to obtain a court's authorization to collect a previous judgment that has not been paid. In this sense it seems quite out of place here; but the procedure at Lyktos might not have been exactly the same, and it could perhaps refer e.g. to the releasing of people (i.e. foreigners) being held illegally.

For fines calculated in cauldrons (*lebetes*), see Introd. 7D. At Gortyn 100 cauldrons is the largest, five cauldrons the smallest fine. On the significance of the cauldron as a standard value unit (of silver), see Kroll 2001: 87–8.

7–9 HMVE compare the otherwise unattested *eszikaiōteres* ('avengers', cf. *ekdikeō* 'to avenge') with the *titai*, officials who collect fines or ensure that fines are collected at Gortyn (see comm. ad **G14**g–p1) and later at Lato (*IC* 1.16.1, lines 31–4). They suggest that these officials were responsible for ensuring compliance with the law and possibly with executing fines, and propose restoring a verb in 7–8 meaning 'ensure' or 'fine' (see n. ad loc.).

9–10 The plural verbal ending -*ōntai* points to the *eszikaiōteres* as subject.

B

[Θιο]ί̣. | ἔϜαδε | Λυκτίοισι· | τᾶς κοι- ←
ναΘνίας | καὶ τᾶ(ς) συνκρίσιος | τ̣[ῶν π]-
[ροβ]άτΘν | καὶ τῶν καρταιπόδΘν | καὶ
τᾶν ὑῶν | ὅρο(ν) μὲν ἦμεν | τόνδε· | Δητ̣[2–3]
[2–3] ἆι ἀ ὀδὸς | ἀ εἰθεῖα | μετ' Ἀμαρτεια̣-
[ζ]ε | καὶ τῶνυ | ἆι ἀ ὀδὸς ἐπὶ τὸ Το[2–3]
[1–2 | κ]αὶ τῶνυ | ἆι ἀ ὀδὸς | ἐς Παλαισείαν | [ἆ]-
ι ἀ ὀδὸς | ὑπανπέτιν | μετ' ἐς Πυλ̣ε̣[2–3]
[. .] ἆι ἀ ὀδὸς | ἐ̣[ς 8–9]ρεα | καὶ τῶνυ | ἆ[ι]
ἀ̣ ὀδὸς | καταν̣[c.4 ὑπανπ (?)]έτιν | Ἐ[.]
[. .]τ̣ο | καὶ τ[c.6–7 | καὶ τῶ]νυ | ἆι ἀ ὀδὸς
[ἀ] παρὰ Να̣[c.5 | καὶ τῶνυ | ἆ]ι ἀ ὀδ[ὸς]
[ἐς] Μαλ[c.25]
[2–3]δ̣ο̣[c.21]ο̣νο[—].

1–4 Gods. The Lyktians decided. The boundary of the pooling together and sorting of the small and large animals and the pigs is to be the following.

4–13 Dēt[4–6], where (there is) the straight path as far as Amarteia; and from there, where (there is) the path to To[3–5]; and from there, where (there is) the path to Palaiseia ('Old Seia'?), where the path (goes) underneath (?) as far as Pyle[4–5]; (and from there ?) the path to [8–9]rea; and from there the underneath (?) path opposite E[3]tos (?); and [c.6–7]; and from there, where (there is) the path beside Na[c.5]; and from there, where (there is) the path to Mal[—].

---

1 ι̣: the lower loop is visible.
2 τ̣: the horizontal stroke at the left is visible.

FIG. 67. **Lyktos1B**

4 τ̣: the horizontal stroke at the left is visible.
4–5 *Δητ*[4–6]: *Δητ*[2–3 *θεν*] Chadwick 1987: 333–4, a specific location that served as the starting point for the description of the limits of the area. Possibly *Δητ*[*άληθεν*] or *Δητ*[*αλλαι*]. VER: a region, possibly Lasithi, wherein the pooling together and separating apart took place. Cf. [*κῆς*] *τὰν Δαττ*[*άλλαν*] in a description of the border between Lato and Olous (*IC* 1.16.5, line 64, second century).
5 α̣: the lower tip of the right oblique stroke is visible.
5–6 *'Αμαρτεια̣*[*ζ*]*ε*: HMVE p. 170, ' "(le lieu-dit) *Les Fauts* ou *Les Deviations* (?)", c'est-à-dire "jusqu'au Carrefour" ("up to the crossroads")'.
6 *τôνυ* = *τοῦδε*; see n. ad **L4**.7.
8 λε̣: the upper tip of vertical stroke and intersecting bit of an oblique stroke of the *lambda* are visible followed by the lower half of the *epsilon*. VER and others write *Πυτ̣*. [. .].
ὑπαντέτιν, otherwise unattested, is taken to mean 'underneath' (*par-dessous*) by HMVE, Bile, VER, and K (*abwärts*); Chadwick 1987: 333 has 'which is not straight'. See also Bile 211.
μετ' = *μέστα* (Attic *μέχρι*). See n. ad **G72**.9.48–9.
9 ε̣: the upper horizontal stroke and intersecting tip of the vertical are visible.
10 α̣: the lower tip of the right oblique is visible.
καταν̣[*c*.4]: an adverb (e.g. *καταν*[*τίον*], *καταν*[*τικρύ*] 'right opposite'); or *κατὰ ν̣*[*c*.4].
11 τ̣: the tip of the horizontal stroke at left is visible.
12 α̣: the apex is visible; it could also be *delta* or (unlikely following a *nu*) *gamma*.
παρὰ Να̣[—]: *παρ' Ἀνα̣*[—] is also possible.
14 δο̣: the upper part of a triangular letter followed by the upper part of a circular letter are visible.
ο̣: the upper part of a circular letter is visible.

B specifies the boundaries of an area where sheep, goats, cattle, and pigs are to be pooled together and sorted out, probably for summer pasturage; the area where this is to be done is delimited by a series of paths.

1–4 HMVE 184–5 (followed by VER, Guizzi 1997: 48) suggest that **Lyktos1B** concerns the reassignment of livestock from private to public ownership. More plausible, however, is Chaniotis' interpretation (1995: 46–8; 1999b: 192–7) that the provision specifies the place where privately owned herds would be brought together in preparation for seasonal migrations, at the end of which the pooled herds would be brought back and separated out again into individual herds.

For animal husbandry in Crete, see Introd. 7C (also 7A). Although Athenaeus (9.375g–376a) says that the Cretans abstained from eating pork at sacrificial meals, pig bones were found in sacrificial debris at Kommos and at the sanctuary of Demeter and Kore at Knossos (Shaw 2000b: 685).

4–14 Each segment circumscribing the area where livestock are to be pooled is described as a path or road (*odos*). The descriptions of nine such segments survive, but with the possible exception of *Dēt*[—] in 4–5 (see below), none of the places mentioned can be identified. HMVE argue that the reliance upon roadways in this description indicates that the area was probably not far from a nucleated settlement, somewhere in the suburbs or lowlands rather than in the uplands to the south and southeast of Lyktos; but these 'roadways' were probably only paths leading to a small village or a natural landmark.

4–5 HMVE 182 propose to restore Dēt[al(l)a], a variant of Datala; this is possible, though we do not know exactly where Datala was (see Datala. Site).

As HMVE note, **A** and **B** share a number of features in addition to physical proximity and similarities in writing. Both begin with the invocation 'gods', followed by the identical enactment formula 'the Lyktians decided' and a word or words indicating the subject of the enactment: foreigners in **A** and the pooling and sorting of livestock in **B**. Whether or not the same historical context motivated both texts (see below), these formal similarities suggest that they were related, perhaps in that they were both enacted at the same meeting of the Lyktians.

HMVE also identify **A** as a law and **B** as a decree, largely on the basis of their syntax: a conditional sentence indicates a law, an infinitive indicates a decree. Yet, the first provision of **A** almost certainly has an infinitive in 3 ([2–3]*en*) as its main verb, as do many other laws (such as **G72**.1.2–3); such a distinction, in other words, is unsupportable.

HMVE 184–5 propose that both **A** and **B** were enacted in response to the same historical context: social and political strife between an elite minority and an impoverished majority in a community dependent upon pastoralism. The elite, they speculate, had hired foreigners to oversee intensive grazing on the vast lands they had accumulated, and the impoverished Lyktians responded by confiscating and pooling together the elite's livestock, sorting them by species, and reassigning them as common property (**B**), and by forbidding the introduction of foreigners into the community (**A**). Not surprisingly, Chadwick 1987, K, and Chaniotis 1995: 46–8, 1999b: 192–7 reject this view; only VER accept it. Not only would this sort of confiscation and communalization of elite property by the people be unparalleled and (judging from everything we know about sixth-century Crete) inherently unlikely, but as Chaniotis observes, according to this view the pooling and sorting of livestock described in **B** would happen just once, whereas the text suggests a recurring activity.

Site

The post-Bronze Age settlement of Phaistos was established in the western Mesara on the same ridge with three low hills (from west to east: Christos Effendi, Acropoli Mediana, and Palace Hill) as the Minoan palace and town. At the start of the Iron Age, a fortified settlement was established on Acropoli Mediana (Cucuzza 1998: 62, 65; Coutsinas 2013: 426–7 no. 30). By the end of the eighth century the settlement had expanded onto Palace Hill where Doro Levi uncovered the remains of two substantial residential quarters, one to the southwest of the palace and another at the base of the ridge to the southeast of the palace at Chalara.[431] One group of rooms in the residential quarter southwest of the palace is particularly conspicuous and has been identified as a locus of banqueting (chieftain's house or *andreion*, Cucuzza 1998: 65–6). Archaeological remains of the seventh-century town indicate substantial growth both on the ridge (stretching east from Christos Ephendi across Acropoli Mediana to Agia Photini) and in the plain to the south.[432] Occupation at Chalara probably continued during the seventh century (Cucuzza 1998: 63), but the residential district southwest of the palace was abandoned around 700. A monumental stone temple, perhaps belonging to the goddess Leto (Cucuzza 1993), was established in the vicinity of the abandoned residential district late in the seventh century (La Rosa 1996).[433] The remains of other monumental buildings dating to the seventh century were found on the summit of Acropoli Mediana and at Phalandra near the church of Agios Georgios.

Archaeologists detect an abrupt change in the material record of the western Mesara, the town of Phaistos in particular, late in the seventh century. At Phaistos the change is marked by the relocation of the settlement to the plain, although at present there is little positive evidence for this presumptive move down from the ridge to the plain below. Traces of the sixth- and fifth-century town have been difficult to identify in part because of uncertainties concerning the chronology of

[431] Residential district southwest of the palace: Levi 1957–8: 265–74; 1961–2: 397–418; Rocchetti 1974–5; Chalara: Levi 1961–2: 477–504; 1967–8. For overviews of the protogeometric–geometric settlement (ninth–eighth centuries), see Cucuzza 1998; Watrous and Hadzi-Vallianou 2004a: 311–13.

[432] For the seventh-century settlement, see Palermo 1992; La Rosa 1996; Watrous and Hadzi-Vallianou 2004a: 314–15. Longo et al. 2014 suggest that Christos Ephendi served as the acropolis of the early settlement; votive material from the hill dating to the fifth and fourth centuries indicates the location of a sanctuary of Athena.

[433] Cucuzza 1998: 67 notes that the mid-seventh-century date of the bronze shields and cauldron found beneath the floor of the temple suggest that its construction may be pushed back a generation or so earlier than La Rosa suggests.

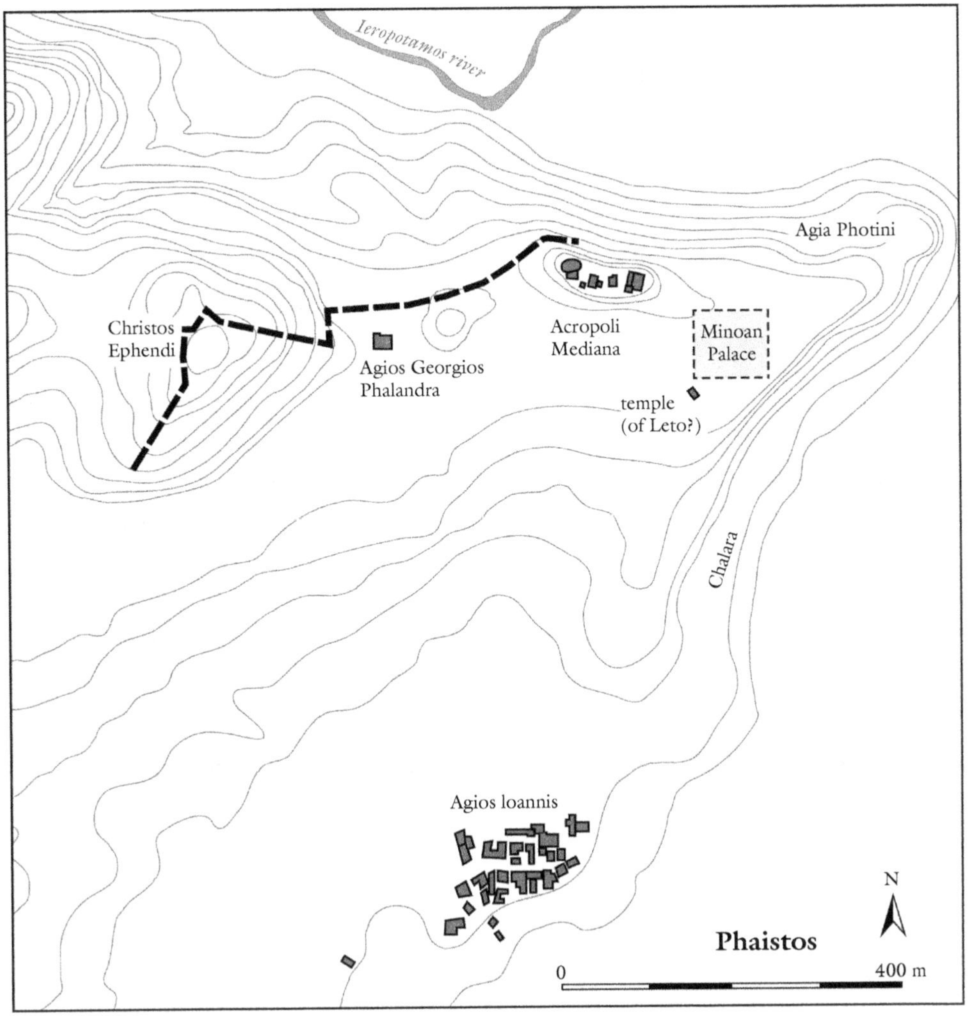

IG. 68. Plan of Phaistos

the local ceramic sequences and the dearth of dateable imports.[434] The remains of monumental buildings (wall blocks and foundations) possibly of the sixth century have been found at Chalara and further to the south near the village of Agios Ioannis. **Ph1**, inscribed *c.*500 on a wall block from Chalara, preserves the term *agora*. We take the term to mean 'meeting place' rather than 'meeting', but the location of the *agora* is not known. At least two wall blocks recovered near Agios Ioannis are reported to bear boustrophedon inscriptions (see further below).

[434] For the paucity of evidence for the archaic settlement (sixth–early fifth centuries), see Palermo 1992; Cucuzza 1997: 77–8; 2001; Watrous and Hadzi-Vallianou 2004a: 318.

Text

Writing in Greek is attested at Phaistos perhaps as early as the late eighth century. A graffito on a storage pithos may be the earliest Greek text discovered thus far on Crete.[435] The dossier of public inscriptions from Phaistos is larger than the single text included below. A small fragment of limestone preserving a few letters from five lines of what was likely a public inscription (a law?) was found among the Hellenistic remains of the residential neighborhood at Chalara (*SEG* 23.556). As noted above, two unpublished inscriptions, described as written in boustrophedon and so presumably archaic, were recovered near the village of Agios Ioannis (Pariente 1994: 825). Archaic inscriptions from Crete written on wall blocks and consisting of more than one or two lines are more than likely laws or legal in nature. We note as well the existence of two unpublished archaic inscriptions, one certainly a law and the other probably legal in nature, that may come from Phaistos. Similarities in the letter-forms (a distinctive *rho* in particular) suggest that they may have come from the same community. One of these inscriptions is built into the wall of the tenth-century Church of Agios Pavlos near the town of ancient Phaistos. It mentions Gortynians and possibly Phaistians.[436] It is, of course, possible that the block was brought there from somewhere else (e.g. Gortyn).

Ph1 (Di Vita and Cantarella 1978 (*SEG* 32.908), Bile 32 no. 11, VER II.39). Fragment of a law concerning inheritance, *c.*550–500. Archaeological Museum of Heraklion (Inv. no. 369). FIG. 69

Six lines of text inscribed boustrophedon on a large limestone block with preserved upper and lower edges. The block is broken at left and right. The treatment of the upper and lower edges of the block (anathyrosis) indicates that there was at least one course of blocks above and one course below this block. The block was discovered together with other uninscribed blocks in the plain below the south end of the palace of Phaistos near Chalara (see above, Site). Di Vita 1978 attributes the blocks to one or more public buildings.

435 *SEG* 26.1050 *Ἐρπετιδάμο Παιδοπίλας ὅδε* 'This (is the vase) of Erpetidamos, son of Paidopila'. For other interpretations of this short text, see *SEG* 29.831; 33.739; 45.1332. Most scholars date the graffito to *c.*700, but cf. Johnston in Jeffery 1990: 468, no. 8a, who suggests eighth to sixth century.

436 The inscription is mentioned by Watrous et al. 1993: 238. If the text does mention the Phaistians together with the Gortynians (we read the letters *ΠΑ* following [*Γο*]*ρτυνιοι*), it likely records an agreement of some kind. If so, it supports the view of Cucuzza that Phaistos and Gortyn were closely linked politically by a formal agreement of some kind, referred to in the scholarship as a *sympoliteia* ('shared constitution'), by the beginning of the fifth century (Cucuzza 1997: 78–81; Watrous and Hadzi-Vallianou 2004a: 324–5). Without epigraphic evidence of this sort, the strongest argument offered in support of formal political ties — namely that the earliest coins (mid-fifth century) of both communities used the same obverse and reverse coin types — does not require a political explanation.

FIG. 69. **Ph1**

Line 1 begins 0.075 m below the upper edge of the block, indicating that it is probably the first line of the text. The letters of line 6 rest on the lower edge of the block and so it is not possible to determine if the text ends there or continued below onto the next course of blocks. The text continued to the right and the left.

[— Ϝ]εῖπαι | ἐν ἀγορ[ᾶι —]	←	— speak out in the agora —
[—]μ̣α | αἰ λείοι σ̣[—]		— if he wishes —
[—] τ̣ὰ δὲ ματρô[ια —]		— the maternal estate —
[— δια (?)]κατίους | σ[τατῆρανς (?) —]		— [two- (?)]hundred staters —
[— αἰ δέ κ]α | μὴ διδô[ι —]		— and if he] does not give —
[—]ς | ἀναιρε[—]		— takes up —

1 [Ϝ]εῖπαι: the compound verbs [ἀνϜ]εῖπαι 'proclaim' or 'give notice' (**Elt2**.3), [ἀποϜ]εῖπαι 'speak out' or 'refuse' (e.g. **G72**.9.37–8; **G73A4**; **Pr7**), [προϜ]εῖπαι 'declare' or 'tell beforehand' (e.g. **G72**.11.50–1; **G90**; **L1**), and possibly [διαϜ]εῖπαι 'declare' or 'tell fully' (attested in the middle in the sense of 'make an agreement', **G72**.9.27) are also possible. VER prefer [ἀποϜ]εῖπαι and translate 'renounce', but this meaning is securely attested only in the middle (ἀποϜειπάθθο **G72**.11.11–12).

2 μ̣ could be *nu*.

3 τ̣: tip of crossbar is preserved.

4 [δια (?)]κατίους: other numbers are of course possible. It is worth noting that multiple 'hundreds' are not otherwise attested in the epichoric laws from Crete.

σ[τατῆρανς]: the *san* could be the first letter of many other words, but in this context, this supplement is likely.

5 [ὄς κ]α is also possible, as are other words ending in -α. Di Vita records a *lambda* following the *alpha*, but what he reads as the short oblique stroke of the *lambda* is clearly not an inscribed stroke but damage.

διδô[ι]: διδόμεν is the only other attested form of the verb in the epichoric inscriptions from Crete (**A1**.14 and **A9**.12). If κα is right, a finite verb (e.g. λῆι) is necessary.

6 ἀναιρε[—] from ἀναιρέω with only middle forms attested in the epichoric inscriptions from Crete (ἀναιρêται ind. or subj. pres. (**A10**B), ἀναιρêσθ[αι] pres. inf. (**G20**), ἀναιλêθθαι (**G72**.5.24–5)). Cantarella, followed by VER, proposes a distinction in the significance of the verbs *anairesthai* 'to take up for oneself' and *eken* 'to have', the former used to express the rights of close relatives to inherit, the latter of more distant relatives (*epiballontes*). The use of these verbs in **G72** does not support this distinction (see n. ad **G72**.5.24–5), although *anairesthai* is limited to inheritance while *eken* is more general.

---

1 An *agora* is otherwise attested in the epichoric inscriptions from Crete at Rhitten (**G80**.14) and Gortyn (**G13**h–g2; 1; **G72**.10.34, 11.10–14; **G75A**; **G81**.7–11). There, as here, the *agora* is specified as the location where a legal proceeding (a declaration of some kind) is to take place.

3 The term *ta matroia* 'maternal estate', otherwise attested on Crete only at Gortyn (**G20**; **G72**.4.44; **G72**.6.34 and 45, 11.44–5) indicates that this law concerns inheritance. VER identify **Ph1** as a law on adoption, more specifically the renunciation of an adoption. They base their view on the restoration of [*apow*]*eipai* (line 1) and **G72**.11.11–12, the latter providing that the renunciation (*apoweipatho*) of an adoption is to be made *kat' agorai*. While it is the case that the section of **G72** on adoption (**G72**.10.33–11.23) focuses on inheritance, the verb 'let him renounce' is in the middle voice while [*apow*]*eipai* is in the active voice. We might also note that **G20**, a fragment of an earlier law concerning inheritance, refers to *oi gnēsioi* 'natural children' and *ta matroia* and preserves the verb *anairesth*[*ai*] 'to take up (an inheritance)' (cf. *anaire*[—] in line 6). The reference to *oi gnēsioi* in **G20** implies other categories of heir, e.g. adopted children. VER's suggestion is possible, but by no means certain.

4 The context of the large sum of money (two hundred? staters) is unclear. **G72**.10.17–20 allows exceptions for gifts in excess of one hundred staters on the part of heirs to their mother and perhaps to the wife of the deceased.

PRINIAS

Site

The settlement on Patela Priniàs, a high (*c.*680 m.) triangular-shaped plateau strategically located at the junction of two valleys connecting the northern and southern coasts, was established in the thirteenth century and continued until sometime in the sixth, when it was abandoned. The earliest excavations (1906–8) brought to light the seventh-century Temple A with its magnificent architectural sculpture and a second, earlier building, the so-called 'Temple B' (Pernier 1914). Scientific exploration resumed in 1969 and has revealed sections of the urban center, including residential blocks and a spacious piazza, that attest a degree of town planning (Rizza 2008), a cemetery contemporary with the life of the settlement 500 m. northwest of Patela Priniàs at Siderospilia that remains largely unpublished, and a pottery workshop (established *c.*700) near Mandra di Gipari on a hillock opposite the west side of the plateau (Rizza, Palermo, and Tomasello 1992).[437] Since 2000 exploration of the central area of the settlement in the vicinity of Temples A and B has continued. Among the many notable discoveries of this latest phase of exploration are the monumental building VA/VD (22 x 6 m.), comprising a main hall (VB) with central hearth and a separate room (VD) with a trilithic structure and clear evidence of ritual activity (Palermo 2007; 2008), and the large structure to its north with room VE that appears to have served as a repository for cups, cooking utensils, and dining debris associated with banqueting (Gigli Patanè in Palermo et al. 2007: 288–92; 2008: 188–94); both structures date to the later eighth century or beginning of the seventh. See Fig. 70.

The ancient name of the settlement is not known. Early editors identified it as Rhitten, a community with which Gortyn concluded an agreement sometime during the first half of the fifth century (**G80**), in part on the basis of *IC* 1.28.2, which preserves a few letters that could perhaps be from the name 'Rizenia', and most scholars since have agreed (e.g. Guarducci 1935: 294; van Effenterre 1993b; VER).[438] A major obstacle to this identification, however, is that Patela Priniàs was abandoned during the fifth century and part of the sixth (Rizza 2008: 301–5). Faure (1963: 22–4; 1993: 70) argues that Rhitten was located south of the Mesara in the Asterousia mountains near Apesokari at the foot of a chain of hills known as 'Lower Riza' (*hē Katō Riza*). This site has not been excavated, but the surface remains date to the Classical and Hellenistic periods (Faure 1963: 24).

[437] Perhaps the earliest writing from Prinias is the signature of a potter (*kerameus*) written prior to firing on the neck of a large ceramic storage jar: [—] . ετεο κεραμεύς, possibly '[X, son of]etes, (the) potter' (Rizza 2008: 92).

[438] The letters *ZENIA* are clear. See *IC* 1.28.2 photo.

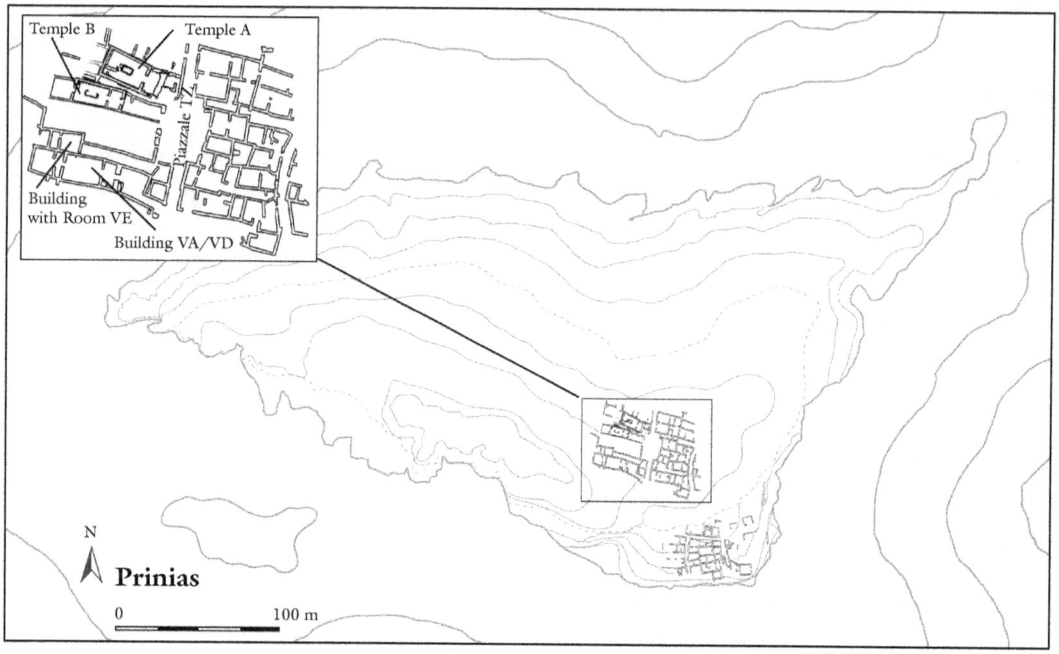

FIG. 70. Plan of Patela Prinià̀s

Text

In addition to **Pr7**, some sixteen early inscriptions each preserving a few rather large (0.05–0.13 m.), carefully formed, and deeply inscribed letters have been found on Patela Prinià̀s or in its vicinity, including fourteen published by Guarducci (*IC* 1.28.2–15) and two discovered since (Rizza 2008: 41 and 77). As a group they are quite different from the small (0.01–0.04 m) and inexpertly written letters of *IC* 1.28.1, a collection of scribblings that are clearly not public in nature. All of the texts preserving a few letters probably come from wall blocks. We do not know the location of the building or buildings from which these blocks originally came,[439] but being inscribed on wall blocks in large letters, they were probably public texts, and since they most likely date to some time before *c.*550, they were probably legal in nature.

Pr7 (VER I.63). *c.* 600–575. Archaeological Museum of Heraklion (Inv. no. 427). FIG. 71

Ten lines of text written vertically on four sides of a limestone pillar that is broken at the bottom and at the top. The lines are traditionally numbered A1–4, B1–2, C1,

[439] Biondi in Palermo et al. 2007: 304–12; and in Pautasso et al. 2010: 68–71, suggests that *IC* 1.28.9–12 come from the walls of a temple located on the southwestern edge of the plateau in the vicinity of the Hellenistic fort built in the late third or early second century.

and D1–3. There is an empty space to the left of C1 with room for three lines of text, making it likely that C1, which begins *ai de tis* ('but if someone'), is the start of a new provision. G reports that the pillar was damaged in the earthquake of 1926. It is currently fitted with a cement base obscuring its lower edges and side B has been patched with cement obscuring part of B1. For discussions of the identification of this inscribed monument as a *kyrbis*, see Guarducci 1931a and Jeffery 1990: 52–5.

FIG. 71. **Pr7**

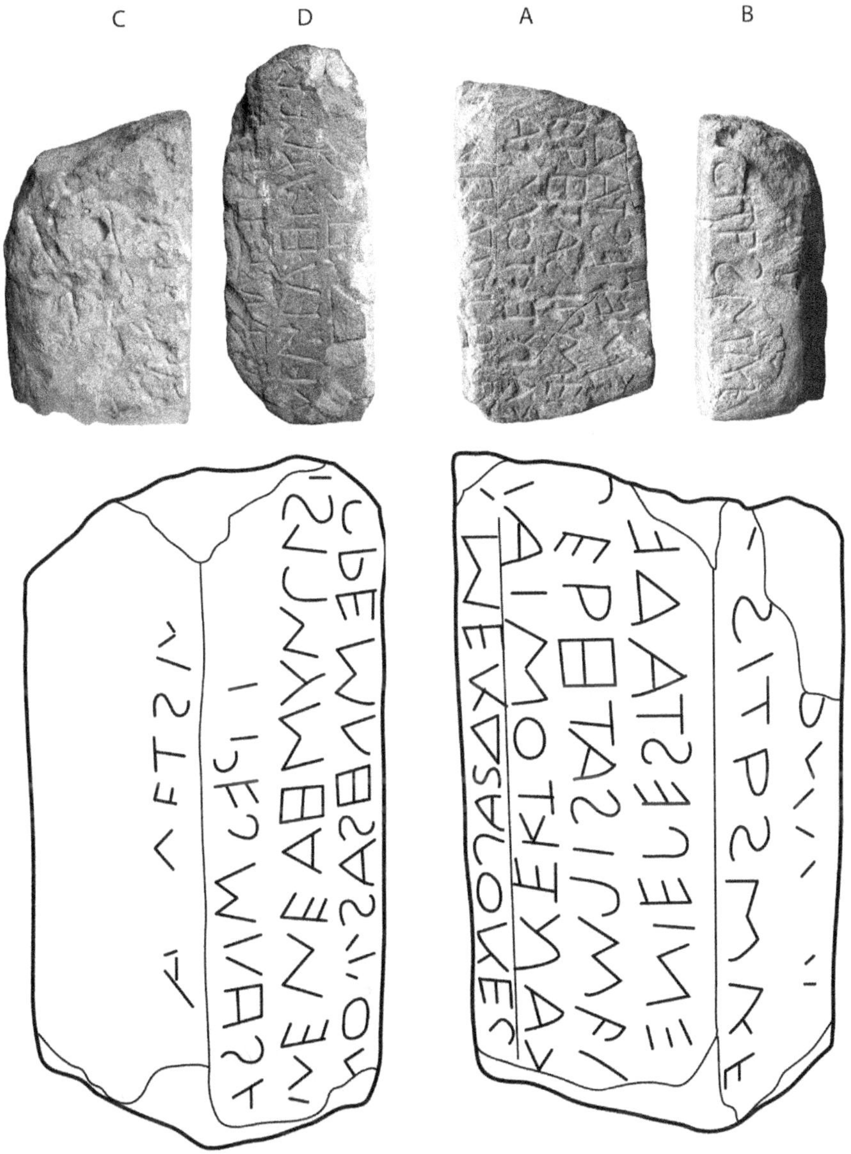

The layout of the text on the stone is complex. All ten lines are written vertically, but one group of five contiguous lines (A2–4, B1–2) has one orientation, requiring a reader to tilt his head to the right, while the other five (C1, D1–3, A1), also contiguous, have the opposite orientation. In the first group, A2 runs up from the bottom of the stone and A3–4 and B1–2 continue in boustrophedon order. In the second group, C1 begins near the bottom of the stone, and D1–3 continue in a boustrophedon pattern; the boustrophedon pattern is broken, however, with A1, which runs top to bottom like D3.

A vertical line, narrower and shallower than the strokes that form the letters, is clearly inscribed between A1 and A2. Located, as it is, between the two lines where the different orientations meet, this line (as G suggests) is probably meant to be an aid to the reader rather than a guideline for the mason. G (followed by VER) suggests that the text is continuous — A2–4, B1–2, C1 (plus any lines now lost on C), D1–3, A1— and that the vertical line separates the first line of the text (A2) from the last (A1).

We think it more likely that we have two separate texts, one beginning with B2 (or perhaps with a line lost on C, contiguous to it) and ending with A2, and the other beginning with C1 (or perhaps with another lost line on C) and ending with A1. Most likely there was at least some empty space on C separating the two texts. The first lines of both texts read from bottom to top. The reader faced one direction to read the first text, and then changed to face in the other direction when he read the second text. We do not know which text was inscribed first.

In accordance with this understanding, our text BA below reverses the order of the lines as printed in G and VER.

Apart from the *digamma* used also at Lyktos and Axos, the alphabet resembles that of the earliest inscriptions from Gortyn (**G1–40**). All *iotas* face left. Arrows indicate bottom to top (←) and top to bottom (→).

BA

B2 [—]...*νο*[—] ←

B1 [—] . *ι* | *τρὶς ϝε*[—] → — three —

A4 [—]*εν* | *ἐπεὶ τάδε* [—] ← — when these —

A3 [—] *πέρηται* | *πσε* . [—] → — he carries off —

A2 [—]*κα ϝέκτος* | *α* . [—] ← — sixth —

CDA

C1 [—] *αἰ δέ τις* [—] → — but if someone —

D1 [—] *π̣ρεισγήια* [—] ← — elders (?) —

D2 [—]*μ̣ενεα ἢ συνπλι* . [—] → — or —

D3 [—] *πρεσγήιαι* | *ο* . [—] ← — to the] elders (?) —

A1 [—] . *σεϝδὶ ἀποϝει*[*π* —] ← — speak out?/deny?/renounce? —

BA

B2 There are traces of three letters before the *nu*: the lower tip of an oblique stroke; the lower tip of a vertical stroke; the lower half of *alpha*, *gamma*, or *digamma*.

B1 The tip of an oblique stroke resembling the lower oblique of a *kappa* is visible before the first *iota*.

ϝε[—]: possibly a form of ϝέ[τος] 'year' or a compound, e.g. τριαϝε[τηρίαν]; cf. *IC* 4.146.7.

A3 There is an oblique stroke after the second *epsilon* consistent with *gamma*, *digamma*, *mu*, *nu*, or *san*.

πσε: σφε G, or possibly a form of the reflexive pronoun πσεϝ̣[αυτ—]; see Bile 208–9.

ϝέκτος: 'sixth' (Bile 218); VER ignore the *digamma* and translate 'outside' (*au dehors*).

A2 There is an oblique stroke after the second *alpha* consistent with *gamma*, *digamma*, *mu*, *nu*, or *san*.

CDA

D1 π̣: lower tip of the vertical is visible.

π̣ρειαγήια: both πρεια- and πρεσ- (D3) are attested elsewhere on Crete (Bile 341).

D2 μ̣: three short oblique strokes are visible; *nu* is also possible.

μ' ἐνέα (= μὴ ἐννέα) is possible but unlikely.

Halbherr's drawing (1910: 95) records the lower part of a vertical stroke after the *iota*.

συνπλι . [—]: perhaps σύνπλιε̣[ς] 'several together'; but σὺν πλι . [—] is also possible. VER write σὺν πλί[οσι] 'with more (people)' (*avec plus [de gens]*).

D3 The drawings of Halbherr (1910: 95) and JP record two strokes, most likely from *mu*, *nu*, or *san*, after the *omicron*.

A1 The drawings of Halbherr 1910: 95 and JP record the lower tip of an oblique stroke before the *san* consistent with a triangular letter or *san*, but not with *nu*.

[παν]σεϝδί: = πανδυδί (G, VER), perhaps 'with all force' or 'with one force' (i.e. 'unanimous'), but *nu* is not epigraphically possible (see preceding note). [πα]σ̣σεϝδὶ is possible, but assimilation is not likely this early (cf. e.g. **D2**: συνπλι[—]).

ἀποϝει[π—]: could be active 'speak out' (**G72**.9.37–8), 'refuse' (**G73A** 4), or middle 'renounce' (**G72**.11.11–12); see n. ad **G72**.9.37–8. VER also suggest a form of ἀπειλεῖν, 'stay out of' (*tenir à l'écart*).

The difficulty in discerning any continuous sense, apart from the repetition of *pre(i)sgēia* (D1, D3) and the numbers 'three' (B1), 'sixth' (A2), and possibly 'nine' (see n. ad D2), indicates that a considerable amount of text has been lost at both ends.

D1, D3: 'elders' (*pre(i)sgēia*): Bile understands *pre(i)sgēia* as 'embassy'. This is possible, but G's suggestion (also VER) of a council (*coetus virorum*) may be preferable; cf. *tons preigistons*, 'the elders', in **G80**.11, where the context suggests a defined group. The word does not occur again until the Hellenistic period.

A1: the break in the boustrophedon pattern suggests a new provision.

Bibliography

JOURNAL ABBREVIATIONS

AA	*Archäologischer Anzeiger*
AAA	*Archaiologika analekta ex Athēnōn. Athens annals of archaeology*
AE	*Archaiologike ephemeris*
AJA	*American Journal of Archaeology*
AR	*Archaeological Reports*
ArchDelt	*Archaiologikon Deltion*
ASA(Atene)	*Annuario della Scuola archeologica di Atene e delle missioni italiane in Oriente*
ASNP	*Annali della Scuola normale superiore di Pisa, Classe di lettere e filosofia,* Ser. 3
Ath. Mitt.	*Mitteilungen des Deutschen Archäologischen Instituts, Athenische Abteilung*
BCH	*Bulletin de correspondance hellénique*
BSA	*Annual of the British School at Athens*
EHHD	*Epeteris tou Kentrou Ereunes tes Istorias tou Ellenikou Dikaio*
GRBS	*Greek, Roman, and Byzantine Studies*
KrChr	*Kretika Chronika*
MAL	*Memorie della Reale Accademia Nazionale dei Lincei, Classe di scienze morali, storiche e filologiche*
Mon. Ant.	*Monumenti Antichi*
Mus. It.	*Museo italiano di antichità classica*
PAAH	*Praktika tes en Athenais Archaiologikes Etaireius*
RAL	*Rendiconti della Reale Accademia Nazionale dei Lincei, Classe di scienze morali, storiche e filologiche*
RFIC	*Rivista di filologia e di istruzione classica*
ZPE	*Zeitschrift für Papyrologie und Epigraphik*
ZSS	*Zeitschrift der Savigny-Stiftung für Rechtsgeschichte, romanistische Abteilung*

Agelarakis, Anagnostis. 2005. *The anthropology of Tomb A1K1 of Orthi Petra in Eleutherna: A Narrative of the bones: Aspects of the Human Condition in Geometric-Archaic Eleutherna*. Athens.

Alexiou, Stylianos. 1952. 'Tête archaïque en poros du Musée de Candie'. *BCH* 76: 1–17.

Alexiou, Stylianos. 1971. 'Chronika 1970'. *Kretica Chronica* Ser. 2, 3: 494–9.

Allegro, Nunzio. 1991. 'Gortina, l'abitato geometrico di Profitis Ilias'. In Musti et al. 1991: 321–30.

Allegro, Nunzio. 2010. '*Οι πρόσφατες έρευνης στο γεωμετρικό και αρχαϊκό οικισμό στη θέση Προφήτης Ηλίας της Γόρτυνας*'. In Andrianakis and Tzachili 2010: 327–35.

Allegro, Nunzio. 2012. '*Γόρτυνα—Προφήτης Ηλίας: νέα δεδομένα από τις ανασκαφικός περιόδους 2009–2010*'. *Αρχαιολογικό έργο Κρήτης 2. Πρακτικά της 2ης Συναντήσης Ρέθυμνο, 26–28 Νοεμβρίου 2010*, 241–5. Rethymno.

Andrianakis, Michalis, and Tzachili, Iris, eds. 2010. *Αρχαιολογικό έργο Κρήτης 1. Πρακτικά της 1ης Συνάντησης Ρέθυμνο, 28–30 Νοεμβρίου 2008*. Rethymno.

Aubet, Maria Eugenia. 2001. *The Phoenicians and the West: Politics, Colonies, and Trade*, 2nd edn. Cambridge.

Aversa, Gregoric, and Monaco, Maria Chiara. 2006. '*Οαξος. Νέα στοιχεία και παρατηρήσεις για τις ιταλικές ανασκαφές του 1899*'. In *Πεπραγμένα του Θ′ Διεθνούς Κρητολογικού Συνεδρίου. Τόμος Α.5. Αρχαία ελληνική και ρωμαική περίοδος. Ελουντα 1–6 Οκτωβρίου 2001*, 43–54. Heraklion.

Avramovič, Sima. 1990. 'Die "Epiballontes" als Erben im Gesetz von Gortyn'. *ZSS* 107: 363–70.

Babington, Churchill. 1865. 'Appendix VII. On the Greek Inscriptions Found in Crete'. In Spratt 1865, II: 411–35.

Barozzi, Francesco. 1577. *Descrittione dell'isola di Creta.*

Baunack, Johannes, and Baunack, Theodor. 1885. *Die Inschrift von Gortyn.* Leipzig.

Beattie, Arthur J. 1975. 'Some Notes on the Spensitheos Decree'. *Kadmos* 14: 8–47.

Bechtel, Friedrich. 1923. 'Der kretische Dialekt'. In *Die Griechischen Dialekte,* vol. 2, 657–795. Berlin.

Beck, Hans, ed. 2013. *A Companion to Ancient Greek Government.* Malden, MA.

Bejor, Giorgio, and Sena Chiesa, Gemma. 2003. 'Gortyna (Creta). Campagna 2002. I lavori sull'acropoli'. *ASA (Atene)* 81: 827–35.

Bennet, John, Grammatikaki, Eva, Vasilakis, Andonis, and Whitelaw, Todd. 2008. 'The Knossos urban landscape project 2005. Preliminary results'. In Louis Godart and Anna Sacconi, eds., *Pasiphae. Rivista di Filologia e Antichità Egee*, I.103–9. Rome.

Berthiaume, Guy. 1982. *Les rôles du mágeiros. Étude sur la boucherie, la cuisine et le sacrifice dans la Grèce ancienne.* Leiden.

Bile, Monique. 1988. *Le dialecte crétois ancien. Étude de la langue des inscriptions. Recueil des inscriptions postérieures aux IC.* Paris.

Bile, Monique. 1997. 'Une inscription d'Eltynia: *IC* I–X 2'. In Claude Brixhe, ed. *Poikila Epigraphika* (Études d'Archéologie Classique 9), 113–22. Paris.

Bile, Monique. 2000. '*IC* 4.41 et le sens de ἐπιδίομαι'. In Lévy 2000: 161–74.

Bile, Monique. 2002. 'Quelques aperçus de la société gortynienne d'après les lois de Gortyne VI 56 – VII 10. In *Mélanges en l'honneur Panayotis Dimakis: Droits antiques et société*, 115–31. Athens.

Bile, Monique. 2012. 'Prolégomènes aux lois de Gortyne I: statut de la femme et ordre social'. In Claude Brixhe and Guy Vottéro, eds. *Folia graeca in honorem Edouard Will, I Linguistica*, 7–63. Nancy.

Bile, Monique. p.c. = personal communication.

Biondi, Giacomo. 2011. 'Recinto funerario in località Dodeka Apostoloi (Priniàs)'. In *Πεπραγμένα του Γ' Διεθνούς Κρητολογικού Συνεδρίου, Χανιά, 1–8 Οκτοβρίου 1996, Α.4. Ιστορικοί Χρόνοι*, 311–20. Chania.

Blass, Friedrich. 1905. 'Die kretischen Inschriften'. In Hermann Collitz and Friedrich Bechtel, eds. *Sammlung der griechischen Dialekt-Inschriften*, III.2.227–423. Göttingen.

Blitzer, Harriet. 2004. 'Agriculture and Subsistence in the Late Ottoman and Post-Ottoman Mesara'. In Watrous et al. 2004: 111–217.

Blümel, Wolfgang. 1992. *Die Inschriften von Knidos. I. Inschriften griechischer Städte aus Kleinasien*, 41. Bonn.

Borgna, Elisabetta. 2003. *Il complesso di ceramica Tardominoico III dell'Acropoli Mediana di Festòs* (Studi di Archeologia Cretese 3). Padua.

Brause, Johannes. 1914. '*ΓΟΡΤΥΝΙΩΝ ΟΡΚΟΣ ΝΟΜΙΜΟΣ*'. *Hermes* 49: 102–9.

Bravo, Benedetto. 1980. 'Sulân. Représailles et justice privée contre des étrangers dans les cités grecques'. *ASNP* 10: 766–987.

Bredaki, Maria, Longo, Fausto, and Benzi, Mario. 2009 (2011). 'Progetto Festòs. Ricognizioni archeologiche di superficie: le campagne 2007–09'. *ASA (Atene)* 87: 935–78.

Bredaki, Maria, Longo, Fausto, and Benzi, Mario. 2012. 'Phaistos Project: preliminary results of the 2009–2010 survey campaigns', *Αρχαιολογικό έργο Κρήτης 2. Πρακτικά της 2ης Συνάντησης Ρέθυμνο, 26–28 Νοεμβρίου 2010*, 274–87. Rethymno.

Bredaki, Maria, Vasilakis, Andonis, and Whitelaw, Todd. 2010. '*Πρόγραμμα Επιφανειακής Έρευνας Περιοχής Κνωσού—Προκαταρκτική έκθεση για την εργασία των ετών* 2005–2007'. In *Αρχαιολογικό έργο Κρήτης 1. Πρακτικά της 1ης Συνάντησης Ρέθυμνο, 28–30 Νοεμβρίου 2008*, 294–301. Rethymno.

Brixhe, Claude. 1982. 'Palatalisations en grec et en phrygien. Problèmes phonétiques et graphiques'. *Bulletin de la Société de linguistique de Paris* 77: 209–49.

Brixhe, Claude, ed. 1991. *Sur la Crète antique: histoire, écritures, langues.* Nancy.

Brixhe, Claude. 1999. 'La circulation des biens dans les *Lois* de Gortyne'. In Catherine Dobias-Lalou, ed. *Des dialectes grecs aux lois de Gortyne*, 75–116. Nancy.

Brulé, Pierre. 1978. *La piraterie crétoise hellénistique.* Paris.

Bücheler, Franz, and Zitelmann, Ernst. 1885. *Das Recht von Gortyn* (Rheinisches Museum, Ergänzungsheft 14). Frankfurt.

Buck, Carl Darling. 1955. *The Greek Dialects.* Chicago.

Callaghan, Peter J. 1978. 'KRS 1976: Excavations at a Shrine of Glaukos, Knossos'. *BSA* 73: 1–40.

Cantarella, Eva. 2005. 'La condizione femminile alla luce della grande iscrizione'. In Greco and Lombardo 2005: 71–83.

Cataudella, Michele R. 1976. 'Aspetti del diritto agrario greco. L'affrancazione'. *Iura* 27: 88–101.

Cavanagh, William. G., and Curtis, Mike, eds. 1998. *Post-Minoan Crete. Proceedings of the First Colloquium* (BSA Studies, vol. 2). London.

Chadwick, John. 1987. 'Some Observations on Two New Inscriptions from Lyktos'. In Lenia Kastrinaki, Georgia Orphanou, and Nikos Giannadakis, eds. *Ειλαπίνη. Τόμος τιμητικός γιά τόν Καθηγητή Νικόλαο Πλάτωνα*, I.329–34. Heraklion.

Chaniotis, Angelos. 1992. 'Die Geschichte von Amnisos von Homer bis zur Eroberung Kretas durch die Türken'. In Schäfer 1992b: 73–128.

Chaniotis, Angelos. 1995. 'Problems of "Pastoralism" and "Transhumance" in Classical and Hellenistic Crete'. *Orbis Terrarum* 1: 39–89.

Chaniotis, Angelos. 1996. *Die Verträge zwischen kretischen Poleis in der hellenistischen Zeit.* Stuttgart.

Chaniotis, Angelos, ed. 1999a. *From Minoan Farmers to Roman Traders. Sidelights on the Economy of Ancient Crete* (Heidelberger Althistorische Beiträge und Epigraphische Studien 29). Stuttgart.

Chaniotis, Angelos. 1999b. 'Milking the Mountains. Economic Activities on the Cretan Uplands in the Classical and Hellenistic Period'. In Chaniotis 1999a: 181–200.

Chaniotis, Angelos. 2005. 'The Great Inscription, its Political and Social Institutions and the Common Institutions of the Cretans'. In Greco and Lombardo 2005: 175–94.

Chantraine, Pierre. 1948. *Grammaire Homérique* I: *Phonétique et Morphologie.* Paris.

Chantraine, Pierre. 1972. 'A propos du nom des Phéniciens et des noms de la pourpre'. *Studii Clasice* 14: 7–15.

Chantraine, Pierre. 1980. *Dictionnaire étymologique de la langue grecque. Histoire des mots.* Paris.

Chatzi-Vallianou, Despina. 1980. '*Σμάρι Πεδιάδας: ένα απομονομένα κέντρο Υστερομινοικού-Πρωτοελληνικού πολιτισμού Κρήτη*'. *AAA* 13: 20–60.

Chatzi-Vallianou, Despina. 2000. '*Η λατρεία της Αθήνας στην Ακρόπολη Σμαρίου*'. In *Πεπραγμένα του Η΄ Διεθνούς Κρητολογικού Συνεδρίου*. A.3, 505–36. Heraklion.

Chatzi-Vallianou, Despina. 2004. '*Ομηρικά στοιχεία στην Ακρόπολη Σμαριού*'. In Nikolaos Stampolidis and Angeliki Giannikouri, eds. *Το Αιγαίο στην Πρώιμη Εποχή του Σιδήριου. Πρακτικά του Διεθνούς Συμποσίου, Ρόδος, 1–4 Νοεμβρίου 2002*, 105–27. Athens.

Clay, Diskin. 2004. *Archilochos Heros. The Cult of Poets in the Greek Polis.* Cambridge, MA.

Cohen, David. 1983. *Theft in Athenian Law* (Münchener Beiträge zur Papyrusforschung und antiken Rechtsgeschichte 74). Munich.

Coldstream, John N. 1973a. *Knossos: The Sanctuary of Demeter* (*BSA* Suppl. 8). London.

Coldstream, John N. 1973b. 'Knossos 1951–1961: Orientalizing and Archaic Pottery from the Town'. *BSA* 68: 33–63.

Coldstream, John N. 1977. *Geometric Greece.* London.

Coldstream, John N. 1999. 'Knossos 1951–1961: Classical and Hellenistic Pottery from the Town'. *BSA* 94: 321–51.

Coldstream, John N. 2000. 'Evans's Greek Finds: The Early Greek Town of Knossos, and its Encroachment of the Borders of the Minoan Palace'. *BSA* 95: 259–99.

Coldstream, John N. 2006. 'Knossos in Early Greek Times'. In Sigrid Deger-Jalkotzy and I. S. Lemos, eds., *Ancient Greece: from the Mycenaean palaces to the age of Homer*, 581–96. Edinburgh.

Coldstream, John N. 2013. 'Geometric and Archaic Crete. A hunt for the elusive polis'. In Niemeier, Pilz, and Kaiser 2013: 341–53.

Coldstream, John N., and Hatzaki, Eleni. 2003. 'Knossos: Early Greek Occupation under the Roman Villa Dionysus'. *BSA* 98: 279–306.

Coldstream, John N., and Huxley, George L. 1999. 'Knossos: The Archaic Gap'. *BSA* 94: 289–307.

Coldstream, John N., and Macdonald, Colin F. 1997. 'Knossos: Area of South-West Houses, Early Hellenic Occupation'. *BSA* 92: 191–245.

Comparetti, Domenico. 1893. 'Le leggi di Gortyna e le altre iscrizioni arcaiche cretesi. Oaxos, Eleutherna, Lyttos, Knossos, Itanos, Praesos etc'. *Mon. Ant.* 3: 1–490.

Comparetti, Domenico. 1916–20. 'Iscrizioni inedite di Gortyna'. *ASA (Atene)* 3: 193–202.

Comparetti, Domenico. 1927. 'Iscrizioni greche arcaiche di Eltynia e Gortyna in Creta e della città di Teos nella Ionia'. *MAL* Ser. 6, 2: 245–76.

Comparetti, Domenico, and Halbherr, Federico. 1888. 'Epigrafi arcaiche di varie città cretesi'. *Mus. It.* 2: 129–78.

Coutsinas, Nadia. 2013. *Défenses crétoises: fortifications urbaines et défense du territoire en Crète aux époques classique et hellénistique. Cahiers archéologiques de Paris* 1, no. 3. Paris.

Cross, Malcolm. 2011. *The Creativity of Crete: City States and the Foundations of the Modern World*. Oxford.

Cucuzza, Nicola. 1993 (1995). 'Leto e il cosiddetto tempio di Rhea di Festòs'. *Quaderni dell'Istituto di Archeologia della Facoltà di Lettere e Filosofia Università di Messina* 8: 21–7.

Cucuzza, Nicola. 1997. 'Considerazioni su alcuni culti nella Messarà di epoca storica e sui rapporti territoriali fra Festòs e Gortina'. *RAL* Ser. 9, 8: 63–93.

Cucuzza, Nicola. 1998. 'Geometric Phaistos: a survey'. In Cavanagh and Curtis 1998: 62–8.

Cucuzza, Nicola. 2005. 'Festòs "post-minoica": Note di topografia e di storia'. *Creta Antica* 6: 285–332.

Cucuzza, Nicola. 2011, 'Tombe e costumi funerari nella Festòs della Dark Age: qualche osservazione'. In Giovanni Rizza, ed. *Identità culturale, etnicità, processi di trasformazione a Creta fra Dark Age e Arcaismo. Per i cento anni di Priniàs* (Convegno di Studi, Atene 9–12 novembre 2006), 359–71. Catania.

D'Acunto, Matteo. 2001. 'Il "gorgoneion" in pietra da Axòs e la modificazione del tipo a Creta tra modelli orientali e greci'. *AION* (archeol) 20: 47–63, 246 (English résumé).

D'Acunto, Matteo. 2002. 'Gortina, il santuario protoarcaico sull'acropoli di Haghios Ioannis: una riconsiderazione'. *ASA (Atene)* Ser. 3, 2: 183–229.

D'Acunto, Matteo. 2002–3. 'Il tempio di Apollo a Dreros: il culto e la cucina del sacrificio'. *AION* (archeol) 9–10: 9–62.

D'Acunto, Matteo. 2008. 'La lissé petre in Od. III, 293–296 ed i territori di Gortina e di Festòs in epoca arcaica'. *Creta Antica* 9: 265–85.

D'Agata, Anna Lucia. 1998. 'Changing patterns in a Minoan and post-Minoan sanctuary: the case of Agia Triada'. In Cavanagh and Curtis 1998: 19–26.

D'Agata, Anna Lucia, and Van de Mortel, Aleydis, eds. 2009. *Archaeologies of Cult. Essays on Ritual and Cult in Crete in Honor of Geraldine C. Gesell* (*Hesperia* Suppl. 42). Princeton.

Dareste, Rodolphe, Haussoullier, Bernard, and Reinach, Théodore. 1891–1904. *Recueil des inscriptions juridiques grecques*. 2 Volumes. Paris.

Davaras, Costis. 1960. '*Ἐπιγραφαὶ ἐκ Κρήτης* I'. *KrChr* 14: 457–65.

Davaras, Costis. 1980 (1982). '*Κρητικὲς ἐπιγραφές* III'. *AE* 1980: 1–42.

Davies, John K. 1996. 'Deconstructing Gortyn: When is a Code a Code?' In Lin Foxhall and Andrew D. E. Lewis, eds. *Greek Law in its Political Setting: Justifications Not Justice*, 33–56. Oxford.

Davies, John K. 2005. 'Gortyn within the Economy of Archaic and Classical Crete'. In Greco and Lombardo 2005: 154–74.

Davies, John K. 2009. 'The Historiography of Archaic Greece'. In Raaflaub and van Wees 2009: 3–21.

Day, Leslie Preston, and Glowacki, Kevin T., et al. 2012. *Kavousi IIB: The Late Minoan IIIC Settlement at Vronda. The Buildings on the Periphery* (Prehistory Monographs 39). Philadelphia.

Day, Leslie Preston, Klein, Nancy L., and Turner, Lee Ann. 2009. *Kavousi IIA: The Late Minoan IIIC Settlement at Vronda. The Buildings on the Summit* (Prehistory Monographs, 26). Philadelphia.

Demargne, Pierre, and van Effenterre, Henri. 1937a. 'Recherches à Dréros'. *BCH* 61: 5–32.

Demargne, Pierre. and van Effenterre, Henri. 1937b. 'Recherches à Dréros, II. Les inscriptions archaïques'. *BCH* 61: 333–48.

De Sanctis, Gaetano. 1907. 'Nuovi studi e scoperte in Gortyna II. Iscrizioni I. Iscrizioni del Pythion'. *Mon. Ant.* 18: cols. 297–318.

De Sanctis, Gaetano. 1908–10. Notebook no. 52. Scuola Archeologica Italiana di Atene.

Descat, Raymond. 2001. 'Monnaie multiple et monnaie frappée en Grèce archaïque'. *Revue Numismatique* 157: 69–81.

Dimitrova, Nora Mitkova, ed. 2008. *Theoroi and Initiates in Samothrace: The Epigraphical Evidence*. Princeton.

Dittenberger, Wilhelm. 1915–24. *Sylloge Inscriptionum Graecarum*. 3rd edn. 4 vols. Leipzig.

Dittenberger, Wilhelm, and Purgold, Karl. 1896. *Die Inschriften von Olympia. Olympia* 5. Berlin.

Di Vita, Antonino, ed. 1988. *Gortina* I (Monografie della Scuola Archeologica di Atene e delle Missioni Italiane in Oriente 3). Rome.

Di Vita, Antonino. 2005. 'La Grande Iscrizione: dal monumento greco all'Odeion romano'. In Greco and Lombardo 2005: 13–40.

Di Vita, Antonino. 2010. *Gortina di Creta: quindici secoli di vita urbana*. Rome.

Di Vita, Antonino, and Cantarella, Eva. 1978 [1982]. 'Iscrizione arcaica giuridica da Festòs'. *ASA (Atene)* 56: 429–35.

Doublet, Georges. 1889. 'Inscriptions de Crète'. *BCH* 13: 47–77.

Duhoux, Yves. 1982. *L'étéocrétois. Les textes, la langue*. Amsterdam.

Eaby, Melissa. 2011. 'Regionalism in Early Iron Age Cretan Burials'. In Joanne M. A. Murphy, ed. *Prehistoric Crete. Regional and Diachronic Studies on Mortuary Systems*, 165–202. Philadelphia.

Ebbinghaus, Susanne. 2005. 'Protector of the City, or the Art of Storage in Early Greece'. *Hesperia* 74: 51–72.

Edwards, G. Patrick, and Edwards, Ruth B. 1974. 'Red Letters and Phoenician Writing'. *Kadmos* 13: 48–57.

Edwards, G. Patrick, and Edwards, Ruth B. 1977. 'The Meaning and Etymology of ποινικαστάς'. *Kadmos* 16: 131–40.

Ehrenberg, Victor. 1943. 'An Early Source of Polis-Constitution'. *Classical Quarterly* 37: 14–18.

Engels, Johannes. 1998. *Funerum sepulcrorumque magnificentia* (Hermes Einzelschriften 78). Stuttgart. (51–3 on Gortyn).

Erickson, Brice L. 2000. 'Late Archaic and Classical Crete. Island Pottery Styles in an Age of Historical Transition, ca. 600–400 B.C.'. Diss., University of Texas, Austin.

Erickson, Brice L. 2001. 'Historical Greek Pottery from the Excavations of the Odeion, Gortyn'. *ASA (Atene)* 76–8: 236–45.

Erickson, Brice L. 2002. 'Aphrati and Kato Syme. Pottery, Continuity, and Cult in Late Archaic and Classical Crete'. *Hesperia* 71: 41–90.

Erickson, Brice L. 2004. 'Eleutherna and the Greek World, ca. 600–400 B.C'. In Lesley Preston Day, Margaret S. Mook, and James D. Muhly, eds. *Crete beyond the Palaces: Proceedings of the Crete 2000 Conference*, 199–212. Philadelphia.

Erickson, Brice L. 2006. 'Cretan Austerity in the Sixth Century BC'. In *Πρακτικά του Συνεδρίου Ο Μυλοπόταμος από την Αρχαιότητα ώς Σήμερα. IV. Ελεύθερνα-Αξός, Πάνορμο 2003*, 69–101. Rethymno.

Erickson, Brice L. 2009. 'Roussa Ekklesia, Part I: Religion and Politics in East Crete'. *American Journal of Archaeology* 113: 353–404.

Erickson, Brice L. 2010a. *Crete in Transition: Pottery Styles and Island History in the Archaic and Classical Periods.* Princeton.

Erickson, Brice L. 2010b. 'Priniatikos Pyrgos and the Classical Period in Eastern Crete: Feasting and Island Identities'. *Hesperia* 79: 305–49.

Erickson, Brice L. 2011. 'Public Feasts and Private Symposia in the Archaic and Classical Periods'. In Glowacki et al. 2011: 381–91.

Evans, Arthur J. 1928. *The Palace of Minos*, vol. ii. London.

Fabricius, E. 1885. 'Alterthümer auf Kreta. III. Archaische Inschriften'. *Ath. Mitt.* 10: 91–6.

Faure, Paul. 1959. 'La Crète aux cent villes'. *KrChr* 13: 171–217.

Faure, Paul. 1963. 'Nouvelles localisations de villes crétoises'. *KrChr* 17: 16–26.

Faure, Paul. 1967. 'Aux frontières de l'État de Lato: 50 toponymes'. In William C. Brice, ed. *Europa. Studien zur Geschichte und Epigraphik der frühen Aegaeis. Festschrift für Ernst Grumach*, 94–112. Berlin.

Faure, Paul. 1993. 'Nouvelles identifications d'antiques localités crétoises'. *Kadmos* 32: 67–74.

Ferruti, Francesco. 2004. 'Un ginnasio a Gortina in un'iscrizione del V sec. A.C'. *Creta Antica* 5: 283–94.

Fisher, Nicolas, and van Wees, Hans, eds. 1998. *Archaic Greece: New Approaches and New Evidence.* Swansea.

Forsdyke, Sara. 2005. *Exile, Ostracism, and Democracy: The Politics of Expulsion in Ancient Greece.* Princeton.

Fraser, Peter M., and Matthews, Elaine, eds. 1987. *A Lexicon of Greek Personal Names I. The Aegean Islands, Cyprus, Cyrenaica.* Oxford.

Frederiksen, Rune. 2011. *Greek City Walls of the Archaic Period, 900–480 BC.* Oxford.

French, Elizabeth B. 1993. 'Archaeology in Greece 1992–93', *AR* 39: 3–84.

Frisone, Flavia. 1995. 'Una legislazione funeraria a Gortina?' *Studi di Antichità* 8.1: 55–68.

Frisone, Flavia. 2000. *Leggi e Regolamenti funerari nel Mondo Greco.* I. *Le Fonti Epigrafiche.* Galatina.

Gagarin, Michael. 1982. 'The Organization of the Gortyn Law Code'. *GRBS* 23: 129–46.

Gagarin, Michael. 1984. 'The Testimony of Witnesses in the Gortyn Laws'. *GRBS* 25: 345–9.

Gagarin, Michael. 1986. *Early Greek Law*, Berkeley, Los Angeles, London.

Gagarin, Michael. 1988. 'The First Law of the Gortyn Code'. *GRBS* 29: 335–43.

Gagarin, Michael. 1989. 'The Function of Witnesses at Gortyn'. In Thür 1989: 29–54.

Gagarin, Michael. 1994. 'The Economic Status of Women at Gortyn: Retroactivity and Change'. In Gerhard Thür, ed. *Symposion 1993*, 61–71. Cologne.

Gagarin, Michael. 1995. 'The First Law of the Gortyn Code Revisited'. *GRBS* 36: 7–15.

Gagarin, Michael. 2001. 'The Gortyn Code and Greek Legal Procedure'. In Eva Cantarella and Gerhard Thür, eds. *Symposion 1997*, 41–51. Cologne.

Gagarin, Michael. 2004. 'The Rule of Law in Gortyn'. In Edward M. Harris and Lene Rubinstein, eds. *The Law and the Courts in Ancient Greece*, 173–83. London.

Gagarin, Michael. 2005a. 'The Unity of Greek Law'. In Gagarin and Cohen 2005: 29–40.

Gagarin, Michael. 2005b. 'Early Greek Law'. In Gagarin and Cohen 2005: 82–94.

Gagarin, Michael. 2008a. *Writing Greek Law*. Cambridge.

Gagarin, Michael. 2008b. 'Women and Property at Gortyn'. *Dike* 11: 5–25.

Gagarin, Michael. 2010a. 'Slaves and Serfs at Gortyn'. *ZSS* 127: 14–31.

Gagarin, Michael. 2010b. 'Legal Procedure at Gortyn'. In Thür 2010b: 127–45.

Gagarin, Michael. 2011. 'Writing Sacred Laws in Archaic and Classical Crete'. In André P. M. H. Lardinois, Josine H. Blok, and Mark G. M. van der Poel, eds. *Sacred Words: Orality, Literacy and Religion*, 101–11. Leiden.

Gagarin, Michael. 2012a. 'The Laws of Crete'. In Bernard Legras, ed. *Transferts culturels et droits dans le monde grec et hellénistique*, 17–29. Paris.

Gagarin, Michael. 2012b. 'Women and the Law in Gortyn'. *Index* 40 (Studies for Eva Cantarella): 57–67.

Gagarin, Michael, and Cohen, David, eds. 2005. *The Cambridge Companion to Ancient Greek Law*. Cambridge.

Gaignerot-Driessen, Florence. 2013. *De l'occupation postpalatiale à la cité grecque: le cas du Mirambello (Crete)*. Vol. I. *Exploration archéologique et géographique de la région* (unpublished doctoral diss.). Université Paris-Sorbonne, Paris.

Gaignerot-Driessen, Florence, and Driessen, Jan, eds. 2014. *Cretan Cities: Formation and Transformation* (*Aegis* 7). Louvain.

Gallant, Thomas W. 1991. *Risk and Survival in Ancient Greece: Reconstructing the Rural Domestic Economy*. Cambridge.

Gallavotti, Carlo. 1977. 'Scrittura della Sicilia ed altre epigrafi arcaiche'. *Helikon* 17: 97–136. (130–5 on Dreros).

Garland, Robert. 1989. 'The Well-Ordered Corpse: An Investigation into the Motives behind Greek funerary Legislation'. *BICS* 36: 1–15. (10–11 on Gortyn).

Gehrke, Hans-Joachim. 1997. 'Gewalt und Gesetz. Die soziale und politische Ordnung Kretas in der Archaischen und Klassischen Zeit'. *Klio* 79: 23–68.

Gehrke, Hans-Joachim. 2009. 'States'. In Raaflaub and van Wees 2009: 395–410.

Genevrois, Gérard. 2012. 'D'Axos à Olympie: sur les traces de la racine *AL-*', *Revue des études anciennes* 114: 279–300.

Glowacki, Kevin. 2007. 'House, household and community at LM IIIC Vronda, Kavousi'. In Westgate, Fisher, and Whitley 2007: 129–41.

Glowacki, Kevin T., and Vogeikoss-Brogan, Natalia, eds. 2011. *ΣΤΕΓΑ. The Archaeology of Houses and Households in Ancient Crete* (*Hesperia* Suppl. 4). Princeton.

Gorlin, Catherine E. 1988. 'The Spensithios Decree and Archaic Cretan Civil Status'. *ZPE* 74: 159–65.

Greco, Emanuele, and Lombardo, Mario, eds. 2005. *La Grande Iscrizione di Gortyna. Centoventi anni dopo la scoperta. Atti del I Convegno Internazionale di Studi sulla Messarà. Scuola Archaeologica Italiana di Atene, Atene-Haghii Deka 25–28 maggio 2004* (TRIPODES 4). Athens.

Gschnitzer, Fritz. 1974. 'Bemerkungen zum Arbeitsvertrag des Schreibers Spensithios'. *ZPE* 13: 265–75.

Guarducci, Margherita. 1931a. 'Studi di epigrafia cretese'. *Historia* 5: 218–35.

Guarducci, Margherita. 1931b. 'Iscrizioni inedite del Museo di Rettimo'. *Rivista dell'Istituto Nazionale di Archeologia e Storia dell'Arte* 3: 27–30.

Guarducci, Margherita. 1935. *Inscriptiones Creticae. Opera et Consilio Friderici Halbherr Collectae* I. *Tituli Cretae Mediae Praeter Gortynios.* Rome.

Guarducci, Margherita. 1936. 'Intorno ai perieci di Creta'. *RFIC* 64: 356–63.

Guarducci, Margherita. 1939. *Inscriptiones Creticae. Opera et Consilio Friderici Halbherr Collectae* II. *Tituli Cretae Occidentalis.* Rome.

Guarducci, Margherita. 1941. 'Note di epigrafia cretese'. *RFIC* 19: 20–35.

Guarducci, Margherita. 1942. *Inscriptiones Creticae. Opera et Consilio Friderici Halbherr Collectae* III. *Tituli Cretae Orientalis.* Rome.

Guarducci, Margherita. 1950. *Inscriptiones Creticae. Opera et Consilio Friderici Halbherr Collectae* IV. *Tituli Gortynii.* Rome.

Guarducci, Margherita. 1967. *Epigrafia Greca I.* Rome.

Guizzi, Francesco. 1997. 'Terra comune, pascolo e contributo ai "syssitia" in Creta arcaica e classica'. *AION* ns 4: 45–51.

Guizzi, Francesco. 2011. 'Houses in the Household I: Ownership and Use of Dwelling Places in Gortynian Inscriptions'. In Glowacki et al. 2011: 394–9.

Haggis, Donald C. 2005. *Kavousi I: The Archaeological Survey of the Kavousi Region* (Prehistory Monographs, 16). Philadelphia.

Haggis, Donald C. 2013. 'Social Organization and Aggregated Settlement Structure in an Archaic Greek City on Crete (ca. 600 BC)'. In Jennifer Birch, ed. *From Prehistoric Villages to Cities. Settlement Aggregation and Community Transformation*, 63–86. New York and London.

Haggis, Donald C. 2014. 'Azoria and Archaic Urbanization'. In Gaignerot-Driessen and Driessen 2014: 119–39.

Haggis, Donald C., and Mook, Margaret S. 2011. 'The Archaic Houses at Azoria'. In Glowacki et al. 2011: 367–80.

Haggis, Donald C., Mook, Margaret S., Coulson, William D. E., Tobin, Jennifer L. 1997. 'Excavations on the Kastro at Kavousi: An Architectural Overview', *Hesperia* 66: 315–90.

Haggis, Donald C., Mook, Margaret S., Scarry, C. Margaret, Snyder, Lynn M., and West, William C. III. 2004. 'Excavations at Azoria, 2002'. *Hesperia* 73: 339–400.

Haggis, Donald C., Mook, Margaret S., Fitzsimons, Rodney D., Scarry, C. Margaret, Snyder, Lynn M., Stefanakis, Manolis I., and West, William C. III, 2007. 'Excavations at Azoria, 2003–2004, Part I: The Archaic Civic Complex'. *Hesperia* 76: 243–321.

Haggis, Donald C., Mook, Margaret S., Fitzsimons, Rodney D., Scarry, C. Margaret, Snyder, Lynn M., and West. William C. 2011a. 'Excavations in the Archaic Civic Buildings at Azoria in 2005–2006'. *Hesperia* 80: 1–70.

Haggis, Donald C., Mook, Margaret S., Fitzsimons, Rodney D., Scarry, C. Margaret, Snyder, Lynn M. 2011b. 'The Excavation of Archaic Houses at Azoria in 2005–2006'. *Hesperia* 80: 431–89.

Halbherr, Federico. ? Notebook no. 4. Scuola Archeologica Italiana di Atene.

Halbherr, Federico. 1884a. Notebook no. 5. Scuola Archeologica Italiana di Atene.

Halbherr, Federico. 1884b. Notebook no. 22. Scuola Archeologica Italiana di Atene.

Halbherr, Federico. 1885. Notebook no. 26. Scuola Archeologica Italiana di Atene.

Halbherr, Federico. 1893–4. Notebook no. 17. Scuola Archeologica Italiana di Atene.

Halbherr, Federico. 1896. 'Cretan Expedition I. Inscriptions from Various Cretan Cities'. *AJA* 11: 539–601.

Halbherr, Federico. 1897. 'Cretan Expedition III. Epigraphical Researches in Gortyna'. *AJA* n.s. 1: 159–238.

Halbherr, Federico. 1899. Notebook no. 53. Scuola Archeologica Italiana di Atene.

Halbherr, Federico. 1899–1900. Notebook no. 51bis. Scuola Archeologica Italiana di Atene.

Halbherr, Federico. 1901a. 'Cretan Expedition XI. Three Cretan Necropoleis: Report on the Researches at Erganos, Panaghia, and Courtes', *AJA* 5: 259–93.

Halbherr, Federico. 1901b. 'Lavori eseguiti dalla missione archeologica Italiana nell'Agora di Gortyna e nell'Asclepieo di Lebena'. *RAL* 10: 291–306.

Halbherr, Federico. 1910. Notebook no. 15. Scuola Archeologica Italiana di Atene.

Halbherr, Federico. 1913. Notebook no. 63. Scuola Archeologica Italiana di Atene.

Halbherr, Federico. 1914. Notebook no. 61. Scuola Archeologica Italiana di Atene.

Halbherr, Federico. ? Notebook no. 65. Scuola Archeologica Italiana di Atene.

Halbherr, Federico, and Fabricius, E. 1885. *Leggi antiche della città di Gortyna*. Florence.

Hansen, Mogens Herman, and Fischer-Hansen, Tobias. 1994. 'Monumental Political Architecture in Archaic and Classical *Poleis*: Evidence and Historical Significance'. In D. Whitehead, ed. *From Political Architecture to Stephanus Byzantius: Sources for the Ancient Greek Polis. Papers from the Copenhagen Polis Centre*, 1 (Historia Einzelschriften 87), 23–90. Stuttgart.

Hansen, Mogens Herman, and Nielsen, Thomas Heine. 2004. *An Inventory of Archaic and Classical* Poleis. Oxford.

Harris, William V. 1989. *Ancient Literacy*. Cambridge, MA.

Harrison, A. R. W. 1968. *The Law of Athens*. Vol. 1: *The Family and Property*. Oxford.

Harrison, A. R. W. 1971. *The Law of Athens*. Vol. 2: *Procedure*. Oxford.

Haussoullier, B. 1880. 'Inscriptions archaïques de Gortyne (Crète)'. *BCH* 4: 460–71.

Haussoullier, B. 1885. 'Inscriptions de Crète'. *BCH* 9: 1–28.

Hawke, Jason. 2011. *Writing Authority: Elite Competition and Written Law in Early Greece*'. DeKalb, IL.

Hayden, Barbara J. 1995. 'Rural Settlement of the Orientalizing through Early Classical Period: The Meseleroi Valley, Eastern Crete'. *Aegean Archaeology* 2: 93–144.

Haysom, Matthew. 2011. 'The strangeness of Crete. Problems for the protohistory of Greek religion'. In Matthew Haysom, and Jenny Wallensten, eds. *Current approaches to religion in ancient Greece. Papers presented at a symposium at the Swedish Institute at Athens, 17–19 April 2008*, 95–110. Stockholm.

Heisserer, Andrew J. 1980. *Alexander the Great and the Greeks: The Epigraphic Evidence.* Norman, OK.

Herrmann, Peter. 1981. 'Teos und Abdera im 5. Jahrhundert v. Chr. Ein neues Fragment der Teiorum Dirae'. *Chiron* 11: 1–30.

Hodkinson, Stephen. 1998. 'Laconian Artistic Production and the Problem of Spartan Austerity'. In Fisher and van Wees 1998: 93–117.

Hodkinson, Stephen. 2000. *Property and Wealth in Classical Sparta.* London.

Hoffmann, Herbert. 1972. *Early Cretan Armorers.* Mainz on Rhine.

Hölkeskamp, Karl-Joachim. 1999. *Schiedsrichter, Gesetzgeber und Gesetzgebung im archaischen Griechenland* (Historia Einzelschriften 131). Stuttgart.

Hood, Sinclair, and Smyth, David. 1981. *Archaeological Survey of the Knossos Area* (*BSA* Suppl. 14). London.

Hood, Sinclair, Warren, Peter, and Cadogan, Gerald. 1964. 'Travels in Crete, 1962'. *BSA* 59: 50–99.

Hornblower, Simon, Spawforth, Anthony, and Eidinow, Esther. 2012. *Oxford Classical Dictionary.* 4th edn. Oxford.

Ikonomaki, Androniki. 2010. *Τα τοπικά αλφάβητα της Κρήτης στην αρχαϊκή και κλασική περίοδο* (diss. The University of Crete, Rethymno).

Jacoby, Felix. 1923–58. *Die Fragmente der griechischen Historiker.* Berlin.

Jakab, Eva. 1989. 'Zwei Kaufvorschriften im Recht von Gortyn: *IC* IV 41 col. VII 1–19 und 72 col. VII 10–15'. *ZSS* 86: 535–44.

Jameson, Michael H. 1988. 'Sacrifice and animal husbandry in classical Greece'. In Charles R. Whittaker, ed. *Pastoral Economies in Classical Antiquity*, 87–119. Cambridge.

Jeffery, Lilian H. 1949. 'Comments on Some Archaic Greek Inscriptions'. *Journal of Hellenic Studies* 69: 25–38.

Jeffery, Lilian H. 1990. *The Local Scripts of Archaic Greece.* 2nd edn. with a Supplement by A. W. Johnston. Oxford (1st edn. 1961).

Jeffery, Lilian H., and Morpurgo-Davies, Anna. 1970. '*Ποινικαστάς* and *Ποινικάζεν*: BM 1969. 4–2. 1, a New Archaic Inscription from Crete'. *Kadmos* 9: 118–54.

Johannowsky, Werner. 2002. *Il Santuario sull'Acropoli di Gortina*, vol. II (Monografie della Scuola Archeologica di Atene e delle Missioni Italiane in Oriente 16). Athens.

Johnston, Alan. 2013. 'Writing in and around Archaic Crete'. In Niemeier, Pilz, and Kaiser 2013: 427–36.

Jones, Donald W. 2000. *External relations of early Iron Age Crete, 1100–600 B.C.* (Archaeological Institute of America Monographs ns 4). Dubuque, IA.

Jones, Nicholas F. 1987. *Public Organization in Ancient Greece. A Documentary Study.* Philadelphia.

Kaczynska, Elwira. 2001. 'Hesychius on *λυκόφρων*'. *Emerita* 69: 263–7.

Kalpaxis, Athanasios. 1991. 'Ανασκαφικά δεδομένα'. In A. Kalpaxis, ed. *Ελεύθερνα II.1. Επιγραφές από το Πυργί και το Νησί*, 11–15. Rethymno.

Kalpaxis, Athanasios. 1994. ''Η πόλη τῆς ἀρχαίας 'Ελεύθερνας καί ἡ ἐγγύτερη οἰκιστική της περιοχή'. In *ΕΛΕΥΘΕΡΝΑ* II.2: 17–21. Rethymno.

Kalpaxis, Athanasios. 2004. 'The Acropolises. Central Excavation, Sector III'. In Stampolidis, ed. 2004c: 104–15.

Kalpaxis, Athanasios, Furtwängler, Andreas, and Schnapp, Alain, eds. 1994. *ΕΛΕΥΘΕΡΝΑ* II.2. *ΕΝΑ ΕΛΛΗΝΙΣΤΙΚΟ ΣΠΙΤΙ* ('*ΣΠΙΤΙ Α*') *ΣΤΗ ΘΕΣΗ ΝΗΣΙ*. Rethymno.

Kanta, Athanasia. 1994. 'The post-palatial period in the area of Amari. Trade and communication between the north and south coasts of Crete'. In Luigi Rocchetti, ed. *Sybrita: la valle di Amari fra bronzo e ferro* (Incunabula Graeca 96), 67–74. Rome.

Karabélias, Evangélos. 2004. *Recherches sur la condition juridique et sociale de la fille unique dans le monde grec ancien excepté Athènes.* Athens.

Kennell, Nigel Martin. 1995. *The Gymnasium of Virtue: Education and Culture in Ancient Sparta.* Chapel Hill, NC.

Kennell, Nigel Martin. 2013. 'Age-Class Societies in Ancient Greece?' *Ancient Society* 43: 1–73.

Kern, Otto. 1967. repr. *Die Inschriften von Magnesia am Maeander.* Berlin.

Keyser, Paul. 1987. 'Numerals on the Gortynian Law-Codes (*IC* IV 72 + 73)'. *ZPE* 69: 283–90.

Kim, Henry S. 2001. 'Archaic coinage as evidence for the use of money'. In Andrew Meadows and Kirsty Shipton, eds. *Money and its Uses in the Ancient Greek World*, 7–21. Oxford.

Klein, Nancy L., and Glowacki, Kevin T. 2009. 'From Kavousi Vronda to Dreros: Architecture and Display in Cretan Cult Buildings'. In D'Agata and Van de Mortel 2009: 153–67.

Koerner, Reinhard. 1981. 'Vier frühe Verträge zwischen Gemeinwesen und Privatleuten auf griechischen Inschriften'. *Klio* 63: 179–206.

Koerner, Reinhard. 1987. 'Zur Landaufteilung in griechischen Poleis in älterer Zeit'. *Klio* 69: 443–9.

Koerner, Reinhard. 1993. *Inschriftliche Gesetzestexte der frühen griechischen Polis.* Cologne, Weimar, Vienna.

Kohler, Josef, and Ziebarth, Erich. 1912. *Das Stadtrecht von Gortyn und seine Beziehungen zum gemeingriechischen Rechte.* Göttingen.

Kotsonas, Antonis. 2002. 'The Rise of the Polis in Central Crete'. *Eulimene* 3: 37–74.

Kotsonas, Antonis. 2008. *The archaeology of Tomb A1K1 of Orthi Petra in Eleutherna: The Early Iron Age pottery.* Heraklion.

Kotsonas, Antonis. 2011. 'Quantification of Ceramics from Early Iron Age Tombs'. In Samuel Verdan, Thierry Theurillat, and Anne Kenzelmann Pfyffer, eds. *Early Iron Age Pottery: A Quantitative Approach. Proceedings of the International Round Table Organized by the Swiss School of Archaeology in Greece (Athens, November 28–30, 2008)* (British Archaeological Reports International Series 2254), 129–38. Oxford.

Kotsonas, Antonis. 2013. 'Orientalizing ceramic styles and wares of Early Iron Age Crete. Aspects of production, dissemination and consumption'. In Niemeier, Pilz, and Kaiser 2013: 233–52.

Kotsonas, Antonis. Forthcoming. 'O Federico Halbherr *και η αρχαϊκή Ελεύθερνα*', *Πεπραγμένα του 11ου Διεθνούς Κρητολογικού Συνεδρίου, Ρέθυμνο, 21–27 Οκτωβρίου 2011.*

Kotsonas, Antonis, Vasilakis, Andonis, and Whitelaw, Todd. 2012. '*Η Κνωσός της Πρώιμης Εποχής του Σιδήρου: τα νέα δεδομένα από το πρόγραμμα επιφανειακής έρευνας* (KULP)'. *Αρχαιολογικό έργο Κρήτης 2. Πρακτικά της 2ης Συνάντησης Ρέθυμνο, 26–28 Νοεμβρίου 2010*, 219–29. Rethymno.

Kotsonas, Antonis, Whitelaw, Todd, Vasilakis, Andonis, and Bredaki, Maria. Forthcoming. 'Early Iron Age Knossos: An overview from the Knossos Urban Landscape Project (KULP)', *Πεπραγμένα του 11ου Διεθνούς Κρητολογικού Συνεδρίου, Ρέθυμνο, 21–27 Οκτωβρίου 2011.*

Kristensen, Karen Rørby. 1994. 'Men, Women and Property in Gortyn: The Karteros of the Law Code'. *Classica et Mediaevalia* 45: 5–26.

Kristensen, Karen Rørby. 2002. 'On the Gortynian *Πυλά* and *Σταρτός* of the 5th Century BC'. *Classica et Mediaevalia* 53: 65–80.

Kristensen, Karen Rørby. 2004. 'Gortynian Debt Bondage: Some New Considerations on IC IV 41 IV–VII, 47 and 72.I.56–II.2, X.25–32'. *ZPE* 149: 73–9.

Kritzas, Charilambos. 2000. '*Νέα επιγραφικά στοιχεία για την ετυμολογία του Λασυθίου*'. *Πεπραγμένα τοῦ Η' Διεθνοῦς Κρητολογικοῦ Συνεδρίου, Ηράκλειο, 9–14 Σεπτεβρίου 1996*, A.2, 81–97. Heraklion.

Kritzas, Charilambos. 2010. '*Φοινικήια γράμματα: Νέα Αρχαϊκή Επιγραφή απο την 'Ελτυνα*'. In Giorgos Rhethemiotakis and Maria Englezou, *Το γεωμετρικό Νεκροταφείο Ελτύνας*, 3–23. Heraklion.

Kroll, John H. 2001. 'Observations on Monetary Instruments in Pre-Coinage Greece'. In Miriam S. Balmuth, ed. *Hacksilber to Coinage: New Insights into the Monetary History of the Near East and Greece*, 77–91. New York.

Kroll, John H. 2008. 'The Monetary Use of Weighed Bullion in Archaic Greece'. In William V. Harris, ed. *The Monetary Systems of the Greeks and Romans*, 12–37. Oxford.

Kroll, John H. 2011. 'The Monetary Background of Early Coinage'. In William E. Metcalf, ed. *The Oxford Handbook of Greek and Roman Coinage*, 33–42. Oxford.

Lacey, Walter K. 1968. *The Family in Classical Greece.* London.

Lanni, Adriaan. Forthcoming. *Law and Order in Ancient Athens.* Cambridge.

La Rosa, Vincenzo. 1996. 'Per la Festòs di età arcaica'. *Studi Miscellanei. Studi in memoria di Lucia Guerrini*, 30: 63–87.

La Rosa, Vincenzo. 2005. 'Nuovi dati sulla via di ascesa alla collina del Palazzo festio dall'età minoica alla geometrica'. *Creta Antica* 6: 227–84.

La Rosa, Vincenzo. 2013. 'A New Protogeometric Road in the Settlement of Phaistos'. In Niemeier, Pilz, and Kaiser 2013: 43–57.

Larsen, Jakob A. O. 1936. 'Perioeci in Crete'. *Classical Philology* 31: 11–22.

Larsen, Jakob A. O. 1949. 'The Origin and Significance of the Counting of Votes'. *Classical Philology* 44: 164–81.

La Torre, Gioacchino. 1988–9. 'Contributo preliminare alla conoscenza del territorio di Gortina'. *ASA(Atene)* 66–7: 277–322.

Lavrencic, Monika. 1988. 'Andreion'. *Tyche* 3: 147–61.

Lebessi, Angeliki. 1970. 'Αρχαιότητες και μνημεία Κεντρικής και Ανατολικής Κρήτης: Αφρατι'. *ArchDelt* 24, 1969, B´ 2 [1970], 415–18.

Lebessi, Angeliki. 1973. 'Αρχαιότητες και μνημεία Κεντρικής και Ανατολικής Κρήτης: Αφρατι'. *ArchDelt* 25, 1970, B´ 2 [1973], 455–60.

Lebessi, Angeliki. 1975a. 'Αρχαιότητες και μνημεία Κεντρικής και Ανατολικής Κρήτης: Λύττος'. *ArchDelt* 26, 1971, B´ 2 [1975], 493–9.

Lebessi, Angeliki. 1975b. ''Ιερον 'Ερμοῦ και Ἀφροδίτης εἰς Σύμην Βιάννου'. *PAAH* 1973 (1975): 188–99.

Lebessi, Angeliki. 1976. *Οι στήλες του Πρινιά*. Athens.

Lebessi, Angeliki. 1980. 'Αρχαιότητες και μνημεία Κεντρικής και Ανατολικής Κρήτης: Λύττος'. *ArchDelt* 29, 1973–1974, B´ 3, [1980], 886–7.

Lebessi, Angeliki. 1983. 'Αρχαιότητες και μνημεία Κεντρικής Κρήτης: Ανασκαφές'. *ArchDelt* 30, 1975, B´ 2 [1983], 341–2.

Lefèvre-Novaro, Daniela, Pautasso, Antonella, Rizza, Salvatore, and Lamaze, Jérémy. 2013. 'Dreros e Priniàs: nuovi dati e prospettive di ricerca sulla polis a Creta'. *Thiasos. Rivista di Archeologia e Architettura Antica* 2: 3–20.

Le Rider, Georges. 1966. *Monnaies crétoises du Ve au 1er siècle av. J.-C.* (Études crétoises, 15). Paris.

Levi, Doro. 1927–9 (1931). 'Arkades. Una città cretese all'alba della civiltà ellenica'. *ASA (Atene)* 10–12: 1–710.

Levi, Doro. 1930–1 (1933). 'I bronzi di Axos'. *ASA(Atene)* 13–14: 43–146.

Levi, Doro. 1957–8 (1958). 'Gli scavi a Festòs nel anni 1956 e 1957'. *ASA(Atene)* ns 19–20: 193–361.

Levi, Doro. 1961–2 (1963). 'Gli scavi a Festòs negli anni 1958–1960'. *ASA(Atene)* ns 23–4: 377–504.

Levi, Doro. 1967–8 (1969). 'L'abitato di Festòs in località Chalara'. *ASA(Atene)* ns 29–30: 55–164.

Lévy, Edmond. 1997. 'Libre et non-libres dans le code de Gortyne'. In Pierre Brulé and Jacques Ouhlen, eds. *Esclavage, guerre, économie en Grèce ancienne: Hommages à Yvon Garlan*, 25–41. Rennes.

Lévy, Edmond, ed. 2000. *La codification des lois dans l'antiquité: Actes du Colloque de Strasbourg 27–29 novembre 1997*. Strasbourg.

Lewis, David. 2013. 'Slave Marriages in the Laws of Gortyn: A Matter of Rights?' *Historia* 62: 390–416.

Liddell, H. G., Scott, R., and Jones, H. Stuart. 1940. *Greek–English Lexicon*. 9th edn. Oxford.

Link, Stefan. 1994a. *Das griechische Kreta. Untersuchungen zu seiner staatlichen und gesellschaftlichen Entwicklung vom 6. bis zum 4. Jahrhundert v. Chr.* Stuttgart.

Link, Stefan. 1994b. 'Die Ehefrau als Erbtochter im Recht von Gortyn'. *ZSS* 111: 414–20.

Link, Stefan. 1997. 'Versprochene Töchter? Noch einmal zur Ehefrau als Erbtochter im Gesetz von Gortyn'. *ZSS* 114 : 378–91.

Link, Stefan. 2003a. 'Kosmoi, Startoi und Iterationsverbote'. *Dike* 6: 139–49.

Link, Stefan. 2003b. 'Female Inheritance in Cretan Gortyn'. Unpublished conference paper.

Link, Stefan. 2004a. 'Zur frühgriechischen kyrieia'. *ZSS* 121: 44–93.

Link, Stefan. 2004b. 'Die Nötigung des Mündels in Gortyn (IC 4.72, col. 2, 16–20)'. *Dike* 7: 169–78.

Longo, Fausto, Greco, Alessandro, and Rossi, Amedeo, 2014. 'Festòs. La città di Radamante'. *Archeologia Viva* 33: 12–27.

Lupu, Eran, 2005. *Greek Sacred Law: A Collection of New Documents.* Leiden.

Luraghi, Nino. 2006. 'Traders, Pirates, Warriors: The Proto-History of Greek Mercenary Soldiers in the Eastern Mediterranean'. *Phoenix* 60: 21–47.

Luraghi, Nino. 2010. 'The Local Scripts from Nature to Culture'. *Classical Antiquity* 29: 68–91.

Maas, Paul. 1931. 'Zum Gesetz von Gortys'. *Zeitschrift für vergleichende Sprachforschung* 58: 266–8.

McDonald, William A. 1956. 'Note on a Fragment of an Archaic Inscription from Dreros'. *Hesperia* 25: 69–72.

Maffi, Alberto. 1983. *Studi di epigrafia giuridica greca.* Milan.

Maffi, Alberto. 1984–5. 'Le Leggi sulle Donne IC. 4, 72, 16–20, Plut. Sol. 23. 1–2'. *Sodalitas. Scritti in onore di Antonio Guarino*, 1553–67. Naples.

Maffi, Alberto. 1987. 'Le mariage de la patrôoque "donnée" dans le Code de Gortyne (col. VIII, 20–30)'. *Revue Historique de Droit Français et Étranger* 65: 507–25.

Maffi, Alberto. 1988. 'Chreos nel Codice di Gortina'. *Atti del Seminario sulla problematica contrattuale in diritto romano. Cisalpino-Goliardica* 1: 273–87.

Maffi, Alberto. 1990. 'Chronique II: Monde grec'. *Revue Historique de Droit Français et Étranger* 68: 106–26.

Maffi, Alberto. 1995. 'Encore une fois le mariage de la patrôoque donnée dans le Code de Gortyne'. *Revue Historique de Droit Français et Étranger* 73: 221–6.

Maffi, Alberto. 1997a. *Il diritto di famiglia nel Codice di Gortina.* Milan.

Maffi, Alberto. 1997b, 'Droit et épigraphie dans la Grèce archaïque. A propos d'un ouvrage récent'. *Revue Historique de Droit Français et Étranger* 75: 435–46. (Review of van Effenterre and Ruzé 1994–5).

Maffi, Alberto. 1997c. 'Processo di libertà e rivendicazione in proprietà dello schiavo a Gortina e ad Atene'. In Gerhard Thür and Julie Vélissaropoulos-Karakostas, eds. *Symposion 1995*, 17–25. Cologne.

Maffi, Alberto. 2003a. 'Studi recenti sul Codice di Gortina'. *Dike* 6: 161–226.

Maffi, Alberto. 2003b. 'La legittimità a stare in giudizio del kosmos gortinio (IC IV 72 I 51–55 e IC IV 41 IV 6–16)'. In Thür and Nieto 2003: 37–56.

Maffi, Alberto. 2007. 'Quarant' anni di studi sul processo greco (I)'. *Dike* 10: 185–267.

Maffi, Alberto. 2011. 'Giudice e mezzi di prova nel diritto di Gortina'. *Processo civile e processo penale nell'esperienza giuridica nel mondo antico: atti del convegno in memoria di Arnaldo Biscardi, Siena, Certosa di Pontignano, 13–15 dicembre 2001*, 153–60. Milan. Web publication:) <http://www.ledonline.it/rivistadirittoromano/index.html?/rivistadirittor omano /attipontignano.html>.

Maffi, Alberto. 2012. 'Lo statuto dei "beni materni" nella Grecia classica'. *Index* 40 (Studies for Eva Cantarella): 91–111.

Magnelli, Adalberto. 1999. 'Disposizioni legislative riguardanti il regime della terra in tre inediti frammenti da Gortyna (Creta)'. *Dike* 2: 143–60.

Magnelli, Adalberto. 2001. 'Iscrizioni'. In *Gortina V.3: Lo scavo del Pretorio (1989–1995)*. ed. Antonino Di Vita, vol. 2, 626–54. Padua.

Magnelli, Adalberto. 2008. 'Gortina VII. Le Iscrizioni dall'età arcaica all'istituzione della provincia Romana'. *RAL* Ser. 9, 19: 233–334.

Maiuri, A. 1911. 'Studi sull' onomastica cretese, II'. *RAL* 20: 631–75.

Malkin, Irad. 1994. *Myth and Territory in the Spartan Mediterranean*. Cambridge.

Mandalaki, Aikaterini. 2010. '*Κριτικές παρατηρήσεις στην επιγραφή* ICret I x (*Ελτυνία*) 2'. *EHHD* 42: 9–42.

Manganaro, Giacomo. 1965. 'Nuove iscrizioni della Creta centrale ed orientale'. *Atti della Academia Nazionale dei Lincei* 20: 295–307.

Manganaro, Giacomo. 1974. 'Epigrafia e istituzioni di Creta'. In *Antichità Cretesi. Studi in onore di Doro Levi* II: 39–58, Catania.

Marangou-Lerat, Antigone. 1995. *Le vin et les amphores de Crète de l'époque classique à l'époque impériale* (Études crétoises 30). Paris.

Marginesu, Giovanni. 2005a. *Gortina di Creta. Prospettive epigrafiche per lo studio della forma urbana*. Athens.

Marginesu, Giovanni. 2005b. 'La Grande Iscrizione e le problematiche topografiche connesse'. In Greco and Lombardo 2005: 115–28.

Marginesu, Giovanni. 2006 (2008). 'Prestigio dello scriba e autenticità dello scritto: il caso di Spensithios'. *ASA (Atene)* (Ser. 3, 6) 1: 381–416.

Marginesu, Giovanni. 2014. 'Use, Re-Use and Erasure of Archaic and Classical Gortynian Inscriptions'. In Pilz and Seelentag 2014: 2007–18.

Marinatos, Spyriden. 1936. 'Le temple géométrique de Dréros'. *BCH* 60: 214–85.

Martínez-Fernández, Ángel. 1983. 'Nota a la terminología jurídica cretense: ἀνκεμολία (*I.C.* IV.21.3 y 44.7)'. In *Unidad y pluralidad en el mundo antiquo. Actas del VI Congreso español de estudios clásicos (Sevilla, 6–11 de abril de 1981)*, II: *Comunicaciones*. Madrid 143–52.

Martini, Remo. 1999. 'Considerazioni comparatistiche in tema di *sacramentum*'. In Jean-François Gerkens et al., eds. *Mélanges Fritz Sturm*, 1.381–94. Liège.

Masson, Olivier, 1983. *Les inscriptions chypriotes syllabiques. Recueil critique et commenté*. Paris: École française d'Athènes.

Mazarakis Ainian, Alexander. 1997. *From Rulers' Dwellings to Temples. Architecture, Religion and Society in Early Iron Age Greece (1100–700 B.C.)* (Studies in Mediterranean Archaeology 121). Jonsered.

Meiggs, Russell, and Lewis, David. 1969. *A Selection of Greek Historical Inscriptions*. Oxford.

Meister, Richard M. E. 1908. 'Eideshelfer im griechischen Rechte'. *Rheinisches Museum* 63: 559–86.

Merkelbach, Reinhold. 1972. 'Die Rechte des lyttischen *ποινικαστάς*'. *ZPE* 9: 102–3.

Metzger, Rainer R. 1973. *Untersuchungen zum Haftungs- und Vermögensrecht von Gortyn*. Basel.

Meyer-Laurin, Harald. 1969. Review of Willetts 1967. *Gnomon* 41: 160–9.

Missiou, Anna. 2011. *Literacy and Democracy in Fifth-Century Athens*. Cambridge.

Mitchell, Lynette G., and Rhodes, Peter J., eds. 1997. *The Development of the Polis in Archaic Greece*. London.

Möller, Astrid. 2007. 'Classical Greece: Distribution'. In Scheidel et al. 2007: 362–84.

Morris, Ian. 1990. 'The Gortyn Code and Greek Kinship'. *GRBS* 31: 233–54.

Morris, Ian. 1998. 'Archaeology and Archaic Greek History'. In Fisher and van Wees 1998: 1–91.

Morris, Ian. 2007. 'Early Iron Age Greece'. In Scheidel et al. 2007: 211–41.

Morrow, Glenn R. 1960. *Plato's Cretan City: A Historical Interpretation of the* Laws. Princeton.

Mulliez, Dominique. 2011. 'Le Mirambello.—Latô, Dréros, l'Anavlochos 2010'. Chronique des fouilles en ligne (<http://chronique.efa.gr/index.php/fiches/voir/1957/>).

Musti, Domenico, et al., eds. 1991. *La Transizione dal Miceneo all'Alto Arcaismo. Dal Palazzo alla Città. Atti del Convegno Internazionale Roma, 14–19 Marzo 1988*. Rome.

Myers, J. Wilson, Myers, Eleanor Emlen, and Cadogan, Gerald eds. 1992. *The Ariel Atlas of Ancient Crete*. Berkeley.

Niemeier, Wolf-Dietrich, Pilz, Oliver and Kaiser, Ivonne, eds. 2013. *Kreta in der geometrischen und archaischen Zeit: Akten des Internationalen Kolloquiums am Deutschen Archäologischen Institut, Abteilung Athen, 27.–29. Januar 2006*. Munich.

Nowicki, Krzysztof. 2000. *Defensible Sites in Crete c.1200–800 B.C.* (*LM IIIB/IIIC through Early Geometric*), (Aegaeum 21). Liège, Austin.

Osborne, Robin. 1997. 'Law and Laws: How do we join the dots?' In Mitchell and Rhodes 1997: 74–82.

Osborne, Robin. 2007. 'Archaic Greece'. In Scheidel et al. 2007: 277–301.

Osborne, Robin. 2009. *Greece in the Making 1200–479 BC*. 2nd edn. London.

Palermo, Dario. 1992. 'L'officina dei pithoi di Festòs: un contributo alla conoscenza della città in età arcaica'. *Cronache di Archeologia. Università di Catania Istituto di Archeologia* 31: 35–53.

Palermo, Dario. 2001. 'Il periodo protogeometrico e geometrico a Festòs: la documentazione ceramica'. In *I centi anni dello scavo di Festòs. Roma 13–14 dicembre 2000. Atti dei Convegni Lincei* 173: 299–308. Rome.

Palermo, Dario, Pautasso, Antonella and Gigli Patanè, Rossella, 2007. 'Lo scavo del 2005 sulla Patela di Priniàs. Relazione Preliminare'. *Creta Antica* 8: 265–314.

Palermo, Dario, Pautasso, Antonella. and Gigli Patanè, Rossella. 2008. 'Lo scavo del 2007 sulla Patela di Priniàs. Relazione Preliminare'. *Creta Antica* 9: 179–208.

Panagiotakis, Nikos. 2003. 'L'évolution archéologique de la Pédiada (Crète centrale): premier bilan d'une prospection'. *BCH* 127: 327–430.

Papadopoulos, Jeanette. 1988. 'Ceramica Geometrica'. In Di Vita 1988: 165–7.

Papakonstantinou, Zinon. 1996. 'The Cretan Apokosmos'. *ZPE* 111: 93–6.

Papakonstantinou, Zinon. 2002. 'Written Law, Literacy and Social Conflict in Archaic and Classical Crete'. *Ancient History Bulletin* 16: 135–50.

Pariente, Anne. 1994. 'Chroniques des fouilles et découvertes archéologiques en Grèce en 1993'. *BCH* 118: 695–866.

Pautasso, Antonella, Gigli Patanè, Rossella, Biendi, Giacomo, Rizza, Salvatore, Romano, Paolo, and Pappalardo, Lighea. 2010. 'Priniàs (Creta): nuovi scavi e prospettive di ricerca'. In Gaetana Marchesini, Giuseppe Nicoletti, and Orazio Pulvirenti, eds. *Il Dialogo dei Saperi*, 59–78. Naples.

Pautasso, Antonella. 2013. 'New Research in the Area of Temple A'. In Niemeier, Pilz, and Kaiser 2013: 179–86.

Pautasso, Antonella. 2014. 'Prinias. Une cité de l'Age du Fer et son histoire'. In Gaignerot-Driessen and Driessen 2014: 59–77.

Pébarthe, Christophe. 2006. *Cité, démocratie et écriture: Histoire de l'alphabétisation d'Athènes à l'époque classique*. Paris.

Peek, Werner. 1941. *Kerameikos. Ergebnisse der Ausgrabungen*. III. *Inschriften, Ostraka, Fluchtafeln*. Berlin.

Pelloso, Carlo. 2009–10. '"Astreintes" e regime probatorio nel processo gortinio: considerazioni in margine a IC IV 72 I, 15–35'. *Dike* 12–13: 91–169.

Perlman, Paula. 1992. 'One-Hundred Citied Crete and the Cretan *Politeia*'. *Classical Philology* 87: 193–205.

Perlman, Paula. 1996. '*Πόλις Ὑπήκοος*. The Dependent *Polis* and Crete'. In Mogens Herman Hansen, ed. *Introduction to an Inventory of* Poleis (Acts of the Copenhagen Polis Centre, vol. 3), 233–87. Copenhagen.

Perlman, Paula. 1999. '*KRĒTES AIEI LĒISTAI*? The Marginalization of Crete in Greek Thought and the Role of Piracy in the Outbreak of the First Cretan War'. In Vincent Gabrielsen, Per Bilde, Troels Engberg-Pedersen, Lisa Hannestad, and Jan Zahle, eds. *Hellenistic Rhodes: Politics, Culture and Society* (*Studies in Hellenistic Civilization* 9), 110–34. Aarhus.

Perlman, Paula. 2000a. 'Gortyn. The First Seven Hundred Years (Part I)'. In Pernille Flensted–Jensen, Thomas Heine Nielsen, and Lene Rubinstein, eds. *Polis and Politics: Studies in Ancient Greek History Presented to Mogens Hansen on His Sixtieth Birthday, August 20, 2000*, 59–89. Copenhagen.

Perlman, Paula. 2000b. *City and Sanctuary in Ancient Greece: The* Theorodokia *in the Peloponnese* (Hypomnemata 121). Göttingen.

Perlman, Paula. 2002. 'Gortyn. The First Seven Hundred Years (Part II): The Laws from the Temple of Apollo Pythios'. In Thomas Heine Nielsen, ed. *Even More Studies in the Ancient Greek* Polis (Papers of the Copenhagen Polis Center, vol. 6). (*Historia* Einzelschriften 162), 187–227. Stuttgart.

Perlman, Paula. 2004a. 'Tinker, Tailor, Soldier, Sailor: The Economies of Archaic Eleutherna, Crete'. *Classical Antiquity* 23: 95–137.

Perlman, Paula. 2004b. 'Crete'. In Hansen and Nielsen 2004: 1144–95.

Perlman, Paula. 2004c. 'Writing on the Walls. The Architectural Context of Archaic Cretan Laws'. In Leslie Preston Day, Margaret S. Mook, and James D. Muhly, eds. *Crete beyond the Palaces: Proceedings of the Crete 2000 Conference*, 181–97. Philadelphia.

Perlman, Paula. 2005. 'Imagining Crete'. In Mogens Herman Hansen, ed. *The Imaginary Polis. Acts of the Copenhagen Polis Centre* vol. 7, 282–334. Copenhagen.

Perlman, Paula. 2010. 'Of Battle, Booty, and (Citizen) Women: A "New" Inscription from Archaic Axos, Crete'. *Hesperia* 79: 79–112.

Perlman, Paula. 2014. 'Reading and Writing Archaic Cretan Society'. In Pilz and Seelentag 2014: 177–206.

Perna, Katia. 2007. 'La ceramica LM IIIC dai livelli sottostanti l'edificio'. In Palermo, Pautasso, and Gigli Patanè 2007: 299–302.

Pernier, Luigi. 1914. 'Templi arcaici sulla Patela di Priniàs. Contributo allo studio dell'arte dedalica'. *ASA(Atene)* 1: 19–111.

Pernier, Luigi. 1925–6 (1929). 'L'odeion nell'agora di Gortina presso il Leteo'. *ASA (Atene)* 8–9: 1–69.

Petroulakis, Eustathios N. 1914. '*Ἐλευθέρνης ἐπιγραφαί*'. *AE* 225–9.

Pilz, Oliver. 2011. *Frühe matrizengeformte Terrakotten auf Kreta. Votivpraxis und Gesellschaftsstruktur in spätgeometrischer und früharchaischer Zeit* (Beiträge zur Archäologie Griechenlands 2). Möhnesee.

Pilz, Oliver. 2014. 'Narrative Art in Archaic and Classical Crete'. In Pilz and Seelentag 2014: 246–61.

Pilz, Oliver, and Seelentag, Gunnar, eds. 2014. *Cultural Practices and Material Culture in Archaic and Classical Crete. Proceedings of the International Conference, Mainz, May 20–21, 2011*. Berlin.

Platon, Nikolaos. 1954. '*Ἀνασκαφή Ὀνυθέ Γουλεδιανῶν Ρεθύμνης*'. *PAAH* 1954: 377–82.

Platon, Nikolaos. 1955. '*Ἀνασκαφή Ὀνυθέ Γουλεδιανῶν Ρεθύμνης*'. *PAAH* 1955: 298–305.

Platon, Nikolaos. 1956. '*Ανασκαφή εις Γουλεδιανά Ρεθύμνης*'. *PAAH* 1956: 226–8.

Platon, Nikolaos. 1957. '*Χρονικά*: Ἡ *ἀρχαιολογική κίνησις ἐν Κρήτῃ κατὰ τὸ ἔτος* 1957'. *KrChr* 11: 326–40.

Pounder Robert L. 1984. 'The Origin of *θεός* as Inscription-Heading'. In *Studies Presented to Sterling Dow on his Eightieth Birthday* (GRBS Monograph 10) 243–50. Durham, NC.

Prent, Mieke. 1996–7. 'The 6th Century BC in Crete: The Best Candidate for Being a Dark Age?' In Marianne Maaskant-Kleibrink and Marja Vink, eds. *Debating Dark Ages*, 35–46. Groningen.

Prent, Mieke. 2005. *Cretan Sanctuaries and Cults: Continuity and Change from Late Minoan IIIC to the Archaic Period*. Leiden.

Prent, Mieke. 2007. 'Cretan Early Iron Age hearth temples and the articulation of sacred space'. In Westgate, Fisher, and Whitley 2007: 141–8.

Price, Martin J. 1981. 'The Beginnings of Coinage in Crete'. In *Πεπραγμένα τοῦ Δ' Διεθνοῦς Κρητολογικοῦ Συνεδρίου*, Ἡράκλειο 1976, A2, 461–6. Athens.

Pringsheim, Fritz. 1950. *The Greek law of sale*. Weimar.

Raaflaub, Kurt A., and van Wees, Hans eds. 2009. *A Companion to Archaic Greece*. Malden, MA.

Raubitschek, Anthony E. 1972. 'A Mitra Inscribed with a Law'. In Hoffmann 1972: 47–9. Mainz.

Reed, Charles M. 2003. *Maritime Traders in the Ancient Greek World*. Cambridge.

Reese, David S. 2005. 'Faunal Remains from Greek Sanctuaries: A Survey (Abstract)'. In Robin Hägg and Brita Alroth, eds. *Greek Sacrificial Ritual, Olympian and Chthonian*. Proceedings of the Sixth International Seminar on Ancient Greek Cult, Goteborg University, 25–27 April 1997, 121–3. Stockholm.

Rethemiotakis, Giorgos. 1986. 'Nomos Irakleiou: Lyktos'. *ArchDelt* 41.2: 222–4.

Rethemiotakis, Giorgos, and Englezou, Maria. 2010. *Το γεωμετρικό νεκροταφείο της Ἔλτυνας* (Archaiologiko Instituto Kritologikon Spoudon, vol. 4). Heraklion.

Rhodes, Peter J., with Lewis, David M. 1997. *The Decrees of the Greek States.* Oxford.

Ricciardi, Maria. 1986–7 (1991). 'Il tempio di Apollo Pizio a Gortina'. *ASA (Atene)* ns 64–5: 7–131.

Rizza, Giovanni. 1967–8. 'Le terrecotte di Axòs'. *ASA (Atene)* 65–6 (ns 29–30): 211–302.

Rizza, Giovanni. 1991. 'Priniàs. La città arcaica sulla Patela'. In Musti et al. 1991: 331–47.

Rizza, Giovanni. 2008. *Priniàs, la città arcaica sulla Patela: scavi condotti negli anni 1969–2000* (Studi e Materiali di Archeologia Greca 8.1). Catania.

Rizza, Giovanni, and Rizzo, Maria A. 1984. 'Prinias'. In *Creta Antica. Cento anni di archeologia italiana (1884–1984)*, 227–56. Rome.

Rizza, Giovanni, Palermo, Dario, and Tomasello, Francesco. 1992. *Mandra di Gipari. Una officina protoarcaica di vasai nel territorio di Prinias* (Studi e Materiali di Archeologia Greca 5). Catania.

Rocchetti, Luigi. 1974–75. 'La ceramica dell'abitato geometrico di Festòs a occidente del palazzo minoico'. *ASA (Atene)* 52–3: 169–300.

Rosivach, Vincent J. 1994. *The System of Public Sacrifices in Fourth-Century Greece.* Atlanta, GA.

Rosén, Haiim B. 1982. 'Questions d'interprétation de textes juridiques grecs de la plus ancienne époque'. In Joseph Modrzejewski and Detlef Liebs, eds. *Symposion 1977*, 9–32. Cologne.

Rougemont, Françoise. 2007. 'Flax and Linen Textiles in the Mycenaean Palatial Economy'. In Carole Gillis and Marie-Louise B. Mosch, eds. *Ancient Textiles: Production, Craft and Society. Proceedings of the conference held in Lund/Falsterbo, Sweden, and Copenhagen, Denmark, on 19–23 March 2003*, 46–9. Oxford.

Rubinstein, Lene. 1993. *Adoption in IV. Century Athens.* Copenhagen.

Russo, Joseph, Fernandez-Galiano, Manuel, and Heubeck, Alfred. 1992. *A Commentary on Homer's Odyssey.* Vol. 3. (Books XVII–XXIV). Oxford.

Ruzé, Françoise. 1983. 'Les tribus et la décision politique dans les cités grecques archaïques et classiques'. *Ktema* 8: 299–306.

Ruzé, Françoise. 1988, 'Aux débuts de l'écriture politique: le pouvoir de l'écrit dans la cité'. In Marcel Detienne, ed. 1988. *Les savoirs de l'écriture en Grèce ancienne*, 82–94. Lille.

Sackett, L. Hugh, ed. 1992. *Knossos: From Greek City to Roman Colony: Excavations at the Unexplored Mansion*, vol. ii (BSA Suppl. 21). Oxford.

Santaniello, Emanuela. 2004. 'Produzione ceramica a Gortina tra età orientalizzante e arcaica. I Rinvenimenti dell'Oikopedo SAIA'. *ASA (Atene)* 82: 443–75.

Schäfer, Jörg. 1992a. 'Die Ausgrabungen. Area D: Das "Heiligtum des Zeus Thenatas"'. In Schäfer 1992b: 159–85.

Schäfer, Jörg, ed. 1992b. *Amnisos. Nach dem archäologischen, historischen und epigrafischen Zeugnissen des Altertums und der Neuzeit.* Berlin.

Schaps, David M. 1979. *Economic Rights of Women in Ancient Greece.* Edinburgh.

Scheidel, Walter, Morris, Ian, and Saller, Richard, eds. 2007. *The Cambridge Economic History of the Greco-Roman World.* Cambridge.

Schiering, Wolfgang. 1982. 'Landbegehungen in Rethymno und Umgebung'. *Archäologischer Anzeiger*, 15–54.

Sealey, Raphael. 1994. *The Justice of the Greeks.* Ann Arbor.

Seelentag, Gunnar. 2009a. 'Regeln für den Kosmos. Prominenzrollen und Institutionen im archaischen Kreta'. *Chiron* 39: 65–99.

Seelentag, Gunnar. 2009b. 'Der Abschluss der Ephebie im archaischen Kreta. Bemerkungen zu einer Gesetzesinschrift aus Dreros'. *ZPE* 168: 149–60.

Shaw, Joseph. W. 2000a. 'The Architecture of the Temples and Other Buildings'. In Shaw and Shaw 2000: 1–100.

Shaw, Joseph W. 2000b. 'Ritual and Development in the Greek Sanctuary'. In Shaw and Shaw 2000: 669–731.

Shaw, Joseph W. 2006. *Kommos: A Minoan Harbor Town and Greek Sanctuary in Southern Crete*. Princeton.

Shaw, Joseph W., and Shaw, Maria C., eds. 2000. *Kommos: An Excavation on the South Coast of Crete*. IV, Part 1, *The Greek Sanctuary*. Princeton.

Sjögren, Lena. 2001. *Sites, Settlements and Early Poleis on Crete (800–500 BC)*. Stockholm.

Sjögren, Lena. 2003. *Cretan Locations. Discerning Site Variations in Iron Age and Archaic Crete (800–500 B.C.)* (BAR-IS 1185). Oxford.

Sjögren, Lena. 2008. *Fragments of Archaic Crete. Archaeological Studies on Time and Space* (Boreas 31). Uppsala.

Smyth, Herbert Weir. 1956. *Greek Grammar*. Cambridge, MA.

Snodgrass, Anthony. 1974. 'Cretans in Arcadia'. In *Antichità Cretesi. Studi in onore di Doro Levi*, vol. II: 196–201. Catania.

Snodgrass, Anthony. 1980. *Archaic Greece: The age of experiment*. Berkeley and Los Angeles.

Sokolowski, Franciszek. 1962. *Lois sacrées des cités grecques. Supplement*. Paris.

Sokolowski, Franciszek. 1969. *Lois sacrées des cités grecques*. Paris.

Sommerstein, Alan H. 2013. 'The Judicial Sphere'. In Alan H. Sommerstein and Andrew J. Bayliss, eds. *Oath and State in Ancient Greece*, 57–119. Berlin.

Sporn, Katja. 2002. *Heiligtümer und Kulte Kretas in klassischer und hellenistischer Zeit* (Studien zu antiken Heiligtümern 3). Heidelberg.

Spratt, Thomas A. B. 1865. *Travels and Researches in Crete* I, II. London.

Stampolidis, Nikolaos Chr. 1993. *Ελεύθερνα* III.1: *Γεωμετρικά - αρχαϊκά χρόνια και Οδηγός στην Έκθεση 'Το γεωμετρικό–αρχαϊκό νεκροταφείο της Ορθής Πέτρας'*. Rethymno.

Stampolidis, Nikolaos Chr. 1994. *Ελεύθερνα* III.2: *Από τη γεωμετρική και αρχαϊκή νεκρόπολη. Ταφικές πυρές και ομηρικά έπη*. Rethymno.

Stampolidis, Nikolaos Chr. 1996. *Ελεύθερνα* III.3: *Αντίποινα. Συμβολή στη μελέτη των ηθών και των εθίμων της γεωμετρικής-αρχαϊκής περιόδου*. Rethymno.

Stampolidis, Nikolaos Chr. 2004a. 'The Polis. West Excavation, Sector III'. In Stampolidis 2004c: 82–103.

Stampolidis, Nikolaos Chr. 2004b. 'The Necropolises. West Excavation, Sector III'. In Stampolidis 2004c: 116–43.

Stampolidis, Nikolaos Chr. ed. 2004c. *Eleutherna: Polis – Acropolis – Necropolis*, tr. A. Doumas and T. Cullen. Athens.

Stampolidis, Nikolaos Chr., and Ikonomaki, Androniki. 2009. '*Τρία Λίθινα Ενεπίγραφα Σπαράγματα από την Ελεύθερνα*'. In Christos Loukos, Napoleon Xipharas, and Kleanthi

Pateraki, eds. *Ubi dubium ibi libertas. Τιμητικός τόμος για τον καθηγητή Νικόλα Φαράκλα, Εκδόσεις Φιλοσοφικής Σχολής Πανεπιστημίου Κρήτης*, 293–319. Rethymno.

Stefanakis, Manolis I. 1998. 'A Mid-Fourth Century Alliance Coinage on Crete? The Case of Kytaion Reassessed'. In Cavanagh and Curtis 1998: 145–56.

Stefanakis, Manolis I. 1999. 'The Introduction of Coinage in Crete and the Beginning of Local Minting'. In Chaniotis 1999a: 247–68.

Svoronos, Joannes N. 1890. *Numismatique de la Crète ancienne*. Paris.

Szegedy-Maszak, Andrew. 1978. 'Legends of the Greek Lawgivers'. *GRBS* 19: 199–209.

Talamanca, Mario. 1979. 'Dikazein e krinein nelle testimonanze greche piu antiche'. In Arnaldo Biscardi, ed. *Symposion 1974*, 103–35. Cologne.

Talamo, Clara. 1987. 'Il sissizio a Creta'. *Miscellanea Greca e Romana* 12: 9–26.

Taramelli, A. 1899. 'Ricerche archeologiche cretesi'. *Mon. Ant.* 9: 307–20.

Tegou, Eva. 2010. '*Αρχαιολογικό Έργο στην Αξό Δήμου Κουλούκωνα*'. In Andrianakis and Tzachili 2010: 490–7.

Tegou, Eva. 2013. '*Αξός. Στοιχεία τοπογραφίας της αρχαίας πόλης και παρατηρήσεις σχετικά με την έρευνα της ιταλικής αποστολής του* 1899'. In Niemeier, Pilz, and Kaiser 2013: 87–101.

Tegou, Eva. 2014. 'Archaic and Classical Axos'. In Pilz and Seelentag 2014: 41–65.

Teza, Emilio. 1883. 'La iscrizione di Oaxós'. *RFIC* 11: 340–6.

Themelis, Petros. 2002. *Αρχαία Ελεύθερνα. Ανατολικός τομέας*. Athens.

Themelis, Petros. 2004. 'The Polis. East Excavation, Sector I'. In Stampolidis 2004c: 46–81.

Themelis, Petros. 2009a. 'Eleutherna, Sector I. The Historical Background'. In Themelis 2009b: 47–92.

Themelis, Petros, ed. 2009b. *Ancient Eleutherna, Sector I*, vol. I. Athens.

Thenon, Louis. 1863. 'Une inscription archaïque de Gortyne'. *Revue Archéologique* ns 8: 441–7, Pl. 16.

Thür, Gerhard. 1970. 'Zum *dikazein* bei Homer'. *ZSS* 87: 426–44.

Thür, Gerhard, ed. 1989. *Symposion 1985*. Cologne.

Thür, Gerhard. 2002. 'Eigentumsstreit und Statusprozess in der grossen Gesetzesinschrift aus Gortyn'. *Dike* 5: 95–109.

Thür, Gerhard. 2003. 'Sachverfolgung und Diebstahl in den griechischen Poleis'. In Thür and Nieto 2003: 57–96.

Thür, Gerhard. 2006. 'Die Einheit des "griechischen Rechts". Gedanken zum Prozessrecht in den griechischen Poleis'. *Dike* 9: 23–62.

Thür, Gerhard. 2009. Review of Gagarin, 2008a. *ZSS* 126: 482–94.

Thür, Gerhard. 2010a. 'Legal Procedure in the Gortyn Code: Response to Michael Gagarin'. In Thür 2010b: 147–50.

Thür, Gerhard, ed. 2010b. *Symposion 2009*. Vienna.

Thür, Gerhard, and Nieto, Francisco Javier Fernández, eds. 2003. *Symposion 1999*. Cologne.

Thür, Gerhard, and Taeuber, Hans, ed. 1994. *Prozessrechtliche Inschriften der griechischen Poleis: Arkadien* (*IPArk*). Vienna.

Tommasello, Francesco. 1996. 'Fornaci a Festòs ed Haghia Triada dall'età mediominoica alla geometrica'. In *Κεραμικαί Εργαστηίρια στην Κρηίτη αποί την αρχαιοίτητα ως σήμερα* (*Πρακτικαί ημεριίδας. Μαργαριίτες, 30 Σεπτεμβριίου 1995*), 27–37. Rethymno.

Treister, Michail. J., and Shelov-Kovedyayev, Theodore V. 1989. 'An Inscribed Conical Clay Object from Hermonassa'. *Hesperia* 58: 289–96.

Triantaphyllopoulos, Jean. 1964. 'Varia Graeco-Romana'. In Antonio Guarino and Luigi Labruna, eds. *Synteleia Vincenzo Arangio-Ruiz. Raccolta di studi di diritto romano, di filologia classica e di vario diritto*, 903–8. Naples.

Trümpy, Catherine. 1997. *Untersuchungen zu den altgriechischen Monatsnamen und Monatsfolgen*. Heidelberg.

Tzifopoulos, Yannis Z. 1998. '"Hemerodromoi" and Cretan "Dromeis": Athletes or Military Personnel? The Case of the Cretan Philonides'. *Nikephoros* 11: 137–70.

Tzifopoulos, Yannis Z. 2004. 'Inscriptions'. In Stampolidis 2004c, 155.

Tzifopoulos, Yannis Z. 2009. 'The Inscriptions'. In Themelis 2009b, 103–52.

van Effenterre, Henri. 1946a. 'Inscriptions archaïques crétoises'. *BCH* 70: 588–606.

van Effenterre, Henri. 1946b. 'Une bilingue étéocrétoise?' *Revue de Philologie* 20: 131–8.

van Effenterre, Henri. 1961. 'Pierres inscrites de Dreros'. *BCH* 85: 544–68.

van Effenterre, Henri. 1973. 'Le contract de travail du scribe Spensithios'. *BCH* 97: 31–46.

van Effenterre, Henri. 1979. 'Le statut comparé des travailleurs étrangers en Chypre, Crète et autres lieux à la fin de l'archaïsme'. *Acts of the International Archaeological Symposium. The Relations between Cyprus and Crete, ca. 2000–500 B.C.*, 279–93. Nicosia.

van Effenterre, Henri. 1982. 'Les "Epiballontes"'. *Studi Biscardi* 3: 459–62.

van Effenterre, Henri. 1983. 'Le droit et la langue à propos du code de Gortyne'. In Panayotis Dimakis, ed. *Symposion 1979*, 115–28. Cologne.

van Effenterre, Henri. 1984. 'Problèmes d'épigaphie juridique grecque. A propos d'un livre d'Alberto Maffi'. *Revue Historique de Droit Français et Étranger* 62: 47–52.

van Effenterre, Henri. 1985. 'DAMOS, DAMIOI et DAMIORGOI'. In *Πεπραγμένα του Ε΄ Διεθνοῦς Κρητολογικοῦ Συνεδρίου, Αγίου Νικολάου, 25 Σεπτεβρίου–1 Οκτωβρίου* 1981, A. 2.81–97. Heraklion.

van Effenterre, Henri. 1991a. 'Loi archaïque sur le excès de boisson'. In van Effenterre et al. 1991: 17–21.

van Effenterre, Henri. 1991b. 'Les deux inscriptions de Nési'. In van Effenterre et al. 1991: 24–30.

van Effenterre, Henri. 1991c. 'Fragment de stèle relatif à l'artisanat du cuir?' In van Effenterre et al. 1991: 22–3.

van Effenterre, Henri. 1992. 'Dreros'. In Myers, Myers, and Cadogan 1992: 86–90.

van Effenterre, Henri. 1993a. 'Modernité du droit grec: un patrimoine'. *Cahiers du Centre G. Glotz* 4: 1–11.

van Effenterre, Henri. 1993b. 'Le pacte Gortyne-Rhittèn'. *Cahiers du Centre G. Glotz* 4: 13–21.

van Effenterre, Henri. 2009. *La Nécropole de Dréros* (Études crétoises, VIII/2), ed. Massimo Perna. Athens and Naples.

van Effenterre, Henri, et al., eds. 1991. *ΕΛΕΥΘΕΡΝΑ* II.1. *ΕΠΙΓΡΑΦΕΣ ΑΠΟ ΤΟ ΠΥΡΓΙ ΚΑΙ ΤΟ ΝΗΣΙ*. Rethymno.

van Effenterre, Henri, and Gondiccas, Daphné. 1999. 'Lyttos, ville fantôme?'. In Martine Bellancourt-Valdher and Jean-Nicolas Corvisier, eds. *La démographie historique antique*, (Cahiers Scientifiques de l'Université d'Artois 11), 127–39. Artois.

van Effenterre, Henri, and Ruzé, Françoise. 1994–5. *Nomima: recueil d'inscriptions politiques et juridiques de l'archaïsme grec.* 2 vols. Rome.

van Effenterre, Henri, and van Effenterre, Micheline. 1985. 'Nouvelles lois archaiques de Lyttos'. *BCH* 109: 157–88.

van Effenterre, Henri, and van Effenterre, Micheline. 1988. 'Le contrôle des étrangers dans la cité grecque'. In Giuseppe Nenci and Gerhard Thür, eds. *Symposion 1988*, 251–9. Cologne.

van Effenterre, Henri, and van Effenterre, Micheline. 1995. 'Les "Lois de Minos"'. In Robert Laffineur and Wolf-Dietrich Niemeier, eds. *POLITEIA. Society and State in the Aegean Bronze Age.* Proceedings of the 5th International Aegean Conference, University of Heidelberg, Archäologisches Institut, 10–13 April 1994 (Aegaeum 12), 335–9. Liège and Austin.

van Effenterre, Henri, and van Effenterre, Micheline. 2000. 'La codification Gortynienne, mythe ou réalité?' In Lévy 2000: 175–84.

Vasilakis, Andonis (*Βασιλακης*, *Ἀντωνης*). 2010. '*Υστερομινωικοί νεώσοικοι Κατσαμπά Ηραλείου*'. In Andrianakis and Tzachili 2010: 285–93.

Viviers, Didier. 1994. 'La cité de Dattalla et l'expansion territoriale de Lyktos en Crète centrale'. *BCH* 118: 229–59.

Viviers, Didier. 1995. 'Hérodote et la neutralité des Crétois en 480 avant notre ère: La trace d'un débat Athénien?' *Hermes* 123: 257–69.

Viviers, Didier. 1999. 'Economy and Territorial Dynamics in Crete from the Archaic to the Hellenistic Period'. In Chaniotis 1999a: 221–33.

Vlassopoulos, Kostas. 2011. 'Greek Slavery: From Domination to Property and Back Again'. *Journal of Hellenic Studies* 131: 115–30.

Vollgraff, W. 1948. *Le décret d'Argos relatif à un pacte entre Knossos et Tylissos.* Amsterdam.

Von Reden, Sitta. 1997. 'Money, Law and Exchange: Coinage in the Greek Polis'. *Journal of Hellenic Studies* 117: 154–76.

Wallace, Robert W. 2013. 'Councils in Greek Oligarchies and Democracies'. In Beck 2013: 191–204.

Wallace, Saro. 2010a. *Ancient Crete: from successful collapse to democracy's alternatives, 12th to 5th centuries BC.* Cambridge.

Wallace, Saro. 2010b. 'The Roots of the Polis. Surface Evidence for the History of Large Settlements in Central Crete'. *AA* 13–90.

Warren, Peter. 1984–5. 'Knossos: Stratigraphical Museum Excavation, 1978–1982, Part III'. *AR* 31: 124–9.

Watrous, Livingston Vance. 1982. *Lasithi. A history of settlement on a highland plain in Crete* (Hesperia Suppl. XVIII). Princeton.

Watrous, Livingston Vance. 1996. *The Cave Sanctuary of Zeus at Psychro. A Study of Extra-Urban Sanctuaries in Minoan and Early Iron Age Crete.* (Aegaeum 15). Liège.

Watrous, Livingston Vance, Hadzi-Vallianou, Despoina, Pope, Kevin, Mourtzas, Nikes, Shay, Jennifer, Shay, C. Thomas, Bennet, John, Tsougarakis, Dimitris, Angelomati-

Tsougaraki, Eleni, Vallianos, Christophosis, and Blitzer, Harriet. 1993. 'A Survey of the Western Mesara Plain in Crete: Preliminary Report of the 1984–1987 Field Seasons'. *Hesperia* 62: 191–248.

Watrous, Livingston Vance, and Hadzi-Vallianou, Despoina. 2004a. 'The Polis of Phaistos: Development and Destruction (Late Minoan IIIC–Hellenistic)'. In Watrous, Hadzi-Vallianou, and Blitzer 2004: 307–38.

Watrous, Livingston Vance, and Hadzi-Vallianou, Despoina. 2004b. 'Creation of a Greek City-State (Late Minoan IIIC-Orientalizing)'. In Watrous, Hadzi-Vallianou, and Blitzer 2004: 339–50.

Watrous, Livingston Vance, Hadzi-Vallianou, Despoina, and Bennet, John. 2004. 'The Field Survey. In Watrous, Hadzi–Vallianou, and Blitzer 2004: 3–17.

Watrous, Livingston Vance, Hadzi-Vallianou, Despoina, and Blitzer, Harriet, eds. 2004. *The Plain of Phaistos. Cycles of Social Complexity in the Mesara Region of Crete* (Institute of Archaeology 23). Los Angeles.

Westbrook, Raymond. 2010. 'The Early History of Law: A Theoretical Essay'. *ZSS* 127: 1–13.

Westgate, Ruth. 2007. 'House and Society in Classical and Hellenistic Crete: A Case Study in Regional Variation'. *American Journal of Archaeology* 111: 423–57.

Westgate, Ruth, Fisher, Nicolas, and Whitley, James, eds. 2007. *Building Communities: House, Settlement and Society in the Aegean and, Beyond. Proceedings of the Conference held at Cardiff University, 17–21 April 2001* (BSA Studies, 15). London.

Whitley, James. 1997. 'Cretan Laws and Cretan Literacy'. *AJA* 101: 635–61.

Whitley, James. 2001. *The Archaeology of Ancient Greece.* Cambridge.

Whitley, James. 2003. 'Archaeology in Greece, 2002–2003', *AR* 49: 1–88.

Whitley, James. 2005. 'Before the Great Code: Public Inscriptions and Material Practice in Archaic Crete'. In Greco and Lombardo 2005: 41–56.

Whitley, James. 2009. 'Crete'. In Raaflaub and van Wees 2009: 273–93.

Whitley, James. 2011. 'Praisos V: A Preliminary Report on the 2007 Excavation Season', *BSA* 106: 3–45.

Whitley, James. 2013. 'The Cretan Orientalizing. A comparative perspective'. In Niemeier, Pilz, and Kaiser 2013: 409–26.

Willetts, Ronald F. 1955. *Aristocratic Society in Ancient Crete.* London.

Willetts, Ronald F. 1962. *Cretan Cults and Festivals.* London.

Willetts, Ronald F. 1967. *The Law Code of Gortyn. Kadmos* Suppl. 1. Berlin.

Willetts, Ronald F. 1972. 'The Cretan Inscription BM 1969. 4—2. 1: Further Provisional Comments'. *Kadmos* 11: 96–8.

Wilson, John-Paul. 2009. 'Literacy'. In Raaflaub and van Wees 2009: 542–63.

Wolff, Hans Julius. 1946. 'The Origin of Judicial Litigation among the Greeks'. *Traditio* 4: 31–87.

Wolff, Hans Julius. 1968. Review of Willetts 1967. *ZSS* 85: 418–28.

Xanthoudides, Stephanos. 1918. '*Γ' ἀρχαιολογικὴ περιφέρεια*'. *ArchDelt* 4: 18–32.

Xanthoudides, Stephanos. 1920. '*Κρητικαὶ ἐπιγραφαί*'. *AE* 75–88.

Youni, Maria Stephanos. 2010. '*Polis* and Legislative Procedure in early Crete'. In Thür 2010b: 151–60.

Zelnick-Abramovitz, Rachel. 2005. *Not Wholly Free: The Concept of Manumission and the Status of Manumitted Slaves in the Ancient Greek World*. Leiden.

Zographaki, Vaso, and Farnoux, Alexandre. 2010. 'Mission franco-hellénique de Dréros'. *BCH* 134: 594–600.

LOCATION OF INSCRIPTIONS

NB We include here only those inscriptions we have seen ourselves.

AXOS

A1 (Aa, B) .... on site
A12 .... Heraklion Museum
Axos1 .... Heraklion Museum
Axos2 .... Rethymno Museum

DATALA

Da1 .... London, British Museum

DREROS

Dr1 .... Neapolis Museum
Dr3 .... Neapolis Museum
Dr4 .... Neapolis Museum
Dr5 (fragment from left) .... Neapolis Museum
Dr7 (fragment from left) .... Heraklion Museum

ELEUTHERNA

Ele3 .... Rethymno Museum
Ele4 .... Rethymno Museum
Ele9 .... Rethymno Museum
Ele11 .... Rethymno Museum
Ele13 .... Rethymno Museum
Ele14 (A) .... Rethymno Museum
Ele15 (A, C) .... Rethymno Museum
Ele16 .... Rethymno Museum
Ele17 .... Rethymno Museum
Eleutherna1 .... Rethymno Museum
Eleutherna2 .... Rethymno Museum
Eleutherna3 .... Rethymno Museum

Eleutherna4 .... Rethymno Museum
Eleutherna5 .... Rethymno Museum

ELTYNIA

Elt2 .... Heraklion Museum
Eltynia1 .... Heraklion Museum

GORTYN

G1 (a) .... Italian School, Agii Deka
G1 (b, f) .... Gortyn, Pythion
G1 (e) .... Heraklion Museum
G3 (a) .... Gortyn, Pythion
G4 .... Heraklion Museum
G8 (c, d, e, f, i, n) .... Heraklion Museum
G9 (n*) .... Heraklion Museum
G10 (c, d, e, f, h, i, l, n, o, r, u, v, h*, i*, l*, p*) .... Heraklion Museum
G10 (g*, k*) .... Italian School, Agii Deka
G10 (s) .... Gortyn, Pythion
G10 (c*) .... Gortyn, Old Museum
G11 (b, d, e) .... Heraklion Museum
G11 (h) .... Gortyn, Pythion
G12 (d) .... Heraklion Museum
G12 (s) .... Italian School, Agii Deka
G13 (a, c, e, g, i, l, m) .... Heraklion Museum
G13 (b) .... Gortyn, Pythion
G13 (d) .... Italian School, Agii Deka
G14 (i, l, m, n, p, s) .... Heraklion Museum
G15 (a, b) .... Heraklion Museum
G18 .... Gortyn, Pythion
G20 .... Heraklion Museum
G21 .... Gortyn, Pythion
G22 .... Gortyn, Pythion
G23 .... Gortyn, Pythion
G28 .... Heraklion Museum
G29 .... Heraklion Museum
G41 .... Gortyn, Odeion
G42 .... Gortyn, Odeion
G43 .... Gortyn, Odeion
G44 .... Gortyn, Odeion
G45 .... Gortyn, Odeion
G46 .... Gortyn, Odeion

G47 .... Gortyn, Odeion
G48 .... Gortyn, Odeion
G51 .... Gortyn, Odeion
G52 .... Heraklion Museum
G53 .... Italian School, Agii Deka
G54 .... Italian School, Agii Deka
G59 .... Heraklion Museum
G60 .... Gortyn, Odeion
G61 .... Gortyn, Odeion
G62 .... Heraklion Museum
G64 (left block) .... Heraklion Museum
G65 .... Heraklion Museum
G66 .... Gortyn, Old Museum
G69 .... Italian School, Agii Deka
G72 .... Gortyn, Odeion
G72.11.1–15 .... Paris, Louvre
G73 .... Gortyn, Odeion
G75 .... Gortyn, Odeion
G76 (right block) .... Italian School, Agii Deka
G77 .... Gortyn, Odeion
G78 .... Gortyn, Pythion
G80 (right block) .... Italian School, Agii Deka
G81 .... Heraklion Museum
G82 .... Gortyn, Old Museum
G83 .... Heraklion Museum
G84 .... Gortyn, Odeion
G85 .... Gortyn, Odeion
G86 .... Italian School, Agii Deka
G90 .... Heraklion Museum
G91 .... Italian School, Agii Deka
G92 .... Heraklion Museum
G97 .... Gortyn, Odeion
G102 .... Gortyn, Odeion
G106 .... Gortyn, Odeion
Gortyn1 .... Heraklion Museum
Gortyn2 .... Italian School, Agii Deka
Gortyn3 .... Italian School, Agii Deka
Gortyn4 .... Italian School, Agii Deka
Gortyn5 .... Italian School, Agii Deka
Gortyn6 .... Italian School, Agii Deka
Gortyn7 .... Italian School, Agii Deka

LYKTOS

L2 .... Heraklion Museum
L4 .... Heraklion Museum
Lyktos1 .... Heraklion Museum

PHAISTOS

Ph1 .... Heraklion Museum

PRINIAS

Pr7 .... Heraklion Museum

INDEX OF GREEK WORDS

We have included all Greek words except αἰ, δέ, κα, καί, μέ, μέν, ὁ, ὅς, τε, τις.

Some of the forms listed below as nom. sing. or first pers. sing. indicative are hypothetical.

Variant spellings are generally combined under the most common form, and cross-references are given in some cases.

We give column numbers for most texts with more than one column; we give line numbers only for **G72**.

Round brackets () with a number indicates the number of occurrences of a word in the same inscription, column, or line. Round brackets with a question mark (?) indicates words we print in the text or suggest in the textual notes but that are not certain. Round brackets with a number and a question mark indicates that one or more of the words in that inscription, column, or line are uncertain.

Square brackets [] around words or reference numbers indicate words read by many scholars but not by us.

INDEX LOCORUM

Authors

Inscriptions in this volume

NB For texts in this volume, we do not include the presentation of the text itself, only significant references (not mere cross-references) to it in other parts of the book.

Other inscriptions

Other

SUBJECT INDEX

NB For references to Greek words, see Index of Greek Words.

The manufacturer's authorised representative in the EU for product safety is Oxford University Press España S.A. of el Parque Empresarial San Fernando de Henares, Avenida de Castilla, 2 – 28830 Madrid (www.oup.es/en or product.safety@oup.com). OUP España S.A. also acts as importer into Spain of products made by the manufacturer.

www.ingramcontent.com/pod-product-compliance
Lightning Source LLC
Chambersburg PA
CBHW082153250926
52123CB00029B/1099
* 9 7 8 0 1 9 8 8 3 2 5 1 5 *